Edgar E. Schaetzing / Karl Englisch
Fachwörterbuch für Hotellerie & Gastronomie
deutsch-englisch/english-german

Edgar E. Schaetzing/Karl Englisch

FACH WÖRTERBUCH

für Hotellerie & Gastronomie

deutsch-englisch/english-german

Unter Mitarbeit von
Antje Haritage und Fritz Neske

Deutscher Fachverlag

Die Deutsche Bibliothek – CIP-Einheitsaufnahme

Schaetzing, Edgar E.:
Fachwörterbuch für Hotellerie & Gastronomie : deutsch-englisch ; English-German / Edgar E. Schaetzing ; Karl Englisch. Unter Mitarb. von Antje Haritage und Fritz Neske. – 4., völlig überarb. und erw. Aufl. – Frankfurt am Main : Dt. Fachverl., 1994
   Bis 3. Aufl. u.d.T.: Schaetzing, Edgar E.: Fachwörterbuch Hotellerie & Gastronomie, Reisebüros & Reiseveranstalter
   ISBN 3-87150-460-2
NE: Englisch, Karl:

4. Auflage
ISBN 3-87150-460-2

© 1994 by Deutscher Fachverlag GmbH, Frankfurt am Main.
Alle Rechte vorbehalten. Nachdruck, auch auszugsweise,
nur mit Genehmigung des Verlages.

Umschlaggestaltung: Art + Work, Frankfurt am Main
Satz, Registersortierung und Filmherstellung: fm Frohberg GmbH, Freigericht
Druck und Bindung: fgb, Freiburg

Inhaltsverzeichnis

Vorwort
Preface 7

Teil I
Deutsch-Englisch
Part I
German-English 9

Teil II
Englisch-Deutsch
Part II
English-German 139

Teil III
Verzeichnis aller Aufwendungen (USAH)
Deutsch-Englisch
Part III
Expense and Payroll Dictionary (USAH)
German-English 279

Teil IV
Verzeichnis aller Aufwendungen (USAH)
Englisch-Deutsch
Part IV
Expense and Payroll Dictionary (USAH)
English-German 299

Anhang
Regelungsinstitutionen (Bilanzrecht) in den USA
Appendix
Regulatory Bodies (accounting legislation) in the USA 321

Vorwort

Das vorliegende Fachwörterbuch ist für Mitarbeiter von Hotels und Restaurants, für Beratungsgesellschaften sowie für die Aus- und Weiterbildung im Gastgewerbe bestimmt.

Das Erfassen der heutzutage gängigen Branchenterminologie und deren übersichtliche Zusammenstellung war natürlich das Hauptanliegen bei der Überarbeitung und Ergänzung der vorliegenden 4. Auflage. Auch galt es, eine genaue und zutreffende Übersetzung der wichtigsten Fachausdrücke des Rechnungswesens anzubieten, die auf dem neuesten Stand und für das Verständnis des „Uniform System of Accounts for Hotels" erforderlich sind. In einer Zeit, in der sich die europäische Hotellerie und Gastronomie – auch die mittleren Betriebe – anschickt, sich mit diesem Kostenrechnungssystem vertraut zu machen, scheint ein Wörterbuch, das dessen komplexe Fachterminologie behandelt, besonders am Platz zu sein.

Das „Expense and Payroll Dictionary" wurde erstellt, um den Fachleuten im Rechnungswesen eine Orientierungshilfe für die Kontierung der zahlreichen Aufwandspositionen zu geben, mit denen sie täglich zu tun haben.

Wer sich für das amerikanische Bilanzrecht interessiert, findet im Anhang des Wörterbuches genaue Informationen über die wichtigsten Regelungsinstitutionen in den USA.

Die Fachterminologie ist einem ständigen Wandel unterworfen, und eine Sammlung der gebräuchlichsten Fachausdrücke kann niemals „fertig" werden. Bewußt haben wir dieses Fachwörterbuch für die Hotellerie und Gastronomie nicht nach philologischen Richtlinien zusammengestellt; es setzt deshalb auch Grundkenntnisse in beiden Sprachen voraus.

Für die Übersetzung verschiedener Fachausdrücke sind wir Herrn Prof. Wolfgang Leiderer sehr verbunden. Besonderer Dank gilt auch Herrn Prof. Robert A. Beck, Dekan der Cornell University und Herrn John P. Daschler, Director Industry Relations des Amerikanischen Hotel- und Motelverbandes, die mit wertvollen Ratschlägen bei einer Reihe von Übersetzungsschwierigkeiten zur Fertigstellung des Wörterbuches beigetragen haben. Danken möchte ich meiner Frau Ilsa Schaetzing, die die Kartei für die gastronomischen Fachausdrücke erstellt hat.

Für Anregungen zur Verbesserung und Ergänzung sind wir besonders verbunden.

Edgar E. Schaetzing
Karl Englisch

Preface

This dictionary is meant for the staff of hotels and restaurants, for consulting companies and students majoring in hotel and restaurant administration.

One of our major concerns in the revision and complementation of this 4th edition was to compile contemporary professional terminology and present it in a succintly comprehensible manner. It was also important to provide accurate and up-to-date translations of accounting terms which are necessary for an understanding of the revised "Uniform System of Accounts for Hotels". At a time in which the European hotel and restaurant business — even the medium sized business — is trying to become familiar with this accounting system, a dictionary dealing with its complex terminology seems to be particularly seasonable.

The "Expense and Payroll Dictionary", in particular, is designed to help accountants classify the numerous expense items encountered in his or her daily work.

Anyone interested in US accounting legislation will find accurate information in regard to the American Regulatory Bodies in the appendix of this dictionary.

The hotel and restaurant terminology is under constant change and a collection of the most common terms can never be "completed". We would like to point out that we have refrained from applying linguistic considerations; the use of the dictionary, therefore, requires basic knowledge in both languages.

We are greatly indebted to Prof. Wolfgang Leiderer for a large number of English terms and wish to express our gratitude to Prof. Robert A. Beck, Dean of the Cornell University, and Mr. John P. Daschler, Director Industry Relations — Educational Institute of the American Hotel & Motel Association whose valuable advice in a number of difficult translations have contributed so much to the completion of this dictionary. I should like to thank my wife Ilsa Schaetzing who prepared the card index of food and beverage terms.

Any suggestions for improvements and additions are welcome.

Edgar E. Schaetzing
Karl Englisch

Teil I
Deutsch – Englisch

Part I
German – English

Teil I: **Deutsch-Englisch**
Part I: German-English

Anmerkung:
Die Angabe der Umsatzbereiche bzw. der Service Center gilt für das „Uniform System of Accounts for Hotels".

Note:
All schedules mentioned apply for the "Uniform System of Accounts for Hotels".

A

Aal eel
Aal grün boiled eel
Aal in Dill eel in dillsauce
Aal in Gelee eel jellied
ab Schiff ex ship
abändern modify
Abänderung modification
abbestellen cancel
Abbestellung cancellation
abbiegen turn off
Abbildung figure
Abbildungstreue (Rechnungslegung) representational faithfulness
Abbruchkosten costs of raizing plant
ABC-Flug (verbilligter Flug) abc-flight (advanced booking flight)
abdrucken imprint
Abendessen dinner, supper
Abendessen mit Tanz dinner dance
Abendkleidung evening dress
Abendkonzert evening concert
Abendmusikparade tattoo
Abendvorstellung (Theater) evening performance
Abfahrt departure
Abfahrt (Schiff) sailing
Abfahrt (Ski) downhill course, downhill trail, trail, run
Abfahrtshang ski slope
Abfahrtslauf downhill race
Abfahrtsstelle place of departure
Abfahrtsstrecke run
Abfahrtafel departure timetable
Abfahrtstag (Schiff) sailing date
Abfahrtszeit time of departure
Abfahrtszeit (Schiff) sailing time
Abfall rubbish, waste
Abfallbeseitigung (Service Center 12) removal of waste matter (schedule 12)
abfallen fall of
Abfallverwertung (Umsatzbereich 6) salvage (schedule 6)
Abfertigung (Flug etc.) check-in, check-out, registration
Abfertigungsformalitäten check-in formality

Abfertigungsschalter counter
abfinden, sich put up
Abfindungsverpflichtung indemnity liability
Abflug departure, start, take-off
Abflugtag day of departure
Abflugzeit time of departure
Abfluß drain
abgabefrei duty-free
Abgangsbahnhof departure station
abgegrenzt accrued
abgelegen off the beaten track, out of the way, remote
abgenutzt worn out
abgrenzbar accruable
Abgrenzung von Zinsaufwand (-ertrag) accrued interest expense (income)
Abhang slope
abhängen von depend on
Abhebung (Bank) withdrawal
Abhilfe remedy
Abhilfemaßnahme relieve measure
abkochen (Milch) scald
Abkürzung short cut
Ablagefach pigeon hole
Ablagekorb tray
Ablaufdiagramm flow chart
ablaufen expire
Ablauforganisation method and procedures
ablegen (Akte) file
ablehnen refuse
Ablehnung refusal
ablenken von distract from
Abmagerungskur reducing diet, slimming diet treatment
abmelden, sich check out
Abmeldung notice of departure
Abnahme decline, decrease
Abnahme (Entgegennahme) acceptance
abnehmen decrease
abnehmen (entgegenehmen) accept
abnutzen (abschreiben) depreciate
Abnutzung durch Gebrauch wear and tear
Abnutzung (Abschreibung) depreciation
Abonnement subscription
abonnieren subscribe

Abraumbeseitigung, rückständige
backlog repair and maintenance
abräumen clear away
Abreise departure
Abreisedatum date of departure
abreisen (Hotel) check out
abreisen, vorzeitig dump
Abreisetag day of departure
Abruf call
abrunden round off
Absage denial
Absatzstelle sales outlet
Abschaffung abolition
abschalten turn off
abschätzen evaluate
Abschied farewell
Abschiedsessen farewell dinner
abschlagen (Golf) tee, tee off
Abschlagstelle (Golf) tee
Abschleppdienst payment car-tow, recovery service
abschleppen take in tow, tow
Abschleppseil tow-rope
Abschleppwagen breakdown lorry, wrecking car
abschließen negotiate
abschließend final
Abschluß (Vereinbarung) closing, negotiation
Abschluß-, Prüfungs- und Beratungskosten accounting, audit and consulting fees
Abschlußbilanz financial statements
Abschlußbuchung closing entry
Abschlußprüfer auditor
Abschlußübersicht work sheet
Abschlußvergütung volume bonus
Abschmierdienst greasing service
abschmieren grease
Abschnitt coupon
abschöpfen skim off
abschreiben (immaterielle Vermögensgegenstände) amortize, write off
Abschreibung amortization
Abschreibung, beschleunigte accelerated depreciation
Abschreibungsmethode, lineare straight line depreciation

Abschreibung, planmäßige regular depreciation
Abschreibung auf abgegrenzte Finanzierungskosten (Service Center 14) amortization of deferred financing costs (schedule 14)
Abschreibung wegen Substanzverzehr depletion
Abschreibungsmethode method of amortization
abschüssig slopy
abseilen rope down
abseits der Straße off the road
absenden send (off), dispatch
absetzen deduct
Absetzung (Nachlaß) deduction
absinken fall of
absperren lock off
Absprache briefing
abspülen wash up
Abstammung origin, ancestry
Abstecher detour
absteigen put up
Absteigequartier house of accomodation
Abstieg descent
abstimmen reconcile
Abstimmung reconciliation
Abstinenzler teetotaller
Abteil compartment
Abteil zweiter Klasse second-class compartment
Abteilung department, division
Abteilung, technische engineering department
Abteilungskoch chef de partie
Abteilungsleiter department head
abtreten (Amt) assign
abtrocknen dry, wipe
abwälzen pass on
Abwaschküche dishwashing area
Abwasserkanal sewer
abwechseln vary
abwechslungsreich diversified, lively
abweichend vom üblichen out-of-line
Abweichung variance
Abwertung devaluation
Abwesender absentee

Abwesenheit absenteeism
Abwesenheitsrate absence rate
abziehen deduct, discount, subtract
Abzug allowance, deduction, discount, subtraction
Abzug (Druck) print
abzugsfähig deductible
abzugsfähig, nicht nondeductible
Achse (Auto) axle
Achselhöhle armpit
Achterdeck after-deck
Achtung attention
Administration administration
Adreßbuch address book, directory
Adresse address
adressieren address
Adressiermaschine addressing machine
Adressliste mailing list
Aerosoltherapie treatment with aerosols
Affinitätsgruppe affinity group
Afrika Africa
Agentur agency, travel agency
Agenturkosten (Werbung und PR) (Service Center 11) agency fees (schedule 11)
Agio bei Ausgabe einer Schuldverschreibung bond premium
Ahornsirup maple syrup
Akkreditiv letter of credit
Akte file, record
Aktenmappe briefcase
Aktenschrank filing cabinet
Aktentasche briefcase
Aktie(n) stock
Aktie, nicht sofort dividendenberechtigte deferred stock
Aktie, ursprünglich festgesetzter Wert einer (USA) stated value (capital stock)
Aktien, ausgegebene issued shar
Aktien, im Umlauf befindliche outstanding shares
Aktien, (eigene) eines Unternehmens treasury stock
Aktiendividende corporate dividen
Aktiengattung class of stock
Aktiengesellschaft mit breiter Streuung des Aktienbesitzes public corporation
Aktion campaign
Aktionär stockholder
Aktiva assets
Aktiva netto, sonstige other assets, net
Aktiva, transitorische deferred income
aktivieren capitalize
Aktivierung capitalization
Aktivseite (Bilanz) asset side
aktualisieren bring up to date
aktuell up-to-date
akzeptieren accept
akzeptieren (Kreditkarte) honor (credit card)
Alarmglocke alarm bell
Ale (Bier), dunkles mild ale
Ale (Bier), helles bitter ale, pale ale
Alkohol alcohol, liquor, spirits
Alkoholausschankzeiten licensed hours, licensing hours
alkoholfrei non-alcoholic
alkoholfreies Getränk soft drink
alkoholisches Getränk alcoholic drink
Allee avenue, boulevard
allergisch allergic
Allerheiligen All Saints' Day
Allerlei mixture (of food)
alles inbegriffen all included, everything included
allgemeine Bilanzierungsgrundsätze general accounting principles
Allgemeiner Deutscher Automobilklub (ADAC) German Automobile Club
Almwiese alpine meadow
Alpenpaß pass in the Alps
Alpenstraße alpine road
Alpinist alpine climber
Alse shad
alt old
Altar altar
Altersheim home for old people
altmodisch old-fashioned
Altschnee base snow, old snow
Altstadt old town

am Apparat (Telefon) bleiben hold on, hold the line
Amateur amateur
Amerika America
Amerikaner American
Amerikanerin American
amerikanisch American
Amerikanische Gesellschaft der Reiseagenturen American Society of Travel Agents (ASTA)
Amerikanischer Hotel- und Motelverband American Hotel and Motel Association
amerikanisches Frühstück American breakfast
Aminosäure amino-acid
Amortisation amortization
Amortisationsfonds sinking fund
amtlich official
Analyse analysis
analysieren analyze
Ananas pine-apple
Ananaseis pine-apple ice cream
Ananassaft pine-apple-juice
anbieten bid, offer
Anblick sight
anbraten parboil, sear
Anchovis anchovy
Anchovisbutter anchovy-butter
Anchovispaste anchovy-paste
Andenkengeschäft souvenir shop
ändern alter, amend, change
Änderung alteration, amendment, change
Änderungen vorbehalten subject to alteration
Andrang rush, throng of people
Aneignung occupancy
anerkennen acknowledge, recognize
anerkennen, dankbar appreciate
Anerkennung acknowledg(e)ment, recognition
Anfahrtsweg approach road
Anfall attack
Anfängerhang ski nursery slope
Anfängerkurs course for beginners
Anfangsbuchstabe initial
Anfangsgehalt initial salary
anfassen touch, handle
anfechten (Vertrag) avoid
Anfechtung avoidance

anfliegen land at
Anforderung requisition
Anfrage inquiry
angeben, im Anhang mention in the notes
Angebot bid, offer, supply
Angebot, verstecktes hidden offer
Angebotserweiterung diversification
angebrannt burnt
Angelegenheit concern, fact, matter
Angelfischerei line-fishing
Angelgelegenheit fishing facility
Angelgerät fishing-gear, fishing-tackle
Angeln angling, fishing
angeln angle, fish
Angelpunkt hub
Angelschein fishing license
Angelsport fishing
angemessen adequate, fair, reasonable, appropriate
Angemessenheit adequacy
angespannt tense
Angestelltenverpflegung employees meals
Angestellter employee
Angestellter, leitender executive (of the company), top executive
Anglerverein angling club, fishing club
Angliederung affiliation
angrenzend adjacent
Anhang appendix, notes
Anhängezettel tag
Anis anise
Anisplätzchen aniseed cooky
Anker lichten weigh anchor
Anker werfen cast anchor
Anklage accusation
ankleiden dress
ankochen parboil
ankommen arrive
Ankunft arrival
Ankunftsbuch arrival book
Ankunftsdatum date of arrival
Ankunftshalle arrival hall
Ankunftstafel arrival time-table
Ankunftstag day of arrival
Ankunftstermin date of arrival
Ankunftszeit, voraussichtliche probable time of arrival

ankündigen announce
Ankündigung announcement
Ankünfteanzahl number of arrivals
Anlage appendix
Anlage (Beifügung) enclosure
Anlage (Geld) investment
Anlage von flüssigen Mitteln cash investment
Anlage, bauliche structure
Anlagegegenstände, abnutzbare depreciable assets
Anlagen, elektrische und maschinelle (Service Center 12) electrical and mechanical equipment (schedule 12)
Anlagen, im Bau befindliche construction in progress
Anlagen, kurzfristige (Geld) short-term investments
Anlagespiegel analysis of fixed assets
Anlagevermögen fixed assets
Anlagevermögen, zu Anschaffungs- bzw. Herstellkosten property, plant and equipment, at cost
anlaufen (Seefahrt) call at
Anlaufhafen port of call
Anlegehafen port of call
Anlegen (Schiff) make fast, moor
anlegen (Schiff) mooring
Anlegeplatz landing dock
Anlegestelle landing-place, mooring pier
Anleihe debenture
Anleiheemission bond issue
Anlernen training
anlernen train
Anmeldeformular registration form
anmelden declare, register
anmelden, sich (Hotel) check-in
Anmeldung declaration, registration
Anmeldung (Hotel) reception
Anmerkungen zum Jahresabschluß notes accompanying the financial statements
Annahme (Entgegennahme) acceptance
Annahme (Vermutung) assumption
annehmen (aufnehmen) adopt

annehmen (entgegen-, hinnehmen) accept
annehmen (Kreditkarte) honor (credit card)
annehmen (vermuten) assume
Annehmlichkeit amenity
Annonce advertisement (Abk.: ad)
Anorak anorak, parka
anordnen arrange, direct
Anordnung arrangement, direction
Anordnung, räumliche layout
Anpassungsfähigkeit flexibility
anregen suggest
anregen (Appetit) whet
Anregung suggestion
Anreise journey
Anreisemöglichkeit possibility of travelling
Anreisetag day of arrival
Anreiz incentive
Anruf call
Ansager announcer
ansammeln accumulate
Anschaffungs- und Herstellungskosten, ursprüngliche original historical acquisition or production costs
Anschaffungskosten, fortgeschriebene durchschnittliche moving average acquisition costs
Anschlagbrett bill-board, bulletin board
Anschlagtafel poster board
anschließend an adjoining
Anschluß connection
Anschlußfahrt connection
Anschlußflug connecting flight
Anschlußstrecke connecting line, connecting route
Anschlußzug connecting train
anschnallen bitte! fasten seat belts
Anschuldigung accusation
Ansehen reputation
Ansichtskarte greetings card, picture postcard
Ansporn incentive
ansprechen auf respond to
Anspruch claim, demand, requirement, right
anspruchsvoll pretentious

anstatt in lieu of, instead of
anstelle von instead of
anstellen employ, engage
Anstellung employment, engagement
ansteuern head for
anstrahlen floodlight
Antenne aerial, antenna
Antiquität antique
Antiquitätengeschäft antique shop
Antrag application, proposal
Antragsformular application form
Antwort answer, reply
antworten answer, reply
Antwortschein, internationaler international reply coupon
anweisen direct, instruct
Anweisung direction, instruction
anwendbar applicable
Anwendbarkeit applicability
anwendbar, nicht inapplicable
anwenden apply
Anwendersoftware application software
Anwesenheit attendance
Anzahlung advance deposit
Anzahlungen, geleistete advances to suppliers, prepayments
Anzeige (Inserat) advertisement (Abk.: ad)
anzeigen (inserieren) advertise
Anzeigenspalte avertisement column
Anzeigentarif advertising rate
Anzeigenwerbung press advertising
anzeigepflichtig notifiable
Anziehungskraft appeal, attraction
Anzug suit
anzünden kindle, light
Aperitif aperitif
Apfel apple
Apfel im Ofen gebacken baked apple, ovenbaked apple
Apfel im Schlafrock baked apple in puff, paste apple turnover
Apfelauflauf apple soufflé
Apfelgelee apple jelly
Apfelkompott stewed apples
Apfelkonfiture apple jam
Apfelkuchen apple pie
Apfelküchlein apple fritter

Apfelmus apple-sauce, apple-purée
Apfelreis apple rice
Apfelsaft apple juice, sweet cider
Apfelsine orange
Apfelspalte apple fritter
Apfelstrudel apple strudel, covered apple pie
Apfelstückchen gewürfelt diced apples
Apfeltasche apple-stuffed turnover
Apfeltorte apple tart
Apfelwein cider, hard cider
Apotheke chemist's shop, pharmacy
Apparat (Telefon) line
Appartement self-contained flat
Appartement, möbliertes furnished self-contained flat
Appartementhaus apartment house, block of flats
Appartementhotel apart-hotel
Appetit appetite
Appetitanreger appetizer, whet
appetitlich appetizing
Applaus applause
Après-Ski après-ski
Aprikose apricot
Aprikosenauflauf apricot soufflé
Aprikosenröllchen, warmes baked aprikot roll
Arbeit job, labo(u)r, work
Arbeiter blue collar worker
Arbeitgeber employer
Arbeitgeberverband employers' association
Arbeitnehmer employee
Arbeitnehmervertrag employees' representative
Arbeitsablauf flow of work
Arbeitsablaufanalyse flow process chart, work flow analysis
Arbeitsablaufbogen flow process chart
Arbeitsablaufdiagramm process chart
Arbeitsanalytiker job analyst
Arbeitsanreicherung job enrichment
Arbeitsanweisung instruction card
Arbeitsbedingung working condition
Arbeitsbedingungen work terms
Arbeitsbelastung work load
Arbeitsbereich work area

Arbeitsbewertung job evaluation
Arbeitsbogen work sheet
Arbeitserlaubnis work permit
Arbeitsersparnis labor saving
Arbeitserweiterung job enlargement
Arbeitsfähigkeit ability to work
Arbeitsgemeinschaft association
Arbeitsgriff grasp
Arbeitsgruppe task force
Arbeitsgruppe team
Arbeitshäufung peak load
Arbeitskraft manpower
Arbeitskräfte labor force, work force
Arbeitskräfte, gelernte skilled manpower
Arbeitsleistung output
arbeitslos unemployed
Arbeitsmarkt labor market
Arbeitsmoral employee morale
Arbeitspapiere working papers
Arbeitsplatz work place
Arbeitsplatzbeschreibung job description, job specification
Arbeitsplatzbewertung performance appraisal
Arbeitsplatzgestaltung work place layout
Arbeitsplatzrotation job rotation
Arbeitsplatzsicherheit job security
Arbeitsplatzstandardisierung job standardization
Arbeitsproduktivität labor productivity
Arbeitsstreitigkeit labor dispute
Arbeitsstudie job analysis
Arbeitsstunde man hour
Arbeitsstunden, geleistete hours worked
Arbeitstag man-day
arbeitsunfähig (dauernd) disabled
Arbeitsunterlage work sheet
Arbeitsunterlagen working papers
Arbeitsunterweisung job instruction
Arbeitsvereinfachung work simplification
Arbeitsvertrag employment contract
Arbeitszufriedenheit job satisfaction, work satisfaction
Architektur architecture
Arena arena, circus-ring
ärgern annoy

Argument argument
argumentieren argue
Arie aria
Arkade arcade
Arm arm
Ärmelkanal und Irische See narrow seas
Aroma aroma, flavo(u)r
aromatisch aromatic, spicy
Arrest arrest
Art kind
Artikel commodity
Artischocke artichoke
Artischockenboden bottom of artichoke
Artischockenherz heart of artichoke
ärztliche Betreuung medical care
ärztliches Attest doctor's certificate
ärztliches Zeugnis medical certificate
Arzt, behandelnder doctor in attendance
Arzt, diensttuender doctor on duty
Asche ash
Äsche grayling
Aschenbecher ashtray
Aspik aspic, jelly
Assistent assistant
Assistent der Geschäftsleitung (Empfang) assistant manager (front)
Asthma asthma
Atemgymnastik breathing exercises
Atmosphäre atmosphere
Attraktion attraction, appeal, feature
Au-pair-Aufenthalt au pair stay
Auerhahn mountain-cock, wood grouse, grouse, black cock
auf Bundesebene federal
Aufbau structure
Aufbewahrung von Wertgegenständen safe deposit of valuables
Aufbewahrungsschein baggage check
Aufbewahrungsstelle checkroom
aufbrechen set off
Aufenthalt stay, stop, halt
Aufenthaltsdauer period of stay, time of stay, duration of the stay, length of stay

Aufenthaltserlaubnis residence permit
Aufenthaltsgenehmigung residence permit
Aufenthaltsgutschein board and lodging voucher
Aufenthaltskosten cost of board and lodging
Aufenthaltsort residence, whereabouts
Aufenthaltsraum day-room, lounge, hotel lounge
Aufenthaltstag day of stay
Aufenthaltsverlängerung extension of stay
Aufenthaltsvisum temporary residence visa
auferlegen impose on
Auffahrt upward journey
Auffahrunfall nose-to-tail collision
auffordern request
Aufforderung request
Aufführung performance
Aufgabe task
Aufgabe, entscheidende pivotal role
Aufgang way up
aufgeben quit, renounce, give up, forego
aufgeben (Post) mail
aufgebracht angry
aufgeschoben deferred
aufgliedern itemize
Aufguß infusion
aufheben lift up
aufheben (ungültig machen) cancel
aufhören cease
aufklären (Wetter) clear up
Aufklebezettel sticker
Auflauf soufflé
Auflauf aus Hackfleisch und Kartoffeln shepherd's pie
auflaufen (ansammeln) accumulate
Auflaufkartoffeln puffed potatoes, soufflé-potatoes
Auflaufomelett omelet soufflé
Auflösung solution
Aufmachung make up
aufmerksam attentive
Aufmerksamkeit attention

Aufmerksamkeiten für Gäste guests' supplies
Aufnahme reception
Aufnahmekapazität capacity of accomodation
aufnehmen raise
aufprägen imprint
aufräumen clean-up
aufrechterhalten maintain
Aufregung worry
aufrichtig sincere
aufrunden round up
aufschieben postpone, defer
Aufschlag surcharge, extra charge, additional charge, increment
aufschließen (Schloß) unlock
Aufschnitt assorted cold meat
Aufschnitt gemischt selection of cold cuts, selection of cold meat
Aufschnitt kalt cold cuts, cold meat
Aufschub delay
Aufschwung, geschäftlicher boom
Aufsicht supervision
Aufsichtsorgan supervisory body
Aufsichtsperson supervisor
aufstehen arise, get up
Aufstellkosten installation costs
Aufstellung schedule, statement
Aufstieg ascent, rise
Auftauen thaw
auftauen thaw
aufteilen subdivide
Aufteilung subdivision
Auftrag order, commission
Auftrag erteilen place an order
auftragen (Speisen) serve
Auftragsgröße lot size
aufwachen wake up
aufwärmen reheat
aufwendig expensive
aufwerten up-value
aufzählen enumerate
aufzeichnen note
Aufzeichung note
aufziehen wind up
Aufzug elevator, lift
Aufzugsschacht elevator shaft
Augenkontakt eye contact
Augenzeuge eye-witness

Aus- und Weiterbildung (Service Center 9) training (schedule 9)
ausbessern repair, darn
ausbilden train, educate
Ausbilder trainer, training manager
Ausbildung training, education
Ausbildung am Arbeitsplatz training on the job
Ausbildungsleiter training manager
Ausbildungsmethode training method
Ausbildungsvertrag contract of apprenticeship
Ausbildungszeit apprenticeship
ausbuchen write off
ausdrücken, etwas geschickt in Worten verbalize
auseinandergehen part
auserlesen exquisite
Ausfahrt outing, way out, exit
Ausfall deficit, deficiency
Ausfallbürgschaft deficiency (or deficit) guarantee; indemnity bond
ausfindig machen trace
Ausflug outing, excursion
Ausflugsdampfer excursion steamer
Ausflugsfahrpreis excursion fare
Ausflugsgebiet tour region, excursion area
Ausflugskarte tour ticket, excursion ticket
Ausflugslokal roadside café
Ausflugsmöglichkeiten touring facilities, excursion facilities
Ausflugsort place of interest
Ausflugsprogramm tour program, excursion program
Ausflugstarif excursion rate
Ausflugsverkehr tourist traffic, holiday traffic
Ausflugsziel day-trippers' goal, excursionists' goal
Ausflügler tourist, tripper, day-tripper, excursionist
Ausfuhr export
Ausfuhrbewilligung export permit
Ausfuhrsperre embargo
Ausfuhrzoll export duty
ausführen accomplish
ausführen (Ware) export

ausfüllen fill in
Ausgabe issue
Ausgabe (Geld) expenditure
Ausgabebüro issuing office
Ausgaben einschränken curtail one's expenses
Ausgaben, persönliche personal expenses
Ausgabetag day of issue
Ausgang way out, exit
Ausgangsinterview exit-interview
Ausgangsort point of origin, starting-point
Ausgangspunkt starting-point
ausgeben issue
ausgeben (Geld) spend
ausgebucht full
ausgelassen (Fett) melted
ausgenommen exempt
ausgestattet mit equipped with
ausgesucht assorted
ausgezeichnet excellent
ausgleichen balance
Ausgleichsposten für Anteile im Fremdbesitz minority interests
Ausgleichszahlung compensation payment
Ausgrabung excavation
aushändigen hand over
Aushangfahrplan train indicator
Aushilfe extra help, parttimer
Aushilfskellner extra waiter
Aushilfskellner für Veranstaltungen banquet extra waiter
auskernen stone
Auskunft auf Anfrage information on application
Auskunft erteilt information given
Auskunftsstelle inquiry office
ausladen unload
Ausland foreign country
Ausland, im abroad
Ausländer alien, foreigner
ausländisch foreign
Auslandsaufenthalt stay abroad
Auslandsflug international flight
Auslandsgast foreign guest, foreign visitor
Auslandsgast oversea(s) visitor
Auslandskrankenversicherung health insurance for abroad

Auslandsreise

Auslandsreise journey abroad, trip abroad
Auslandsreisender tourist abroad
Auslandstarif foreign rate
Auslandstelegramm oversea(s) telegram
Auslandstourist foreign tourist, oversea(s) tourist
Auslandswerbung advertising abroad, publicity campaign abroad
Auslaß outlet
auslasten utilize fully
auslaufen (ausrinnen) leak
auslaufen (Schiff) put up to sea, leave port
Auslegung construction
ausleihen lend
Ausleihungen an verbundene Unternehmen loans receivable from affiliated companies
Auslöser shutter-release, trigger
Ausnahme exception
ausnehmen exempt
auspacken unpack
ausreichend satisfying
Ausreise, bei der on leaving the country
Ausreisesichtvermerk exit visa
Ausreisevisum exit visa
ausrollen (Teig) roll
Ausrüstung outfit
Ausschank pub, public house, saloon, saloon-bar, tavern
Ausschank alkoholischer Getränke sale of alcoholic drinks
Ausschanklizenz (alkoholische Getränke) licence, fully licensed
ausscheiden eliminate
Ausscheidung elimination
Ausschiffung debarkation
Ausschiffungsgebühr disembarkment charge
ausschreiben write out
Ausschuß committee
ausschütten distribute
Außenbord-Motorboot outboard motor boat
Außendienst field work
Außenkabine outside room
Außenseiter outsider
Außenvertreter outside representative
Außenwerbung outdoor advertising
außer Kraft ineffective
außerhalb exterior
äußerlich exterior
Aussicht view
Aussichtsfenster observation window, wide-vision window
Aussichtsturm observation tower
Ausspannen relaxation
Ausstattung equipment, make-up, outfit
Aussteigebahnhof arrival station
aussteigen alight, get off
aussteigen (Flugzeug) deplane
ausstellen display, exhibit
ausstellen (Dokument) issue
Aussteller exhibitor
Ausstellung exhibition
Ausstellung (Dokument) issue
Ausstellungsgelände exhibition grounds
Ausstellungsort (Dokument) place of issue
Ausstellungsstand exhibition stand
Austausch exchange
austauschen swap
Austauschgutschein exchange voucher
Auster oyster
Austernbank oyster-bank, oysterbed
Austernpark oyster-farm
Australien Australia
Ausverkauf sale, sellout
ausverkauft sold out
Auswahl assortment, choice, range, selection
auswählen select
auswärts outward
Ausweichangebot alternative offer
Ausweichstelle passing-place
Ausweis admission card, identification card, legitimation, membership card
Ausweis beim Jahresabschluß financial statement presentation
ausweisen disclose
Ausweispapier identification paper
Ausziehbett pull-out bed
ausziehen (Mantel) take off
ausziehen, sich undress

Auszubildender apprentice, trainee
Auszug abstract
Auto car, motor-car
Autoabfahrtsstelle town terminal
Autoanhänger trailer
Autoausfahrt exit drive
Autobahn driveway, freeway, motorway
Autobahnausfahrt exit road
Autobahneinfahrt access road
Autobahngebühr motorway toll, toll
Autobahnhotel motorway hotel
Autobahnraststätte motorway restaurant
Autobahnzubringer feeder road, motorway feeder road
Autobeförderung conveyance of cars
Autobus bus
Autobusbetrieb, städtischer urban bus service
Autodach-Gepäckträger roof rack
Autoeinfahrt way in
Autofähre car ferry
Autofahrer motorist
Autofahrt car ride, motor ride, motoring trip
Autoführer motoring guide
Autogepäckträger luggage rack
Autohilfe motorist's roadside assistance service
Autohupe hooter
Autokarte road map
Autokino drive-in cinema
Automat penny-in-the-slot, slot machine
Automatenrestaurant self-service restaurant with slot machines
Automatenverkauf automatic selling
Automation automation
automatisieren automate
Automobilclub motor club
Automobildienst automobile service
Autonummernschild licence plate
Autorally motor-rally
Autoreise motoring journey, motoring trip
Autoreisender motoring tourist
Autoreisezug car-carrier train
Autoreisezug (Schlafwagen) car sleeper train

Autoreisezug-Service motorail
Autorennen motor race
Autoschlüssel car key
Autostraße driveway, motor road
Autotour motoring trip
Autounfall motor accident
Autoverkehr automobile traffic, car traffic, motor traffic
Autoverladung (bei Schiffen) roll on – roll off, car-loading
Autoverleih car hire (rental) service
Autovermietung an Selbstfahrer self-drive car hire service
avisieren advise, inform, notify
Avocadobirne avocado pear

B

Babysitter baby-sitter
Babytragekorb infant's carrying basket
Bachforelle brook-trout
Backblech baking tin
backen bake, fry
backen, in der Schale bake in their jackets
Bäcker baker
Backhuhn fried chicken
Backofen oven
Backpflaume prune
Backpulver baking powder
Bad, medizinisches medicinal bath
Bad (Wanne) bath
Badeanlage bathing facility
Badeanstalt bathing establishment, swimming-pool
Badeanzug bathing costume, bathing suit, bathing suit, swimsuit
Badearzt spa doctor
Badebucht cove for bathing
Badefreuden seaside pleasures
Badegast bather, wateringplace visitor
Badehaube bathing cap
Badehose bathing shorts, bathing trunks, slips, trunks
Badekur course of treatment at a spa, cure at a spa
Bademantel bathing-gown, bathrobe
Badematte bath mat

**Bademeister swimming master
Bademeister (Heilbad)** bath attendant
Bademütze bathing cap
Baden verboten! bathing prohibited
baden (i. Freien) bath
Badeort bathing resort, spa, watering-place
Badeplatz bathing place
Bäderbehandlung balneotherapy
Bäderwesen balneology
Badesaison bathing season
Badesteg bathing pier
Badestrand bathing beach
Badetasche beach-bag
Badetuch bath towel
Badewanne bathtub
Badewärter beach-guard, life-guard
Badezimmer bathroom
Badezimmer, gemeinsames shared bathroom
Bahn- oder Busanschluß surface connection
Bahn-Bus-Verkehr surface transport
Bahn-Schiffsreise railsteamer journey
Bahnbus railway bus
Bahnfahrt railway journey, train journey
Bahnhof railway station
Bahnhofsaufsicht station superintendent
Bahnhofsbuchhandlung railway bookstall
Bahnhofsgaststätte station restaurant
Bahnhofshalle station hall
Bahnhofshotel station hotel
Bahnhofsmission Traveller's Aid Office
Bahnhofsvorstand stationmaster
Bahnhofsvorsteher stationmaster
Bahnnetz railway network
Bahnpersonal railroad staff, railway staff
Bahnpostamt station post office
bahnpostlagernd poste restante railway station
Bahnreise railway journey, train journey

Bahnschalter rail-ticket office, ticket office
Bahnstation railway station
Bahnsteig platform
Bahnsteigkarte platform ticket
Bahnsteigschaffner ticket-collector
Bahnsteigsperre ticket barrier
Bahnstrecke railway line
Bahnübergang grade crossing, railway level, level crossing
Bahnverbindung rail connection
Baiser meringue
Balkon balcony
Balkonzimmer room with balcony
Ballettaufführung ballet performance
Ballsaal ballroom
Banane banana
Bananen flambiert flamed bananas
Band (Buch) volume
Bandnudeln ribbon maccaroni
Bank bank
Bankett banquet
Bankettgeschäft banquet business
Bankettinformation function sheet
Bankettküche banquet kitchen
Bankettleiter banquet manager
Bankettoberkellner banquet headwaiter
Bankettumsätze, verschiedene (Umsatzbereich 2) miscellaneous banquet income (schedule 2)
Bankfeiertag bank holiday
Bankguthaben cash in banks
Bar bar
bar cash
bar bezahlen pay cash
Barauslage out-of-pocket expense
Barbe barbel
Bareinkauf cash purchase
Bargeld cash on hand
Bargeldkasse petty cash
Bargerät bar utensil
Barhocker stool
Barkasse launch, motor launch
Barkellner cocktail bar tender
Barmann barman
Barometer barometer
Barsch perch
Barscheck open check
Bartheke bar counter
Barverkauf cash sale

Barwert present value, (actual) cash value
Barzahlung cash payment
Barzahlung bei Ankunft (des Gastes) paid in advance (pia)
Basilika basilica
Basilikum basil
Basis basis
Bau construction
Bau, im under construction
Bauch stomach
Bauerngulasch beef stew peasant style
Bauernhaus farmhouse
Bauernhof farm
Bauernschinken farmer's ham
Bauernstube farmhouse room
Baugenehmigung building permit
Baumaterialien und Baustoffe (Service Center 12) building and supplies (schedule 12)
Baummelone pawpaw
Bauplatz building lot, building site
Baustelle construction site
Bauwerk, historisches historical building
Bauwert building cost
Bayern Bavaria
beachten mind
beachten, nicht ignore
beanspruchen claim
beanstanden object to
Beanstandung objection
beantragen apply for, propose
Bearbeitungsgebühr charge for handling
beaufsichtigen supervise
beauftragen charge, order
Beauftragter representative, agent
Béchamelsoße béchamel sauce
Becher mug
Bedarf need
Bedarfshaltestelle request stop
Bedarfsmeldung purchase requisition
Bedarfsschätzung estimate of demand
bedauern regret
Bedeutung meaning
bedienen attend, serve, wait on
Bedienung waitress, attendance

Bedienung inbegriffen service included
Bedienungsgeld service, service charge
Bedienungspersonal service staff
Bedienungszuschlag service charge, extra charge for service
bedingen condition
Bedingung condition
Bedrohung, tätliche assault
Bedürfnis requirement, want, need
Beefsteak beefsteak, steak
Beefsteak à la Meier beefsteak with fried egg
Beefsteak à la tartare beefsteak tartare style
Beefsteak, doppeltes double-sized steak
Beefsteakpastete beef pie
beeindrucken impress
beeinflussen influence
beeinträchtigen impair, interfere, disturb
Beeinträchtigung disturbance
beendigen terminate
Beendigung termination
Beere berry
befähigen qualify
befahrbar passable, usable
Befahrbarkeit navigability, passability
befahren (Schiff) navigate
befolgen follow
befördern forward
Beförderung transport, carriage, conveyance
Beförderung auf dem Luftweg air carriage
Beförderungsbedingung condition of conveyance
Beförderungskosten transport charges
Beförderungsmittel conveyance, means of transportation
Beförderungspreis transport charge
befreien (Pflicht) relieve
befreit exempt
befriedigen satisfy
befriedigend satisfying
Befugnis authority
begebbar negotiable

Begebbarkeit negotiability
begeben, sich go to
begießen, mit Fett baste
Begleitbrief couvering letter
begleiten accompany
begleitende Kinder accompanying children
Begleitperson accompanying person
begrenzen limit
begrenzt restricted
Begrenzung limitation
Begrüßungstechnik encounter technique
behaglich snug, cosy
Behaglichkeit cosiness
Behälter container
Behandlung treatment
behaupten affirm, assert
Behauptung statement, affirmation, assertion
beherbergen lodge, put up, accomodate
Beherbergungsabteilung rooms department
Beherbergungsbereich room division department
Beherbergungsbetrieb establishment of the hotel trade
Beherbergungskapazität accomodation capacity
Beherbergungsstatistik rooms statistic
Beherbergungsvertrag contract of accomodation
bei (Adresse) care of (c/o)
bei Durchsicht at sight
Beifahrer assistant driver
Beifall applause
Beifuß tarragon
beifügen annex, attach, enclose
Beigeschmack aftertaste, tang
Beilage side dish, trimmings
Beilagenwerbung insert advertising
Bein leg
Beinfleisch rib of beef boiled
Beisammensein gathering
beistehen assist
beitragen (beisteuern) contribute (to)
beitreten join, enter
beiwohnen attend

Bekannter acquaintance
Bekanntgabe notice, notification
bekanntgeben notice, announce
Bekanntmachung announcement
Bekanntschaft acquaintance
Beköstigung board
belasten (Konto) debit, charge to (an account)
belästigen molest, annoy, disturb
Belästigung molestation, nuisance, annoyance, disturbance
Belastungsspitze peak load
belaufen auf, sich amount to
belebt animated, busy
Beleg voucher
Belegschaft work force
belegt (Telefon) busy
Belegung occupancy, reservation
Belegungsprozentsatz percentage of occupancy
beleidigen insult, offend
Beleidigung affront, insult
beleuchten illuminate
Beleuchtung lighting
belichten (Foto) expose
Belichtungsmesser exposure meter
Beliebtheitsgrad popularity rate
belohnen reward, award
Belohnung reward, award
bemängeln complain
bemühen, sich solicit
benachbart adjacent
benachrichtigen inform, advise
Benachrichtigung notification, advice
Benehmen behavio(u)r, performance
benehmen, sich behave
benennen name
Benutzer user
Benzin petrol, fuel, gasoline
Benzinkanister petrol can, gasoline can
Benzinschein petrol voucher, gasoline coupon
Benzintank petrol tank, fuel tank
Benzinverbrauch petrol consumption
beobachten observe
Beobachtung observation
bequem comfortable
Bequemlichkeit comfort
beraten advise

Berater advisor, consultant
Beratungsdienst advisory service
berechnen invoice, bill, calculate, charge
Berechnung calculation
berechtigen justify
berechtigen, j-n enable
Berechtigung justification, right
Bereich range
bereisen travel, tour
bereit ready
bereitstellen provide, supply
Berg mountain
Berg- und Talfahrt upward and downward journey
bergauf uphill
Bergausrüstung climbing equipment
Bergbahn mountain railway
Bergdorf mountain village
Bergfahrt upward journey
Bergführer mountain guide
Berggasthof mountain inn
Berggipfel mountain peak, mountain top
Berghotel mountain hotel, mountain lodge
Berghütte mountain cabin, mountain hut
Bergpaß mountain pass, defile
Bergrestaurant mountain restaurant
Bergschuh climbing boot
Bergsee mountain lake
Bergstation top terminal, unloading station
Bergsteigen mountaineering, rock-climbing
Bergsteiger mountain climber, mountaineer
Bergsteigerausrüstung mountaineering equipment
Bergsteigerschule mountaineering school
Bergstraße mountain road
Bergtour mountain tour
Bergwacht mountain rescue service
Bergwanderung mountain hike
Bergwiese mountain meadow
Bericht report
berichten report, advise
berichtigen adjust, correct

Berichtigung adjustment
Berichtigungsbuchung adjusting entry
Berieselungsapparat sprinkler
Berliner Pfannkuchen Berlin doughnut
Berner Platte sauerkraut or string beans with meat and sausage
Bernstein amber
Beruf occupation, profession
Berufsausbildung vocational training
Berufskrankheit occupational illness
beruhigend reassuring, satisfying
beruhigen, j-n put at ease
beruhigen, sich calm down
besänftigen calm
Besatzung crew
beschädigen injure
Beschaffenheit quality
beschäftigen employ, engage
beschäftigt busy
Beschäftigung employment, engagement, occupation, volume
Beschäftigung, saisonale seasonal employment
Beschäftigungsgrad operating rate, utilization of capacity, volume, activity level
Bescheidenheit modesty
Bescheinigung certificate
beschlagnahmen confiscate
beschleunigen accelerate
beschließen decide
Beschließerin matron
Beschluß decision
Beschränkung restriction
beschreiben describe
Beschreibung description, specification
Beschwerde complaint, grievance
Beschwerdebuch complaints book
beschweren aggrieve
beschweren, sich complain
beseitigen remove
Besen broom
besetzt full, occupied, taken
besetzt (Telefon) busy, engaged
besichtigen inspect, perambulate
Besichtigungsfahrt sightseeing excursion

Besichtigungsreise perambulation
Besitz, ungestörter undisturbed possession
Besitzerin landlady
Besitzgesellschaft holding company
Besitzwechsel notes receivable
besonder(er, e, es, s) extra
besonnen discreet
besorgt anxious
Besprechung conference
Bestand on hand (amount)
Bestandsaufnahme der Warenvorräte, körperliche physical inventory count
Bestandskonto balance sheet account, real account
Bestandteil part
bestätigen acknowledge, affirm, confirm, reconfirm, verify
Bestätigung acknowledg(e)ment, affirmation, confirmation, reconfirmation, verification
Bestattungsunternehmen undertaker
bestechen bribe
Bestechung bribe
Bestechungsgeld bribe
Besteck cutlery
bestehen auf insist (on, upon)
bestehen aus consist of
Besteigung ascent
Bestellaufnahme ordertaking
bestellen order
bestellen, telefonisch book by telephone
Bestellformular order form
Bestellhäufigkeit ordering rate
Bestellkopie order copy
Bestellkosten, jährliche annual ordering costs
Bestellmenge order quantity
Bestellmenge, Berechnung der wirtschaftlichen calculation of an economic order quantity
Bestellscheinblock order pad
Bestellung booking, order, requisition
Bestellung, telefonische order by telephone
Bestellungen, Anzahl der jährlichen annual placing of orders

Bestellverfahren ordering procedure, reorder system
besteuern tax
Besteuerung taxation
bestimmen determine
bestimmt definite
Bestimmungsbahnhof destination station
Bestimmungsflughafen airport of destination
Bestimmungshafen port of call
Bestimmungsland country of destination
Bestimmungsort place of destination, destination
Bestrahlung heat therapy
bestreuen powder, sprinkle
Besuch visit
besuchen visit
Besucher visitor
Besucherbalkon observation platform
Besucherkarte visitors' card
Besuchervisum visitors' visa
Besuchszeiten visiting hours
beteiligen, sich participate
Beteiligung investment, participation
Beteiligung, stille silent partnership
Beteiligungsgesellschaft investee company
Beteiligungsunternehmen, nichtkonsolidiertes nonconsolidated subsidiary
betonen emphasize
Betrag amount
Betrag, aufgelaufener accumulated amount
betragen amount
betreten enter
Betreuung care
Betreuung, persönliche individual care
Betrieb business, company, organization
betrieblicher Mittagstisch food service
Betriebs- und Gewerbesteuer (Service Center 14) business and occupation taxes (schedule 14)

Betriebsbesichtigung field trip
Betriebserweiterung increase in capacity, capacity increase
Betriebsferien staff holiday
betriebsfertig ready for use
Betriebsfunktion activity
Betriebsführung management, top management
Betriebsführung, wissenschaftliche scientific management
Betriebsklima working climate
Betriebskosten, laufende current operating expenses
Betriebskreislauf operating cycle
Betriebsmittel working fund
Betriebsordnung company policy
Betriebsrat labor committee
Betriebsschluß closing hour
Betriebsstätte outlet
Betriebsstoffe operating supplies
Betriebssystem operating system
Betriebsübersicht work sheet
Betriebsvereinbarung company policy
Betriebsverlust operating loss
Betriebszeit hours of service, operating months
Betriebszugehörigkeit company seniority
Betrug betrayal
betrügen betray
Bett bed, berth, sleeping-berth
Bettcouch studio couch, bed-couch, divan
Bettüberzug bedspread
Bettvorleger bedside rug
Bettwäsche bed-linen
Bettzeug bedding
Bett, Französisches french bed
Beute quarry
bevollmächtigen authorize
Bevollmächtiger representative
bevorraten keep in stock
bevorschussen advance
bevorzugen prefer
bevorzugt favourite
Bevölkerung population
Bevölkerungsdichte population density
Bewachung guard

bewandert experienced
bewegen move
beweglich movable
Bewegungsstudie motion study
Beweis proof
Bewerber applicant
Bewerbung application, employment application
Bewerbungsbogen application form
bewerten evaluate, value, appraise
Bewertung appraisal, evaluation, valuation
Bewertung des Umlaufvermögens valuation of current assets
Bewertung des Vorratsvermögens valuation of inventory
bewiesen proven
Bewilligung grant
bewirten cater for
bewirten, festlich feast
Bewirtung entertainment
Bewirtungsspesen entertainment expense
Bewohner resident
bewölkt cloudy
bezahlen pay
Bezahlung payment
bezeichnen describe
bezeichnend significant
Bezeichnung description
beziehen auf, sich refer
Beziehung relation
Beziehungen, zwischenmenschliche human relations
Bezirk area, district
Bezugnahme reference
bezugsfertig ready for occupancy
bezweifeln doubt
Bibliothek library
Bidet bidet
Bier beer
Bier vom Faß beer on tap, beer on draft, beer on draught
Bier (Lager-) lager
Bier, deutsches helles (dunkles) German light (dark) beer
Bier, dunkles dark beer, porter
Bier, dunkles (schwächeres) stout beer
Bier, englisches ale (pale ale)
Bier, helles light beer, pale ale

Bier, offenes beer on tap, beer on draft, beer on draught
Bierausschank ale-house, beer-shop
Bierfest beer festival
Biergarten beer-garden
Bierkeller beer-cellar
Bierkrug (in Form eines Mannes) toby jug
Bierlokal public house
Bierstube beer saloon, taproom
bieten bid
Bilanz balance, statement of financial position, balance sheet
Bilanz, konsolidierte consolidated balance sheet
Bilanzansatz balance sheet value
Bilanzfrisur window dressing
Bilanzgewinn unappropriated surplus, unappropriated retained earnings
Bilanzgewinnentwicklungsrechnung statement of retained earnings
Bilanzgleichung balance sheet equation
Bilanzierung financial accounting
Bilanzierungsgrundsätze accounting principles
Bilanzierungszeitraum balance sheet period
Bilanzkennzahlen balance sheet ratios
Bilanzposition balance sheet item
Bilanzstichtag balance (sheet) date
Bilanzvermerk parenthetical disclosure
Bilanzwert balance sheet value
Bildprospekt illustrated booklet
Bildschirm screen
Bildungsaufenthalt educational stay
Bildungsreise educational tour
Bildungsurlaub educational holiday, sabbatical leave
Billardzimmer billiard-room
Billett ticket
billig cheap, inexpensive, low-priced, reasonable
billigen approve, authorize
Bindeglied link
bindend obligatory
Binnenflugverkehr domestic air traffic

Binnenhafen inland harbour, river port
Binnenland interior
Binnenschiffahrt inland navigation
Binnentarif internal tariff
Binnenverkehr inland carriage
Birchermüsli Swiss porridge with fresh fruit
Birkhahn heath-cock, black-cock
Birkhenne heath-hen, moor-hen
Birkhuhn black grouse
Birne pear
bis heute up-to-date
Biskotten lady finger cake
Biskuit mit Weinschaum biscuit in wine sauce
Biskuittorte fancy-cake of biscuit
Bismarckhering marinated herring, soused herring
Bitte request
Bitte anschnallen! fasten seat belts
Bitte nicht berühren! please do not touch
Bitte nicht stören! do not disturb
bitten request
bitten um ask for
bitter bitter
Blankofahrschein blank ticket
Bläßhuhn water hen
Blatt leaf, sheet
Blätterteig puff-paste
Blätterteiggebäck puff pastry
Blätterteigpastetchen patty, puff-paste patty
Blätterteigpastete filled puff pastry, large patty, large puff-paste pie, vol-au-vent
Blätterteigpastete mit Geflügelfüllung large puff-paste pie stuffed with chicken and mushrooms
Blätterteigstengelchen puff-paste stick
Blaupause blue print
Bleibegast (Gast, der seinen Aufenthalt verlängert) stay over
bleiben, am Apparat (Telefon) hold on, hold the line
bleiben, auf dem laufenden keep up to date
Blick look, view

Blick auf overlooking
blicken look
Blickfang eye appeal
Blitz lightning
Blitzlichtbirne flash cube
Blumenhändler florist
Blumenkohl cauliflower
Blumenkohl gratiniert cauliflower browned
Blumenkohlcremesuppe cream of cauliflower
Blumenkohlsalat cauliflower salad
Blumenkohlsuppe cauliflower soup
Blumenladen flower shop
Blumenschale jardiniere
Blumenstand flower stand
Blumenständer jardiniere
Blumenstrauß bunch of flowers (bouquet)
blutig gebraten rare, underdone
Blutübertragung blood transfusion
Blutvergiftung blood poisoning
Blutwurst black pudding
Bob bob
Bobbahn bob run
Bobschlitten bobsled
Bobsport bobsledding
Boccia-Bahn boccie-court
Boden ground
Bodenrenke blue char
Bodensatz sediment
Bodenschätze natural resources
Bodenseefelchen felchen from Lake Constance
Bodenstewardeß ground hostess
Bö gust
Bogenschießen archery
Bohne bean
Bohne, dicke broad bean
Bohne, grüne flageolet, French bean, green bean, haricot bean, runner bean
Bohne, rote red bean
Bohne, weiße white bean
Bohneneintopf, brasilianischer Brazilian bean-stew
Bohnenkaffee, gemahlener ground coffee
Bohnenpüree puree of beans
Bohnensalat, grüner French beans salad

Bohnensuppe haricot soup, soup with white beans
Bohnensuppe, weiße white bean-soup
Bon coupon
Bonität credit standing
Boom boom
Boot boat
Bootfahren boating
Bootsanhänger (Auto) boat trailer
Bootsdeck boat deck
Bootsfahrt boat-ride, boat trip, row
Bootshaus boat-house
Bootssteg landing-stage
Bootsverleih boat-hire
Bord (Schiff) board
Bord, an on board
Bordausweis boarding pass (card)
Bordbuch log-book
Bordeauxwein claret
Bordfest festivity on board (ship)
Bordkarte boarding pass (card)
Bordmechaniker flight engineer
Bordpersonal crew
Bordspiel ship game, deck game
Bordzeitung ship's newspaper
Botanischer Garten Botanical Garden
Botengang errand
Botschaft message
Botschaft (Diplomatie) embassy
Bouillon broth, clear soup, hot broth
Bouillon mit Ei beef broth with egg
Bouillon mit gebackenen Erbsen soup with fried peas
Boutique boutique
Bowle claret-cup, wine soup, cold punch
Bowling bowling
Branchentelefonbuch classified telephone directory
Brandschutzbestimmungen fire regulations
Brandung surf
Brandungsreiten surf-riding
brasilianischer Bohneneintopf Brazilian bean-stew
Brasse sea-bream
braten fry
braten, auf dem Rost barbecue
braten, zu stark overcook

Braten joint, roast
Bratenplatte platter
Bratensoße gravy
Brathähnchen roast chicken
Brathuhn roast chicken
Brathühnchen broiler
Bratkartoffeln fried potatoes, sauté potatoes
Bratkartoffeln mit Zwiebeln butterfried potatoes with onions
Bratofen oven
Bratpfanne frying-pan, skillet
Bratwurst butterfried sausage, pan fried pork sausage, roast sausage
Bratwürstchen fried sausage
Bratwürstchen mit Sauerkraut grilled sausages with sauerkraut
Brauch custom, usage
brauchbar usable
Bräuche manners
brauchen require
Brauchtum folklore
Brauerei brewery
bräunen bask
Braunschweiger Wurst Brunswick sausage
Brause pop
Brause (Dusche) shower
Brauselimonade fizzed lemonade
Brechbohne, junge string bean
Brechreiz nausea
Brei mash, pap
breiig pappy
Breite width
Breitling whitebait
Brennöl kerosene
Brennpunkt focus
Bretzel pretzel
Briefkasten letter-box, mailbox
Brieflocher letter punch
Briefmarke postal stamp, stamp
Briefmarkenautomat stamp machine
Briefordner letter file
Briefpapier letter-paper, note-paper
Brieftasche wallet
Briefträger mailman (USA), postman
Briefumschlag envelope
Briefversand letter service
Briefwechsel correspondence
Brise breeze
Britischer Hotel- und Gaststättenverband British Hotels and Restaurants Association
brodeln lassen simmer
Brokkoli brokkoli
Brombeere blackberry, brambleberry
Broschüre booklet, brochure, pamphlet
Brot bread
Brot, altbackenes stale bread
Brot, belegtes sandwich
Brot, belegtes einfaches open sandwich
Brot, dunkles brown bread
Brot geröstet mit heißem Käse Welsh rabbit (rarebit)
Brot und Butter bread and butter
Brotkorb bread-basket
Brotlaib loaf of bread
Brotpudding bread and butter pudding
Brotscheiben hart geröstet Melbatoast
Brotschnitte geröstet und garniert canape
Brotzeit elevenses, midmorning snack
Brötchen bun, roll
Bruch (Geschirr) breakage
Bruchlandung crash landing
Brunch brunch
Brunnen fountain, spring
Brunnenkresse nasturtium
Brunnenkur treatment at a spa
Brust breast
Bruststreifen vom Huhn strips of chicken breast
Brust, Bruststück (Küche) brisket
brutto gross
Bruttoergebnis (Gewinn oder Verlust) (Umsatzbereich 2) gross profit (loss) (schedule 2)
Bruttogewicht gross weight
Bruttogewinn gross profit
Brücke bridge
Brückenzoll bridge toll
brühen scald
Buch book
buchen book, enter, make an entry reserve
Buchführung accounting, audit, bookkeeping

Buchführung mit Abgrenzungen, periodengerechte accrual basis of accounting
Buchführungsfehler bookkeeping error
Buchhalter accountant, bookkeeper
Buchhaltungsbeleg bookkeeping voucher
Buchhaltung, doppelte bookkeeping by double entry
Buchhaltung, einfache bookeeping by single entry
Buchhändler bookseller
Buchhandlung bookshop
Buchprüfer auditor
Büchsenfleisch tinned meat
Büchsenöffner tin opener
Bucht bay
Buchung booking, entry, bookkeeping entry
Buchung, garantierte guaranteed payment reservation (guaranteed booking)
Buchungssatz, zusammengesetzter compound entry
Buchweizen buckwheat
Buchwert carrying value, book value
Bückling bloater, kipper
Büffet refreshment bar
Büffetier bartender, barman
Büffetkellner bartender
Büffetmädchen barmaid
Büffetwagen (Eisenbahn) buffet car
Bug bow
Bügel- und Reinigungsdienst und Verkauf von Herrenbekleidung (Umsatzbereich 6) valet (schedule 6)
Bügelbrett ironing-board
bügelfrei drip-dry
Bügelservice pressing service
Büglerei ironing service, pressing service
Bühne stage
Bühnenfestspiele theatre festival
Bullauge porthole
Bummel stroll
Bummelzug accomodation train, slow train
Bündel bunch

Bundesrepublik Deutschland Federal Republic of Germany
Bundesstaat state
Bündner Fleisch air-cured beef of the Grisons
Bungalow bungalow
Bungalowdorf bungalow village
Burg castle, fortress, stronghold
bürgen (für jds. Schulden) guarantee somebody's debt
Bürger citizen
Bürgermeister mayor
Bürgersteig footpath, pavement, sidewalk
Bürgschaft contract of guarantee
Bürgschaftsrisiko risk under guarantee
Burgruine castle ruins
Burgunderwein Burgundy wine
Büro office
Büroangestellter clerk, white collar worker
Büroarbeit paper work
Büroausstattung office equipment
Bürobedarf stationery
Büromaterial office supplies
Büromobiliar, -einbauten und -maschinen office furniture, fixtures, and equipment
Bürste brush
Bus bus, coach, motor coach
Busanhänger bus trailer
Busbahnhof bus and coach station, bus station
Busfahrer bus driver, coach driver
Busfahrt bus trip
Bushaltestelle bus stop, coach stop
Buslinie bus line, coach line
Busreise bus trip
Busreisen bus travel, coach travel
Busschaffner bus conductor, coach conductor
Busunternehmen bus company
Busverbindung bus connection, bus line, coach connection, coach line
Busvermietung bus hire
Butter butter
Butter, braune nut butter
Butter, gebrannte burnt butter
Butter, in cooked in butter
Butter, zerlassene melted butter

Butterbrot buttered slice of bread
Buttermilch buttermilk

C

Café café
campen camp
Camper camper
Campingausrüstung camping equipment
Campingausweis camping permit
Campingbus motor caravan
Campingplatz camping ground
Campingplatz, bewachter guarded camping site
Campingplatz, voll eingerichtet camping site, offering full facilities
Campingtourismus camping tourism
Campingtourist camper
Canneloni canneloni
Caravaner trailtourist
Caerphilly-Käse Caerphilly cheese
Cayennepfeffer Cayenne pepper
Champagner champagne
Champignonomelett omelet with mushrooms
Champignons gebacken fried button mushrooms
charakterisieren feature
Charterflug charter flight
Chartermaschine charter aircraft
chartern charter
Chateaubriand Chataubriand
Chaudeau sabayon
Checkliste check list
Cheddarkäse Cheddar cheese
Chef de rang assistant headwaiter
Chefkoch chef
Chefsekretärin executive secretary
Chefsteward chief steward
Chesterkäse Cheshire cheese
Chinakohl chinese cabbage
Chip (Elektronik) chip
Cocktail cocktail
Cocktailempfang cocktail reception
Cognacschwenker brandyglass
Computer computer
Concierge concierge
Container container
Containerzug freightliner train

Cordon bleu cheese and ham stuffed veal steak
Cornflakes cornflakes
Couch couch
Couchtisch club table
Couvert cover
Creme (Speise) mousse
Cremeschnitte cream slice
Cremespeise mousse
Cremetorte fancy-cake with cream
Cremetörtchen mit Johannisbeergelee red currant-tartlets
Creme, bayrische molded cream
Creme, bayrische gestürzte Bavarian cream
Cumberlandsoße Cumberland sauce
Curling curling
Curry curry
Currypulver curry powder

D

D-Zug express train
Dachgarage roof garage
Dachgarten roof-garden
Dachkammer attic, garret
Dachwohnung penthouse
Damenfriseur ladies' hairdresser
Damentoilette ladies' lavatory, ladies' room
Damenwahl ladies' choice
Damen(toilette) Ladies
Damhirsch fallow-deer
Damm dike, embankment
Dämmerung dawn
Dampfbad Russian bath, vapour bath
Dampfbügeln steam-ironing
Dampfer steamer, steamship
Dampfkartoffeln steamed potatoes
Dampfnudeln steamed noodles with vanilla-cream
Darstellungsform format
darübergießen pour over
Daten, historische historical data
Datenbank data bank
Datenbankanbieter host
Datenendstation terminal
Datenverarbeitung data processing
datieren date

Dattel date
Dattelmuschel piddock
Datum date
Dauer duration
Dauerabonnement season ticket
Dauerausweis all-year round admission ticket
Dauergast permanent resident
Dauerkarte commutation ticket
Dauerlauf jogging
dauernd permanent
Dauerwurst hard sausage
Daunendecke eider-down
Debitoren accounts receivable
Deck deck
Deckel lid
Deckelkrug tankard
decken secure
Deckoffizier warrant officer
Deckplatz place on deck
Decksteward deck steward
Deflation deflation
Deich dike
Dekoration decorations
delegieren delegate
Denkmal memorial, monument
Denkmalspflege preservation of monuments
denkwürdig (Hotelaufenthalt) memorable (stay)
Dependance annex
deponieren deposit
Depositenzertifikat certificate of deposit
Derby-Käse Derby cheese
des Pudels Kern heart of the matter
Dessert dessert, sweet dish
Dessertwein dessert wine
destillieren distil
deutlich distinct
Deutsche Bundesbahn (DB) German Federal Railways
Deutsche Schlaf- und Speisewagengesellschaft (DSG) Dining Car Company
Deutsche Zentrale für Fremdenverkehr Central Office of German Travel
Deutscher Camping Club (DCC) German Camping Club

Deutscher Fremdenverkehrsverband German Tourist Association
Deutscher Hotel- und Gaststättenverband German Hotel and Catering Association
Devise (Geld) foreign currency, foreign exchange
Devisenbestimmungen currency regulations
Devisenbewirtschaftung currency control, currency restrictions, exchange control
Devisenfreigrenze currency allowance
Devisenkontrolle currency control, exchange control, foreign currency control
Devisenkurs rate of exchange
Devisenvorschriften currency regulations, exchange regulations
Devisenzuteilung allocation of foreign exchange
Diagramm chart
Diapositiv slide, transparency
Diät diet
Diätkost diet, dietary cooking, dietary foods
Diätkur diet cure, dietic treatment
Diätküche dietary cooking, diet kitchen
Diätnahrung dietary foods
Diätplan diet plan
dicht dabei near at hand
Dickmilch curds and whey
Diebstahl pilferage, theft
Diebstahlversicherung theft insurance
dienen serve
dienlich appropriate
Dienst duty, service
Dienstalter length of service
Dienstalter (im Betrieb) company seniority
Dienstanweisung working instructions
Dienstanweisungs-Handbuch instruction manual
Dienstleistung service
Dienstleistungen, sonstige other catering operations

Dienstleistungsgewerbe 34

Dienstleistungsgewerbe service trade
Dienstmädchen maid
Dienstplan, gestaffelter staggering scheduling
Dienstprogramm service program, utility program
dienstunfähig (dauernd) disabled
Dienstvertrag employment contract
Differenz difference
Differenzierung diversification
diktieren dictate
Dill dill
Diner dinner
Diner mit Show dinner with floor show
Diner, förmliches (festliches) formal dinner
Direktflug through flight
Direktionsvertreter während der Nacht night manager
Direktor manager
Direktor (oder leitender Angestellter) einer AG corporate executive
Direktor, stellvertretender executive assistant manager
Direktverbindung through connection
Direktwerbung direct mail advertising
Disagio disagio, discount, mark down
Disagio bei Ausgabe von Schuldverschreibungen bond discount
Diskette diskette
Diversifikation diversification
Dividende, kumulative cumulative dividend
Dividende genehmigen declare a dividend
Dividendenausschüttung distribution of income, distribution of the dividend
Dividendenertrag dividend yield
Dobostorte fancy-cake with caramel
Docht wick
Dom cathedral
donnern thunder
Doppelbett double bed
Doppellendenstück double tenderloin

Doppelzimmer double-room, twin-bedded room
Doppelzimmer mit einem großen Bett double
Doppelzimmer mit zwei großen Betten twin double
Dorf village
Dorfgasthaus country inn, village inn, wayside inn
Dorfschenke country pub, village pub
Dörrpflaume prune
Dorsch cod
Dosenbier canned beer, tinned beer
Drachenfisch dragon fish
Drahtseilbahn aerial railway
Dreibettabteil three-berth compartment
Dreibettkabine three-berth room
Dreibettzimmer triple room, three-bed room
dreifach triplicate
Dreimeilenzone three-mile zone
Dreiminutenei three-minute egg
dringen auf insist (on, upon)
dringend urgent
Drink drink
Drogist druggist
Druck pressure
Druck- und Büromaterial printing and stationery
drucken print
Drucker printer
Drucksache printed matter
Duft odour
Dumping dumping
Dunkelheit darkness
dunstig hazy
durchdrehen mince
Durcheinander mess
Durchfahrt passage
durchführbar feasible
Durchführbarkeit feasibility
durchführen accomplish
Durchgang pass
Durchgangsland transit country
Durchgangsreisender through passenger
Durchgangsstraße thoroughfare
Durchgangsverkehr through traffic, transit traffic

durchgebraten well done
durchgehend geöffnet permanently open, open all day
Durchreisender chance guest, temporary hotel guest, transient guest
Durchreisevisum transit visa
Durchschnitt average
durchsehen revise
durchseihen strain
durchsuchen search
durchwandern perambulate
Durchwanderung perambulation
Durst thirst
durstig thirsty
Duschanlage showers
Dusche shower, shower-bath
Dusche, medizinische douche
Duschkabine shower-bath cubicle
Duschnische shower stall
Duschraum shower-room
Dutzend dozen (doz.)
Düne dune
Dünnbier near beer
Düsenflugzeug jet, jet plane
Düsenmaschine jet
Düsentriebwerk jet propulsion unit
Düsenverkehrsflugzeug jet liner

E

Eberfleisch brawn
Echtzeit real time
Eckplatz corner seat
Edamer Käse Dutch cheese, Edam cheese
Edelkastanie chestnut
Edelpilz mushroom
Ehefrau wife
Eheleute couple, spouses
Ehemann husband
eher (als) prior to
Ehrenmal cenotaph
ehrlich honest, sincere
Ei egg
Ei (hart und in Teig eingehüllt) Scotch egg
Ei, hartgekochtes hard-boiled egg
Ei, verlorenes poached egg
Ei, verlorenes auf Toast poached egg on toast

Ei, weichgekochtes soft boiled egg
Eiche oak
Eidotter yolk
Eier gefüllt stuffed eggs
Eier im Glas eggs in a glass
Eier im Näpfchen eggs in cocotte
Eier in Öl gebacken deep-fried eggs
Eier mit Speck bacon and eggs
Eierbecher egg-cup
Eierbrot egg sandwich
Eierfrucht egg-plant
Eiergerichte egg-dishes
Eiersalat egg-salad
Eiersandwich egg sandwich
Eierteig gebacken Yorkshire pudding
eifrig zealous
Eigelb egg yolk, yolk
Eigendeckung self insurance
Eigendünkel self-esteem
Eigenkapital owner's equity, stockholder's equity, net worth
Eigenkapitalausweis statement of owner's equity
Eigenkapitalentwicklung (von Personenunternehmen) statement of partners' equity
Eigenkapitalspiegel statement of stockholders' equity
Eigentum ownership, property
Eigentumsrecht property right
Eigentümer owner
Eigentümergesellschaft owning company
Eigenverbrauch own consumption
Eignung qualification
Eilauftrag rush order
Eile haste, rush
Eilgüterzug fast freight train
Eimer bucket
Ein-Zimmer-Suite junior suite
einarmiger Bandit (Spielautomat) one-armed bandit
Einbahnstraße one-way street
Einbaukosten installation cost
Einbauschrank built-in cupboard (wardrobe)
Einbauten (oder Ausbauten) in gemieteten Räumen leasehold improvements

Einbettabteil single-berth compartment
Einbettzimmer single bedroom, single room
einbeziehen involve
Einbrecher burglar
einbringen yield
Einbringung contribution
Einbruch burglary
Einbruchsversicherung burglary insurance
einbüßen lose
einfach plain, simple, single
einfach (Vorgang) straightforward (process)
Einfahrt driveway, entrance
Einfahrt verboten! no entry
einfetten grease
Einflugschneise air corridor
Einfluß influence
Einfuhrbeschränkung import restriction
Einfuhrgenehmigung import license
Einfuhrhandel import trade
Einfuhrzoll import duty
einfühlend empatic
Einfühlungsvermögen empathy
Einfühlungsvermögen zeigen empathize
einführen implement, introduce
einführen (Außenhandel) import
Einführung (Amt) introduction
Einführungsschulung introduction training, orientation training
Einführungswerbung initial advertising
Eingabe input
Eingabeaufforderung prompt
Eingang entrance, entry, input
Eingangsmeldung receiving report
eingeboren native
eingedickt jellied
Eingemachtes preserves
eingeschneit snow-bound, snowed up
eingeschränkt restricted
eingleisig single track
einheimisch national, native
Einheimischer native
Einheit unit
einheitlich uniform
Einheitsklasse standard class
Einheitspreis flat price
einholen overtake
Einkauf, zentraler central buying
einkaufen buy, purchase, shopping
Einkäufer buyer, purchasing agent
Einkaufsabteilung purchasing department
Einkaufspolitik purchasing policy
Einkaufspreis cost price
Einkaufsrichtlinien purchasing specifications
Einkaufsverfahren purchasing procedure
Einkaufszentrum shopping center
Einkommen earnings, income, revenue
Einkommensteuer income tax
einladen invite
Einladung invitation
Einladungsbrief letter of invitation
Einlage deposit
Einlagen investments by owners
Einlagen, ausstehende capital not paid-in
Einlagenzertifikat certificate of deposit
Einlaß admission
Einlaufsuppe clear soup with beaten egg
einlösen cash
einmachen pot
Einmannbetrieb one-man operation
einmischen interfere
Einnahme receipts
einordnen rank
einordnen, sich get in lane
Einreise entry, entry into the country
Einreisegenehmigung entry permit
einreisen (in ein Land) enter a country
Einreisevisum entry visa
einrichten organize
Einrichtung equipment, facility, feature, organization
Einrichtungsgegenstände furniture and fixtures
Einrichtungsplanung facilities planning
Eins-A-Hotel high-class hotel

Einsatz input
einschalten turn on
einschiffen embark
Einschiffung embarkation
einschließen include, involve
einschließlich inclusive
einschließlich Bedienung und Abgaben inclusive of service and taxes
Einschränkung limitation, restriction
Einschreibebrief registered letter
einschreiben register
Einsicht understanding
Einspänner black coffee with whipped cream
Einstandspreis cost price
einstecken plug
Einsteigekarte boarding pass (card)
einsteigen get in
Einsteigen! all aboard
Einstellung attitude
Einstellung der Arbeitnehmer zum Betrieb employee attitude
Einstellungspolitik hiring policy
Einstellungsverfahren hiring procedure
einstufen classify
Einstufung classification
einstweilig interim
eintauchen dip
einteilen part
Eintopfgericht hot-pot
Eintopfsuppe soup with egg dough drops
eintragen enroll, enter, record, register
einträglich advantageous, lucrative
Eintragung enrollment, entry, record, registration
eintreten enter, join
eintreten ohne anzuklopfen enter without knocking
Eintritt entry
Eintritt frei! admission free
Eintritt verboten! keep out, no entry
Eintrittsgelder (Umsatzbereich 2) cover charges (schedule 2)
Eintrittskarte admission card, admission ticket, ticket of admission
einverstanden sein agree with
Einverständnis accord

Einwanderer immigrant
Einwanderung immigration
einweichen soak
einwilligen approve
Einwilligung approval
Einwirkung impact
Einwohner inhabitant, resident
einzahlen deposit
Einzahlung deposit
Einzahlungen in einen Tilgungsfonds sinking fund payments
Einzelangaben particulars
Einzelbad private bath
Einzelflugpauschale inclusive single fare
Einzelkabine single cabin, single room
Einzelkaufmann proprietorship
einzeln individual
Einzelpauschalreise individual inclusive journey
Einzelreise individual journey
Einzelreisender individual traveller, single passenger, single tourist
Einzelrückfahrt individual return
Einzelzimmer single, single room
Einzelzimmerzuschlag single room supplement
einziehen confiscate
Einziehung von Außenständen collection of outstanding debts
Einziehung (Geld) collection
Einziehungskosten collection expenses
Einzimmerappartement one-room flat
Eis ice
Eis, gemischtes mixed ice, mixed-ice-cream
Eis, halbgefrorenes parfait
Eisauflauf ice-cream soufflé
Eisbaiser ice-cream meringue
Eisbecher coupe, ice-cream cup, ice-cream sundae, sundae
Eisbecher mit heißer Schokoladensoße ice-cream cup with hot chocolate sauce
eisbedeckt ice-coated
Eisbein pickled pork, pickled shank of pork, pickled pork trotters,

Eisdiele   38

salted pig's knuckle, salted pig's trotter
Eisdiele ice-bar, ice-cream parlour, ice-parlour
Eisenbahn railroad, railway
Eisenbahnendstation railway terminus
Eisenbahnfähre train ferry
Eisenbahnfahrkarte rail ticket, railway ticket
Eisenbahnfahrplan railroad schedule, railway timetable
Eisenbahngütertransport rail transport
Eisenbahnknotenpunkt railway junction
Eisenbahnnetz railway system
Eisenbahntarif railway rates
Eisenbahnübergang railroad grade crossing
Eisenbahnverkehr rail traffic, railway traffic
Eisenbahnwagen railroad car, railway carriage, railway coach, waggon
eisfrei free from ice, ice-free
eisgekühlt iced
Eishalle skating-rink
Eishockey ice-hockey
eisig icy
Eiskaffee coffee ice-cream, ice-cream coffee
Eiskunstlauf figure skating
Eiskübel bucket, ice-pail
Eislauf ice-skating, skating
Eislaufen ice-skating, skating
eislaufen skate
Eisläufer skater
Eismaschine ice machine
Eismeringe ice-cream meringue
Eisomelett baked Alaska
Eisschnellauf speed skating
Eisschnitte brick of ice-cream
Eisschokolade iced chocolate
Eisschrank ice-box
Eissegeln ice-yachting
Eisstadion ice stadium
Eistee iced tea
Eistorte ice-cream cake
Eistüte ice-cone
Eisverkäufer ice man

Eiswaffel ice-cream wafer
Eiswasser ice water
Eiswürfel ice-cube
Eiszapfen icicle
elegant elegant, fashionable
Elektriker electrician
elektronische Datenverarbeitung einsetzen computerize
Elektronische Datenverarbeitung (EDV) Electronic Data Processing (EDP)
Elektrotherapie electrotherapy
Elimination elimination
eliminieren eliminate
Embargo embargo
Emissionsbank underwriter
Emissionsübernahme underwriting
emittieren issue
Empfang reception
Empfänger addressee, recipient, endorsee
Empfangsabteilung front office department
Empfangsbestätigung receipt
Empfangsbüro reception office
Empfangschef front office manager
Empfangsdame receptionist, room clerk
Empfangshalle lobby, reception hall
Empfangsherr desk clark, receptionist, room clerk
Empfangspersonal front office staff
Empfangspult front desk, reception desk
Empfangssekretär reception clerk
empfehlen recommend
Empfehlung recommendation
Empfehlungsbrief letter of recommendation
empfindlich queasy, sensitive
Empfindlichkeit responsiveness
endgültig definite, final
Endhaltestelle terminal point
Endivie endive
Endiviensalat endive salad
Endstation terminal, terminal point, terminus
Endtermin final day
Endwert accumulated amount
Energiekosten (Service Center 13) energy costs (schedule 13)

Energieversorgung power supply
eng narrow
englischer Cocktail Gin and It
englischer Kuchen sultana (fruit) cake
Engpaß bottleneck
Enlastungszug relief train
Entdeckung discovery
Entdeckungsfahrt exploration
Ente duck
Ente, junge duckling
Ente gebraten roast duck
entfernen remove
entfernt distant, far, remote
Entfernung distance
Entfernung (in Meilen) milage
Entfernungsmesser range finder
Entfernungstabelle table of distances
entgegengesetzt adverse, opposite
entlassen dismiss
entlassen, fristlos fire
Entlassung dismissal
Entlassungsinterview exit-interview
entlasten relieve
entleihen borrow
Entnahme (Bank) withdrawal
entnehmen withdraw
entschädigen compensate
Entschädigung compensation
entschärfen defuse
entscheiden decide, determine, rule
entscheidend crucial
Entscheidung decision, determination
Entschluß decision
entschuldbar excusable
entschuldigen excuse
entschuldigen, sich apologize
Entschuldigung apology, excuse
entspannen relax
Entspannungskur relaxation cure
entsprechen match
entsteinen stone
entwenden pilfer
entwerten depreciate
Entwicklung development
Entwicklung des Eigenkapitals statement of owner's equity
Entwicklungsland country in development
Entwicklungsrichtung tendency

entzündlich, leicht inflammable
erblicken view
Erbpacht leasehold
Erbse pea
Erbse, gelbe yellow pea
Erbse, grüne green pea
Erbsenpüree puree of peas, pea mash
Erbsensuppe pea soup
Erbsensuppe, grün cream of green pea soup
Erdbeere strawberry
Erdbeereis strawberry ice-cream
Erdgeschoß ground-floor
Erdnuß peanut
Erdnußbutter peanut butter
erfahren experience, experienced
Erfahrung experience
erfassen, gesondert (z. B. Strom) submeter
erfolglos inefficient
Erfolgskonto nominal account
Erfolgsplanung, langfristige long-range profit
erfordern require
Erfordernis requirement
erforschen explore
erfreuen, j-n please
erfrischend refreshing
erfrischt refreshed
Erfrischung refreshment
Erfrischungshalle soda fountain
Erfrischungskiosk refreshment stall
Erfrischungsraum refreshment bar, refreshment room
erfüllen fulfill, meet
erfüllend, noch zu executory
Erfüllung fulfilment
Erfüllungsort place of delivery, place of performance
ergänzen complete, add
Ergänzung supplement
Ergänzungsbehandlung supplementary treatment
ergeben submissive
Ergebnis result
Ergiebigkeitsgrad, relativer rate potential percentage
erhalten (bewahren) maintain
Erhaltung maintenance
Erhebung survey

Erhebungsbogen survey sheet
erholen relax, get well again, recover
erholsam refreshing, restful
Erholung convalescence, recovery, recreation, relaxation
Erholungsanlage recreational facility
Erholungsaufenthalt rest-cure
Erholungsgebiet recreational area
Erholungsheim convalescent home, rest-home
Erholungskur rest-cure
Erholungsmöglichkeit recreational facility
Erholungsort holiday resort
Erholungspark recreational park
Erholungspause rest pause
Erholungsprogramm recreation program
Erholungsreise convalescent trip
Erholungsurlaub convalescent leave, holiday leave, recreational holiday
Erholungszeit relaxation time
Erholungszentrum recreation centre
erhöhen increase, raise, rise, advance
Erhöhung increase, rise
erinnern remind
Erinnerung reminder
Erinnerungsposten pro memoria item
Erinnerungswerbung reminder advertising
erkennbar visible
erkennen identify
Erkennen recognition
erkennen recognize
erkennen, nicht ignore
Erklärung assurance, declaration, statement; solution
Erklärungstag (Tag, an dem der Vertragsentwurf für den Käufer bindend wird) option date
Erkrankung illness
Erkundigung enquiry
erlangen acquire
erlauben allow, permit
Erlaubnis permission, permit
Erläuterungen im Anhang explanation in the notes

erleben experience
erleichtern facilitate
Erleichterung facilitation, relief
ermächtigen enable
ermäßigen reduce
Ermäßigung reduction
Ermäßigung für Hausgäste reduction for hotel guests
Ermessen discretion
ermitteln ascertain
ermutigend reassuring
ermüden fatigue
ermüdet fatigued, weary
Ermüdung fatigue
ernähren feed, nourish
Ernährung nutrition
erneuern render a service, renew, renovate, revalidate
Erneuerung renewal, renovation
ernsthaft (Angelegenheit) serious (matter)
Ernte crop, harvest
Erntedankfest harvest thanksgiving, Thanksgiving Day
Eröffnung opening
erprobt experienced
erregen provoke
errichten erect
Ersatz compensation, substitute
Ersatzteil spare part
erscheinen appear
Erscheinen appearance
Erscheinung appearance
Erschließungskosten exploration expenses
erschöpft weary
Erschöpfung fatigue
ersetzen compensate, reimburse, replace, substitute
Erstaufführung first performance
erste Hilfe first aid
erste Kategorie first class catagory
erste Klasse first class
erste Klasse (Vermerk auf Flugscheinen) F (= First)
erste Wahl prime choice
Ersteklassetarif first class fares
Erstellung (von Jahresabschlüssen) compilation
erster Rang (Theater) dresscircle
erstklassig first class, prime

erstreben solicit
Ertrag income, revenue, yield
Ertragssteuer income tax
Ertragssteuern, latente deferred income tax
erwachsen adult
Erwachsener adult, grown-up
erwärmen warm
erwarten await, expect
Erwartung expectation
erweitern expand, extend
Erweiterung expansion, extension
erwerben buy, purchase, acquire
Erzeugnis product
Erzeugnisse, fertige finished goods
Erzeugnisse, unfertige work in process
erziehen educate
Esel donkey
Espresso espresso coffee
Espressobar espresso bar
essen eat
Essen meal
Essen à la carte meals à la carte
Essen kostenlos ausgeben furnished meal without charge
Essenabonnement luncheon voucher arrangement, meal ticket arrangement
Essenbon luncheon voucher
Essengutschein luncheon voucher, meal ticket
Essensbon meal ticket
Essensgedeckeanzahl number of food covers
Essenszeit meal-time
Eßgeschirr crockery
Essig vinegar
Essig- und Ölständer cruetstand
Essiggemüse mixed pickles
Essiggemüse scharf gewürzt piccalilli
Essiggurke gherkin, pickle
Essigsoße (zum Einlegen) pickle, vinaigrette
Essigsoße, grüne green vinegar sauce
Eßlokal eating-place
Eßlöffel table-spoon
Eßzimmer dining-room
Estragon tarragon

Etage floor
Etagenbad public bath-room
Etagenbeschließerin floor housekeeper
Etagendiener floor houseman, valet
Etagengouvernante floor housekeeper
Etagenhausdame floor housekeeper
Etagenhausdiener floor houseman
Etagenkellner floor waiter, room service waiter
Etagenoberkellner room service headwaiter
Etagenpersonal floor staff
Etagenservice room service
Etikett label
Etikette tag
etikettieren label
EU-Richtlinie EC directive
Eventualverbindlichkeit contingent liability
Exkursion outing, study trip
expandieren expand
Expansion expansion
Expedient shipping clerk
Export export
exportieren export
Express express
extra extra
Extrakellner extra waiter

F

Fachkenntnis skill
Fachmesse trade fair
Fachwerkhaus half-timbered house
Fachwissen job knowledge, knowhow
fade insipid, tasteless
Fadennudeln vermicelli
fähig capable
Fähigkeit ability, capability, capacity, skill
Fahrbahn carriageway, roadway
Fahrbahn, einspurige single file traffic
Fahrbahn, zweispurige dual carriageway
Fahrdamm roadway
Fähre ferry, ferry-boat

fahren (Auto) drive, go by car
Fahrgast fare, passenger
Fahrgäste aussteigen lassen set down passengers
Fahrgeld fare
Fahrgestell (Flugzeug) landing-gear
Fahrkarte ticket
Fahrkarte, einfache single ticket
Fahrkarte, ermäßigte cheap ticket, reduced-fare ticket
Fahrkarte zum halben Preis half-fare ticket
Fahrkarte zum vollen Preis general-tariff ticket
Fahrkartenausgabe booking office
Fahrkartenautomat automatic ticket machine, ticket machine
Fahrkartenschalter booking office, ticket office, ticket office window
Fahrkilometer voyage distance
fahrlässig careless
Fahrlässigkeit carelessness
Fährmann ferryman
Fahrplan schedule, timetable
Fahrplan (Ankünfte-Abreisen) arrivals and departures table
fahrplanmäßig regular, scheduled
fahrplanmäßig fahren run at regular times
Fahrpreis fare
Fahrpreisermäßigung fare reduction, reduced fare
Fahrpreisermäßigung für Reisegesellschaften reduced fares for tourist groups, fare reduction for tourist parties
Fahrrad bicycle
Fahrradausflug bicycle excursion
Fahrradständer cycle-stand
Fahrradvermietung bicycle hire
Fahrradweg cycle path
Fahrrinne navigation channel
Fahrschein ticket
Fahrscheinheft booklet of coupons (tickets)
Fahrscheinkontrolle ticket inspection
Fahrspur lane
Fahrstuhl elevator, lift
Fahrstuhlführer elevator boy, lift-boy

Fahrt journey, sailing, trip, voyage
Fahrt, auf der en route
Fahrt ins Blaue mystery tour
Fahrtkosten car fare
Fahrtroute itinerary
Fahrtunterbrechung break of journey, intermediate stop
Fahrverkehr vehicle traffic
Fahrzeit journey time, running time, travel time
Fahrzeug automobile, vehicle
fakultativ optional
fallen lassen drop
fallen, ins Auge eye catching
fällig due, payable
fällig werden fall due
Fälligkeitstermin maturity date
Falschbuchung irregular entry
Falscher Hase forcemeat roasted
Faltboot faltboat
Familienbad mixed bathing
Familienbetrieb family business, family run firm
Familieneinkommen family income
Familienferien family holiday, family vacation
Familienferienhotel family guesthouse
Familienferienort family holiday resort
Familienkarte family ticket
Familienname surname
Familienpaß joint passport
Familienpension family boarding house, residential hotel
Familienpreis (kostenlose Unterbringung von Kindern im Zimmer der Eltern) Family Plan
Familienstand family status, marital status, personal status
Familientourismus family tourism
Familienzulage family allowance
Fang catch
fangen catch
Fangobehandlung mud treatment
Fangopackung mud pack
Fangotherapie mud therapy
Farbabzug (Foto) colour print
Fasan pheasant
Fasan gebraten roast pheasant
Faschingsdienstag Shrove Tuesday

Faschingskrapfen carnival fritter
Faschingszeit carnival season
Faß barrel
Faßbier draught
Fäßchen keg
Faßhahn tap
Fassung (Lampe) socket
fast roh underdone
Fastenzeit Lent
Fastnacht carnival
Fastnachtsdienstag Mardigras
Fastnachtszeit Shrovetide
faul lazy
faul (verdorben) rotten
Fauna fauna
Fausthandschuh mitten
Federball shuttle cock
Federballspiel badminton
Federwild feathered game
Fehlbetrag deficit, deficiency, shortage
Fehlen absenteeism, miss
fehlend missing
Fehler defect, error, fault
Fehler aufdecken locate errors
fehlerhaft defective, faulty
fehlleiten misguide
Fehlstunden hours absent
feiern celebrate
Feiertag holiday
Feiertag, gesetzlicher legal holiday, public holiday
Feiertagslohn holiday pay
Feige fig
fein fine
Feinkosthändler provision dealer
Feinschmecker gourmet
Feinschmeckeressen gourmet's meal
Feinschmeckerrestaurant gourmet restaurant
Felchen white fish
Feldbett camp cot
Feldflasche water-bottle
Feldweg country lane, field path
Felsen rock
felsig rocky
Fenchel fennel
Fenster window
Fensterladen window shade
Fensterplatz window seat
Fensterputzer window cleaner
Fensterscheibe window pane, pane
Fenstertechnik windowing technique
Ferien machen take a holiday
Feriendorf holiday village
Ferienfahrkarte holiday ticket
Ferienflugpreis excursion fare
Ferienführer holiday guide
Feriengast holiday guest
Feriengebiet holiday region
Ferienhaus cottage, holiday house
Ferienhotel holiday hotel
Ferieninsel holiday island
Ferienkurs holiday course, summer school
Ferienlager holiday camp
Ferienland holiday country
Feriennetzkarte holiday runabout ticket, holiday season ticket, guest pass
Ferienordnung vacation schedule
Ferienort holiday resort
Ferienplakat travel poster
Ferienprogramm vacation program(me)
Ferienreise holiday trip
Feriensonderzug holiday train
Ferienstaffelung staggered holidays
Ferientag holiday
Ferienunterkunft holiday flat, vacation apartment
Ferienverkehr holiday traffic
Ferienwohnung holiday flat, vacation apartment
Ferienzeit holiday season
Ferkel porkling
Fernbleiben absenteeism
Fernblick distant view
Ferndurchwahl direct distance dialing
Fernfahrplan long-distance time-table
Ferngespräch long-distance call, trunk-call
Ferngespräch anmelden place a long-distance call
Fernglas binoculars, telescope
Fernlaster long-distance lorry
fernschnellzug limited express train, long-distance express
Fernschreiber teleprinter, teletype
Fernschreibercode teleprinter code

Fernschreibnetz telex
Fernsehapparat television set
Fernsehen television
Fernsehgerät television set
Fernsehraum television room
Fernsehturm television tower
Fernsprechamt telephone exchange, trunk exchange
Fernsprechzelle call-box, telephone booth, telephone box
Fernsprechzelle, öffentliche public call-room
Fernverkehr long-distance traffic
Fernverkehrsstraße arterial road, highway, trunk road
fertig ready
Fertigerzeugnis finished good, finished product
Fertiggericht ready-to-serve dish
Fertiggerichtsysteme convenience foods
fest fixed
Festausschuß festival committee
Festbeleuchtung festive illumination
festellen fix
Festessen anniversary dinner, banquet, gala dinner
festgelegt (festgesetzt) fixed
Festhalle banqueting hall, festival hall
festlegen fix
Festmahl feast
festnehmen arrest
Festpreis fixed price
Festsaal banqueting hall, banquet room, festival hall
festsetzen (Zahlungsmodus) establish (method of payment)
Festspiele festival
feststellen ascertain
Festtag anniversary
Festumzug pageant
Festung fortress, stronghold
Festvorstellung gala performance
Festwertspeicher read-only memory (rom)
Festwiese fair ground
Festwoche festival week
Festwochen festival
Festzelt fair-ground tent
Festzug festive procession
fett fat, fatty

Fett shortening, suet
Fett, tierisches animal fat
Fettgebackenes fritters
fettlos without fat
Fettpapier greaseproof paper
feucht damp, humid, moist
Feuchtigkeit humidity, moisture
Feuer fire
feuergefährlich inflammable
Feuerhaken poker
Feuerleiter fire escape
Feuerlöschbrause sprinkler
Feuerlöscher fire-extinguisher
Feuermelder fire-alarm
Feuerversicherung fire insurance
Feuerwehr fire-brigade, fire department
Feuerwerk fire-works
Feuerzeug cigarette lighter, lighter
Feuerzeugbenzin lighter fuel
Finanz- und Rechnungswesen (i.w.S.) financial accounting
Fieber fever, temperature
Fifo-Wert FIFO value
Figur figure
Filet fillet
Filet Wellington roast fillet of beef in puff-paste
Filetbraten in Rahmsoße fillet of beef in cream-sauce
Filetgulasch in Sauerrahmsoße beef Stroganoff
Filetsteak fillet-mignon
Filetsteak (Chateaubriand) Chateaubriand
Filetstück, kleines mignonette
Filialbetrieb chain
Filiale branch office
Film film
Film (Kino) movie
filmen film
Filmfestspiele film festival
Filmprogramm cinema program, movie program
Filmschauspieler film actor
Filmtheater movie theater
Filmvorführung movie performance
Filmvorstellung movie performance, movie show
Filterkaffee filter coffee
filtern (Kaffee etc.) percolate

Filterzigarette filter-tipped cigarette
Finanz-Leasingvertrag capital lease
Finanzanlagen financial assets
Finanzanlagevermögen financial assets
Finanzbuchhaltung financial accounting
Finanzhilfe financial aid
Finanzlage financial position
Finanzplan budget
Finderlohn finder's reward
Firmenbetreuung firm service
Firmenpreis commercial rate, company rate
Firmenwert goodwill
Firn firn
Firnschnee neve
First-class-Hotel first class hotel
Fisch fish
Fisch, marinierter pickled fish
Fisch gebraten mit Pommes frites fish and chips
Fisch in Öl gebacken deep-fried fish
Fischbesteck fish knife and fork
Fische und Schalentiere fishes and crustaceous animals
Fischeintopfgericht pot-stew of fish
fischen fish
Fischen fishing
Fischer fisherman
Fischerboot fishing-boat
Fischerdorf fishing-village
Fischfilet fillet of fish
Fischfrikadelle fishcake
Fischhandlung fishmonger
Fischmayonnaise mayonnaise of fish
Fischrestaurant fish and chip shop
Fischsalat fish salad
Fischsuppe fishsoup, French fish soup
Fitness-Studio health club
fixe (feste) Kosten (Service Center 14) fixed charges (schedule 14)
Fizz fizz
FKK nudism
Flageolet flageolet
Flagge flag
flambieren flame
flambiert flambé, flamed
Flannell-Tafel flannel-board

Flasche bottle
Flaschenbier bottled beer
Flaschenöffner bottle-opener
Flaschenpfand bottle deposit
Flaschenwein bottled wine
flaumig fluffy
Fleisch meat
Fleisch, durchwachsenes marbled meat
Fleisch in Streifen schneiden und dörren jerk
Fleisch vom Grill grilled meat
Fleisch vom Holzkohlengrill charcoal broiled mixed grill, barbecued meat
Fleischallerlei gekocht mixed boiled meat, assorted boiled meat
Fleischanhänger meat tag
Fleischbrühe beeftea, meat broth
Fleischbrühe mit Nudeleinlage broth with noodles
Fleischbrühe mit Reiseinlage broth with rice
Fleischer butcher
Fleischfondue (Rindfleisch) beef fondue
fleischig meaty
Fleischkäse meat-pudding
Fleischklößchen meat-ball
Fleischklöße, gebraten rissole
Fleischknödel meat dumpling, quenelle
Fleischpastete meat pie
Fleischschnitte grilliert slice of grilled (beef) meat
Fleischspeise meat dish
Flieger aviator
Flip Chart flip chart
Flitterwochen honeymoon
Floppydisk floppy disk
Flora flora
Floß raft
Flosse flipper
Flotte fleet
Flug air-journey, flight
Flug, planmäßiger scheduled flight
Flug ohne Zwischenlandung non-stop flight
Flug-Bus-Verbindung bus-air service, coach-air service

Flug-Eisenbahn-Verkehr

Flug-Eisenbahn-Verkehr airrail transport
Flug-Schiffs-Reise air-steamer voyage
Flugbuchung air booking
Fluggast air passenger
Fluggastgebühr airport service charge
Fluggastversicherung aircraft passenger insurance
Fluggeschwindigkeit flying speed
Fluggesellschaft airline
Flughafen aerodrome, airport
Flughafenbus airport bus, shuttle
Flughafenempfangsgebäude airport terminal building
Flughafenrestaurant airport restaurant
Flughafensteuer airport tax
Flughafenzollamt airport customs office
Fluginformation flight information
Flugkapitän captain, flight captain
Flugkarte airline ticket, airticket, plane ticket
Fluglinie airline
Flugnetz route network
Flugpauschale all-in air fare, inclusive air fare
Flugpauschalreise inclusive air journey
Flugplan flight schedule, schedule, timetable
Flugplatz aerodrome, airfield
Flugplatzbahnhof town terminal
Flugplatzreservierung air reservation
Flugpreis airfare
Flugreise air-journey
Flugschein airline ticket, air-ticket, plane ticket
Flugschein pilot's licence
Flugschein, offener open-air ticket
Flugscheinverkaufsstelle air-ticket issuing office
Flugscheinvermerk für Touristenklasse y
Flugsicherheit flying safety
Flugsicherung air traffic control
Flugsteig gate, gateway
Flugstrecke air route
Flugtouristik air tourism, holiday air travel
Flugverbindung connecting flight
Flugverkehr air services
Flugzeit flight time, flying time
Flugzettel flyer
Flugzeug aircraft, airplane, plane
Flugzeug, einmotoriges single-engined aircraft
Flugzeug besteigen board a plane
Flugzeug der Touristenklasse air coach
Flugzeug verlassen deplane
Flugzeugabsturz plane crash
Flugzeugankunft arrival by air
Flugzeugbesatzung aircrew
Flugzeugentführung hijacking
Flugzeugführer aircraft pilot
Flugzeughalle hangar
Flugzeugladung plane load
Flugzeugmotor aircraft engine
Flugzeugrumpf fuselage
Flunder flounder, fluke
Fluß river
Fluß, schiffbarer navigable river
Flußdampfer river steamer
Flußforelle river-trout, stream trout
Flußhotel riverside hotel
Flußkarte river map
Flußschiffahrt river traffic
Flügel wing
Flügel (Musikinstrument) grand piano
Flügelspitze vom Huhn chicken winglet, chicken wing, winglet
flüssig liquid
Fogosch (Zander) perch-pike
Folgeerscheinung after-effect
folgen keep track of, follow
folgerichtig consistent
Folgerichtigkeit consistency
Folio folio
Folklore folklore
Fonds funds
Fondue Bourgignonne fondue Bourgignonne
Food und Beverage-Manager food and beverage manager
Footballspiel football match
Förderband conveyer belt
fordern claim, demand

fördern promote
Forderung claim
Forderung, dubiose doubtful account
Forderungen receivables, accounts receivable
Forderungen, langfristige noncurrent receivables
Forderungen, nach dem Alter aufgegliederte aged receivables
Forderungen, noch nicht fällige current receivables
Forderungen, uneinbringliche bad debts
Forderungen, zweifelhafte doubtful accounts
Forderungen abzüglich der uneinbringlichen Forderungen net receivables
Forderungen aus noch nicht abgerechneten Leistungen accrued receivables, unbilled receivables
Forderungen aus Warenlieferungen und Leistungen an Dritte accounts receivables – trade
Forderungen gegenüber Konzerngesellschaften accounts receivables – affiliates
Forderungen insgesamt total receivables
Forelle trout
Forelle blau blue boiled trout
Forelle in Butter gebraten butterfried trout
Forelle in Champagner trout in champagne
Forellenfischen trout fishing
Form der Darstellung form of presentation
formal formal
Formalität formality
Formel formular
förmlich formal
Formular blank, form
formulieren formulate
forschen research
Forschung research
Forschung und Entwicklung research and development
Forschungsabteilung research department

Forsthaus forester's house
Fortbildungsseminar workshop
Fortgang progress
Foto photo
Fotoausrüstung photographic equipment
fotografieren take a photo
Fotografieren verboten! photographing not allowed
Fotosafari photo safari
Foyer foyer, lobby
Fracht cargo, carriage, freight
Frachtbrief consignment note
Frachtbuch cargo book
Frachtflugzeug airfreighter, cargo aircraft, freight aircraft
Frachtschiff freighter
Frachtführer carrier
Frachtgebühr freightage
Frachtkosten freight charges
Frachtrechnung freight bill
Frachtschiff freighter
Frachtsendung cargo consignment
Frachttarif goods tariff
Frack tailcoat
Frage question
Fragebogen questionary, questionnaire, survey sheet
Franchise vergeben franchise
Franchise-Geber franchisor
Franchise-Gebühr franchise fee
Franchise-Nehmer franchisee
Franchise-Unternehmer franchise operator
Franchise-Vertrag franchise-agreement
Franchising franchising
Frankfurter Würstchen Frankfurter, Frankfurter sausage
frankieren stamp
Frankiermaschine franking machine, postage meter
frankiert post-paid
franko post-paid
Frankreich France
Fräulein miss
frei disengaged, free vacant
frei an Bord free on board (f.o.b.)
frei Eisenbahn free on rail (f.o.r.)
frei Kai free on quai (f.o.q.)
frei Waggon free on truck (f.o.t.)

Freibad bathing place, lido, open-air bath, open-air swimming-pool, outdoor bath
Freibetrag allowance
Freifahrtkarte complimentary ticket
Freigepäck free baggage allowance
freigestellt optional
freigiebig generous
Freigrenze allowance
Freihafen free port
Freihalten! keep clear
Freihandelszone Free Trade Area
Freikarte free ticket
Freikörperkultur (FKK) nudism, naturism
Freiluftbühne open-air stage, open-air theatre
Freilufttheater open-air theatre
freimachen (räumen) vacate
Freisein vacancy
Freistempler franking machine
freiwillig voluntary
Freizeit leisure time, spare time, off time
Freizeitbeschäftigung leisure time activity
fremd unfamiliar, alien
Fremdenbuch visitors' book
Fremdenfeindlichkeit xenophobia
Fremdenführer guide
Fremdenführer, deutschsprachiger German-speaking guide
Fremdenheim boarding-house, guest-house
Fremdenregister hotel register
Fremdenverkehr tourism, tourist trade, tourist traffic
Fremdenverkehrsamt touristboard, tourist office
Fremdenverkehrsbetrieb tourist trade establishment
Fremdenverkehrsbüro tourist office
Fremdenverkehrsforschung travel research
Fremdenverkehrsförderung promotion of the tourist trade
Fremdenverkehrsgebiet tourist region
Fremdenverkehrsindustrie hotel and tourist industry, touristic industry
Fremdenverkehrskampagne tourist campaign
Fremdenverkehrsland holiday country, tourist country
Fremdenverkehrsort tourist centre, tourist resort
Fremdenverkehrspolitik tourist policy
Fremdenverkehrsprospekt travel booklet
Fremdenverkehrssaison tourist season
Fremdenverkehrsstadt tourist town
Fremdenverkehrsstatistik tourist trade statistics, travel statistics
Fremdenverkehrsstreuung staggering of tourist traffic
Fremdenverkehrsträger tourist traffic institution
Fremdenverkehrsverband tourist association
Fremdenverkehrswerbung tourist advertising, tourist publicity
Fremdenverkehrswesen tourism
Fremdenverkehrswirtschaft tourist economy
Fremdenverkehrszeitschrift tourist journal
Fremdenverkehrszentrale central office of tourism
Fremdenzimmer guest-room, spare room
Fremdenzimmer! rooms to let
Fremder stranger
Freude joy
freundlich kind
Freundlichkeit kindness
Friedhof cemetery, churchyard
friedlich peaceful
Frikadelle beefburger, fricadelle, meat croquet
Frikassee fricassee
frisch fresh
frisch gestrichen wet paint
Frischling young wild boar
Frischwarenverzeichnis market list
Frischwasser fresh water
Friseur hairdresser

Frisiersalon hairdresser's saloon, barber shop
Frisiertisch dressing-table, dresser
Frist time limit
Frisur hair-style
Fronleichnam Corpus Christi
Frosch frog
Froschschenkel frog-leg
Frost frost
frostig chilly
Frostschutzmittel anti-freezing mixture
Frottiertuch Turkish towel
fröhlich jolly
Fröhlichkeit gaiety
Frucht fruit
Fruchtbrei squash
Fruchteiscreme fruit sundae
fruchtig fruity
Fruchtsaft fruit juice, squash
Früchte fruit, fruits
Früchtekorb fruit-basket
Früchte, eingemachte preserves
Früchte, gehackte (zur Pastetenfüllung) mincemeat
früh early
früher prior to
Frühjahr spring
Frühjahrsferien spring holiday
Frühjahrsmesse spring trade fair
Frühjahrsputz spring cleaning
Frühkonzert morning concert
Frühling spring
Frühlingsgemüse early vegetable
Frühstück breakfast
Frühstück, englisches English breakfast
Frühstück, komplettes complete breakfast
Frühstück, zweites elevenses, mid-morning snack
Frühstücksausgabestelle pontry
Frühstücksfleisch luncheon meat
Frühstückspause mid-morning break
Frühstückspension residential hotel
Frühstückstablett breakfast tray
Frühstückszimmer breakfast room, tea-room
frühzeitig in good time
Frühzug morning train
Fuhrlohn cartage

führend leading
Führerschaft leadership
Führerschein driver's license, driving license
Führerschein, internationaler international driving permit (IDP)
Führer, mehrsprachiger multilingual guide
Fuhrpark fleet of trucks
Führung (Reise) guided visit
Führung übernehmen take the lead
Führungsentscheidung management decision
Führungsfähigkeit leadership-ability
Führungskraft executive
Führungskräfteausbildung executive development
Führungskräfteentwicklung management development
Führungsprovision management fee
Führungsverantwortung managerial responsibility
Führungszeugnis certificate of conduct
Füllsel (Füllung) forcemeat, stuffing
Fundbüro lost-property office
Fundgegenstand found article
Fünfuhrtee five-o'clock-tea
Funktaxi radio taxi
Funktion function
funktionieren operate
Fusion merger
fusionieren merge
Fuß (Längenmaß = 0.3048m) foot
Fußball (europ. Sport) soccer
Fußgängerbrücke footbridge
Fußgängertunnel subway
Fußgängerübergang peel
Fußwanderung hike

G

Gabel fork
gähnen yawn
Galerie gallery
Gallone gallon
Gang passage
Gang (Essen) course
Gangschaltung gear-change

Gang, erster first course
Gans goose
Gänse geese
Gänsebraten roast goose
Gänsebraten mit Sauerkraut roast goose with sauerkraut
Gänseklein giblets of goose
Gänseleber goose liver
Gänselebermoussee gooseliver-mousse
Gänseleberpastete gooseliver patty, gooseliver pie, pate de foie gras
ganz quite; whole, entire
Ganzjahresbetrieb year-round service
ganzjährig geöffnet open all the year round
ganzjährig in Betrieb operating all the year round
Garage garage, garageparking lot
Garage, verschließbare lockup garage
Garage und Parkplatz (Umsatzbereich 5) garage and parking (schedule 5)
Garantie guarantee, guaranty
garantieren guarantee, ensure
garantiert warranted
Garantieverpflichtung product warranty
Garautomat automatic cooker
Garderobe checkroom, cloakroom, wardrobe
Garderobenfrau checkroom girl, cloakroom attendant
Garderobenmarke cloakroom ticket
gären (lassen) ferment
Garküche cook-shop
Garn yarn
Garnele prawn, shrimp
garnieren garnish
garniert garnished
Garnierung dressing, garnishing
Gärten und Parkanlagen (Pflege) (Service Center 12) grounds and landscaping (schedule 12)
Gartencafé open-air café
Gartenfest garden party
Gartenlokal open-air restaurant
Gartenrestaurant open-air restaurant, tea garden

Gartenschau horticulture show
Gartenstadt garden city
Gärtner gardener
Gas geben accelerate
Gasfeuerzeug gas lighter
Gashahn gas tap
Gasherd gas cooker, gas range
Gaspedal accelerator
Gasse lane
Gassenschenke off-licence inn
Gast guest, patron, pax
Gast, zahlender paying guest
Gastaufnahmevertrag contract of accomodation
Gäste bedienen serve, attend, wait on
Gästeanzahl guest count
Gästeanzahlung, verlorene (Umsatzbereich 6) forfeited advance deposit (schedule 6)
Gästebegrüßung guest encounter
Gästebuch visitors' book
Gästefragebogen guest questionnaire
Gästegeschenke guests' supplies
Gästehaus guest-house
Gästeregistrierung guest registration
Gästeverzeichnis hotel register
Gästewäsche guest laundry
Gästezahlung guest count
Gästezimmer guest-room, sitting-room, spare room
Gastfamilie host family
gastfreundlich hospitable
Gastfreundschaft hospitality
Gastgeber host
Gastgeberin hostess
Gastgewerbe catering business, hotel and restaurant business
Gasthaus café, hotel, inn, pub
Gasthof inn
Gastland host country
gastlich hostible
Gastronom hotel-keeper, innkeeper
Gastronomie gastronomy
Gastronomiebereich food and beverage department
Gastspiel guest performance
Gaststättenbesitzer restaurant-keeper
Gastwirt innkeeper, landlord, restaurant-keeper
Gastwirtschaft inn, saloon

Gastzimmer dining-room, parlour, spare-room
Gatte husband
Gattung kind
Gaumen palate
gebacken baked
Gebäck pastry, pastries
Gebäck, kleines cookie, cooky
Gebäude building
Gebäudeeinrichtung und -ausstattung building fixtures and equipment
Gebiet area, territory, zone
Gebirge mountains
Gebirgsklima mountain climate
Gebirgswelt mountains
gebraten roast, roasted, sauteed
Gebrauch use
gebrauchen make use of, apply
gebräuchlich customary
Gebrauchsanweisung instruction for use
gebrauchsfertig ready-to-use
Gebrauchsgegenstand, persönlicher personal belonging
gebraucht used, second hand
Geburt birth
Geburtsdatum date of birth
Geburtsname maiden name
Geburtsort birthplace, place of birth
Geburtsurkunde birth certificate
Gebühr fee
Gebühr erheben levy a charge
Gebühren für öffentliche Versorgungsbetriebe (Service Center 14) utility taxes (schedule 14)
gedämpft (kochen) steamed, stewed
Gedeck cover
Gedeck, trockenes cover charge
Gedeckpreis cover charge
gedünstet braised, steamed
geeignet appropriate
Gefahr danger, jeopardy, risk
Gefahr laufen run the risk
gefährden jeopardize
Gefährdung hazard, jeopardy
gefährlich dangerous, risky
Gefälle hill
gefallen, j-m please
Gefäß jar

Geflügel fowl, poultry
Geflügel kalt cold fowl
Geflügelbrust breast of chicken
Geflügelklein giblets of chicken
Geflügelkleinsuppe giblet soup
Geflügelkroketten croquettes of fowl
Geflügelleber chicken liver
Geflügelpastete warm chicken pie
Geflügelragout ragout of chicken
Geflügelrahmragout chicken à la king
Geflügelrahmsuppe (Mulligatawny) curried chicken-cream soup
Geflügelreis chicken rice
Geflügelsalat chicken salad
Geflügelsuppe soup with fowl
Geflügelsuppentopf chicken noodle soup
gefräßig greedy
Gefriergut frozen food
gefroren iced, frozen
Gefühl emotion
gefüllt filled, stuffed
Gegenbuchung contra entry
Gegend region
Gegengift antidote
Gegenkonto contra account
Gegenrechnung contra account
gegenseitig mutual
Gegenstand object
Gegenteil opposite
gegenüber facing, opposite
Gegenüberstellung von Aufwand und Ertrag, periodengerechte matching
Gegenverkehr oncoming traffic, two-way traffic
Gegenwartswert present value, realizable value
Gegenwert equivalent
gegrillt broiled, barbecued
gehackt chopped, fricasseed, hashed
Gehalt pay, salary
Gehälter und Löhne, noch nicht ausbezahlte accrued salaries and wages
Gehaltsscheck pay check
gehaltvoll meaty
gehen go, walk
gehen, an Bord go on board

gehen, an Land debark, go ashore
gehen, vor Anker anchor
gehen lassen forego
Gehen Sie geradeaus! go straight on
Gehilfe assistant
gehorsam submissive
Gehweg footpath
Geisteszustand state of mind
gekocht cooked, plain boiled
Geländefahrt cross-country drive
Gelbfilter yellow filter
Geld, nicht verfügbares restricted money
Geldbetrag, bei öffentlichen Versorgungsbetrieben hinterlegter security deposit
Geldbeutel purse
Geldeinlage eines Gesellschafters money contributed by a partner
Geldkassette cash box
Geldmittel funds
Geldstrafe fine, penalty
Geldstrafe auferlegen impose a fine upon
Geldwechsel currency conversion, exchange of money
Geldwechselautomat change-giving machine
Geldwertänderung change in value of currency
Gelee jelly
Gelegenheit occasion
Gelegenheitsarbeiter casual worker
Gelegenheitswerbung opportunity advertising
geliert jellied
geltend machen assert
Geltungsdauer validity
Gemäldegalerie picture gallery
gemälzt, nicht non-maltet
gemein rotten
Gemeinde community
Gemeindesteuer community tax
Gemeinkosten overhead cost, overhead expenses
gemeinsam joint
Gemeinschaft community
gemeinschaftlich teamwork
Gemeinschaftsbadezimmer communal bathroom
Gemeinschaftsküche communal canteen, communal kitchen
Gemeinschaftsraum recreation room
Gemeinschaftsverkaufsförderung group business promotion
Gemeinschaftsverpflegung communal feeding, communal provisions
Gemeinschaftswerbung associate advertising, cooperative advertising, group advertising
gemischt assorted, mixed
Gemischtwarenhandlung general store
Gemse chamois
Gemüse vegetable
Gemüse, gemischtes mixed vegetable
Gemüse in Essig eingelegt pickles
Gemüsecremesuppe cream of vegetable
Gemüsegericht vegetable dish
Gemüseplatte vegetable plate
Gemüsesalat vegetable salad
Gemüsesuppe julienne, vegetable broth
Gemüsesuppe gekühlt chilled vegetable soup, grits
Gemüsesuppe klar clear soup with vegetables
Gemüsesuppe (mit Fleisch), dicke pottage
Gemüsesuppe (mit Hammelfleisch), Scotch broth
gemütlich cosy, snug
Gemütlichkeit cosiness, leisureliness
genau exact
genau bestimmen pinpoint
Genauigkeit accuracy
genehmigen approve
Genehmigung approval, permit
Generaldirektor general manager
Generalüberholung overhauls, reconditioning
genießen enjoy
Genußschein participating certificate
Genüsse, kulinarische pleasures of the table
geöffnet open
Gepäck baggage, luggage
Gepäck, Bestätigung für abhanden gekommenes send luggage in

advance prosperity irregularity report (PIR)
Gepäck, sperriges bulky baggage
Gepäck aufgeben check-in baggage, register luggage
Gepäckabfertigung baggage registration counter, checking of baggage, luggage office, luggage registration counter, registering of luggage, registration of luggage
Gepäckabholung collection of luggage
Gepäckablage baggage rack, luggage rack
Gepäckanhänger baggage label, luggage label
Gepäckanhänger (Auto) baggage trailer
Gepäckannahme receipt of baggage to be deposited
Gepäckannahmeschalter receipt of baggage to be deposited
Gepäckaufbewahrung check-room, left-luggage office
Gepäckaufbewahrungsschein receipt for registered luggage
Gepäckaufgabestelle baggage office, luggage office
Gepäckausgabe handing out of baggage
Gepäckbahnsteig baggage platform, luggage platform
Gepäckbeförderung conveyance of luggage
Gepäckdienst baggage service, luggage service
Gepäckgebühr je Stück charge per piece of baggage
Gepäckkontrolle examination of luggage
Gepäcknetz baggage rack, luggage rack
Gepäckraum luggage compartment, luggage room
Gepäckraum (Bahn) baggage compartment
Gepäckraum (Flugzeug) baggage hold
Gepäckraum (Schiff) baggage room
Gepäckschalter deposit counter

Gepäckschein baggage check, consignment note, left-luggage ticket, luggage receipt, luggage-ticket
Gepäckschließfach baggage locker, luggage locker, station locker
Gepäckträger luggage porter, porter, redcap
Gepäcktransfer luggage transfer
Gepäckversicherung baggage insurance
Gepäckwagen baggage car, luggage van
Gepäckzustellung delivery of baggage
gepflegt well-groomed
gepökelt pickled, salted
Gerät appliance, implement, tool
Gerätschaften equipment
geräuchert smoked
geräumig roomy
Geräusch noise
gerecht fair
gereizt irate
Gericht (Essen) dish, meal
Gericht, fleischloses meatless dish
geringwertig low valued
gerinnen curdle
gern essen relish
gern haben like
geröstet toasted, roast
Gerste barley
Gerstenmehlkuchen (dreieckig) scone
Gerstenschleimsuppe barley soup
Geruch odour, smell, fragrance
Gerücht gossip, grapevine
gesalzen salted
Gesamtbetrag aggregate amount
Gesamteinkommen comprehensive income
Gesamtplanung master scheduling
Gesamtstreckenfahrpreis through fare
Geschäft business, concern, deal, dealing, transaction
Geschäft durch gegenseitige Empfehlung referral business
Geschäftsbank (USA) commercial bank (money center)
Geschäftsbrief business letter

geschäftsfähig capable of contracting
Geschäftsfreund business friend
Geschäftsführer manager
Geschäftsführung management, top management
Geschäftsleben business life
Geschäftsleitung management
Geschäftsmann businessman
Geschäftspolitik business policy
Geschäftsräume business premises
Geschäftsreise business trip (tour)
Geschäftsrückgang business recession
Geschäftsschluß closing hour
Geschäftsstelle branch office
Geschäftsstellenleiter branch manager
Geschäftsstraße shopping street
Geschäftsumfang business volume
Geschäftsverbindung business relation
Geschäftsverkehr dealing, traffic
Geschäftsviertel business district, downtown, shopping center
Geschäftsvorfall business transaction (event)
Geschäftswagen business car
Geschäftszeit business hours, office hours
Geschäftszyklus operating cycle
geschält peeled
geschehen happen
Geschenk gift, gratuity, present
Geschenkartikel gift articles, fancy goods
Geschenkgutschein gift token
Geschenkladen gift shop
geschickt experienced
Geschirr dishes
Geschirrspülmaschine dishwashing machine
Geschirrtuch tea-towel, dish-towel
geschlossen closed
Geschmack flavour, taste
geschmacklos insipid, tasteless
Geschmacklosigkeit tastelessness
Geschmackseigenschaft attribute of taste
Geschmacksreichtum tastefulness
geschmackvoll tasteful

geschmolzen melted
geschmort braised
Geschnetzeltes shredded meat
geschützt sheltered, protected
Geschwätz gossip
Geschwindigkeit speed
Geschwindigkeitsbegrenzung speed limit
Gesellschaft association, society, company
Gesellschaft, geschlossene private party
Gesellschaft des bürgerlichen Rechts (GbR) partnership
Gesellschaft mit beschränkter Haftung (GmbH) limited liability company (Ltd.)
Gesellschafter, beschränkt haftender limited partner
Gesellschafter, stiller silent partner
Gesellschafter, unbeschränkt (persönlich) haftender general partner
Gesellschaftsabend social evening
Gesellschaftsanteil corporate stock
Gesellschaftsfahrt party outing, party trip
Gesellschaftsflug party flight
Gesellschaftskleidung formal dress, evening dress
Gesellschaftsraum lounge, private room
Gesellschaftsreise conducted tour, escorted tour, guided tour, organized tour, party tour
Gesellschaftsreisen party travel
Gesellschaftsreiseverkehr group travel
Gesellschaftsspiel parlour game, party game
Gesellschaftszimmer function room
gesetzlich lawful, legal, legitimate
gesetzmäßig legitimate
gespannt tense
gespickt mit Speck larded
Gesprächsstoff topics of conversation
Gestalt figure
gestatten let, permit
Gestehungskosten cost price
gestern yesterday

gesund healthy, wholesome
Gesundheit health
Gesundheitsbestimmungen public health regulations
Gesundheitsvorschriften sanitary regulations
Gesundheitszeugnis health certificate
Gesundheitszustand health
Getränk beverage, drink
Getränk, alkoholfreies non-alcoholic beverage
Getränk, mit Eis(würfel) on the rocks
Getränke nicht inbegriffen drinks extra
Getränke und kalte Speisen im Zug drinks and snacks on board
Getränkeautomat bellcaptain, drink dispenser
Getränkekarte list of beverages
Getränkekellner wine-butler
Getreide cereals
Getreideflocken cereals
Getriebe (Fahrzeug) transmission
Getriebe, automatisches automatic transmission
getrocknet dried
getrüffelt truffled
gewähren allow, grant
gewährleisten ensure
Gewährleistung ohne rechtliche Verpflichtung warranties without legal obligations
Gewand garment
Gewässerverschmutzung pollution of the waters
Gewerbe trade
Gewerkschaft labo(u)r union, union
Gewicht weight
Gewinn gain, profit, surplus
Gewinnbeteiligung (Tantiemen) profit sharing plan
gewinnbringend profitable
gewinnen (erhalten) benefit, gain
Gewinnrücklagen machen appropriations of retained earnings
Gewinnvortrag einschließlich freie Rücklagen retained earnings
Gewitter eletric storm, thunderstorm
Gewohnheit custom, habit

gewöhnen an accustom to, become used to
gewöhnlich ordinary
gewöhnt an accustomed
Gewürz spice
Gewürzgurke pickle, pickled gherkin
Gewürznelke cloves
Gezeiten tides
gezuckert sugared
gierig greedy
gießen pour
giftig toxic(al)
Gin gin
Gipfel (Gebäck) crescent
Girant endorser
Girat endorsee
Giro endorsement
Girokonto checking account, current account
glänzend glossy
Glas glass
Gläschen tot
Gläser glassware
Gläsergestell rack
Glasfaserski glass fibre ski
Glasgeschirr glassware
Glasur icing
Glaswaren glassware
glatt slippery
Glatteis glazed frost
Glaubersalzquelle sodium sulphate spring
gleich equal
gleichbedeutend equivalent
gleichgültig casual
gleichkommend quasi
gleichmäßig equal
gleichwertig equivalent
Gleis line, track
Gleise rails
Gletscher glacier
Gletschereis glacial ice
Gletschersee glacial lake, glacier lake
Gletscherspalte crevasse
Gletscherwanderung glacier travel
Glied member
Gliederungsschema der Bilanz balance sheet format
Global-Versicherungspolice insurance-general

Globetrotter globetrotter
Glocke bell
Glücksspiel gambling, game of chance
Glühbirne bulb, electric bulb
Glühwein hot claret with cinnamon and clove, hot wine, mulled claret, mulled wine
gnädige Frau, gnädiges Fräulein madam
Go-Kart-Sport karting
Goldbarsch dorado
Goldmakrele blue fish, gilt head, golden mackerel
Golfausrüstung golf equipment
Golfplatz golf course, links
Golfspieler golfer
Gondel cable car, gondola
Gondelfahrt gondola ride
Gorgonzola Gorgonzola
Gottesdienst divine service, service, mass
Gourmet gourmet
Graben moat
Grad degree
grafisch darstellen chart
Granatapfel pomegranate
Grapefruit grapefruit
Grapefruit eisgekühlt chilled grapefruit
Grapefruitsaft grapefruit juice
Gratifikation bonus, gratuity
gratiniert browned, gratinated
Gratisaktie bonus stock (shares)
Gratiszimmer complimentary room
Gremium committee
Grenzbahnhof frontier station
Grenze überschreiten cross the frontier
Grenzformalitäten frontier formalities
Grenzgebiet border area, frontier area
Grenzkostenrechnung direct costing
Grenzstadt border town, frontier town
Grenzstein landmark
Grenzübergang border crossing, frontier crossing
Grenzübergangsstelle border crossing point, frontier crossing point

Grenzübertritt border crossing, frontier crossing
Grenzverkehr border traffic
Grenzzone border zone, frontier zone
Griechenland Greece
Grieß semolina
Grießklößchen gratiniert baked semolina, dumplings
Grießklößchensuppe soup with semolina dumplings
Grießpudding semolina pudding
Grießpudding kalt cold semolina pudding
Grießstrudel semolina pie
Grießsuppe semolina soup
Griff handle
Griff- und Bewegungsstudie micromotion study
Grill grill
Grill, vom grilled
Grillbar grill-bar
Grillrestaurant grill-room
Grillstube grill-room
Grippe influenza
Grog grog, toddy
Grog mit Rum hot rum grog
Großabnehmer outlet
großartig magnificent
Großhandelsrabatt wholesale discount
Großmast main mast
Großreparaturen general overhaul
Großsegel main sail
Großwildreservat big-game reservation
großzügig generous
Grotte grotto
Grund cause, reason
Grund (Boden) ground
Grundfahrpreis basic fare
Grundgehalt basic salary
Grundkapital capital stock
Grundlage basis
Grundlagenforschung basic research
Grundlohn basic pay
grundlos gratuitous
Grundpreis basic price
Grundsatz der Bewertungsstetigkeit consistency in valuation

Grundsätze ordnungsmäßiger Buchführung und Bilanzierung generally accepted accounting principles
grundsätzlich underlying
Grundstück land
Grundstücke und Gebäude, geleaste leasehold
Grundstückseinrichtungen land improvements
Grundstücksmakler estate agent
Grundzubereitung pre-preparation
Gruppenbesichtigung group visit
Gruppenermäßigung group discount
Gruppenfahrt party outing, party trip
Gruppenleiter group leader
Gruppenreise group journey, party tour
Gruppenreisen party travel
Gruppentarif party rate
Gruppenversicherung group insurance
Gruß greeting
Grußkarte greetings card
Gruyèrekäse Gruyère cheese
gründen establish, from
Gründling goby
Gründonnerstag Maundy Thursday
Gründung establishment, foundation
Grüne Versicherungskarte international motor insurance card
Grünfläche open space
Grünkohl green cabbage, kale
Grütze, rote red grits
Gugelhupf plain circle cake, Vienna plum pudding
Gulasch brown stew, goulash
Gulasch, ungarisches Hungarian goulash
Gulaschsuppe goulash soup
Gummilinse zoom lens
Gummistiefel gum boots, rubber boots
Gurke cucumber
Gurke, saure pickled cucumber
Gurkensalat cucumber salad
gut good, well
gut eingerichtet well-furnished
gutbürgerlich plain
gutbürgerlich (Küche) homely
gute Nacht good night

guten Abend good evening
guten Morgen good morning
guten Tag good afternoon
guter Glaube good faith
Gutschein coupon, give-away, voucher
Gutschein, noch nicht eingelöster matured coupon
gutschreiben credit
Gutschrift credit entry, credit
gültig valid
Gültigkeit validity
Gültigkeitsdauer period of validity
Gültigkeitserklärung validation
Gürtel, grüner green belt
Güte (Qualität) quality
Güteklasse grade
Güter goods
Güterbahnhof freight station, goods station
Güterkraftverkehr road haulage
Güterverkehr freight traffic, goods traffic
Güterwagen freight car, goods waggon
Güterzug freight train, goods train
Gütezeichen quality label
Gymnastik gymnastics, setting-up exercises

H

Haarbürste hairbrush
Haarklemme hair-grip
Haarnadel hairpin
Haarnadelkurve hairpin bend
Haarnetz hair-net
Haarschnitt hair-cut
Haarspange hair-slide
Haarwasser hair lotion
Haarwild furred game
Habensaldo credit balance
Habenseite (eines Kontos) credit side
Hackbeefsteak Hamburger, Hamburger steak, hashed steak Russian style
Hackbraten hashed meat, meat-loaf
Hackbrett chopping board
hacken mince

Hackfleisch ground meat, minced beef, minced meat
Hackfleisch mit braunen Bohnen chili con carne
Hackfleischkotelett vom Kalb chopped veal cutlet
Hackmaschine (für Fleisch) mincer, mincing machine
Hackmesser chopping knife, chopper
Hafen harbour, harbor, port
Hafen am offenen Wasser open-water port
Hafenanlagen docks, port installations
Hafenausfahrt harbour mouth
Hafenbahnhof harbour station, marine railway station
Hafeneinfahrt entrance to a harbour, harbour mouth, port entrance
Hafengebühren harbour dues, keelage
Hafengeld port dues
Hafenpolizei harbour police
Hafenrundfahrt circular tour of port
Hafenschlepper harbour tug
Hafenviertel dock area, dock quarter
Hafer oat
Haferbrei porridge
Haferflocken oats, oat flakes
Hafermehl oatmeal
Haferschleim gruel
Haferschleimsuppe oatmeal cream soup
Haft arrest
haftbar responsible
Haftpflicht third-party liability
Haftpflichtdeckung liability insurance coverage
haftpflichtig liable
Haftpflichtversicherung liability insurance, third-party insurance
Haftung responsibility, liability, contingent liability
Haftungsverhältnisse contingencies
Hagebutte hip
Hagebuttentee hip-tea
Hagelversicherung hail insurance
Hahn cock, rooster
Hähnchen (oder Suppenhuhn) und Lauch cock-a-leekie

Haifischflossen shark's fins
Haifischflossensuppe shark's fins soup
Haken hook
halb durch rare
halbe Flasche, eine half a bottle
halbe Portion, eine half a portion
halber Preis half-fare
halbes Backhuhn, ein half a fried chicken
Halbfabrikate goods in process
Halbinsel peninsula
halbjährlich semiannual
halbmonatlich semi-monthly
Halbmondpastetchen gefüllt stuffed half-moon patty
Halbpension demi-pension, half pension
halbtags half-day
Halbtagsausflug half-day excursion
Hallenschwimmbad indoor swimming-pool
Hallensport indoor sport
Hallentennis covered-court tennis
Halskette necklace
Halt halt
Halt, planmäßiger scheduled halt, scheduled stop
Halt – Vorfahrt beachten halt at major road ahead
halten halt, stop
halten an, sich follow
Haltestelle stop
Halteverbot no stopping, prohibition to stop
Halteverbot, heute auf dieser Straßenseite no stopping this side today
Haltung attitude
Hamburger Hamburger, Hamburger steak
Hammel mutton
Hammel-, Rindfleisch- und Kartoffeleintopf Lancashire hot pot
Hammelkeule leg of mutton
Hammelragout mutton-stew
Hammelragout irische Art Irish stew
Hammelrippchen mutton chop
Hammelrücken saddle of mutton

Hammelspießchen mutton on skewers
Hand hand
Hand- und Maschinenwerkzeuge tools and dies
handbetrieben hand-operated
Handblasebalg hand bellows
Handbremse hand brake
Handbuch manual
Handel bargain, deal, trade, traffic
Handeln bargain, deal, trade
Handelsbrauch trade custom, usage of trade
Handelsgesetzbuch (HGB) commercial code
Handelsschiff merchant ship, trading vessel
Handelssperre embargo
Handelsvertreter traveller
Handelsware merchandise
Handelswechsel notes receivable trade
Handgepäck hand luggage, portable luggage
handhaben handle
Handhabung (z. B. von Gästebeschwerden) handling (of guest complaints)
Handkoffer suitcase
Handlung action
Handlungsreisender commercial travel(l)er
Handschuh glove
Handserviette hand-napkin
Handtasche handbag
Handtuch towel
Handtuchhalter towel-rack
Handwerk handicraft
Handwerker craftsman
Hang slope
Hangar hangar
Hängematte hammock
Hardware hardware
Harpune harpoon
hart hard
hart am Wind segeln sail near to the wind
hartgekocht hard-boiled, hard-cooked
Häschen leveret
Hase hare

Haselhuhn hazel-ben
Haselhuhnragout brown hazel-hen-stew
Haselnuß hazelnut
Haselnußtorte hazelnut tart
Hasenbraten roast hare
Hasenpfeffer jugged hare
Hasenrücken saddle of hare
Hase, junge leveret
häßlich ugly
Hast haste
Haube hood
häufig frequent
Häufigkeit frequency
Hauptbahnhof central station, main station
Hauptbuch general ledger
Hauptbüro head office, main office
Hauptdeck main deck
Haupteingang main entrance
Hauptfleischgang main joint, main meat course
Hauptgang (Speisen) main course, main joint, main meat course
Hauptgericht main course, main dish
Hauptmahlzeit main meal
Hauptreiseverkehr peak tourist traffic
Hauptreisezeit peak tourist season
Hauptsaisonflugpreis peak season fare
Hauptschlüssel pass-key, master-key
Hauptspeise main dish
Hauptstadt capital, metropolis
Hauptstraße main road, main street
Hauptteil bulk
Hauptverkehrsstraße highway
Hauptverkehrszeit rush hours
Hauptversammlung annual meeting
Hauptverwaltung headquarter
Haus, möbliertes furnished house
Haus-zu-Haus-Gepäckbeförderung door-to-door pick up and delivery service
Hausdame executive housekeeper, housekeeper, matron
Hausdiener bell captain
Hausdiener bellman, houseman, valet
Hauseigentümer landlord
Hausgast resident guest, border, resident

hausgemacht home-made
Haushaltsgüter household goods
Haushaltspackung family size package
Haushaltsrechnung family budget
Hausmannskost plain fare
Hausmantel housecoat
Hausmeister janitor
Hausnummer house number
Hausordnung house rules, regulations of the house, rules of residents
Hausreinigung spring cleaning
Hausreinigungsabteilung housekeeping department
Hausschlüssel house key
Hausschuh slipper
Haustelefon house telephone
Haustier pet
Haustür front door
Hauszeitung house organ
Haut skin, peeling
Haxe knuckle
Hecht jack, pike
Hechtklößchen pike dumplings
Heck stern
Hecke hedge
Hefe leaven, yeast
Hefeextrakt yeast extract
Hefeteigkuchen mit Früchten fruit savarin
Hefter folder
Heide heath, pagan
Heidelbeere bilberry
Heilanzeige indication
Heilbad health resort, spa
Heilbadekur balneation, course of treatment at a spa
Heilbäder nehmen bathe
Heilbäderwesen balneation
Heilbutt halibut
Heilfaktor curative factor
Heilfaktor, natürlicher natural curative factor
Heilgymnastik physiotherapy
Heilklima curative climate, wholesome climate
Heilkraft curative power
Heilmethode method of treatment
Heilmittel remedy

Heilmoor curative-mud
Heilquelle medicinal spring, mineral spring, spa
Heilschlamm curative-mud
Heilstätte sanatorium
Heilung cure
Heilwasser medicinal mineral water
Heim hostel
Heimat home country
Heimatabend folkloristic evening
Heimatanschrift home address
Heimathafen home port, port of registry
Heimatstadt native town
Heimcomputer home computer
Heimkehr return home
Heimreise homeward journey, journey home, voyage home
heiß hot
Heißluftbad hot-air bath
Heißwasser hot water
Heißwasserboiler water-heater
Heiterkeit gaiety
Heizöl fuel
Heizung heating
helfen aid, assist, help
Helikopter helicopter
Helikopterflugplatz helicopterport
Heliotherapie sun-light treatment
Henne hen
herablassend reden (mit einem Gast) talk down (to a guest)
herabsetzen reduce
Herabsetzung reduction
herausfordern challenge
Herausforderung challenge
herb dry, tart
Herberge hostel
Herbst autumn, fall
Herbstferien autumn holiday, fall vacation
Herbstmesse autumn tradefair
Herd range
Herd, elektrischer electric range
Hering geräuchert smoked herring
Heringssalat herring salad
Herkunft origin
Herrenfriseur barber, gentlemen's hairdresser, men's hairdresser
Herrennachthemd night shirt

Herrentoilette gentlemen's cloakroom, gentlemen's lavatory, men's lavatory
herstellen produce
Herstellungskosten, fortgeschriebene durchschnittliche moving average production costs
hervorheben highlight
hervorragend outstanding
hervorrufen provoke
Herz heart
herzhaft hearty
herzlich hearty
Herzoginnenkartoffeln dutchess potatoes
Heu hay
Heuhaufen haystack
heute today
Hilfe aid, help
Hilfe leisten assist
Hilfs- und Betriebsstoffe supplies
Hilfsdienst auxiliary service
Hilfskoch assistant cook, junior cook
Hilfsquelle resource
Himbeere raspberry
Himbeereis raspberry ice
Himbeersaft raspberry juice
Himmel sky
Himmelfahrtstag Ascension Day
Himmelsrichtung direction
Himmelsrichtungen, die vier cardinal directions
Hin- und Rückfahrschein roundabout ticket, return ticket
Hin- und Rückflug outward and inward flight, outward and return flight
Hin- und Rückreise outward and homeward voyage, outward and homeward journey
Hin- und Rückreisepreis return fare
hinausgehen über exceed
Hinfahrt outward journey, outward voyage
Hinflug outward flight, outward journey
hinreichend adequate
Hinreise outward journey, outward voyage
Hintergrundmusik background music

Hinterland hinterland
Hinterlegung deposit
Hinterlegungsbestätigung certificate of deposit
Hinweis reference
hinzufügen add
Hinzufügung addition
Hirn brains
Hirnsuppe calf's brains soup
Hirsch deer, stag, venison
Hirse millet
hissen hoist
Hitze heat
hitzig passionately
Hobelkäse shaved cheese
Hoch (Wetter) anticyclone
Hochbahn overhead railway
Hochbetrieb great bustle
Hochgarage multi-storey garage
Hochgebirge high mountains
Hochkonjunktur boom
Hochplateau high plateau
Hochsaison height of the season, high season, peak season
hochschätzen appreciate
hochseetüchtig ocean-going
Hochstraße mountain road
Hochtourist mountaineer
Hochtouristik mountaineering
Hochwasserversicherung wave damage insurance
hochwertig high value
Hochzeit wedding
Hochzeitsreise honeymoon
hochziehen hoist
Hof court, courtyard, yard
Hofzimmer back room
Hoheitsgewässer territorial waters
Holding holding company
Holland Holland
Holländische Sauce Dutch sauce
Holsteiner Schnitzel veal collop with fried egg
Holundertee elderberry-tea
Holz wood
Holzfeuer wood fire
Holzkohle charcoal
Holzkohlen-Grillgericht barbecue
Holzkohlenfeuer, vom charcoal broiled
Holzzucker xylose

Honig honey
Honorar fee
Hopfen hop
Hopfensprossen hop sprouts
Hoppel-poppel veal stew with scrambled eggs
Horizont skyline
Horsd'oeuvre horsd'oeuvre
Hospiz hospice
Hostess hostess
Hot dog hot dog
Hotel hotel
Hotel der gehobenen Mittelklasse upper-bracket hotel
Hotel erster Klasse first class hotel
Hotel für Durchreisende transient hotel
Hotel garni residential hotel, lodging-house
Hotel internationaler Klasse hotel of international standard
Hotel- und Gaststättenführer hotel and restaurant guide
Hotel- und Gaststättengewerbe hotel and catering trade
Hotelangestellter hotel employee
Hotelanzeiger hotel directory
Hotelbelegung hotel booking, hotel occupancy, occupancy
Hotelbesitzer hotel owner
Hotelbetrieb hotel operation
Hotelbetriebsführung operational management
Hotelbett hotel bed
Hotelbettenüberschuß hotel bedrooms surplus
Hotelboy hotel bellboy, boy
Hotelbüro hotel office
Hoteldiener bellman, porter
Hoteldirektion hotel management
Hoteldirektor hotel manager, resident manager
Hoteleigenschaft hotelhood
Hoteleinstufung classification of hotels
Hotelempfangshalle hotel lobby
Hotelfach hotel business
Hotelfachschule hotel training school, school of hotel management
Hotelfriseur haidresser at the hotel
Hotelführer hotel guide

Hotelführung hotel-keeping
Hotelgast hotel guest
Hotelgebäude hotel building
Hotelgelände hotel side
Hotelgröße hotel size
Hotelgrundstück hotel site
Hotelgutschein hotel voucher
Hotelhalle entrance hall, hotel entrance hall, hotel foyer, hotel vestibule, lobby, lounge
Hotelier hotel-keeper
Hotelkapazität hotel capacity
Hotelkette hotel chain
Hotelklassifizierung classification of hotels
Hotelleitung hotel management
Hotellerie hotel and catering trade, hotel industry, hotel trade
Hotelmanagement, praktisches operational management
Hotelmanager property manager
Hotelnachweis hotel broker
Hotelnebenkosten incidental charges
Hotelordnung hotel rules and regulations
Hotelpage bellboy, bellhop, hotel pageboy
Hotelpension private hotel
Hotelpersonal hotel staff
Hotelportier hall porter
Hotelrechnung hotel bill
Hotelrepräsentant hotel representative
Hotelreservierung hotel booking
Hotelrestaurant hotel dining-room
Hotelstammgast regular hotel guest
Hoteltelegrafenschlüssel, internationaler international hotel code
Hotelunterbringung hotel accomodation
Hotelunterkunft hotel accomodation
Hotelverband hotel association
Hotelvertrag hotel contract
Hotelwesen hotel-keeping, innkeeping, hotel trade
Hotelzettel (Gepäck) hotel label
Hotelzimmer hotel room
Hotel, auf einen bestimmten Gästetyp spezialisiertes single market property

Hotel, erstklassiges high-class hotel
Hotel, gutgeführtes hotel under good management
Höchstbesetzung mit Personal maximum manning
Höchstgebot highest bid
Höchstgeschwindigkeit maximum speed, top speed
Höchstkredit credit line
Höchstpreis maximum price
höflich polite
Höflichkeit courtesy
Höhe height
Höhenbegrenzung height restriction
Höhenklima mountain climate
Höhenlage high altitude
Höhenluft mountain air
Höhenluftkurort high altitude health resort
Höhenrestaurant mountain restaurant
Höhensonne ultra-violet lamp
Höhenunterschied vertical drop
höhere Gewalt act of God
Höhle cave
Hörensagen hearsay
Hörnchen (Gebäck) half moons
Hörnchennudeln elbow macaroni
Hubschrauber helicopter
Hubschrauberflugplatz helicopterport
Hubschrauberlandeplatz air-stop
Huckpackverkehr road-rail service
Huhn chicken
Huhn in Aspik chicken in jelly
Huhn in Tomatensauce mit Pilzen und Eiern chicken stew
Hummer lobster
Hummercocktail lobster cocktail
Hummermayonnaise lobster mayonnaise
Hund dog
Hunde sind an der Leine zu halten! dogs must be kept on the lead
Hunger hunger
Hupe horn
hupen honk, hoot
Hupen verboten! no honking, no hooting
Husten cough
Hutkoffer hatbox

Hutzucker loaf sugar
hübsch handsome
Hüfte hip
Hügel hill
Hühnchen baby chicken, hen-chicken, pullet
Hühnchen spring-chicken
Hühnerbrust chicken breast
Hühnerbrühe chicken-broth
Hühnerkeule chicken leg
Hülsenfrucht legume
Hülsenfrüchte pulse
Hütte hut
Hütte, bewirtschaftete serviced hut
Hüttenkäse cottage cheese
Hüttenzelt umbrella tent
Hypothek mortgage

I

identifizieren identify
Identifizierung identification
im Widerspruch stehen (zu, mit) disagree (with)
Imbiß luncheonette, snack
Imbißbar (im Restaurant) lunch-counter
Imbißpaket box meal, food pack, lunch packet
Imbißstube café, luncheonette, snack-bar, snack-counter, tea-shop
Immobilien immovables
Impfbestimmungen inoculation requirements
impfen vaccinate
Impfung inoculation, vaccination
Impfzeugnis certificate of vaccination
Import import
importieren import
in die Praxis umsetzen implement
in Übereinstimmung mit consistent with
Index index
Indisches Geflügelgericht chicken curry
individuell individual
Indossament endorsement
Indossamentverbindlichkeiten contingent liabilities from endorsements

Indossant endorser
Indossatar endorsee
indossierbar negotiable
Indossierbarkeit negotiability
Industrieausstellung industrial fair
Industriegebiet industrial area
Industriemesse industry fair
Information information
Information und Betreuung
    reception and information office
Informationsbüro information bureau, inquiry office
Informationsdienst information service
Informationsquelle source of information
Informationsreise information trip
informieren brief, inform
Ingenieur engineer
Ingwer ginger
Ingwerbier ginger beer
Ingwerkuchen pepper cake
Ingwerlimonade ginger ale
Ingwerpudding ginger pudding
Inhaber holder, keeper
Inhalation inhalation
Inhalationsapparat inhaler
Inhalationskur inhalation therapy
Inkassospesen collection expenses
inkognito incognito
inländisch domestic
Inlandpostgebühren inland postage rates
Inlandsflug domestic flight
Inlandsgast national tourist
Inlandsstrecke domestic route
Inneneinrichtung interior equipment
Innenhof inner courtyard
Innenkabine inside room
Innenrevision administrative audit
Innenstadt city, town centre, downtown
Innereien offals
Insekt insect
Insel island, isle
Inserat advertisement (Abk.: ad)
Installateur plumber
instandhalten maintain
Instandhaltung maintenance
Instandhaltung und Wartung – Hardware/Software (Service Center 8) maintenance – hardware/software (schedule 8)
Instandhaltungsauftrag maintenance work order
Instandhaltungskosten maintenance cost
instandsetzen repair
Instandsetzung reconditioning
instruieren brief, instruct
Instrument, begebbares (z. B. Wechsel, Scheck etc.) negotiable instrument
Intercity-Zug Inter-City train
Interessengruppe der Jahresabschlußverwender user group
Internationale Fachausstellung für das Hotel- und Gaststättengewerbe International Exhibition of the Hotel and Catering Trade
Internationale Vereinigung der Fremdenverkehrszentralen International Union of Touristic Centers
Internationale Zivil-Luftfahrt-Organisation International Civil Aviation Organization (ICAO)
Internationaler Automobilverband International Automobile Federation
Internationaler Hotelverband International Hotel Association (IHA)
Internationaler Luftverkehrsverband International Air Transport Association (IATA)
Internationaler Verband der Jugendherbergen International Youth Hostel Federation (IYHF)
Internationaler Verband der Reisebüros Federation of Travel Agencies (FIAV)
Internationales Impfzeugnis International Vaccination Certificate
Interpreter (Datenverarbeitung) interpreter
Interzonenverkehr interzonal traffic
Interzonenzug interzonal train
invalide disabled

Inventar inventory list
Inventarbücher fixed assets records
Inventur, permanente cycle count of inventories
Inventuraufnahmeblatt tally sheet
Inventurzettel inventory tag
investieren invest
Investition investment
inzwischen meanwhile
Irische See und Ärmelkanal narrow seas
Irland Ireland
irreführend misleading
irren mistake, err
Irrtum error, mistake
Irrtümer und Änderungen vorbehalten errors and alterations excepted
Island Iceland
Ist-Kosten actual cost
Italien Italy
Italienischer Salat Italian Salad
ivriert liveried

J

Jacht cabin cruiser, yacht
Jachthafen marina
Jacke jacket, jerkin
Jagd hunt, hunting, shooting
Jagdaufseher gamekeeper
Jagdgebiet hunting ground
Jagdhütte hunting box, shooting box, shooting lodge
Jagdreise shooting trip
Jagdreservat game reserve
Jagdrevier hunting ground, shoot
Jagdsaison hunting season, open season, shooting season
Jagdschein game licence, shooting licence
Jagdzeit open season, shooting season
jagen hunt, shoot
Jahr, im per annum
Jahres- oder Monatsabschluß financial statements
Jahresabschreibung, anteilige pro rata depreciation
Jahresbedarf annual usage

Jahrestag anniversary
Jahrestemperatur, mittlere mean annual temperature
Jahresurlaub annual holiday (vacation)
Jahresüberschuß net income, net profit
Jahresverbrauch annual usage
Jahresverdienst annual earnings
Jahresversammlung annual meeting
Jahreszeit season
Jahreszeitsalat season's salad
jährlich annual, per annum, yearly
Jahrmarkt fun-fair
Jakobsmuschel scallop St. Jacques
Jalousien Persian blinds
Jamaikapfeffer pimento
Japan Japan
Jodquelle iodine spring
Joggen jogging
Joghurt yoghourt
Johannisbeere currant
Johannisbeere, rote red currant
johlen maffick
Jolle dinghy, sailing dinghy
Joule joule
Journal journal
Journalbuchung journal entry
Jubiläumsgeschenk anniversary present
Jubiläumszuwendung anniversary gratuity
Jugend youth
Jugendfahrpreis youth fare
Jugendgruppenreise youth group journey
Jugendherberge youth hostel
Jugendherbergsausweis Youth Hostel Association Membership Card
Jugendklub youth club
jugendlich juvenile
Jugendlicher youth
Jugendreise youth travel
Jumbo Jet jumbo jet
jung young
Jungfernbraten fillet of pork roasted
Junggeselle bachelor
Jungkellner waiter apprentice
Jungkoch junior cook
Jungschwein baby pig

Juwelen 66

Juwelen jewellery, jewelery
Juwelier jeweller, jeweler

K

Kabarett cabaret
Kabel cable, line cord
Kabeljau hake
kabeln cable
Kabine cabin
Kabine (Seilbahn) cable car
Kabinengepäck cabin luggage
Kabinenkoffer trunk
Kabinenseilbahn cabin cable railway
Kaffee coffee
Kaffee koffeinfrei coffee without caffeine, decaffeinated coffee
Kaffee mit einem Schuß Branntwein lace-coffee
Kaffee mit Sahne coffee with cream
Kaffee türkisch Turkish coffee
Kaffeecremetorte fancy-cake with coffee cream
Kaffeekanne coffee-pot
Kaffeemühle coffee-mill
Kaffeepause coffee break
Kaffeetasse coffee cup
Kaffee(filter)maschine coffee percolator
Kahn boat
Kahnfahrt boat-ride, boat trip
Kai quay, wharf
Kai, am on the quay
Kaianlagen quayage
Kaigebühren quay dues
Kaigeld quayage
Kaiserschmarrn pancake Emperor style
Kajak kayak
Kajüte cabin
Kakao cocoa
Kakifrucht kaki
Kakipflaume persimmon
Kalb calf, veal
Kalbfleisch veal
Kalbfleisch, eingemachtes stewed veal
Kalbfleisch geschnetzelt chipped veal

Kalbfleisch kalt in Thunfischsoße veal with tuna
Kalbfleischröllchen veal birds, veal olives
Kalbfleischwürstchen small veal sausage
Kalbsbraten roast loin of veal, roast of veal
Kalbsbries sweetbreads
Kalbsbries gebacken calf's sweetbread baked
Kalbsbrust calf's breast
Kalbsbrust gefüllt stuffed breast of veal, roast stuffed breast of veal
Kalbsbrustknorpel calf's gristle
Kalbsfilet fillet of veal
Kalbsfricandeau fricandeau of veal
Kalbsfrikassee fricassee of veal
Kalbsfüße calf's feet
Kalbsgulasch mit Klößen stew of veal with dumplings
Kalbshaxe calf's knuckle, knuckle of veal
Kalbshaxenscheibe sliced knuckle of veal
Kalbsherz calf's heart
Kalbshirn calf's brain
Kalbshirn gebacken calf's brains fried
Kalbskarreebraten rib roast of veal
Kalbskeule leg of veal
Kalbskopf calf's head
Kalbskopf en tortue calf's head with turtle sauce
Kalbskopf gebacken calf's head fried
Kalbskopf in Essigsoße calf's head vinaigrette
Kalbskotelett veal chop, veal cutlet
Kalbskotelett natur plain veal cutlet
Kalbsleber calf's liver, liver of veal
Kalbsleber gebacken calf's liver fried
Kalbsleber geröstet calf's liver roasted
Kalbsleber geschnetzelt shredded calf's liver
Kalbsleberscheiben sliced calf's liver
Kalbsleberspießchen calf's liver on skewers

Kalbslunge calf's lights
Kalbsmedaillon medaillon of veal
Kalbsnieren kidney of veal
Kalbsnierenbraten roast loin of veal with kidney
Kalbsnierensteak kidney steak
Kalbsnuß kernel of veal
Kalbsnüßchen small veal steak
Kalbsragout brown veal stew, veal stew
Kalbsroulade rolled veal steak, veal roll
Kalbsröllchen am Spieß rolled veal on skewers
Kalbsrücken saddle of veal
Kalbsschlegel leg of veal
Kalbsschnitzel veal collop, veal scallop
Kalbsschnitzel gefüllt cheese- and ham stuffed veal steak, stuffed veal collop
Kalbsschnitzel paniert breaded veal steak
Kalbsschnitzelchen gespickt larded veal collops
Kalbsschulter shoulder of veal
Kalbssteak veal steak
Kalbszunge calf's tongue
Kalkulation calculation
kalkulieren calculate
Kalorientabelle table of calorific values
kalt cold
kalte Speisen cold dished
kaltes Büffet cold buffet
Kamera camera
Kamille camomile
Kamillentee camomile tea
Kamin chimney, fireplace, fire-side
Kaminecke inglenook
Kamm comb
Kammuschel scallop
Känguruhschwanzsuppe kangoroo tail soup
Kaninchen rabbit
Kännchen jug, pannikin
Kanne pitcher
Kantine (mit großem Warenangebot) commissare store
Kanu canoe
Kanzel (Flugzeug) cockpit

Kapaun capon
Kapazität capacity
Kapazitätsausnutzung utilization of capacity
Kapazitätsausweitung capacity increase, increase in capacity
Kapelle (Kirche) chapel
Kapelle (Musik) band
Kapellmeister bandleader
Kaper caper
Kapernsauce caper sauce
Kapital capital, funds, stockholder's equity
Kapital, eingebrachtes contributed capital
Kapital, eingezahltes paid-in capital
Kapitalbedarf capital demand, capital requirements
Kapitaleinlage contribution
Kapitalgesellschaft (etwa: Aktiengesellschaft (AG)) corporation
Kapitalrückfluß amortization
Kapitalrücklage additional paid-in capital
Kapitalrückzahlung principal payment
Kapuzinerkresse nasturtium
Karaffe carafe, decanter
Karamelpudding caramel custard, caramel pudding, cup custard, custard pudding
Karfiolsuppe cauliflower soup
Karfreitag Good-Friday
Karnevalszeit carnival season, Shrovetide
Karotte carrot
Karpfen carp
Karriere career
Karte map
Kartei file
Karteikarte file card
Kartenspiel (Gemeinsame Kasse) kitty
Kartenverkauf sale of tickets
Kartoffel potato
Kartoffel, süße sweet potato
Kartoffelbrei creamed potatoes, mashed potatoes, potatomash
Kartoffelchips potato chips
Kartoffelknödel potato dumpling

Kartoffelkörbchen potato basket, potato nest
Kartoffelkroketten croquettes potatoes, potato-croquettes
Kartoffeln geröstet broiled potatoes
Kartoffeln in der Schale potatoes in their jackets
Kartoffeln, gebacken baked potatoes
Kartoffeln, neue new potatoes
Kartoffelpuffer potato pancake
Kartoffelsalat potato salad
Kartoffelscheiben gebacken potato crips
Kartoffelstäbchen gebacken French fried potatoes
Kartoffelstampfer potato masher
Kartoffelsuppe potato soup, soup with potatoes
Karussell merry-go-round, roundabout
Käse cheese
Käse, geriebener grated cheese
Käseauflauf cheese souffle
Käsebrot chesse sandwich
Käsefondue cheese fondue
Käsekuchen cheese cake, cheese pie
Käsekuchen, süßer sweet cheese cake
Käseplatte selection of cheese
Käseschnitte toasted cheese
Käseschnitte geröstet Welsh rabbit (rarebit)
Käsetörtchen cheese tartlet
Kasse petty cash
Kasse (Kino etc.) box office
Kasseler Rippenspeer smoked pork ribs, roast smoked spare rib of pork
Kassenbericht, täglicher daily cash report
Kassenbestand cash on hand
Kasseneinnahmen, tägliche daily cash receipts
Kasse, kleine petty cash
kassieren charge
Kassierer cashier
Kastanienpüree chestnut-vermicelli
Kategorie category
Kater (Katzenjammer) hangover
Katerfrühstück hangover breakfast
Kathedrale cathedral
kauen chew

Kauf purchase
Kauf, vorteilhaftester best buy
kaufen buy
Kaufentschluß buying decision
Käufer buyer
Käufermarkt buyer's market
Kaufgewohnheiten buying habits
Kaufkraft buying power
Kaufvertrag agreement of purchase and sale, contract of sale
Kaufvertrag unter Eigentumsvorbehalt conditional sale agreement
Kaviar caviar
Kaviarbrötchen caviar sandwich
Kedgeree (Reisgericht mit Fisch, Eiern, Zwiebeln) kedgeree
Kefir kefir
Kegel ninepin, skittle
Kegelbahn bowling-alley, skittle-alley
Kegeln bowling
kegeln bowl, play ninepins, play skittles
Kehrrichteimer dustbin
kehrtmachen turn back
Keilkissen bolster
Keilriemen wedge strap
Kein Eintritt! no admittance, no entry
Keine Durchfahrt! no through road
Keks, dünner cracker
Keller cellar
Kellerbar dive bar, underground bar
Kellergeschoß basement
Kellerlokal beer-cellar, underground restaurant
Kellner waiter
Kellnerin waitress
Kellnerlehrling waiter apprentice
kennenlernen experience
Kenntnis knowledge
Kenntnisse, praktisch verwertbare working knowledge
Kennzahl index figure
Kennzeichen mark
Kennzeichen, besondere distinguishing marks
kennzeichnen feature
Kennziffer key number, ratio
Keramik pottery
Kerbel chervil
Kern kernel, stone

Kern der Sache, der eigentliche heart of the matter
Kerosin kerosene
Kerzenabend evening by candlelight
Kerzenlicht candle light
Kerzenständer candlestick
Kessel kettle
Kessel, elektrischer electric kettle
Ketchup ketchup
Kette chain
Keule haunch
Keule (Fleisch) leg
Kichererbse chick-pea
Kiebitz lapwing, pewit, plover
Kiebitzeier plover's eggs
Kiesstrand pebbly beach
Kilometer kilometre
Kinderausweis child's travel document
Kinderbecken children's pool
Kinderbetreuung child care
Kinderbett child's bed, cot, crib
Kinderbrei pap
Kindererholungsheim recreational center for children
Kinderermäßigung reduction for children
Kinderfahrkarte child's ticket
Kindermädchen nursemaid
Kinderspeisesaal children's dining-room
Kinderspielplatz children's playground
Kinderspielzimmer children's playroom
Kinderzimmer nursery
Kino movie theater
Kinokarte cinema ticket, movie ticket
Kinoprogramm cinema program, movie program
Kinosaal movie room
Kiosk news stand
Kirchenkonzert church concert
Kirchensteuer church tax
Kirchturm steeple
Kirchweih local fair
Kirsche cherry
Kirschkuchen cherry cake
Kirschlikör cherry brandy
Kirschtorte cherry tart
Kissen cushion

Kissenbezug pillow-case, pillow-slip
Kiste case
Kitsch trash
Klage complaint
Klage (Gericht) action
klagen complain
klagen (Gericht) sue
Klappbett fold-away bed, folding bed
Klappsitz folding seat, tip-up seat
Klapptisch fold-away table, folding table, pull-down table
klären clarify, clear
Klärung solution
Klasse category
Klassifikation grading
klassifizieren classify, grading
Klassifizierung classification
Klausel clause
Klausel (in Gesetzen, Verträgen etc.) provision
Klavier piano
Klebstoff glue
Kleid dress, gown
Kleiderablage hall stand
Kleiderbügel clothes-hanger, coat-hanger, hanger
Kleiderbürste clothes-brush
Kleiderschrank wardrobe
Kleiderständer coat-rack
Kleidung clothing
Kleinanzeige small ad
Kleinbus microbus, minibus
kleingehackt minced
Kleingeld change, coppers
Kleintaxi minicab
Klemptner plumber
Kletterausrüstung climbing equipment
Klettern mountain-climbing
Klettersport mountain-climping
Klettertour climbing tour
Klima climate
Klima, gemäßigtes moderate climate
Klima, mildes mild climate
Klima, rauhes severe climate
Klimaanlage air conditioning
Klimakurort climatic health resort
Klimastation climatological station
Klimaverhältnisse climatic conditions
Klingel bell

Klingelknopf button
Klinik clinic
Klipper clipper
klopfen knock
Klopfen knock
Kloß dumpling
Klößchen small dumpling
Kloster monastery
Klub club
Klubabend club evening
Klubhaus clubhouse
Klumpen lump
Knackwurst saveloy
Kneipe pub, saloon-bar
Kneipenbummel pub crawl
Kneippanlagen facilities for hydropathic treatment
Kneippkur hydropathic treatment
Knoblauch garlic
Knoblauchsoße garlic sauce
Knochen bone
Knöchel ankle
Knödel dumpling
Knödelsuppe soup with dumpling
Knollensellerie celeriac
Knoten knot
Knurrfisch gurnet
Knurrhahn gurnard
knusprig crisp
Koch cook
kochen boil, cook
Kochen cooking
Kochen in Folie paper bag cooking
Kochgelegenheit cooking-facilities
Kochgeschirr cooking utensils, mess-tin
Kochkessel kettle
Kochkunst art of cooking, culinary art
Kochnische kitchenette
Kochschrank kitchenette
Kochstelle cooking stove
Kochtopf cooking-pot, saucepan
Kodenummer code number
Koffer suitcase
Kofferanhänger baggage label, luggage label
Kofferaufkleber suitcase label
Kofferradio portable radio
Kofferraum (Auto) boot, trunk
Kohl cabbage

Kohlfisch whiting
Kohlrabi kohlrabi
Kohlroulade rolled stuffed cabbage leave
Kohlsprossen broccoli, sprouts
Koje (Schiff) berth, bunk
Kokosnuß coconut
Kolonialwarengeschäft grocery store
Kolonie colony
Kombiwagen estate car, station wagon
Komfort, moderner luxurious fittings
Kommanditist limited partner
Kommode chest of drawers
Kommunikationssystem, internes internal communicating system
Kompetenz authority
Komplementär general partner
Kompott preserved fruit, stewed fruit
Kondensmilch condensed milk
Konditor confectioner
Konditorei sweet shop
Konfekt confections
Konferenz conference, meeting
Konferenzraum conference room
Konfitüre jam, preserves
Konfitürenomelett jam-omelett
Kongreß congress
Kongreßberatung congress information service
Königinsuppe cream of chicken
Königsberger Klopse meat-balls in white caper sauce
Konkurrent competitor
Konkurrenz competition
Konkurrenz, scharfe keen competition
konkurrieren compete
Konkurs bankruptcy
Konservatismus conservatism
Konserven preserves, tinned food
Konservenbüchse can, tin
Konsortialbank underwriter
Konsulat consulate
Konsum consumption
Konsument consumer
konsumieren consume
Konten für Kunden (z.B. Firmen) city ledger
Kontenblatt ledger card, ledger sheet

Kontengliederung account classification
Kontenplan chart of accounts
Kontenrahmen chart of accounts
kontieren classify
Kontingent quota
Konto account
Konto, laufendes current account
Konto abschließen close an account
Konto eröffnen open an account
Kontoauszug abstract account
Kontoform account format
Kontokorrent account current (A/C), current account
Kontokorrenteinlage demand deposit
Kontokorrentguthaben current balance
Kontokorrentkonto checking account
Kontroll-Liste check list
Kontrolle control
Kontrolle, eingebaute built-in check
Kontrolle, genaue close control
Kontrolle, scharfe close control
Kontrolle durch Planung budgetary control
Kontrolleur ticket inspector
kontrollieren control
Kontrollspanne span of control
Kontrollturm control tower
konvertieren convert
Konzernabschluß consolidated financial statements
Konzernbilanz consolidated balance sheet
Konzernumlage-Kosten management fee
Konzertpavillon bandstand
Konzertsaal concert-hall
Konzession (Umsatzbereich 6) concession (schedule 6)
Kooperation cooperation
Kopf head
Kopfkissen pillow
Kopfsalat cabbage lettuce, lettuce
Kopfschmerz headache
Kopiergerät copier
Kopilot co-pilot
Kopplungsverkauf combination sale, tie-in sale
Korinthe currant

Kork cork
Korkenzieher bottle screw, corkscrew
Korkgeschmack corky taste
Körperschaft corporation
Körperschaft, nicht handeltreibende nontrading corporation
Korrespondenzqualität letter quality
Korridor corridor
kosher (rein nach jüdischen Speisegesetzen) kosher
Kosmetik beauty culture
Kosmetikartikel cosmetics
Kosmetikerin beautician
Kosmetiksalon beauty parlour
Kost, abwechslungsreiche varied diet
Kost, leichte light food
Kost, vegetarische vegetarian diet
Kosten, sonstige direkte (Umsatzbereiche 1–5 im USASH) expenses (schedules)
Kosten der verkauften Erzeugnisse cost of goods sold
Kosten der vermittelten Telefongespräche (Umsatzbereich 3) cost of calls (schedule 3)
Kosten für die Buchführung accounting costs
Kosten pro Bestellung cost per order
Kosten-Nutzen Analyse cost-benefit-analysis
kostenlos complimentary, gratuitous
Kostenstellenrechung departmental costing
köstlich delicious, lovely
Kostüm suit
Kostümball fancy-dress ball
Kotelett cutlet, rib steak
Kotelett (ohne Knochen) chop
Krabbe crab, prawn, shrimp
Krabben hard-shell crabs
Krabbencocktail prawn cocktail
Krabbenfleisch crabmeat
Kraftbrühe clear soup
Kraftfahrer motorist
Kraftfahrzeug motor vehicle
Kraftfahrzeugbenutzer motor vehicle user

Kraftfahrzeugversicherung motor insurance, motor vehicle insurance
Kraftstrom electric power, power current
Kragen collar
krank ill
Kranken- und Unfallversicherung health and accident insurance
Krankengymnast physiotherapist
Krankengymnastik physiotherapy, remedial gymnastics
Krankenhaus hospital
Krankenhauskostenversicherung hospitalization insurance
Krankenschwester nurse
Krankenurlaub sick leave
Krankenversicherung health insurance, sickness insurance
Krankenwagen ambulance, motor ambulance
Krankheit illness
Krankheit, ansteckende contagious desease
Krankheitsrate illness frequency rate
Krapfen doughnut, fritter
Kraut herb
Kräuter, feingehackte fines herbes
Kräuterbutter butter with fine herbs
Kräuteressig aromatic vinegar
Kräuterkäse green cheese
Kräuteromelett omelet with fine herbes
Kräutertee infusion of herbs
Krautfleisch boiled pork with pickled cabbage
Krautsalat cabbage salad, cole slaw
Krawall affray
Kreativität creativeness
Krebs crawfish, crayfish
Krebsrahmsuppe bisque of crayfish, crayfish cream soup
Krebsschwanzsalat crayfish salad
Krebssuppe crayfish soup
Kredit credit
Kredit, langfristiger long-term credit
Kredit, nicht in Anspruch genommener unused credit
Kredit gewähren grant a credit
Kreditbeschaffung credit supply
Kreditbürgschaft loan guarantee
Kreditgeschäft credit operation
Kreditgrenze limit of credit, credit line
Kreditkartenprovision credit card commission
Kreditkauf credit purchase
Kreditlinie credit line
Kreditmöglichkeiten credit facilities
Kreditquellen credit resources
Kreditrichtlinien credit standards
Kreditverkauf credit sale
Kreditverkäufe charge sales
Kreditverlust loss of credit
Kreditwürdigkeit credit rating, credit standing
Kredtikarteninhaber credit card holder
Kreisverkehr roundabout, traffic circle
Kresse cress, water-cress
Kreuzfahrt cruise, crisscross journey, zigzag cruise
Krickente teal
Kricketspiel cricket match
kritischer Weg (Netzplantechnik) critical path
Kroketten croquettes
Krug jar, jug, mug, pitcher
Krustentiere crustaceans
Küche cuisine, kitchen
Küche, gutbürgerliche plain cooking
Kuchen cake
Küchenbenutzung kitchen privileges
Küchenbrigade kitchen brigade
Küchenbuffet kitchen cupboard, kitchen dresser
Küchenchef chef, executive chef
Küchenchef, stellvertretender sous-chef
Kücheneinrichtung, maschinelle mechanical kitchen equipment
Küchengerät kitchen utensil
Küchengeruch kitchen smell
Küchenherd kitchen range
Küchenhilfe cook's assistant, kitchen help, pantry girl
Küchenjunge kitchen-boy
Küchenkraut pot-herb
Küchenmädchen kitchenmaid
Küchenpersonal kitchen personnel, kitchen staff

Küchenplanung kitchen layout planning
Küchlein fritters
kühl chilly, cool, fresh
kühlen chill
Kühler (Auto) radiator
Kühlhaus cold storage
Kühlhauslagerung cold storage
Kühlschrank fridge, refrigerator
Kühltasche insulated picnic bag
Kühlwagen refrigerator car
Kühlwasser cooling-water
Kühlwasser nachfüllen top up the radiator
Küken poussin, young chicken
kulinarische Genüsse culinary delights
Kulturzentrum cultural centre
Kümmel caraway (seed)
Kummer grief, worry
kumuliert zum Datum month-do-date
Kunde customer, patron
Kundendienst-Gebühren (Service Center 8) service bureau fees (schedule 8)
Kundengruppe type of customers
Kundenkreis type of customers
kündigen give notice, withdraw, terminate
Kündigung resignation, termination
Kündigungsquote quit rate
Kündigungsrate labor turnover
Kündigungsschutz dismissal restrictions
Kunstfliegen aerobatics
Kunstgalerie art gallery
Künstler artist
Kunsthändler art dealer
Kunsthonig artifical honey
Kunstmuseum art museum
Kunstreise art historical journey
Kunstsammlung art collection
Kunstschatz art treasure
Kunstzentrum art centre
Kur course of treatment, treatment
Kur, zusätzliche supplementary course of treatment, supplementary cure
Kurarzt spa doctor
Kuraufenthalt stay at a spa

Kurbehandlung cure, spa treatment
Kurbetrieb, ganzjähriger spa open all the year round
Kürbis pumpkin
Kureinrichtungen therapeutical facilities
Kurhaus spa house
Kurkonzert spa concert
Kurmittel treatment
Kurorchester spa orchestra
Kurort health resort, spa
Kurpark spa park
Kurpatient health resort patient
Kurpfuscher quack doctor
Kurs course, rate of exchange
Kursbuch railway guide, timetable
Kursmaschine scheduled plane
Kursnotierung quotation
Kurswagen through-carriage
Kurtaxe tax de sejour, visitors' tax
Kurve bend
Kurve, scharfe sharp bend
Kurzarbeiter part-timer
kurzfristig short term
Kurzparker short-term parker
Kurzparkzone zoned street, limited parking zone
Kurzstreckenflug short-distance flight
Kurzwarenladen haber-dasher
Kürzung reduction
Küste coast, seaside, shore
Küstengebiet coastal area
Küstenkreuzfahrt coastal cruise
Küstenschiffahrt coastal shipping
Küstenstraße coastal road
Kutteln tripe
Kutteln, gedämpfte potstew of tripes
Kutteln in Weißwein gekocht tripe à la mode de Caen
Kuttelnsuppe tripes soup

L

Lachs salmon
Lachsforelle salmon trout
Ladefähigkeit loading capacity
Ladeluke loading hatch
laden take shippings
Ladentisch counter

Laderaum hold
Ladeschein carrier's receipt
Ladung cargo
Lage locality, position
Lage, in der capable
Lage, in ruhiger quietly located
Lager camp
Lager (Waren) stock, store, storeroom
Lager, allgemeines general store
Lageranforderung requisition, storeroom requisition
Lagerhalter storekeeper
Lagerhaus warehouse
lagern keep in stock, store
lagern, im Kühlhaus coldstore
Lagerort location of goods
Lagerraum storage space
Lagerung storage
Lagerverwalter für Lebensmittel food storekeeper
Lagune lagoon
Laie layman
Laken sheet
Lamm lamb, yeanling
Lammbraten roast lamb
Lammbrust lamb breast
Lammkeule leg of lamb
Lammkotelett lamb cutlet
Lammragout lamb stew
Lammschulter lamb shoulder
Lampe lamp
Lancashirekäse Lancashire (cheese)
Land country
Land, an ashore
Land, ans on shore
Landaufenthalt stay in the country
Landausflug outing in the country, shore excursion
Landbezirk rural district
Landebahn landing-runway, runway
Landegeschwindigkeit landing speed
landen in land at
Landeplatz landing-field, landing-strip
Landesgrenze frontier
Landesspezialität local speciality
Landessprache national language
landesüblich conventional, in accordance with local customs

Landeswährung national currency
Landfriedensbruch affray
Landgasthof country inn
Landhaus cottage, country house
Landkarte map
ländlich rural
Landluft country air
Landpachtrecht (Mietrecht), dingliches leasehold
Landschaft landscape, scenery
Landschaft, natürliche nature
landschaftlich schön scenic
Landschaftsschutz protection of places of natural beauty
Landschinken country ham
Landseite, zur facing inland
Landspitze cape
Landstraße country road
Landstreicher tramp, tramper
Landung landing
Landungsbrücke gangway, jetty, landing-pier, landing-stage
Landungssteg jetty
Landwein local wine
lang long
Länge length
langfristig in the long run, longrange, long-term
Langlauf jogging
Langlauf (Ski) cross-country skiing, langlauf
Langsam fahren! drive slowly, reduce speed now
Langstreckendienst long-distance service
Langstreckenflug long-distance flight
Langstreckenflugzeug longrange plane
Languste rock lobster, spiny lobster
Lappen rag
Lärm noise
Lärmbekämpfung noise control
lärmend feiern maffick
lassen let
Lastenaufzug freight elevator, goods elevator
Lastwagenanhänger truck trailer
Last(kraft)wagen lorry, truck
Lateinamerika Latin America

Laterne lantern
Laubengang arcade
Laubenpromenade mall
Lauch leek
Lauchgemüse leeks
Lauchsuppe leek soup
Laufbahn career
Laufgang walkway
Laufkundschaft occasional customers
Laufzeit duration
Laufzeit des Kredits credit period
Laune fancy
lauwarm lukewarm
lawinengefährdet exposed to avalanches
lawinensicher safe from avalanches
Leasing leasing
Leasing-Bilanzierungsvorschriften capital lease requirements
Leasing-Geber lessor
Leasing-Nehmer lessee
Leasing-Objekte leased objects
Leasingrate lease payment
Leasingvertrag, aktivierungspflichtiger capital lease
Lebensart manners, way of living
Lebensgewohnheit living habit
Lebenshaltungskosten cost of living
Lebenslauf curriculum vitae
Lebensmittel provisions
Lebensmittelhändler grocer
Lebensmittellagerraum food store
Lebensmittelvergiftung food-poisoning
Lebensstandard living standard, standard of living
Lebensversicherung life insurance
Leber liver
Leberkäse leberkaese
Leberknödel liver dumpling
Leberknödelsuppe hot broth with liver dumplings, soup with liver dumplings
Leberpüreesuppe liver puree soup
Leberreissuppe soup with liver rice
Leberwurst liver sausage, leberwurst
Leberwurst mit Sauerkraut liver sausage with sauerkraut

lebhaft animated
Lebkuchen ginger bread
lecken leak
ledig single, unmarried
leer empty
Leerlaufzeit idle time
leerstehend unoccupied
Legitimation legitimation
Lehnstuhl arm-chair, easy chair
Lehrfilm training film
Lehrling apprentice
Lehrmethode teaching method, training method
Lehrvertrag contract of apprenticeship, indenture of apprenticeship
Lehrzeit apprenticeship
Leicesterkäse Leicester
leicht mild, readily
leicht erreichbar easy to get to
Leichtathletik athletics
leihen borrow, lend
Leihgebühr lending-fee
Leihwagen hired car
Leihwagendienst car hire (rental) service
Leinkuchen linseed-cake
Leinsamen linseed
Leipziger Allerlei Leipzig hodge-podge
leisten, sich afford
Leistung efficiency, pace, performance, productivity
Leistungen öffentlicher Versorgungsbetriebe (z. B. Strom, Gas, Wasser) utilities
Leistungsbeurteilung merit rating
Leistungsbewertung performance appraisal
Leistungseinheit production standard
leistungsfähig efficient
Leistungsfähigkeit efficiency
Leistungsgrad performance
Leistungskontrolle performance control
Leistungsmaßstab performance standard, production standard, standard of performance
Leistungsmessung measurement of performance

Leistungsstandard standard of performance
Leistungsvermögen capacity
leiten manage
leitender Angestellter executive
Leiter manager
Leiter, technischer engineer
Leiter der Beherbergungsabteilung rooms division manager
Leiter der Wareneinsatzkontrolle (Speisen u. Getränke) food and beverage controller
Leiter der Wareneinsatzkontrolle (Speisen) food cost controller
Leiter des Rechnungswesens comptroller
Leiter der Hausdamenabteilung executive housekeeper
Leiter der Reservierungsabteilung reservation supervisor
Leitkarte guide
Leitung control
Leitungsentscheidung administrative decision
Lende loin
Lendenschnitte fillet-mignon, fillet of beef, tenderloin steak
Lendenstück loin
Lendenstück, zartes tenderloin
Lerche lark
Lernender learner
Leseraum reading-room
Lesespeicher read-only memory
Lesezimmer reading-room
letztendlich ultimative
Leuchtreklame electric sign advertising
Leuchtturm lighthouse
Licht light
Lichtbildervortrag lecture with slides
Lichteffekt lighting effect
Lichthupe flashing signal
Lichtschalter switch
lieblich lovely
Lieblingsgericht favourite dish
Lieferant supplier
Lieferbedingungen terms of delivery
Lieferer supplier
liefern deliver, supply

Lieferschein delivery note, delivery slip
Liefertermin delivery date
Lieferung delivery, supply
Lieferzeit delivery time, time of delivery
Liege couch
Liege, fahrbare roll-a-way
Liegegeld quay dues
Liegehalle open-air veranda
Liegekur open-air rest cure, rest-cure
liegen, in der Sonne bask
Liegeplatz couchette
Liegeplatzgebühr couchette charge
Liegestuhl deck-chair
Liegetag layday
Liegeterrasse rest-cure terrace
Liegewiese gardens, rest-cure lawn, sun-bathing lawn
Lifo- und Fifo-Verbrauchsfolgenunterstellungen LIFO and FIFO cost flow assumptions
Lifo-Wert LIFO value
Lift elevator, lift
Liftboy elevator boy, lift-boy
Likör liqueur
Limit limit
Limonade lemonade
Limone lime
Limonensaft lime juice
Lindenblütentee linden flowers tea
Linie line
Linienbus scheduled bus, town bus
Linienfluggesellschaft scheduled airline
Linienflugzeug airliner, liner
Linienfunktion line function
Linienmaschine scheduled plane
Linienschiff liner
Linienstelle line position
Linienverkehr regular traffic
Links fahren! keep left
Linksverkehr left-hand traffic
Linnen linen
Linse (Gemüse) lentil
Linsensuppe lentil soup
Linzenzinhaber licensee
Linzer Torte fancy-cake with Linz nut, trellis cake

Lippenstift lipstick
Liptauer Käse garniert Liptauer garnished
Liquidität liquidity
Liquiditätsgesichtspunkten, nach in the order of their liquidity
Liquiditätslage liquidity position, cash position
Liste list
Listenpreis list price
Lizensgeber licensor
Lizenz right, licence
Lockenwickler curler
locker casual, loosely, fluffy
Löffel spoon
Logan-Beere (Brombeerenart) loganberry
Loge (Theater) box
Logiergast temporary guest
Logierhaus lodging-house
Logiernacht room night
Logierzimmer guest-room
Logis lodging
Lohn pay, wage
Lohnanreiz wage incentive
Lohnerhöhung increase of wages, wage increase
Lohnsteuer und Sozialabgaben, einbehaltene payroll deductions
lokal local
Lokal tavern
Lokalkolorit local colour
Lokomitivführer engine-driver
Lorbeer laurel
Lorbeerblatt bay-leaf
lose loosely
lösen (ein Problem) resolve (a problem)
Losgröße lot size
Losgröße, optimale optimal lot size
Lösung solution
loswerden get rid of
Lothringer Specktorte hot bacon tart
Lotse pilot
lotsen pilot
Lotsendienst guide service
Lotsengebühr pilotage
Lücke gap
Luft, reine ozone
Luftbad air-bath
Luftdruck atmospheric pressure

Luftfahrt aviation
Luftfahrtausstellung air display
Luftfahrtgesellschaft airline
Luftfahrtgesellschaft, angeschlossene associated airline
Luftfilter air filter
Luftfracht air cargo, airfreight
Luftfrachtbüro cargo office air
Luftfrachtkosten airfreight charges
Luftfrachtraum airfreight space
Luftfrachtspedition airfreight service
Luftheizung hot-air heating
luftig airy
Luftkarte aviation chart
Luftkissen air cushion
Luftkissenboot hovercraft
Luftkorridor air corridor
luftkrank air-sick
Luftkrankheit air-sickness
Luftkurort air resort, climatic health resort
Luftloch air-hole
Luftmatratze air-mattress
Luftpost air mail
Luftpostkuvert air mail envelope
Luftpostpaket air parcel
Luftpostpapier air mail stationary
Luftpumpe air pump
Luftraum air space
Luftreisedienst air passenger service
Lufttaxi air taxi
Lufttemperatur air-temperature
Lüftung ventilation
Luftverkehr air traffic
Luftverkehrsgesellschaft air transport company
Luftverschmutzung pollution
Luftzug draught
Luke hatch
Lunchpaket box meal, lunch packet, packed lunch
Lunge lights, lungs
lustig jolly
Luxus de luxe, fancy, luxury
Luxusbus luxury bus
Luxusdampfer luxury liner
Luxusgüter luxury goods
Luxushotel luxury hotel
Luxusjacht luxury yacht
Luxuskabine luxury cabin

Luxusreise luxury trip
Luxusrestaurant luxury restaurant

M

Mädchenname maiden name
Madeira (Wein) Madeira
Madeirasoße Madeira sauce
Magenbitter bitters
Magenfahrplan (Luftfahrt) catering arrangements
Magenstärkung pick-me-up
mager lean, meagre
Magermilch skim (med) milk
Magerspeck lean bacon
mähen mow
Mahlzeit meal
Mahlzeit, gemeinsame table d'hote meal
Mahlzeit, reichliche substantial meal
Mahlzeiten an Bord meals on board ship
Mahlzeitengutschein luncheon voucher
Mahnbrief dunning letter
mahnen remind
Mahnung dunning, reminder
Maibaum Maypole
Maifisch shad
Maikräuter woodruff
Mais corn, Indian corn, maize, sweetcorn
Maisbrei hominy
Maisbrot (amerik.) pone
Maisflocken cornflackes
Maisgrütze Italian corn-pudding
Maiskolben corn-cob
Maiskuchen, amerikanischer johnny-cake
Maismehl corn flour
Maisonette (zweistöckige Wohnung) duplex
Maisstärkemehl maizena
Majoran marjoram
Makkaroni macaroni
Makrele mackerel
Makrone macaroon
Malerarbeiten und Dekoration painting and decorating
malerisch picturesque, scenic

Malteser Maltese
Malve mallow
Malz malt
Management, mittleres middle management
Managementgebühren management fee
Managementtraining management training
Manager manager
Managerkrankheit managerial desease
Mandarine mandarine, tangerine
Mandel almond
Mandelgebäck almond pastry
Mandelkuchen almond cake
Mandelpudding almond pudding
Mandelschnitte almond bar
Mandeltorte almond tart, fancy-cake with almonds
Mangel defect, deficiency, fault, lack, want
Mängel shortcomings
Mängelanzeige notice of defects
mangelhaft defective, faulty
mangeln lack
mangels in default of
Mangold chard, spinach beets, Swiss chard
Mangopflaume mango
Maniküre manicure
Manko shortage
männlich male
Mansarde attic, mansard
Mantel overcoat
Manteltarifvertrag overall labor agreement
manuell manual
Margarine margarine
Marillenknödel apricot dumplings
Marinade marinade, souse
marinieren marinade
mariniert marinated
Mark marrow
Markbein marrow-bone
Marke brand, mark
Markenname brand
Markenrecht trademark
Marketing marketing
Marketing Manager marketing manager

Marketingkosten, sonstige (Service Center 11) miscellaneous marketing expenses (schedule 11)
Markise awning, window awning
Markklößchen marrow dumplings
Markknochen marrow-bone
Markstein milestone
Markt market
Markt, freier open market
Marktanalyse market analysis
Marktfähigkeit negotiability
Markthalle market-hall
Marktliste market list
Marktplatz market-place
Marktpreis market price
Marktsättigung market saturation
Marktwirtschaft, freie free enterprise economy
Markt(zeit)wert fair market value
Marmelade jam
Marmeladenbrötchen jam roll
Martini dry Cocktail (ähnlich) Gin and French
Martini Sweet Cocktail (ähnlich) Gin and It
Marzipan marchpane
Maschine (Flugzeug) plane
maschinell mechanical
maschinelle Kücheneinrichtung mechanical kitchen equipment
Maschinen und maschinelle Anlagen machinery and equipment
Maskenball fancy-dress ball, masked ball
Maß measure
Massage massage
Masse bulk
Massenkauf bulk purchase
Massentourismus large-scale tourism
Massenverkehrsmittel large-scale public transport
Massenversammlung rally
Masseur masseur
Masseuse masseuse
Maßnahme measure
Maßstab yardstick
Mast mast
Masthähnchen spring-chicken
Masthuhn fattened chicken
Mastschwein porker
Matinéevorstellung morning performance
Matjeshering red herring, salt(ed) herring
Matratze mattress
Matritze stencil
Matrixdrucker matrix printer
Matrose sailor
matt dim, weary
Mauer wall
Maulbeere mulberry
Maulesel mule
Maultier mule
Maurer mason
Maut toll
Mayonnaise mayonnaise
Mayonnaiseeier eggs in mayonnaise
Mayonnaisesalat mayonnaise salad
Mayonnaisesoße mayonnaise sauce
Mechaniker mechanic(ian)
mechanisch mechanical
mechanisieren mechanize
Medikament medicine, drug
Meer sea
Meeraal conger-eel
Meerästche mullet
Meerbarbe mullet
Meerbarsch sea-perch, white bass
Meerbutt brill
Meerdrachen dragon fish
Meeresfrüchte sea-food
Meereskrebs marine cray fish
Meerfisch salt-water fish, sea-fish
Meerrettich horse-radish
Meerrettichsoße horse-radish sause
Meerwasser sea-water
Meerwasserkur seawater cure, thalassotherapy
Mehl flour
Mehlspeise farinaceous dish
Mehrbenutzersystem multi-user system
Mehrheit majority
Mehrwertsteuer value added tax (V.A.T.)
Mehrzweckraum multi-purpose room
Meilenstein milestone
Meilenzahl milage
Meinung opinion

Meinung, vorläufige tentative conclusion
Meinungsumfrage opinion survey
Meldeamt registration office
Meldebuch hotel register
melden bei der Polizei, sich register with the police
Meldepflicht, polizeiliche obligation to register with the police
meldepflichtig notifiable
Meldeschein registration form
Meldeschluß (Luftfahrt) check-in time, latest check-in time
Meldezeit reporting time
Melone melon
Melone geeist chilled melon
Menge quantity
Menge, kleine dash
mengen mingle
Mengenstandard quantity standard
Mengenvorgabe quantity standard
Menü menu
Menü für Autofahrer menu for motorists
Menü und Preis fest table-d'hote
Menü zu festen Preisen menu at fixed prices
Menüplanung menu planning
Merchandising merchandising
Merkblatt leaflet
Merkmal feature
Messe fair
Messe-Informationsstelle fair information office
Messegelände exhibition grounds, fair ground
Messeleitung fair authorities
Messer knife
Metropole metropolis
Mettwurst smoked sausage
Metzger butcher
Metzgerei butcher's shop
Meunière Soße meunière sauce
Miesmuschel scallop (mussel)
Miet- und sonstige Erträge (Umsatzbereich 6) rentals and other income (schedule 6)
mietbar rentable
Mietbesitz leasehold
Miete hire, rent
Miete, vorausbezahlte prepaid rent

mieten hire, lease, rent
Mieter leaseholder, lessee, tenant, lodger
Mieter tenant
Mieterträge aus der Vermietung von Räumen im Hotel (Umsatzbereich 6) space rentals (schedule 6)
Mietflugzeug air taxi
Mietgebühr rental charge
Mietwagen hired car
mietweise on lease
Mietwohngrundstück apartment house property
Mikrocomputer micro computer
Milch milk
Milch, heiße hot milk
Milch, pasteurisierte pasteurized milk
Milchbar milk bar
Milchbrötchen milk-roll
Milchgelee junket
Milchhändler milkman
Milchkaffee coffee with hot milk, white coffee
Milchkännchen milk-jug
Milchlamm baby lamb
Milchmixgetränk milk shake
Milchreis milk-rice, rice pudding
Milchspeise milk-dish
mild mild
Minderheitsaktionär minority stockholder
minderjährig under age
Minderjähriger infant
Minderjährigkeit age of minority
minderwertig inferior
Mindestaufenthalt minimum stay
Mindestgebot lowest bid
Mindestlohn minimum wage
Mindestpreis minimum rate
Mindestteilnehmerzahl minimum number of participants
Mineralbad mineral bath
Mineralie mineral
Mineralquelle mineral spring, spa
Mineralwasser mineral water, table water
Mineralwasser (halbe Flasche) split
Minestrone minestrone
Minicomputer mini computer

Minigolf miniature golf
Minigolfplatz miniature golf course
Minus shortage
Minzsoße mint sauce
Mirabelle mirabelle plum, yellow plum
mischen merge, mix
mischen, sich mingle
Mischgericht mixture (of food)
Mischkosten semivariable cost
Mischung mix
Mispel medlars
Mißbrauch abuse, misuse
mißbrauchen abuse, misuse
Mißfallen displeasure
mißfallen (an etwas Mißfallen finden) displease (to be displeased with s. th.)
Mißhandlung ill-treatment
mißlingen fail
mißtrauen distrust
Mißverhalten misconduct
Mißverständnis misunderstanding
Mißwirtschaft mismanagement
mit dem Auge wahrnehmbar visible
Mitarbeit cooperation
Mitarbeiter-Beurteilungsskala employee rating scale
Mitarbeiterbefragung employees opinion survey
Mitbesitzer joint owner
Mitbürgschaft joint guaranty, co-surety
Miteigentümer joint proprietor
Mitglied member
Mitglied der Geschäftsleitung officer
Mitglied eines Emissionskonsortiums underwriter
Mitgliederbeitrag membership fee
Mitgliedsaufnahme affiliation
Mitgliedschaft membership
Mitgliedskarte membership card
Mitreisender fellow-passenger
Mittag noon
Mittagessen lunch(eon)
Mittagsgeschäft lunch business
Mittagspause lunch break, lunch hour
Mittagsrestaurant luncheon-bar, lunch-room
Mittagsschlaf siesta
Mittagszeit lunch-hour
mitteilen inform
mitteilen (j-m etwas mitteilen) communicate (to communicate s. th. to s. o.)
Mitteilung note, communication
Mittel funds, means
Mittel, flüssige (Geld) liquid assets, cash, liquid funds
Mittel, vorübergehend angelegte flüssige temporary cash investments
Mittel insgesamt, flüssige total cash
mittel medium
mittelfristig medium term
Mittelmeer Mediterranean
mittelmeerisch Mediterranean
Mittelpunkt focus, hub
Mittelrippenstück (Rind) spiece of the ribs of beef
Mittelstation mid station
Mittelstreckenflug medium-range flight
Mitternacht midnight
Mixed Grill mixed grill
Mobiliar furnishings
möblieren furnish
Mode fancy, fashion
modernisieren modernize
Modernisierungsplan improvement budget
Modeschau fashion show
Modewaren fancy-goods
Modewettbewerb fashion contest
Modezeitschrift fashion magazine
modifizieren modify
Modifizierung modification
modisch fashionable
mögen like
Möglichkeit facility
Mohnbeugel poppy-seed bun
Mokka demi-tasse
Mole jetty, pier, mole
Molkerei dairy
Monatskarte monthly season ticket
Monatsprogramm monthly program
Monatsverbrauch monthly consumption

Mond moon
Mondschein-Bootsfahrt moonlight boat-trip
Moorbad mud bath
Moorbehandlung mud treatment
Moorschnepfe snipe
Moos moss
Moral morale
moralisch moral
Morast quagmire
Morchel morel
morgen tomorrow
Morgenland Orient
Morgenrock dressing gown, robe
Moschee mosque
Moselwein Moselle wine
Moskitonetz mosquito net
Motel motel, motor hotel, tourist court
motivieren motivate
Motorboot motor boat, motor launch
Motorenlärm engine noise
Motorrad motor-cycle
Motorroller motor scooter, scooter
Motorschiff motor vessel (MV), motorship (MS)
Motorschlitten motor sleigh, snowmobile
Möwe sea-gull
Möwenei mew eggs
müde tired, weary
Muffins (engl. Teegebäck) muffin
Müll rubbish
Müllbeseitigung rubbish removal
Mulligatawny curried chickencream soup
Mulligatawny-Suppe (Geflügelrahmsuppe mit Curry) mulligatawny soup
Müllschlucker waste-disposer
multilateral multi-lateral
Multimomentaufnahme work sampling study
Multiplikator multiplier
multiplizieren multiply
mündig of age
mündlich oral, verbal
Mund-zu-Mund-Werbung word of mouth advertising
Mundwasser mouth wash
Münze coin
Münzfernsprecher coin box

mürbe well-cooked
Mürbekuchen (getaucht in Sirup, Sherry etc.) trifle
Mürbeteigkuchen shortcake
Muschel mussel, clam
Muschelsuppe clam broth, clam chowder, mussel soup
Muscheltiere sea-shells
Museum museum
Musical musical
Musik und Unterhaltung music and entertainment
Musikabend evening concert, musical evening
Musikbox juke-box
Musiker musician
Muskatblatt mace
Muskatblüte mace
Muskatellerwein muscatel (wine)
Muskatnuß nutmeg
Muße leisure
Muster draft, pattern
musterhaft exemplary
Muttergesellschaft parent company
Muttersprache native language

N

nach Ankunft upon arrival
nach Verladung when shipped
Nach- und Vorsaison off-peak season
Nachbarland neighbouring country
Nachbarschaft neighbourhood
Nachbehandlung after-treatment
nachbestellen reorder
Nachbestellung reorder
Nachfaßverfahren follow-up system
Nachfrage demand, inquiry
Nachfrage, jährliche annual demand
Nachkur after-treatment, rest after treatment
Nachfragepreis bid price
Nachfrageprognose predict demand
Nachlaß (Rabatt) discount
nachlassen slack off
nachlösen take a supplementary ticket
Nachmittag afternoon
nachmittags p. m.

Nachmittagstee afternoon tea
Nachmittagstee und Abendessen kombiniert high tea
Nachnahme cash on delivery (c.o.d)
Nachprüfbarkeit (Rechnungslegung) verifiability
nachprüfen review
Nachprüfung verification
Nachricht communication, message
Nachsaison after-season, low season
Nachsaisonermäßigung after-season reduction
nachsenden redirect
Nachspeise dessert, sweets
nächste (Entfernung) nearest
Nacht- und Sonntagsdienst night and sunday duty
Nachtarbeit nightwork
Nachtbar night-club
Nachteil disadvantage
Nachtfahrt night trip
Nachtflug night flight
Nachthemd nightdress
Nachtisch dessert, sweets
Nachtklub cabaret, night-club
Nachtleben night life
Nachtlokal night-club
Nachtpiste night run
Nachtportier night concierge
Nachtrag annex
Nachtreinigungspersonal night-cleaner
Nachtruhe night rest
Nachtschicht lobster shift, night shift
Nachtschichtvergütung night shift bonus
Nachtschnellzug overnight express
Nachttarif night rate
Nachttelefonistin night-telephone operator
Nachttisch bedside-table
Nachttopf chamber-pot
Nachtverkehr night service, night traffic
Nachtwächter night-watchman
Nachtzug night train
Nachweis proof
Nachzahlung late payment, post payment, subsequent payment
nahe near, near at hand
Nähe vicinity

Nähe, in der near at hand
Nahrung food, nourishment
Nahrung aufnehmen ingest
Nahrungsaufnahme ingestion
Nahrungsmittel food, nourishment
Nahrungsmittelverfälschung adulteration of food
Nahschnellverkehrszug fast local train
Nahverkehr local traffic, short-distance traffic
Nähzeug sewing kit
Name name
namens on behalf of
Napfkuchen pound-cake
naß humid, moist, wet
Nässe wetness
national national
Nationalfeiertag national holiday
Nationalität nationality
Nationalitätszeichen nationality sign
Nationalpark national park
Nationaltracht national costume
Natron, kohlensaures bicarbonate, natron
Natur nature
Naturalleistung payment in kind
Naturheilbehandlung nature cure
Naturheilkunde naturopathy
Naturheilkundiger naturopath
Naturheilverfahren naturopathy
Naturschätze natural resources
Naturschnitzel plain veal steak
Naturschönheit beauty spot
Naturschutz nature conservation, wildlife conservation
Naturschutzgebiet nature reserve
Nautik navigation
Navelorange navel orange
Navigation navigation
Navigationskarte navigation guide
Navigationskunde navigation
Nebel fog, mist
nebelfrei free from fog
Nebenausgaben extras
Nebenbetriebe other operated departments
nebeneinander liegende Zimmer adjoining rooms
Nebengebäude annex, penthouse
Nebengebühr extra

Nebenkosten additional charge, incidental charges
Nebenstelle branch office
Nebenstraße by-road, by-street
Nebenstrecke branch line
neblig foggy, misty
Negativ negative
nehmen, an Bord take shipping
nennen name
Nennkapital authorized shares
Nennwert face value, par value
nett kind
Nettoeinzahlungsüberschüsse, diskontierte present value of future cash flow
Nettoerlös net revenue
Nettoumsatz net revenue
Netzplantechnik (CPM-Methode) Critical Path Method
Neuheit novelty
Neujahrskreuzfahrt New Year's cruise
Neujahrstag New Year's Day
Neuklassifizierung reclassification
Neunauge lamprey
Neuschnee new fallen snow
Neutralität (Rechnungslegung) neutrality
Nicht berühren! don't touch
nicht erfüllen fail
nicht haben lack
Nicht hinauslehnen! do not lean out
nicht mögen dislike
Nicht öffnen! do not open
nicht unwahrscheinlich reasonably possible
nicht übereinstimmen (mit) disagree (with)
Nichte niece
Nichterfüllung nonfulfillment, failure of performance
Nichtlieferung nondelivery
Nichtraucher non-smoker
Nichtraucherabteil non-smoker compartment
Nichtschwimmer non-swimmer
Nichtschwimmerbecken non-swimmers' pool
Nichtzutreffendes streichen! delete which is inapplicable
Niederlassung establishment

Niederschlag precipitation, rainfall
Niederstwertprinzip at the lower of cost or market
niederträchtig rotten
Niere kidney
Nierstückbraten roast sirloin of beef
nippen sip
Niveau level
Nominalbetrag face value
Nominalkapital authorized shares
Nominalwert par value
Non-Stop-Flug non-stop flight
Nordsalm Scandinavian salmon
Nordwind north wind
Normalarbeitszeit regular time
Normalleistung normal performance
Normung standardization
Not distress
Notadresse emergency address
Notausgang emergency exit
Notbremse communication cord, emergency brake
Notbremse ziehen pull the emergency brake
Notfall emergency
notieren note, quote
Notiz memorandum, note
Notizen machen take notes
Notlage distress
Notlage, finanzielle financial distress
Notlandung emergency landing, forced landing
Notleine communication cord
Notrutsche emergency chute
Notsitz folding seat, tip-up seat
Notstand distress
nötigen compel
nüchtern sober
Nudel noodle
Nudelbrett pastry board
Nudelholz rolling pin
Nudeln, grüne green noodles
Nudeln, hausgemachte home-made noodles
Nudelsuppe noodle soup
null zero
null und nichtig null and void
Nullkontrolle zero balancing
Nummer (Telefon) line
Nummer, fortlaufende consecutive number

Nummernschild number plate
Nuß kernel, nut
Nußbeugel nut bun
Nußbutter browned butter, nut butter
Nußeis nut ice
Nußpudding nut pudding
Nußtorte fancy-cake with nuts, nut tart
Nutzen benefit
Nutzen bringen benefit
nützen benefit
Nutzenschwelle break-even point
Nutzlast pay load
**Nutzungsdauer,
 betriebsgewöhnliche** useful life of the asset

O

Oase oasis
obdachlos homeless
Oberbett upper berth
Oberdeck upper deck
Oberkellner head waiter, maitre
Objektiv lens
Obligation debenture
obligatorisch mandatory
Observatorium observatory
Obst, gemischtes mixed fruit
Obst- und Gemüsehändler greengrocer
Obstgelee fruit jelly
Obsthändler fruiterer
Obstkuchen fruit cake, fruit pie, flan
Obstsalat freh fruit cup, fruit salad
Obstschüssel fruit bowl
Obsttorte fruit flan, fruit tart
Obsttörtchen tartlet
Ochse ox
Ochsenbraten roast beef
Ochsengaumen ox-palate
Ochsenmaulsalat ox-muzzle salad, pickled beef's muzzle, salad of ox-palate
Ochsenrippenstück prime rib of beef, rib of beef
Ochsenschwanz oxtail
Ochsenschwanzragout oxtail stew
Ochsenschwanzsuppe oxtail soup

Ochsenschwanzsuppe gebunden thick oxtailsoup
Ochsenschwanzsuppe klar clear oxtail soup
Ochsenzunge ox-tongue
Ochsenzunge gebraten braised ox-tongue
ofengebacken oven-baked
Ofenheizung stove heating
offen open
Offenlegung disclosure
öffentliche Anlagen public gardens
öffentliche Bekanntmachung public notices
öffentliche Fernsprechzelle public call-room
öffentliche Toilette comfort-station, public convenience, public lavatory
Öffentlichkeit publicity
Öffentlichkeitsarbeit public relations
offerieren offer
Offerte offer
offiziell official
öffnen open
ohne without
ohne Berechnung free of charge
ohne weiteres readily
Ohrenschützer ear-warmers
ökonomisch economical
Öl oil
Ölheizung oil heating
Olive olive
Olive, große grüne queen olive
Olive, reife ripe olive
Olive gefüllt stuffed olive
Olivenöl olive oil
Ölsardinen sardines
Ölstand oil level
Ölwechsel oil-changing
Ölzentralheizung oil-fired central heating
Olympiastadt Olympic city
Olympische Spiele Olympic Games
Omelett omelet
Omelett, einfaches plain omelet
Omelett mit Rum flaming rum-omelet
Omelett Soufflé puff omelet
Omnibus bus, coach, motor coach, omnibus
Open Bar open bar

Oper opera
Operational Management operational management
Operettentheater operetta house
Opernball Opera Ball
Opernhaus opera house
Option option
Optionsrecht option
optisch optical
Orange orange
Orangeade orangeade
Orangeat candied orange peel
Orangeneis orange ice-cream
Orangenlimonade, natürliche orangeade
Orangenmarmelade marmelade
Orchester orchestra
Orchesterplatz bandstand
ordentlich orderly, tidy
Ordnung order, regulation
ordnungsgemäß orderly
Organigramm organization chart
Organisation organization
Organisation, nicht unternehmerisch tätige nonbusiness organization
Organisationsplan organization chart
Organisator organizer
organisieren organize
Orient orient
Orientierungsfeld orientation plan
Ort town, village
örtlich local
Örtlichkeit locality
Ortsbrauch local custom
Ortschaft, geschlossene builtup area
Ortsgespräch local call
Ortstafel place-name sign
Ortstaxe local tax
ortsüblich in accordance with local customs
Ortsverkehr local carriage, local traffic
Ortswerbestempel local advertisement postmark
Ortszeit local time
Osten east
Osterferien Easter holidays
Osterfest Easter
Ostern Easter
Österreich Austria
österreichische Bundesbahn Austrian Federal Railways
Ostwind east wind
Ouvertüre overture
Ozean ocean
Ozeandampfer ocean liner, transatlantic liner
Ozeanflug transatlantic flight
Ozeanreise transoceanic voyage
Ozon ozone
Ozonbad ozonic bath
ozonhaltig ozoniferous
ozonisch ozonic

P

Pacht leasehold, rent
pachtbar rentable
Pachtbesitz leasehold
pachten lease, rent
Pächter leaseholder, lessee, tenant
pachtweise on lease
packen pack
Packpapier kraft paper, wrapping paper
Packung pack, package
Packwagen luggage van
Paddel paddle
Paddelboot canoe, paddling boat
paddeln paddle
Page hotel bellboy, page-boy
Paket package, parcel
Paketkarte dispatch note
Paketpost parcel post
Palatschinken rolled pancake, stuffed pancakes, thin pancakes filled with jam
Palette range
Palmenmark hearts of palm
Palmsonntag Palm Sunday
Pampelmuse grapefruit
Pampelmusensaft grapefruit juice
paniert bread-crumbed
Pannenhilfe breakdown service
Panorama panorama
Papierkorb waste-paper basket
Papierserviette paper napkin
Papierwaren paper supplies
pappig pappy

Pappschnee sticky snow
Paprika paprika
Paprika, gefüllt stuffed green (sweet) peppers
Paprikahühnchen stewed chicken in paprika (cream) sauce
Paprikaschnitzel braised veal cutlet in paprika sauce, veal steak Hungaria style
Parahotellerie (z. B. Privatquartiere, Ferienzentren, Campingplätze, Erholungsheime etc.) supplementary accomodation
Paranuß Brazil nut
Paravent folding screen
Pariser Kartoffeln fried potato balls
Parka parka
Parkdauer bis zu waiting limited to
Parken gebührenfrei free parking
Parken verboten! waiting prohibited
Parkett stall
Parkgelegenheit parking facilities
Parkhochhaus multi-story car park
Parkmöglichkeit parking facilities
Parkplatz car park, garage-parking lot, parking lot, parking place
Parkplatz, bewachter guarded car park
Parkscheibe parking disk
Parkuhr parking meter
Parkverbot no waiting, prohibition to park
Parkwächter parking attendant
Parmesankäse Parmesan cheese
Parterre ground floor
Paß (Ausweis) passport
Paß (Berg) pass
Paßabfertigung passport inspection
Passagenpreis passenger fare
Passagevertrag contract of passage
Passagier passenger, pax
Passagierdampfer liner, passenger steamer
Passagierflugzeug passenger plane
Passagiergepäck passenger's luggage
Passagierschiff passenger ship
Passant chance guest, temporary hotel guest, transient (guest)
Passantenhotel transient hotel
passend appropriate

passend machen match
Paßhöhe altitude of a pass
passieren happen
Passierschein permit
Passiva liabilities and owners' equity
Passiva insgesamt total liabilities and stockholders' equity
passive Zahlungsbilanz adverse balance of payments
Passivierungspflicht accrual mandatory
Passivierungswahlrecht accrual elective
Passivkonto liability account
Passivseite (Bilanz) equity side
Paßkontrolle passport inspection
Paßstelle passport office
Paßvorschriften passport regulations
Pastetchen patty
Pastetchen mit gehackten Früchten gefüllt mince-pie
Pastete pate, pie
Pastetenkruste pie-crust
Pasteurisierung pasteurization
Patent patent
Patentverletzung patent violation
Patissier pastry cook
pauschal flat
Pauschalarrangement inclusive arrangement, inclusive terms
Pauschalbetrag flat sum, lump sum
Pauschale inclusive price, lump sum
Pauschalgebühr inclusive charge
Pauschalpreis inclusive fare, inclusive price
Pauschalpreis für Selbstfahrer inclusive rates for self-drive car hire
Pauschalpreisferien all-in holiday, inclusive holiday
Pauschalreise all-expense trip, all-in journey, inclusive journey, inclusive trip, package tour
Pellkartoffeln potatoes boiled in their skins
Pelzgeschäft furrier
Pelzmantel fur coat
Pemmikan (Dörrfleisch) pem(m)ican
Pendelverkehr shuttle service
Pension guest house, private hotel, boarding house

Pension gehen, in retire
Pension (Rente) retirement
Pension (Übernachtung) boarding-house, guest-house
Pensionsgast boarder, resident
Pensionsplan pension scheme
Pensionspreis board, price for board and lodging
Pensionsrückstellung pension obligation, pension reserve
per Adresse care of (c/o)
per Anhalter reisen hitch-hike
Perkolator percolator
perlend sparkling
Perlhuhn guinea-fowl
Perlwein sparkling wine
Perlzwiebel pearl onion
Person, juristische corporate body
Personal personnel
Personalabteilung personnel department
Personalanforderung personnel requisition
Personalbeschaffung recruitment
Personalbeschreibung personal data
Personalbudget manpower budget
Personalchef personnel manager
Personalcomputer personal computer
Personalpförtner time keeper
Personalplanungsleitfaden manning table
Personalumschlag labor turnover
Personalverpflegung employees' meals
personell übersetzt overstaffed
Personenfähre passenger ferry
Personengesellschaft (etwa: Offene Handelsgesellschaft (OHG)) partnership
Personentransport passenger carriage
Personenverkehr passenger carriage, passenger traffic
Personenwagen passenger car
Personenzahl size of pary
Personenzug passenger train
persönlich individually
persönliche Gebrauchsgegenstände articles for daily use, personal belongings

persönliches Schuldanerkenntnis promissory note
Petersfisch John Dory (fish)
Petersilie parsley
Petersilienkartoffeln parsley potatoes
Petersiliensoße parsley sauce
Petroleum kerosene
Pfad trail
Pfand (Pfandrecht) pledge
Pfandbrief mortgage bond
pfänden attach, pawn
Pfandrecht lien
Pfandrecht, gewährtes pledge of property, asset pledged
Pfännchen pannikin
Pfanne pan
Pfannenstiel panhandle
Pfannkuchen pancake
Pfannkuchensuppe pancake soup
Pfau peacock
Pfeffer pepper
Pfeffer (Fleischgericht) jugged meat
Pfeffer, grüner green pepper
Pfeffergefäß pepper-box
Pfefferkorn pepper-corn
Pfefferkuchen ginger bread
Pfefferminze peppermint
Pfefferminztee mint tea
Pfeffermühle pepper mill
Pfefferschote pepper
Pfefferschote, rote red pepper
Pfefferschoten-Mischgericht French pepper-stew
Pfeffersteak pepper-steak
Pfefferstreuer pepper-caster, pepper-pot
pfeifen whistle
Pferdedroschke hackney-cab
Pferderennen horse-race
Pferdeschlitten horse sleigh
Pferdesport equestrian sport
Pferdeverleih hacking
Pferdewagen horse drawn vehicle
Pfifferling chanterelle
Pfingsten Pentecost, Whitsunday
Pfingstferien Whitsun holidays
Pfirsich peach
Pfirsich Melba peach Melba
Pfirsich-Eis peach ice-cream
Pflanzenfett shortening
Pflanzenöl plant oil

Pflanzenwelt flora
Pflaume plum, prune
pflaumen- od. rosinenreich plummy
Pflaumenkuchen plum flan
Pflicht duty
pflichttreu loyal
Pflichttreue loyality
Pförtner commissionaire, door-keeper
Pfund (engl.: ca. 450 g) pound
Phantasie fancy
Pichelsteiner Fleisch mixed meat-stew with vegetables
Pickles pickles
Picknick picnic
Picknicktasche picnic bag
pikant spicy
Pilgermuscheln cockles
Pilgerreise pilgrimage
Pilot aircraft pilot, pilot
Pilz (allgemein) fungus
Pilz, eßbarer mushroom
Pilzcremesuppe cream of mushroom
Pilze auf Toast mushrooms on toast
Pilzschnitte mushrooms on toast
Pilzsoße mushroom sauce
Pilzsuppe mushroom soup, soup with mushrooms
Pint (Hohlmaß: ca. 0,5 Liter) pint
Piste runway, ski run, slope
Pistenpflege ski run maintenance, slope grooming
Pizza open pie, pizza
Plaid plaid
Plakat poster
Plakatwerbung poster advertising
Plan blue print, forecast, plan
Plane awning
planen schedule
Plankostenrechnung standard-cost system
planmäßig on schedule, scheduled planning
Planschbecken paddling-pool
planschen paddle, splash
Planung planning
Planung der Speisekarte menu planning
Planziel target
Plastikbeutel plastic bag
Platte plate, platter, serving dish

Plattenlaufwerk hard disc
Platz (Ort) square
Platz (Sitz) seat
Platz, besetzter taken seat
Platzanweiser attendant, usher
Platzanweiserin usherette
Platzanzahl, begrenzte limited number of seats
Platzbelegung, elektronische teleregister
Platzbestellung booking of seats, seat reservation
Plätzchen biscuit
Platzkarte reserved seat ticket, ticket for reserved seat
Platzkarten erforderlich seats should be reserved in advance
Platzkartengebühr seat reservation fee
Platzmiete tennis court fee
Platzregen downpour
Platzreservierung seat reservation
Platzzuteilung allocation of seats
Plinsen buckwheat pancakes
Plötze roach
Plumpudding (engl. Weihnachtskuchen) plum pudding
Pockenschutzimpfung variolization
Pokerspiel poker
polieren polish
Politesse meter maid, traffic warden
Politik policy
Politik der offenen Tür open-door policy
Polizei police
Polizeipräsidium policehead quarters
Polizeirevier police station
Polizist constable, policeman
Pommes frites chips, French fried potatoes, chipped potatoes
Popkonzert pop concert
Popmusik pop
Porree leek
Porridge porridge
Portal porch
Porterhousesteak, kleines T-bone steak
Portier bellcaptain, concierge
Portion portion
Portionsgröße portion size

Porto postage
Portogebühr postal rate
Portwein port wine
Porzellan china, porcelain
Porzellan- und Glaswaren china and glassware
Position position
Positionslicht navigation light
Post mail
Postamt post office
Postanweisung postal money order, postal order
Postanweisung, internationale international money order
Postbezirk postal district
Postbus post-office bus
Posten (Rechnung) item
Posten, transitorischer deferred item
Poster poster
Postfach pigeon hole, post-office box
postfertig ready for mail
Postflug mail flight
Postflugzeug mail plane
Postkarte postcard
postlagernd general delivery, poste restante
Postleitzahl postal zone number, zip code
Postliste mailing list
Postscheckamt postal giro office
Postscheckkonto postal check account
Postsparkonto postal savings account
Poststempel postmark
Postzustellung postal delivery
Poularde poulard
Pökelfleisch corned beef, pickles pork
Pökelrindfleisch salted beef
Pökelzunge red beef tongue
prächtig magnificent
Praktikant trainee, intern
praktisch rational
Pralinen chocolates
Prämiensystem incentive system
Präsidenten-Suite presidential suite
Praxis experience
Preis rate

Preis, angemessener reasonable price
Preis, ermäßigter reduced rate
Preis, freier open price
Preis, kontrollierter administered price
Preis anheben jack price
Preis drücken cut price
Preis einschließlich sämtlicher Kosten FAS price
Preis erhöhen raise price
Preis für ein Doppelzimmer, höchster double occupancy rack rate
Preis je Tag und Person price per day and person
Preis pro Einheit unit price
Preis senken cut price
Preisänderungen vorbehalten prices subject to alteration
Preisangabe quotation, quotation of prices
Preisangebot machen quote
Preisanpassung adjustment of prices
Preisbeschränkung rate restriction
Preisdruck dumping
Preise auf Anfrage prices on request, rates on application
Preise einschließlich Bedienungsgeld und Mehrwertsteuer prices include service charge and added-value tax
Preise ohne Gewähr prices without guarantee
Preise schließen die folgenden Leistungen ein prices include the following services
Preiselbeere cranberry, red bilberry
Preiserhöhung advance in price, price increase
Preisermäßigung price cut
Preisfestsetzung pricing
Preisfestsetzungsverfahren, nachfrageorientiertes yield management
preisgeben give up
Preisgefüge price structure
Preisklasse price category
Preislage, mittlere medium priced, moderate rate

Preisliste price list
Preisnachlaß price allowance, rebate
Preisniveau level of prices
Preisnotierung quotation
Preisobergrenze price ceiling
Preispolitik price policy
Preisschild price tag
Preisschwankung fluctuation of price
Preissenkung mark down, reduction of the rates
Preissteigerung advance in price
Preisunterbietung dumping
Presseerklärung press release
Presseinformation press release
Pressemitteilung hand out
Presskopf head cheese, pressed hog's head
Priorität precendence, priority
Prise (Salz) dash, pinch
Privatbadestrand private bathing-beach
Privatbesitz private property
Privatgrundstück private property
Privathaus private house
Privatjacht private yacht
Privatkonto drawing account
Privatsphäre privacy
Privatwagen private car
Privatzimmer private room
pro Tag per day
Probe (Muster) pattern
Probe, auf on trial
Probebilanz trial balance
Probelauf trial run
probieren attempt, try
Produkt product
Produktionsmenge output
Produktionsplanung production planning
Produktionssteuerung production control
Produktivität productivity
professionell professional
Profi professional
Prognose forecast
Prognosefaktor forecast factor
Programm package, program (amerik.), programme (brit.)
Programmänderung change in the program
Programmiersprache programming language
Projektor projector
Promenade promenade
Promenadendeck promenade deck
prompt readily
Propangas propan gas
Propellerflugzeug airscrew-driven aeroplane
Prosit! cheerio, cheers, to your health
Prospekt booklet, brochure, folder, leaflet, prospectus
Prost! bottoms up
Protokoll minutes
Proviant provisions
Proviantkorb luncheon-basket
Provision commission
Provision der Konsortialführerin management fee
Provision gewähren grant a commission
Provisionsertrag (Umsatzbereich 6) commission (schedule 6)
Provisionssatz, zusätzlicher overriding commission
provozieren provoke
Prozeß action, litigation
Prozeßrisiko risk of litigation
prüfen audit, examine, inspect, test
Prüfer auditor
Prüfliste check list
Prüfmeinung opinion
Prüfung test
Prüfung an Ort und Stelle spot check
Prüfung des betrieblichen Finanz- und Rechnungswesens financial auditing
Prünelle prunelle
Pub pub
Public Relations public relations
Publikation publication
Publizität publicity
Pudding pudding
Puder powder
Puderzucker icing sugar
Pufferzeit (Netzplan) buffer time
Puffmais popcorn
Pullmanwagen Pullman (car)
Pult desk
Pulver powder

Pulverschnee powder snow
Pumpernickel Westphalian rye-bread
Punkt, markanter (z.b. bei Wegbeschreibungen) landmark
Punsch punch
Puppe doll
pur neat
Puter turkey
PX (Warenhaus für amerik. Armeeangehörige) PX (post exchange)

Q

Quacksalber quack doctor
Qualifikation qualification
qualifizieren qualify
qualifiziert qualified
Qualität quality
Qualitätsbewertung quality evaluation
Qualitätskennzeichnung grade labelling
Qualitätskontrolle quality control
Qualitätskontrolleur quality checker
Qualitätsprüfung der Speisen food test
Qualitätsstandard quality standard
Qualitätsüberprüfungsprogramm quality assurance program
Qualle jellyfish
Quantität quantity
Quarantäne quarantine
Quark curd cheese
Quarkknödel white cheese dumpling
Quarktaschen pastry envelopes filled with white chese
Quart (1.136 Liter) quart
Quarter (amerik. Münze) quarter
Quartier lodging, quarters
Quartiergeber landlord
Quartiermeister quartermaster
quasi quasi
Quelle fountain, spring
Quellpavillon pump room
Quellwasser spring water
Querulant trouble maker
Querverweis cross-reference
Quitte quince
quittieren receipt

Quittung receipt
Quote quota
Quotient quotient
quotieren quote

R

Rabatt allowance, discount, rebate
Rabatt trade discount
Rad (Fahrrad) bike
Raddampfer paddle-steamer, side-wheeler
Radfahrweg cycle track
Radieschen radish
Radio radio, wireless
Radio in allen Zimmern radio sets in every room
Radioübertragung transmission
Radlermaß shandy
Radonquelle radon spring
Radtourist cycling tourist
Ragout fricassee, hash, ragout, stew
Ragout, weißes white stew
Rahm cream, sweet cream
Rahm, saurer sour cream
Rahmenprogramm für Begleitpersonen spouse program
Rahmkäse cream cheese
Rahmkäsetorte cream cheese tart
Rahmschnitzel creamed veal collop, veal steak in sour cream
Rahmsoße cream sauce
Rahmsuppe cream soup
Rallye rallye
Rampe ramp
Ramschverkauf jumble sale
Rand edge
Rang rank
Rang, zweiter (im Theater) upper circle
rangieren shunt, rank
ranzig rancid
Rapunzelsalat lamb's lettuce-salad
Rasen nicht betreten! keep off the grass
Rasensprenger sprinkler
Rasierapparat, elektrischer electric razor
Rasierwasser after-shave lotion

Rastplatz lay-by
Raststätte road-house
Rat advice
Rate instalment, rate
Ratenzahlung deferred payment
Ratgeber guide
Rathaus city hall, town hall
rationalisieren economize, rationalize
Rationalisierung economizing, rationalization
Rationalisierungsfachmann efficiency expert
Ratschlag advice
Raucher smoker
Raucherabteil smoker, smoking compartment
Räucheraal smoked eel
Räucherhering kippered herring
Räucherhering gebraten fried kipper
Räucherlachs smoked salmon
Räucherschinken gammon, smoked ham
Rauchfleisch smoked beef, smoked beat
Rauchfleisch mit Kraut smoked pork with pickled cabbage
Rauchsalon smoke room
rauh rugged
Rauigote-Soße rauigote sauce
Raum für Säuglingsbetreuung babies' room
Raum in der Hotelhalle lobby space
räumen clear, vacate
Räumung clearance
Reabilitätstest reliability criterion
reagieren auf respond to
Reaktionsfähigkeit responsiveness
Reaktion, gefühlsmäßige emotional reaction
Realisationszeitpunkt recognition
realisieren realize
Rebhuhn partridge
Rebhuhnpastete partridge pie
Rebstock vine
Rechenmaschine calculating machine, calculator
Rechenschaft (od. Rechnung) ablegen über account for
Rechentabelle ready reckoner
rechnen calculate

rechnen mit relevanten Kosten relevant costing
Rechnung bill, calculation, invoice
Rechnung stellen, in bill
Rechnung vorlegen present a bill
Rechnungsabgrenzung, aktive deferred charges, prepaid expenses, accrued revenues, accrued income
Rechnungsabgrenzung, passive accrued expenses
Rechnungsabgrenzung, transitorische prepaid expenses
Rechnungsbetrag invoice amount
Rechnungslegung, externe financial accounting
Recht right
Rechte, grundstücksgleiche real property rights
rechtfertigen justify
Rechtfertigung justification
rechtlich lawful, legal
rechtmäßig lawful, legitimate, rightful
Rechtmäßigkeit rightfulness
Rechts fahren! keep right
Rechtsabbiegen verboten no right turn
Rechtsanspruch legal claim
Rechtsanspruch right
Rechtsanwalt lawyer
Rechtsanwaltsgebühren legal fees and expenses
Rechtsberatung legal services
Rechtsform legal form
rechtsgültig legal
Rechtshilfe legal aid
Rechtsschutzversicherung legal aid insurance
Rechtsstreit litigation
Rechtsverkehr right-hand traffic
rechtswidrig illegal
Reeder ship owner
Reederei shipping company
Regel regulation, rule
regeln control, rule
Regeltarif general tariff
Regelungsinstitution regulatory body
Regelzug scheduled train
Regen rainfall

Regenbogenforelle rainbow trout
regendicht rainproof
Regenerationszentrum health club
Regenmantel mackintosh, raincoat
Regenschauer shower of rain
Regenversicherung rain insurance
Regenzeit rainy season
Registratur registry office
Registrierungsgebühr registration fee
regnerisch pluvial, rainy
Reh deer, roe
Rehbock roebuck
Rehbraten roast venison
Rehragout stew of venison
Rehrücken saddle of venison
Rehrücken flambiert flamed saddle of venison
Rehschlegel leg of venison
Reibeisen grater
Reibekuchen potato-fritters
reiben grate
reichlich ample
reif mature, ripe
Reifen tyre
Reifendruck tyre pressure
Reifenwechsel changing a wheel
Reihe queue
rein clean (sauber), neat (ordentlich)
Reineclaude greengage
Reinertrag net proceeds
Reingewicht net weight
Reingewinn net income, net profit
reinigen clean, cleanse
reinigen, chemisch dry-clean
Reinigung cleaning
Reinigung, chemische dry cleaning
Reinigung der Veranstaltungsräume public space and kitchen cleaning
Reinigungsabteilung stewarding department
Reinigungskraft parlour-maid
Reinigungsmittel cleaning supply
Reinigungspersonal cleaning personnel, housemen
Reinverlust net loss
Reis rice
Reis, gekochter boiled rice
Reis, roher paddy
Reisauflauf soufflé of rice

Reise journey, tour, travel, trip, voyage
Reiseagent tourist agent
Reiseagentur tourist agency
Reiseandenken travel souvenir
Reiseanmeldung final holiday registration
Reiseapotheke portable medicine-case, tourist's medicine-case
Reiseatlas tourist atlas
Reiseauskunft travel information
Reisebedingungen, allgemeine general travel conditions
Reisebeginn start
Reisebegleiter travel companion
Reisebeilage travel supplement
Reisebetreuung travel service
Reisebus tourist bus
Reisebüro tourist agency, travel agency
Reisebüroverband association of travel agencies, International Federation of Travel Agencies
Reisedauer duration of a journey
Reisedichte passenger density
Reiseetappe stage of journey
Reiseführer guide, guide-book, itinerary
Reisegebiet touring area, tourist area, tourist region
Reisegepäck, fehlendes lost luggage
Reisegepäck, verschlepptes wrongly routed luggage
Reisegeschwindigkeit cruising speed
Reisegesellschaft tourist party
Reisegutschein travel voucher
Reiseintensität volume of tourist traffic
Reisekasse travelling funds
Reisekreditbrief traveller's letter of credit
Reiseleiter courier, tour conductor, tour manager, travel supervisor
Reiseleiter, sprachkundiger linguist-courier
Reiseleiterin tour manager
Reiseleitung courier's office, tour management

Reisemarkt tourist market, travel market
Reisemitbringsel holiday gift
Reisemittler tourist agent
reisen travel
reisen, ins Ausland go abroad
reisen, mit dem Zug travel by train
Reisen abwickeln operate
Reisender tourist, traveller, voyager
Reisender (Verkäufer) salesman
Reisepapiere travel documents
Reisepaß passport
Reiseplakat touristic poster, travel poster
Reiseplan itinerary
Reiseprogramm travel program
Reiseprospekt travel booklet
Reiseproviant packet lunch, travelling provisions
Reiseroute itinerary, touring itinerary
Reiseroute festlegen fix the route of a journey
Reiseruf S.O.S. message
Reisescheck traveller's cheque (check)
Reisespesen-Tagessatz per diem allowance
Reisestrecke touring itinerary
Reisetag travelling day
Reisetasche bag, travelling bag
Reiseunfallversicherung travel accident insurance
Reiseunterbrechung stopover
Reiseveranstalter tour operator, travel organizer
Reiseverkehr tourist traffic, travel
Reiseverlauf course of a journey, touring itinerary
Reiseversicherung travel insurance
Reisevorbereitungen travel preparations
Reisewegänderung change of route
Reisewelle travel boom
Reisewetterversicherung tourist weather insurance
Reisezahlungsverkehr payments of travellers
Reisezeit tourist season, travel time
Reiseziel destination
Reisezug passenger train

Reisfleisch meat rice, steamed rice with chopped pork (beef)
Reisgericht (in Form) rice pie, rice timbale
Reisgericht mit Erbsen rice dish with peas
Reisgericht mit Reibkäse rice dish with grated cheese
Reissuppe rice soup
Reißverschluß zip
Reitbahn riding-ring
Reitgelände riding-ground
Reitgelegenheit riding-facilities
Reitklub riding-club
Reitkurs riding-course
Reitpferde zu vermieten horses for hire
Reitschule riding-school
Reitstall riding-stable
Reitweg bridle-path, riding-track
Reiz zest
Reklamation complaint
Reklame advertising
reklamieren complain, reclaim
Rekonvaleszenz convalescence
Relevanz (Rechnungslegung) relevance
Reling rail
Rendite yield
Rennboot racing boat
rennen race
Rennstrecke race course, trail
Rentabilität profitability
Rentenwert (Rente) bond
Ren(tier) reindeer
Reparaturauftrag maintenance work order, repair order
Reparaturdienst service station
Reparaturwerkstätte garage, repair shop
reparieren fix, repair
repariert fixed
Repräsentationswerbung prestige advertising
Reservat national park, nature reserve, reservation
Reservations- und Beschwerdebuch im Restaurant log-book
Reserve reserve, resource
Reserve, eiserne minimum stock

Reservebett spare bed
reservieren reserve
Reservierung reservation
Reservierung, feste guaranteed reservation
Reservierungsdame reservation clerk
Reservierungssystem reservation service, reservation system
Rest remainder, residue
Restaurantbesetzung sitting
Restaurantdeck restaurant deck
Restaurantdirektor restaurant manager
Restaurateur restaurant-keeper
Resultat result
Rettich black radish, radish
Rettungsboot life-boat
Rettungsexpedition rescue expedition
Rettungsgürtel life-belt
Rettungsmannschaft rescue party
Rettungsstation life-guard station, life-saving station
Rettungswagen ambulance, motor ambulance
revidieren revise
Rezept (Küche) recipe
Rezeption reception desk, office
Rhabarber pie-plant (amerik.), rhubarb (brit.)
Rheinsalm Rhine salmon
Rheinwein (weißer) hock, Rhine wine
richten nach, sich act on
richtig correct
Richtlinie regulation
Richtlinien business policy
Richtung direction
Richtungspfeil direction arrow
riechen smell
Riesenslalom giant slalom
Rind (Fleisch) beef
Rinde peeling
Rinderbrust brisket of beef
Rinderschmorbraten potted beef, stewed beef
Rinderschwanzstück geschmort braised aitchbone
Rindfleisch beef
Rindfleisch, gekocht boiled beef

Rindfleisch in Essig und Öl cold beef in vinegar
Rindfleischsalat salad of boiled beef
Rindsbraten joint of beef
Rindsfilet fillet of beef, tenderloin
Rindsfilet im Blätterteig tenderloin of beef 'Wellington'
Rindsgulasch beef stew
Rindslendenbraten roast fillet of beef
Rindsmagen in Milch und Wasser tripe and onions
Rindsragout brown beef stew
Rindsrostbraten top cut roast
Rindsroulade rolled braised beef, beef olive
Rindszunge geräuchert smoked beef tongue
Rind(vieh) cattle
Ringbahn belt line, circle railway
Ringstraße belt highway, circular road, ring road
Rippchen rib
Rippenspeer spare-rib
Risiko hazard, risk
risikoreich risky
Risikoübernahme, volle full coverage
riskieren risk
Roastbeef roast sirloin
Roastbeef, englisches roast beef (English style)
Rochen ray
Rodelbahn toboggan run, toboggan slide
Rodelhang coasting slide, toboggan run, toboggan slide
Rodellift sledge tow, toboggan tow
Rodeln luging, tobogganing
rodeln toboggan
Rogen roe
Roggen rye
Roggenbrot rye-bread
roh raw
Rohertrag gross profit on sales, raw yield
Rohgewinn gross profit, margin
Rohkost vegetarian food

Rohkostplatte salad plate
Rohmaterial raw material
Röhre tube
Rohrpost tube post
Rohschinken raw ham
Rohstoff raw material
Rollbahn runway
Rollbraten rolled beef
Roller scooter
Rollfilm roll film
Rollgeld cartage, wheelage
Rollmops collared herring, rolled herring, rollmop herring
Rollschinken rolled ham
Rollschuhbahn skating-rink
Rollstuhl bath chair, wheel-chair
Rolltreppe escalator
Röntgenaufnahme X-ray photo
Roquefort-Käse Roquefort
Rose rose
Rosenkohl Brussels sprouts
rosig gebraten medium done
Rosine raisin
Rosinenpudding baked sultana pudding
Rosmarin rosemary
Rost grill
Rostbraten boned rips of beef, roast beef
Röstbrot grilled bread
Röstbrotschnitte toast
Röstbrotwürfelchen fried slippets
Rösti hash brown potatoes
rot red
Rotbarbe red mullet
Rotbrasse sea-bream
Rote Beete beet-root
Rote Beete-Salat beet-root salad
rote Grütze red grits
rote Rübe red beet
rotieren rotate
Rotkohl red cabbage
Rotwein red wine
Rotzunge dab, lemon-sole
Roulade collared beef
Routinearbeit routine work
routiniert experienced
Rübe, rote red beet
Rübe, weiße swede, turnip
Rübensuppe, russische rote Russian beetroot soup

Rückantwortkarte reply postcard
Rückbestätigung (über eine erfolgte Buchung) reconfirmation
Rückbürgschaft counter security
Rücken (Fleisch) saddle
Rückenschmerzen backache
Rückenstück saddle
Rückenstück vom Lamm baron of lamb
Rückenwind tail-wind
Rückfahrkarte return ticket, roundabout ticket
Rückfahrt return journey, return trip
Rückflug return flight
Rückgabe return
Rückgang decline
rückgestellt accrued
Rückinformation feed-back
Rückkaufswert von Lebensversicherungen cash surrender value of life insurance
Rückkehr return
Rückkoppelungsqualität (Rechnungslegung) feedback value
Rücklage einschließlich Gewinn- oder Verlustvortrag, freie unappropriated surplus
Rücklagen reserves
Rücklagen, offene unappropriated retained earnings
Rücklagen, stille hidden reserves
Rücklagen, zweckgebundene appropriated retained earnings, appropriated surplus
Rücklagen und Gewinnvortrag stockholder's equity
Rückreise return journey, return trip, return voyage
Rückreiseverkehr homeward tourist traffic
Rückstand, im in arrears
Rückstellung für Ertragssteuer accrual for income tax, income tax reserve
Rückstellungen provision for estimated liabilities, accrued liabilities, loss contingencies, accrual

Rückstellungen, sonstige (Handelsrecht) accrued liabilities
Rücktrittsfrist escape period
Rücktrittsrecht right of rescission
Rückvergütung quantity discount
rückwärtiges Zimmer back room
rückzahlbar repayable
Rückzahlungsbetrag repayment amount
Rückzahlungsverpflichtungen (im Jahresabschluß) sinking fund requirements
Ruder oar
Ruderboot rowboat, rowing-boat
rudern row
Rudersee boating-lake
Ruf reputation
Ruhebank park bench
Ruheraum rest room
Ruhestand retirement
Ruhezeiten hours of rest
Ruhezone zone of rest
ruhig calm, quiet
ruhig werden calm down
Ruine ruin
Rum rum
Rumbaba rhum-baba
Rummelplatz amusement park, fun-fair
Rumpsteak rumpsteak
Rumpsteak am Rost rumpsteak grilled
rund round
Rundblick panorama
Runde round
Rundfahrt circular tour, trip
Rundflug excursion flight, sight-seeing flight
Rundfunk broadcasting, radio
Rundfunkwerbung broadcast advertising
Rundgang tour round, walk round
Rundreise circle trip, circular tour, circular trip, round trip
Rundreisefahrschein circle trip ticket
Rundschreiben circular
Rundsicht panorama
Rundzelt bell tent
Russische Eier eggs Russian style, mayonnaise eggs, Russian eggs

rutschig slippery
Rühreier scrambled eggs

S

Sachanlagevermögen abzüglich Abschreibungen net property and equipment
Sache concern
Sache, bewegliche chattel
Sacheinlage contribution in kind
Sachertorte chocolate cake Sacher style, fancy-cake with chocolate
Sachkenntnis knowhow
Sackgasse blind alley, cul-de-sac
Safari safari, trekking
Safran saffron
Safranreis risotto with saffron, saffron-risotto
Saft juice, sap
Saftgulasch beef stew in juice
saftig juicy
Sahne cream, sweet cream
Sahnebaiser meringue
Saibling char
Saison season
Saison, tote off-season
Saison, vorherige previous season
Saisonaufschlag seasonal price increase
Saisonbetrieb seasonal establishment, seasonal service
Saisoneröffnung opening of the season
Saisongeschäft seasonal business
Saisonhotel seasonal hotel
Saisonhotellerie seasonal hotel trade
Saisonschwankung seasonal fluctuation, seasonal variation
Saisonspitze seasonal peak
Saisonzuschlag seasonal surcharge
Sakko jacket
Salami salami
Salat salad
Salat, gemischter mixed salad, tossed salad
Salat, grüner green salad
Salatschüssel salad bowl
Salatsoße dressing, salad dressing

Salatsoße französisch French dressing
Salbei sage
saldieren net (offset)
saldieren (Konto) balance (an account)
Saldo balance
Saldo ermitteln balance (an account)
Salm salmon
Salm, pochierter boiled salmon
Salmmayonnaise salmon mayonnaise
Salmmittelstück salmon cut, salmon cutlet
Salon parlor
Salon-Schlafwagen Pullman(car)
Salonwagen saloon carriage
Salz salt
Salzbretzel pretzel
Salzburger Nockerl Salzburg sweet dumpling
salzen salt
Salzfäßchen salt-cellar
Salzgurke salted cucumber
Salzkartoffeln boiled potatoes, plain boiled potatoes
Salzmandeln salted almonds
Salzstreuer salt-cellar
Samenkorn kernel
Sammeleinkauf group buying
Sammelfahrschein party ticket
Sammelfahrt party outing
Sammelgarage large-capacity garage, multi-car garage
sammeln collect, rally
Sammelpaß collective passport, group passport
Sammelpunkt meeting-place
Sammelstelle meeting-place, place of assembly
Sammelvisum group visa
Sammlung collection
Sanatorium sanatorium
Sandbad sand-bath
Sandbank sandbank
Sandburgenwettbewerb sand-castle competition
Sanddüne sand-dune
Sandkuchen Madeira cake
Sandsteinfelsen sandstone rock
Sandstrand sandy beach

Sandwich sandwich
sanieren reorganize
sanitäre Anlagen sanitary facilities
Sardelle anchovy
Sardellenbutter anchovy-butter
Sardellenbuttersoße anchovy butter sauce
Sardellensoße anchovy sauce
Sardellenstäbchen anchovy straws
Sardine, große pilchard
Sardinen in Öl sardines in oil
sauber neat, tidy
Säuberung cleaning
Sauce Béarnaise Béarnaise sauce
Sauce Hollandaise Hollandaise sauce
Sauciere sauce-boat
sauer acid, sour
Sauerampfer sorrel
Sauerbraten braised beef marinated, German pot roast, sauerbraten
Sauerkraut pickled cabbage, sauerkraut
Sauerkrautplatte sauerkraut with smoked meat, ham and sausage
Sauerstoffbad oxygen bath
Sauerteig leaven
saufen guzzle, tope
Säuglingsbetreuung baby care
Saum hem
säumig tardy
Sauna sauna
Sauterne Sauterne
Schabkäse, heißer hot Swiss cheese-mush
Schablone template
Schachtel box
Schaden damage, disadvantage, loss
schaden damage, injure
Schadenersatz compensation for damages, damages
Schadenersatz leisten pay damages
Schadenersatzanspruch claim for damages
Schadenersatzklage action for damages
Schadensanzeige notice of claim
Schadensersatzverpflichtung (aus Produkthaftung) product liability claim
Schadensfall event of loss

Schadensfeststellung ascertainment of damage
Schadenshaftung liability for damages
Schadensregulierung loss settlement
schadhaft defective
schädigen aggrieve, damage
Schaffner conductor guard
Schafskäse sheep's cheese, eve cheese
Schale peel, peeling
schälen peel
Schalentier shellfish
schalldicht soundproof
Schallplatte record, grammophone record
Schalotte scallion, shallot
Schalter (z. B. Bank-) window
Schalterbeamter booking clerk, ticket clerk
Schalterhalle booking hall
Schalterstunden der Bank banking hours
Schalthebel gear lever
Schaltjahr leap year
Schalttafel patchboard
Schampus fizz
Schankerlaubnis und Gewerbeaufsicht licenses and inspections
Schankkellner barman, bartender, tapster
Schankkellnerin barmaid
Schankstube taproom
Schanktisch bar
Schankwirt saloonkeeper
Schankwirt tavern-keeper, publican
scharf (gewürzt) delived, highly seasoned, hot, spicy
Schatten shadow
schattig shady
schätzen esteem, estimate, rate
Schätzung appraisal, estimate
Schätzung, grobe rough estimate
schauen look
Schaufensterbummel window-shopping
Schaukasten show case
Schaum bubble-bath
schäumen foam

schäumend (Wein) sparkling
Schaumgefrorenes sponge ice-cream
Schaumlöffel skimmer
Schaumwein sparkling hock
Schauplatz site
Schauspieler actor
Schauspielerin actress
Schauspielhaus playhouse
Scheck cheque
Scheck, bestätigter (gedeckter) certified check
Scheckbuch checkbook, cheque book
Scheckbürgschaft check guarantee
Scheckheft cheque book
Scheckkarte bank card, credit card
Scheibe slice
Scheibenwischer windshield wiper
Scheinwerfer headlight
Schellfisch haddock
Schema scheme, model
Schenke bar, saloon-bar
Schenkung gift
Scherbett sherbet
Scherz joke
Scheuerlappen scouring cloth
Scheuertuch floor cloth
Schicht layer, shift
Schicht, unterbrochene split shift
Schichttorte layer-cake
Schiebedach sliding roof
Schieber (Kinderlöffel) pusher
Schienennetz railway system
Schienenweg railway line
schießen shoot
Schiff ship, vessel
Schiff, auf dem on board (a) ship
Schiff, beladenes fullship
Schiff besteigen board a ship
Schiff-Eisenbahn-Umladeplatz rail and water terminal
Schiffahrt navigation
Schiffahrtsgesellschaft liner company
Schiffahrtskunde navigation
Schiffahrtsverkehr waterborne traffic
schiffbar navigable
Schiffbarkeit navigability
schiffen navigate
Schiffer seaman
Schiffsanlegestelle wharf

Schiffsanschluß steamship connection
Schiffsarzt ship's doctor
Schiffsbau shipbuilding
Schiffskapitän captain, sea-captain
Schiffskarte steamer ticket
Schiffskellner steward
Schiffskoch ship's cook
Schiffsladung cargo
Schiffsmiete charter money
Schiffsraum shipping space
Schiffsreise cruise, voyage
Schiffsrumpf hull
Schiffsschraube screw
Schiffstonnage tonnage
Schiffsverbindung steamer service
Schildkröte turtle
Schildkrötensuppe turtle soup
Schildkrötensuppe, echte real turtle soup
Schildkrötensuppe, falsche mock turtle soup, clear mock turtle soup
Schildkrötensuppe klar clear turtle soup
Schinken ham
Schinken, gekochter boiled ham
Schinken, gepökelter ham cured
Schinken, geräucherter ham smoked
Schinken, roher ham raw
Schinken im Brotteig baked ham in bread crust
Schinkenknödelsuppe soup with ham dumplings
Schinkenomelett ham omelet, omelet with ham
Schirm umbrella
Schlafabteil sleeper section, sleeping-compartment
schlafend asleep
Schlafgelegenheit sleeping accomodation
Schlafkur hypnotherapy, sleeping-cure
Schlafplatz sleeping-berth
Schlafraum dormitory
Schlafsaal dormitory
Schlafsack sleeping-bag
Schlafstelle night's lodging, overnight accomodation
Schlafwagen sleeper

Schlafwagen mit Speisewageneinrichtung hotel car
Schlafwagenkarte sleeping-car ticket
Schlafwagenschaffner sleeping-car attendant
Schlafwagenzuschlag sleeping-car charge
Schlafzimmer bedroom
Schlagbaum turnpike
schlagen knock
Schlägerei affray
Schlaglicht highlight
Schlagloch road-hole
Schlagsahne whipped cream
Schlagteig batter
Schlammbad mud bath
Schlammpackung mud pack
Schlange queue
Schlange stehen queue up
Schlange (an der Rezeption) line (at the front desk)
Schlauchboot pneumatic boat, rubber dinghy
Schleichhandel black market
Schleie tench
schlemmen revel
Schlepper (Schiff) tugboat
Schlepplift rope tow, T-bar tow
Schlesisches Himmelreich boiled smoked bacon Silesian style
Schleudergefahr! slippery when wet
schleudern skid
Schleuse lock, sluice
schlichten adjust
Schlichtung adjustment
Schließfach lock box, locker, safe deposit box
Schlitten luge, sled, toboggan
Schlittenfahrt sleigh-ride
Schlittenlift sledge tow, toboggan tow
Schlittschuhlaufen skate
Schloß (Gebäude) castle
Schloß (Tür) lock
Schloßruine castle ruins
Schlußabrechnung final account
Schlußlicht tail-light
Schlückchen tot
Schlüpfer knickers
schlürfen quaff, sip
Schlüssel key

Schlüsselarbeitskräfte key personnel
Schlüsselposition key position
Schlüsselzahl code number
schmackhaft savoury, tasty
Schmackhaftigkeit tastiness
schmal narrow
Schmalfilm narrow film
Schmalz dripping, lard
schmausen feast
schmecken lassen, sich relish
schmelzen thaw
Schmelzkartoffeln butterfried potatoes
Schmelzkäse cheese spread, cream cheese
schmerzstillend anodyne
Schmorbraten braised beef, pot roast
schmoren casserole
Schmuck jewellery, jewelery
schmuggeln smuggle
schmutzig dirty
schmücken decorate
Schnappschuß snapshot
Schnaps hard liquor
Schnäpschen pick-me-up
Schneeball snowball
schneebedeckt snow-covered
Schneebericht snow report
Schneebesen (egg)beater, whisk
Schneebrille snow-goggles
Schneefall snow-fall
Schneefeld snowfield
schneegeräumt snow-cleared
Schneehuhn snow grouse
Schneeketten snow-chains, tyre chains
Schneelage snow conditions
Schneemann snow man
Schneematsch slush
Schneepflug snow-plough, snowplow (amerik.)
Schneeräumung snow-clearing
schneereich snowy
Schneesaison snowy season
Schneeschmelze snow break
Schneesturm snowstorm
Schneeverhältnisse snow conditions
Schneewehe snowdrift
schneiden cut
Schneider tailor

schnell quick
Schnellbus express coach, high-speed bus
Schnelldampfer fast steamer
Schnellgaststätte quick lunch restaurant, quick service restaurant
Schnellhefter letter file
Schnellimbißstube self-service snack bar
Schnellstraße express road, high-speed road
Schnelltriebwagen express railcar
Schnellverkehr express traffic
Schnellzug express train, fast train
schnell... express
Schnepfe partridge, wood cock
Schnepfen gegrillt grilled snipes
Schnitt cut
Schnitte slice
Schnittlauch chives
Schnittstelle interface
Schnitzel collop, escalope, scallop (of meat)
Schnorchel snorkel
Schnupftabak snuff
Schokolade chocolate
Schokoladenauflauf soufflé of chocolate
Schokoladenbaiser chocolate-meringue
Schokoladeneis chocolate ice-cream
Schokoladenpudding chocolate pudding
Schokoladentorte chocolate cake
Scholle (Fisch) plaice
Schonfaktor sedative factor
Schonkost mild diet
Schonzeit closed season
Schopfbraten skin of pork, spare-rib
Schoppenwein carafe wine, wine by the glass
Schorle shandy, wine with sodawater
Schottenrock kilt
schön beautiful, lovely, picturesque
Schönheitskur cosmetic therapy
Schönheitssalon beauty parlour
Schönheitswettbewerb beauty contest
Schöpflöffel ladle, soup-ladle
Schrank cupboard, wardrobe
Schranke barrier

Schrankkoffer wardrobe trunk
schrecklich awful
Schreibabteil secretarial compartment
Schreibbüro letter service
schreiben, auf Zimmerrechnung charge to the room
Schreibmappe writing case
Schreibmarke corsor
Schreibmaschine typewriter
Schreibpapier note-paper, writing paper
Schreibtisch desk
Schreibzeug writing kit
schriftlich written
Schritt pace
Schritt fahren! slow down
schrumpfen shrink
Schublade drawer
Schuhanzieher shoehorn
Schuhe putzen clean the shoes, shine the shoes
Schuhputzer bootblack, boots (Hotel), showblack
Schuhputzlappen shoe-shining cloth
Schulausflug educational tour, school outing
Schuld debt, liability, obligation, indebtedness
Schuld, antizipative accrued liability
Schuld geben blame
Schulden debts
Schulden machen incur debts
schuldig sein owe
Schuldschein promissory note
Schuldschein, umlauffähiger kurz- bzw. mittelfristiger negotiable note
Schuldverschreibung bond, debenture
Schuldverschreibung (vom Kreditnehmer vorzeitig rückzahlbar) callable bond
Schuldverschreibung, gesicherte collateral trust bond
Schuldwechsel notes payable
Schulferien school holidays
Schulter shoulder
Schulter gefüllt stuffed shoulder
Schulungshotel training hotel
Schund trash
Schuppen shed

Schuß Branntwein in Getränken lace
Schutzhütte refuge
Schutzimpfung protective inoculation, protective vaccination
Schürze apron
Schüssel bowl, dish
schütteln shake
schützen ensure
schützen secure
Schützenfest shooting-match
Schwalbennestersuppe birds nest soup
Schwamm sponge
schwanken fluctuate
Schwankung fluctuation
Schwanz tail
Schwartenmagen pork galantine
Schwarzarbeit illicit work
Schwarzbrot brown bread
schwarze Bohnen black beans
schwarze Johannisbeere black currant
schwarzer Kaffee black coffee
schwarzes Brett bill-board, bulletin board
Schwarzmarkt black market
Schwarzwurzel salsify
Schwebebahn suspension railway
schweben hover
Schwefelquelle sulphur spring
Schwein pig
Schweinebraten roast joint of pork, roast pork
Schweinefleisch pork
Schweinekotelett pork chop, pork cutlet
Schweinekotelett gebacken fried pork cutlet
Schweinekotelett gegrillt grilled pork chop
Schweineschlegel leg of pork
Schweineschnitzel gegrillt grilled pork cutlet
Schweinesülze jelly of pork
Schweinsbrust breast of pork
Schweinsfüße pettitoes, pig's trotters
Schweinsgulasch stew of pork Hungarian style
Schweinshaxe pork knuckles
Schweinskarree rib of pork

Schweinskopf pig's head
Schweinskopfsülze brawn
Schweinsnieren pork kidneys
Schweinsohren geräuchert
  smoked pig's ears
Schweinsrippchen mit Sauerkraut
  smoked rib of pork with sauerkraut
Schweinsschulter shoulder of pork
**Schweinswürstchen in
  gebackenem Eierteig**
  toad-in-the-hole
Schweiß sweat
Schweiz Switzerland
Schweizer Käse Swiss cheese
Schwelle threshold
schwenken wave
Schwenkkartoffeln sauté potatoes, roast potatoes
schwer (Wein) full bodied
Schwerpunkt center
Schwertfisch swordfish
Schwestergesellschaft affiliated company
Schwimmatratze beach mattress
Schwimmbad swimming-bath, swimming-pool
schwimmen float, swim
Schwimmen natation, swimming
schwimmendes Hotel floating hotel
Schwimmer swimmer
Schwimmhalle swimming-hall
Schwimmlehrer swimming instructor
Schwimmluftmatratze inflatable beach mattress
Schwimmunterricht swimming lessons
Schwimmweste life-jacket, life vest
Schwimmweste, aufblasbare Mae West
Schwitzbad hot-air bath, sudatory bath, vapor bath
schwitzen sweat
Schwund shrinkage
Schwundverlust shrinkage
schwül sultry
See lake
See, an der on the sea
See, auf hoher on high seas, in the open sea
See, hohe high seas
See, zur on the sea

See (Meer) sea
See-Luft-Reise sea-air voyage
Seebad sea bath, seaside resort
Seebadekur marinotherapy
Seebarbe mullet
Seebarsch bass, snook
Seebrasse bream
Seeforelle lake trout
Seefracht cargo
Seehafen seaport
Seehecht coal fish, hake, silver hake
Seeheilbad sea bath, seaside health resort
Seehotel sea-front hotel, seaside hotel
Seekarte nautical chart
Seeklima sea-climate
seekrank seasick
Seekrankheit nausea, seasickness
Seemann seaman
Seemeile (1.853 km) nautical mile, knot
Seereise cruise, voyage
Seereisender voyager
Seeroute sea route
Seesack sea bag
Seeschiffahrt maritime shipping
Seestern starfish
Seeteufel angler, frog fish
Seetiere sea-food
Seetourismus sea tourism
Seetourist sea tourist
Seetouristik sea tourism
Seewasser-Badebecken seawater bathing pool
Seeweg sea route
Seezunge sole
Seezungenröllchen rolled fillets of sole
Seezungenstreifen strips of sole fillets
Segel sail
Segelboot sailing-boat, yacht
Segelfliegen glide
Segelfliegen gliding
Segelflugsport gliding
Segelflugzeug glider, sailing-plane
Segeljolle yawl
segeln glide, sail
Segelregatta yacht-race
Segelsaison yachting-season
Segelschule yachting-school

Segelsport yachting
Segeltuch canvas
sehenswert remarkable, worth seeing
Sehenswürdigkeit place of interest, sight
Sehenswürdigkeiten beauty spots, sights
Sehenswürdigkeiten besuchen sight-seeing
Seidenpapier tissue paper
Seilbahn cable railway, rope railway
Seilschwebebahn aerial ropeway
Sekt champagne, sparkling hock
Selbstachtung self-esteem
selbständig self employed, free lance
Selbstbedienung self-service
Selbstbedienungsladen self-service store, supermarket
Selbstbedienungsrestaurant cafeteria, self-service cafeteria, self-service restaurant
selbstbewußt self-assured
Selbstfahrer owner-driver
Selbstkostenpreis cost price
Selbstversicherung, freiwillige self insurance
selbstvertrauend self-assured
Sellerie celery
Selleriesalat celery salad
selten rare
Selterswasser soda-water
Semmel roll
Semmelknödel white bread dumpling
senden forward, send
Sendung transmission
Senf mustard
Senf, englischer English mustard
Senffrüchte pickled fruit
Senfglas mustard pot
Senfgurke gherkin in piccalilly
Senfobst pickled fruit
Senfsoße mustard sauce
senkrecht perpendicular
seriös respectable
Serpentinenstraße switch-back road, winding road
Service service
Service an Bord service on board
Service-Office office
servieren serve, service
Serviererin waitress

Servierleistung service
Serviette napkin, table napkin
Sessel arm-chair, easy chair, seat
Sessellift chairlift
Setzei fried egg
setzen, auf eine Warteliste put on a waiting list
Shake shake
Sherry sherry
Show show
Shuffleboard (Bordspiel) shuffle-board
sich beschäftigen (mit) deal (with)
sicher safe
Sicherheit safety
Sicherheit (Gegenstand) collateral
Sicherheiten, gewährte securities rendered
Sicherheitsbestand buffer stock
Sicherheitsbindung safety binding
Sicherheitsgurt seat belt
Sicherheitsgürtel seat belt
Sicherheitsleistung collaterisation
Sicherheitsvorkehrungen treffen take security precautions
sichern secure
sicherstellen ensure
Sicherung fuse
Sicherungsübereignung chattel mortgage
Sicht visibility
sichtbar apparent, visible
Sichteinlage demand deposit
Sichtvermerk visa
Sieb sieve
sieben (Sieb) sift
sieden, leicht simmer
Silber silver
Silberfelchen silver trout
Silbergeschirr silver
Silvesterdiner New Year's dinner
Silvesterfeier New Year's Eve celebration
Silvesterreise New Year's cruise
Sirup molasses, syrup, treacle
Sitte custom
Sitten manners
Sittenwidrigkeit immorality
sittlich moral
Sitz seat
Sitzbad hip-bath

Sitzplatzkapazität seating-capacity
Sitzung conference, meeting
Sitzungsraum conference room
Sitzungssaal conference hall
Skala scale
Skateboard skateboard
Ski ski
Skilaufen ski
Skiausrüstung ski equipment
Skibindung ski binding
Skibob skibob
Skidorf skiing village
Skifahren skiing
Skifahrer skier
Skiferien skiing holidays
Skiführer ski guide
Skigelände ski grounds
Skigymnastik skiing exercises
Skihang ski slope
Skihose ski trousers
Skihotel ski hotel
Skihütte ski hut, ski lodge
Skikleidung ski wear
Skiklub skiing club
Skilanglauf cross-country running on skis, langlauf
Skilauf skiing
Skiläufer skier
Skilehrer ski-coach, skiing instructor
Skiort ski center, ski resort
Skipaß ski-lift season ticket
Skireise skiing trip
Skirennen ski race
Skischlepplift ski tow
Skischule ski school
Skisport skiing
Skispringen ski-jumping
Skistiefel skiboot
Skistock ski pole, ski stick
Skitagespaß ski-lift day ticket
Skitour ski tour
Skitourist ski tourist
Skiträger ski carrier
Skiunterricht skiing instruction, skiing lessons
Skiurlaub skiing holidays
Skiverleih ski hire, ski rental
Skiwachs ski wax
Skiwanderung hike on skis
Skiwochenende skiing weekend
Skizentrum ski center

Skonto cash discount
Skontoerträge cash discounts earned
Smoking dinner-jacket, tuxedos
Snackbar cafeteria, snackbar
Soda soda
Soda-Himbeer raspberry syrup with soda water
Sodawasser mit Speiseeis ice-soda
sofort instantly
Software software
Sojabohne soy bean
Solawechsel promissory note
Solbad (Kurort) salt-water resort, salt-water bath
Sole salt water
Solebad brine bath
Soll-Saldo debit balance
Sollseite (eines Kontos) debit side
Solquelle salt spring
Sommelier wine-butler
Sommeraufenthalt summer stay
Sommerbad open-air swimming-pool
Sommerendivie romaine
Sommerfahrplan summer timetable
Sommerferien summer holiday, summer vacation
Sommerferiendorf summer holiday village
Sommerfest summer party
Sommerfrische summer resort
Sommergast summer visitor
Sommerhaus holiday house
Sommerkohl savoy cabbage
Sommerkurort summer health resort
Sommermesse summer fair
Sommerreiseverkehr summer tourist traffic
Sommersaison summer season
Sommersitz summer residence
Sommerspiele summer festival
Sommerzeit daylight-saving time, summer time
Sonderabschreibung accelerated depreciation
Sonderbus special bus
Sonderflug extra flight, non-scheduled flight
Sonderflugzeug special plane
Sonderkontingent special quota
Sonderkosten extra cost
Sonderpreis special rate

Sonderprospekt special brochure, special folder
Sonderschicht extra shift
Sondertarif special rate
Sondertour extra tour
Sonderurlaub special leave
Sondervergütung bonus
Sonderzug extra train, relief train
Sonnenaufgang sunrise
Sonnenbad sunbath
Sonnenbad nehmen sunbathe
Sonnenbestrahlung solar radiation
Sonnenblende window screen
Sonnenbrand sunburn
Sonnenbrille sun glasses
Sonnendeck sun deck
Sonneneinstrahlung insolation
Sonnenkur heliotherapy, sun treatment
Sonnenschirm parasol, sunshade, sun umbrella
Sonnenstich sunstroke
Sonnenstrahlung solar radiation
Sonnenterrasse summer terrace, sunterrace
Sonnenuntergang sunset
sonnig sunny
Sonntagsausflug Sunday excursion
Sonntagsfahrkarte Sunday excursion ticket
Sonntagsrückfahrkarte week-end return ticket
sonstige Umsätze, verschiedene (Umsatzbereich 2) miscellaneous other income (schedule 2)
Sorbett sherbet
sorgen für take care of
sorgen, sich worry
Sorgfalt accuracy
sorgfältig careful
Sorte brand, kind
sortieren assort
Sortiment product mix, sales mix
Soße sauce
Soße, milde veloute sauce
Soße, pikant piquant sauce
Soße, pikante fertige Yorkshire relish
Sozialtourismus social tourism
Sozialversicherung social insurance
Sozietät (Anwälte, Ärzte etc.) partnership
Spaghetti mit Hackfleischsoße spaghetti with minced meat-sauce
Spaghetti mit Tomatensoße spaghetti with tomato sauce
Spalte column
Spanferkel suckling pig
Spanien Spain
spanischer Fischeintopf Spanish fish stew
spanischer Suppentopf Spanish meat-pot
spanisches Reisgericht mit Fisch und Fleisch Spanish rice dish with fish and meat
Spanne margin
Spannung voltage
sparen economize
Spargel asparagus
Spargelcremesuppe cream of asparagus
Spargelsalat asparagus salad
Spargelspitzen asparagus tips
Spargelsuppe asparagus soup
Sparkasse savings bank
sparsam thrifty
Spaß fun, joke
spät late
Spätbuchung late booking
Spätsaison after-season
Spätzle dough dumplings, tiny flour dumplings
spazierengehen walk
Spazierfahrt pleasure drive
Spaziergang ramble, walk
Spazierweg walk
Speck bacon
Speckstreifen zum Spicken lardon
Spediteur forwarding agent, carrier
Speicher mit wahlfreiem Zugriff random access memory (RAM)
speichern store
Speise food, meal
Speise- und Weinkarte menu and wine list
Speiseartikel, standardisierter standardized menu item
Speiseeis ice (brit.), ice-cream
Speisefolge menu
Speisekammer larder, pantry

Speisekarte bill of fare, menu
Speisekarte für Kinder children's menu
Speisekürbis pumpkin, vegetable marrow
Speiselokal eating-place
speisen dine, eat, feed
Speisenaufzug service lift
Speisen, frisch gemachte dishes prepared to order
Speisen, warme hot dishes
Speiserest left-over
Speisesaal dining-saloon
Speisewagen diner, dining-car, restaurant-car
Speisezimmer dining-room
Sperre barrier
sperren block
Sperrfrist blocked period
Sperrgebiet prohibited area
Sperrgut bulky goods (freight)
Sperrsitz stall
Sperrstunde closing time
Spesen charge
Spesengast guest on an expense account
Spesenkonto expense account
Spezialarrangement special arrangement
Spezialität des Hauses speciality of the house
Spezialitätenwochen food festival
Spezialpreis für Familien family rate
Spezialpreis für Reiseveranstalter run of the house rate
Spezialslalom special slalom
Spezifikation specification
Spicknadel larding-needle, larding-pin
Spiegel looking-glass, mirror
Spiegel- und Fensterglasversicherung plate glass insurance
Spiegeleier fried eggs, shirred eggs
Spiegeleier mit Schinken ham and eggs
Spiel (Golf) eröffnen tee
Spiel, elektronisches (Umsatzbereich 6) electronic game (schedule 6)

Spielautomat (Umsatzbereich 6) slot machine, one armed bandit (schedule 6)
Spielbank gambling casino, gambling table
spielen gamble
Spieler gambler, player
Spielfilm feature
Spielkasino gambling casino
Spielmarke chip
Spielplatz playground
Spielschuld gambling debt
Spieltisch gambling table
Spielwiese playing-field
Spielzeug toy
Spielzimmer nursery, play-room
Spieß, gebraten am on the spit
Spieß (Fleisch) skewer
Spießchen skewer
Spießchen, am en brochette
Spinat spinach
Spirituose liquor
Spirituosen spirits
Spirituosengeschäft liquor shop
Spirituskocher spirit stove
Spitzenbelastungszeit peak hour
Spitzengehalt top salary
Spitzenverkehr peak hour traffic
Spitzenwein vintage wine
Sportanlagen sports facilities
Sportartikel sports goods
Sportausrüstung sports equipment
Sportdeck game deck
Sportflugzeug sports plane
Sporthalle gym, sports hall
Sporthotel sports hotel
Sportkleidung sports clothes, sportswear
Sportler sportsman
Sportplatz athletic ground, sports field
Sportsegler yachtsman
Sportveranstaltung athletics meeting, sporting event
Sportwagen (Auto) sports car
Sprache language
spracheigentümlich idiomatic
Sprecher announcer, speaker
Springbrunnen fountain
Spritzer dash
Spritzer Soda dash of soda

Sprotte sprat
Sprudelbad effervescent bath
Sprungbrett spring-board, take-off board
sprunghaft volatile
Sprungschanze ski jump
Sprungturm diving-tower, high-diving tower
spülen rinse, wash up
Spüler dish-washer
Spülküche stewarding department
Spülküchenleiter steward
Spülmaschine dish-washer
Spülmaschine für Gläser glass-washing machine
Spur trail
Squash squash
Staat country
Staatsangehöriger citizen, national
Staatsangehörigkeit nationality
Staatsbürgerschaft citizenship
Staatsgrenze state frontier
Staatswald state forest
Stab-Linien-Organisation line and staff organization
Stabsfunktion staff function
Stabsstelle staff position
Stabsverantwortung staff responsibility
Stachelbeere gooseberry
Stadion stadium
Stadt city, town
Stadtautobahn urban freeway
Stadtbahn city railway
Stadtbezirk municipal district
Stadtbüro ticket office, town office
Stadtgebiet city zone, urban area
städtisch municipal, urban
Stadtkoffer overnight bag
Stadtmauer town-wall
Stadtmotel motor inn
Stadtmuseum municipal museum
Stadtplan map of the town, street plan, town plan
Stadtrundfahrt city sight-seeing tour, sight-seeing tour
Stadtrundflug aerial city tour, city sight-seeing flight
Stadtschnellstraße urban express road
Stadttheater municipal theater

Stadtverkehr urban traffic
Stadtviertel quarter
Stadtzentrum town centre
Staffelform report format
staffeln scale
Stahlfach safe deposit box
Stammaktien common stock
Stammeinlagen (GmbH) common shares (of a limited liability company)
Stammgast regular customer
Stammkunde patron
Stammlokal favourite pub
Stammtisch table reserved for regular customers
Stand status
Standard standard
standardisieren standardize
Standardisierung standardization
ständig permanent
Standort location
Stange, von der off the peg
Stangenbohne string bean
Stangensellerie celery sticks
Stangenspargel asparagus sticks
stark hearty, strong
Start start, take-off
Startbahn runway
Station stop
stationär stationary
Stationsoberkellner captain (waiter)
Statistik statistic
statistisch statistical
Stativ tripod
stattfinden take place
Status status
Staub dust
staubsaugen hoover
Staubsauger hoover, vacuum cleaner
Staubtuch duster
Staubzucker icing sugar
Staudamm barrage, dam
Stausee reservoir
Steak steak
Steak- und Nierenpastete (warm) steak and kidney pie
Steckdose outlet, socket, wall plug, wall socket
Steckdose für Elektrorasierer razor point, shaver point
stecken plug

Stecker connector
Steg plank
Stehbierhalle public bar
stehen, auf der Warteliste stand-by
stehen, im Wettbewerb compete
stehlen steal, thieve
Stehplatz standing-place
steigern (Wirkung) intensify
Steigerung rise, increase
Steigerung (Wert) increment
Steigung rise, ascent
steil steep
steil hochziehen zoom
Steilflug zoom
Steilhang steep slope
Steilküste bluff, steep coast
Stein stone
Steinbutt turbot
Steingarten rock garden
Steinhuhn rock partridge
Steinpilz boletus, cep
Steinschlag falling stones
Stelle, freie opening
Stelle, offene vacancy
Stelle, produktionsunabhängige non-production post
Stellenangebot offer of employment, position offered
Stellenbeschreibung job description
Stellenbesetzungsplan staffing schedule
Stellenbezeichnung job title
Stellengruppe job category
Stelleninhaber job holder
Stellung position
Stellvertreter substitute
Stempel stamp
stempeln stamp
Steppdecke quilt
Sterlet sturgeon
Sternfahrt rally
Sternwarte observatory
Steuer helm
Steuer (Abgabe) tax
Steuermann helmsman, navigator
Steuermannsmaat quarter-master
steuern control, pilot, steer
Steuerruder rudder
Steuerstundung deferred income tax
Steuerverbindlichkeiten taxes payable

Steward steward
Stewardeß air hostess, stewardess
Stichprobenprüfung random test
Stichtag cut-off date
Stiefel boot
Stierkampf bull-fight
Stierkämpfer bull-fighter
Stiftung foundation
still calm, quiet
stillschweigend implied
stillstehend idle
Stimmenabgabe, kumulative cumulative voting
Stimmrecht voting right
Stimmung mood
Stimmungsmusik mood music
Stint smelt
Stockfisch dried cod, salt cod, salted codfish
Stockung stoppage
Stockwerk floor
Stoffgeschäft draper's
stopfen (Strümpfe) darn
stornieren cancel
Stornierungsgebühr cancellation fee
Storno cancellation
Stoßarbeit peak load
stoßen push
Stoßverkehr peak hour traffic, rush hour traffic
Stoßzeit peak hour, peak period, rush hour
Stör sturgeon
stören disturb
Störung annoyance, disturbance, interference, nuisance
Strafstoß (Sport) penalty
Strahlen, ultraviolette ultraviolet rays
Strand beach, sea-shore, shore
Strandbad lido
Strandfest seaside gala
Strandgut wreck
Strandhotel beach hotel, seaside hotel
Strandkorb beach-chair
Strandpromenade boardwalk
Strandschirm beach-umbrella
Strandschuhe beach shoes
Strandwärter beach attendant
Straße, breite avenue

Straße, gebührenpflichtige toll road
Straße, gesperrte road closed
Straße, schneegeräumte road cleared of snow
Straße, zweibahnige (zweispurige) two-lane road
Straßenanzug business suit, lounge suit
Straßenatlas road atlas
Straßenbahn streetcar, tram, tramway
Straßenbahnhaltestelle tram stop
Straßenbahnkarte tram ticket
Straßenbahnlinie streetcar line, tram line
Straßenbahnwagen tramcar
Straßenbau road construction
Straßenbauarbeiten road works
Straßenbaustelle road site
Straßenbenutzungsgebühr toll
Straßencafé open-air café, sidewalk café
Straßeneinmündung T-junction
Straßengabel bifurcation
Straßengabelung road fork
Straßengraben road ditch
Straßenhändler street hawker
Straßenkarte road map
Straßenkleidung outdoor dress
Straßenkreuzung intersection, crossing, cross-roads, junction, road junction
Straßenlaterne street-lamp
Straßennetz road network
Straßenschild street sign
Straßenschuhe oxfords, walking shoes
Straßentransportunternehmen highway carrier
Straßentunnel road tunnel
Straßenverengung road narrows
Straßenverkehr road traffic
Straßenzoll toll
Straßenzustand road conditions
Straßenzustandsbericht road report
Strategie strategy
Strauch shrub
Strauß bunch
Strecke course, distance, line, stretch
Strecken, auf kurzen on short routes
Strecke, zurückgelegte distance travelled

Streckenänderung change of route
Streckenführung routing
Streckenkarte route map
Streckennetz airways system, route network
Streckennetz, interkontinentales intercontinental network
streichen cancel
Streichholz match
Streichholzkartoffeln shoestring potatoes
Streichholzschachtel matchbox
Streichung cancellation
Streik strike
streiken strike
Streit argument, quarrel
streiten argue, quarrel
Streithahn trouble maker
streng geheim top secret
Strichliste check list
stricken knit
Strickhemd jersey shirt
Strickjacke jersey dress
Strickleiter rope-ladder
strohgedeckt thatched
Strohhalm straw
Strohkartoffeln potato straws, straw potatoes
Strom electric power
Stromtarif electric rate schedule
Stromverbrauch electric power consumption, power consumption
Strudel (Speise) strudel
Struktur structure
Studentenfahrt student travel, student trip
Studentenreiseverkehr student travel
Studienreise educational trip, study trip
Studienurlaub educational holiday
Stuhl chair
stumpf blunt
Stunde, angemessene reasonable hour
stunden defer
Stundenlohnsatz hourly rate
Stück part, piece
Stück Kuchen piece of cake
Stückgutfracht package freight
stürmisch rough, tempestuous

Substanzverringerung depletion
suchen search
Sucher (Foto) view-finder
Südbalkon balcony facing south
Süden gehen, nach facing south
Südterrasse terrace facing south
Südzimmer room facing south
Suite suite
Sultanine sultana
Sultaninenpudding spotted dick
Sülze aspic, jelly
summieren add up, sum up
Sumpf swamp
Supermarkt supermarket
Suppe soup
Suppe, dicke bisque, chowder, potage
Suppe, legierte thick soup
Suppe klar mit Eierstich clear soup royal
Suppeneinlage garnish
Suppenfleisch mit Meerettich boiled meat with horse-radish
Suppenhuhn boiled chicken
Suppenschüssel soup-tureen, tureen
Suppenteller soup plate
Suppentopf mit Fleischeinlage boiled beef on broth, pot of broth with boiled meat
Suppentopf mit Geflügeleinlage chicken in broth
Surfbrett surf board
süß sweet
süßen sweeten
Süßigkeiten candy, sweets
Süßkartoffel sweet potato
Süßmost sweet cider
Süßspeise dessert, sweet dish
Süßwasserfisch fresh-water fish, sweet water fish
Süßwasserkrebs fresh water crayfish
Süßwasserschwimmbad fresh-water swimming-pool
Süßwein dessert wine, sweet wine
Swimmingpool (Service Center 12) swimming-pool (schedule 12)
Symbol symbol
System system
Szegediner Gulasch Hungarian pork stew, stewed pork and sauerkraut in paprika sauce

T
T-bone steak T-bone steak
Tabak tobacco
Tabakladen tobacconist's shop
Tabakspeife tobacco pipe
Tabaksteuer tobacco tax
Tabelle chart, table
Tabellenkalkulation worksheet calculation
Table d'hôte table d'hote
Tablett tray
Tablett (amerik. drehbares) lazy Susan
tadeln blame
Tafel table
Tafel-Tischmesser table-knife
Tafelsalz table salt
Tafelspitz boiled round of beef
Tafelwasser table-water
Tagesanbruch dawn, daybreak
Tagesankaufskurs spot buying rate
Tagesausflug day excursion, whole-day tour
Tagesfahrt day flight
Tagesgericht ready-to-serve dish, table d'hote meal
Tageskarte day ticket, today's bill of fare, today's menu
Tageskurs current rate
Tageslichtfilm daylight colour film
Tagesordnung agenda
Tagesplatte the day's dish
Tagesprogramm today's program
Tagesraum day-room, sitting-room
Tagesrestaurant day restaurant
Tagesrückfahrkarte day turn ticket
Tagesspezialität today's special dish, today's speciality
Tagessuppe the soup of the day
Tagestour day excursion
Tageswert am Absatzmarkt current market value
Tageszeit time of day
Tageszimmerpreis day rate (use rate)
täglich daily, per day
Tagwerk man-day
Takelung rigging
taktvoll discreet
Tal valley

Talfahrt   downward journey
Talsperre   barrage, dam
Talstation (Bergbahn)   base terminal, loading station
tanken   refuel, take in petrol
Tankstelle   filling station, petrol station, service station
Tankwart   filling station attendant, garage assistant, service station attendant
Tanz   dancing
Tanz im Freien   open-air dance
Tanzabend   dancing-party, evening dance
Tanzbar   dance bar
Tanzdiner   dinner dance
Tanzfläche   dance floor
Tanzkapelle   dance band
Tanzkasino   spa ballroom
Tanzlokal   dance hall
Tanzorchester   dance band
Tanzsaal   ballroom, dance hall
Tanztee   afternoon dance, tea dance
Tanzvorführung   dancing show
Tarif   tariff
Tarif, ermäßigter   reduced rates
Tariflohn   wages according to agreement
Tarifpreis   rack rate
Tarifsenkung   reduction of the rates
Tarifvertrag   collective agreement, labor contract, union agreement
Tarifvorschrift   tariff provision
Tartarensoße   tartare sauce
Tasche   bag
Taschendieb   pickpocket
Taschenfahrplan   pocket train schedule
Taschengeld   pocket money
Taschenlampe   elektric torch, flash light, pocket lamp
Taschenmesser   pen-knife
Taschenrechner   calculator
Taschentuch   handkerchief
Tasse   cup
Tastatur   keyboard
Taste   key
Tastenfeld   keyboard
Tastenknopf   key button
Tat   action, fact
Tatar   minced raw beef

Tätigkeit   activity, function, job
Tätigkeitsbericht   activity report
Tätigkeitsbeschreibung   job-breakdown, job description
Tätigkeitsbezeichnung   job title
Tätigkeitsgebiet   field of activity
Tätigkeitsmerkmal   job attribute
Tatsache   fact
tatsächlich   actual, factual
Taube   pigeon, squab
Tauchbecken   diving-pool
tauchen   dive
Taucherausrüstung   diving equipment
Taucherclub   diving club
Tauen   thaw
tauglich   capable
Tauglichkeit   capability, qualification
Tausch   exchange
tauschen   change, exchange, swap
Tauwetter   thaw
Taxi   cab, taxi
Taxichauffeur   taxi-driver
Taxifahrer   taxi-driver
Taxistand   cab stand, taxi rank
Team   team
Techniker   technician
technischer Leiter   chief engineer
Tee   tea
Tee mit Milch   tea with milk
Tee mit Zitrone   tea with lemon
Tee vor dem Aufstehen   early morning tea
Teebüchse   tea-caddy
Teegebäck   scones, tea cakes
Teegeschirr   tea-service
Teegesellschaft   tea-party
Teehaus   tea-house
Teekanne   tea-pot
Teekessel   tea-kettle
Teelöffel   tea-spoon
Teemaschine   tea-urn
Teerestaurant   tea-shop
Teeservice   tea set
Teestube   tea-room
Teestunde   tea-time
Teetasse   teacup
Teewagen   tea-cart, tea-trolley
Teewärmer   tea-cosy
TEE-Zug   TEE-train (Trans-Europe-Express)

Teich pond
Teig dough, paste
Teigdecke pie-crust
Teiggraupen grape-nuts
Teigtaschen pastry envelopes, stuffed fritters
Teigwaren farinaceous food, paste foods
Teigwaren mit geriebenem Käse noodle dish with grated cheese
Teigwaren-Vorgericht farinaceous sidedish
Teil part, portion
teilen part
teilen, mit j-m ein Zimmer share a room with s. o.
teilhaben participate
Teilhaber associate, participant
Teilmassage partial massage
Teilnahme participation
Teilnahmebedingung condition of participation
teilnehmen attend, participate
teilnehmen an take part in
Teilnehmer participant
Teilnehmerliste list of participants
Teilnehmerzahl number of participants
Teilstornierung partial cancellation
Teilstrecke stage
Teilung division
Teilverpflegung partial board
teilweise partial
Teilzahlung instalment, partial payment, part payment
Teilzahlungskredit instalment credit
Teilzeitarbeiter part-timer
Telefon telephone
Telefonanlage telephone installation
Telefonbuch telephone directory
Telefonhörer telephone receiver
telefonisch bestellen order by telephone, book by telephone
telefonische Telegrammaufnahme telegram by telephone
Telefonistin operator, telephone operator
Telefonleitung line
Telefonvermittlung telephone exchange, trunk exchange

Telefonverzeichnis telephone directory
Telefonzelle call-box, telephone booth, telephone box
Telefonzentrale switchboard
Telegrafenamt telegraph office
telegrafieren cable, wire
telegrafisch telegraphic
telegrafische Anweisung telegraphic order
Telegramm cable, telegram, wire
Telegrammadresse telegraphic address
Telegrammformular telegram form
Telegrammkosten telegram charges
Telekommunikation telecommunication
Teleobjekt telephoto lens
Telex telex
Teller dish, plate
Teller, kleiner (Brot) bread-plate
Tellerwäscher dishwasher
Temperatur temperature
Tempo pace, speed
Tendenz tendency, trend
Tendenz, steigende uptrend
Tennis tennis
Tennisball tennis ball
Tennisklub tennis club
Tennisplatz tennis court
Tennisschläger racket, tennis racket
Tennisschuhe plimsols, tennis shoes
Tennisspiel tennis game
Tennisturnier tennis tournament
Teppich carpet
Termin, letzter deadline
Termineinlage (Geld) term deposit
termingerecht in due time
Terminierung timing
Terminkalender appointment book
Terrainkur terrain treatment
Terrassenrestaurant terrace restaurant
Testat des Wirtschaftsprüfers auditor's report
teuer expensive
Textverarbeitung word processing
Theaterbesucher playgoer
Theaterkarte theatre ticket
Theatersaison theatrical season

Theatervorstellung theatrical performance
Theke bar, counter
therapeutisch therapeutical
Thermalbad thermal baths
Thermalbadehaus hydropathic establishment
Thermalbecken thermal-water pool
Thermalhallenbad thermal indoor swimming-pool
Thermalwasser thermal water
Thermosflasche Thermos flask
Thermotherapie thermotherapy
Thunfisch tuna fish, tunny
Thymian thyme
Tief depression
Tiefe depth
Tiefgarage underground garage
tiefgefroren deep-frozen
tiefgekühlt quick-frozen
Tiefkühlerzeugnis frozen food
Tiegel casserole, pot, saucepan
Tiergarten zoo
Tierwelt fauna
tilgen amortize
Tilgung amortization, principal payment
Tilgungsfonds sinking fund
Tilsiter Käse tilsit cheese
Tintenfisch cuttle-fish, squid
Tisch table
Tisch decken lay the table, set the table
Tisch reservieren reserve a table, book a table
Tischdecke table-cloth, table-cover
Tischdecke, kleine tea-cloth
Tischgeschirr table-ware
Tischgespräch table-talk
Tischkarte place-card
Tischlampe table-lamp
Tischmesser table-knife
Tischnummer table number
Tischplatte table-top
Tischreservierung table reservation
Tischtennis ping-pong, table-tennis
Tischtennishalle ping-pong room, table-tennis room
Tischtuch table-cloth
Tischwein dinner wine, table wine
Tischzeiten meal-times

Tischzeug table-linen
Toast grilled bread, toast
Toaster toaster
Toastmeister toastmaster
Toaströster toaster
Toboggan toboggan
Tochtergesellschaft subsidiary company
Toilette lavatory, rest room, toilet, washroom, water-closet, W.C.
Toilette, öffentliche public convenience, public lavatory
Toilettenpapier toilet-paper
Toilettenseife toilet soap
Toilettentisch dressing-table
Tollwutimpfung antirabic vaccination
Tollwutimpfzeugnis certificate of antirabic vaccination
Tomate tomato
Tomaten gefüllt stuffed tomatoes
Tomatenketchup tomato ketchup
Tomatenmark tomato-pulp
Tomatensaft tomato juice
Tomatensalat tomato salad
Tomatensauce (spanisch) creole sauce
Tomatensoße tomato sauce
Tomatensuppe tomato-soup
Tonic, Tonicwasser tonic, tonic water
Tonwiedergabegeräte sound equipment
Topf jar, pan, pot
Topfenstrudel sweet curds pie
Topiocasuppe soup with topioca
Tor gate
Tor (Sport) goal
Torte fancy-cake, tart
Torwart (Sport) goalkeeper, keeper
Tour excursion, tour
Tourenkarte touristic map
Tourismus tourism
Touristenausweis tourist card
Touristenflugpreis tourist fare
Touristengebiet tourist region
Touristenhotel tourist hotel
Touristenkarte tourist card
Touristenklasse economy class, tourist class
Touristenverkehr tourism, touristic traffic

Touristenvisum

Touristenvisum tourist visa
Touristik tourism
touristisch touristic
Tourist(in) tourist
toxisch toxic(al)
Törtchen tartlet
Trabrennen trotting race
Trachtenfest pageant, show of national costumes
Trachtenumzug procession in national costumes
Tragflächenboot hydrofoil
Trainer coach
trainieren coach, practise, train
Training training
Trainingsanzug training suit
Tramp tramp
trampen tramp
Tramper hitch-hiker
Trampschiff tramp
tranchieren carve
Transfer transfer
Transit transit
Transitgut transit goods
Transitreise transit journey
Transitreisender transit passenger
Transitverkehr transit traffic
Transitvisum transit visa
Transport carriage, transport, transportation
Transportgefahr risk of conveyance
Transportgewerbe transportation
Transporthaftung liability of the carrier
transportierbar transportable
transportieren transport
Transportkosten transportation cost
Transportschäden damages in transit
Transporttarif carriage rates
Transportunternehmen carrier, transport company, motor carrier, transport contractor
Transportversicherung transport insurance
Transportvertrag contract of carriage
Tratsch gossip
Traube grape
Traube, blaue black grape
Traube, weiße white grape
Traubenkur grape cure
Traubensaft grape juice

treffen meet
Treffpunkt meeting-place, place of assembly
treiben compel
Treibstoff fuel
Trekking trekking
Trend trend
trennen disconnect, separate
Trennwand partition
Treppe stairs
Treppenhaus staircase
Tretblasebalg foot pump inflator
treu loyal
Treue loyality
Tribüne grand-stand
Trichter funnel
Triebwagen railcar
Triebwagenzug multiple-unit train
trinkbar drinkable
Trinkei fresh egg
trinken drink, tope
Trinken potation
Trinker alcoholic, dipsomaniac
Trinkgeld tip, gratuity
Trinkgeld geben tip
Trinkhalle (Kur) pump-room
Trinkhalm straw
Trinkkännchen pannikin
Trinkkur pump-room cure
Trinkkur machen drink the waters
Trinkspruch toast
Trinkspruch ausbringen propose a toast
Trinkwasser drinking water
trocken dry
Trockenfleisch air-dried meat, dried meat
Trockengestell rack
Trockenraum drying-room
trocknen drain, dry
Tropen tropics
Tropfen drop
Tropfsteinhöhle limestone cave
tropisch tropical
Trunkenheit drunkenness
Truthahn turkey
Truthahn gebraten roast turkey
Trüffel truffle
Trüsche burbot
Tuch cloth
Tunke sauce

Turbinendampfschiff
    turbo-steamship, TSS
Turbinenschiff turbo-ship, TS
Turm tower
Turmzimmer tower room
Turnhalle gym, gymnasium
Turnschuhe gym shoes, sneakers
Tür door
Tür bitte schließen please close the door
Türanhänger für die Frühstücksbestellung breakfast key
Türkisches Bad Turkish bath
Türklinke door handle
Türsteher usher
Typenrad daisywheel
Typenraddrucker daisy wheelprinter
typisch typical

U

U-Bahn subway, tube, underground
übel (sich...fühlend) qualmish
Übelkeit nausea
üben practise
über via
über dem Nennwert above par
über pari above par
überbacken au gratin, gratinated
Überbevorratung overstocking
überblicken survey
überbringen deliver
Übereinkommen accord
Übereinstimmung consistency
Überfahrt crossing
Überfahrtsdauer crossing time
überfällig overdue, past due
überfordern overcharge
überfüllt crowded, overcrowded
Übergangszeit transition period
übergar overdone
übergeben hand, pass, pass over
übergeben, sich vomit
übergehen pass, pass over
Übergepäck baggage in excess, excess baggage
Übergepäckzuschlag excess baggage fare

überholen overtake
Überholverbot no overtaking, prohibition to overtake
überhöht excessive
Überkapazität excess capacity, overcapacity
überladen overload
überlagern overlap
Überlandverkehr interurban traffic, overland transportation
überlappen overlap
Überlauf overflow
überlaufen overcrowded, touristed
Übernachtung night's lodging, overnight stay
Übernachtungsgast chance guest
Übernachtungshotel transient hotel
Übernachtungsmöglichkeit overnight accomodation
Übernachtungspreis overnight charge
Übernachtungspreis, reiner European Plan
Übernachtungspreis für Durchreisende transient rate
Übernachtungsvertrag contract of accomodation
Übernahme assumption
Übernahme von Schuldverschreibungen corporate underwriting
Überpreis excessive charge, excessive price
Überproduktion overproduction
überprüfen review, verify
Überprüfung review, verification
Überprüfung der Hotels checking of the hotels
Überraschungsinventur spot check
Überraschungsomelette baked Alaska
überschätzen overestimate
Überschätzung overestimate
überschlagen, sich turn upside down
Überschlagsrechnung rough calculation
überschreiten exceed
Überschrift heading
Übersee, in od. nach oversea(s)
Überseefahrt transoceanic voyage
Überseeflugzeug clipper

Überseetransport oversea(s) shipment
übersehen (nicht beachten) ignore
übersetzen translate
übersetzen (Fähre) ferry over
Übersetzer interpreter
Übersetzung translation
Übersicht statement
übersteigen exceed
übersteigen surpass
Überstunden overtime
Überstundenanforderung request for overtime
Übertrag amount carried over, transfer
übertragbar transferable
übertragen assign, delegate, transfer
Übertragung posting
übertreffen surpass
übertreiben exaggerate
übertreten violate
übertrieben excessive
überwachen control
überwachen monitor
Überwachungsstelle supervisory body
überwältigen overwhelm
überweisen remit
überwinden overcome
überzahlen overpay
überziehen overdraw
Überzieher overcoat
überzuckert iced
üblich costumary, usual
Übung exercise
Übungsgelände training ground
Übungshang practice slope
Ufer shore
Uferstraße coastal road, embankment
Uhr clock
Uhrzeigersinn, entgegen dem anticlockwise
Ultraschall ultrasonics, ultrasound
Umberfisch umber
umbuchen change reservations, reclassify, relocate
Umbuchung reclassification, transfer, adjusting entry
umfassen encompass
Umgang mit Gästen (Empfang) guest relations (front office)
Umgebung surroundings
Umgehungsstraße by-pass, diversion
umgruppieren regroup
Umherreisen itinerary
umherreisen itinerate, perigrinate
umkehren turn round
Umkehrpunkt point of turnaround
Umkleidekabine bathing cabin
Umkleideraum changing room
Umkleideraum für das Personal locker room
Umkreis von, im within the radius of
Umladungsgebühr reloading charge
Umlauf circulation
Umlauffähigkeit negotiability
Umlaufvermögen current assets
Umlaufvermögen insgesamt total current assets
Umleitung detour, diversion
Umorganisation reorganization
umorganisieren reorganize
umrechnen convert, translate
Umrechnung translation
Umrechnungskurs rate of exchange
Umrechnungstabelle conversion table
Umrechungsgrundlage für Fremdwährungen conversion method for foreign currency
umreißen outline
Umriß outline
Umsätze, sonstige (Umsatzbereich 2) other income (schedule 2)
Umschlag turnover
Umschlaghafen port of transsshipment
Umschlagplatz transsshipment point
umschließen encompass
umschulen re-educate
Umschulung re-education, retraining
Umsteigebahnhof connecting station
Umsteigekarte transfer, transfer ticket
Umsteigen change of carriage
Umsteigepunkt connecting point
umwandeln convert
Umweg detour, roundabout way
Umwelt environment
Umweltschutz environmental protection

Umzug procession
unabhängig independent
unangemessen inadequate
unangenehm disagreeable
unauffindbarer Gegenstand article not to be found
Unaufmerksamkeit inattention
unbefugt unauthorized
Unbehagen uneasiness
unbekannt unfamiliar, unknown
unbequem uncomfortable
unberechtigt unauthorized
unbesetzt vacant
unbeständig volatile
unbewohnt unoccupied
unbezahlt unpaid
undatiert undated
undeutlich dim
undurchführbar impracticable
unentgeltlich free, gratuitous
unerfahren inexperienced
unerkannt incognito
unerläßlich indispensable
unerlaubt unauthorized
unerschwinglich unattainable
unfähig incapable
Unfall accident
Unfallmeldung notice of accident
Unfallquelle accident hazard
Unfallrisiko accident risk
Unfallschutzkarte medical identification card
Unfallstation casualty department, first-aid post
Unfallverhütungsvorschrift safety regulation
Unfallversicherung accident insurance
unfreundlich unfriendly
Unfug nuisance
ungelernte Arbeitskräfte unskilled manpower
ungemütlich uncomfortable
ungenau loosely
Ungenauigkeit inaccuracy
ungesetzlich illegal, lawless
ungestört peaceful, undisturbed
ungesund insanitary
ungeteilt (Aufmerksamkeit) undivided (attention)
Ungeziefer vermin

Unglücksfall accident
ungültig invalid, void
Uniform uniform
unklar misty
unkompliziert (Vorgang) straightforward (process)
unkonvertierbar inconvertible
unmittelbar direct
unproduktiv idle
Unrecht wrong
unregelmäßig casual
unreif unripe
unrichtig incorrect
Unruhe worry
unsauber unclean
unschmackhaft tasteless
unsittlich immoral
Unsittlichkeit immorality
untätig idle
unter den Tisch reden, (den Gast) talk down (to a guest)
unter pari below par
Unterabteilung subdivision
Unterbett lower berth
unterbewerten underestimate
unterbieten undercut
unterbrechen interrupt
Unterbrechung interruption
unterbringen accomodate, lodge
Unterbringung accomodation
Unterdeck lower deck
Unterführung underpass
Untergebener subordinate
Unterhalt maintenance
unterhalten maintain
unterhaltend amusing
Unterhaltung entertainment
Unterhaltungsabend evening entertainment
Unterhose drawers, underpants
Unterkunft accomodation, lodging, shelter
Unterkunft shelter
Unterkunft, freie (z. B. für Busfahrer, Reiseleiter etc.) free lodging
Unterlage hand out, proof
Unterlagen records
unterlassen fail
Unterlegung eines Kredits durch eine Sicherheit collaterisation

Untermiete sublease
Untermieter sublessee, subtenant
Unternehmen company, concern, establishment
Unternehmen, assoziiertes associated company
Unternehmen, verbundene affiliated entities
unternehmen undertake
Unternehmensberater management consultant
Unternehmensform (des Handelsrechts) business organization
Unternehmensplanung corporate planning
Unternehmenszusammenschlüsse business combinations
Unternehmer employer
Unternehmer, gastgewerblicher entrepreneur of the hotel and catering trade
Unternehmung business
unterordnen subordinate
Unterpacht sublease
Unterpächter sublessee, subtenant
untersagen prohibit
Untersatz table-mat
unterschätzen underestimate
Unterschenkel leg
Unterschied difference
unterschiedlich varying
unterschreiten undercut
Unterschrift signature
Untersetzer mat, saucer
unterstellt sein report to
unterstützen relieve, support
Unterstützung support
untersuchen analyze, examine, test
Untersuchung analysis, inquiry, research, survey, test
Untersuchung, quantitative quantitative analysis
Untertasse saucer
unterteilen subdivide
untervermieten sublet
Untervermieter sublessor
Untervermietung sublease
Untervermietungsrecht right of sublease
unterverpachten sublet
Unterverpächter sublessor

Untervertrag subcontract
Unterwäsche underwear
Unterwasserausrüstung underwater equipment
Unterwassergymnastik underwater exercises
Unterwassermassage underwater massage
Unterwassersport aqua-lunging, scuba diving
unterwegs en route, in transit
Unterwegsaufenthalt stop en route
unterweisen instruct
Unterweisung instruction
Unterweisung, betriebliche job instruction training
unterwürfig submissive
unterzeichnen sign
unübersichtliche Kurve blind bend
unveräußerlich inalienable
unverbindlich without obligation
unverdünnt neat
unvereinbar incompatible
unverheiratet unmarried
unverträglich uncompatible
unverzüglich instant, without delay
unwahrscheinlich remote
Unwetter tempest
unwirksam ineffective
unwirtschaftlich inefficient
unwohl qualmish, queasy
Unze (28, 350g) ounce, o.z.
unzerbrechlich unbreakable
unzufrieden querulous
unzufrieden sein (mit etwas) displease (to be displeased with s. th.)
Unzulänglichkeiten shortcomings
unzulässig inadequate, inadmissible
Upgrading (Verkaufsmethode) upgrading
Upselling (Verkaufsmethode) upselling
Urlaub holidays, leave, vacation
Urlaub, bezahlter paid holiday
Urlaub, gesetzlicher legal holiday
Urlauber holiday-maker, vacationer
Urlauberzug leave-train
Urlaubseinteilung vacation schedule
Urlaubsgeld holiday pay, vacation pay

Urlaubsgeldrückstellung accrual for vacation pay
Urlaubsort holiday centre, holiday place
Urlaubsplan leave schedule
Urlaubsreise holiday trip
Urlaubsreisender holiday-maker
Urlaubsverkehr holiday traffic
Urlaubsversicherung holiday insurance
Urlaubswetter holiday weather
Urlaubszeit holiday season
Ursprung origin
Ursprungsland country of origin
urteilen determine, reason
Urwald virgin forest

V

Vakanz vacancy
Vakanzliste list of vacant rooms
Vanille vanilla
Vanilleauflauf soufflé of vanilla
Vanilleeis vanilla ice, vanilla ice-cream
Vanillepudding blancmange
Vanillesoße custard sauce
variabel variable
Vase vase
Vegetarier vegetarian
Vegetarierrestaurant vegetarian restaurant
vegetarisch vegetarian
Ventil valve
Ventilator fan, ventilator
Venusmuschel clam
Verabredung appointment
Verandadeck veranda deck
veränderlich variable
verändern alter, vary
Veränderung alteration, variance
veranlassen cause, arrange for
Veranstalter organizer
Veranstaltung banquet, event
Veranstaltung, gesellschaftliche social activity
Veranstaltung, jüdische kosher function, kosher party
Veranstaltungsgeschäft banquet business
Veranstaltungsinformation event order
Veranstaltungsleiter banquet manager
Veranstaltungsraum banquet room, function room
verantwortlich liable, responsible
verantwortlich machen hold accountable, blame
Verantwortung liability, responsibility
verärgert angry
verauslagen disburse
Veräußerungsgewinne (oder -verluste) aus dem Verkauf von Anlagevermögen (Service Center 14) gain (or loss) on sale of property (schedule 14)
Veräußerungswert realizable value
Verband der Wirtschaftsdirektoren Food and Beverage Manager Association (FBMA)
Verbandskasten first-aid kit
Verbandszeug dressings, first aid kit
verbessern amend, correct, improve, revise
verbieten prohibit
verbinden (Medizin) bandage
verbinden (vereinigen) associate
verbinden (verpflichten) oblige
Verbindlichkeit liability, obligation
Verbindlichkeiten accounts payable, liabilities
Verbindlichkeiten, kurzfristige current liabilities
Verbindlichkeiten, kurzfristiger Teil langfristiger current maturities (or portion) of long-term debt
Verbindlichkeiten, langfristige long-term liabilities, long-term debt
Verbindung connection, service, link
Verbrauch consumption
verbrauchen consume
Verbraucher consumer, user
Verbrauchsgüter nondurable goods
verbreiten durch Rundfunk broadcast
Verbuchung auf einem Konto posting to an account
verbunden mit related to
verdanken owe

verdauen digest
Verdauung digestion
Verdauungsstörung indigestion
Verderb waste
Verderb (von Waren) spoilage
verderben spoil, waste
verderblich, leicht perishable
verdienen earn
Verdienst (Gehalt) earnings
Verdienst merit
Verdienstausfall loss of earnings
Verdienstspanne profit margin
verdrehen distort
Verdruß worry
verdünnen dilute
Verein association, club
vereinbar mit consistent with
vereinbaren agree upon, agree with, arrange, contract
Vereinbarung agreement, arrangement, contract
vereinheitlichen standardize
Vereinheitlichung standardization
vereinigen join
vereinigen, sich associate
Vereinsmitgliedschaft club membership
Verfahren procedure
Verfalldatum date of expiry
verfallen expire, out of date, waste
Verfallsdatum (Kreditkarte) expiration date (credit card)
Verfalltag expiration date
Verfälschung adulteration
verfault rotten
verfehlen miss
verfolgen follow up
Verfrachtung shipment
verfügbar available, liquid
Verfügbarkeit availability
verfügen über dispose of
Verfügung disposal
vergehen pass
Vergleich accord
Vergleichbarkeit (Rechnungslegung) comparability
Vergleichbarkeit in zeitlicher Hinsicht (Rechnungslegung) consistency
Vergnügen pleasure

Vergnügungsdampfer pleasure boat
Vergnügungsfahrt cruise, pleasure drive
Vergnügungslokal place of entertainment
Vergnügungspark amusement park
Vergnügungsreise pleasure trip
Vergnügungssteuer entertainment tax
Vergnügungszentrum entertainment centre
Vergrößerung enlargement
Vergünstigung benefit, allowance
Vergünstigungen reduced rates
vergüten compensate
Vergütung compensation
verhaften arrest
Verhaftung arrest
Verhalten behavior
verhalten, sich behave
Verhältnis ratio
verhandeln negotiate
Verhandlung negotiation, transaction
verheiratet married
verhindern prevent
Verhinderung prevention
verhüten prevent
verirren, sich get lost
Verjüngungskur rejuvenation cure
Verkauf sale
Verkauf, persönlicher personal selling
verkaufen market, sell
Verkäufer salesman
Verkäufermarkt seller's market
Verkaufsabteilung sales department
Verkaufsargument sales argument
Verkaufsargument an das Gefühl appellierend emotional sales argument
Verkaufsautomat (Umsatzbereich 6) vending machine (schedule 6)
Verkaufsförderung promotion, sales promotion
Verkaufsförderung (durch Ausstellung) visual merchandising
Verkaufsgrundsätze merchandising policy
Verkaufshilfe (Service Center 11) selling aid (schedule 11)

Verkaufshinweise (auf Einrichtungen im Hotel) inhouse sale
Verkaufsleiter marketing manager, sales manager
Verkaufsort point of sale
Verkaufspreis sales price, selling price
Verkaufspreise für Speisen und Getränke food and beverage prices
Verkaufsrepräsentant sales representative
Verkaufssteuerung merchandising
Verkaufsvertreter sales representative
Verkehr traffic
Verkehr, entgegenkommender oncoming traffic
Verkehr, täglicher daily service
verkehren operate
Verkehrsader traffic artery
Verkehrsampel traffic light
Verkehrsamt local tourist office, tourist information office
Verkehrsaufkommen quantity of available traffic
Verkehrsdelikt motoring offence
Verkehrsdichte traffic density
Verkehrseinschränkung traffic restriction
Verkehrsflugzeug airliner, liner
Verkehrsfluß traffic flow
Verkehrsgewerbe transportation industry, carriers
Verkehrsinsel refuge, street island
Verkehrsknotenpunkt junction
Verkehrsmaschine airliner
Verkehrsmittel vehicle
Verkehrsmittel, öffentliche public transport
Verkehrsmittelwerbung transportation advertising
Verkehrsordnung traffic regulation
Verkehrsplanung transport planning
Verkehrspolitik transport policy
Verkehrspolizei traffic police
Verkehrspolizist pointsman
Verkehrsregelung traffic regulation
Verkehrssicherheit road safety, traffic safety
Verkehrsspitze peak days

Verkehrsstau area congestion
Verkehrsstauung traffic congestion
Verkehrsstockung traffic block, traffic hold-up, traffic jam
Verkehrsteilnehmer road user
Verkehrsträger (Fluggesellschaft, Bus, Bahn, Schiff) carrier
Verkehrsunfall traffic accident
Verkehrsüberwachung traffic control
Verkehrsverbindung communication
Verkehrsverbot prohibition of entry of vehicles
Verkehrsverein local tourist association
Verkehrswert fair market value
Verkehrswirtschaft free economy
Verkehrszeichen road sign
verkehrt wrong
verkehrt täglich (Bus etc.) daily service, operates daily
verklagen sue
verknüpfen knit
verknüpft mit related to
verkrampft tense
Verladebahnsteig loading platform
Verladegebühr loading charges
Verladekosten shipping charges
Verladestelle loading point
Verladung embarkation
verlangen demand, require
verlangen insist (on, upon)
verlangen nach ask for
Verlangen, auf on demand
verlängern extend, prolong, renew
Verlängerung extension, prolongation, renewal
Verlängerungsschnur extension cord
Verlängerungstag additional day
Verlängerungswoche additional week, extra week
verlassen quit
verlassen auf, sich depend on, rely on
Verläßlichkeit reliability
Verlauf progress
Verlautbarungsentwurf exposure draft
Verleih hire service, rental service
verleihen lend
Verleihgebühr hire charge

verletzen harm, hurt, violate
Verletzung harm, hurt
verlieren lose
verlieren, an Wert deteriorate
Verlobung engagement
Verlust damage, deficit, loss, net loss
Verlust und Beschädigung von Gasteigentum loss and damage of guest property
Verlustanzeige notification of a loss
Verluste aus schwebenden Geschäften, drohende probable losses from pending transactions
Verlustvortrag losses brought forward
Verlustzeit lost time
vermehren increase
Vermehrung increase
vermeiden avoid
Vermeidung avoidance
Vermerk memorandum
vermerken note
vermieten lease, let, rent
Vermieter hirer, landlord, lessor
vermindern impair, reduce
vermindern, sich shrink
Verminderung decline
vermischen mix
vermischt miscellanious
vermissen miss
vermißt missing
Vermögen insgesamt, sonstiges total other assets
Vermögen zu Anschaffungskosten abzüglich Abschreibungen, sonstiges other assets, at cost less amortization
Vermögensgegenstände, immaterielle intangible assets
Vermögenslage financial position
Vermögensrecht property right
Vermögensteile, liquide liquid assets
Vermögenswerte, immaterielle intangible assets
Vermögenswerte, langfristige noncurrent assets
vernachlässigen neglect
Vernunft reason
vernünftig rational
veröffentlichen bring out, publish

Veröffentlichung publication
verpachten let, rent
Verpächter lessor
verpacken pack, package
Verpackung packing, packaging
Verpackungskosten packaging expenses
verpfänden pledge
Verpflegung board, catering, food, food supply
Verpflegungsbereich food and beverage department
Verpflegungskapazität food supply capacity
verpflichten engage, obligate, oblige
verpflichtend obligatory
verpflichtet bound, indebted, obliged
Verpflichtung commitment
Verpflichtung engagement, obligation
Verrechnungskonto clearing account
verreisen go away on holiday
Verrichtung job, performance
versagen fail
versammeln, sich meet
Versammlung meeting
Versandanzeige advice of dispatch (shipment)
versandfertig ready for shipment
Versandkosten shipping cost, transportation cost
Versandort place of dispatch
versäumen neglect
Versäumnis default
verschieben postpone
Verschiebung postponement
verschiedenartig miscellanious, various
verschiedene sundry
Verschiedenheit variety
verschlafen oversleep oneself, sleep late
verschlechtern, sich deteriorate
verschließen (luftdicht) air-seal
verschlingen gulp
Verschluß shutter
verschmelzen merge
verschneiden (Wein) dilute
Verschneidung (Wein) adulteration
verschneit snow-covered, snowed up
Verschönerung beautification
verschuldet indebted

Verschuldung indebtedness
verschwiegen discreet
Verschwiegenheit discretion
verschwommen hazy
versenden ship
Versendung shipment
versengen sear
Versetzung transfer
Versetzungskosten (Service Center 9) relocation expenses (schedule 9)
versichern insure
versichern (behaupten, bestätigen) affirm
versichern (erklären) assure
Versicherung insurance
Versicherung (Behauptung, Bestätigung) affirmation
Versicherung (Erklärung) assurance
Versicherungsbeitrag insurance charge, insurance contribution
Versicherungsbeiträge, vorausbezahlte unexpired insurance
Versicherungsgesellschaft insurance company
Versicherungsschutz insurance protection
versorgen cater for, supply
verspäten delay
verspätet late
verspätete Ankunft eines Fluggastes late passenger arrival
Verspätung delay
versprechen promise
verstaatlichen nationalize
Verständlichkeit (der Rechnungslegungsinformation) understandability
Verständnis understanding
verstärken intensify
Verstärker amplifier
verstehen understand
verstellbar adjustable
versteuert tax paid
versuchen attempt, try
vertagen postpone, put off
Vertagung postponement
vertauschen swap
verteilen distribute
verteilen (Anschaffungskosten auf Geschäftsjahre) allocate (acquisition costs over the business years)
Verteilung distribution, division
Vertrag agreement, contract
Vertrag, gegenseitiger mutual agreement
vertragen agree with
vertraglich contractual
vertraglich gebunden bound by contract
verträglich mit compatible with
Vertragsbedingung term
Vertragsbestimmung clause, term
Vertragsbruch breach of contract
Vertragsbüro appointed office
Vertragsentwurf tentative agreement
Vertragsgaststätte appointed restaurant, authorized restaurant
Vertragshaftung liability under the contract
Vertragshaus authorized establishment
Vertragshotel appointed hotel, authorized hotel
Vertragsklauseln, einschränkende restrictive covenants
Vertragsstrafe contractual penalty
vertrauenswürdig trustworthy
Vertrauenswürdigkeit trustworthiness
vertraulich confidential
vertretbar justifiable
vertreten represent
Vertreter agent, representative, salesman
Vertreterbesuch call
Vertretung agency, representation
Vertrieb distribution
Vertriebskosten selling expenses
Vertriebsleiter marketing manager
verunglücken meet with an accident
verursachen provoke, cause
verurteilt zu bound to
vervollkommnen improve
verwalten administer, manage
Verwaltung administration
Verwaltungsgebühr management fee
Verwaltungsvertrag management agreement
verwandeln in ein Hotel hotelize
verwandt related

Verwandtenbesuch visit of relatives
Verwandter, nächster next of kin
Verwandte(r) relation, relative
Verwarnung warning, ticket
verwenden apply
verwerten make use of
Verwirrung mess
Verzehr consumption
verzeichnen list
Verzeichnis list, index, register, schedule, statement
Verzeichnis der Sollportionsgrößen portion chart
verzerren distort
Verzicht quitclaim
verzichten give up, quitclaim, renounce
verzichten auf forego
verzieren decorate
verzollen clear, declare
verzollt duty paid
Verzollung clearance
Verzollung einer Schiffsladung clearing
verzögern delay
Verzögerung delay, retardation
Verzug default
Vieh cattle
vielbesucht much-frequented
vielfach multiple
Vielfalt variety
Vielfraß glutton, gourmand
vielseitig multi-lateral
vielsprachig polyglot
Viertel quarter
Vierteljahr quarter
vierteljährlich quarterly
Vierzehntage fortnight
Vinnaigrettesoße vinnaigrette(sauce)
VIP very important person, vip
Visagebühr visa charge
Visum visa
Visumsantrag application for a visa
Vitrine show case
Vizepräsident vice-president
Vogel bird
Volksfest public festival
Volkskunst folk art
Volkslied folk song
Volkstanz folk dance
Volkstracht national costume

voll bezahlt paid-up
voll eingezahlt paid-up
voll im Geschmack full-flavoured
Vollauslastung sell out
Vollbad full bath
vollbelegte Tage sell out days
vollbringen accomplish
vollenden accomplish
Vollhaftung full liability
volljährig full of age, of age
Volljährigkeit age of majority, full age, lawful age
vollklimatisiert fully airconditioned
Vollkornbrot whole(meal)-bread
Vollkostenrechnung actual cost system
Vollmacht authority
Vollmassage full massage
Vollmond full moon
Vollpension board and lodging, board and residence, board residence, full board, full board and lodging, full pension
Vollpreisfahrkarte normal-fare ticket
Vollprüfung audit
vollziehen fulfill
Vollziehung fulfillment
Volumen volume
von Bedeutung significant
von Bord gehen leave the ship
Vor- oder Nachsaison shoulder period, off-peak season
Vor- und Nachsaisonfahrpreis off-peak fare
vorangehen precede
Voranmeldung advance reservation
Voranschlag budget, estimate
voranschlagen estimate
vorausbezahlt prepaid
vorausgehen precede
vorausgehend prior to
vorausplanen budget, forecast
Vorausplanung budget
Voraussagetauglichkeit (Rechnungslegung) predicative value
Vorausschau forecast
voraussehen expect
voraussetzen assume
Voraussetzung prerequisite, assumption

voraus, im in advance
Vorbehalt reservation
vorbereiten prepare
Vorbereitung preparation
vorbestellen book, reserve
Vorbestellung advance booking
Vorbestellung von Plätzen
　reservation of seats in advance
vorbeugend preventive
Vorbeugung prevention
vorbildlich exemplary
Vorbildung education
Vordeck fore deck
Vorderdeck forecastle
Vordersitz front seat
Vorderzimmer front-room
Voreröffnungskosten preopening expenses
Voreröffnungsmanagement
　pre-opening management
Vorfahre ancestor
Vorfahren ancestry
Vorfahrt right-of-way
Vorfahrt beachten! give way
Vorfahrtsstraße major road, priority road
vorfallen happen
Vorführung performance, show
Vorgabe standard, target
Vorgebirge promontory
Vorgericht appetizer, side dish
Vorgericht, pikantes savoury
Vorgesetztenschulung supervisory training
Vorgesetzter superior, supervisor
Vorgesetzter, direkter immediate supervisor
Vorhalle vestibule
Vorhalle, überdachte porch
vorhanden on hand
Vorhang curtain
vorher prior to
vorherbestimmt bound to
vorherrschend predominant
Vorjahr previous year
Vorkalkulation cost estimate
vorkochen pre-cook
vorkühlen pre-cool
Vorlage draft
vorläufig interim, provisional, temporary, tentative

vorlegen produce
Vorleger rug
Vorliebe preference
Vormittag forenoon
vormittags (bei Zeitangabe) a. m.
Vorname Christian name
vornehm distinguished
Vorortzug suburban train
Vorrang precedence, priority
Vorräte stock on hand
Vorräte zum Niederstwert
　inventories, at the lower of cost or market
vorrätig on hand
Vorratsraum storeroom
Vorrecht privilege, precedence
Vorrichtung appliance
Vorruhestand early retirement
Vorsaison low season, preseason
Vorschau preview
vorschießen advance
Vorschlag proposal, suggestion
vorschlagen suggest
Vorschrift provision, regulation, rule
Vorschub leisten promote
Vorschuß advance
Vorschüsse und Kredite an Mitglieder der Geschäftsleitung advances to officers
Vorsicht! caution, take care
Vorsicht Zug! beware of trains
vorsichtig cautious
vorsichtig discreet
Vorsichtsprinzip conservatism
Vorspeise appetizer, cocktail savory, horsd'oeuvre, side dish
Vorspeisen kalt cold side dishes
Vorstand executive board
Vorstands- und Verwaltungsratmitglied
　executive (of the company)
Vorstandsmitglied officer
vorstellen introduce
Vorstellung introduction
Vorstellung, geschlossene private performance
Vorteil advantage, benefit, gain
vorteilhaft advantageous
vorteilhafter Kauf bargain
Vortrag lecture

Vortragsreise lecture tour
vorübergehend temporary
Vorverkauf advance booking
Vorverkaufsstelle (advance) booking office
Vorvertrag preliminary agreement
Vorwahlnummer area code
vorwärmen preheat
vorweg in advance
vorwegnehmen anticipate
vorzeitig in advance
vorziehen prefer
Vorzug preference, priority
Vorzugsaktien preferred stock
Vorzugsaktien, kumulative cumulative preferred stock
Vorzugsbehandlung preferential treatment
Vorzugsfrachtrate (Luftverkehr) commodity rate
Vorzugspreis special price
Vorzüge (z. B. eines Hotelzimmers) amenities
Vögel am Spieß mit Polenta birds on skewer with corn pie

W

Waage scale
wach awake
wach liegen lie awake
Wachmacher eye opener
Wacholder juniper
Wachs wax
Wachsbohne wax bean
Wachsei wax-egg
wachsen (größer werden) grow
wachsen (Wachs) wax
Wachstum growth
Wachstumsrate growth rate
Wachtel quail
Wächter watchman
Waffel wafer, waffle
Waffelkartoffeln fried potato wafers
wagen attempt
Wagen carriage
Wagen (Auto) car, motor-car
Wagenheber jack
Wagenpflege motor-car service
Wagentür carriage door

Waggonfracht carload freight
Waggonfrachtrate carload rate
Waggonladung carload
Wagnis risk
Wahl choice, alternative
wählen (Telefon) dial
wahlfrei optional
wahrnehmbar apparent
wahrnehmen notice
wahrscheinlich probable
Währung currency
Währung, harte hard currency
Währung, konvertierbare convertable currency, free currency
Währungsrisiko foreign exchange risk
Wald forest, wood
Walderdbeere wild strawberry
Waldhuhn wood grouse
Waldmeister woodruff
waldreich well-wooded
Waldspaziergang walk in the woods
Waldweg forest path
Wallfahrtskirche pilgrimage church
Wallfahrtsort place of pilgrimage
Walnuß walnut
Walzer waltz
Wandelhalle pump room
Wandelschuldverschreibung convertible bond
Wanderer hiker, rambler, tramper
Wanderfahrt walking tour
Wanderführer hikers' guide, ramblers' guide
Wandergebiet hiking region
wandern hike, peregrinate, ramble, tramp, walk
Wandern hiking, peregrination, rambling, tramping, walking
Wanderschau touring exhibition
Wandersport hiking, rambling
Wandertourismus hiking, rambling
Wanderung peregrination, ramble, walking tour
Wanderverein rambling association
Wandkarte wall map
Wandschirm folding screen
Wanne tub
Wannenbad tub-bath
Ware commodity, goods, merchandise

Waren, verderbliche perishable goods
Ware, schwimmende goods afloat
Waren unter Zollverschluß goods in bond
Warenannahme receiving department
Warenannehmer receiving clerk
Warenausgabe issuing
Warenbestand stock in trade, merchandise on hand, merchandise inventory
Wareneinstandskosten cost of goods purchased
Warenhaus department store
Warenkosten, bereinigte (Umsatzbereich 2) net cost of food and beverage sales (schedule 2)
Warenkosten, nicht bereinigte (Umsatzbereich 2) cost of food and beverage consumed (schedule 2)
Warenkosten, sonstige (Umsatzbereich 2) other cost of sales (schedule 2)
Warenlager merchandise
Warenvorrat goods in hand
Warenzeichen trademark
warm warm
Wärme warmth
wärmen warm
Wärmflasche hot-water bottle
Warmwasser hot water
Warnschild warning sign
Warnung warning
Warteliste waiting list
warten wait
Wartesaal waiting room
Warteschlange waiting line
Wartestellung stand-by position
Wartezeit waiting period
Wartezeiten delays, waits
Wartezimmer waiting room
Wartung maintenance, servicing
Wartungsvertrag maintenance contract
Wasch- und Toilettenanlagen washing and lavatory facilities
waschbar washable
Waschbecken wash-basin
Wäsche laundry

Wäsche (Umsatzbereich 2) linen (schedule 2)
Wäsche- und Reinigungskosten (Umsatzbereich 2) laundry and dry cleaning (schedule 2)
Wäschebeschließerin linen keeper, linen room attendant
waschecht washable
Wäscherei laundry
Wäschereileiter laundry manager
Wäschesack laundry bag
Wäscheschacht laundry chute
Wäscheschrank linen-closet
Wäscheverleih linen hire
Waschküche (umgangsspr. für dichter Nebel) pea soup
Waschlappen face cloth
Waschmaschine washing-machine
Waschpulver washing powder
Waschraum lavatory, rest room
Waschtisch washstand
Waschwanne washing tub
Wasser water
Wasser, fließendes running water
Wasser, lauwarmes tepid water
Wasser, destilliertes distilled water
Wasserball water-polo
wasserdicht waterproof
Wasserfall waterfall
Wasserfliegen water gliding
Wasserflugzeug hydroplane, seaplane
Wasserglas tumbler
Wasserhahn tap, water-tap
Wasserhuhn coot, water hen
Wasserkur water cure
Wasserleitung water pipes
Wassermelone water-melon
Wasserschaden durch Feuerlöschbrause sprinkler leakage
Wassersegelflugzeug sea glider
Wasserski water-ski
Wasserspiele ornamental fountains
Wassersport aquatic sports, water sports
Wasserstand water level
Wasserstelle watering-place
Wassertemperatur water temperature
Wasserverunreinigung water pollution

Wasserwelle water wave
Watte cotton wool
Wechsel bill of exchange
Wechselbad contrast bath
Wechselbürgschaft guarantee of a bill (of exchange)
Wechselforderungen notes receivable
Wechselgeld change
Wechselgeld behalten! keep the change
Wechselkurs exchange rate
Wechselkursschwankungen fluctuation of the exchange rate
wechseln change, exchange, rotate (Personal)
wechselnd varying
Wechselobligo contingent liabilities from bills of exchange
Wechselobligo aus der Weitergabe von Wechseln (nicht Einlösung) endorsment risks for bills of exchange (notes)
Wechselschicht rotating shift
wechselseitig mutual
Wechselstrom alternating current
Wechselstube exchange office, foreign exchange office
Wechselverbindichkeiten notes payable
Weckdienst waking service
wecken call, wake up
Wecker alarm-clock
weggeben give-away
wegräumen clear away
Wegweiser guidepost, signpost
Wegzeit travel time
weiblich female
weich soft
Weichkäse cream cheese
Weichtier mollusk
Weide pasture
Weideland pasturage
Weigerung refusal
Weiher fishpond
Weihnachten Christmas, X-mas
Weihnachtsferien Christmas holidays, Christmas vacation
Weihnachtsgratifikation Christmas bonus
Weihnachtsmann Santa Claus

Weihnachtspudding Christmas pudding
Weihnachtszeit Christmas period
Wein wine
Wein, abgelagerter mature wine
Wein, alter old wine
Wein, gespritzter spritzer
Wein, hellroter rose wine
Wein, junger new wine
Wein, leichter light wine
Wein, naturreiner vintage wine
Wein, offener open wine, wine by the glass, wine in a carafe
Wein, roter offener red wine from the cask
Wein, schwerer heavy wine
Wein, süßer sweet wine
Wein, trockener dry wine
Weinberg vineyard
Weinbergschnecke edible snail, snail
Weinblume wine bouquet
Weinbrand brandy
Weinbrandglas brandy-glass
Weinfest wine festival
Weinflasche wine bottle
Weingegend wine district
Weinglas wine-glass
Weingut vineyard
Weinhändler wine-merchant
Weinhandlung wine shop
Weinkarte wine-list
Weinkeller wine-cellar
Weinkkraut cabbage in wine, pickled cabbage
Weinkühler ice-pail, wine cooler
Weinlese vintage
Weinlesefest vintage festival
Weinlokal wine-cellar
Weinprobe wine-test
Weinprobiergläschen taster
Weinrebe vine
Weinschenke wine-house
Weinstube wine-tavern
Weißbier white beer
Weißbohnengericht stew of white beans
Weißbrot white bread
Weißkohl white cabbage
Weißkraut white cabbage
Weißling whiting

Weißwein white wine
Weißwein, offener white wine from the cask
Weißwurst white sausage, weisswurst
Weißzeug linen
weit far
weiterfahren set off again
Weiterfahrt continuation of one's journey
Weiterflug onward air journey
weiterreichen pass
Weiterverfolgung (einer Sache) follow up
Weizenbrot wheaten bread
Weizengrießbrei cream of wheat
Weizenmehlkuchen (dreieckig) scone
Welle (Technik) shaft
Welle (Wasser) wave
Wellenbrecher breakwater
Wellenreiter aqua-planing
wellig wavy
Wels sheat-fish
Weltausstellung international exhibition, world exhibition, World Fair
Weltenbummler globe-trotter
Weltruf world-wide fame
Weltverband der Reisebüros World Association of Travel Agencies
Weltzeit Greenwich mean time
wenden turn round
Wenden verboten! no U-turn
weniger less
Wenslaydale-Käse Wenslaydale
Werbeabteilung publicity department, advertising department
Werbeagentur advertising agency
Werbebrief advertising letter, sales letter
Werbebudget advertising budget
Werbeetat advertising budget
Werbefahrt advertising tour
Werbefeldzug advertising campaign, publicity campaign
Werbegeschenk advertising gift, give-away
Werbeidee advertising idea
Werbekampagne advertising campaign, campaign
Werbematerial sales literature
Werbemittel advertising media
werben advertise, promote
Werbeplakat poster
Werbeplan advertising program
Werberundschreiben advertising circular
Werbung advertising, promotion
Werbung durch Drucksachenversand direct mail advertising
Werbung durch Zugaben free gift advertising
Werbung, indirekte indirect advertising
Werbung, lokale local advertising
werfen, über Bord throw over board
Werft wharf
Werkstätte workshop
Werkzeug implement, tool
Wermut(wein) vermo(u)th
Wert value
Wert der verkauften Waren zum Einstandspreis (Umsatzbereich 4) cost of merchandise sold (schedule 4)
Wert legen auf, besonderen emphasize
Wertabnahme deflation
Wertangabe declaration of value
Wertansatz measurement
Wertberichtigung accumulated depreciation, provision
Wertberichtigungen auf Forderungen allowance for doubtful accounts
Wertberichtigungen auf Vorräte inventory valuation adjustments
wertlos worthless
Wertmesser standard
Wertminderung von Beteiligungen impairment (of net assets)
Wertpapier(e) stock
Wertpapiere des Umlaufvermögens marketable securities, short-term investments
Wertpapiere (des Anlagevermögens) investments (held as fixed assets)
Wertsachen valuables

Wesentlichkeit, Kriterium der (Rechnungslegung) materiality
Weste waistcoat
Westeuropäische Zeit (WEZ) Western European time
Wettangeln angling competition
Wettbewerb competition
Wettbewerber competitor
Wettbewerbsbeschränkung restraint of trade
Wettbewerbsmarkt competitive market
Wetteramt meteorological office, weather bureau
Wetterbericht weather forecast
Wetterdienst meteorological services
wetterfest weatherproof
Wetterkarte weather chart
Wettervorhersage weather forecast
Wetterwarte weather station
Whisky whisky, whiskey
wichtig significant
widrig adverse
wie like
Wiederbeschaffungskosten current cost
Wiederbeschaffungswert replacement value
Wiedereinreisevisum re-entry visa
wiedereinschiffen, sich reembark
wiedereinstellen rehire
Wiedererkennen recognition
wiedererkennen recognize
Wiedereröffnung re-opening
wiederherstellen restore
Wiederherstellung restoration
wiederholen repeat
Wiederholung repetition
Wiederholungsauftrag repeated order
Wiederholungsgeschäft repeated business
auf Wiedersehen! good bye
Wiederverkäufer reseller
wiederverwenden reuse
Wiederverwendung reuse
Wiedervorlagemappe follow-up file
Wiedervorlageverfahren follow-up system
wiegen weigh

Wiener Rostbraten rumpsteak with fried onions, steak Vienna style, Vienna steak with fried onions
Wiener Schnitzel fried slice of veal Vienna style, Viennese schnitzel
Wiener Würstchen Wieners
Wiese meadow
wild rugged, wild
Wild (Fleisch) game, venison
Wildbret game
Wildente pintail, wild duck
Wildfleischragout jugged game
Wildgans wild goose
Wildkaninchen wild rabbit
Wildnis wilderness
Wildpastete cold game pie
Wildschwein wild boar
Wildschweinfilet gegrillt grilled fillet of wild boar
Wildschweinkeule wild boar haunch
Wildschweinrücken wild boar saddle
Wildschweinskopf gefüllt head of wild boar, stuffed boar's head
Wille des Unternehmers management's attention
willkommen welcome
Windbeutel cream puff, small cream puff
windgeschützt protected against the wind
windig airy, windy
Windjacke windcheater
Windschutzscheibe windscreen, windshield
Windstärke wind force
Windstoß gust
Windsurfen windsurfing
Windtorte meringue cake
winken wave
Winteraufenthaltsort winter stay
Winterendivie escarole
Winterfahrplan winter time-table
Winterferiendorf winter holiday village
Winterflugplan winter timetable
Winterfreuden joys of winter
Winterfrische winter holiday resort
Wintergarten winter garden
Winterkur winter cure
Winterkurort winter health resort
winterlich wintry

Winterreifen winter tyre
Winterreiseverkehr winter tourist traffic
Wintersaison winter season
Wintersport winter sports
Wintersportarrangement inclusive winter sport terms
Wintersportausrüstung winter sports equipment
Wintersporteinrichtungen winter sports facilities
Wintersportort winter sports centre, winter sports resort
Wintersportreise winter sports trip
Wintersportsaison winter sports season
Wintersportveranstaltung winter sports event
Wintersportzug snow train
Wintertourismus winter tourism
Winzer wine grower
Winzerfest vintagers' festival
Wirbelsturm tornado
wirklich factual
wirksam effective
Wirksamkeit effectiveness
Wirkung impact
Wirsingkohl savoy cabbage
Wirt saloonkeeper
Wirtin landlady
wirtschaftlich economical
Wirtschaftssystem economic system
Wirtshaus public house, tavern
wischen wipe
Wissen knowledge
Wissen, praktisches know-how
wissentlich knowingly
Wochenendausflug weekend excursion
Wochenende week-end
Wochenendfahrt week-end outing, week-end trip
Wochenendpension week-end guest-house
Wochenendreiseverkehr week-end tourist traffic
Wochenendspezialpreis special week-end price
Wochenendtourismus week-end tourism

Wochenmarkt weekly market
Wochenrechnung weekly bill
Wochenschau newsreel
Wochentag week-day
Wodka vodka
wohl well
wohnen dwell, live, reside
Wohngebiet residential area
wohnhaft resident
Wohnhaus apartment house
Wohnort place of residence
Wohnraum living-room
Wohnschlafraum bed-sitter, bed-sitting room
Wohnsitz domicile, residence
Wohnsitz, ständiger permanent residence
Wohnsitz haben reside
Wohnung apartment, flat
Wohnung, möblierte furnished apartment
Wohnungs- und Zimmervermittlung housing bureau
Wohnungsbau housebuilding
Wohnungsgeldzuschuß housing allowance
Wohnwagen caravan, trailer
Wohnwagenanhänger caravan trailer
Wohnwagenfahrer trailerite
Wohnwagentourist caravaner
Wohnzimmer living-room, sitting-room
Wolke cloud
wolkig cloudy
Wolldecke blanket, wool blanket
wollen want
wöchentlich weekly
Wörterbuch dictionary
wörtlich verbal
Wrack wreck
Wurst sausage
Wurstaufschnitt slices of sausage
Wurstplatte assorted sausage
wünschen want
würdigen appreciate
Würfelzucker lump sugar
Würstchen sausage
Würze zest
würzen (Speisen) season
würzig spicy, well-seasoned

wütend irate
W.C. water-closet, W.C.

Y

Yield Management yield management
Yield Management-Team yield management team

Z

zäh tough
Zahl figure
zahlbar payable
zahlen pay
zählen count
Zahlkarte paying-form
Zahlmeister paymaster, purser
Zahlung payment
Zahlungsgewohnheit paying habit
Zahlungsmodus method of payment
Zahlungsort place of payment
Zahlungsweise method of payment
Zahnarzt dentist
Zahnbürste tooth brush
Zahnpaste toothpaste
Zahnstocher toothpick
Zander pike-perch
zanken quarrel
Zapfenstreich tattoo
zart tender
Zebrastreifen zebra crossing
zechen carouse, tipple
Zecherei potation
Zechprellerei bilking, hotel fraud
Zeichen mark, symbol
Zeichenerklärung legend, signs and symbols
zeigen exhibit, show
Zeit time
Zeit, angemessene reasonable time
Zeit, verkehrsarme off-peak period
Zeit totschlagen (vertreiben) kill time
Zeit- und Bewegungsstudie time and motion study
Zeitansage time signal

Zeitaufnahme time exposure
zeitgemäß up-to-date
Zeitkarte commutation ticket, season ticket
Zeitnähe (Rechnungslegung) timeliness
Zeitnahme timing
Zeitplan schedule
Zeitschrift journal, magazine, periodical
Zeitschriftenkiosk bookstall, news stall
Zeitung newspaper
Zeitungsbeilage insert
Zeitungsstand news stand
Zeitungswerbung newspaper advertising
Zeitvorgabe time allowance
zeitweilig temporary
Zeitzeichen time signal
Zelluloid celluloid
Zelt tent
Zelt- und Wohnwagenwesen camping and caravaning
zelten camp, pitch a tent
Zelthering tent-peg
Zeltlager tent camp
Zeltplatz camping ground
Zeltvordach tent awning
zentrale Frage pivotal question
Zentraleinheit central processing unit (CPU)
Zentralheizung central heating
Zentralverwaltung home office
Zentralverwaltungswirtschaft government controlled economy
Zentrum center
zerklüftet rugged
zerlassen melted
zerschneiden carve
zerteilen part
Zervelat(wurst) saveloy
Zeugnis certificate
Zichorie (Salat) chicory
Zicklein kid-goat, yeanling
Ziege goat
Ziegenkäse goat cheese
ziehen pull
ziehen: aus dem Wasser gezogen plain boiled
Ziel goal, objective

Ziel (gegen Ziel liefern) supply on credit
Zielbahnhof destination station
Zielflughafen destination airport
Zielland country of destination
Zielort destination, point of turnaround
Zielsetzung objective
ziemlich quite
Ziffer figure
Zigarette cigarette
Zigarettenverkäufer tobacconist
Zigarillo small cigar
Zigarre cigar
Zigeuner gipsy
Zigeunergulasch beef stew gipsy style
Zimmer room
Zimmer, behindertengerechtes barrier-free room for handicapper accessibility
Zimmer, belegte und freie rooms occupied and vacant
Zimmer, belegte (im Berichtszeitraum) room nights sold
Zimmer, ineinandergehende connecting rooms
Zimmer am Swimmingpool cabana, poolside room
Zimmer frei rooms vacant
Zimmer im voraus bestellen book a room in advance
Zimmer mit Bad oder Dusche room with private bath or shower
Zimmer mit drei Betten triple
Zimmer mit Frühstück bed and breakfast, Continental Plan (CP)
Zimmer mit Halbpension Modified American Plan (MAP)
Zimmer mit Meeresblick room with a view of the sea
Zimmer mit Übernachtung und Frühstück Continental Plan (bed and breakfast)
Zimmer mit Verbindungstür(en) connecting room
Zimmer mit Vollpension American Plan (AP)
Zimmer mit zwei (einzelnen) Betten twin

Zimmer mit zusätzlicher Schlafcouch studio (executive room)
Zimmer ohne Berechnung complimentary room
Zimmer, vorhandene (im Berichtszeitraum) room nights available
Zimmer zu vermieten rooms to let
Zimmer zur Straße room facing the street
Zimmerdecke ceiling
Zimmerfrühstückskarte door knob menu
Zimmerkellner room service waiter
Zimmerlautstärke room loudness
Zimmerliste rooming list
Zimmermädchen chamber-maid, maid
Zimmernachweis accomodation service
Zimmernummer room number
Zimmerpreis room charge, room rate
Zimmerpreis, durchschnittlicher average rate
Zimmerpreis, niedrigster flat rate
Zimmerpreis mit Frühstück charge for bed and breakfast
Zimmerpreis ohne Pension European Plan
Zimmerreservierung hotel reservation
Zimmertelefon room telephone
Zimmervermittlung accomodation service
Zimt cinnamon
Zink zinc
Zins- und Dividendenforderungen interest and dividends receivable
Zinsen interest
Zinsen, kalkulatorische imputed interest
Zitadelle citadel
Zitherspieler zitherist
Zitronat candied lemon peel
Zitrone lemon
Zitronenbaiserpudding lemon meringue pie
Zitroneneis lemon-ice
Zitronenlimonade lemon soda, lemonade

Zitronenpresse lemon-squeezer
Zitronensaft lemon juice
Zitronenschale lemon rind
Zivilflughafen commercial airport
Zündholz match
Zündholzkartoffeln matchstick potatoes
Zündholzschachtel matchbox
Zoll customs, duty
Zoll- und Paßabfertigung passport and customs examination
Zollabfertigung custom clearance, customs clearing
Zollabfertigungsgebühren clearance charges
Zollabfertigungshalle customs examination hall
Zollbeamter customs officer
Zollbehörde customs authorities
Zolldurchlaßschein transire
Zollerhöhung increase of customs
Zollerklärung customs declaration
Zollerstattung duty drawback
zollfrei duty-free
Zollfreiheit exemption from duty
Zollgebiet customs territory
Zollhinterziehung evasion of customs
Zollkontrolle customs inspection
Zollnummer (Auto) customs number
zollpflichtig dutiable, liable to customs, liable to duty
zollpflichtig, nicht non-dutiable
Zolltarif customs tariff, tariff
Zollverschluß, unter in bond
Zollvorschriften customs regulations
Zollwert customs assessment value
Zone range, zone
Zoo zoo
zoologischer Garten zoological garden
zoomen zoom
Zoomobjektiv zoom lens
Zorn an j-m auslassen, seinen take it out on s.o.
zornig angry, irate
zu tun haben (mit) deal (with)
zu verkaufen for sale
zu vermieten for hire
zu (allzu) too
zu (Richtung) to

Zubehörteile accessory parts
zubereiten prepare
zubereitet am Tisch prepared at (guest's) table
zubereitet in Butter buttered, prepared with butter
Zubereitung preparation
zubilligen award
Zubilligung award
Zubringerbus airport bus
Zubringerdienst (Bus) bus service
Zubringerflugzeug feeder-service aircraft
Zubringerstraße feedway
Zubringerverkehr road transport connection
Zuchtforelle farm trout
Zucker sugar
Zuckerbäcker pastry cook
Zuckerdose sugar-basin
Zuckererbse sugar pea
Zuckerglasur, mit iced
Zuckerguß icing
Zuckermelone cantoloupe
Zuckerschale sugar-bowl
Zuckerzange sugar-tongs
Zufahrtstraße approach road
Zufall chance, coincidence
Zufall, unabwendbarer circumstances beyond control
Zufallsstichprobenuntersuchung random sampling
zufrieden content
zufriedenstellend satisfactory
Zug train
Zug, durchgehender through train
Zug besteigen board train
Zug mit Schiffsanschluß boat train
Zug versäumen miss the train
Zug-Schiffs-Reise kombiniert rail and steamship travel
Zugabe addition, free gift
Zugabewerbung free gift advertising
Zugang access, pass
Zugänge (Geld) additions
zugänglich, leicht (für) accessible (to)
Zuganschluß rear of the train
Zugauskunft railway inquiry office
Zugbegleiter conductor, guard, train conductor

Zugbrücke drawbridge
Zugnummer train number
zugrundeliegend underlying
Zugschaffner guard, railway guard
Zugsekretärin secretary rail
Zugspitze head of a train
Zugteil train set
Zugtelefon telephone on the train
Zugverbindung rail connection
Zugverspätung delay of a train
Zugwagen motor lorry, truck
Zugzeiten train timings
Zugzusammensetzung train formation
zuhören listen
Zulage extra pay
zulässig allowable
Zulassung admission, motor vehicle licence
Zuleitung plumbing
Zulieferindustrie supplying industry
zum halben Preis half price
zum Schweigen bringen (den Gast) talk down (to a guest)
Zum Wohl! cheers
zum Nennwert at par
Zunahme (Wert) increment
Zuname surname
Zunge tongue
zur Folge haben involve
zur Schau stellen display
zurechenbar attributable
zurückbehalten retain
zurückerstatten refund, reimburse, repay
zurückgeben return
zurückgestellt deferred
zurückkaufen reacquire
zurückkommen return
zurückrechnen reckon back
zurücktreten renounce, retire
zurückverfolgen trace
zurückvergüten reimburse
zurückweisen refuse
zurückzahlen refund, repay
Zusage confirmation
zusagen, j-m please
zusammenfassen sum up
Zusammenfassung recapitulation, summary
zusammenstellen compile, reconcile

Zusammenstoß collision
Zusatz addition, admixture
Zusatzbett extra bed
Zusatzfahrkarte supplementary ticket
Zusatzgeschäft additional business
zusätzlich additional, extra
Zusatzzoll additional duty
Zuschlag extra, supplement, supplementary charge, supplementary fare, additional charge
Zuschlagssatz rate of mark up
Zuschuß subsidy
Zusteigemöglichkeit picking-up point
Zustelldienst delivery service
Zustimmung agreement, approval
Zustrom rush
Zutat ingredient
zuteilen allocate, allot
Zuteilung allocation, allotment
Zutritt access, admission
Zutritt verboten! off limits, no admittance
zuverlässig reliable
Zuverlässigkeit reliability
zuviel berechnen overcharge
Zuwachs (Wert) increment
zuweisen allocate
Zuweisung allocation
Zuweisung eines Zimmers (an den Gast) rooming (the guest)
zwanglos informal, unconventional
zweckmäßig rational
zweckmäßig (ratsam) advisable
Zweibettabteil double-berth compartment, two-berth compartment
Zweibettkabine two-berth room
Zweibettzimmer double room, room with two beds
Zweifel doubt
zweigleisige Strecke double-track line
Zweigstelle branch office
zweijährlich biennial
zweimonatlich bimonthly
zweistöckig double deck
zweite Klasse second class
zweiter Gang second course
zweiter Rang (Theater) upper circle
zweiwöchentlich biweekly
Zwergkürbis summer-squash

Zwetschge damson, plum, prune
Zwetschgenknödel plum dumpling
Zwieback rusk
Zwiebel onion
Zwiebel, kleine spring onion
Zwiebelfleisch beef stew with onions
Zwiebelmus onion mash
Zwiebelrostbraten braised filet of beef with onions, sirloin steak with onions
Zwiebelsoße onion sauce
Zwielicht twilight
zwingen force, compel
zwingend forcible, mandatory
Zwischenabrechnung interim bill, interim invoice
Zwischenaufenthalt intermediate stop
Zwischendeck between decks, steerage
Zwischengericht entree
Zwischenhafen intermediate port
Zwischenlandung stop en route, stopover
Zwischenübernachtung overnight stay en route
Zwischenrippenstück sirloin
Zwischenrippenstück mit Filet porterhouse steak
Zwischenrippenstück mit grünem Pfeffer sirloin steak with green pepper
Zwischensaison intermediate season
Zwischenstation intermediate station
Zwischenstecker adaptor
Zwischenstock mezzanine

Teil II
Englisch – Deutsch

Part II
English – German

Teil II: **Englisch-Deutsch**
Part II: English-German

Gender labels   m : Masculinum (der)
                      f : Femininum (die)
                      n : Neutrum (das)
                      pl.: Plural (die)

Note:
All schedules mentioned apply for the "Uniform System of Accounts for Hotels".

Anmerkung:
Die Angabe der Umsatzbereiche bzw. der Service Center gilt für das „Uniform System of Accounts for Hotels".

A

à la carte à la carte
abc-airline-guide Verzeichnis *(n)* der Flughäfen *(pl.m)* und Luftverkehrsgesellschaften *(pl.f)* im Linienverkehr *(m)*
abc-flight (advanced booking charter) ABC-Flug *(m)* (verbilligter Flug)
ability Fähigkeit *(f)*
ability to work Arbeitsfähigkeit *(f)*
abolition Abschaffung *(f)*
above par über Pari *(m)*, über dem Nennwert *(m)*
abroad im Ausland *(n)*
absence rate Abwesenheitsrate *(f)*
absentee Abwesender *(m)*
absenteeism Abwesenheit *(f)*, Fernbleiben *(n)*, Fehlen *(n)*
abstract Auszug *(m)*
abuse Mißbrauch *(m)*, mißbrauchen
accelerate Gas *(n)* geben, beschleunigen
accelerated depreciation beschleunigte Abschreibung *(f)*
accelerated depreciation Sonderabschreibung *(f)*
accelerator Gaspedal *(n)*
accept annehmen, akzeptieren, abnehmen
acceptance Annahme *(f)*, Akzept *(n)*, Abnahme *(f)*
access Zugang *(m)*, Zutritt *(m)*
access road (Autobahn-) Einfahrt *(f)*
accessible (to) leicht zugänglich (für)
accessory parts Zubehörteile *(pl.n)*
accident Unfall *(m)*, Unglücksfall *(m)*
accident hazard Unfallquelle *(f)*, Unfallrisiko *(n)*
accident insurance Unfallversicherung *(f)*
accommodate unterbringen, beherbergen
accommodation Unterbringung *(f)*, Unterkunft *(f)*
accommodation capacity Beherbergungskapazität *(f)*
accommodation service Zimmervermittlung *(f)*, Zimmernachweis *(m)*
accommodation train Bummelzug *(m)*
accompanied luggage Handgepäck *(n)*
accompany begleiten
accompanying children begleitende Kinder *(pl.n)*
accompanying person Begleitperson *(f)*
accomplish ausführen, durchführen, vollenden, vollbringen
accord Übereinkommen *(n)*, Einverständnis *(n)*; Vergleich *(m)* (zwischen Schuldner und einzelnen Gläubigern)
account Konto *(n)*
account classification Kontengliederung *(f)*
account for Rechenschaft *(f)* (od. Rechnung) ablegen über
account format Kontoform *(f)*
accounting costs Kosten *(pl.)* für die Buchführung *(f)*
accounting principles Bilanzierungsgrundsätze *(pl.m)*
accounting, audit, and consulting fees Abschluß-, Prüfungs- und Beratungskosten *(pl.)*
accounts payable Verbindlichkeiten *(pl.f)*
accounts receivable Forderungen *(pl.f)*, Debitoren *(pl.m)*
accounts receivables – affiliates Forderungen *(pl.f)* gegenüber Konzerngesellschaften *(pl.f)*
accounts receivables – trade Forderungen *(pl.f)* aus Warenlieferungen *(pl.f)* und Leistungen *(pl.f)* an Dritte *(pl.m)*
accrual passive Rechnungsabgrenzung *(f)*, Rückstellung *(f)*
accrual basis of accounting periodengerechte Buchführung *(f)* mit Abgrenzungen *(pl.f)*
accrual elective Passivierungswahlrecht *(n)*
accrual for income tax Rückstellung *(f)* für Ertragssteuer *(f)*

accrual for interest expense (interest income) Abgrenzung (f) von Zinsaufwand (m) (-ertrag)
accrual for vacation pay Urlaubsgeldrückstellung (f)
accrual mandatory Passivierungspflicht (f)
accrued rückgestellt, abgegrenzt; aufgelaufen
accrued expenses passive Rechnungsabgrenzung (f)
accrued income aktive Rechnungsabgrenzung (f)
accrued interest expense (interest income) Abgrenzung (f) von Zinsaufwand (m) (-ertrag)
accrued liabilities Rückstellungen (pl.f), sonstige Rückstellungen (pl.f) (Handelsrecht)
accrued receivables Forderungen (pl.f) aus noch nicht abgerechneten Leistungen (pl.f)
accrued revenues aktive Rechnungsabgrenzung (f)
accrued salaries and wages noch nicht ausbezahlte Löhne (pl.m) und Gehälter (pl.n)
accumulate auflaufen, ansammeln
accumulated amount Endwert (m), aufgelaufener Betrag (m)
accumulated depreciation Wertberichtigung (f)
accuracy Genauigkeit (f), Sorgfalt (f)
accusation Anklage (f), Anschuldigung (f)
accustomed gewöhnt an
accustom to gewöhnen an
acid sauer
acknowledge anerkennen, bestätigen
acknowledg(e)ment Anerkennung (f), Bestätigung (f)
acquaintance Bekannter (m), Bekanntschaft (f)
acquire erwerben, erlangen, anschaffen
act of God höhere Gewalt (f)
act on sich richten nach
action Tat (f), Handlung (f), Klage (f), Prozeß (m)
action for damages Schadenersatzklage (f)

activity Tätigkeit (f), Betriebsfunktion (f)
activity level Beschäftigungsgrad (m)
activity report Tätigkeitsbericht (m)
actor Schauspieler (m)
actress Schauspielerin (f)
actual tatsächlich, Ist (n)
actual cost Ist-Kosten (pl.), tatsächlich entstandene Kosten (pl.)
actual cost system Vollkostenrechnung (f)
adaptor Zwischenstecker (m)
add hinzufügen, ergänzen
add up summieren
addition Hinzufügung (f), Zugabe (f), Zusatz (m)
additional zusätzlich
additional business Zusatzgeschäft (n)
additional charge Zuschlag (m), Aufschlag (m), Nebenkosten (pl.)
additional charge for single room Einzelzimmerzuschlag (m)
additional cost Zusatzkosten (pl.)
additional day Verlängerungstag (m)
additional duty Zusatzzoll (m)
additional paid-in capital Kapitalrücklage (f)
additional reservation Zubuchung (f)
additional week Verlängerungswoche (f)
additions Zugänge (pl.m) (Geld)
address Adresse (f), adressieren
address book Adreßbuch (n)
addressee Empfänger (m)
addressing machine Adressiermaschine (f)
adequacy Angemessenheit (f)
adequate angemessen, hinreichend
adjacent angrenzend, benachbart
adjoining anschließend an
adjoining rooms nebeneinander liegende Zimmer (pl.n)
adjust berichtigen, schlichten
adjustable verstellbar
adjusting entry Berichtigungsbuchung (f), Umbuchung (f)
adjustment Berichtigung (f), Schlichtung (f)
administer verwalten
administration Verwaltung (f)

administrative decision Leitungsentscheidung *(f)*
admission Zulassung *(f)*, Zutritt *(m)*, Einlaß *(m)*
admission card Ausweis *(m)*, Eintrittskarte *(f)*
admission free Eintritt *(m)* frei!
admission ticket Eintrittskarte *(f)*
admixture Zusatz *(m)*
adopt annehmen, beitreten
adult Erwachsener *(m)*, erwachsen
adulteration Verfälschung *(f)*, Verschneidung *(f)*
adulteration of food Verfälschung *(f)* von Nahrungsmitteln *(pl. n)*
advance vorschießen, bevorschussen, erhöhen, Vorschuß *(m)*, Steigerung *(f)*
advance booking Vorbestellung *(f)*, Vorverkauf *(m)*
advance booking office (Karten-) Vorverkaufsstelle *(f)*
advance deposit Anzahlung *(f)*
advance in price Preissteigerung *(f)*, Preiserhöhung *(f)*
advance reservation Voranmeldung *(f)*
advances to officers Vorschüsse *(pl. m)* und Kredite *(pl. m)* an Mitglieder *(pl. n)* der Geschäftsleitung *(f)*
advances to suppliers geleistete Anzahlungen *(pl. f)*
advantage Vorteil *(m)*
advantageous vorteilhaft, einträglich
adverse entgegengesetzt, widrig
advertise anzeigen, werben
advertisement column Anzeigenspalte *(f)*
advertisement, ad Annonce *(f)*, Inserat *(n)*
advertising Werbung *(f)*, Reklame *(f)*
advertising abroad Auslandswerbung *(f)*
advertising agency Werbeagentur *(f)*
advertising budget Werbebudget *(n)*, Werbeetat *(m)*
advertising campaign Werbefeldzug *(m)*, Werbekampagne *(f)*
advertising circular Werberundschreiben *(n)*
advertising gift Werbegeschenk *(n)*
advertising idea Werbeidee *(f)*
advertising letter Werbebrief *(m)*
advertising media Werbemittel *(pl. n)*
advertising program Werbeplan *(m)*
advertising rate Anzeigentarif *(m)*
advertising tour Werbefahrt *(f)*
advice Rat *(m)*, Ratschlag *(m)*, Benachrichtigung *(f)*
advice of dispatch Versandanzeige *(f)*
advisable zweckmäßig
advise beraten, avisieren
advisor Berater *(m)*
advisory service Beratungsdienst *(m)*
affiliated entities verbundene Unternehmen *(pl. n)*
affiliation Mitgliedsaufnahme *(f)*, Angliederung *(f)*
affinity group Affinitätsgruppe *(f)* (Reisegruppe mit bestimmtem Reisezweck)
affirm behaupten, bestätigen, versichern
affirmation Behauptung *(f)*, Bestätigung *(f)*, Versicherung *(f)*
afford sich leisten
affray Krawall *(m)*, Schlägerei *(f)*, Landfriedensbruch *(m)*
affront Beleidigung *(f)*
after-deck Achterdeck *(n)*
after-effect Folgeerscheinung *(f)*
after-season Nachsaison *(f)*, Spätsaison *(f)*
after-season reduction Nachsaisonermäßigung *(f)*
after-shave lotion Rasierwasser *(n)* nach der Rasur *(f)*
after-treatment Nachkur *(f)*, Nachbehandlung *(f)*
afternoon Nachmittag *(m)*
afternoon dance Tanztee *(m)*
afternoon tea Nachmittagstee *(m)*
aftertaste Beigeschmack *(m)*
age Alter *(n)*
age group Altersgruppe *(f)*
age limit Altersgrenze *(f)*
age of majority Volljährigkeit *(f)*
age of minority Minderjährigkeit *(f)*
aged receivables nach dem Alter *(n)* aufgegliederte Forderungen *(pl. f)*

agency Vertretung *(f)*, Agentur *(f)*
agency commission
　Agenturprovision *(f)*
agency fees (schedule 11)
　(Werbe-)Agenturkosten *(pl.)*
　(Service Center 11)
agency representative
　Agenturvertreter *(m)*
agenda Tagesordnung *(f)*
agent Beauftragter *(m)*, Vertreter *(m)*
aggregate amount Gesamtbetrag *(m)*
aggrieve beschweren, schädigen
agree upon vereinbaren
agree with einverstanden sein, vereinbaren, vertragen
agreeable angenehm
agreement Zustimmung *(f)*, Abkommen *(n)*, Vereinbarung *(f)*, Vertrag *(m)*
agreement of purchase and sale
　Kaufvertrag *(m)*
aid helfen, Hilfe *(f)*
air-bath Luftbad *(n)*
air booking Buchung *(f)* eines Fluges *(m)*
air bus terminal Air-Terminal *(m)*
air cargo Luftfracht *(f)*
air carriage Beförderung *(f)* auf dem Luftweg *(m)*
air charter Charterfluggesellschaft *(f)*
air coach Passagierflugzeug *(n)* der Touristenklasse *(f)*
air-conditioned mit Klimaanlage *(f)*
air-conditioning Klimaanlage *(f)*
air corridor Luftkorridor *(m)*, Einflugschneise *(f)*
aircraft Flugzeug *(n)*
aircraft departure time Abflugzeit *(f)*
aircraft engine Flugzeugmotor *(m)*
aircraft passenger insurance
　Fluggastversicherung *(f)*
aircraft pilot Pilot *(m)*, Flugzeugführer *(m)*
aircrew Flugzeugbesatzung *(f)*
air-cured beef of the Grisons
　Bündnerfleisch *(n)*
air cushion Luftkissen *(n)*
air display Luftfahrtausstellung *(f)*
air-dried meat Trockenfleisch *(n)*
airfare Flugpreis *(m)*

airfield Flugplatz *(m)*
air filter Luftfilter *(m)*
airfreight Luftfracht *(f)*
airfreight charges Luftfrachtkosten *(pl.)*
airfreight space Luftfrachtraum *(m)*
airfreighter Frachtflugzeug *(n)*
air hostess Stewardeß *(f)*
air-journey Flug *(m)*, Flugreise *(f)*
airline Fluggesellschaft *(f)*, Fluglinie *(f)*, Luftfahrtgesellschaft *(f)*
airline desk Abfertigungsschalter *(m)*
airline ticket Flugkarte *(f)*, Flugschein *(m)*
airliner Verkehrsflugzeug *(n)*, Verkehrsmaschine *(f)*, Linienflugzeug *(n)*
air mail Luftpost *(f)*
air mail envelope Luftpostkuvert *(n)*
air mail stationery Luftpostpapier *(n)*
air-mattress Luftmatratze *(f)*
air parcel Luftpostpaket *(n)*
air passenger Fluggast *(m)*
air passenger service
　Luftreisedienst *(m)*
airplane Flugzeug *(n)*
air pocket Luftloch *(n)*
air pollution Luftverschmutzung *(f)*
airport Flughafen *(m)*
airport bus Flughafenbus *(m)*, Zubringerbus *(m)*
airport customs office
　Flughafenzollamt *(n)*
airport of destination
　Bestimmungsflughafen *(m)*
airport of dispatch
　Abfertigungsflughafen *(m)*
airport restaurant
　Flughafenrestaurant *(n)*
airport service charge
　Fluggastgebühr *(f)*
airport tax Flughafensteuer *(f)*
airport terminal building
　Flughafenempfangsgebäude *(n)*
air pump Luftpumpe *(f)*
air-rail transport
　Flug-Eisenbahn-Verkehr *(m)*
air reservation
　Flugplatzreservierung *(m)*
air resort Luftkurort *(m)*

air route Flugstrecke *(f)*
airscrew-driven aeroplane Propellerflugzeug *(n)*
air-seal luftdicht verschließen
air services Flugverkehr *(m)*
air-sick luftkrank
air-sickness Luftkrankheit *(f)*
air space Luftraum *(m)*
air-steamer voyage Flug- und Schiffs-Reise *(f)*
air-stop Hubschrauberlandeplatz *(m)*
air taxi Mietflugzeug *(n)*, Lufttaxi *(n)*
air-temperature Lufttemperatur *(f)*
air-ticket Flugkarte *(f)*, Flugschein *(m)*
air-ticket issuing office Flugscheinverkaufsstelle *(f)*
air-tourism Flugtouristik *(f)*
air traffic Luftverkehr *(m)*
air traffic control Flugsicherung *(f)*
air transport company Luftverkehrsgesellschaft *(f)*
airways system Streckennetz *(n)*
airy luftig, windig
alarm bell Alarmglocke *(f)*
alarm-clock Wecker *(m)*
alcohol Alkohol *(m)*
alcoholic alkoholisch, Alkoholiker *(m)*
alcoholic drink alkoholisches Getränk *(n)*
ale (pale ale) englisches Bier *(n)*
ale-house Bierausschank *(m)*
alien Ausländer *(m)*, fremd
alight aussteigen
all additional costs will be borne by the traveller sämtliche Mehrkosten *(pl.)* gehen zu Lasten *(pl.f)* des Reisenden *(m)*
all board einsteigen!
all-expense trip Pauschalreise *(f)*
all-in air fare Flugpauschale *(f)*
all-in holiday Pauschalpreisferien *(pl.)*
all-in journey Pauschalreise *(f)*
all included alles inbegriffen
All Saints' Day Allerheiligen
all-year round admission ticket Dauerausweis *(m)*
allergic allergisch
allocate (acquisition costs over the business years) verteilen (Anschaffungskosten auf Geschäftsjahre), zuteilen, zuweisen
allocation Zuteilung *(f)*, Zuweisung *(f)*
allocation of foreign exchange Devisenzuteilung *(f)*
allocation of seats Platzzuteilung *(f)*
allot zuteilen
allotment Zuteilung *(f)*, Kontingent *(n)*
allow erlauben, gewähren
allowable zulässig
allowance Rabatt *(m)*, Abzug *(m)*, Nachlaß *(m)*, Freibetrag *(m)*, Freigrenze *(f)*
allowance for doubtful accounts Wertberichtigungen *(pl.f)* auf Forderungen *(pl.f)*
almond Mandel *(f)*
almond bar Mandelschnitte *(f)*
almond cake Mandelkuchen *(m)*
almond pastry Mandelgebäck *(n)*
almond pudding Mandelpudding *(m)*
almond tart Mandeltorte *(f)*
alpine climber Alpinist *(m)*
alpine hut Berghütte *(f)*
alpine meadow Almwiese *(f)*
alpine road Alpenstraße *(f)*
altar Altar *(m)*
alter (ver)ändern
alteration Änderung *(f)*, Veränderung *(f)*
alternating current Wechselstrom *(m)*
alternative Wahl *(f)*, Alternative *(f)*
alternative offer Ausweichangebot *(n)*
altitude of a pass Paßhöhe *(f)*
amateur Amateur *(m)*
a.m. vormittags (bei Zeitangabe)
amber Bernstein *(m)*
ambulance Krankenwagen *(m)*, Rettungswagen *(m)*
amend ergänzen, ändern, verbessern
amenities Vorzüge *(pl.m)*, Reize *(pl.m)* (z.B. eines Hotelzimmers)
amenity Annehmlichkeit *(f)*
America Amerika *(n)*
American Amerikaner *(m)*, Amerikanerin *(f)*, amerikanisch
American breakfast üppiges

Frühstück *(n)* (Schinken, Eier, Pfannkuchen, Toast, Fruchtsaft etc.)
American Hotel and Motel Association Amerikanischer Hotel- und Motelverband *(m)*
American Society of Travel Agents (ASTA) Amerikanische Gesellschaft *(f)* der Reiseagenturen *(pl.f)*
amino-acid Aminosäure *(f)*
amortization Tilgung *(f)*, Amortisation *(f)*; Abschreibung *(f)* (auf immaterielle Anlagewerte); Rückfluß *(m)* des investierten Kapitals *(n)*
amortization of deferred financing costs (schedule 14) Abschreibung *(f)* auf abgegrenzte Finanzierungskosten *(pl.)* (Service Center 14)
amortize abschreiben (immaterielle Vermögensgegenstände), tilgen, abzahlen, amortisieren
amount betragen, Betrag *(m)*
amount to sich belaufen auf
ample reichlich
amplifier Verstärker *(m)*
amusement park Vergnügungspark *(m)*, Rummelplatz *(m)*
amusing unterhaltend
analysis Analyse *(f)*, Untersuchung *(f)*
analysis of fixed assets Anlagespiegel *(m)*
analyze untersuchen, analysieren
ancestor Vorfahre *(m)*
ancestry Vorfahren *(pl.m)*, Abstammung *(f)*
anchor vor Anker gehen
anchovy Sardelle *(f)*
anchovy-butter Anchovisbutter *(f)* (Sardellenbutter)
anchovy butter sauce Sardellenbuttersoße *(f)*
anchovy-paste Anchovispaste *(f)*
anchovy sauce Sardellensauce *(f)*
anchovy straws Sardellenstäbchen *(pl.n)*
angle angeln
angler Angler *(m)*
angling Angeln *(n)*
angling club Anglerverein *(m)*
angling competition Wettangeln *(n)*
angry verärgert, aufgebracht, zornig
animal fat tierisches Fett *(n)*
animated belebt, lebhaft
anise Anis *(n)*
aniseed cooky Anisplätzchen *(n)*
ankle Knöchel *(m)*
annex beifügen, Nachtrag *(m)*, Nebengebäude *(n)*, Dependance *(f)*
anniversary Jahrestag *(m)*, Festtag *(m)*
anniversary dinner Festessen *(n)*
anniversary gratuity Jubiläumszuwendung *(f)*
anniversary present Jubiläumsgeschenk *(n)*
announce ankündigen, bekanntgeben
announcement Ankündigung *(f)*, Bekanntmachung *(f)*
announcer Ansager *(m)*, Sprecher *(m)*
annoy ärgern, belästigen
annoyance Störung *(f)*, Belästigung *(f)*
annual jährlich
annual demand jährliche Nachfrage *(f)*
annual earnings Jahresverdienst *(m)*
annual holiday (or vacation) Jahresurlaub *(m)*
annual meeting Jahresversammlung *(f)*, Hauptversammlung *(f)*
annual ordering costs jährliche Bestellkosten *(f)*
annual placing of orders Anzahl *(f)* der jährlichen Bestellungen *(pl.f)*
annual usage Jahresbedarf *(m)*, Jahresverbrauch *(m)*
anodyne schmerzstillend
anorak Anorak *(m)*
answer Antwort *(f)*, antworten
antenna Antenne *(f)*
anticipate vorwegnehmen
anticlockwise entgegen dem Uhrzeigersinn *(m)*
anticyclone Hoch *(n)* (Wetter)
antidote Gegengift *(n)*
anti-freezing mixture Frostschutzmittel *(n)*
antique Antiquität *(f)*, antik
antique shop Antiquitätengeschäft *(n)*

antirabic vaccination
  Tollwutimpfung *(f)*
anxious besorgt
AP (American Plan) Zimmer *(n)* mit Vollpension *(f)*
apart-hotel Appartementhotel *(n)*
apartment Wohnung *(f)*
apartment house Appartementhaus *(n)*, Wohnhaus *(n)*
apartment house property Mietwohngrundstück *(n)*
aperitif Aperitif *(m)*
apologize sich entschuldigen
apology Entschuldigung *(f)*
apparent sichtbar, wahrnehmbar
appeal Anziehungskraft *(f)*, Attraktion *(f)*
appear erscheinen
appearance Erscheinung *(f)*, Erscheinen *(n)*
appendix Anhang *(m)*, Anlage *(f)*
appetite Appetit *(m)*
appetizer Vorspeise *(f)*, Vorgericht *(n)*, Appetitanreger *(m)*
appetizing appetitlich
applause Beifall *(m)*
apple Apfel *(m)*
apple fritter Apfelspalte *(f)*, Apfelküchlein *(n)*
apple jam Apfelkonfitüre *(f)*
apple jelly Apfelgelee *(n)*
apple juice Apfelsaft *(m)*
apple pie Apfelkuchen *(m)*
apple purée Apfelmus *(n)*
apple rice Apfelreis *(m)*
apple sauce Apfelmus *(n)*
apple soufflé Apfelauflauf *(m)*
apple strudel Apfelstrudel *(m)*
apple-stuffed turnover Apfeltasche *(f)*
apple tart Apfeltorte *(f)*
apple turnover Apfel *(m)* im Schlafrock *(m)*
appliance Gerät *(n)*, Vorrichtung *(f)*
applicability Anwendbarkeit *(f)*
applicable anwendbar
applicant Bewerber *(m)*
application Bewerbung *(f)*, Antrag *(m)*
application for visa Visumsantrag *(m)*

application form Antragsformular *(n)*, Bewerbungsbogen *(m)*
application software Anwendersoftware *(f)*
apply verwenden, anwenden, gebrauchen
apply for beantragen, sich bemühen (um)
appointed hotel Vertragshotel *(n)*
appointed office Vertragsbüro *(n)*
appointed restaurant Vertragsgaststätte *(f)*
appointment Verabredung *(f)*
appointment book Terminkalender *(m)*
appraisal Schätzung *(f)*, Bewertung *(f)*
appraise bewerten
appreciate dankbar anerkennen, würdigen, hochschätzen
apprentice Auszubildender *(m)*, Lehrling *(m)*
apprenticeship Ausbildungszeit *(f)*, Lehrzeit *(f)*
approach road Zufahrtsstraße *(f)*, Anfahrtsweg *(m)*
appropriate passend, geeignet, angemessen, dienlich
appropriated retained earnings zweckgebundene Rücklagen *(pl.f)*
appropriated surplus zweckgebundene Rücklagen *(pl.f)*
appropriations of retained earnings Gewinnrücklagen *(pl.f)* machen
approval Einwilligung *(f)*, Zustimmung *(f)*, Genehmigung *(f)*
approve einwilligen, billigen, genehmigen
après-ski Après-Ski *(n)*
apricot Aprikose *(f)*
apricot dumplings Marillenknödel *(pl.m)*
apricot soufflé Aprikosenauflauf *(m)*
apron Schürze *(f)*
aqualunging Unterwassersport *(m)*
aquaplaning Wellenreiten *(n)*
aquatic sports Wassersport *(m)*
arcade Arkade *(f)*, Laubengang *(m)*
archery Bogenschießen *(n)*
architecture Architektur *(f)*

area Bezirk *(m)*, Gebiet *(n)*
area code Vorwahlnummer *(f)*
area congestion Verkehrsstau *(m)*
arena Arena *(f)*
argue streiten, argumentieren
argument Streit *(m)*, Argument *(n)*
aria Arie *(f)*
aerial Antenne *(f)*
aerial city tour Stadtrundflug *(m)*
aerial railway Drahtseilbahn *(f)*
aerial ropeway Seilschwebebahn *(f)*
arise aufstehen
arm Arm *(m)*
arm-chair Lehnstuhl *(m)*, Sessel *(m)*
armpit Achselhöhle *(f)*
aerobatics Kunstfliegen *(n)*
aerodrome Flugplatz *(m)*, Flughafen *(m)*
aroma Aroma *(n)*
aromatic aromatisch
aromatic vinegar Kräuteressig *(m)*
arrange anordnen, vereinbaren
arrangement Anordnung *(f)*, Vereinbarung *(f)*
arrest verhaften, festnehmen, Arrest *(m)*, Haft *(f)*, Verhaftung *(f)*
arrival Ankunft *(f)*
arrival book Ankunftsbuch *(n)*
arrival by air Flugzeugankunft *(f)*
arrival hall Ankunftshalle *(f)*
arrival station Aussteigebahnhof *(m)*
arrival time Ankunftszeit *(f)*
arrival time-table Ankunftstafel *(f)*
arrivals and departures table Fahrplan *(m)* (Ankünfte – Abreisen)
arrive ankommen
art centre Kunstzentrum *(n)*
art collection Kunstsammlung *(f)*
artdealer Kunsthändler *(m)*
art gallery Kunstgalerie *(f)*
art historical journey Kunstreise *(f)*
art museum Kunstmuseum *(n)*
art of cooking Kochkunst *(f)*
art shop Kunsthandlung *(f)*
art treasure Kunstschatz *(m)*
arterial road Fernverkehrsstraße *(f)*, Hauptverkehrsader *(f)*
artichokes Artischocken *(pl. f)*
artichoke bottoms Artischockenböden *(pl. m)*

article not to be found unauffindbarer Gegenstand *(m)*
articles for daily use persönliche Gebrauchsgegenstände *(pl. m)*
artifical honey Kunsthonig *(m)*
artist Künstler *(m)*
Ascension Day Himmelfahrtstag
ascent Aufstieg *(m)*, Besteigung *(f)*
ascertain feststellen, ermitteln
ascertainment of damage Schadensfeststellung *(f)*
ash Asche *(f)*
ashore an Land *(n)*
ashtray Aschenbecher *(m)*
ask for verlangen nach, bitten um
asleep schlafend
asparagus Spargel *(m)*
asparagus salad Spargelsalat *(m)*
asparagus soup Spargelsuppe *(f)*
asparagus sticks Stangenspargel *(pl. m)*
asparagus tips Spargelspitzen *(pl. f)*
aspic Aspik *(n)*, Sülze *(f)*
assault tätliche Bedrohung *(f)*
assert geltend machen, behaupten
assertion Behauptung *(f)*
asset side Aktivseite *(f)* (Bilanz)
assets Aktiva *(pl.)*
assets pledged gewährte Pfandrechte *(pl. n)*
assign übertragen, abtreten
assignment Abtretung *(f)*, Übertragung *(f)*, Auftrag *(m)*
assist helfen, beistehen, Hilfe *(f)* leisten
assistance Hilfe *(f)*, Unterstützung *(f)*, Beihilfe *(f)*
assistant Gehilfe *(m)*, Assistent *(m)*
assistant cook Hilfskoch *(m)*, Jungkoch *(m)*
assistant driver Beifahrer *(m)*
assistant head-waiter Chef de rang *(m)*
assistant manager (front) Assistent *(m)* der Geschäftsleitung *(f)* (Empfang)
associate sich vereinigen, verbinden, Teilhaber *(m)*
associate advertising Gemeinschaftswerbung *(f)*

associated airline angeschlossene Luftfahrtgesellschaft (f)
associated company assoziiertes Unternehmen (n)
association Arbeitsgemeinschaft (f), Verein (m), Gesellschaft (f)
association of travel agencies Reisebüroverband (m)
assort sortieren
assorted ausgesucht, gemischt
assorted biscuits gemischte Plätzchen (pl.n)
assorted boiled meat gekochtes Fleischallerlei (n)
assorted cold meat Aufschnitt (m)
assorted sausage Wurstplatte (f)
assorted stewed fruit gemischtes Kompott (n)
assortment Auswahl (f), Sortiment (n)
assume annehmen, voraussetzen
assumption Annahme (n), Voraussetzung (f), Übernahme (f)
assurance Versicherung (f), Erklärung (f)
assure versichern
asthma Asthma (n)
at par zum Nennwert (m)
at sight bei Durchsicht (f)
at the lower of cost or market Niederstwertprinzip (n)
athletic ground Sportplatz (m)
athletics Leichtathletik (f)
athletics meeting Sportveranstaltung (f)
atmosphere Atmosphäre (f)
atmospheric pressure Luftdruck (m)
attach beifügen, pfänden
attack Anfall (m)
attempt versuchen, probieren, wagen
attend teilnehmen, beiwohnen, bedienen
attendance Anwesenheit (f), Bedienung (f)
attendant Platzanweiser (m)
attention Aufmerksamkeit (f), Achtung (f)
attentive aufmerksam
attic Dachkammer (f), Mansarde (f)
attitude Haltung (f), Einstellung (f)

attraction Anziehungskraft (f), Attraktion (f)
attributable zurechenbar
attribute of taste Geschmackseigenschaft (f)
au gratin überbacken
au pair stay Au-pair-Aufenthalt (m)
audit Vollprüfung (f)
auditor Prüfer (m), Abschlußprüfer (m), Buchprüfer (m)
auditor's report Testat (n) des Wirtschaftsprüfers (m)
Austria Österreich
Austrian Federal Railways Österreichische Bundesbahn (f)
authority Vollmacht (f), Befugnis (f), Kompetenz (f)
authorize bevollmächtigen, billigen
authorized establishment Vertragshaus (n)
authorized hotel Vertragshotel (n)
authorized restaurant Vertragsgaststätte (f)
authorized shares alle zur Ausgabe (f) zugelassenen Aktien (pl.f); Nennkapital (n), Nominalkapital (n)
automate automatisieren
automatic cooker Garautomat (m)
automatic selling Automatenverkauf (m)
automatic ticket machine Fahrkartenautomat (m)
automatic transmission automatisches Getriebe (n)
automation Automation (f)
automobile Fahrzeug (n)
automobile service Automobildienst (m)
automobile traffic Autoverkehr (m)
autumn Herbst (m)
autumn holiday Herbstferien (pl.)
autumn trade-fair Herbstmesse (f)
auxiliary service Hilfsdienst (m)
availability Verfügbarkeit (f), Gültigkeit (f), Gültigkeitsdauer (f)
available verfügbar, gültig
avenue breite Straße (f), Allee (f)
average Durchschnitt (m)
average room rate durchschnittlicher Zimmerpreis (m)
aviation Luftfahrt (f)

aviation chart Flugkarte *(f)*
aviator Flieger *(m)*
avocado (pear) Avocado *(f)* (Birne)
avoid aufheben, vermeiden, anfechten
avoidance Vermeidung *(f)*, Anfechtung *(f)*, Aufhebung *(f)*
await erwarten
awake wach, wecken, aufwachen
award belohnen, zubilligen, Belohnung *(f)*, Zubilligung *(f)*
awful schrecklich
awning Plane *(f)*, Markise *(f)*
axle Achse *(f)* (Auto)

B

babies' room Raum *(m)* für Säuglingsbetreuung *(f)*
baby care Säuglingsbetreuung *(f)*
baby chicken Hühnchen *(n)*
baby lamb Milchlamm *(n)*
baby pig Jungschwein *(n)*
baby-sitter Babysitter *(m)*
bachelor Junggeselle *(m)*
back-ache Rückenschmerzen *(pl. m)*
back pay Lohnnachzahlung *(f)*
back room Hofzimmer *(n)*, rückwärtiges Zimmer *(n)*
background music Hintergrundsmusik *(f)*
backlog repair and maintenance rückständige Abraumbeseitigung *(f)*
bacon Speck *(m)*
bacon and eggs Eier *(pl. n)* mit Speck *(m)*
bad debts uneinbringliche Forderungen *(pl. f)*
badminton Federballspiel *(n)*
bag Tasche *(f)*, Reisetasche *(f)*
baggage Gepäck *(n)*
baggage car Gepäckwagen *(m)*
baggage check Gepäckschein *(m)*, Aufbewahrungsschein *(m)*
baggage compartment Gepäckraum *(m)* (Bahn)
baggage hold Gepäckraum *(m)* (Flugzeug)
baggage in excess Übergepäck *(n)*
baggage insurance Gepäckversicherung *(f)*
baggage label Gepäckanhänger *(m)*, Kofferanhänger *(m)*
baggage locker Gepäckschließfach *(n)*
baggage office Gepäckaufgabestelle *(f)*
baggage platform Gepäckbahnsteig *(m)*
baggage rack Gepäckablage *(f)*, Gepäcknetz *(n)*
baggage registration counter Gepäckabfertigung *(f)*
baggage room Gepäckraum *(m)* (Schiff)
baggage service Gepäckdienst *(m)*
baggage trailer Gepäckanhänger *(m)* (Auto)
bake backen
baked Alaska Überraschungsomelett *(n)*, Eisomelett *(n)*
baked apple im Ofen *(m)* gebackener Apfel *(m)*
baked apple dumplings Äpfel *(pl. m)* im Schlafrock *(m)*
baked apple in puff paste Apfel *(m)* im Schlafrock *(m)*
baked apricot roll warmes Aprikosenröllchen *(n)*
baked ham in bread crust Schinken *(m)* im Brotteig *(m)*
baked in their jackets in der Schale *(f)* gebacken
baked potatoes Pellkartoffeln *(pl. f)* amerikanische Art *(f)*
baked semolina dumplings gratinierte Grießklößchen *(pl. n)*
baked sultana pudding Rosinenpudding *(m)*
baker Bäcker *(m)*
baking tin Backblech *(n)*
balance Saldo *(m)*, Bilanz *(f)*
balance (an account) saldieren, den Saldo *(m)* ermitteln
balance sheet Bilanz *(f)*
balance sheet account Bestandskonto *(n)*
balance sheet equation Bilanzgleichung *(f)*
balance sheet format Gliederungsschema *(n)* der Bilanz *(f)*

balance sheet item Bilanzposition *(f)*
balance sheet period
 Bilanzierungszeitraum *(m)*
balance sheet ratios
 Bilanzkennzahlen *(pl.f)*
balance sheet value Bilanzwert
 (m), Bilanzansatz *(m)*
balance (sheet) date Bilanzstichtag
 (m)
balcony Balkon *(m)*
balcony facing south Südbalkon *(m)*
ballet performance
 Ballettaufführung *(f)*
ballroom Ballsaal *(m)*, Tanzsaal *(m)*
balneation Heilbadekur *(f)*,
 Heilbäderwesen *(n)*
balneology Bäderwesen *(n)*
balneotherapy Bäderbehandlung *(f)*
banana Banane *(f)*
band Kapelle *(f)*
bandage verbinden, Verband *(m)*
bandleader Kapellmeister *(m)*
bandstand Konzertpavillon *(m)*,
 Orchesterplatz *(m)*
bank Bank *(f)*
bank card Scheckkarte *(f)*
bank holiday Bankfeiertag *(m)*
banking hours Schalterstunden
 (pl.f) der Bank *(f)*
banquet Bankett *(n)*, Veranstaltung
 (f), Festessen *(n)*
banquet business
 Veranstaltungsgeschäft *(n)*,
 Bankettgeschäft *(n)*
banquet extra waiter
 Aushilfskellner *(m)* für
 Veranstaltungen *(pl.f)*
banquet headwaiter
 Bankettoberkellner *(m)*
banquet kitchen Bankettküche *(f)*
banquet manager
 Veranstaltungsleiter *(m)*,
 Bankettleiter *(m)*
banquet room Festsaal *(m)*,
 Veranstaltungsraum *(m)*
banqueting hall Festhalle *(f)*,
 Festsaal *(m)*
bar Schanktisch *(m)*, Theke *(f)*, Bar
 (f), Schenke *(f)*
bar counter Bartheke *(f)*
bar utensil Bargerät *(n)*

barbecue braten auf dem Rost *(m)*,
 Holzkohlen-Grillgericht *(n)*
barbel Barbe *(f)*
barber Herrenfriseur *(m)*
bargain Handel *(m)*, handeln,
 vorteilhafter Kauf *(m)*
barkeeper Barmann *(m)*, Buffetier
 (m)
barley Gerste *(f)*
barley soup Gerstenschleimsuppe *(f)*
barmaid Schankkellnerin *(f)*,
 Büffetmädchen *(n)*
barman Barmann *(m)*, Schankkellner
 (m), Buffetier *(m)*
barometer Barometer *(n)*
baron of lamb Rückenstück *(n)* vom
 Lamm *(n)*
barrage Staudamm *(m)*, Talsperre *(f)*
barrel Faß *(n)*
barrier Schranke *(f)*, Sperre *(f)*
barrier-free room for handicapper
 accessibility
 behindertengerechtes Zimmer *(n)*
bartender Schankkellner *(m)*,
 Büffetkellner *(m)*, Büffetier *(m)*
base pay Grundlohn *(m)*
base salary Grundgehalt *(n)*
base snow Altschnee *(m)*
base terminal Talstation *(f)*
 (Bergbahn)
basement Kellergeschoß *(n)*
basic grundlegend
basic fare Grundfahrpreis *(m)*
basic pay Grundlohn *(m)*
basic price Grundpreis *(m)*
basic research
 Grundlagenforschung *(f)*
basic salary Grundgehalt *(n)*
basil Basilikum *(n)*
basilica Basilika *(f)*
basis Grundlage *(f)*, Basis *(f)*
bask in der Sonne *(f)* liegen, bräunen
bass Seebarsch *(m)*
baste mit Fett *(n)* begießen
bath Bad *(n)* (Wanne), baden (im
 Freien)
bath attendant Bademeister *(m)*
bath chair Rollstuhl *(m)*
bather Badegast *(m)*
bathing beach Badestrand *(m)*
bathing cabin Umkleidekabine *(f)*

bathing cap Bademütze *(f)*,
  Badehaube *(f)*
bathing costume Badeanzug *(m)*
bathing establishment Badeanstalt
  (f)
bathing facilities Badeanlagen *(pl.f)*
bathing-gown Bademantel *(m)*
bathing pier Badesteg *(m)*
bathing place Badeplatz *(m)*,
  Freibad *(n)*
bathing prohibited Baden *(n)*
  verboten!
bathing resort Badeort *(m)*
bathing season Badesaison *(f)*
bathing shorts Badehose *(f)*
bathing suit Badeanzug *(f)*
bathing trunks Badehose *(f)*
bath mat Badematte *(f)*
bathrobe Bademantel *(m)*
bathroom Badezimmer *(n)*
bath towel Badetuch *(n)*
bathtub Badewanne *(f)*
batter Schlagteig *(m)*
Bavarian cream gestürzte Creme *(f)*,
  Bayrische Creme *(f)*
bay Bucht *(f)*
bay-leaf Lorbeerblatt *(n)*
beach Strand *(m)*
beach attendant Strandwärter *(m)*
beach-bag Badetasche *(f)*
beach-chair Strandkorb *(m)*
beach-guard Badewärter *(m)*
beach hotel Strandhotel *(n)*
beach mattress Schwimmatratze *(f)*
beach shoes Strandschuhe *(pl.m)*
beach-umbrella Strandschirm *(m)*
bean Bohne *(f)*
Béarnaise sauce Sauce Béarnaise *(f)*
beautician Kosmetikerin *(f)*
beautification Verschönerung *(f)*
beauty contest
  Schönheitswettbewerb *(m)*
beauty culture Kosmetik *(f)*
beauty parlour Kosmetiksalon *(m)*,
  Schönheitssalon *(m)*
beauty spot Naturschönheit *(f)*,
  Sehenswürdigkeit *(f)*
béchamel sauce Béchamelsoße *(f)*
bed Bett *(n)*
bed and breakfast Zimmer *(n)* mit
  Frühstück *(n)*

bed-couch Bettcouch *(f)*
bed-linen Bettwäsche *(f)*
bed-sitter, bed-sitting room
  Wohnschlafraum *(m)*
bedding Bettzeug *(n)*
bedroom Schlafzimmer *(n)*
bedside rug Bettvorleger *(m)*
bedside-table Nachttisch *(m)*
bedspread Bettüberzug *(m)*
beef Rind *(n)*
beef broth with egg Bouillon mit
  Ei *(f)*
beef fondue Fleischfondue *(n)*
  (Rindfleisch)
beef olive Rindsroulade *(f)*
beef pie Beefsteakpastete *(f)*
beef stew Rindsgulasch *(f)*
beef stew gipsy style
  Zigeunergulasch *(n)*
beef stew in juice Saftgulasch *(n)*
beef stew peasant style
  Bauerngulasch *(n)*
beef stew with onions
  Zwiebelfleisch *(n)*
beef Stroganoff Filetgulasch in
  Sauerrahmsauce *(n)*
beefburger Frikadelle *(f)*
beefsteak Beefsteak *(n)*
beefsteak tartare style Beefsteak à
  la tartare *(n)*
beefsteak with fried egg Beefsteak
  à la Meier *(n)*
beeftea Fleischbrühe *(f)*
beer Bier *(n)*
beer-cellar Bierkeller *(m)*,
  Kellerlokal *(n)*
beer festival Bierfest *(n)*
beer-garden Biergarten *(m)*
beer on draft (draught) offenes
  Bier *(n)*, Bier *(n)* vom Faß *(n)*
beer on tap Bier vom Faß *(n)*
beer saloon Bierstube *(f)*
beer-shop Bierausschank *(m)*
beet-root Rote Beete *(f)*
beet-root salad Rote Beete-Salat
  (m)
behave sich benehmen, sich verhalten
behavio(u)r Verhalten *(n)*,
  Benehmen *(n)*
bell Glocke *(f)*, Klingel *(f)*
bellboy Hotelpage *(m)*

bellcaptain Portier *(m)*;
Getränkeautomat *(m)*
bellhop Hotelpage *(m)*
bellman Hausdiener *(m)*,
Hoteldiener*(m)*
bell tent Rundzelt *(n)*
below par unter pari
belt highway Ringstraße *(f)*
belt line Ringbahn *(f)*
bend Kurve *(f)*
benefit gewinnen, nützen, Nutzen
(m), Vorteil *(m)*, Vergünstigung *(f)*
Berlin doughnut Berliner
Pfannkuchen *(m)*
berry Beere *(f)*
berth Koje *(f)*, Bett *(n)*
best buy vorteilhaftester Kauf *(m)*
betray betrügen
betrayal Betrug *(m)*
between-decks Zwischendeck *(n)*
beverage Getränk *(n)*
beverage-tax Getränkesteuer *(f)*
beware of trains Vorsicht, Zug!
biannual halbjährlich, zweimal
jährlich
bicarbonate Natron *(n)*
bicycle Fahrrad *(n)*
bicycle excursion Fahrradausflug
(m)
bicycle hire Fahrradvermietung *(f)*
bid anbieten, bieten, Angebot *(n)*
bid price Nachfragepreis *(m)*
bidet Bidet *(n)*
biennial zweijährlich, alle zwei Jahre
(pl.n) eintretend
bifurcation Straßengabel *(f)*
big-game reservation
Großwildreservat *(n)*
bike Rad *(n)*
bilberry Heidelbeere *(f)*
bilking Zechprellerei *(f)*
bill Rechnung *(f)*, in Rechnung *(f)*
stellen, berechnen
bill of exchange Wechsel *(m)*
bill of fare Speisekarte *(f)*
bill-board Anschlagbrett *(n)*,
Anschlagtafel *(n)*, schwarzes Brett
(n)
billiard-room Billardzimmer *(n)*
bimonthly zweimonatlich
binoculars Fernglas *(n)*

bird Vogel *(m)*
birds nest soup
Schwalbennestersuppe *(f)*
birds on skewer with corn pie
Vögel am Spieß mit Polenta *(pl.m)*
birth Geburt *(f)*
birth certificate Geburtsurkunde *(f)*
birthplace Geburtsort *(m)*
biscuit Plätzchen *(n)*
biscuit in wine sauce Biskuit mit
Weinschaum *(m)*
bisque dicke Suppe *(f)*
bisque of crayfish Krebsrahmsuppe
(f)
bitter bitter
bitter ale helles Ale *(n)*
bitters Magenbitter *(m)*
biweekly zweiwöchentlich
black bean schwarze Bohne *(f)*
black cock Auerhahn *(m)*, Birkhahn
(m)
black coffee schwarzer Kaffee *(m)*
black coffee with whipped cream
Einspänner *(m)*
black currant schwarze
Johannisbeere *(f)*
black grapes blaue Trauben *(pl.f)*
black grouse Birkhuhn *(n)*
black market Schwarzmarkt *(m)*,
Schleichhandel *(m)*
black pudding Blutwurst *(f)*
black radish Rettich *(m)*
blackberry Brombeere *(f)*
blame tadeln, verantwortlich machen,
die Schuld *(f)* geben
blancmange Vanillepudding *(m)*
blank Formular *(n)*
blank ticket Blankofahrschein *(m)*
blanket Wolldecke *(f)*
blind alley Sackgasse *(f)*
blind bend unübersichtliche Kurve *(f)*
bloater Bückling *(m)*
block sperren
block of flats Appartementhaus *(n)*
blocked period Sperrfrist *(f)*
blood poisoning Blutvergiftung *(f)*
blood transfusion Blutübertragung
(f)
blue boiled trout Forelle blau *(f)*
blue char Bodenrenke *(f)*
blue collar worker Arbeiter *(m)*

blue fish Goldmakrele *(f)*
blue print Blaupause *(f)*, Plan *(m)*
bluff Steilküste *(f)*
blunt stumpf
board Verpflegung *(f)*, Beköstigung *(f)*, Pensionspreis *(m)*; Bord *(m)* (Schiff)
board a plane sich an Bord *(m)* eines Flugzeugs *(n)* begeben
board and lodging voucher Aufenthaltsgutschein *(m)*
board and residence Vollpension *(f)*
board residence Vollpension *(f)*
boarding house Pension *(f)*
boarding pass (card) Bordausweis *(m)*, Bordkarte *(f)*, Einsteigekarte *(f)*
boardwalk Strandpromenade *(f)*
boat Boot *(n)*, Kahn *(m)*
boat deck Bootsdeck *(n)*
boat-hire Bootsverleih *(m)*, Bootsvermietung *(f)*
boat-house Bootshaus *(n)*
boating Bootfahren *(n)*
boating-lake Rudersee *(m)*
boat-ride Bootsfahrt *(f)*, Kahnfahrt *(f)*
boat trailer Bootsanhänger *(m)* (Auto)
boat train Zug *(m)* mit Schiffsanschluß *(m)*
boat-trip Bootsfahrt *(f)*, Kahnfahrt *(f)*
bob Bob *(m)*
bob run Bobbahn *(f)*
bobsled Bobschlitten *(m)*
bobsledding Bobsport *(m)*
boccie, boccia Boccia *(n)*
boccie court Boccia-Bahn *(f)*
boiled gekocht
boiled beef gekochtes Rindfleisch *(n)*
boiled beef in broth Suppentopf mit Fleischeinlage *(m)*
boiled chicken Suppenhuhn *(n)*
boiled eel Aal grün *(m)*
boiled ham gekochter Schinken *(m)*
boiled pork with horse-radish Suppenfleisch *(n)* mit Meerrettich *(m)*
boiled pork with pickled cabbage Krautfleisch *(n)*
boiled potatoes Salzkartoffeln *(pl.f)*
boiled rice gekochter Reis *(m)*
boiled round of beef Tafelspitz *(m)*
boiled salmon pochierter Salm *(m)*

boiled smoked bacon Silesian style Schlesisches Himmelreich *(n)*
boletus Steinpilz *(m)*
bolster Keilkissen *(n)*
bond Rente *(f)*, Rentenwert *(m)*, Bond *(m)*, Schuldverschreibung *(f)*
bond discount Disagio *(n)* bei Ausgabe *(f)* von Schuldverschreibungen *(pl.f)*
bond issue Anleiheemission *(f)*
bond premium Agio *(n)* bei Ausgabe *(f)* einer Schuldverschreibung *(f)*
bone Knochen *(m)*
boned rips of beef Rostbraten *(m)*
bonus Gratifikation *(f)*, Sondervergütung *(f)*
bonus stock (shares) Gratisaktie *(f)* (Form der Selbstfinanzierung)
book buchen, vorbestellen; Buch *(n)*
book a room in advance ein Zimmer *(n)* im voraus bestellen
book a table einen Tisch *(m)* reservieren (Restaurant)
book by telephone telefonisch bestellen
booking Bestellung *(f)*, Buchung *(f)*
booking clerk Schalterbeamter *(m)*
booking hall Schalterhalle *(f)*
booking of seats Platzbestellung *(f)*
booking office Fahrkartenschalter *(m)*, Fahrkartenausgabe *(f)*, Vorverkaufsstelle *(f)*
bookkeeping by double entry doppelte Buchhaltung *(f)*
bookkeeping by single entry einfache Buchhaltung *(f)*
bookkeeping voucher Buchhaltungsbeleg *(m)*
booklet Broschüre *(f)*, Prospekt *(m)*
booklet of coupons (tickets) Fahrscheinheft *(n)*
bookseller Buchhändler *(m)*
bookshop Buchhandlung *(f)*
book-stall Zeitschriftenkiosk *(m)*
book value Buchwert *(m)*
boom geschäftlicher Aufschwung *(m)*, Hochkonjunktur *(f)*, Boom *(m)*
boot Stiefel *(m)*, Kofferraum *(m)* (Auto)

bootblack Schuhputzer *(m)*
boots Hausdiener *(m)* (Hotel)
border Grenze *(f)*, Landesgrenze *(f)*; Pensionsgast *(m)*, Hausgast *(m)*
border area Grenzgebiet *(n)*
border crossing Grenzübergang *(m)*, Grenzübertritt *(m)*
border crossing point Grenzübergangsstelle *(f)*
border town Grenzstadt *(f)*
border traffic Grenzverkehr *(m)*
border zone Grenzzone *(f)*
borrow leihen, entleihen
Botanical Garden Botanischer Garten *(m)*
bottle Flasche *(f)*
bottle deposit Flaschenpfand *(m)*
bottle screw Korkenzieher *(m)*
bottle-opener Flaschenöffner *(m)*
bottled beer Flaschenbier *(n)*
bottled wine Flaschenwein *(m)*
bottleneck Engpaß *(m)*
bottoms of artichoke Artischockenböden *(pl. m)*
bottoms up Prost!
boulevard Allee *(f)*
bound to vorherbestimmt, verurteilt zu
bound (by contract) verpflichtet, vertraglich gebunden
bouquet Blumenstrauß *(m)*
boutique Boutique *(f)*
bow Bug *(m)*
bowl kegeln; Schüssel *(f)*
bowling Bowling *(n)*, Kegeln *(n)*
bowling-alley Kegelbahn *(f)*
box Loge *(f)* (Theater); Schachtel *(f)*
box meal Lunchpaket *(n)*, Imbißpaket *(n)*
box office Kasse *(f)* (Kino, Theater)
boy Hotelboy *(m)*
brains Hirn *(n)*
braised gedünstet, geschmort
braised aitchbone Rinderschwanzstück geschmort *(n)*
braised beef Schmorbraten *(m)*
braised beef marinated Sauerbraten *(m)*
braised filet of beef with onions Zwiebelrostbraten *(m)*

braised ox-tongue Ochsenzunge gebraten *(f)*
braised veal cutlet in paprika sauce Paprikaschnitzel *(n)*
brambleberry Brombeere *(f)*
branch line Nebenstrecke *(f)*
branch manager Geschäftsstellenleiter *(m)*
branch office Nebenstelle *(f)*, Zweigstelle *(f)*, Filiale *(f)*, Geschäftsstelle *(f)*
brand Marke *(f)*, Sorte *(f)*, Markenname *(m)*
brandy Weinbrand *(m)*
brandy-glass Weinbrandglas *(n)*, Cognacschwenker *(m)*
brawn Eberfleisch *(n)*, Schweinskopfsülze *(f)*
Brazil nut Paranuß *(f)*
Brazilian bean-stew brasilianischer Bohnen-Eintopf *(m)*
breach of contract Vertragsbruch *(m)*
bread Brot *(n)*
bread and butter Brot *(n)* und Butter *(f)*
bread and butter pudding Brotpudding *(m)*
bread-crumbed paniert
bread-plate kleiner Teller *(m)* (Brot)
breadbasket Brotkorb *(m)*
breaded paniert
breaded veal steak paniertes Kalbsschnitzel *(n)*
break of journey Fahrtunterbrechung *(f)*
breakage Bruch *(m)* (Geschirr)
breakdown lorry Abschleppwagen *(m)*
breakdown service Pannenhilfe *(f)*
breakfast Frühstück *(n)*
breakfast key Türanhänger *(m)* für die Frühstücksbestellung *(f)*
breakfast room Frühstückszimmer *(n)*
breakfast tray Frühstückstablett *(n)*
breakwater Wellenbrecher *(m)*
bream Seebrasse *(f)*
breast Brust *(f)*
breast of chicken Geflügelbrust *(f)*
breast of pork Schweinsbrust *(f)*

breathing exercises
  Atemgymnastik (f)
breeze Brise (f)
brewery Brauerei (f)
bribe bestechen, Bestechung (f), Bestechungsgeld (n)
brick of ice-cream Eisschnitte (f)
bridge Brücke (f); Bridge (n)
bridge toll Brückenzoll (m)
bridle-path Reitweg (m), Saumpfad (m)
brief instruieren, informieren; kurz
briefcase Aktenmappe (f), Aktentasche (f)
briefing Absprache (f)
brill Meerbutt (m)
brine bath Solebad (n)
bring out veröffentlichen
bring up-to-date aktualisieren
brisket Brust (f) (Stück)
brisket of beef Rinderbrust (f)
British Hotels and Restaurants Association Britischer Hotel- und Gaststättenverband (m)
British Travel and Holiday Association Britischer Verband für Reise- und Urlaubswesen (m)
broad bean dicke Bohne (f)
broadcast Rundfunk (m), durch Rundfunk (m) verbreiten
broadcast advertising Rundfunkwerbung (f)
broccoli Brokkoli (pl.), Kohlsprossen (pl.f)
brochure Prospekt (m), Broschüre (f)
broiled gegrillt
broiled potatoes geröstete Kartoffeln (pl.f)
broiler Brathähnchen (n)
brook-trout Bachforelle (f)
broom Besen (m)
broth Bouillon (f)
broth with rice Fleischbrühe (f) mit Reiseinlage (f)
broth with vermicelli Fleischbrühe (f) mit Nudeleinlage (f)
brown beef stew Rindsragout (n)
brown bread dunkles Brot (n), Schwarzbrot (n)
brown hazel-hen-stew Haselhuhnragout (n)

brown stew Gulasch (n)
brown veal stew Kalbsragout (n)
browned gratiniert
browned butter Nußbutter (f)
brunch Brunch (m)
Brunswick sausage Braunschweiger Wurst (f)
brush Bürste (f)
Brussels sprouts Rosenkohl (m)
bubble-bath Schaumbad (n)
bucket Eimer (m), Eiskübel (m)
buckwheat Buchweizen (m)
buckwheat pancakes Plinsen (pl.f)
buffer stock Sicherheitsbestand (m)
buffer time Pufferzeit (f) (Netzplan)
buffet car Büffetwagen (m) (Eisenbahn)
building Gebäude (n)
building and supplies (schedule 12) Baumaterialien (pl.n), Baustoffe (pl.m) (Service Center 12)
building cost Bauwert (m)
building fixtures and equipment Gebäudeeinrichtung (f) und -ausstattung (f)
building lot Bauplatz (m)
building permit Baugenehmigung (f)
building site Bauplatz (m)
built-in check eingebaute Kontrolle (f)
built-in control automatische Kontrolle (f)
built-in cupboard (wardrobe) Einbauschrank (m)
built-up area geschlossene Ortschaft (f)
buiscuit Plätzchen (n)
bulb Glühbirne (f)
bulk Masse (f), Hauptteil (m)
bulk purchase Massenkauf (m)
bulky baggage sperriges Gepäck (n)
bulky goods (or freight) Sperrgut (n)
bull-fight Stierkampf (m)
bull-fighter Stierkämpfer (m)
bulletin board Anschlagbrett (n), schwarzes Brett (n)
bun Brötchen (n)
bunch Bündel (n), Strauß (m)
bunch of flowers Blumenstrauß (m)

bungalow Bungalow *(m)*
bungalow village Bungalowdorf *(n)*
bunk Koje (Schiff) *(f)*
burbot Trüsche *(f)*
burglar Einbrecher *(m)*
burglary Einbruch *(m)*
burglary insurance
    Einbruchsversicherung *(f)*
Burgundy wine Burgunderwein *(m)*
burnt angebrannt
burnt butter gebrannte Butter *(f)*
bus Bus *(m)*, Autobus *(m)*, Omnibus *(m)*
bus-air service
    Bus-Flug-Verbindung *(f)*
bus and coach station Busbahnhof *(m)*, Autobahnhof *(m)*
bus company Busunternehmen *(n)*
bus conductor Busschaffner *(m)*
bus connection Busverbindung *(f)*
bus driver Busfahrer *(m)*
bus hire Busvermietung *(f)*
bus line Buslinie *(f)*, Busverbindung *(f)*
bus rental Busvermietung *(f)*
bus service Busverbindung *(f)*
bus service Zubringerdienst (Bus) *(m)*
bus station Busbahnhof *(m)*
bus stop Bushaltestelle *(f)*
bus trailer Busanhänger *(m)*
bus travel Busreisen *(pl.f)*
bus trip Busreise *(f)*, Busfahrt *(f)*
business Geschäft *(n)*, Betrieb *(m)*, Unternehmung *(f)*
business and occupation taxes (schedule 14) Betriebs- und Gewerbesteuer *(f)* (Service Center 14)
business car Geschäftswagen *(m)*
business combinations
    Unternehmenszusammenschlüsse *(pl.m)*
business district Geschäftsviertel *(n)*
business friend Geschäftsfreund *(m)*
business hours Geschäftszeit *(f)*
business letter Geschäftsbrief *(m)*
business life Geschäftsleben *(n)*
businessman Geschäftsmann *(m)*

business organization
    Unternehmensform *(f)* des Handelsrechts *(n)*
business policy Geschäftspolitik *(f)*, Richtlinien *(pl.f)*
business premises Geschäftsräume *(pl.m)*
business recession
    Geschäftsrückgang *(m)*
business relation
    Geschäftsverbindung *(f)*
business suit Straßenanzug *(m)*
business transaction (event)
    Geschäftsvorfall *(m)*
business trip (tour) Geschäftsreise *(f)*
business volume Geschäftsumfang *(m)*
busy belebt, belegt (Telefon), beschäftigt
butcher Metzger *(m)*, Fleischer *(m)*
butcher's shop Metzgerei *(f)*, Fleischerei *(f)*
butter Butter *(f)*
butter with fine herbs Kräuterbutter *(f)*
buttered in Butter zubereitet
buttered slice of bread Butterbrot *(n)*
butterfried potatoes
    Schmelzkartoffeln *(pl.f)*
butterfried potatoes with onions
    Bratkartoffeln *(pl.f)* mit Zwiebeln *(pl.f)*
butterfried sausage Bratwurst *(f)*
butterfried trout in Butter *(f)* gebratene Forelle *(f)*
buttermilk Buttermilch *(f)*
button Klingelknopf *(m)*
buy kaufen, einkaufen, erwerben
buyer Käufer *(m)*, Einkäufer *(m)*
buyer's market Käufermarkt *(m)*
buying decision Kaufentschluß *(m)*
buying habits Kaufgewohnheiten *(pl.f)*
buying power Kaufkraft *(f)*
by-pass Umgehungsstraße *(f)*
by-road Nebenstraße *(f)*
by-street Nebenstraße *(f)*

C

cab Taxi (n)
cab stand Taxistand (m)
cabana Zimmer (n) am Swimmingpool (m)
cabaret Kabarett (n), Nachtklub (m)
cabbage Kohl (m)
cabbage in wine Weinkraut (n)
cabbage lettuce Kopfsalat (m)
cabbage salad Krautsalat (m)
cabin Kabine (f), Kajüte (f)
cabin cable railway Kabinenseilbahn (f)
cabin cruiser Jacht (f)
cabin luggage Kabinengepäck (n)
cable kabeln, telegrafieren, Kabel (n), Telegramm (n)
cable car Gondel (f), Kabine (f)
cable railway Seilbahn (f)
cafeteria Selbstbedienungsrestaurant (n), Snackbar (f)
café Imbißstube (f), Café (n), Gasthaus (n)
cake Kuchen (m)
calculate rechnen, berechnen, kalkulieren
calculating machine Rechenmaschine (f)
calculation Rechnung (f), Berechnung (f), Kalkulation (f)
calculation of an economic order quantity Berechnung (f) der wirtschaftlichen Bestellmenge (f)
calculator Rechenmaschine (f), Taschenrechner (m)
calf (veal) Kalb (n)
calf's brain Kalbshirn (n)
calf's brain fried Kalbshirn (n) gebacken
calf's brain soup Hirnsuppe (f)
calf's breast Kalbsbrust (f)
calf's feet Kalbsfüße (pl. m)
calf's gristle Kalbsbrustknorpel (m)
calf's head Kalbskopf (m)
calf's head fried Kalbskopf (m) gebacken
calf's head vinaigrette Kalbskopf (m) in Essigsoße (f)
calf's head with turtle sauce Kalbskopf „en tortue" (m)
calf's heart Kalbsherz (n)
calf's knuckle Kalbshaxe (f)
calf's lights Kalbslunge (f)
calf's liver Kalbsleber (f)
calf's liver fried Kalbsleber (f) gebacken
calf's liver on skewers Kalbsleberspießchen (n)
calf's liver roasted Kalbsleber (f) geröstet
calf's sweetbread baked Kalbsbries (n) gebacken
calf's tongue Kalbszunge (f)
call Abruf (m), Anruf (m), Vertreterbesuch (m), wecken
call at anlaufen (Seefahrt)
call-box Telefonzelle (f), Fernsprechzelle (f)
callable bond vom Kreditnehmer (m) vorzeitig rückzahlbare Schuldverschreibung (f)
calm beruhigen, besänftigen, still, ruhig
calm down sich beruhigen, ruhig werden
camera Kamera (f)
camomile Kamille (f)
camomile tea Kamillentee (m)
camp Lager (n), campen, zelten
camp fire Lagerfeuer (n)
camp out Feldbett (n)
campaign Werbekampagne (f), Aktion (f)
camper Camper (m), Campingtourist (m)
camping Camping (n), Campingtourismus (m)
Camping and caravaning Zelt- und Wohnwagenwesen (n)
camping equipment Campingausrüstung (f)
camping ground Campingplatz (m), Zeltplatz (m)
camping permit Campingausweis (m)
camping site offering full facilities eingerichteter Campingplatz (m)
can Konservenbüchse (f)
canapé geröstete Brotschnitte (f) garniert

cancel stornieren, streichen, abbestellen
cancellation Abbestellung *(f)*, Storno *(m)*, Streichung *(f)*
cancellation fee Stornierungsgebühr *(f)*, Anullierungsgebühr *(f)*
candied lemon peel Zitronat *(n)*
candied orange peel Orangeat *(n)*
candle light Kerzenlicht *(n)*
candlestick Kerzenständer *(m)*
candy Süßigkeiten *(pl.f)*
canned in Konservenbüchse *(f)*
canned beer Dosenbier *(n)*
canneloni Canneloni *(pl.)*
canoe Kanu *(n)*, Paddelboot *(n)*
cantaloupe Zuckermelone *(f)*
canvas Segeltuch *(n)*
capability Fähigkeit *(f)*, Tauglichkeit *(f)*
capable fähig, tauglich, in der Lage *(f)*
capacity Kapazität *(f)*, Fähigkeit *(f)*, Leistungsvermögen *(n)*
capacity increase Betriebserweiterung *(f)*, Kapazitätsausweitung *(f)*
capacity of accommodation Aufnahmekapazität *(f)*
cape Landspitze *(f)*
caper Kaper *(f)*
caper sauce Kapernsauce *(f)*
capital Kapital *(n)*, Betriebskapital *(n)*; Hauptstadt *(f)*
capital lease Variante *(f)* eines Finanz-Leasingvertrages *(m)*, aktivierungspflichtiger Leasingvertrag *(m)*
capital lease requirements Leasing-Bilanzierungsvorschriften *(pl.f)*
capital not paid-in nicht eingezahltes Grund- oder Stammkapital *(n)*; ausstehende Einlagen *(pl.f)*
capital stock Grundkapital *(n)*
capitalization Aktivierung *(f)*
capitalize aktivieren
capon Kapaun *(m)*
captain Schiffskapitän *(m)*, Flugkapitän *(m)*
captain (waiter) Stationsoberkellner *(m)*

car Wagen *(m)*, Auto *(n)*
car-carrier train Autoreisezug *(m)*
car ferry Autofähre *(f)*
car hire service Autoverleih *(m)*, Leihwagendienst *(m)*
car key Autoschlüssel *(m)*
car-loading Autoverladung *(f)*
car park Parkplatz *(m)*
car rental service Autoverleih *(m)*
car ride Autofahrt *(f)*
car-sleeper train Autoreisezug *(m)* (Schlafwagen)
car-tow Abschleppdienst *(m)*
car traffic Autoverkehr *(m)*
carafe Karaffe *(f)*
carafe wine Schoppenwein *(m)*
caramel custard Karamelpudding *(m)*
caramel pudding Karamelpudding *(m)*
caravan Wohnwagen *(m)*
caravan trailer Wohnwagenanhänger *(m)*
caravaner Wohnwagentourist *(m)*
caraway-seed Kümmel *(m)*
cardinal directions die vier Himmelsrichtungen *(pl.f)*
care Betreuung *(f)*
care fare Fahrtkosten *(pl.)*
care of (c/o) per Adresse *(f)*, bei
career Karriere *(f)*, Laufbahn *(f)*
careful sorgfältig
careless fahrlässig
carelessness Fahrlässigkeit *(f)*
cargo Ladung *(f)*, Schiffsladung *(f)*, Fracht *(f)*, Seefracht *(f)*
cargo aircraft Frachtflugzeug *(n)*
cargo book Frachtbuch *(n)*
cargo consignment Frachtsendung *(f)*
cargo office air Luftfrachtbüro *(n)*
carload Waggonladung *(f)*
carload freight Waggonfracht *(f)*
carload rate Waggonfrachtrate *(f)*
carnival fritter Faschingskrapfen *(m)*
carnival season Karnevalszeit *(f)*, Faschingszeit *(f)*
carouse zechen
carp Karpfen *(m)*
carpet Teppich *(m)*
Caerphilly cheese Caerphilly-Käse *(m)*

carriage Beförderung (f), Transport (m), Fracht (f), Wagen (m)
carriage door Wagentür (f)
carriage rates Transporttarif (m)
carriageway Fahrbahn (f)
carrier Frachtführer (m), Spediteur (m), Transportunternehmen (n), Verkehrsträger (m) (Fluggesellschaft, Bus, Bahn, Schiff)
carrier's receipt Ladeschein (m)
carriers Verkehrsgewerbe (n)
carrot Karotte (f)
carrying value Buchwert (m)
cartage Rollgeld (n), Fuhrlohn (m)
carve tranchieren, zerschneiden
case Koffer (m), Kiste (f)
cash kassieren, einlösen, bar, Bargeld (n), flüssige Mittel (pl. n)
cash balances pledged to secure letters of credit Gelder (pl. n), die als Sicherheit (f) zur Abdeckung (f) eines Akkreditivs (n) abgetreten sind
cash basis of accounting Buchführung (f), die nur Ausgaben (pl. f) und Einnahmen (pl. f) festhält
cash box Geldkassette (f)
cash discount Skonto (m)
cash discounts earned Skontoerträge (pl. m)
cash in banks Bankguthaben (n)
cash investments Anlage (f) von flüssigen Mitteln (pl. n)
cash on delivery (c.o.d.) Nachnahme (f)
cash on hand Kassenbestand (m), Bargeld (n), Kleine Kasse (f)
cash position Liquiditätslage (f)
cash restricted for payment of long-term liabilities flüssige Mittel (pl. n), die für die Bezahlung (f) von langfristigen Verbindlichkeiten (pl. f) vorgesehen sind
cash surrender value of life insurance Rückkaufswert (m) von Lebensversicherungen (pl. f)
cash value Barwert (m)
cashier Kassierer (m)

casserole Tiegel (m), schmoren
cast anchor den Anker (m) werfen
castle Burg (f), Schloß (n)
castle ruins Schloßruine (f), Burgruine (f)
casual gleichgültig, locker, unregelmäßig
casual worker Gelegenheitsarbeiter (m)
casualty department Unfallstation (f)
catch Fang (m), fangen
category Klasse (f), Kategorie (f)
cater for versorgen, bewirten
catering Verpflegung (f)
catering arrangements Magenfahrplan (Luftfahrt) (m)
catering business Gastgewerbe (n)
catering industry Catering-Industrie (f)
catering trade Gastgewerbe (n), Gaststättengewerbe (n)
cathedral Dom (m), Kathedrale (f)
cattle Rindvieh (n), Vieh (n)
cauliflower Blumenkohl (m)
cauliflower browned Blumenkohl gratiniert (m)
cauliflower salad Blumenkohlsalat (m)
cauliflower soup Karfiolsuppe (f), Blumenkohlsuppe (f)
cause veranlassen, verursachen, Anspruch (m), Grund (m)
caution Vorsicht!
cautious vorsichtig
cave Höhle (f)
caviar Kaviar (m)
caviar sandwich Kaviarbrötchen (n)
Cayenne pepper Cayennepfeffer (m)
cease aufhören
ceiling Zimmerdecke (f)
celebrate feiern
celeriac Knollensellerie (m)
celery Sellerie (m)
celery salad Selleriesalat (m)
celery sticks Stangensellerie (m)
cellar Keller (m), Weinkeller (m)
celluloid Zelluloid (n)
cemetery Friedhof (m)
cenotaph Ehrenmal (n)
center Zentrum (n), Schwerpunkt (m)

central buying zentraler Einkauf *(m)*
central heating Zentralheizung *(f)*
Central Office of German Travel
  Deutsche Zentrale *(f)* für
  Fremdenverkehr *(m)*
central processing unit (CPU)
  Zentraleinheit *(f)*
central station Hauptbahnhof *(m)*
cep Steinpilz *(m)*
cereals Getreide *(n)*, Getreideflocken
  (pl.f)
certificate Bescheinigung *(f)*,
  Zeugnis *(n)*
certificate of antirabic vaccination
  Tollwutimpfzeugnis *(n)*
certificate of conduct
  Führungszeugnis *(n)*
certificate of deposit
  Hinterlegungsschein *(m)*,
  Hinterlegungsbestätigung *(f)*;
  Depositenzertifikat *(n)*,
  Einlagenzertifikat *(n)*
certificate of vaccination
  Impfzeugnis *(n)*
certified check (von der bezogenen
  Bank als gedeckt) bestätigter
  Scheck *(m)*
certified financial statement
  Jahresabschluß *(m)*, versehen mit
  dem Bestätigungsvermerk *(m)* des
  Wirtschaftsprüfers *(m)*
Certified Public Accountant (CPA)
  amerikanischer Wirtschaftsprüfer
  (m)
chain Kette *(f)*, Filialbetrieb *(m)*
chair Stuhl *(m)*
chairlift Sessellift *(m)*
chairman of the board
  Aufsichtsratvorsitzender *(m)*
challenge herausfordern,
  Herausforderung *(f)*
chamber-maid Zimmermädchen *(n)*
chamber-pot Nachttopf *(m)*
chamois Gemse *(f)*
champagne Sekt *(m)*, Champagner
  (m)
chance Zufall *(m)*
chance guest Durchreisender *(m)*,
  Passant *(m)*, Übernachtungsgast *(m)*
change Kleingeld *(n)*, Wechselgeld
  (n), wechseln, ändern, tauschen

change in the program
  Programmänderung *(f)*
change in value of currency
  Geldwertänderung *(f)*
change of carriage Umsteigen *(n)*
change of route Änderung *(f)* des
  Reiseweges *(m)*, Steckenänderung
  (f)
change reservations umbuchen
change-giving machine
  Geldwechselautomat *(m)*
changing a wheel Reifenwechsel
  (m)
changing room Umkleideraum *(m)*
chanterelle Pfifferling *(m)*
chapel Kapelle *(f)*
char Saibling *(m)*
charcoal Holzkohle *(f)*
charcoal broiled vom
  Holzkohlenfeuer *(n)*
charcoal broiled mixed grill
  Fleisch *(n)* vom Holzkohlengrill *(m)*
chard Mangold *(m)*
charge Berechnung *(f)*, Spesen *(pl.)*
charge for bed and breakfast
  Zimmerpreis *(m)* mit Frühstück *(n)*
charge for handling
  Bearbeitungsgebühr *(f)*
charge for service
  Bedienungszuschlag *(m)*,
  Bedienungsgeld *(n)*
charge per piece of baggage
  Gepäckgebühr *(f)* je Stück *(n)*
charge sales Kreditverkäufe *(pl.m)*
charge to (account) belasten
  (Konto)
charge to the room auf
  Zimmerrechnung *(f)* schreiben
chart grafisch darstellen, Tabelle *(f)*,
  Diagramm *(n)*
chart of accounts Kontenrahmen
  (m), Kontenplan *(m)*
charter chartern
charter aircraft Chartermaschine *(f)*
charter flight Charterflug *(m)*
charter money Schiffsmiete *(f)*
Chateaubriand Filetsteak *(n)*,
  Chateaubriand
chattel bewegliche Sache *(f)*
chattel mortgage
  Sicherungsübereignung *(f)*

cheap billig
cheap ticket ermäßigte Fahrkarte *(f)*
checkbook Scheckbuch *(n)*
check guarantee Scheckbürgschaft *(f)*
check list Kontroll-Liste *(f)*, Prüfliste *(f)*, Checkliste *(f)*
check (amerik.) Scheck *(m)*
check-in Abfertigung *(f)* (Flug), sich anmelden (Hotel)
check-in baggage Gepäck *(n)* aufgeben
check-in formality Abfertigungsformalität *(f)*
check-in time Eincheckzeit *(f)*, Meldeschluß *(m)* (Luftfahrt)
check-out sich abmelden, abreisen (Hotel), Abfertigung *(f)*
checked baggage aufgegebenes Gepäck *(n)*
checking account Kontokorrentkonto *(n)*, Girokonto *(n)*
checking of baggage Gepäckabfertigung *(f)*
checking of the hotels Überprüfung *(f)* der Hotels *(pl. n)*
checkroom Garderobe *(f)*, Gepäckaufbewahrung *(f)*, Aufbewahrungsstelle *(f)*
checkroom girl Garderobenfrau *(f)*
Cheddar cheese Cheddarkäse *(m)*
cheers Zum Wohl! Prosit!
cheese Käse *(m)*
cheese and ham stuffed veal steak gefülltes Kalbsschnitzel *(n)*, Cordon bleu *(n)*
cheese cake Käsekuchen *(m)*
cheese fondue Käsefondue *(n)*
cheese pie Käsekuchen *(m)*
cheese sandwich Käsebrot *(n)*
cheese soufflé Käseauflauf *(f)*
cheese spread Schmelzkäse *(m)*
cheese tartlet Käsetörtchen *(n)*
chef Küchenchef *(m)*, Chefkoch *(m)*
chef de partie Abteilungskoch *(m)*
chemist's shop Apotheke *(f)*
cheque (brit.) Scheck *(m)*
cheque book (brit.) Scheckbuch *(n)*, Scheckheft *(n)*
cherry Kirsche *(f)*

cherry brandy Kirschlikör *(m)*
cherry cake Kirschkuchen *(m)*
cherry tart Kirschtorte *(f)*
chervil Kerbel *(m)*
Cheshire cheese Chesterkäse *(m)*
chest of drawers Kommode *(f)*
chestnut Edelkastanie *(f)*
chestnut-vermicelli Kastanienpüree *(n)*
chew kauen
chick-pea Kichererbse *(f)*
chicken Huhn *(n)*
chicken à la King Geflügelrahmragout *(n)*
chicken breast Hühnerbrust *(f)*
chicken broth Hühnerbrühe *(f)*
chicken curry indisches Geflügelgericht *(n)*
chicken in broth Suppentopf mit Geflügeleinlage *(m)*
chicken in jelly Huhn in Aspik *(n)*
chicken leg Hühnerkeule *(f)*
chicken liver Geflügelleber *(f)*
chicken noodle soup Geflügelsuppentopf *(m)*
chicken pie warme Geflügelpastete *(f)*
chicken rice Geflügelreis *(m)*
chicken salad Geflügelsalat *(m)*
chicken stew Huhn *(n)* in Tomatensauce *(f)* mit Pilzen *(pl. m)* und Eiern *(pl. n)*
chicken winglet Flügelspitze *(f)* vom Huhn *(f)*
chicken, fried Backhuhn *(n)*
chicken, roast Brathuhn *(n)*
chicory Zichorie *(f)* (Salat)
chief conductor Zugführer *(m)*
chief engineer Technischer Leiter *(m)*
chief steward Chefsteward *(m)*
child care Kinderbetreuung *(f)*
child's bed Kinderbett *(n)*
child's ticket Kinderfahrkarte *(f)*
child's travel document Kinderausweis *(m)*
children's dining-room Kinderspeisesaal *(m)*
children's menue Speisekarte *(f)* für Kinder *(pl. n)*
children's playground Kinderspielplatz *(m)*

children's playroom Kinderspielzimmer *(n)*
children's pool Kinderbecken *(n)*
chili con carne Hackfleisch *(n)* mit braunen Bohnen *(pl.f)*
chill kühlen
chilled grapefruit Grapefruit *(f)* eisgekühlt
chilled melon geeiste Melone *(f)*
chilled vegetable soup gekühlte Gemüsesuppe *(f)*
chilly kühl, frostig
chimney Kamin *(m)*
china Porzellan *(n)*
china and glassware Porzellan- und Glaswaren *(pl.f)*
chinese cabbage Chinakohl *(m)*
chip Chip *(m)* (Elektronik)
chipped veal geschnetzeltes Kalbfleisch *(n)*
chips Pommes frites *(pl.f)*
chives Schnittlauch *(m)*
chocolate Schokolade *(f)*
chocolate cake Schokoladentorte *(f)*
chocolate cake Sacher style Sachertorte *(f)*
chocolate ice-cream Schokoladeneis *(n)*
chocolate-meringue Schokoladenbaiser *(n)*
chocolate pudding Schokoladenpudding *(m)*
chocolates Pralinen *(pl.f)*
choice Auswahl *(f)*, Wahl *(f)*
chop Kotelett (ohne Knochen) *(n)*
chopped gehackt
chopped veal cutlet Hackfleischkotelett vom Kalb *(n)*
chopper Hackmesser *(n)*
chopping board Hackbrett *(n)*
chopping knife Hackmesser *(n)*
chowder dicke Suppe *(f)*
Christian name Vorname *(m)*
Christmas Weihnachten *(n)*
Christmas bonus Weihnachtsgratifikation *(f)*
Christmas holidays (vacation) Weihnachtsferien *(pl.)*
Christmas period Weihnachtszeit *(f)*
Christmas pudding Weihnachtspudding *(m)*

church concert Kirchenkonzert *(n)*
church tax Kirchensteuer *(f)*
churchyard Friedhof *(m)*
cider Apfelwein *(m)*
cigar Zigarre *(f)*
cigarette Zigarette *(f)*
cigarette lighter Feuerzeug *(n)*
cinema program Kinoprogramm *(n)*, Filmprogramm *(n)*
cinema ticket Kinokarte *(f)*
cinnamon Zimt *(m)*
circle railway Ringbahn *(f)*
circle trip Rundreise *(f)*
circle trip ticket Rundreisefahrschein *(m)*
circular Rundschreiben *(n)*
circular road Ringstraße *(f)*
circular tour Rundfahrt *(f)*, Rundreise *(f)*
circular tour of port Hafenrundfahrt *(f)*
circular trip Rundreise *(f)*
circulation Umlauf *(m)*
circumstances beyond control unabwendbarer Zufall *(m)*
circus-ring Arena *(f)*
citadel Zitadelle *(f)*
citizen Bürger *(m)*, Staatsangehöriger *(m)*
citizenship Staatsbürgerschaft *(f)*
city Stadt *(f)*, Innenstadt *(f)*
city-airport transfer Zubringerdienst *(m)*
city hall Rathaus *(n)*
city ledger Konten *(pl.n)* für Kunden *(pl.m)* (z.B. Firmen)
city railway Stadtbahn *(f)*
city sightseeing flight Stadtrundflug *(m)*
city sightseeing tour Stadtrundfahrt *(f)*
city zone Stadtgebiet *(n)*
claim fordern, beanspruchen, Anspruch *(m)*, Forderung *(f)*
claim for damages Schadenersatzanspruch *(m)*
clam Venusmuschel *(f)*
clam broth Muschelsuppe *(f)*
clam chowder Muschelsuppe *(f)*
claret Bordeauxwein *(m)*
claret-cup Bowle *(f)*

clarify erklären
class of stock Aktiengattung (f)
classification Klassifizierung (f), Einstufung (f)
classification of hotels Hoteleinstufung (f), Hotelklassifizierung (f)
classified balance sheet Bilanzen (pl.f), die in kurz- oder langfristige Aktiva bzw. Passiva gegliedert werden
classified telephone directory Branchentelefonbuch (n)
classify klassifizieren, einstufen, kontieren
clause Klausel (f), Vertragsbestimmung (f)
clean reinigen, rein, sauber
cleaning Reinigung (f), Säuberung (f)
cleaning personnel Reinigungspersonal (n)
cleaning supplies Reinigungsmittel (pl.n)
cleanse reinigen
clean-up aufräumen
clear klären, verzollen, räumen
clear away abräumen, wegräumen
clear mock turtle soup falsche Schildkrötensuppe (f)
clear oxtail soup klare Ochsenschwanzsuppe (f)
clear port auslaufen (Schiffahrt)
clear soup Bouillon (f), Kraftbrühe (f)
clear soup royal klare Suppe (f) mit Eierstich (m)
clear soup with beaten egg Einlaufsuppe (f)
clear soup with vegetables klare Gemüsesuppe (f)
clear turtle soup klare Schildkrötensuppe (f)
clear up aufklären (Wetter)
clearance Verzollung (f), Räumung (f)
clearance charges Zollabfertigungsgebühren (pl.f)
clearing Verzollung (f) einer Schiffsladung (f)
clerk Büroangestellter (m)
climate Klima (n)

climatic conditions Klimaverhältnisse (pl.n)
climatic health resort Luftkurort (m), Klimakurort (m)
climatological station Klimastation (f)
climbing boot Bergschuh (m)
climbing equipment Bergausrüstung (f), Kletterausrüstung (f)
climbing tour Klettertour (f)
clinic Klinik (f)
clipper Atlantikflugboot (n)
cloakroom Garderobe (f)
cloakroom attendant Garderobenfrau (f)
cloakroom ticket Garderobenmarke (f)
clock Uhr (f)
close an account Konto (n) abschließen
close control genaue (scharfe) Kontrolle (f)
closed geschlossen
closed season Schonzeit (f)
closing Abschluß (m)
closing entry Abschlußbuchung (f)
closing hour Geschäfts- oder Betriebsschluß (m)
closing time Sperrstunde (f)
cloth Tuch (n)
clothes-brush Kleiderbürste (f)
clothes-hanger Kleiderbügel (m)
clothing Kleidung (f)
cloud Wolke (f)
cloudy bewölkt, wolkig
cloves Gewürznelke (f)
club Verein (m)
club evening Klubabend (m)
club membership Vereinsmitgliedschaft (f)
club-table Couchtisch (m)
clubhouse Klubhaus (n)
co-pilot Kopilot (m)
co-surety Mitbürgschaft (f)
coach Bus (m), Omnibus (m); Trainer (m), trainieren
coach conductor Busschaffner (m)
coach connection Busverbindung (f)
coach driver Busfahrer (m)
coach line Buslinie (f), Busverbindung (f)

coach stop Bushaltestelle (f)
coach travel Busreisen (pl.f)
coach-air service
  Bus-Flug-Verbindung (f)
coal fish Seehecht (m)
coast Küste (f)
coastal area Küstengebiet (n)
coastal cruise Küstenkreuzfahrt (f)
coastal road Küstenstraße (f),
  Uferstraße (f)
coastal shipping Küstenschiffahrt (f)
coasting slide Rodelhang (m)
coat-hanger Kleiderbügel (m)
coat-rack Kleiderständer (m)
cock Hahn (m)
cock-a-leekie Hähnchen (n) oder
  Suppenhuhn (n) und Lauch (m)
cockles Pilgermuscheln (pl.f)
cockpit Kanzel (f) (Flugzeug)
cocktail Cocktail (m)
cocktail bar tender Barkellner (m)
cocktail reception Cocktailempfang (m)
cocktail savory Vorspeise (f)
cocoa Kakao (m)
coconut Kokosnuß (f)
cod Dorsch (m)
cod fish Dorsch (m)
code number Schlüsselzahl (f),
  Kodenummer (f)
coffee Kaffee (m)
coffee break Kaffeepause (f)
coffee cup Kaffeetasse (f)
coffee ice-cream Eiskaffee (m)
coffee-mill Kaffeemühle (f)
coffee-pot Kaffeekanne (f)
coffee percolator
  Kaffee(filter)maschine (f)
coffee with cream Kaffee mit
  Sahne (m)
coffee with hot milk Milchkaffee (m)
coffee without caffeine
  koffeinfreier Kaffee (m)
coin Münze (f)
coin box Münzfernsprecher (m)
coincidence Zufall (m)
cold kalt
cold beef in vinegar Rindfleisch (n)
  in Essig (m) und Öl (n)
cold buffet kaltes Büffet (n)
cold cuts kalter Aufschnitt (m)

cold cuts on plate Aufschnitt-Teller (m)
cold dishes kalte Speisen (pl.f)
cold fowl Geflügel kalt (n)
cold game pie Wildpastete (f)
cold meat kalter Aufschnitt (m)
cold punch Bowle (f)
cold semolina pudding kalter
  Grießpudding (m)
cold side dishes kalte Vorspeisen (pl.f)
cold-storage Kühlhaus (n),
  Kühlhauslagerung (f)
coldstore im Kühlhaus (n) lagern
cole slaw Krautsalat (m)
collar Kragen (m)
collared beef Roulade (f)
collared herring Rollmops (m)
collateral Sicherheit (f),
  Sicherungsgegenstand (m),
  Sicherungsgut (n)
collateral trust bond gesicherte
  Schuldverschreibung (f)
collaterisation Sicherheitsleistung
  (f), Unterlegung (f) eines Kredits
  (m) durch eine Sicherheit (f)
collect sammeln
collection Einziehung (f) (Geld)
collection expenses Inkassospesen
  (pl.), Einziehungskosten (pl.)
collection of luggage
  Gepäckabholung (f)
collection of outstanding debts
  Einziehung (f) von Außenständen
  (pl.m)
collective agreement Tarifvertrag (m)
collective passport Sammelpaß (m)
collision Zusammenstoß (m)
collop Schnitzel (n)
colony Kolonie (f)
colour print Farbabzug (m) (Foto)
column Spalte (f)
comb Kamm (m)
combination sale Kopplungsverkauf (m)
comfort Bequemlichkeit (f)
comfortable bequem
comfortstation öffentliche Toilette (f)
commercial airport Zivilflughafen (m)

commercial bank (money center) Geschäftsbank *(f)* (USA)
commercial code Handelsgesetzbuch (HGB) *(n)*
commercial rate Firmenpreis *(m)*
commercial travel(l)er Handelsreisender *(m)*
commissary store Kantine *(f)* (mit großem Warenangebot)
commission (schedule 6) Provisionsertrag *(m)* (Umsatzbereich 6)
commissionaire Pförtner *(m)*
commitment Verpflichtung *(f)*
committee Ausschuß *(m)*, Gremium *(n)*
commodity Ware *(f)*, Artikel *(m)*
commodity rate Vorzugsfrachtrate *(f)* (Luftverkehr)
common shares (of a limited liability company) Stammeinlagen *(pl. f)* (GmbH)
common stock Stammaktien *(pl. f)*
communal bath room Gemeinschaftsbadezimmer *(n)*
communal canteen Gemeinschaftsküche *(f)*
communal feeding Gemeinschaftsverpflegung *(f)*
communal kitchen Gemeinschaftsküche *(f)*
communal provisions Gemeinschaftsverpflegung *(f)*
communicate (s. th. to s. o.) mitteilen (j-m etwas mitteilen)
communication Mitteilung *(f)*, Nachricht *(f)*, Verkehrsverbindung *(f)*
communication cord Notbremse *(f)*
community Gemeinde *(f)*, Gemeinschaft *(f)*
community tax Gemeindesteuer *(f)*
commutation ticket Zeitkarte *(f)*, Dauerkarte *(f)*
company Unternehmen *(n)*, Betrieb *(m)*, Gesellschaft *(f)*
company policy Betriebsordnung *(f)*, Betriebsvereinbarung *(f)* (bei Rückstellungen)
company rate Firmenpreis *(m)*
company seniority Betriebszugehörigkeit *(f)*, Dienstalter *(n)* im Betrieb *(m)*
comparability Vergleichbarkeit *(f)* (Rechnungslegung)
compartment Abteil *(n)*
compatible with verträglich mit
compel zwingen, nötigen, treiben
compensate entschädigen, ersetzen, vergüten
compensation Ersatz *(m)*, Entschädigung *(f)*, Vergütung *(f)*
compensation for damages Schadenersatz *(m)*
compensation payment Ausgleichszahlung *(f)*
compete konkurrieren, im Wettbewerb *(m)* stehen
competition Konkurrenz *(f)*, Wettbewerb *(m)*
competitive market Wettbewerbsmarkt *(m)*
competitor Konkurrent *(m)*, Wettbewerber *(m)*
compilation Erstellung *(f)* (von Jahresabschlüssen)
complain reklamieren, bemängeln, sich beschweren
complaint Beschwerde *(f)*, Reklamation *(f)*, Klage *(f)*
complaints book Beschwerdebuch *(n)*
complete breakfast komplettes Frühstück *(n)*
complimentary kostenlos
complimentary room Gratiszimmer *(n)*, Zimmer *(n)* ohne Berechnung *(f)*
complimentary ticket Freifahrkarte *(f)*
compound entry zusammengesetzter Buchungssatz *(m)*
comprehensive income Gesamteinkommen *(n)*
comptroller Controller *(m)*, (staatlicher) Rechnungsprüfer *(m)*
computer Computer *(m)*
computerize elektronische Datenverarbeitung *(f)*
conceptual framework Ausformulierung *(f)* wesentlicher Rechnungslegungsgrundsätze

(pl.m); Theorie *(f)* der Rechnungslegung *(f)*
concern Unternehmung *(f)*, Angelegenheit *(f)*, Geschäft *(n)*, Sache *(f)*
concert hall Konzertsaal *(m)*
concession (schedule 6) Konzession *(f)* (Umsatzbereich 6)
concierge Portier *(m)*, Concierge *(m, f)*
condensed milk Kondensmilch *(f)*
condition bedingen, Bedingung *(f)*
condition of conveyance Beförderungsbedingung *(f)*
condition of participation Teilnahmebedingung *(f)*
conducted tour Gesellschaftsreise *(f)*
conductor Schaffner *(m)*, Zugbegleiter *(m)*
confectioner Konditor *(m)*
confections Konfekt *(n)*
conference Sitzung *(f)*, Konferenz *(f)*, Besprechung *(f)*
conference hall Sitzungssaal *(m)*
conference room Konferenzraum *(m)*, Sitzungsraum *(m)*
confidential vertraulich
confirm bestätigen
confirmation Bestätigung *(f)*, Zusage *(f)*
confiscate beschlagnahmen, einziehen
conger-eel Meeraal *(m)*
congress Kongreß *(m)*
congress hall Kongreßhalle *(f)*
congress information service Kongreßberatung *(f)*
connecting flight Flugverbindung *(f)*, Anschlußflug *(m)*
connecting line (or route) Anschlußstrecke *(f)*
connecting point Umsteigepunkt *(m)*
connecting rooms ineinandergehende Zimmer *(pl.n)*
connecting station Umsteigebahnhof *(m)*
connecting train Anschlußzug *(m)*
connection Anschluß *(m)*, Verbindung *(f)*, Anschlußfahrt *(f)*
connector Stecker *(m)*

consecutive number fortlaufende Nummer *(f)*
conservatism Konservatismus *(m)*; Vorsichtsprinzip *(n)*
consignment note Frachtbrief *(m)*; Gepäckschein *(m)*
consist of bestehen aus
consistency Folgerichtigkeit *(f)*, Übereinstimmung *(f)*
consistency Vergleichbarkeit *(f)* in zeitlicher Hinsicht *(f)* (Rechnungslegung)
consistency in valuation Grundsatz *(m)* der Bewertungsstetigkeit *(f)*
consistent folgerichtig; ohne Widerspruch *(m)*
consistent with vereinbar mit, in Übereinstimmung *(f)* mit
consolidated balance sheet Konzernbilanz *(f)*, konsolidierte Bilanz *(f)*
consolidated financial statements Konzernabschluß *(m)*
constable Polizist *(m)*
construction Bau *(m)*, Auslegung *(f)*
construction in progress im Bau *(m)* befindliche Anlagen *(pl.f)*
construction site Baustelle *(f)*
consulate Konsulat *(n)*
consultant Berater *(m)*
consume verbrauchen, konsumieren
consumer Verbraucher *(m)*, Konsument *(m)*
consumption Verbrauch *(m)*, Konsum *(m)*, Verzehr *(m)*
contagious disease ansteckende Krankheit *(f)*
container Behälter *(m)*
content zufrieden
continental breakfast einfaches Frühstück *(n)*
Continental Plan (CP) (bed and breakfast) Zimmer *(n)* mit Übernachtung *(f)* und Frühstück *(n)*
contingencies Haftungsverhältnisse *(pl.n)*
contingent liabilities from bills of exchange Wechselobligo *(n)*
contingent liabilities from endorsements Indossamentverbindlichkeiten *(pl.f)*

contingent liability
Eventualverbindlichkeit *(f)*,
Haftung *(f)*
continuation of one's journey
Weiterfahrt *(f)*
contra account Gegenkonto *(n)*,
Gegenrechnung *(f)*
contra entry Gegenbuchung *(f)*
contract vereinbaren, Vertrag *(m)*,
Vereinbarung *(f)*
contract of accommodation
Beherbergungsvertrag *(m)*,
Gastaufnahmevertrag *(m)*,
Übernachtungsvertrag *(m)*
contract of apprenticeship
Ausbildungsvertrag *(m)*,
Lehrvertrag *(m)*
contract of carriage
Transportvertrag *(m)*
contract of guarantee Bürgschaft *(f)*
contract of passage Passagevertrag *(m)*
contract of sale Kaufvertrag *(m)*
contractual vertraglich
contractual penalty Vertragsstrafe *(f)*
contrast bath Wechselbad *(n)*
contribute (to) beitragen, beisteuern
contributed capital eingebrachtes Kapital *(n)*
contribution Kapitaleinlage *(f)*, Einbringung *(f)*
contribution in kind Sacheinlage *(f)*
contributory pension plan
Pensionsplan *(m)*, bei dem Arbeitgeber *(m)* und Arbeitnehmer *(m)* gemeinsam Beiträge *(pl. m)* leisten
control kontrollieren, überwachen, steuern, regeln, Kontrolle *(f)*, Leitung *(f)*
control tower Kontrollturm *(m)*
convalescence Erholung *(f)*, Rekonvaleszenz *(f)*
convalescent home Erholungsheim *(n)*
convalescent leave
Erholungsurlaub *(m)*
convalescent trip Erholungsreise *(f)*
convenience foods
Fertiggerichtesysteme *(pl. n)*
conventional landesüblich

conversion Umwandlung *(f)* eines Interessenten *(m)* in einen Hotelgast *(m)*
conversion method for foreign currency Umrechnungsgrundlage *(f)* für Fremdwährungen *(pl. f)*
conversion table
Umrechnungstabelle *(f)*
convert umrechnen, umwandeln, konvertieren
convertible bond
Wandelschuldverschreibung *(f)*
convertible currency konvertierbare Währung *(f)*
conveyance Beförderung *(f)*, Beförderungsmittel *(n)*
conveyance of cars
Autobeförderung *(f)*
conveyance of luggage
Gepäckbeförderung *(f)*
conveyer belt Förderband *(n)*
cook Koch *(m)*, kochen
cook-shop Garküche *(f)*
cooked gekocht
cooked in butter in Butter
cookie kleines Gebäck *(n)*
cooking Kochen *(n)*, Kochkunst *(f)*
cooking-facilities Kochgelegenheit *(f)*
cooking-pot Kochtopf *(m)*
cooking stove Kochstelle *(f)*
cooking utensils Kochgeschirr *(n)*
cook's assistant Küchengehilfe *(m)*
cooky kleines Gebäck *(n)*
cool kühl
cooling-water Kühlwasser *(n)*
cooperation Kooperation *(f)*, Mitarbeit *(f)*
cooperative advertising
Gemeinschaftswerbung *(f)*
coot Wasserhuhn *(n)*
copier Kopiergerät *(n)*
coppers Kleingeld *(n)*
cork Kork *(m)*
corkscrew Korkenzieher *(m)*
corky taste Korkgeschmack *(m)*
corn Mais *(m)*
corn flour Maismehl *(n)*
corncob Maiskolben *(m)*
corned beef Pökelfleisch *(n)*

corner seat Eckplatz *(m)*
cornflakes Maisflocken *(pl.f)*, Cornflakes *(pl.)*
corporate body juristische Person *(f)*
corporate dividend Aktiendividende *(f)*
corporate executive Direktor *(m)* (oder leitender Angestellter) einer AG *(f)*
corporate officer etwa: Vorstandsmitglied *(n)*
corporate planning Unternehmensplanung *(f)*
corporate stock Gesellschaftsanteil *(m)*
corporate underwriting Übernahme *(f)* von Schuldverschreibungen *(pl.f)*
corporation Körperschaft *(f)*, (Kapital-)Gesellschaft *(f)*, etwa: Aktiengesellschaft (AG) *(f)*
Corpus Christi Fronleichnam
correct richtig, berichtigen, verbessern
corridor Korridor *(m)*, Gang *(m)*
cosiness Behaglichkeit *(f)*, Gemütlichkeit *(f)*
cosmetic therapy Schönheitskur *(f)*
cosmetics Kosmetikartikel *(pl.m)*
cost-benefit-analysis Kosten-Nutzen-Analyse *(f)*
cost of calls (schedule 3) Kosten *(pl.)* der vermittelten Telefongespräche *(pl.n)* (Umsatzbereich 3)
cost of food and beverage consumed (schedule 2) nicht bereinigte Warenkosten *(pl.)* (Umsatzbereich 2)
cost of goods purchased Wareneinstandskosten *(pl.)*
cost of living Lebenshaltungskosten *(pl.)*
cost of merchandise sold (schedule 4) Wert *(m)* der verkauften Waren *(pl.f)* zum Einstandspreis *(m)* (Umsatzbereich 4)
cost price Selbstkostenpreis *(m)*, (Netto-)Einkaufspreis *(m)*, Einstandspreis *(m)*; Gestehungskosten *(pl.)*

cost reduction Kostensenkung *(f)*
costs of raizing plant Abbruchkosten *(pl.)*
cosy behaglich, gemütlich
cot Kinderbett *(n)*
cottage Ferienhaus *(n)*, Landhaus *(n)*
cottage cheese Hüttenkäse *(m)*
cotton wool Watte *(f)*, Rohbaumwolle *(f)*
couch Couch *(f)*, Liege *(f)*
couchette Liegeplatz *(m)*
couchette charge Liegeplatzgebühr *(f)*
cough Husten *(m)*
count zählen
counter Abfertigungsschalter *(m)*, Ladentisch *(m)*, Theke *(f)*
counter security Rückbürgschaft *(f)*
country Land *(n)*, Staat *(m)*
country air Landluft *(f)*
country ham Landschinken *(m)*
country house Landhaus *(n)*
country in development Entwicklungsland *(n)*
country inn Dorfgasthaus *(n)*, Landgasthof *(m)*
country lane Feldweg *(m)*
country of destination Bestimmungsland *(n)*, Zielland *(n)*
country of origin Ursprungsland *(n)*
country pub Dorfschenke *(f)*
country road Landstraße *(f)*
coupe (Eis-)Becher *(m)*
couple Eheleute *(pl.)*
coupon Gutschein *(m)*, Abschnitt *(m)*, Bon *(m)*
courier Reiseleiter *(m)*
courier's office Reiseleitung *(f)*
course Kurs *(m)*, Strecke *(f)*, Gang *(m)* (Essen)
course for beginners Anfängerkurs *(m)*
course of a journey Reiseverlauf *(m)*
course of treatment Kur *(f)*
course of treatment at a spa Heilbadekur *(f)*, Bäderkur *(f)*, Badekur *(f)*
court Hof *(m)*
courtesy Höflichkeit *(f)*
courtyard Hof *(m)*

cove for bathing Badebucht *(f)*
cover Gedeck *(n)*, Couvert *(n)*
cover charge Gedeckpreis *(m)*,
trockenes Gedeck *(n)*
cover charges (schedule 2)
Eintrittsgelder *(pl.n)*
(Umsatzbereich 2)
covered apple pie Apfelstrudel *(m)*
covered-court tennis Hallentennis *(n)*
covering letter Begleitbrief *(m)*
CP (Continental Plan) Zimmer *(n)* mit Übernachtung *(f)* und Frühstück *(n)*
crab Krabbe *(f)*
crabmeat Krabbenfleisch *(n)*
cracker dünner Keks *(m)*
craftsman Handwerker *(m)*
cranberry Preiselbeere *(f)*
crash landing Bruchlandung *(f)*
crawfish, crayfish Krebs *(m)*
crayfish cream soup Krebsrahmsuppe *(f)*
crayfish salad Krebsschwanzsalat *(m)*
crayfish soup Krebssuppe *(f)*
cream Rahm *(m)*, Sahne *(f)*
cream cheese Rahmkäse *(m)*, Weichkäse *(m)*, Schmelzkäse *(m)*
cream cheese tart Rahmkäsetorte *(f)*
cream of asparagus Spargelcremesuppe *(f)*
cream of cauliflower Blumenkohlcremesuppe *(f)*
cream of chicken Königinsuppe *(f)*
cream of green pea soup grüne Erbsensuppe *(f)*
cream of mushroom Pilzcremesuppe *(f)*
cream of vegetable Gemüsecremesuppe *(f)*
cream of wheat Weizengrießbrei *(m)*
cream puff Windbeutel *(m)*
cream sauce Rahmsauce *(f)*
cream slice Cremeschnitte *(f)*
cream soup Rahmsuppe *(f)*
creamed potatoes Kartoffelbrei *(m)*
creamed veal collop Rahmschnitzel *(n)*
creativeness Kreativität *(f)*
credit gutschreiben, Kredit *(m)*, Gutschrift *(f)*

credit balance Habensaldo *(n)*
credit card Kreditkarte *(f)*
credit card commission Kreditkarten-Provision *(f)*
credit card holder Kreditkarteninhaber *(m)*
credit entry Habenbuchung *(f)*, Gutschrift *(f)*
credit facilities Kreditmöglichkeiten *(pl.f)*
credit line Kreditlinie *(f)*, Kreditgrenze *(f)* (Höchstkredit)
credit operation Kreditgeschäft *(n)*
credit period Laufzeit *(f)* des Kredits *(m)*
credit purchase Kreditkauf *(m)*
credit rating Kreditwürdigkeit *(f)*
credit resources Kreditquellen *(pl.f)*, Kreditmöglichkeiten *(pl.f)*
credit sale Kreditverkauf *(m)*
credit side Habenseite *(f)* eines Kontos *(n)*
credit standards Kreditrichtlinien *(pl.f)*
credit standing Kreditwürdigkeit *(f)*, Bonität *(f)*
credit supply Kreditbeschaffung *(f)*
creole sauce Tomatensoße *(f)* (spanisch)
crescent Gipfel *(m)* (Gebäck)
cress Kresse *(f)*
crevasse Gletscherspalte *(f)*
crew Besatzung *(f)*, Bordpersonal *(n)*
crib Kinderbett *(n)*
cricket match Kricketspiel *(n)*
crisp knusprig
crisscross journey Kreuz-und-Querfahrt *(f)*
critical path kritischer Weg *(m)*
Critical Path Method Netzplantechnik *(f)* (Methode des kritisches Weges)
crockery Eßgeschirr *(n)*
crop Ernte *(f)*
croquette potatoes Kartoffelkroketten *(pl.f)*
croquettes Kroketten *(pl.f)*
croquettes of fowl Geflügelkroketten *(pl.f)*
cross the frontier die Grenze *(f)* überschreiten

cross-country drive Geländefahrt *(f)*
cross-country skiing Skilanglauf *(m)*
cross-roads Straßenkreuzung *(f)*
crossing Straßenkreuzung *(f)*, Überfahrt *(f)*
crossing time Überfahrtsdauer *(f)*
crowded überfüllt
crucial entscheidend
cruet-stand Essig- und Ölständer *(m)*
cruise Schiffsreise *(f)*, Seereise *(f)*, Kreuzfahrt *(f)*, Vergnügungsfahrt *(f)*
cruising speed Reisegeschwindigkeit *(f)*
crustaceans Krustentiere *(pl. n)*
cucumber Gurke *(f)*
cucumber salad Gurkensalat *(m)*
cuisine Küche *(f)*, Kochkunst *(f)*
cul-de-sac Sackgasse *(f)*
culinary art Kochkunst *(f)*
culinary delights kulinarische Genüsse *(pl. m)*
cultural centre Kulturzentrum *(n)*
cumulative dividend kumulative Dividende *(f)*
cumulative preferred stock kumulative Vorzugsaktien *(pl. f)*
cumulative voting kumulative Stimmenabgabe *(f)* (Mittel für die Minderheitenvertretung)
cup Tasse *(f)*
cup custard Karamelpudding *(m)*
cupboard Schrank *(m)*
curative climate Heilklima *(n)*
curative factor Heilfaktor *(m)*
curative-mud Heilmoor *(n)*, Heilschlamm *(m)*
curative power Heilkraft *(f)*
curd cheese Quark *(m)*
curdle gerinnen
curds and whey Dickmilch *(f)*
cure Kurbehandlung *(f)*, Heilung *(f)*
cure at a spa Bäderkur *(f)*, Badekur *(f)*
curler Lockenwickler *(m)*
curling Curling *(n)*
currant Johannisbeere *(f)*, Korinthe *(f)*
currency Währung *(f)*
currency allowance Devisenfreigrenze *(f)*
currency control Devisenkontrolle *(f)*

currency conversion Geldwechsel *(m)*
currency regulations Devisenbestimmungen *(pl. f)*, Devisenvorschriften *(pl. f)*
currency restrictions Devisenbeschränkung *(f)*
current account laufendes Konto *(n)*, Girokonto *(n)*, Kontokorrent *(n)*
current assets Umlaufvermögen *(n)*
current balance Kontokorrentguthaben *(n)*
current cost Wiederbeschaffungskosten *(pl.)*
current liabilities kurzfristige Verbindlichkeiten *(pl. f)*
current market value Tageswert *(m)* am Absatzmarkt *(m)*
current maturities (or portion) of long-term debt kurzfristiger Teil *(m)* langfristiger Verbindlichkeiten *(pl. f)*
current operating expenses laufende Betriebskosten *(pl.)*
current rate Tageskurs *(m)*
current receivables noch nicht fällige Forderungen *(pl. f)*
curriculum vitae Lebenslauf *(m)*
curried chickencream soup Geflügelrahmsuppe mit Curry *(f)*, Mulligatawny-Suppe *(f)*
curry Curry *(m)*
curry powder Currypulver *(n)*
cursor Schreibmarke *(f)*
curtail one's expenses seine Ausgaben *(pl. f)* einschränken
curtain Vorhang *(m)*
cushion Kissen *(n)*
custard pudding Karamelpudding *(m)*
custard sauce Vanillesoße *(f)*
custom Sitte *(f)*, Gewohnheit *(f)*, Brauch *(m)*
customary gebräuchlich, üblich
customer Kunde *(m)*
customs Zoll *(m)*, Zölle *(pl. m)*
customs assessment value Zollwert *(m)*
customs authorities Zollbehörde *(f)*
customs clearance (clearing) Zollabfertigung *(f)*

customs declaration Zollerklärung *(f)*
customs examination hall Zollabfertigungshalle *(f)*
customs inspection Zollkontrolle *(f)*
customs number Zollnummer *(f)*
customs officer Zollbeamter *(m)*
customs regulations Zollvorschriften *(pl.f)*
customs tarif Zolltarif *(m)*
customs territory Zollgebiet *(n)*
cut schneiden, Schnitt *(m)*
cut price Preis *(m)* drücken, Preis *(m)* senken
cut-off date Stichtag *(m)*
cutlery Besteck *(n)*
cutlet Schnitzel *(n)*
cuttle-fish Tintenfisch *(m)*
cycle count of inventories permanente Inventur *(f)*
cycle path Fahrradweg *(m)*
cycle track Radfahrweg *(m)*
cycle-stand Fahrradständer *(m)*
cycling tourist Radtourist *(m)*

D

dab Rotzunge *(f)*
daily täglich
daily cash receipts tägliche Kasseneinnahmen *(pl.f)*
daily cash report täglicher Kassenbericht *(m)*
daily service täglicher Verkehr *(m)*, verkehrt täglich
dairy Molkerei *(f)*
daisywheel Typenrad *(n)*
daisywheelprinter Typenraddrucker *(m)*
dam Staudamm *(m)*, Talsperre *(f)*
damage schaden, schädigen, Schaden *(m)*, Verlust *(m)*
damages Schadenersatz *(m)*
damages in transit Transportschäden *(pl.m)*
damp feucht
damson Zwetschge *(f)*
dance band Tanzorchester *(n)*, Tanzkapelle *(f)*
dance bar Tanzbar *(f)*

dance hall Tanzsaal *(m)*, Tanzlokal *(n)*
dancefloor Tanzfläche *(f)*
dancing Tanz *(m)*
dancing show Tanzvorführung *(f)*
dancing-party Tanzabend *(m)*
danger Gefahr *(f)*
dangerous gefährlich
dark beer dunkles Bier *(n)*
darkness Dunkelheit *(f)*
darn stopfen, ausbessern
dash Prise *(f)*, kleine Menge *(f)*, Spritzer *(m)*
dash of soda Spritzer Soda *(m)*
data bank Datenbank *(f)*
data processing Datenverarbeitung *(f)*
date datieren, Datum *(n)*; Dattel *(f)*
date of arrival Ankunftsdatum *(n)*, Ankunftstermin *(m)*
date of birth Geburtsdatum *(n)*
date of departure Abreisedatum *(n)*
date of expiry Verfalldatum *(n)*
dawn Dämmerung *(f)*, Tagesanbruch *(m)*
daybreak Tagesanbruch *(m)*
day excursion Tagesausflug *(m)*, Tagesfahrt *(f)*, Tagestour *(f)*
day flight Tagesflug *(m)*
day of arrival Ankunftstag *(m)*, Anreisetag *(m)*
day of departure Abreistag *(m)*, Abflugtag *(m)*
day of issue Ausgabetag *(m)*
day rate (use rate) Tageszimmerpreis *(m)*
day restaurant Tagesrestaurant *(n)*
day return ticket Tagesrückfahrkarte *(f)*
day-room Tagesraum *(m)*, Aufenthaltsraum *(m)*
day ticket Tageskarte *(f)*
day-tripper Ausflügler *(m)*
day-trippers' goal Ausflugsziel *(n)*
daylight colour film Tageslichtfilm *(m)*
daylight-saving time Sommerzeit *(f)*
de luxe Luxus *(m)*
deadline letzter Termin *(m)*
deal handeln, Handel *(m)*, Geschäft *(n)*

deal (with) sich befassen, sich beschäftigen, zu tun haben (mit)
dealing Geschäft *(n)*, Geschäftsverkehr *(m)*
debark an Land gehen, ausschiffen
debarkation Ausschiffung *(f)*
debenture Obligation *(f)*, Schuldverschreibung *(f)*, Anleihe *(f)*
debit (an account) belasten (Konto)
debit balance Soll-Saldo *(n)*
debit side Sollseite *(f)* eines Kontos *(n)*
decaffeinated coffee koffeinfreier Kaffe *(m)*
decanter Karaffe *(f)*
decide entscheiden
decision Entscheidung *(f)*, Entschluß *(m)*, Beschluß *(m)*
decision usefulness entscheidungsbezogene Kriterien *(pl.n)* für die Rechnungslegung *(f)*
deck Deck *(n)*
deck game Bordspiel *(n)*
deck steward Decksteward *(m)*
deck-chair Liegestuhl *(m)*
declaration Erklärung *(f)*, Anmeldung *(f)*
declaration of value Wertangabe *(f)*
declare anmelden, verzollen
declare a dividend eine Dividende *(f)* genehmigen
decline Abnahme *(f)*, Rückgang *(m)*, Verminderung *(f)*
declining balance depreciation degressive Abschreibung *(f)*
decorate schmücken, verzieren
decoration Dekoration *(f)*
decrease abnehmen, Abnahme *(f)*
deduct abziehen, absetzen
deductible abzugsfähig
deduction Abzug *(m)*, Absetzung *(f)*
deep-fried eggs in Öl *(n)* gebackene Eier *(pl.n)*
deep-fried fish in Öl *(n)* gebackener Fisch *(m)*
deep-frozen tiefgefroren
deer Hirsch *(m)*, Reh *(n)*
default Verzug *(m)*, Versäumnis *(n)*
defect Fehler *(m)*, Mangel *(m)*
defective mangelhaft, fehlerhaft, schadhaft

defer aufschieben, stunden
deferred zurückgestellt
deferred charges aktive Rechnungsabgrenzung *(f)* (langfristig)
deferred compensation Vergütungen *(pl.f)* oder Leistungen *(pl.f)*, die erst bei der effektiven Auszahlung *(f)* steuerpflichtig werden
deferred income transitorische Aktiva *(pl.)*
deferred income tax aufgeschobene Einkommenssteuerverbindlichkeiten *(pl.f)*; Steuerstundung *(f)*
deferred item transitorischer Posten *(m)*
deferred payment Ratenzahlung *(f)*, Abzahlung *(f)*
deferred stock nicht sofort dividendenberechtigte Aktie *(f)*
deficiency Mangel *(m)*, Defizit *(n)*, Fehlbetrag *(m)*, Ausfall *(m)*
deficiency (deficit) guarantee Ausfallbürgschaft *(f)*
deficit Ausfall *(m)*, Fehlbetrag *(m)*, Defizit *(n)*, Verlust *(m)*
defile Bergpaß *(m)*
definite bestimmt, endgültig
deflation Deflation *(f)*, Wertabnahme *(f)*
defuse entschärfen
degree Grad *(m)*
delay verzögern, verspäten, Verzögerung *(f)*, Aufschub *(m)*, Verspätung *(f)*
delay of a train Zugverspätung *(f)*
delays Wartezeiten *(pl.f)*
delegate delegieren, übertragen
delete which is inapplicable Nichtzutreffendes *(n)* streichen
delicious köstlich
deliver liefern, überbringen
delivery Lieferung *(f)*
delivery date Liefertermin *(m)*
delivery note Lieferschein *(m)*
delivery of baggage Gepäckzustellung *(f)*
delivery service Zustelldienst *(m)*
delivery slip Lieferschein *(m)*
delivery time Lieferzeit *(f)*

demand verlangen, fordern, Anspruch *(m)*, Nachfrage *(f)*
demand deposit Sichteinlage *(f)*, Kontokorrenteinlage *(f)* (Einlage, über die jederzeit verfügt werden kann)
demand oriented approach (yield management) nachfrageorientiertes Preisfestsetzungsverfahren *(n)* (Yield Management)
demi-pension Halbpension *(f)*
demi-tasse Mokka *(m)*
denial Absage *(f)*
dentist Zahnarzt *(m)*
department Abteilung *(f)*
department store Warenhaus *(n)*
departmental costing Kostenstellenrechnung *(f)*
departure Abreise *(f)*, Abfahrt *(f)*, Abflug *(m)*
departure station Abgangsbahnhof *(m)*
departure time Abfahrtszeit *(f)*, Abflugzeit *(f)*
departure timetable Abfahrtstafel *(f)*
depend on abhängen von, sich verlassen auf
deplane das Flugzeug *(n)* verlassen, aussteigen
depletion Substanzverringerung *(f)*, Abschreibung *(f)* wegen Substanzverzehr *(m)*
deposit einzahlen, deponieren
deposit Einzahlung *(f)*, Einlage *(f)*, Anzahlung *(f)*, Einlieferung *(f)*, Hinterlegung *(f)*
deposit counter Gepäckschalter *(m)*
depreciable assets abnutzbare Anlagegegenstände *(pl. m)*
depreciate abschreiben, entwerten, abnutzen
depreciation Abschreibung *(f)*, Abnutzung *(f)*
depression Tief *(n)*
depth Tiefe *(f)*
Derby-cheese Derby-Käse *(m)*
descent Abstieg *(m)*
describe bezeichnen, beschreiben
description Beschreibung *(f)*, Bezeichnung *(f)*

desk Pult *(n)*, Schreibtisch *(m)*
desk clerk Empfangschef *(m)*
despatch absenden
dessert Dessert *(n)*, Nachtisch *(m)*, Nachspeise *(f)*, Süßspeise *(f)*
dessert wine Dessertwein *(m)*, Süßwein *(m)*
destination Bestimmungsort *(m)*, Zielort *(m)*, Reiseziel *(n)*
destination airport Zielflughafen *(m)*
destination station Bestimmungsbahnhof *(m)*, Zielbahnhof *(m)*
deteriorate (sich) verschlechtern, an Wert *(m)* verlieren
determination Entscheidung *(f)*
determine bestimmen, entscheiden, urteilen
detour Umleitung *(f)*, Umweg *(m)*, Abstecher *(m)*
devaluation Abwertung *(f)*
development Entwicklung *(f)*
deviled scharf gewürzt
dial wählen (Telefon)
diced apples gewürfelte Apfelstückchen *(pl. n)*
dictate diktieren
dictionary Wörterbuch *(n)*
diet Diät *(f)*, Diätkost *(f)*
diet cure Diätkur *(f)*
diet plan Diätplan *(m)*
dietary cooking Diätkost *(f)*, Diätküche *(f)*
dietary foods Diätkost *(f)*, Diätnahrung *(f)*
dietic kitchen Diätküche *(f)*
dietic treatment Diätkur *(f)*
difference Unterschied *(m)*, Differenz *(f)*
digest verdauen
digestion Verdauung *(f)*
dike Deich *(m)*, Damm *(m)*
dill Dill *(m)*
dilute verschneiden, verdünnen
dim matt, undeutlich
dine speisen, zu Abend *(m)* essen
diner Speisewagen *(m)*
dinghy Jolle *(f)*
dining-car Speisewagen *(m)*
dining-room Eßzimmer *(n)*, Speisezimmer *(n)*, Gastzimmer *(n)*

dining-saloon Speisesaal *(m)*
dinner Abendessen *(n)*, Diner *(n)*
dinner dance Abendessen *(n)* mit Tanz *(m)*, Tanzdiner *(n)*
dinner-jacket Smoking *(m)*
dinner wine Tischwein *(m)*
dinner with floor show Diner *(n)* mit Show *(f)*
dip eintauchen
dipsomaniac Trinker *(m)*
direct unmittelbar, anweisen, anordnen
direct costing Grenzkostenrechnung *(f)*
direct distance dialing Ferndurchwahl *(f)*
direct mail advertising Direktwerbung *(f)*, Werbung *(f)* durch Drucksachenversand *(m)*
direction Anweisung *(f)*, Anordnung *(f)*, Richtung *(f)*
directional arrow Richtungspfeil *(m)*
directory Adreßbuch *(n)*
dirty schmutzig
disabled (dauernd) dienstunfähig, arbeitsunfähig, invalide
disadvantage Nachteil *(m)*, Schaden *(m)*
disagio Disagio *(n)*
disagree (with) nicht übereinstimmen (mit), im Widerspruch *(m)* stehen (zu, mit)
disagreeable unangenehm
disburse bezahlen, auszahlen, auslegen (Geld)
discerning anspruchsvoll
disclose ausweisen
disclosure Offenlegung *(f)*
disconnect trennen
discount abziehen, diskontieren, Diskont *(m)*, Rabatt *(m)*, Abzug *(m)*, Nachlaß *(m)*
discovery Entdeckung *(f)*
discreet vorsichtig, besonnen, taktvoll, verschwiegen
discretion Verschwiegenheit *(f)*, Ermessen *(n)*
disembarkation charge Ausschiffungsgebühr *(f)*
disengaged frei

dish Gericht *(n)*, Speise *(f)*, Teller *(m)*, Schüssel *(f)*
dish towel Geschirrtuch *(n)*
dish-washer Spüler *(m)*, Tellerwäscher *(m)*, Spülmaschine *(f)*
dish-washing area Abwaschküche *(f)*
dish-washing machine Geschirrspülmaschine *(f)*
dishes Geschirr *(n)*
dishes prepared to order frischgemachte Speisen *(pl.f)*
diskette Diskette *(f)*
dislike nicht mögen
dismiss entlassen
dismissal Entlassung *(f)*
dismissal restrictions Kündigungsschutz *(m)*
dispatch absenden
dispatch note Paketkarte *(f)*
dispatcher Einsatz *(m)* der Zimmerfrauen *(pl.f)*
display ausstellen, zur Schau *(f)* stellen
displease (to be displeased with s.th.) mißfallen, unzufrieden sein (mit etwas)
displeasure Mißfallen *(n)*
disposal Verfügung *(f)*
dispose of verfügen über
distance Entfernung *(f)*, Strecke *(f)*
distance travelled zurückgelegte Strecke *(f)*
distant entfernt
distant view Fernblick *(m)*
distil destillieren
distilled water destilliertes Wasser *(n)*
distinctly deutlich
distinguished vornehm
distinguishing marks besondere Kennzeichen *(pl.n)*
distort verdrehen, verzerren
distract from ablenken von
distress Not *(f)*, Notlage *(f)*, Notstand *(m)*
distribute verteilen, ausschütten
distribution Verteilung *(f)*, Vertrieb *(m)*
distribution channel Absatzweg *(m)*
distribution of income Ausschüttung *(f)* einer Dividende *(f)*

distribution of the dividend
Ausschüttung *(f)* der Dividende *(f)*
district Bezirk *(m)*
distrust mißtrauen, Mißtrauen *(n)*
disturb stören, belästigen, beeinträchtigen
disturbance Störung *(f)*, Belästigung *(f)*, Beeinträchtigung *(f)*
divan Bettcouch *(f)*
dive tauchen
dive bar Kellerbar *(f)*
diversification Differenzierung *(f)*, Angebotserweiterung *(f)*, Diversifikation *(f)*
diversified abwechslungsreich
diversion Umleitung *(f)*, Umgehungsstraße *(f)*
dividend payable Verbindlichkeiten *(pl.f)* gegenüber den Gesellschaftern *(pl.m)* (aus erklärter, aber noch nicht bezahlter Dividende)
dividend yield Dividendenertrag *(m)*
divine service Gottesdienst *(m)*
diving club Taucherclub *(m)*
diving equipment Taucherausrüstung *(f)*
diving-pool Tauchbecken *(n)*
diving-tower Sprungturm *(m)*
division Abteilung *(f)*, Teilung *(f)*, Verteilung *(f)*
do not disturb bitte nicht stören!
do not lean out nicht hinauslehnen!
do not open nicht öffnen!
dock area Hafenviertel *(n)*
dock quarter Hafenviertel *(n)*
docks Hafenanlagen *(pl.f)*
doctor in attendance behandelnder Arzt *(m)*
doctor on duty diensttuender Arzt *(m)*
doctor's certificate ärztliches Attest *(n)*
dog Hund *(m)*
dogs must be kept on the lead Hunde *(pl.m)* sind an der Leine *(f)* zu halten
doll Puppe *(f)*
domestic inländisch
domestic air traffic Binnenflugverkehr *(m)*
domestic flight Inlandsflug *(m)*

domestic route Inlandsstecke *(f)*
domicile Wohnsitz *(m)*
donkey Esel *(m)*
don't touch nicht berühren!
door Tür *(f)*
door handle Türklinke *(f)*
door-keeper Pförtner *(m)*
door knob menu Zimmerfrühstückskarte *(f)*
door-to-door pick up and delivery service Haus-zu-Haus-Gepäckbeförderung *(f)*
dorado Goldbarsch *(m)*
dormitory Schlafraum *(m)*, Schlafsaal *(m)*
double Doppelzimmer *(n)* mit einem großen Bett *(n)*
double bed Doppelbett *(n)*
double-bedded room Zimmer *(n)* mit zwei Betten
double-berth compartment Zweibettabteil *(n)*
double-deck zweistöckig
double-entry bookkeeping doppelte Buchführung *(f)*
double occupancy rack rate höchster Preis *(m)* für ein Doppelzimmer *(n)*
double room Doppelzimmer *(n)*, Zweibettzimmer *(n)*
double-sized steak doppeltes Beefsteak *(n)*
double tenderloin Doppellendenstück *(n)*
double-track line zweigleisige Strecke *(f)*
doubt bezweifeln, Zweifel *(m)*
doubtful accounts zweifelhafte Forderungen *(pl.f)*
douche Dusche *(f)*
dough Teig *(m)*
dough dumplings Spätzle *(pl.)*
doughnut Krapfen *(m)*
downhill course Abfahrt *(f)*
downhill race Abfahrtslauf *(m)*
downhill trail Abfahrt *(f)*
downpour Platzregen *(m)*
downstream sales unrealisierte konzerninterne Gewinne *(pl.m)*, die aus Verkäufen *(pl.m)* der Mutter- an die Tochtergesellschaft *(f)* resultieren

downtown Geschäftsviertel *(n)*, Innenstadt *(f)*
downward journey Talfahrt *(f)*
dozen (doz.) Dutzend *(n)*
draft Muster *(n)*, Vorlage *(f)*
dragon fish Drachenfisch *(m)*, Meerdrachen *(m)*
drain trocknen, Abfluß *(m)*
draper's Stoffgeschäft *(n)*
draught Luftzug *(m)*
draught beer Faßbier *(n)*, offenes Bier *(n)*
drawbridge Zugbrücke *(f)*
drawer Schublade *(f)*
drawers Unterhose *(f)*
dress Kleid *(n)*, ankleiden
dress-circle erster Rang *(m)* (Theater)
dressing Garnierung *(f)*, Salatsoße *(f)*; Verbandszeug *(n)*
dressing gown Morgenrock *(m)*
dressing-table Frisiertisch *(m)*, Toilettentisch *(m)*
dried getrocknet
dried cod Stockfisch *(m)*
dried meat Trockenfleisch *(n)*
drink Getränk *(n)*, Drink *(m)*, trinken
drink dispenser Getränkeautomat *(m)*
drink the waters eine Trinkkur *(f)* machen
drinkable trinkbar
drinking water Trinkwasser *(n)*
drinks and snacks on board Getränke *(pl.n)* und kalte Speisen *(pl.f)* im Zug *(m)*
drinks extra Getränke *(pl.n)* nicht inbegriffen
drip-dry bügelfrei
dripping Schmalz *(n)*
drive fahren (einen Wagen)
drive slowly langsam fahren!
drive-in cinema Autokino *(n)*
driver's license Führerschein *(m)*
driveway Autostraße *(f)*, Einfahrt *(f)*, Autobahn *(f)*
driving licence Führerschein *(m)*
drop Tropfen *(m)* fallen lassen
drug Medikament *(n)*
druggist Drogist *(m)*
drunkenness Trunkenheit *(f)*
dry trocken, herb, (ab)trocknen
dry cleaning chemische Reinigung *(f)*

dry wine trockener Wein *(m)*
dry-clean chemisch reinigen
drying-room Trockenraum *(m)*
dual carriageway zweispurige Fahrbahn *(f)*
duck Ente *(f)*
duckling junge Ente *(f)*
due fällig
dump vorzeitig abreisen
dumping Preisdruck *(m)*, Preisunterbietung *(f)*, Dumping *(n)*
dumpling Kloß *(m)*, Knödel *(m)*
dune Düne *(f)*
dunning Mahnung *(f)*
dunning letter Mahnbrief *(m)*
duplex Maisonette *(f)* (zweistöckige Wohnung)
duration Dauer *(f)*, Laufzeit *(f)*
duration of a journey Reisedauer *(f)*
duration of the stay Aufenthaltsdauer *(f)*
dust Staub *(m)*
dustbin Kehrichteimer *(m)*
duster Staubtuch *(n)*
Dutch Cheese Edamer Käse *(m)*
Dutch sauce holländische Soße *(f)*
dutchess potatoes Herzoginnenkartoffeln *(pl.f)*
dutiable zollpflichtig
duty Pflicht *(f)*, Dienst *(m)*; Zoll *(m)*
duty drawback Zollerstattung *(f)*
duty-free zollfrei, abgabefrei
duty-free shop Verkaufsstand *(m)* für zollfreie Waren *(pl.f)*
duty paid verzollt
dwell wohnen

E

ear-warmers Ohrenschützer *(pl.m)*
early früh
early morning tea Tee *(m)* vor dem Aufstehen *(n)*
early retirement Vorruhestand *(m)*
early vegetable Frühlingsgemüse *(n)*
earn verdienen
earnings Verdienst *(m)*, Einkommen *(n)*
east wind Ostwind *(m)*
Easter Ostern, Osterfest *(n)*

Easter holidays Osterferien *(pl.)*
easy to get to leicht erreichbar
easy-chair Sessel *(m)*, Lehnstuhl *(m)*
eat essen, speisen
eating-place Eßlokal *(n)*, Speiselokal *(n)*
EC directive EU-Richtlinie *(f)*
economical wirtschaftlich, ökonomisch
economy class Touristenklasse *(f)*
Edam cheese Edamer Käse *(m)*
edge Rand *(m)*
edible snail Weinbergschnecke *(f)*
educate ausbilden, erziehen
education Ausbildung *(f)*, Vorbildung *(f)*
educational holiday Bildungsurlaub *(m)*, Studienurlaub *(m)*
educational stay Bildungsaufenthalt *(m)*
educational tour Bildungsreise *(f)*, Schulausflug *(m)*
educational trip Studienreise *(f)*
eel Aal *(m)*
eel in dill-sauce Aal *(m)* in Dill *(m)*
eels jellied Aal *(m)* in Gelee *(n)*
effective wirksam
effectiveness Wirksamkeit *(f)*
effervescent bath Sprudelbad *(n)*
efficiency Leistung *(f)*, Leistungsfähigkeit *(f)*
efficiency expert Rationalisierungsfachmann *(m)*
efficient leistungsfähig
egg Ei *(n)*
egg and bacon Eier mit Speck *(pl. n)*
eggbeater Schneebesen *(m)*
egg-cup Eierbecher *(m)*
egg-dishes Eiergerichte *(pl. n)*
egg-plant Eierfrucht *(f)*, Aubergine *(f)*
egg-salad Eiersalat *(m)*
egg-sandwich Eiersandwich *(n)*, Eierbrot *(n)*
eggs, fried Spiegeleier *(pl. n)*, Setzeier *(pl. n)*
eggs in a glass Eier im Glas *(pl. n)*
eggs in cocotte Eier im Näpfchen *(pl. n)*
eggs in mayonnaise Mayonnaiseeier *(pl. n)*

eggs Russian style russische Eier *(pl. n)*
egg yolk Eigelb *(n)*
eiderdown Daunendecke *(f)*
elbow macaroni Hörnchennudeln *(pl. f)*
elderberry-tea Holundertee *(m)*
electric bulb Glühbirne *(f)*
electric kettle elektrischer Kessel *(m)*
electric power Strom *(m)*, Kraftstrom *(m)*
electric power consumption Stromverbrauch *(m)*
electric range elektrischer Herd *(m)*
electric rate schedule Stromtarif *(m)*
electric razor elektrischer Rasierapparat *(m)*
electric sign advertising Leuchtreklame *(f)*, Leuchtwerbung *(f)*
electric storm Gewitter *(n)*
electric torch Taschenlampe *(f)*
electrical and mechanical equipment (schedule 12) elektrische und maschinelle Anlagen *(pl. f)* (Service Center 12)
electrician Elektriker *(m)*
Electronic Data Processing (EDP) Elektronische Datenverarbeitung (EDV) *(f)*
electronic game (schedule 6) elektronisches Spiel *(n)* (Umsatzbereich 6)
electrotherapy Elektrotherapie *(f)*
elegant elegant
elevator Fahrstuhl *(m)*, Aufzug *(m)*, Lift *(m)*
elevator boy Fahrstuhlführer *(m)*, Liftboy *(m)*
elevator shaft Aufzugsschacht *(m)*
elevenses zweites Frühstück *(n)*, Brotzeit *(f)*
eliminate eliminieren, ausscheiden
elimination Elimination *(f)*, Ausscheidung *(f)*
embankment Uferstrafe *(f)*, Damm *(m)*
embargo Ausfuhrsperre *(f)*, Handelssperre *(f)*, Embargo *(n)*
embark einschiffen
embarkation Verladung *(f)*, Einschiffung *(f)*

embassy Botschaft *(f)*
emergency Notfall *(m)*
emergency address Notadresse *(f)*
emergency brake Notbremse *(f)*
emergency chute Notrutsche *(f)*
emergency exit Notausgang *(m)*
emergency landing Notlandung *(f)*
emotion Gefühl *(n)*
emotional reaction gefühlsmäßige Reaktion *(f)*
emotional sales argument an das Gefühl *(n)* appellierendes Verkaufsargument *(n)*
empathize Einfühlungsvermögen *(n)* zeigen
empathy Einfühlungsvermögen *(n)*
empatic einfühlend
emphasize (nachdrücklich) betonen, Nachdruck *(m)* legen auf, besonderen Wert *(m)* legen auf
employ beschäftigen, anstellen
employee Angestelle(r) *(f,m)*, Arbeitnehmer *(m)*
employee attitude Einstellung *(f)* der Arbeitnehmer *(pl.m)* zum Betrieb *(m)*
employee moral Arbeitsmoral *(f)*
employee rating scale Mitarbeiter-Beurteilungsskala *(f)*
employees' meals Angestelltenverpflegung *(f)*, Personalverpflegung *(f)*
employees' opinion survey Mitarbeiterbefragung *(f)*
employees' representative Arbeitnehmervertreter *(m)*
employer Unternehmer *(m)*, Arbeitgeber *(m)*
employers' association Arbeitgeberverband *(m)*
employment Beschäftigung *(f)*, Anstellung *(f)*
employment application Bewerbung *(f)*
employment contract Arbeitsvertrag *(m)*, Dienstvertrag *(m)*
employment contract Arbeitsvertrag *(m)*
empty leer
en brochette am Spießchen *(n)*

en route unterwegs, auf der Fahrt *(f)*
enable j-n berechtigen, ermächtigen
enclose beifügen
enclosure Anlage *(f)*
encompass umfassen, umschließen
encounter technique Begrüßungstechnik *(f)*
endive Endivie *(f)*
endive salad Endiviensalat *(m)*
endorsee Indossatar *(m)*, Girat *(m)*, Empfänger *(m)*
endorsement Indossament *(n)*, Giro *(n)*
endorsement risks for bills of exchange (notes) Wechselobligo *(n)* aus der Weitergabe *(f)* von Wechseln *(pl.m)* (Nichteinlösung)
endorser Indossant *(m)*, Girant *(m)*
energy costs (schedule 13) Energiekosten *(pl.)* (Service Center 13)
engage anstellen, beschäftigen, verpflichten
engaged besetzt (Telefon)
engagement Anstellung *(f)*, Beschäftigung *(f)*, Verpflichtung *(f)*; Verlobung *(f)*
engine-driver Lokomotivführer *(m)*
engine noise Motorenlärm *(m)*
engineer Ingenieur *(m)*, technischer Leiter *(m)*
engineering department technische Abteilung *(f)*
English breakfast englisches Frühstück *(n)*
English mustard englischer Senf *(m)*
enjoy genießen
enlargement Vergrößerung *(f)*
enquiry Erkundigung *(f)*
enroll eintragen
enrollment Eintragung *(f)*
ensure sicherstellen, schützen, garantieren, gewährleisten
enter betreten, buchen, eintragen, eintreten, beitreten
enter a country in ein Land *(n)* einreisen
enter without knocking eintreten ohne anzuklopfen
entertainment Bewirtung *(f)*, Unterhaltung *(f)*

entertainment centre
Vergnügungszentrum (n)
entertainment tax
Vergnügungssteuer (f)
entrance Eingang (m), Einfahrt (f)
entrance hall Hotelhalle (f)
entrance to a harbour
Hafeneinfahrt (f)
entrepreneur of the hotel and catering trade gastgewerblicher Unternehmer (m)
entry Buchung (f), Eingang (m), Einreise (f), Eintragung (f), Eintritt (m)
entry into the country Einreise (f)
entry permit Einreisegenehmigung (f)
entry visa Einreisevisum (n)
entrée Zwischengericht (n)
enumerate aufzählen
envelope Briefumschlag (m)
environment Umwelt (f)
environmental protection Umweltschutz (m)
equal gleich, gleichmäßig
equestrian sport Pferdesport (m)
equipment Einrichtung (f), Ausstattung (f), Gerätschaften (pl.f)
equipped with ausgestattet mit
equity side Passivseite (f) (Bilanz)
equivalent gleichwertig, gleichbedeutend, Gegenwert (m)
erect errichten
err irren
errand Botengang (m)
error Fehler (m), Irrtum (m)
errors and alterations excepted
Irrtümer (pl.m) und Änderungen (pl.f) vorbehalten
escalator Rolltreppe (f)
escalope Schnitzel (n)
escape period Rücktrittsfrist (f)
escarole Winterendivie (f)
escorted tour Gesellschaftsreise (f)
espresso bar Espressobar (f)
espresso coffee Espresso (m)
establish gründen
establish (method of payment) festsetzen (Zahlungsmodus)
establishment Gründung (f), Unternehmen (n), Niederlassung (f)

establishment of the hotel trade
Beherbergungsbetrieb (m)
establishment of the tourist trade
Fremdenverkehrsbetrieb (m)
estate agent Grundstücksmakler (m)
estate car Kombiwagen (m)
esteem schätzen
estimate schätzen, veranschlagen, Schätzung (f), Voranschlag (m)
European Plan (EP) reiner Übernachtungspreis (m)
evaluate bewerten, abschätzen
evaluation Bewertung (f), Auswertung (f)
evasion of customs
Zollhinterziehung (f)
eve-cheese Schafskäse (m)
evening by candlelight
Kerzenabend (m)
evening concert Abendkonzert (n), Musikabend (m)
evening dance Tanzabend (m)
evening dress Abendkleidung (f)
evening entertainment
Unterhaltungsabend (m)
evening gown Abendkleid (n)
evening performance
Abendvorstellung (f) (Theater)
event Veranstaltung (f), Ereignis (n)
event of loss Schadensfall (m)
event order Veranstaltungsinformation (f)
everything included alles inbegriffen
ex ship ab Schiff (n)
exact genau
exaggerate übertreiben
examination of luggage
Gepäckkontrolle (f)
examine prüfen, untersuchen
excavation Ausgrabung (f)
exceed überschreiten, übersteigen, hinausgehen über
excellent ausgezeichnet
excess baggage Übergepäck (n)
excess baggage fare Zuschlag (m) für Übergepäck (n)
excess capacity Überkapazität (f)
excessive überhöht, übertrieben
excessive charge Überpreis (m)
excessive price Überpreis (m)

exchange wechseln, tauschen, Austausch *(m)*
exchange control Devisenkontrolle *(f)*
exchange of money Geldwechsel *(m)*
exchange office Wechselstube *(f)*
exchange rate Wechselkurs *(m)*
exchange regulations Devisenvorschriften *(pl.f)*
exchange voucher Austauschgutschein *(m)*
exclusive agency Alleinvertretung *(f)*
excursion Ausflug *(m)*, Tour *(f)*
excursion area Ausflugsgebiet *(n)*
excursion facilities Ausflugsmöglichkeiten *(pl.f)*
excursion fare Ausflugsfahrpreis *(m)*, Ferienflugpreis *(m)*
excursion flight Rundflug *(m)*
excursion program Ausflugsprogramm *(n)*
excursion rate Ausflugstarif *(m)*
excursion steamer Ausflugsdampfer *(m)*
excursion ticket Ausflugskarte *(f)*
excursionist Ausflügler *(m)*
excursionist's goal Ausflugsziel *(n)*
excusable entschuldbar
excuse entschuldigen, Entschuldigung *(f)*
executive Vorstands- und Verwaltungsratmitglied *(n)*, leitender Angestellter *(m)*, Führungskraft *(f)*
executive assistant manager stellvertretender Direktor *(m)*
executive board Vorstand *(m)*
executive chef Küchenchef *(m)*
executive development Ausbildung *(f)* von Führungskräften *(pl.f)*
executive housekeeper Leiterin *(f)* der Hausdamenabteilung *(f)*, Hausdame *(f)*
executive secretary Chefsekretärin *(f)*
executory noch auszuführend, zu erfüllend
exemplary musterhaft, vorbildlich
exempt ausgenommen, befreit, ausnehmen

exemption from duty Zollfreiheit *(f)*
exeption Ausnahme *(f)*
exercise Übung *(f)*
exhibit ausstellen, zeigen
exhibition Ausstellung *(f)*
exhibition grounds Ausstellungsgelände *(n)*, Messegelände *(n)*
exhibition stand Ausstellungsstand *(m)*
exhibitor Aussteller *(m)*
exit Ausgang *(m)*, Ausfahrt *(f)*
exit drive Autoausfahrt *(f)*
exit-interview Entlassungsinterview *(n)*, Ausgangsinterview *(n)*
exit road Autobahnausfahrt *(f)*
exit visa Ausreisevisum *(n)*, Ausreisesichtvermerk *(m)*
expand erweitern, expandieren
expansion Erweiterung *(f)*, Expansion *(f)*
expect erwarten, voraussehen
expectation Erwartung *(f)*
expenditure Ausgabe *(f)*
expenses (schedules) sonstige direkte Kosten *(pl.)* (Umsatzbereiche 1–5 im USASH)
expensive teuer, aufwendig
experience erfahren, kennenlernen, erleben, Erfahrung *(f)*, Praxis *(f)*
experienced erfahren, bewandert, erprobt, routiniert, geschickt
expiration date (credit card) Verfallsdatum *(n)* (Kreditkarte)
expire ablaufen, verfallen
explanation in the notes Erläuterungen *(pl.f)* im Anhang *(m)*
exploration Entdeckungsfahrt *(f)*
exploration expenses Erschließungskosten *(pl.)*
explore erforschen
export ausführen, exportieren, Ausfuhr *(f)*, Export *(m)*
export duty Ausfuhrzoll *(m)*
export permit Ausfuhrbewilligung *(f)*
expose belichten (Foto)
exposed to avalanches lawinengefährdet
exposure draft Verlautbarungsentwurf *(m)*

exposure meter Belichtungsmesser *(m)*
express Express *(m)*, Schnellzug *(m)*
express coach Schnellbus *(m)*
express railcar Schnelltriebwagen *(m)*
express road Schnellstraße *(f)*
express traffic Schnellverkehr *(m)*
express train Schnellzug *(m)*, D-Zug *(m)*
exquisite auserlesen
extend verlängern, erweitern
extension Verlängerung *(f)*, Erweiterung *(f)*
extension cord Verlängerungsschnur *(f)*
extension of stay Aufenthaltsverlängerung *(f)*
exterior äußerlich, außerhalb
extra Zuschlag *(m)*, Nebengebühr *(f)*; besonders
extra bed Zusatzbett *(n)*
extra charge Aufschlag *(m)*
extra charge for service Bedienungszuschlag *(m)*
extra flight Sonderflug *(m)*
extra help Aushilfe *(f)*
extra pay Zulage *(f)*
extra shift Sonderschicht *(f)*
extra tour Sondertour *(f)*
extra train Sonderzug *(m)*
extra waiter Extrakellner *(m)*, Aushilfskellner *(m)*
extra week Verlängerungswoche *(f)*
extras Nebenausgaben *(pl. f)*
eye appeal Blickfang *(m)*
eye catching ins Auge *(n)* fallend
eye contact Augenkontakt *(m)*
eye opener Überraschung *(f)*, Entdeckung *(f)*
eye-witness Augenzeuge *(m)*

F

F (=first) Erste Klasse *(f)* (Vermerk auf Flugscheinen)
face cloth Waschlappen *(m)*
face of the balance sheet Bilanz *(f)*
face value Nominalbetrag *(m)*, Nennwert *(m)*

facilitate erleichtern
facilitation Erleichterung *(f)*
facilities for hydropathic treatment Kneippanlagen *(pl. f)*
facilities planning Einrichtungsplanung *(f)*
facility Einrichtung *(f)*, Möglichkeit *(f)*
facing gegenüber
facing inland zur Landseite *(f)*
facing south nach Süden gehend
fact Wahrheit *(f)*, Tatsache *(f)*
factual tatsächlich, wirklich
fail unterlassen, nicht erfüllen, versagen, mißlingen
failure of performance Nichterfüllung *(f)*
fair Messe *(f)*, angemessen, gerecht
fair authorities Messeleitung *(f)*
fair information office Messe-Informationsstelle *(f)*
fair market value Marktwert *(m)*, Verkehrswert *(m)*, Martkzeitwert *(m)*
fair-ground Messegelände *(n)*, Festwiese *(f)*
fair-ground tent Festzelt *(n)*
fall Herbst *(m)*
fall due fällig werden
fall off abfallen, absinken
fall vacation Herbstferien *(pl.)*
falling stones Steinschlag *(m)*
fallow-deer Damhirsch *(m)*
faltboat Faltboot *(n)*
family allowance Familienzulage *(f)*
family boardinghouse Familienpension *(f)*
family budget Haushaltsrechnung *(f)*
family business Familienbetrieb *(m)*
family guesthouse Familienferienhotel *(n)*
family holiday Familienferien *(pl.)*
family holiday resort Familienferienort *(m)*
family income Familieneinkommen *(n)*
Family Plan Familienpreis *(m)* (kostenlose Unterbringung von Kindern im Zimmer der Eltern)
family rate Spezialpreis *(m)* für Familien *(pl. f)*
family-run firm Familienbetrieb *(m)*

family size package Haushaltspackung *(f)*
family status Familienstand *(m)*
family ticket Familienkarte *(f)*
family tourism Familientourismus *(m)*
family vacation Familienferien *(pl.)*
fan Ventilator *(m)*
fancy Phantasie *(f)*, Mode *(f)*, Luxus *(m)*, Laune *(f)*
fancy-cake Torte *(f)*
fancy-cake of biscuit Biskuittorte *(f)*
fancy cake with almonds Mandeltorte *(f)*
fancy cake with caramel Dobostorte *(f)*
fancy-cake with chocolate Sachertorte *(f)*
fancy-cake with coffee cream Kaffeecremetorte *(f)*
fancy-cake with cream Cremetorte *(f)*
fancy-cake with Linz nut Linzer Torte *(f)*
fancy cake with nuts Nußtorte *(f)*
fancy-dress ball Kostümball *(m)*, Maskenball *(m)*
fancy goods Modewaren *(pl.f)*, Geschenkartikel *(pl.m)*
far weit, entfernt
fare Fahrgeld *(n)*, Fahrpreis *(m)*
fare reduction Fahrpreisermäßigung *(f)*
fare reductions for tourist parties Fahrpreisermäßigungen *(pl.f)* für Reisegesellschaften *(pl.f)*
farewell Abschied *(m)*
farewell dinner Abschiedsessen *(n)*
farinaceous dish Mehlspeise *(f)*
farinaceous food Teigwaren *(pl.f)*
farinaceous sidedish Teigwaren-Vorgericht *(n)*
farm Bauernhof *(m)*
farm trout Zuchtforelle *(f)*
farmer's ham Bauernschinken *(m)*
farmhouse Bauernhaus *(n)*
farmhouse room Bauernstube *(f)*
FAS price Preis *(m)* einschließlich sämtlicher Kosten *(pl.)* bis zum Schiff *(n)*
fashion Mode *(f)*

fashion contest Modewettbewerb *(m)*
fashion magazine Modezeitschrift *(f)*
fashion show Modeschau *(f)*
fashionable modisch, elegant
fast freight train Eilgüterzug *(m)*
fast local train Nahschnellverkehrszug *(m)*
fast steamer Schnelldampfer *(m)*
fast train Schnellzug *(m)*
fasten seat belts bitte anschnallen!
fat Fett *(n)*
fatigue Ermüdung *(f)*, Erschöpfung *(f)*, ermüden
fattened chicken Masthuhn *(n)*
fatty fett
fault Fehler *(m)*, Mangel *(m)*
faulty fehlerhaft, mangelhaft
favourite bevorzugt
favourite dish Lieblingsgericht *(n)*
favourite pub Stammlokal *(n)*
feasible durchführbar
feast Festmahl *(n)*, festlich bewirten, schmausen
feathered game Federwild *(n)*
feature Attraktion *(f)*, Einrichtung *(f)*, Merkmal *(n)*, Spielfilm *(m)*
federal auf Bundesebene *(f)*
Federation of Travel Agencies (FIAV) Internationaler Verband *(m)* der Reisebüros *(pl.n)*
fee Gebühr *(f)*
feed ernähren, speisen
feed-back Rückinformation *(f)*
feedback value Rückkoppelungsqualität *(f)* (Rechnungslegung)
feeder road Autobahnzubringer *(m)*
feeder-service aircraft Zubringerflugzeug *(n)*
feedway Zubringerstraße *(f)*
feet *(pl.)*, siehe **foot**
Felchen from Lake Constance Bodenseefelchen *(n)*
fellow-passenger Mitreisender *(m)*
female weiblich
fennel Fenchel *(m)*
ferment gären (lassen)
ferry Fähre *(f)*
ferry over übersetzen
ferry-boat Fähre *(f)*
ferryman Fährmann *(m)*

festival Festspiele *(pl.n)*, Festwochen *(pl.f)*
festival committee Festausschuß *(m)*
festival hall Festhalle *(f)*, Festsaal *(m)*
festival week Festwoche *(f)*
festive illumination Festbeleuchtung *(f)*
festive procession Festzug *(m)*
festivity on board ship Bordfest *(n)*
fever Fieber *(n)*
field of activity Tätigkeitsgebiet *(n)*
field path Feldweg *(m)*
field trip Betriebsbesichtigung *(f)*
field work Außendienst *(m)*
FIFO value Fifo-Wert *(m)*
fig Feige *(f)*
figure Zahl *(f)*, Ziffer *(f)*, Abbildung *(f)*
figure skating Eiskunstlauf *(m)*
filbert Haselnuß *(f)*
file ablegen; Akte *(f)*, Kartei *(f)*
file card Karteikarte *(f)*
filing cabinet Registratur *(f)*, Aktenschrank *(m)*
fill in ausfüllen
filled gefüllt
filled puff pastry Blätterteigpastete *(f)*
fillet Filet *(n)*
fillet of beef Lendenschnitte *(f)*
fillet of beef with cream-soup Filetbraten in Rahmsauce *(m)*
fillet of beef, tenderloin Rindsfilet *(n)*
fillet of fish Fischfilet *(n)*
fillet of pork roasted Jungfernbraten *(m)*
fillet of veal Kalbsfilet *(n)*
fillet-mignon Filetsteak *(n)*, Lendenschnitte *(f)*
fillingstation Tankstelle *(f)*
fillingstation attendant Tankwart *(m)*
film Film *(m)*, filmen
film actor Filmschauspieler *(m)*
film festival Filmfestspiele *(pl.n)*
filter coffee Filterkaffee *(m)*
filter(-tipped) cigarette Filterzigarette *(f)*
final endgültig, abschließend
final day Endtermin *(m)*

final holiday registration Reiseanmeldung *(f)*
financial accounting (externe) Rechnungslegung *(f)*, Bilanzierung *(f)*; Finanzbuchhaltung *(f)*; i.w. S.: Finanz- und Rechnungswesen *(n)*
financial aid Finanzhilfe *(f)*
financial assets Finanzanlagen *(pl.f)*, Finanzanlagevermögen *(n)*
financial auditing Prüfung *(f)* des betrieblichen Finanz- und Rechnungswesens *(n)*
financial distress finanzielle Notlage *(f)*
financial position Vermögenslage *(f)*, Finanzlage *(f)*
financial statement presentation Ausweis *(m)* beim Jahresabschluß *(m)*
financial statements Abschlußbilanz *(f)*, einschließlich Ertragsrechnung *(f)* und Rechnung *(f)* des Bilanzgewinns *(m)*, der Anmerkungen sowie der Mittelherkunfts- und Verwendungsrechnung; Jahres- oder Monatsabschluß *(m)*
finder's reward Finderlohn *(m)*
fine Geldstrafe *(f)*; fein
fines herbes feingehackte Kräuter *(pl.n)*
finished goods fertige Erzeugnisse *(pl.n)*
finished product Fertigerzeugnis *(n)*
fire fristlos entlassen; Feuer *(n)*
fire-alarm Feuermelder *(m)*
fire-brigade Feuerwehr *(f)*
fire department Feuerwehr *(f)*
fire escape Feuerleiter *(f)*
fire-extinguisher Feuerlöscher *(m)*
fire insurance Feuerversicherung *(f)*
fireplace Kamin *(m)*
fire regulations Brandschutzbestimmungen *(pl.f)*
fire-side Kamin *(m)*
fire-works Feuerwerk *(n)*
firm service Firmenbetreuung *(f)*
firn Firn *(m)*
first aid erste Hilfe *(f)*
first-aid kit Verbandszeug *(n)*, Verbandskasten *(m)*

first-aid post Unfallstation *(f)*
first class erste Klasse *(f)*, erstklassig
first class category erste Kategorie *(f)*
first class fares Ersteklassetarif *(m)*
first class hotel Hotel *(n)* erster Klasse *(f)*
first course erster Gang *(m)*
first performance Erstaufführung *(f)*
fish angeln, fischen, Fisch *(m)*
fish and chips gebratener Fisch *(m)* mit Pommes frites *(pl.)*
fish and chips shop Fischrestaurant *(n)*
fish knife and fork Fischbesteck *(n)*
fish salad Fischsalat *(m)*
fish soup Fischsuppe *(f)*
fishcake Fischfrikadelle *(f)*
fisherman Fischer *(m)*
fishes and crustaceous animals Fische *(pl. m)* und Schalentiere *(pl. n)*
fishing Angeln *(n)*, Fischen *(n)*, Angelsport *(m)*
fishing-boat Fischerboot *(n)*
fishing club Anglerverein *(m)*
fishing facility Angelgelegenheit *(f)*
fishing-gear Angelgerät *(n)*
fishing licence Angelschein *(m)*
fishing-tackle Angelgerät *(n)*
fishing village Fischerdorf *(n)*
fishmonger Fischhandlung *(f)*
fishpond Weiher *(m)*
five-o'clock tea Fünfuhrtee *(m)*
fix feststellen, festsetzen
fix the route of a journey Reiseroute *(f)* festlegen
fixed fest, festgesetzt, festgelegt
fixed assets Anlagevermögen *(n)*
fixed assets records Inventarbücher *(pl. n)*
fixed charges (schedule 14) fixe (feste) Kosten *(pl.)* (Service Center 14)
fixed price Festpreis *(m)*
fizz Fizz *(m)*, Schampus *(m)*
fizzi lemonade Brauselimonade *(f)*
flag Flagge *(f)*
flageolet Bohne *(f)*, grüne
flambé flambiert

flame flambieren
flamed flambiert
flamed bananas flambierte Bananen *(pl. f)*
flamed saddle of venison flambierter Rehrücken *(m)*
flaming-rum-omelet Omelett mit Rum *(n)*
flan Obstkuchen *(m)*
flannel board Flanell-Tafel *(f)*
flash bulb Blitzlichtbirne *(f)*
flash cube Blitzwürfel *(m)*
flash light Taschenlampe *(f)*; Blitzlicht *(n)*
flashing signal Lichthupe *(f)*
flat pauschal, Wohnung *(f)*
flat price Einheitspreis *(m)*
flat rate niedrigster Zimmerpreis *(m)*
flat sum Pauschalbetrag *(m)*
flavour Aroma *(n)*, Geschmack *(m)*
fleet Flotte *(f)*
fleet of trucks Fuhrpark *(m)*
flexibility Anpassungsfähigkeit *(f)*
flight Flug *(m)*
flight captain Flugkapitän *(m)*
flight engineer Bordmechaniker *(m)*
flight information Fluginformation *(f)*
flight schedule Flugplan *(m)*
flight time Flugzeit *(f)*
flip chart Flip Chart *(n)*
flipper Flosse *(f)*
float schwimmen
floating hotel schwimmendes Hotel *(n)*
floodlight anstrahlen
floor Stock(werk) *(n)*, Etage *(f)*
floor cloth Scheuertuch *(n)*
floor housekeeper Etagenbeschließerin *(f)*, Etagenhausdame *(f)*, Etagengouvernante *(f)*
floor houseman Etagendiener *(m)*, Etagenhausdiener *(m)*
floor staff Etagenpersonal *(n)*
floor waiter Etagenkellner *(m)*
floppy disk Floppy disk *(f)*
florist Blumenhändler *(m)*
flounder Flunder *(f)*
flour Mehl *(n)*
flow chart Ablaufdiagramm *(n)*

flow of work Arbeitsablauf *(m)*
flow process chart
   Arbeitsablaufbogen *(m)*,
   Arbeitsablaufanalyse *(f)*
flower shop Blumenladen *(m)*
flower stand Blumenstand *(m)*
fluctuate schwanken
fluctuation Schwankung *(f)*
fluctuation of price
   Preisschwankung *(f)*
fluctuations of the exchange
   Wechselkursschwankungen *(pl.f)*
fluffy flaumig, locker
fluke Flunder *(f)*
flyer Flugzettel *(m)*
flying safety Flugsicherheit *(f)*
flying speed Fluggeschwindigkeit *(f)*
flying time Flugzeit *(f)*
foam Schaum *(m)*, schäumen
focus Brennpunkt *(m)*, Mittelpunkt *(m)*
fog Nebel *(m)*
foggy neblig
fold-away bed Klappbett *(n)*
fold-away table Klapptisch *(m)*
folder Hefter *(m)*, Prospekt *(m)*
folding bed Klappbett *(n)*
folding screen Wandschirm *(m)*, Paravent *(m)*
folding seat Klappsitz *(m)*, Notsitz *(m)*
folding table Klapptisch *(m)*
folio Blatt *(n)*, Folio *(n)*
folk art Volkskunst *(f)*
folk dance Volkstanz *(m)*
folk song Volkslied *(n)*
folklore Folklore *(f)*, Brauchtum *(n)*
folkloristic evening Heimatabend *(m)*
follow folgen, befolgen, sich halten an
follow up verfolgen
follow up Weiterverfolgung *(f)* (einer Sache)
follow-up file Wiedervorlagemappe *(f)*
follow-up system
   Wiedervorlageverfahren *(n)*,
   Nachfaßsystem *(n)*
food Speisen *(pl.f)*, Verpflegung *(f)*, Nahrung *(f)*
food and beverage controller
   Leiter *(m)* der
   Wareneinsatzkontrolle *(f)* (Speisen und Getränke)
food and beverage department
   Verpflegungsbereich *(m)*,
   Gastronomiebereich *(m)*
food and beverage manager Food und Beverage-Manager *(m)*
Food and Beverage Manager Association (FBMA) Verband *(m)* der Wirtschaftsdirektoren *(pl.m)*
food and beverage prices
   Verkaufspreise *(pl.m)* für Speisen *(pl.f)* und Getränke *(pl.n)*
food cost controller Leiter *(m)* der Wareneinsatzkontrolle *(f)* (Speisen)
food festival Spezialitätenwochen *(pl.f)*
food pack Imbißpaket *(n)*
food-poisoning
   Lebensmittelvergiftung *(f)*
food service betrieblicher Mittagstisch *(m)*
food store Lebensmittellagerraum *(m)*
food storekeeper Lagerverwalter *(m)* für Lebensmittel
food supply Verpflegung *(f)*
food supply capacity
   Verpflegungskapazität *(f)*
food test Qualitätsüberprüfung *(f)* der Speisen *(pl.f)*
foot Fuß (= 0,3048m) *(m)*
foot pump inflator Tretblasebalg *(m)*
football match Fußballspiel *(n)*
footbridge Steg *(m)*, Fußgängerbrücke *(f)*
footpath Gehweg *(m)*, Bürgersteig *(m)*, Fußweg *(m)*
for hire zu vermieten
for sale zu verkaufen
force zwingen
forced landing Notlandung *(f)*
forcemeat Füllung *(f)*, Füllsel *(n)*
forcemeat, roasted falscher Hase *(m)*
forcible zwingend
fore deck Vordeck *(n)*
forecast vorausplanen, Prognose *(f)*, Plan *(m)*, Vorausschau *(f)*
forecast factor Prognosefaktor *(m)*

forecastle Vorderdeck *(n)*
forego verzichten auf, gehen lassen, aufgeben
foreign ausländisch
foreign country Ausland *(n)*
foreign currency Devisen *(pl.f)*
foreign currency control Devisenkontrolle *(f)*
foreign exchange Devisen *(pl.f)*
foreign exchange office Wechselstube *(f)*
foreign exchange risk Währungsrisiko *(n)*
foreign guest Auslandsgast *(m)*
foreign rate Auslandstarif *(m)*
foreign tourist Auslandstourist *(m)*
foreign visitor Auslandsgast *(m)*
foreigner Ausländer *(m)*
forenoon Vormittag *(m)*
forest Wald *(m)*
forest path Waldweg *(m)*
forester's house Forsthaus *(n)*
forfeited advance deopsit (schedule 6) verlorene Gästeanzahlung *(f)* (Umsatzbereich 6)
fork Gabel *(f)*
form Formular *(n)*
form of presentation Darstellungsform *(f)*
formal förmlich, formal
formal dinner förmliches, festliches Diner *(n)*
formal dress Gesellschaftskleidung *(f)*
formality Formalität *(f)*
format Darstellungsform *(f)*
formula Formel *(f)*
formulate formulieren
fortnight vierzehn Tage *(pl. m)*
fortress Festung *(f)*, Burg *(f)*
forward befördern, senden
forwarding agency Spedition *(f)*
forwarding agent Spediteur *(m)*
found article gefundener Gegenstand *(m)*
foundation Gründung *(f)*; Stiftung *(f)*
fountain Quelle *(f)*, Springbrunnen *(m)*, Brunnen *(m)*
fowl Geflügel *(n)*
foyer Foyer *(n)*
fragrance Geruch *(m)*

France Frankreich
franchise in Franchise vergeben
franchise fee Franchise-Gebühr *(f)*
franchise operator Franchise-Unternehmer *(m)*
franchise-agreement Franchise-Vertrag *(m)*
franchisee Franchise-Nehmer *(m)*
franchising Franchising *(n)*
franchisor Franchise-Geber *(m)*
Frankfurter sausage Frankfurter Würstchen *(n)*
Frankfurters Frankfurter Würstchen *(pl. n)*
franking machine Freistempler *(m)*, Frankiermaschine *(f)*
free frei, unentgeltlich
free baggage allowance Freigepäck *(n)*
free currency konvertierbare Währung *(f)*
free economy Verkehrswirtschaft *(f)*
free enterprise economy freie Marktwirtschaft *(f)*
free from fog nebelfrei
free from ice eisfrei
free gift Zugabe *(f)*
free gift advertising Werbung *(f)* durch Zugaben *(pl.f)*, Zugabewerbung *(f)*
free lance selbständig
free lodging freie Unterkunft *(f)* (z.B. für Busfahrer, Reiseleiter etc.)
free of charge ohne Berechnung *(f)*
free on board (f.o.b.) frei an Bord *(m)*
free on quay (f.o.q.) frei Kai *(m)*
free on rail (f.o.r.) frei Eisenbahn *(f)*
free on truck (f.o.t.) frei Waggon *(m)*
free parking gebührenfreies Parken *(n)*
free port Freihafen *(m)*
free sale Verkauf *(m)* ohne Einschränkung *(f)* hinsichtlich Zeitraum *(m)* und Umfang *(m)*
free ticket Freikarte *(f)*
Free Trade Area Freihandelszone *(f)*
freeway Autobahn *(f)*
freight Fracht *(f)*
freight aircraft Frachtflugzeug *(n)*
freight bill Frachtrechnung *(f)*

freight car Güterwagen *(m)*
freight charges Frachtkosten *(pl.)*
freight elevator Lastenaufzug *(m)*
freight service Luftfrachtspedition *(f)*
freight station Güterbahnhof *(m)*
freight traffic Güterverkehr *(m)*
freight train Güterzug *(m)*
freightage Frachtgebühr *(f)*
freighter Frachtschiff *(n)*
freightliner train Containerzug *(m)*
French bean grüne Bohne *(f)*
French beans salad grüner Bohnensalat *(m)*
french bed Französisches Bett *(n)*
French dressing französische Salatsoße *(f)*
French fish soup Fischsuppe *(f)*
French fried potatoes Pommes frites *(pl.)*, gebackene Kartoffelstäbchen *(pl. n)*
French pepper-stew Pfefferschoten-Mischgericht *(n)*
frequency Häufigkeit *(f)*
frequent häufig
frequented vielbesucht
fresh frisch, kühl
fresh egg Trinkei *(n)*
fresh fruit cup Obstsalat *(m)*
fresh water Frischwasser *(n)*
fresh water crayfish Süßwasserkrebs *(m)*
fresh-water fish Süßwasserfisch *(m)*
fresh-water swimming pool Süßwasserschwimmbad *(n)*
fricadelle Frikadelle *(f)*
fricandeau of veal Kalbsfricandeau *(n)*
fricasee of veal Kalksfrikassee *(n)*
fricassee Frikassee *(n)*, Ragout *(n)*
fricasséed gehackt
fridge Kühlschrank *(m)*
fried gebraten, in Öl *(n)* gebacken
fried button mushrooms gebackene Champignons *(pl. m)*
fried chicken Brathuhn *(n)*
fried eggs Setzeier *(pl. n)*, Spiegeleier *(pl. n)*
fried kipper gebratener Räucherhering *(m)*
fried pork cutlet gebackenes Schweinekotelett *(n)*

fried potato balls Pariser Kartoffeln *(pl. f)*
fried potato wafers Waffelkartoffeln *(pl. f)*
fried potatoes Bratkartoffeln *(pl. f)*
fried sausage Bratwürstchen *(n)*
fried sippets Röstbrotwürfelchen *(pl. n)*
fried slice of veal Vienna style Wiener Schnitzel *(n)*
fritter Fettgebackenes *(n)*, Krapfen *(m)*, Küchlein *(n)*
fritters arme Ritter *(pl. m)*
frog Frosch *(m)*
frog fish Seeteufel
frog-leg Froschschenkel *(m)*
front desk Empfangspult *(m)*
front door Haustür *(f)*
front office department Empfangsabteilung *(f)*
front office manager Empfangschef *(m)*
front office staff Empfangspersonal *(n)*
front-room Vorderzimmer *(n)*
front seat Vordersitz *(m)*
frontier Grenze *(f)*, Landesgrenze *(f)*
frontier area Grenzgebiet *(n)*
frontier crossing Grenzübergang *(m)*, Grenzübertritt *(m)*
frontier crossing point Grenzübergangsstelle *(f)*
frontier formalities Grenzformalitäten *(pl. f)*
frontier station Grenzbahnhof *(m)*
frontier town Grenzstadt *(f)*
frontier zone Grenzzone *(f)*
frost Frost *(m)*
frozen gefroren
frozen food Tiefkühlerzeugnis *(n)*, Gefriergut *(n)*
fruit Frucht *(f)*, Früchte *(pl. f)*, Obst *(n)*
fruit-basket Früchtekorb *(m)*
fruit bowl Obstschüssel *(f)*
fruit cake Obstkuchen *(m)*
fruit flan Obsttorte *(f)*
fruit jelly Obstgelee *(n)*
fruit juice Fruchtsaft *(m)*
fruit pie Obstkuchen *(m)*
fruit salad Obstsalat *(m)*

fruit savarin Hefeteigkuchen mit Früchten *(m)*
fruit sundae Fruchteiscreme *(f)*
fruit tart Obsttorte *(f)*
fruiterer Obsthändler *(m)*
fruits Früchte *(pl. f)*
fruity fruchtig
fry braten, backen
frying-pan Bratpfanne *(f)*
fuel Heizöl *(n)*, Treibstoff *(m)*, Benzin *(n)*
fuel tank Benzintank *(m)*
fulfill erfüllen, vollziehen
fulfilment Erfüllung *(f)*, Vollziehung *(f)*
full besetzt, ausgebucht, ausverkauft
full bath Vollbad *(n)*
full board Vollpension *(f)*
full board and lodging Vollpension *(f)*
full-bodied schwer (Wein)
full coverage volle Risikoübernahme *(f)*
full-flavoured voll im Geschmack *(m)*
full liability Vollhaftung *(f)*
full massage Vollmassage *(f)*
full moon Vollmond *(m)*
full pension Vollpension *(f)*
full ship beladenes Schiff *(n)*
fullage volljährig
fully air-conditioned vollklimatisiert
fully licensed Ausschankberechtigung *(f)* alkoholischer Getränke *(pl. n)*
fun Spaß *(m)*
fun-fair Rummelplatz *(m)*, Jahrmarkt *(m)*
function Tätigkeit *(f)*, Funktion *(f)*
function room Veranstaltungsraum *(m)*, Gesellschaftszimmer *(n)*
function sheet Bankettinformation *(f)*
funds Geldmittel *(pl. n)*, Kapital *(n)*
funds Kapital *(n)*, Fonds *(m)*, Mittel *(pl.)*
funnel Trichter *(m)*
fur coat Pelzmantel *(m)*
furnish bereitstellen, möblieren
furnish meals without charge kostenlos Essen *(n)* ausgeben
furnished apartment möblierte Wohnung *(f)*

furnished house möbliertes Haus *(n)*
furnished selfcontained flat möbliertes Appartement *(n)*
furnishings and equipment Mobiliar *(n)* und Ausstattungsgegenstände *(pl. m)*
furniture and fixtures Einrichtungsgegenstände *(pl. m)*
furniture, fixtures, equipment, and decor (schedule 12) Möbel *(pl. n)*, Einbauten *(pl.)*, Ausstattung *(f)* und Dekor *(n)* (Service Center 12)
furred game Haarwild *(n)*
furrier Pelzgeschäft *(n)*
fuse Sicherung *(f)*
fuselage Flugzeugrumpf *(m)*

G

gaiety Heiterkeit *(f)*, Fröhlichkeit *(f)*
gain Gewinn *(m)*, Vorteil *(m)*, gewinnen
gain contingencies unsichere Ansprüche *(pl. m)*
gain (or loss) on sale of property (schedule 14) Veräußerungsgewinne *(pl. m)* (oder -verluste) aus dem Verkauf *(m)* von Anlagevermögen *(n)*
gala dinner Festessen *(n)*
gala performance Festvorstellung *(f)*
gallery Galerie *(f)*
gallon Gallone *(f)*
gamble spielen
gambler Spieler *(m)*
gambling Glücksspiel *(n)*
gambling casino Spielkasino *(n)*, Spielbank *(f)*
gambling debt Spielschuld *(f)*
gambling table Spieltisch *(m)*
game Wildbret *(n)*, Wildfleisch *(n)*
gamekeeper Jagdaufseher *(m)*
game licence Jagdschein *(m)*
game of cards Kartenspiel *(n)*
game of chance Glücksspiel *(n)*
game reserve Jagdreservat *(n)*
games deck Sportdeck *(n)*
games room Spielzimmer *(n)*
gammon Räucherschinken *(m)*

gangway Landungsbrücke *(f)*
gap Lücke *(f)*
garage Garage *(f)*,
Reparaturwerkstätte *(f)*
garage and parking (schedule 5)
Garage *(f)* und Parkplatz *(m)*
(Umsatzbereich 5)
garage assistant Tankwart *(m)*
garage-parking lot Garage *(f)*,
Parkplatz *(m)*
garden city Gartenstadt *(f)*
garden party Gartenfest *(n)*
gardener Gärtner *(m)*
gardens Liegewiese *(f)*
garlic Knoblauch *(m)*
garlic sauce Knoblauchsoße *(f)*
garment Gewand *(n)*
garnish garnieren, Suppeneinlage *(f)*
garnished garniert
garnishing Garnierung *(f)*
garret Dachkammer *(f)*
gas cooker Gasherd *(m)*
gas-cooker range Gasherd *(m)*
gas lighter Gasfeuerzeug *(n)*
gas tap Gashahn *(m)*
gasoline Benzin *(n)*
gasoline can Benzinkanister *(m)*
gasoline coupon Benzinschein *(m)*
gastronomy Gastronomie *(f)*
gate Tor *(n)*, Flugsteig *(m)*
gateway Flugsteig *(m)*
gathering Beisammensein *(n)*
gear-change Gangschaltung *(f)*
gear lever Schalthebel *(m)*
geese Gänse *(pl.f)*
general accounting principles
allgemeine Bilanzierungsgrundsätze *(pl.m)*
general delivery postlagernd
general ledger Hauptbuch *(n)*
general manager Generaldirektor *(m)*
general overhaul
Generalüberholung *(f)*,
Großreparatur *(f)*
general partner unbeschränkt
(persönlich) haftender Gesellschafter *(m)*, Komplementär *(m)*
general store
Gemischtwarenhandlung *(f)*,
allgemeines Lager *(n)*

general tariff Regeltarif *(m)*
general travel conditions
allgemeine Reisebedingungen *(pl.f)*
general-tariff ticket Fahrkarte *(f)*
zum vollen Preis *(m)*
generally accepted accounting principles Grundsätze *(pl.m)*
ordnungsmäßiger Buchführung *(f)*
und Bilanzierung *(f)*
generous freigiebig, großzügig
gentlemen's cloak-room
Herrentoilette *(f)*
gentlemen's hairdresser
Herrenfriseur *(m)*
gentlemen's lavatory Herrentoilette *(f)*
German Automobile Club
Allgemeiner Deutscher
Automobilclub ADAC *(m)*
German Camping Club Deutscher
Camping-Club (DCC) *(m)*
German Federal Railways
Deutsche Bundesbahn (DB) *(f)*
German Hotel and Catering Association Deutscher Hotel- und Gaststättenverband (DEHOGA) *(m)*
German light (dark) beer deutsches
helles (dunkles) Bier *(n)*
German pot roast Sauerbraten *(m)*
German Sleeping and Dining Car Company Deutsche Schlaf- und Speisewagengesellschaft (DSG) *(f)*
German-speaking guide
deutschsprechender Fremdenführer *(m)*
German Tourist Association
Deutscher
Fremdenverkehrsverband, (DFV) *(m)*
get in einsteigen
get in lane sich einordnen
get lost sich verirren
get off aussteigen
get rid of loswerden
get up aufstehen
get well again sich erholen
gherkin Essiggurke *(f)*
gherkin in picca-lilli Senfgurke *(f)*
giant slalom Riesenslalom *(m)*
giblet soup Geflügelkleinsuppe *(f)*

giblets of chicken Geflügelklein *(n)*
giblets of goose Gänseklein *(n)*
gift Geschenk *(n)*, Schenkung *(f)*
gift article Geschenkartikel *(m)*
gift shop Geschenkladen *(m)*
gift token Geschenkgutschein *(m)*
gilt head Goldmakrele *(f)*
gin Gin *(m)*
Gin and French englischer Cocktail (Martini dry Cocktail)
Gin and It englischer Cocktail (Martini sweet ähnlich)
ginger Ingwer *(m)*
ginger beer Ingwerbier *(n)*
ginger pudding Ingwerpudding *(m)*
gingerale Ingwerlimonade *(f)*
gingerbread Lebkuchen *(m)*, Pfefferkuchen *(m)*
gipsy Zigeuner *(m)*
giro Postscheck *(m)*
give notice kündigen
give up aufgeben, preisgeben, verzichten
give way Vorfahrt beachten!
give-away weggeben; Werbegeschenk *(n)*, Gutschein *(m)*
glacial ice Gletschereis *(n)*
glacial lake Gletschersee *(m)*
glacier Gletscher *(m)*
glacier lake Gletschersee *(m)*
glacier travel Gletscherwanderung *(f)*
glass Glas *(n)*
glass fibre ski Glasfaserski *(m)*
glass-washing machine Abwaschmaschine *(f)* für Gläser *(pl. n)*
glassware Glaswaren *(pl. f)*, Gläser *(pl. n)*
glazed frost Glatteis *(n)*
glide segelfliegen, segeln
glider Segelflugzeug *(n)*
gliding Segelfliegen *(n)*, Segelflugsport *(m)*
globe-trotter Weltenbummler *(m)*, Globetrotter *(m)*
glossy glänzend
glove Handschuh *(m)*
glue Klebstoff *(m)*
glutton Vielfraß *(m)*
go gehen
go abroad ins Ausland *(n)* reisen
go ashore an Land *(n)* gehen

go away on holiday verreisen
go by car mit dem Auto *(n)* fahren
go on board an Bord *(m)* gehen
go straight on gehen Sie geradeaus!
goal Ziel *(n)*, Tor *(n)* (Sport)
goalkeeper Torwart *(m)*
goat Ziege *(f)*
goat cheese Ziegenkäse *(m)*
goby Gründling *(m)*
golden mackerel Goldmakrele *(f)*
golf course Golfplatz *(m)*
golf equipment Golfausrüstung *(f)*
golfer Golfspieler *(m)*
gondola Gondel *(f)*
gondola ride Gondelfahrt *(f)*
good afternoon Guten Tag!
good evening Guten Abend!
good faith guter Glaube *(m)*
Good Friday Karfreitag *(m)*
good morning Guten Morgen!
good night Gute Nacht!
good-bye Auf Wiedersehen
goods Waren *(pl. f)*, Güter *(pl. n)*
goods afloat schwimmende Ware *(f)*
goods elevator Lastenaufzug *(m)*
goods in bond Waren *(pl. f)* unter Zollverschluß *(m)*
goods in hand Warenvorrat *(m)*
goods in process Halbfabrikate *(pl. n)*
goods station Güterbahnhof *(m)*
goods tariff Frachttarif *(m)*
goods traffic Güterverkehr *(m)*
goods train Güterzug *(m)*
goods waggon Güterwagen *(m)*
goodwill Firmenwert *(m)*
goose Gans *(f)*
goose liver Gänseleber *(f)*
gooseliver-mousse Gänselebermousse *(f)*
goose liver pie Gänseleberpastete *(f)*
gooseberry Stachelbeere *(f)*
Gorgonzola Gorgonzola *(m)*
gossip Gerücht *(n)*, Tratsch *(m)*, Geschwätz *(n)*
goulash Gulasch *(n)*
goulash soup Gulaschsuppe *(f)*
gourmand Vielfraß *(m)*
gourmet Feinschmecker *(m)*
gourmet restaurant Feinschmeckerrestaurant *(n)*

gourmet's meal Feinschmeckeressen *(n)*
government controlled economy Zentralverwaltungswirtschaft *(f)*
gown Kleid *(n)*
grade Güteklasse *(f)*; Steigung *(f)*
grade crossing Bahnübergang *(m)*
grade labelling Qualitätskennzeichnung *(f)*
gradient Steigung *(f)*
grading klassifizieren, Klassifikation *(f)*
grand piano Flügel *(m)*
grand-stand Tribüne *(f)*
grand total Endsumme *(f)*, Abschlußsumme *(f)*
grant gewähren; Bewilligung *(f)*
grant a commission Provision *(f)* gewähren
grant a credit einen Kredit *(m)* gewähren
grape Traube *(f)*
grape cure Traubenkur *(f)*
grape juice Traubensaft *(m)*
grape-nuts Teiggraupen *(pl.f)*
grapefruit Pampelmuse *(f)*, Grapefruit *(f)*
grapefruit juice Pampelmusensaft *(m)*, Grapefruitsaft *(m)*
grapevine Weinstock *(m)*; Gerücht *(n)*
grasp Arbeitsgriff *(m)*
grate reiben
grated cheese geriebener Käse *(m)*
grater Reibeisen *(n)*
gratinated gratiniert, überbacken
gratuitous grundlos, kostenlos, unentgeltlich
gratuity Geschenk *(n)*, Gratifikation *(f)*, Trinkgeld *(n)*
gravy Bratensoße *(f)*
grayling Äsche *(f)*
grease einfetten, abschmieren
greaseproof paper Fettpapier *(n)*
greasing service Abschmierdienst *(m)*
great bustle Hochbetrieb *(m)*
greedy gierig, gefräßig
green beans grüne Bohnen *(pl.f)*
green belt grüner Gürtel *(m)*
green cabbage Grünkohl *(m)*

green cheese Kräuterkäse *(m)*
green noodles grüne Nudeln *(pl.f)*
green pea grüne Erbse *(f)*
green pepper grüne Paprikaschote *(f)*
green salad grüner Salat *(m)*
green vinegar sauce grüne Essigsoße *(f)*
greengage Reineclaude *(f)*
greengrocer Obst- und Gemüsehändler *(m)*
Greenwich mean time Weltzeit *(f)*
greeting Gruß *(m)*
greetings card Grußkarte *(f)*, Ansichtskarte *(f)*
grief Kummer *(m)*
grievance Beschwerde *(f)*, Mißstand *(m)*
grill Grill *(m)*, Rost *(m)*
grill-bar Grillbar *(f)*
grill-room Grillstube *(f)*, Grillrestaurant *(n)*
grilled vom Grill *(m)*
grilled bread Toast *(m)*, Röstbrot *(n)*
grilled fillet of wild boar gegrilltes Wildschweinfilet *(n)*
grilled meat Fleisch vom Grill *(n)*
grilled pork chop gegrilltes Schweinekotelett *(n)*
grilled pork cutlet gegrilltes Schweineschnitzel *(n)*
grilled sausages with sauerkraut Bratwürstchen *(pl.n)* mit Sauerkraut *(n)*
grilled snipes gegrillte Schnepfen *(pl.f)*
grits gekühlte Gemüsesuppe *(f)*
grocer Lebensmitteleinzelhändler *(m)*
grocery story Kolonialwarengeschäft *(n)*
grog Grog *(m)*
gross brutto
gross profit (loss) (schedule 2) Bruttoergebnis *(n)* (Gewinn oder Verlust) (Umsatzbereich 2)
gross weight Bruttogewicht *(n)*
grotto Grotte *(f)*
ground Boden *(m)*, Grund *(m)*
ground coffee gemahlener Bohnenkaffee *(m)*
ground floor Erdgeschoß *(n)*, Parterre *(n)*

ground hostess Bodenstewardeß *(f)*
ground meat Hackfleisch *(n)*
grounds and landscaping (schedule 12) (Pflege von) Gärten *(pl. m)* und Parkanlagen *(pl. f)* (Service Center 12)
group advertising Gemeinschaftswerbung *(f)*
group business promotion Gemeinschaftsverkaufsförderung *(f)*
group buying Sammeleinkauf *(m)*
group discount Gruppenermäßigung *(f)*
group insurance Gruppenversicherung *(f)*
group journey Gruppenreise *(f)*
group leader Gruppenleiter *(m)*
group passport Sammelpaß *(m)*
group travel Gesellschaftsreiseverkehr *(m)*
group visa Sammelvisum *(n)*
group visit Gruppenbesichtigung *(f)*
grouse Auerhahn *(m)*
grouse, black Birkhuhn *(n)*
grow wachsen (größer werden)
grown-up Erwachsener *(m)*
growth Wachstum *(n)*
growth rate Wachstumsrate *(f)*
gruel Haferschleim *(m)*
Gruyère cheese Gruyèrekäse *(m)*
guarantee garantieren, Garantie *(f)*
guarantee of a bill (of exchange) Wechselbürgschaft *(f)*
guarantee somebody's debt für jds. Schulden *(pl. f)* bürgen
guaranteed booking garantierte Buchung *(f)*
guaranteed payment reservation garantierte Buchung *(f)*
guaranteed reservation feste Reservierung *(f)*
guard Bewachung *(f)*, Schaffner *(m)*, Zugbegleiter *(m)*, Zugschaffner *(m)*
guarded camping-site bewachter Campingplatz *(m)*
guarded car park bewachter Parkplatz *(m)*
guest Gast *(m)*
guest count Gästeanzahl *(f)*, Gästezählung *(f)*
guest encounter Gästebegrüßung *(f)*

guest house Pension *(f)*
guest laundry Gästewäsche *(f)*
guest on an expense account Spesengast *(m)*
guest pass Feriennetzkarte *(f)*
guest performance Gastspiel *(n)*
guest questionnaire Gästefragebogen *(m)*
guest registration Gästeregistrierung *(f)*
guest relations (front office) Umgang *(m)* mit Gästen *(pl. m)* (Empfang)
guest-room Gästezimmer *(n)*, Fremdenzimmer *(n)*, Logierzimmer *(n)*
guests' supplies Gästegeschenke *(pl. n)*, Aufmerksamkeiten für Gäste *(pl. m)*
guide Reiseführer *(m)*, Fremdenführer *(m)*; Ratgeber *(m)*, Leitkarte *(f)*
guide-book Reiseführer *(m)*
guide service Lotsendienst *(m)*
guided tour Gesellschaftsreise *(f)*
guided visit Führung *(f)*
guidepost Wegweiser *(m)*
guinea-fowl Perlhuhn *(n)*
gulp verschlingen
gum boots Gummistiefel *(pl. m)*
gurnard Knurrhahn *(m)*
gurnet Knurrfisch *(m)*
gust Bö *(f)*, Windstoß *(m)*
guzzle saufen
gym Sporthalle *(f)*, Turnhalle *(f)*
gym shoes Turnschuhe *(pl. m)*
gymnasium Turnhalle *(f)*
gymnastics Gymnastik *(f)*

H

haberdasher Kurzwarenladen *(m)*
habit Gewohnheit *(f)*
hacking Pferdeverleih *(m)*
hackney-cab Pferdedroschke *(f)*
haddock Schellfisch *(m)*
hail insurance Hagelversicherung *(f)*
hair-cut Haarschnitt *(m)*
hair-grip Haarklemme *(f)*
hair lotion Haarwasser *(n)*

hair-net Haarnetz *(n)*
hair-slide Spange *(f)*
hair-style Frisur *(f)*
hairbrush Haarbürste *(f)*
hairdresser at the hotel
 Hotelfriseur *(m)*
hairdresser's saloon Frisiersalon *(m)*
hairpin Haarnadel *(f)*
hairpin bend Haarnadelkurve *(f)*
hake Kabeljau *(m)*, Seehecht *(m)*
half a bottle eine halbe Flasche *(f)*
half a fried chicken ein halbes Backhuhn *(n)*
half a portion eine halbe Portion *(f)*
half moons Hörnchen *(n)* (Gebäck)
half-day halbtags
half-day excursion Halbtagsausflug *(m)*
half-fare halber Preis *(m)*
half-pension Halbpension *(f)*
half-price zum halben Preis *(m)*
half-timbered house Fachwerkhaus *(n)*
halibut Heilbutt *(m)*
hall porter Hotelportier *(m)*
hall-stand Kleiderablage *(f)*
halt Aufenthalt *(m)*, Halt *(m)*, halten
halt at major road ahead Halt-Vorfahrt *(f)* beachten
ham Schinken *(m)*
ham and eggs Spiegeleier *(pl.n)* mit Schinken *(m)*
ham, boiled gekochter Schinken *(m)*
ham cured Schinken gepökelt *(m)*
ham omelet Schinkenomelett *(n)*
ham raw roher Schinken *(m)*
ham smoked geräucherter Schinken *(m)*
Hamburger Hamburger *(m)*, Hackbeefsteak *(n)*
Hamburger steak Hamburger *(m)*, Hackbeefsteak *(n)*
hammock Hängematte *(f)*
hand Hand *(f)*, aushändigen
hand bellows Handblasebalg *(m)*
hand brake Handbremse *(f)*
hand luggage Handgepäck *(n)*
hand out Unterlage *(f)*, Pressemitteilung *(f)*
hand-napkin Handserviette *(f)*
hand-operated handbetrieben

handbag Handtasche *(f)*
handicraft Handwerk *(n)*
handing out of baggage
 Gepäckausgabe *(f)*
handkerchief Taschentuch *(n)*
handle anfassen, Griff *(m)*, handhaben
handling (of guest complaints) Handhabung *(f)* (z.B. von Gästebeschwerden)
handover aushändigen, übergeben
handsome hübsch
hangar Flugzeughalle *(f)*, Hangar *(m)*
hanger Kleiderbügel *(m)*
hangover Kater *(m)*, Katzenjammer *(m)*
hangover breakfast Katerfrühstück *(n)*
happen geschehen, vorfallen, passieren
harbour dues Hafengebühren *(pl.f)*
harbour mouth Hafenausfahrt *(f)*, Hafeneinfahrt *(f)*
harbour police Hafenpolizei *(f)*
harbour station Hafenbahnhof *(m)*
harbour tug Hafenschlepper *(m)*
harbour (harbor) Hafen *(m)*
hard hart
hard cider Apfelwein *(m)*
hard-boiled hartgekocht
hard-boiled eggs hartgekochte Eier *(pl.n)*
hard-cooked hartgekocht
hard currency harte Währung *(f)*
hard disc Plattenlaufwerk *(n)*
hard liquor Schnaps *(m)*
hard sausage Dauerwurst *(f)*
hard-shell crabs Krabben *(pl.f)*
hardware Maschinen *(pl.f)* eines elektronischen Datenverarbeitungssystems *(n)*, Hardware *(f)*
hare Hase *(m)*
haricot bean grüne Bohne *(f)*
haricot soup Bohnensuppe *(f)*
harm verletzen, Verletzung *(f)*
harpoon Harpune *(f)*
harvest Ernte *(f)*
harvest thanksgiving Erntedankfest *(n)*
hash Ragout *(n)*
hash brown potatoes Rösti *(f)*

hashed gehackt
hashed meat Hackbraten *(m)*
hashed steak Russian style
  Hackbeefsteak *(n)* in Rahmsoße *(f)*
haste Eile *(f)*, Hast *(f)*
hatbox Hutkoffer *(m)*
hatch Luke *(f)*
haunch Keule *(f)*
haunch of vension Rehkeule *(f)*
hay Heu *(n)*
haystack Heuhaufen *(m)*
hazard Risiko *(n)*, Gefährdung *(f)*
hazel-hen Haselhuhn *(n)*
hazelnut Haselnuß *(f)*
hazelnut tart Haselnußtorte *(f)*
hazy dunstig, verschwommen
head Kopf *(m)*
head cheese Preßkopf *(m)*
head for ansteuern
head of a train Zugspitze *(f)*
head of wild boar
  Wildschweinskopf (gefüllt)
head office Hauptbüro *(n)*, Zentrale *(f)*
head waiter Oberkellner *(m)*
headache Kopfschmerz *(m)*
heading Überschrift *(f)*
headlight Scheinwerfer *(m)*
headquarter Hauptverwaltung *(f)*
health Gesundheit *(f)*, Gesundheitszustand *(m)*
health certificate
  Gesundheitszeugnis *(n)*
health club Fitness-Studio *(n)*, Regenerationszentrum *(n)*
health insurance
  Krankenversicherung *(f)*
health insurance for abroad
  Auslandskrankenversicherung *(f)*
health resort Kurort *(m)*, Heilbad *(n)*
health resort patient Kurpatient *(m)*
hearsay Hörensagen *(n)*
heart Herz *(n)*
heart of artichoke Artischockenherz *(n)*
heart of the matter der eigentliche Kern *(m)* der Sache *(f)*, des Pudels Kern *(m)*
hearts of palm Palmenmark *(n)*
hearty stark, herzhaft, herzlich
heat Hitze *(f)*

heat therapy Bestrahlung *(f)*
heath Heide *(f)*
heath cock Birkhahn *(m)*
heath hen Birkhuhn *(n)*
heating Heizung *(f)*
heavy wine schwerer Wein *(m)*
hedge Hecke *(f)*
height Höhe *(f)*
height of the season Hochsaison *(f)*
height restriction Höhenbegrenzung *(f)*
helicopter Helikopter *(m)*, Hubschrauber *(m)*
helicopterport
  Hubschrauberflugplatz *(m)*
heliotherapy Sonnenkur *(f)*
helm Steuer *(n)*
helmsman Steuermann *(m)*
help Hilfe *(f)*, helfen
hem Saum *(m)*
hen Henne *(f)*
hen-chicken Hühnchen *(n)*
herb Kraut *(n)*
herring salad Heringssalat *(m)*
hidden offer verstecktes Angebot *(n)*
hidden reserves stille Rücklagen *(pl.f)*
high altitude Höhenlage *(f)*
high altitude health resort
  Höhenluftkurort *(m)*
high-class hotel 1a-Hotel *(n)*, erstklassiges Hotel *(n)*
high-diving tower Sprungturm *(m)*
high mountains Hochgebirge *(n)*
high plateau Hochplateau *(n)*
high seas hohe See *(f)*
high season Hochsaison *(f)*
high-speed bus Schnellbus *(m)*
high-speed road Schnellstraße *(f)*
high tea Nachmittagstee *(m)* und Abendessen *(n)* kombiniert
high value hochwertig
highest bid Höchstgebot *(n)*
highlight Schlaglicht *(n)*, hervorheben
highly seasoned scharf gewürzt
highway Hauptverkehrsstraße *(f)*
highway carrier
  Straßentransportunternehmen *(n)*
hijacking Flugzeugentführung *(f)*
hike wandern, Fußwanderung *(f)*
hike on skis Skiwanderung *(f)*

hiker Wanderer *(m)*
hikers' guide Wanderführer *(m)*
hiking Wandern *(n)*, Wandertourismus *(m)*, Wandersport *(m)*
hiking region Wandergebiet *(n)*
hill Steigung *(f)*, Gefälle *(n)*
hinterland Hinterland *(n)*
hip Hagebutte *(f)*; Hüfte *(f)*
hip-bath Sitzbad *(n)*
hip-tea Hagebuttentee *(m)*
hire mieten, Miete *(f)*
hire charge Verleihgebühr *(f)*
hire service Verleih *(m)*
hired car Leihwagen *(m)*, Mietwagen *(m)*
hirer Vermieter *(m)*
hiring policy Einstellungspolitik *(f)*
hiring procedure Einstellungsverfahren *(n)*
historical building historisches Bauwerk *(n)*
historical data historische Daten *(pl.)* (Daten der Vergangenheit)
hitch-hike per Anhalter *(m)* reisen
hitch-hiker Tramper *(m)*
hock Rheinwein *(m)*
hoist hissen, hochziehen
hold Laderaum *(m)*
hold accountable verantwortlich machen
hold on am Apparat *(m)* (Telefon) bleiben
hold the line am Apparat *(m)* (Telefon) bleiben
holder Inhaber *(m)*
holding company Dachgesellschaft *(f)*, Besitzgesellschaft *(f)*, Holding *(f)*
holiday Feiertag *(m)*, Ferientag *(m)*
Holiday air travel Flugtouristik *(f)*
holiday camp Ferienlager *(n)*
holiday country Ferienland *(n)*, Fremdenverkehrsland *(n)*
holiday course Ferienkurs *(m)*
holiday flat Ferienunterkunft *(f)*, Ferienwohnung *(f)*
holiday gift Reisemitbringsel *(n)*
holiday guest Feriengast *(m)*
holiday guide Ferienführer *(m)*
holiday hotel Ferienhotel *(n)*
holiday house Ferienhaus *(n)*, Sommerhaus *(n)*
holiday insurance Urlaubsversicherung *(f)*
holiday island Ferieninsel *(f)*
holiday leave Erholungsurlaub *(m)*
holiday-maker Urlaubsreisender *(m)*, Urlauber *(m)*
holiday pay Feiertagslohn *(m)*, Urlaubsgeld *(n)*
holiday place Urlaubsort *(m)*
holiday region Feriengebiet *(n)*
holiday resort Ferienort *(m)*, Erholungsort *(m)*
holiday runabout ticket Feriennetzkarte *(f)*
holiday season Urlaubszeit *(f)*, Ferienzeit *(f)*
holiday season ticket Feriennetzkarte *(f)*
holiday ticket Ferienfahrkarte *(f)*
holiday traffic Urlaubsverkehr *(m)*, Ferienverkehr *(m)*, Ausflugsverkehr *(m)*
holiday train Feriensonderzug *(m)*
holiday trip Ferienreise *(f)*, Urlaubsreise *(f)*
holiday village Feriendorf *(n)*
holiday weather Urlaubswetter *(n)*
holidays Urlaub *(m)*
Holland Holland
hollandaise sauce Sauce Hollandaise *(f)*
home address Heimatanschrift *(f)*
home computer Heimcomputer *(m)*
home country Heimat *(f)*
home for old people Altersheim *(n)*
homeless obdachlos
homely gutbürgerlich (Küche)
home-made hausgemacht
home-made noodles hausgemachte Nudeln *(pl.f)*
home office Zentrale *(f)*
home port Heimathafen *(m)*
homeward journey Heimreise *(f)*
homeward tourist traffic Rückreiseverkehr *(m)*
hominy Maisbrei *(m)*
honest ehrlich
honey Honig *(m)*
honeymoon Hochzeitsreise *(f)*, Flitterwochen *(pl.)*
honking Hupen *(n)*

honor (credit card) akzeptieren, annehmen (Kreditkarte)
hood Haube *(f)*
hook Haken *(m)*
hooter Autohupe *(f)*
hoover Staubsauer *(m)*, staubsaugen
hop Hopfen *(m)*
hop sprouts Hopfensprossen *(pl.f)*
horn Hupe *(f)*
hors d'oeuvre Vorspeise *(f)*, Hors-d'oeuvre *(n)*
horse sleigh Pferdeschlitten *(m)*
horse-drawn vehicle Pferdewagen *(m)*
horse-race Pferderennen *(n)*
horse-radish Meerrettich *(m)*
horse-radish sauce Meerrettichsoße *(f)*
horses for hire Reitpferde *(pl.n)* zu vermieten
horticultural show Gartenschau *(f)*
hospice Hospiz *(n)*
hospitable gastlich, gastfreundlich
hospital Krankenhaus *(n)*
hospital benefits Krankenhauskostenzuschuß *(m)*
hospitality Gastfreundschaft *(f)*
hospitalization insurance Krankenhauskostenversicherung *(f)*
host Gastgeber *(m)*, Wirt *(m)*; Datenbankanbieter *(m)*
host country Gastland *(n)*
host family Gastfamilie *(f)*
hostel Herberge *(f)*, Heim *(n)*
hostess Hosteß *(f)*, Gastgeberin *(f)*
hot heiß
hot-air bath Schwitzbad *(n)*, Heißluftbad *(n)*
hot-air heating Luftheizung *(f)*
hot bacon tart Lothringer Specktorte *(f)*
hot broth Bouillon *(f)*
hot broth with liver dumplings Leberknödelsuppe *(f)*
hot claret with cinnamon and clove Glühwein *(m)*
hot dishes warme Speisen *(pl.f)*
hot dog Hot dog *(m)*
hot milk heiße Milch *(f)*
hot pot Eintopfgericht *(n)*
hot rum grog Grog mit Rum *(m)*

hot slices of Swiss cheese heißer Schabkäse *(m)*
hot Swiss cheesemush Käsefondue *(n)*
hot water Warmwasser *(n)*, Heißwasser *(n)*
hot-water bottle Wärmflasche *(f)*
hot wine Glühwein *(m)*
hotel Hotel *(n)*, Gasthaus *(n)*
hotel accommodation Hotelunterbringung *(f)*, Hotelunterkunft *(f)*
hotel and catering trade Hotellerie *(f)*, Hotel- und Gaststättengewerbe *(n)*
hotel and restaurant business Gastgewerbe *(n)*
hotel and restaurant guide Hotel- und Gaststättenführer *(m)*
hotel and tourist industry Fremdenverkehrsindustrie *(f)*
hotel and tourist trade Fremdenverkehrsgewerbe *(n)*
hotel association Hotelverband *(m)*
hotel bed Hotelbett *(n)*
hotel bedrooms surplus Hotelbettenüberschuß *(m)*
hotel bellboy Hotelboy *(m)*, Page *(m)*
hotel bill Hotelrechnung *(f)*
hotel booking Hotelreservierung *(f)*
hotel bookings Hotelbelegung *(f)*
hotel broker Hotelnachweis *(f)*
hotel building Hotelgebäude *(n)*
hotel business Hotelfach *(n)*
hotel capacity Hotelkapazität *(f)*
hotel car Schlafwagen *(m)* mit Speisewageneinrichtung *(f)*
hotel chain Hotelkette *(f)*
hotel contract Hotelvertrag *(m)*
hotel dining-room Hotelrestaurant *(n)*
hotel directory Hotelanzeiger *(m)*
hotel employee Hotelangestellter *(m)*
hotel entrance hall Hotelhalle *(f)*
hotel foyer Hotelhalle *(f)*
hotel fraud Zechprellerei *(f)*
hotel guest Hotelgast *(m)*
hotel guide Hotelführer *(m)*
hotelhood Hoteleigenschaft *(f)*
hotel industry Hotellerie *(f)*
hotelize in ein Hotel *(n)* verwandeln

hotel-keeper Hotelier *(m)*,
  Gastronom *(m)*
hotel-keeping Hotelführung *(f)*,
  Hotelwesen *(n)*
hotel label Hotelzettel *(m)* (Gepäck)
hotel lobby Hotelempfangshalle *(f)*
hotel lounge Aufenthaltsraum *(m)*
hotel management Hotelleitung *(f)*,
  Hoteldirektion *(f)*
hotel manager Hoteldirektor *(m)*
hotel occupancy Hotelbelegung *(f)*
hotel of international standard
  Hotel *(n)* internationaler Klasse *(f)*
hotel office Hotelbüro *(n)*
hotel operation Hotelbetrieb *(m)*
hotel owner Hotelbesitzer *(m)*
hotel pageboy Hotelpage *(m)*
hotel register Gästeverzeichnis *(n)*,
  Meldebuch *(n)*, Fremdenregister *(n)*
hotel representative
  Hotelrepräsentant *(m)*
hotel reservation
  Zimmerreservierung *(f)*
hotel room Hotelzimmer *(n)*
hotel rules and regulations
  Hotelordnung *(f)*
hotel side Hotelgelände *(n)*,
  Hotelgrundstück *(n)*
hotels information service
  Hotelnachweis *(m)*
hotel size Hotelgröße *(f)*
hotel staff Hotelpersonal *(n)*
hotel trade Hotelwesen *(n)*,
  Hotellerie *(f)*
hotel training school
  Hotelfachschule *(f)*
hotel under good management
  gutgeführtes Hotel *(n)*
hotel vestibule Hotelhalle *(f)*
hotel voucher Hotelgutschein *(m)*
hourly rate Stundenlohnsatz *(m)*
hours absent Fehlstunden *(pl.f)*
hours of rest Ruhezeiten *(pl.f)*
hours of service Betriebszeit *(f)*
hours worked geleistete
  Arbeitsstunden *(pl.f)*
house key Hausschlüssel *(m)*
house number Hausnummer *(f)*
house of accommodation
  Absteigequartier *(n)*
house organ Hauszeitung *(f)*

house rules Hausordnung *(f)*
house telephone Haustelefon *(n)*
housebuilding Wohnungsbau *(m)*
housecoat Hausmantel *(m)*
household goods Haushaltsgüter
  (pl.n)
housekeeper Hausdame *(f)*
housekeeping department
  Hausdamenbereich *(m)*,
  Hausreinigungsabteilung *(f)*
houseman Hoteldiener *(m)*,
  Reinigungspersonal *(n)*
housing allowance
  Wohnungsgeldzuschuß *(m)*
housing bureau Wohnungs- und
  Zimmervermittlung *(f)*
hover schweben
hovercraft Luftkissenboot *(n)*
hub Mittelpunkt *(m)*, Angelpunkt *(m)*
hull Schiffsrumpf *(m)*
human relations zwischenmenschliche Beziehungen *(pl.f)*
humid feucht, naß
humidity Feuchtigkeit *(f)*
Hungarian goulash ungarisches
  Gulasch *(n)*
Hungarian pork stew Szegediner
  Gulasch *(n)*
hunger Hunger *(m)*
hunt jagen, Jagd *(f)*
hunting Jagd *(f)*
hunting box Jagdhütte *(f)*
hunting ground Jagdrevier *(n)*,
  Jagdgebiet *(n)*
hunting season Jagdsaison *(f)*
hurt verletzen, Verletzung *(f)*
husband Gatte *(m)*, Mann *(m)*
hut Hütte *(f)*
hydrofoil Tragflächenboot *(n)*
hydropathic establishment Kur-
  badehaus *(n)*, Thermalbadehaus *(n)*
hydropathic treatment Kneippkur *(f)*
hydroplane Wasserflugzeug *(n)*
hypnotherapy Schlafkur *(f)*

I

ice Eis *(n)*, Speiseeis *(n)*
ice-bar Eisdiele *(f)*
ice-box Eisschrank *(m)*

ice-coated eisbedeckt
ice-cone Eistüte *(f)*
ice-cream Speiseeis *(n)*
ice-cream cake Eistorte *(f)*
ice-cream coffee Eiskaffee *(m)*
ice-cream cup Eisbecher *(m)*
ice-cream cup with hot chocolate-sauce Eisbecher mit heißer Schokoladensauce *(m)*
ice-cream meringue Eisbaiser *(m)*, Eismeringe *(f)*
ice-cream soufflè Eisauflauf *(m)*
ice-cream sundae Eisbecher *(m)*
ice-cream wafer Eiswaffel *(f)*
ice-cube Eiswürfel *(m)*
iced tea Eistee *(m)*
ice-free eisfrei
ice-freezer Eismaschine *(f)*
ice-hockey Eishockey *(n)*
ice machine Eismaschine *(f)*
ice man Eisverkäufer *(m)*
ice pail Eiskübel *(m)*, Weinkühler *(m)*
ice-parlo(u)r Eisdiele *(f)*
ice-skating Eislauf *(m)*, Eislaufen *(n)*
ice-soda Sodawasser *(n)* mit Speiseeis *(n)*
ice stadium Eisstadion *(n)*
ice water Eiswasser *(n)*
ice-yachting Eissegeln *(n)*
iced eisgekühlt, gefroren, überzuckert, mit Zuckerglasur *(f)*
iced chocolata Eisschokolade *(f)*
icicle Eiszapfen *(m)*
icing Zuckerguß *(m)*, Glasur *(f)*
icing sugar Puder-, Staubzucker *(m)*
icy eisig
idel untätig, stillstehend, unproduktiv
idel time Leerlaufzeit *(f)*
identification Identifizierung *(f)*
identification card Ausweis *(m)*
identification paper Ausweispapier *(n)*
identify identifizieren, erkennen
idiomatic spracheigentümlich
ignore übersehen, nicht beachten, nicht erkennen
ill krank
ill-treatment Mißhandlung *(f)*
illegal ungesetzlich, rechtswidrig
illicit work Schwarzarbeit *(f)*
illness Krankheit *(f)*, Erkrankung *(f)*

illness frequency rate Krankheitsrate *(f)*
illuminate beleuchten
illustrated booklet Bildprospekt *(m)*
immediate supervisor direkter Vorgesetzter *(m)*
immigrant Einwanderer *(m)*
immigrate einwandern
immigration Einwanderung *(f)*
immoral unsittlich
immorality Unsittlichkeit *(f)*, Sittenwidrigkeit *(f)*
immovables Immobilien *(pl.f)*
impact Wirkung *(f)*, Einwirkung *(f)*
impair vermindern, beeinträchtigen
impairment (of net assets) Wertminderung *(f)* (von Beteiligungen)
implement einführen, in die Praxis *(f)* umsetzen
implement Gerät *(n)*, Werkzeug *(n)*
implied stillschweigend
import einführen, importieren, Import *(m)*
import duty Einfuhrzoll *(m)*
import license Einfuhrgenehmigung *(f)*
import restriction Einfuhrbeschränkung *(f)*
import trade Einfuhrhandel *(m)*
impose a fine upon eine Geldstrafe *(f)* auferlegen
impose on auferlegen
impracticable undurchführbar
impress beeindrucken
imprint aufprägen, abdrucken
improper falsch
improve verbessern, vervollkommnen
improvement budget Modernisierungsplan *(m)*
imputed interest kalkulatorische Zinsen *(pl.)*
in accordance with local customs ortsüblich, landesüblich
in advance vorweg, im voraus, vorzeitig
in arrears im Rückstand *(m)*
in bond unter Zollverschluß *(m)*
in default of mangels
in due time termingerecht
in lien of anstatt

in the long run langfristig
in the open sea auf hoher See *(f)*
in the order of their liquidity nach Liquiditätsgesichtspunkten *(pl. m)*
in transit unterwegs
inaccuracy Ungenauigkeit *(f)*
inadequate unzulässig, unangemessen
inadmissible unzulässig
inalienable unveräußerlich
inapplicable nicht anwendbar
inattention Unaufmerksamkeit *(f)*
incapable unfähig
incentive Anreiz *(m)*, Ansporn *(m)*
incentive system Prämiensystem *(n)*
incidental charges Hotelnebenkosten *(pl.)*
incidental charges Nebenkosten *(pl.)*
include einschließen
inclusive einschließlich
inclusive air fare Flugpauschale *(f)*
inclusive air journey Flugpauschalreise *(f)*
inclusive arrangement Pauschalarrangement *(n)*
inclusive charge Pauschalgebühr *(f)*
inclusive fare Pauschalpreis *(m)*
inclusive holiday Pauschalpreisferien *(pl.)*
inclusive journey Pauschalreise *(f)*
inclusive of service and taxes einschließlich Bedienung *(f)* und Abgaben *(pl. f)*
inclusive price Pauschale *(f)*, Pauschalpreis *(m)*
inclusive rates for self-drive car hire Pauschalpreise *(pl. m)* für Selbstfahrer *(pl. m)*
inclusive single fare Einzelflugpauschale *(f)*
inclusive terms Pauschalarrangement *(n)*
inclusive trip Pauschalreise *(f)*
inclusive winter sports terms Wintersportarrangement *(n)*
incognito unerkannt, inkognito
income Einkommen *(n)*, Ertrag *(m)*
income tax Ertragssteuer *(f)*
income tax reserve Rückstellung *(f)* für Ertragssteuer *(f)*
incompatible unverträglich, unvereinbar

inconvertible unkonvertierbar
incorrect unrichtig
increase erhöhen, vermehren, Erhöhung *(f)*, Aufschlag *(m)*, Vermehrung *(f)*
increase in capacity Betriebserweiterung *(f)*, Kapazitätsausweitung *(f)*
increase of customs Zollerhöhung *(f)*
increase of wages Lohnerhöhung *(f)*
increment Zunahme *(f)*, (Wert-)Zuwachs *(m)*, (Wert-)Steigerung *(f)*; Aufschlag *(m)*
incur debts Schulden *(pl. f)* machen, in Schulden *(pl. f)* geraten
indebtedness Verschuldung *(f)*, Schuld *(f)*, Schuldenlast *(f)*
indemnity bond Ausfallbürgschaft *(f)*
indemnity liability Abfindungsverpflichtung *(f)*
indenture of apprenticeship Lehrvertrag *(m)*
independent unabhängig
index Verzeichnis *(n)*
index figure Kennzahl *(f)*
Indian corn Mais *(m)*
indication Heilanzeige *(f)*
indigestion Verdauungsstörung *(f)*
indirect advertising indirekte Werbung *(f)*
indispensable unerläßlich
individual einzeln, individuell
individual care persönliche Betreuung *(f)*
individual inclusive journey Einzelpauschalreise *(f)*
individual journey Einzelreise *(f)*
individual return Einzelrückfahrt *(f)*
individual traveller Einzelreisender *(m)*
individually persönlich
indoor sport Hallensport *(m)*
indoor swimmingpool Hallenschwimmbad *(n)*
induction Einführung *(f)*
induction training Einführungsschulung *(f)*
industrial area Industriegebiet *(n)*
industrial fair Industrieausstellung *(f)*
industry fair Industriemesse *(f)*

ineffective außer Kraft *(f)*, unwirksam
inefficient unwirtschaftlich, erfolglos
inexpensive billig, nicht teuer
inexperienced unerfahren
infant Säugling *(m)*; Minderjähriger *(m)*
infant's carrying basket Babytragekorb *(m)*
inferior minderwertig
inflammable leicht entzündlich, feuergefährlich
inflatable beach mattress Schwimmluftmatratze *(f)*
influence beeinflussen, Einfluß *(m)*
influenza Grippe *(f)*
inform benachrichtigen, mitteilen, informieren, avisieren
informal zwanglos
information Information *(f)*
information apply to Auskunft *(f)* erteilt
information bureau Informationsbüro *(n)*
information on application Auskünfte *(pl.f)* auf Anfrage *(f)*
information service Informationsdienst *(m)*
information trip Informationsreise *(f)*
infusion Aufguß *(m)*
infusion of herbs Kräutertee *(m)*
ingest Nahrung *(f)* aufnehmen
ingestion Nahrungsaufnahme *(f)*
inglenook Kaminecke *(f)*
ingredient Zutat *(f)*
inhabitant Einwohner *(m)*
inhalation Inhalation *(f)*
inhalation therapy Inhalationskur *(f)*
inhaler Inhalationsapparat *(m)*
inhouse sale Verkaufshinweise *(pl.m)* auf Einrichtungen *(pl.f)* im Hotel *(n)*
initial Anfangsbuchstabe *(m)*; unterzeichnen
initial advertising Einführungswerbung *(f)*
initial salary Anfangsgehalt *(n)*
injure schaden, beschädigen
inland carriage Binnenverkehr *(m)*
inland harbour Binnenhafen *(m)*
inland navigation Binnenschiffahrt *(f)*

inland postage rates Inlandspostgebühren *(pl.f)*
inn Gasthaus *(n)*, Gasthof *(m)*, Gastwirtschaft *(f)*
inner courtyard Innenhof *(m)*
innkeeper Gastwirt *(m)*, Gastronom *(m)*
innkeeping Hotelwesen *(n)*
inoculation Impfung *(f)*
inoculation requirement Impfbestimmung *(f)*
input Eingabe *(f)*, Einsatz *(m)*, Eingang *(m)*
inquiry Anfrage *(f)*, Nachfrage *(f)*, Untersuchung *(f)*
inquiry office Auskunftsstelle *(f)*, Informationsbüro *(n)*
insanitary ungesund
insect Insekt *(n)*
insert Zeitungsbeilage *(f)*
insert advertising Beilagenwerbung *(f)*
inside room Innenkabine *(f)*
insipid fade, geschmacklos
insist (on, upon) dringen auf, bestehen auf, verlangen
insolation Sonneneinstrahlung *(f)*
insolvent zahlungsunfähig
inspect prüfen, besichtigen
installation cost Einbaukosten *(pl.)*, Aufstellungskosten *(pl.)*
instalment credit Teilzahlungskredit *(m)*
instant sofort, unverzüglich
instead of anstatt, an Stelle von
instruct anweisen, unterweisen, instruieren
instruction Anweisung *(f)*, Unterweisung *(f)*
instruction card Arbeitsanweisung *(f)*
instruction for use Gebrauchsanweisung *(f)*
instruction manual Dienstanweisungs-Handbuch *(n)*
insulated picnic bag Kühltasche *(f)*
insult beleidigen, Beleidigung *(f)*
insurance Versicherung *(f)*
insurance charge Versicherungsbeitrag *(m)*
insurance company Versicherungsgesellschaft *(f)*

insurance contribution
Versicherungsbeitrag *(m)*
insurance protection
Versicherungsschutz *(m)*
insurance – building and contents Versicherung – Gebäude *(n)* und Einrichtungen *(pl.f)*
insurance – general
Global-Versicherungspolice *(f)*
insure versichern
intangible assets immaterielle Vermögenswerte *(pl.m)*
intensify verstärken, steigern; Intensität *(f)*, (hoher) Grad *(m)*
Inter-City train Intercity-Zug *(m)*
intercontinental network
interkontinentales Streckennetz *(n)*
interest Zinsen *(pl.m)*
interest and dividends receivable
Zins- und Dividendenforderungen *(pl.f)*
interest on capital leases
Zinsanteile *(pl.m)*, die in den Leasingraten *(pl.f)* enthalten sind
interface Schnittstelle *(f)*
interfere einmischen, beeinträchtigen
interference Störung *(f)*
interim vorläufig, einstweilig
interim bill Zwischenrechnung *(f)*
interim invoice Zwischenrechnung *(f)*
interior Binnenland *(n)*
interior equipment Inneneinrichtung *(f)*
intermediate season
Zwischensaison *(f)*
intermediate port Zwischenhafen *(m)*
intermediate station
Zwischenstation *(f)*
intermediate stop
Fahrtunterbrechung *(f)*, Zwischenaufenthalt *(m)*
internal communicating system
internes Kommunikationssystem *(n)*
internal tariff Binnentarif *(m)*
International Air Transport Association (IATA)
Internationaler Luftverkehrsverband *(m)*
International Automobile Federation Internationaler Automobil-Verband *(m)*
International Civil Aviation Organization (ICAO)
Internationale Zivil-Luftfahrt-Organisation *(f)*
international driving permit (IDP)
internationaler Führerschein *(m)*
international exhibition
Weltausstellung *(f)*
International Exhibition of the Hotel and Catering Trade
Internationale Fachausstellung *(f)* für das Hotel- und Gaststättengewerbe *(n)*
International Federation of Travel Agencies Reisebüroverband *(m)*
international flight Auslandsflug *(m)*
International Hotel Association (IHA) Internationaler Hotelverband *(m)*
international hotel code
internationaler Hoteltelegrafenschlüssel *(m)*
international money order
internationale Postanweisung *(f)*
international motor insurance card internationale grüne Versicherungskarte *(f)*
international reply coupon
internationaler Antwortschein *(m)*
International Union of Tourist Centers Internationale Vereinigung *(f)* der Fremdenverkehrszentralen *(pl.f)*
International Vaccination Certificate internationales Impfzeugnis *(n)*
International Youth Hostel Federation (IYHF)
Internationaler Verband *(m)* der Jugendherbergen *(pl.f)*
interpreter Dolmetscher *(m)*, Interpreter *(m)*
interrupt unterbrechen
interruption Unterbrechung *(f)*
intersection Straßenkreuzung *(f)*
interurban traffic Überlandverkehr *(m)*
interzonal traffic Interzonenverkehr *(m)*

interzonal train Interzonenzug *(m)*
introduce einführen, vorstellen
introduction Einführung *(f)*, Vorstellung *(f)*
invalid ungültig
inventories, at the lower of cost or market Vorräte *(pl.m)*, zum Niederstwert *(m)*
inventory list Inventar *(n)*
inventory tag Inventurzettel *(m)*
inventory valuation adjustments Wertberichtigungen *(pl.f)* auf Vorräte *(pl.m)*
invest investieren, anlegen
investee company Beteiligungsgesellschaft *(f)*
investment Investition *(f)*; (Kapital-, Geld-, Wertpapier-, Vermögens-) Anlage *(f)*, Beteiligung *(f)*
investments by owners Einlagen *(pl.f)*
investments (held as fixed assets) Wertpapiere *(pl.n)* (des Anlagevermögens)
invitation Einladung *(f)*
invite einladen
invoice Rechnung *(f)*, berechnen
invoice amount Rechnungsbetrag *(m)*
involve einbeziehen, einschließen, zur Folge *(f)* haben
iodine spring Jodquelle *(f)*
irate zornig, wütend, gereizt
Irish stew Hammelragout irische Art *(n)*
ironing service Büglerei *(f)*
ironing-board Bügelbrett *(n)*
irregular entry Falschbuchung *(f)*
island Insel *(f)*
isle Insel *(f)*
issue ausgeben, ausstellen, Ausgabe *(f)*, Ausstellung *(f)*
issue emittieren, auflegen, ausgeben, ausstellen
issue Problemkreis *(m)*, der bei Verlautbarungen *(pl.f)* behandelt wird
issued shares alle ausgegebenen Aktien *(pl.f)*
issuing Warenausgabe *(f)*
issuing office Ausgabebüro *(n)*

Italian cornpudding Maisgrütze *(f)*
Italian salad italienischer Salat *(m)*
Italy Italien
item (Rechnungs-)Posten *(m)*, Gegenstand *(m)*
itemize aufgliedern, spezifizieren
itinerancy Umherreisen *(n)*
itinerary Fahrtroute *(f)*, Reiseroute *(f)*, Reiseplan *(m)*, Reiseführer *(m)*
itinerate umherreisen

J

jack Wagenheber *(m)*; Hecht *(m)*
jack price Preis *(m)* anheben
jacket Jacke *(f)*, Sakko *(m, n)*
jam Marmelade *(f)*, Konfitüre *(f)*
jam roll Marmeladenbrötchen *(n)*
jam-omelet Konfitürenomelett *(n)*
janitor Hausmeister *(m)*
jar Gefäß *(n)*, Topf *(m)*, Krug *(m)*
jardiniére Blumenschale *(f)*, Blumenständer *(m)*
jellied eingedickt, in Gelee *(n)*, geliert
jellied eels Aal in Gelee *(m)*
jelly Aspik *(m)*, Gelee *(n)*, Sülze *(f)*
jelly of pork Schweinesülze *(f)*
jellyfish Qualle *(f)*
jeopardize gefährden
jeopardy Gefahr *(f)*, Gefährdung *(f)*
jerk Fleisch *(n)* in Streifen *(pl.m)* schneiden und dörren
jerkin Jacke *(f)*
jersey dress Strickkleid *(n)*
jersey shirt Strickhemd *(n)*
jet Düsenflugzeug *(n)*, Düsenmaschine *(f)*
jet liner Düsenverkehrsflugzeug *(n)*
jet plane Düsenflugzeug *(n)*
jet propulsion unit Düsentriebwerk *(n)*
jetty Landungsbrücke *(f)*, Landungssteg *(m)*, Mole *(f)*
jewel(le)ry Schmuck *(m)*, Juwelen *(pl.m)*
jewel(l)er Juwelier *(m)*
job Tätigkeit *(f)*, Arbeit *(f)*, Verrichtung *(f)*
job analysis Arbeitsstudie *(f)*

job analyst Arbeitsanalytiker *(m)*
job attribute Tätigkeitsmerkmal *(n)*
job breakdown Tätigkeitsbeschreibung *(f)*
job category Stellengruppe *(f)*
job description Stellenbeschreibung *(f)*, Tätigkeitsbeschreibung *(f)*, Arbeitsplatzbeschreibung *(f)*
job enlargement Arbeitserweiterung *(f)*
job enrichment Arbeitsanreicherung *(f)*
job evaluation Arbeitsbewertung *(f)*
job holder Stelleninhaber *(m)*
job instruction Arbeitsunterweisung *(f)*
job instruction training betriebliche Unterweisung *(f)*
job knowledge Fachwissen *(n)*
job rotation Arbeitsplatzrotation *(f)*
job satisfaction Arbeitszufriedenheit *(f)*
job security Arbeitsplatzsicherheit *(f)*
job specification Arbeitsplatzbeschreibung *(f)*
job standardization Arbeitsplatzstandardisierung *(f)*
job title Stellenbezeichnung *(f)*, Tätigkeitsbezeichnung *(f)*
jogging Dauerlauf *(m)*, Langlauf *(m)*, Joggen *(n)*
John Dory (fish) Petersfisch *(m)*
johnny-cake amerik. Maiskuchen *(m)*
join vereinigen, eintreten, beitreten
joint gemeinsam, gemeinschaftlich; Braten *(m)*
joint guaranty (USA) Mitbürgschaft *(f)*
joint of beef Rindsbraten *(m)*
joint owner Mitbesitzer *(m)*
joint passport Familienpaß *(m)*
joint proprietor Miteigentümer *(m)*
joke Spaß *(m)*, Scherz *(m)*
jolly lustig, fröhlich
joule Joule *(n)*
journal entry Journalbuchung *(f)*
journal voucher Buchungsbeleg *(m)*
journey Reise *(f)*, Fahrt *(f)*, Anreise *(f)*
journey abroad Auslandsreise *(f)*
journey home Heimreise *(f)*

journey time Fahrzeit *(f)*
joy Freude *(f)*
joys of winter Winterfreuden *(pl.f)*
jug Kännchen *(n)*, Krug *(m)*
jugged game Wildfleischragout *(n)*
jugged hare Hasenpfeffer *(m)*
jugged meat Pfeffer-Fleischgericht *(n)*
juice Saft *(m)*
juicy saftig
juke-box Musikbox *(f)*
julienne Gemüsesuppe *(f)*
jumble sale Ramschverkauf *(m)*
jumbo jet Jumbo Jet *(m)*
junction Straßenkreuzung *(f)*, Verkehrsknotenpunkt *(m)*
junior cook Jungkoch *(m)*, Hilfskoch *(m)*
junior suite Ein-Zimmer-Suite *(f)*
juniper Wacholder *(m)*
junket Milchgelee *(n)*
justifiable vertretbar
justification Berechtigung *(f)*, Rechtfertigung *(f)*
justify berechtigen, rechtfertigen
juvenile jugendlich

K

kaki Kakifrucht *(f)*
kale Grünkohl *(m)*
kangaroo tail soup Känguruhschwanzsuppe *(f)*
karting Go-kart-Sport *(m)*
kayak Kajak *(m)*
kedgeree Kedgeree *(n)* (Reisgericht mit Fisch, Eiern, Zwiebeln)
keelage Hafengebühren *(pl.f)*
keen competition scharfe Konkurrenz *(f)*
keep books Bücher *(pl.n)* führen
keep clear freihalten!
keep in stock lagern, bevorraten
keep left links fahren!
keep off the grass Rasen *(m)* nicht betreten!
keep out Eintritt *(m)* verboten!
keep right rechts fahren!
keep the change Wechselgeld *(n)* behalten!

keep track of folgen, mitgehen mit
keep up-to-date auf dem laufenden bleiben
keeper Inhaber *(m)*
kefir Kefir *(m)*
keg Fäßchen *(n)*
kernel Kern *(m)*, Nuß *(f)*, Samenkorn *(n)*
kernel of veal Kalbsnuß *(f)*
kerosene Petroleum *(n)*, Brennöl *(n)*
ketchup Ketchup *(m, n)*
kettle (Koch-)Kessel *(m)*
key Schlüssel *(m)*, Taste *(f)*
key board Tastatur *(f)*, Tastenfeld *(n)*
key button Tastenknopf *(m)*
key number Kennziffer *(f)*
key personnel Schlüsselarbeitskräfte *(pl.f)*
key position Schlüsselposition *(f)*, Schlüsselstellung *(f)*
keying mit Kennziffern *(pl.f)* versehen
kid-goat Zicklein *(n)*
kidney Niere *(f)*
kidney steak Kalbsnierensteak *(n)*
kidneys of veal Kalbsnieren *(pl.f)*
kill time Zeit totschlagen, vertreiben
kilometre Kilometer *(m)*
kilt Schottenrock *(m)*
kind Art *(f)*, Gattung *(f)*, Sorte *(f)*; nett, freundlich
kindle anzünden
kindness Freundlichkeit *(f)*
kipper Bückling *(m)*
kippered herring Räucherhering *(m)*
kitchen Küche *(f)*
kitchen-boy Küchenjunge *(m)*
kitchen brigade Küchenbrigade *(f)*
kitchen cupboard Küchenbuffet *(n)*
kitchen dresser Küchenbuffet *(n)*
kitchen help Küchenhilfe *(f)*
kitchen layout planning Küchenplanung *(f)*
kitchen personnel Küchenpersonal *(n)*
kitchen privileges Küchenbenutzung *(f)*
kitchen range Küchenherd *(m)*
kitchen smell Küchengeruch *(m)*
kitchen staff Küchenpersonal *(n)*
kitchen utensil Küchengerät *(n)*

kitchenette Kochnische *(f)*, Kochschrank *(m)*
kitchenmaid Küchenmädchen *(n)*
kitty Kartenspiel (gemeinsame Kasse) *(n)*
knickers Schlüpfer *(m)*
knife Messer *(n)*
knit stricken, verknüpfen
knock Klopfen *(n)*, schlagen, klopfen
knot Knoten *(m)*, Seemeile *(f)*
know-how Fachwissen *(n)*, Sachkenntnis *(f)*, praktisches Wissen *(n)*
knowingly wissentlich
knowledge Wissen *(n)*, Kenntnis *(f)*, Kenntnisse *(pl.)*
knuckle Haxe *(f)*
knuckle of veal Kalbshaxe *(f)*
kohlrabi Kohlrabi *(m)*
kosher koscher (nach jüdischen Speisegesetzen)
kosher party jüdische Veranstaltung *(f)*
kraft paper Packpapier *(n)*

L

label Etikett *(n)*, etikettieren
labor Arbeit *(f)*
labor committee Betriebsrat *(m)*
labor contract Tarifvertrag *(m)*
labor dispute Arbeitsstreitigkeit *(f)*
labor force Arbeitskräfte *(pl.f)*
labor market Arbeitsmarkt *(m)*
labor productivity Arbeitsproduktivität *(f)*
labor saving Arbeitsersparnis *(f)*
labor turnover Personalumschlag *(m)*, Kündigungsrate *(f)*
labor union Gewerkschaft *(f)*
lace Schuß *(m)* (in Getränken), Branntwein *(m)*
lace-coffee Kaffee *(m)* mit einem Schuß *(m)* Branntwein *(m)*
lack mangeln, nicht haben, Mangel *(m)*
Ladies Damen(toilette) *(f)*
ladies' choice Damenwahl *(f)*
ladies' hairdresser Damenfriseur *(m)*
ladies' lavatory Damentoilette *(f)*
ladies' room Damentoilette *(f)*

ladle Schöpflöffel *(m)*
lady finger cake Biskottentorte *(f)*
lady fingers Biskotten *(pl.f)*
lager Bier (Lager) *(n)*
lagoon Lagune *(f)*
lake See *(m)*
lake trout Seeforelle *(f)*
lamb Lamm *(n)*
lamb breast Lammbrust *(f)*
lamb cutlet Lammkotelett *(n)*
lamb shoulder Lammschulter *(f)*
lamb stew Lammragout *(n)*
lamb's lettuce-salad Rapunzelsalat *(m)*
lamp Lampe *(f)*
lamprey Neunauge *(n)*
Lancashire hot-pot Hammel-, Rindfleisch und Kartoffel-Eintopf *(m)*
Lancashire(-cheese) Lancashire-Käse *(m)*
land Grundstück *(n)*
land at anfliegen, landen in
land improvements Grundstückseinrichtungen *(pl.f)*
land safely sicher landen
landing Landung *(f)*
landing dock Anlegeplatz *(m)*
landing field Landeplatz *(m)*
landing gear Fahrgestell *(n)*
landing pier Landungsbrücke *(f)*
landing place Anlegestelle *(f)*
landing runway Landebahn *(f)*
landing speed Landegeschwindigkeit *(f)*
landing stage Bootssteg *(m)*, Landungsbrücke *(f)*
landing strip Landeplatz *(m)*
landlady Besitzerin *(f)*, Wirtin *(f)*
landlord Hauseigentümer *(m)*, Gastwirt *(m)*, Vermieter *(m)*, Quartiergeber *(m)*
landmark markanter Punkt *(m)* (z. B. bei Wegbeschreibungen), Grenzstein *(m)*
landscape Landschaft *(f)*
lane Fahrspur *(f)*, Gasse *(f)*
langlauf Skilanglauf *(m)*
language Sprache *(f)*
lantern Laterne *(f)*
lapwing Kiebitz *(m)*
lard Schmalz *(m)*

larded gespickt mit Speck *(m)*
larded veal collops gespickte Kalbsschnitzelchen *(pl.n)*
larder Speisekammer *(f)*
larding needle Spicknadel *(f)*
larding pin Spicknadel *(f)*
lardon Speckstreifen zum Spicken *(m)*
large-capacity garage Sammelgarage *(f)*
large patty Blätterteigpastete *(f)*
large puff-paste patty stuffed with chicken and mushrooms (vol-au-vent) Blätterteigpastete mit Geflügelfüllung *(f)*
large puff-paste pie Blätterteigpastete *(f)*
large-scale public transport Massenverkehrsmittel *(n)*
large-scale tourism Massentourismus *(m)*
lark Lerche *(f)*
late spät, verspätet
late booking Spätbuchung *(f)*
late passenger arrival verspätete Ankunft *(f)* eines Fluggastes *(m)*
late payment Nachzahlung *(f)*
latest check-in time Meldeschluß *(m)*
launch Barkasse *(f)*
laundry Wäsche *(f)*, Wäscherei *(f)*
laundry and dry cleaning (schedule 2) Wäsche- und Reinigungskosten *(pl.)* (Umsatzbereich 2)
laundry bag Wäschesack *(m)*
laundry chute Wäscheschacht *(m)*
laundry manager Wäschereileiter *(m)*
laurel Lorbeer *(m)*
lavatory Toilette *(f)*, Waschraum *(m)*
lawful rechtlich, rechtmäßig, gesetzlich
lawful age Volljährigkeit *(f)*
lawless ungesetzlich
lawyer Rechtsanwalt *(m)*
lay the table Tisch *(m)* decken
lay-by Rastplatz *(m)*
layday Liegetag *(m)*
layer Schicht *(f)*
layer-cake Schichttorte *(f)*
layman Laie *(m)*
layout räumliche Anordnung *(f)*
lazy faul

lazy Susan amerik. drehbares Tablett *(n)*
leadership Führerschaft *(f)*
leadership ability Führungsfähigkeit *(f)*
leading führend
leaf Blatt *(n)*
leaflet Merkblatt *(n)*, Prospekt *(m)*
leak auslaufen, lecken
lean mager
lean bacon Magerspeck *(m)*
leap year Schaltjahr *(n)*
learner Lernender *(m)*
lease payment Leasingrate *(f)*
leased object Leasing-Objekt *(n)*
leasehold dingliches Landpacht- bzw. Mietrecht *(n)*, Erbpacht *(f)*; geleaste Grundstücke *(pl. n)* und Gebäude *(pl. n)*, Mietbesitz *(m)*
leasehold improvements Einbauten *(pl.)* oder Ausbauten *(pl.)* in gemieteten Räumen *(pl. m)*
leaseholder Mieter *(m)*, Pächter *(m)*
leave Urlaub *(m)*
leave port auslaufen
leave schedule Urlaubsplan *(m)*
leave the ship von Bord *(m)* gehen
leave-train Urlauberzug *(m)*
leaven Sauerteig *(m)*, Hefe *(f)*
leberkaese Leberkäse *(m)*
lecture Vortrag *(m)*
lecture tour Vortragsreise *(f)*
lecture with slides Lichtbildervortrag *(m)*
ledger card (ledger sheet) Kontenblatt *(n)*
leek Lauch *(m)*, Porree *(m)*
leek soup Lauchsuppe *(f)*
leeks Lauchgemüse *(n)*
left-hand traffic Linksverkehr *(m)*
left-luggage office Gepäckaufbewahrung *(f)*
left-luggage ticket Gepäckschein *(m)*
left-over Speiserest *(m)*
leg Bein *(n)*, Keule (Fleisch) *(f)*, Unterschenkel *(m)*
leg of lamb Lammkeule *(f)*
leg of mutton Hammelkeule *(f)*
leg of pork Schweineschlegel *(m)*
leg of veal Kalbskeule *(f)*, Kalbsschlegel *(m)*

leg of vension Rehschlegel *(m)*
legal rechtsgültig, gesetzlich
legal aid Rechtshilfe *(f)*
legal aid insurance Rechtsschutzversicherung *(f)*
legal claim Rechtsanspruch *(m)*
legal fees and expenses Rechtsanwaltsgebühren *(pl. f)*
legal form Rechtsform *(f)*
legal holiday gesetzlicher Feiertag *(m)*, gesetzlicher Urlaub *(m)*
legal services Rechtsberatung *(f)*
legend Zeichenerklärung *(f)*
legitimate gesetzmäßig, gesetzlich, rechtsmäßig
legitimation Ausweis *(m)*, Legitimation *(f)*
legume Hülsenfrucht *(f)*
Leicester Leicester-Käse *(m)*
Leipzig hodge-podge Leipziger Allerlei *(n)*
leisure Muße *(f)*
leisure time Freizeit *(f)*
leisure time activity Freizeitbeschäftigung *(f)*
leisureliness Gemütlichkeit *(f)*
lemon Zitrone *(f)*
lemon-ice Zitroneneis *(n)*
lemon juice Zitronensaft *(m)*
lemon meringue pie Zitronenbaiserpudding *(m)*
lemon rind Zitronenschale *(f)*
lemon sole Rotzunge *(f)*
lemon squash Zitronenlimonade *(f)*
lemon squeezer Zitronenpresse *(f)*
lemonade Limonade *(f)*
lend leihen, verleihen, ausleihen
lending-fee Leihgebühr *(f)*
length Länge *(f)*
length of service Diensthalter *(n)*
length of stay Aufenthaltsdauer *(f)*
lens Objektiv *(n)*
Lent Fastenzeit *(f)*
lentil Linse *(f)*
lentil soup Linsensuppe *(f)*
less weniger
lessee Leasing-Nehmer *(m)*, Mieter *(m)*, Pächter *(m)*
lessor Leasing-Geber *(m)*, Vermieter *(m)*, Verpächter *(m)*

let gestatten, lassen; vermieten, verpachten
letter box Briefkasten *(m)*
letter file Briefordner *(m)*, Schnellhefter *(m)*
letter of credit Akkreditiv *(n)*
letter of invitation Einladungsbrief *(m)*
letter of recommendation Empfehlungsbrief *(m)*
letter punch Brieflocher *(m)*
letter quality Korrespondenzqualität *(f)*
letter service Briefversand *(m)*, Schreibbüro *(n)*
letter-paper Briefpapier *(n)*
lettuce Kopfsalat *(m)*
level Niveau *(n)*
level crossing Bahnübergang *(m)*
level of prices Preisniveau *(n)*
leveret Häschen *(n)*, junger Hase *(m)*
levy a charge Gebühr *(f)*, erheben
liabilities Verbindlichkeiten *(pl.f)*
liabilities and owners' equity Verbindlichkeiten *(pl.f)* und Eigenkapital *(n)*; Passiva *(pl.)*
liability for damages Schadenshaftung *(f)*
liability insurance Haftpflichtversicherung *(f)*
liability insurance coverage Haftpflichtdeckung *(f)*
liability of the carrier Transporthaftung *(f)*
liability under the contract Vertragshaftung *(f)*
liable verantwortlich, haftpflichtig
liable of charges gebührenpflichtig
liable to customs zollpflichtig
liable to duty zollpflichtig
library Bibliothek *(f)*
licence, license Ausschanklizenz *(f)*, Konzession *(f)*
licence plate Autonummernschild *(n)*
licensed hours Alkoholausschankzeiten *(pl.f)*
licensee Lizenzinhaber *(m)*
licenses and inspections Schankerlaubnis *(f)* und Gewerbeaufsicht *(f)*

licensing hours Alkoholausschankzeiten *(pl.f)*
licensor Lizenzgeber *(m)*
lid Deckel *(m)*
lido Freibad *(n)*, Strandbad *(n)*
lie awake wach liegen
lien Pfandrecht *(n)*
life-belt Rettungsgürtel *(m)*
life-boat Rettungsboot *(n)*
life-guard Badewärter *(m)*
life-guard station Rettungsstation *(f)*
life insurance Lebensversicherung *(f)*
life-jacket Schwimmweste *(f)*
life-saving station Rettungsstation *(f)*
life vest Schwimmweste *(f)*
LIFO or FIFO cost flow assumptions Lifo- oder Fifo-Verbrauchsfolgeunterstellungen *(pl.f)*
LIFO value Lifo-Wert *(m)*
lift Aufzug *(m)*, Fahrstuhl *(m)*
lift up aufheben
lift-boy Fahrstuhlführer *(m)*, Liftboy *(m)*
light leicht; Licht *(n)*, anzünden
light beer helles Bier *(n)*
light food leichte Kost *(f)*
light wine leichter Wein *(m)*
lighter Feuerzeug *(n)*
lighter fuel Feuerzeugbenzin *(n)*
lighthouse Leuchtturm *(m)*
lighting Beleuchtung *(f)*
lighting effect Lichteffekt *(m)*
lightning Blitz *(m)*
lights Lunge *(f)*
like gern haben, mögen; wie
lime Limone *(f)*; Linde *(f)*
lime juice Limonensaft *(m)*
lime tea Lindenblütentee *(m)*
limestone cave Tropfsteinhöhle *(f)*
limit begrenzen, Limit *(n)*, Grenze *(f)*
limit of credit Kreditgrenze *(f)*
limitation Begrenzung *(f)*, Einschränkung *(f)*
limited express train Fernschnellzug *(m)*
limited liability company Gesellschaft *(f)* mit beschränkter Haftung *(f)*
limited number of seats begrenzte Platzanzahl *(f)*

limited parking zone Kurzparkzone *(f)*
limited partner beschränkt haftender Gesellschafter *(m)*, Kommanditist *(m)*
linden flowers tea Lindenblütentee *(m)*
line Linie *(f)*, Strecke *(f)*, Gleis *(n)*; Teleph.: Leitung *(f)*, Apparat *(m)*, Nummer *(f)*
line and staff organization Stablinienorganisation *(f)*
line cord Kabel *(n)*
line function Linienfunktion *(f)*
line position Linienstelle *(f)*
line (at the front desk) Schlange *(f)* (an der Rezeption)
line-fishing Angelfischerei *(f)*
linen (schedule 2) Wäsche *(f)* (Umsatzbereich 2)
linen-closet Wäscheschrank *(m)*
linen hire Wäscheverleih *(m)*
linen keeper Wäschebeschließerin *(f)*
linen room attendant Wäschebeschließerin *(f)*
liner Passagierdampfer *(m)*, Linienschiff *(n)*, Verkehrsflugzeug *(n)*, Linienflugzeug *(n)*
liner company Schiffahrtsgesellschaft *(f)*
linguist-courier sprachkundiger Reiseleiter *(m)*
link Bindeglied *(n)*, Verbindung *(f)*
links Dünen *(pl.f)*, Golfplatz *(m)*
linseed Leinsamen *(m)*
linseed cake Leinkuchen *(m)*
lipstick Lippenstift *(m)*
Liptauer, garnished Liptauer-Käse garniert *(m)*
liqueur Likör *(m)*
liquid flüssig
liquid assets Bargeld *(n)* sowie sonstige Vermögensteile *(pl. m)*, die jederzeit verflüssigt werden können; liquide Vermögensteile *(pl. m)*
liquid funds flüssige Mittel *(pl. n)*
liquidity Liquidität *(f)*, flüssige Mittel *(pl. n)*
liquidity position Liquiditätslage *(f)*
liquo(u)r Spirituose *(f)*, Alkohol *(m)*
liquor shop Spirituosengeschäft *(n)*

list verzeichnen; Liste *(f)*, Verzeichnis *(n)*
list of beverages Getränkekarte *(f)*
list of participants Teilnehmerliste *(f)*
list of travel agencies Agenturverzeichnis *(n)*
list of vacant rooms Vakanzliste *(f)*
list price Listenpreis *(m)*
listen zuhören
litigation Prozeß *(m)*, Rechtsstreit *(m)*
live leben, wohnen
lively abwechslungsreich
liver Leber *(f)*
liver dumpling Leberknödel *(m)*
liver of veal Kalbsleber *(f)*
liver puree soup Leberpüreesuppe *(f)*
liver sausage Leberwurst *(f)*
liver sausage with pickled cabbage Leberwurst *(f)* mit Sauerkraut *(n)*
liveried livriert
living habit Lebensgewohnheit *(f)*
living-room Wohnzimmer *(n)*, Wohnraum *(m)*
living standard Lebensstandard *(m)*
loading capacity Ladefähigkeit *(f)*
loading charges Verladegebühr *(f)*
loading hatch Ladeluke *(f)*
loading platform Verladebahnsteig *(m)*
loading point Verladestelle *(f)*
loading station Talstation *(f)*
loaf of bread Brotlaib *(m)*
loaf sugar Hutzucker *(m)*
loan guarantee Bürgschaft *(f)* für ein Darlehen *(n)*, Kreditbürgschaft *(f)*
loans receivable from affiliated companies Ausleihungen *(pl.f)* an verbundene Unternehmen *(pl. n)*
lobby Empfangshalle *(f)*, Foyer *(n)*, Hotelhalle *(f)*
lobby space Raum *(m)* in der Hotelhalle *(f)*
lobster Hummer *(m)*
lobster cocktail Hummercocktail *(m)*
lobster mayonnaise Hummermayonnaise *(f)*
lobster shift Nachtschicht *(f)*
local lokal, örtlich

local advertisement postmark
Ortswerbestempel *(m)*
local advertising lokale Werbung *(f)*
local call Ortsgespräch *(n)*
local carriage Ortsverkehr *(m)*
local colour Lokalkolorit *(n)*
local custom Ortsbrauch *(m)*
local fair Kirchweih *(f)*
local festival Heimatfest *(n)*
local speciality Landesspezialität *(f)*
local tax Ortstaxe *(f)*
local time Ortszeit *(f)*
local tourist association
Verkehrsverein *(m)*
local tourist office Verkehrsamt *(n)*
local traffic Ortsverkehr *(m)*, Nahverkehr *(m)*
local wine Landwein *(m)*
locality Örtlichkeit *(f)*, Lage *(f)*
locate errors Fehler *(pl. m)* aufdecken
location Standort *(m)*
location of goods Lagerort *(m)*
lock Schloß *(n)* (Türen), Schleuse *(f)*
lock box Schließfach *(n)*
lock off absperren
lock-up garage verschließbare Garage
locker Schließfach *(n)*
locker room Umkleideraum *(m)* für das Personal *(n)*
lodge beherbergen, unterbringen; Jagdhütte *(f)*
lodger Mieter *(m)*
lodging Unterkunft *(f)*, Quartier *(n)*, Logis *(n)*
lodging-house Hotel garni *(n)*, Logierhaus *(n)*
log-book Bordbuch *(n)*, Reservations- und Beschwerdebuch *(n)* im Restaurant *(n)*
log-hut Blockhütte *(f)*
loganberry Logan-Beere *(f)*
loin Lendenstück *(n)*, Lende *(f)*
long lang
long-distance call Ferngespräch *(n)*
long-distance express
Fernschnellzug *(m)*
long-distance flight
Langstreckenflug *(m)*
long-distance lorry Fernlaster *(m)*

long-distance service
Langstreckendienst *(m)*
long-distance time-table
Fernfahrplan *(m)*
long-distance traffic Fernverkehr *(m)*
long-range langfristig
long-range plane
Langstreckenflugzeug *(n)*
long-range profit planning
langfristige Erfolgsplanung *(f)*
long-term langfristig
long-term credit langfristiger Kredit *(m)*
long-term debt langfristige Verbindlichkeiten *(pl. f)*
long-term liabilities langfristige Verbindlichkeiten *(pl. f)*
look Blick *(m)*, schauen, blicken
looking-glass Spiegel *(m)*
loosely lose, locker, ungenau
lorry Lastkraftwagen *(m)*
lose verlieren, einbüßen
loss Verlust *(m)*, Schaden *(m)*
loss and damage to guest property Verlust *(m)* und Beschädigung *(f)* von Gasteigentum *(n)*
loss contingencies Verpflichtungen *(pl. f)*, die nicht nur der Höhe *(f)*, sondern auch der Wahrscheinlichkeit *(f)* ihres Eintretens nach mit Unsicherheiten *(pl. f)* behaftet sind
loss of credit Kreditverlust *(m)*
loss of earnings Verdienstausfall *(m)*
loss settlement Schadensregulierung *(f)*
losses brought forward
Verlustvortrag *(m)*
lost luggage fehlendes Reisegepäck *(n)*
lost profit entgangener Gewinn *(m)*
lost-property office Fundbüro *(n)*
lost time Verlustzeit *(f)*
lot size Losgröße *(f)*, Auftragsgröße *(f)*
lounge Aufenthaltsraum *(m)*, Gesellschaftsraum *(m)*, Hotelhalle *(f)*
lounge suit Straßenanzug *(m)*
lovely köstlich, lieblich, schön

low-priced billig
low season Vorsaison *(f)*, Nachsaison *(f)*
low valued geringwertig
lower berth Unterbett *(n)*
lower deck Unterdeck *(n)*
lowest bid Mindestgebot *(n)*
loyal treu, pflichttreu
loyality Treue *(f)*, Pflichttreue *(f)*
lucrative einträglich
luge Schlitten *(m)*
luggage Gepäck *(n)*
luggage compartment Gepäckraum *(m)*
luggage insurance Gepäckversicherung *(f)*
luggage label Gepäckanhäger *(m)*, Kofferanhänger *(m)*
luggage locker Gepäckschließfach *(n)*
luggage office Gepäckabfertigung *(f)*, Gepäckaufgabestelle *(f)*
luggage platform Gepäckbahnsteig *(m)*
luggage porter Gepäckträger *(m)*
luggage rack Gepäckablage *(f)*, Gepäcknetz *(n)*, Autogepäckträger *(m)*
luggage receipt Gepäckschein *(m)*
luggage registration counter Gepäckabfertigung *(f)*
luggage room Gepäckraum *(m)*
luggage service Gepäckdienst *(m)*
luggage-ticket Gepäckschein *(m)*
luggage transfer Gepäcktransfer *(m)*
luggage van Gepäckwagen *(m)*, Packwagen *(m)*
lukewarm lauwarm
lump Klumpen *(m)*, Stück *(n)*
lump sugar Würfelzucker *(m)*
lump sum Pauschale *(f)*, Pauschalbetrag *(m)*
lunch break Mittagspause *(f)*
lunch business Mittagsgeschäft *(n)*
lunch-counter Imbißbar (in Restaurants) *(f)*
lunch-hour Mittagszeit *(f)*, Mittagspause *(f)*
lunch packet Lunchpaket *(n)*, Imbißpaket *(n)*
lunch-room Mittagsrestaurant *(n)*

lunch(eon) Mittagessen *(n)*
luncheon-bar Mittagsrestaurant *(n)*
luncheon-basket Proviantkorb *(m)*
luncheon meat Frühstücksfleisch *(n)*
luncheon voucher Essenbon *(m)*, Essensgutschein *(m)*, Mahlzeitengutschein *(m)*
luncheon voucher arrangement Essensabonnement *(n)*
luncheonette Imbiß *(m)*, Imbißstube *(f)*
lungs Lunge *(f)*
luxurious fittings moderner Komfort *(m)*
luxury Luxus *(m)*
luxury bus Luxusbus *(m)*
luxury cabin Luxuskabine *(f)*
luxury goods Luxusgüter *(pl.n)*
luxury hotel Luxushotel *(n)*
luxury liner Luxusdampfer *(m)*
luxury restaurant Luxusrestaurant *(n)*
luxury trip Luxusreise *(f)*
luxury yacht Luxusjacht *(f)*

M

Mae West aufblasbare Schwimmweste *(f)*
macaroni Makkaroni *(pl.f)*
macaroon Makrone *(f)*
mace Muskatblüte *(f)*, Muskatblatt *(n)*
machinery and equipment Maschinen *(pl.f)* und maschinelle Anlagen *(pl.f)*
mackerel Makrele *(f)*
mackintosh Regenmantel *(m)*
madam gnädige Frau (Anrede) *(f)*, gnädiges Fräulein *(n)*
Madeira Madeira *(m)* (Wein)
Madeira cake Sandkuchen *(m)*
Madeira sauce Madeira-Sauce *(f)*
maffick lärmend feiern, johlen
magazine Zeitschrift *(f)*
magnificent prächtig, großartig
maid Dienstmädchen *(n)*, Zimmermädchen *(n)*
maiden name Mädchenname *(m)*, Geburtsname *(m)*
mail aufgeben (Post), Post *(f)*

mail flight Postflug *(m)*
mail plane Postflugzeug *(n)*
mailbox Briefkasten *(m)*
mailing list Postliste *(f)*,
   Adressenliste *(f)*
mailman Briefträger (amerik.) *(m)*
main course Hauptgang *(m)*
   (Speisen), Hauptgericht *(n)*
main deck Hauptdeck *(n)*
main dish Hauptgericht *(n)*,
   Hauptspeise *(f)*
main entrance Haupteingang *(m)*
main joint Hauptfleischgang *(m)*,
   Hauptgang *(m)*
main mast Großmast *(m)*
main meal Hauptmahlzeit *(f)*
main meat course Hauptgang *(m)*,
   Hauptfleischgang *(m)*
main office Hauptbüro *(n)*, Zentrale
   (f)
main road Hauptstraße *(f)*
main sail Großsegel *(n)*
main station Hauptbahnhof *(m)*
main street Hauptstraße *(f)*
maintain instandhalten, unterhalten,
   erhalten, aufrechterhalten
maintain records Bücher *(pl. n)*
   führen
maintenance Instandhaltung *(f)*,
   Unterhalt *(m)*, Erhaltung *(f)*,
   Wartung *(f)*
**maintenance – hardware/software
   (schedule 8)** Instandhaltung *(f)*
   und Wartung *(f)* – Hardware/
   Software (Service Center 8)
maintenance contract
   Wartungsvertrag *(m)*
maintenance cost
   Instandhaltungskosten *(pl.)*
maintenance work order
   Instandhaltungsauftrag *(m)*,
   Reparaturauftrag *(m)*
maitre Oberkellner *(m)*
maize Mais *(m)*
maizena Maisstärkemehl *(n)*
major road Vorfahrtsstraße *(f)*
majority Mehrheit *(f)*
make an order buchen
make fast anlagen
make up Aufmachung *(f)*,
   Ausstattung *(f)*

make use of gebrauchen, verwerten
male männlich
mall Laubenpromenade *(f)*
mallow Malve *(f)*
malt Malz *(n)*
Maltese Malteser *(m)*
man-day Arbeitstag *(m)*, Tagewerk
   (n)
man hour Arbeitsstunde *(f)*
manage leiten, verwalten
management Geschäftsleitung *(f)*,
   Betriebsführung *(f)*,
   Geschäftsführung *(f)*
management agreement
   Verwaltungsvertrag *(m)*
management consultant
   Unternehmensberater *(m)*,
   Betriebsberater *(m)*
management decision
   Führungsentscheidung *(f)*
management development
   Führungskräfteentwicklung *(f)*
management fee
   Managementgebühren *(pl. f)*;
   Führungsprovision, Provision *(f)*
   der Konsortialführerin *(f)*;
   Verwaltungsgebühr *(f)*; Regiekosten
   (pl.), Konzernumlage-Kosten *(pl.)*
management training
   Führungsausbildung *(f)*,
   Managementtraining *(n)*
management's attention Wille *(m)*
   des Unternehmers *(m)*
manager Leiter *(m)*, Direktor *(m)*,
   Geschäftsführer *(m)*, Manager
   (m)
managerial disease
   Managerkrankheit *(f)*
managerial responsibility
   Führungsverantwortung *(f)*
mandarine Mandarine *(f)*
mandatory obligatorisch, zwingend
mango Mangopflaume *(f)*
manicure Maniküre *(f)*
manners Sitten *(pl. f)*, Bräuche
   (pl. m), Lebensart *(f)*
manning guide
   Personalplanungsleitfaden *(m)*
manning table
   Stellenbesetzungsplan *(m)*
manpower Arbeitskraft *(f)*

manpower budget Personalbudget *(n)*
mansard Mansarde *(f)*
manual Handbuch *(n)*, manuell
manual of instructions Dienstanweisungshandbuch *(n)*
map Landkarte *(f)*, Karte *(f)*
map of the town Stadtplan *(m)*
maple syrup Ahornsirup *(m)*
marbled meat durchwachsenes Fleisch *(n)*
marchpane Marzipan *(n)*
Mardigras Fastnachtsdienstag *(m)*
margarine Margarine *(f)*
margin Spanne *(f)*, Rohgewinn *(m)*
marina Jachthafen *(m)*
marinade Marinade *(f)*, marinieren
marinated mariniert
marinated herring Bismarckhering *(m)*
marine cray fish Meereskrebs *(m)*
marine railway station Hafenbahnhof *(m)*
marinotherapy Seebadekur *(f)*
marital status Familienstand *(m)*
maritime shipping Seeschiffahrt *(f)*
marjoram Majoran *(m)*
mark kennzeichnen, Zeichen *(n)*, Marke *(f)*
mark down Preissenkung *(f)*; Disagio *(n)*
market verkaufen, absetzen, Markt *(m)*, Absatzgebiet *(n)*
market analyses Marktanalyse *(f)*
market hall Markthalle *(f)*
market list Marktliste *(f)*, Frischwarenverzeichnis *(n)*
market-place Marktplatz *(m)*
market price Marktpreis *(m)*
market research Marktforschung *(f)*
market saturation Marktsättigung *(f)*
marketable security Wertpapier *(n)* des Umlaufvermögens *(n)*
marketing Absatzlehre *(f)*, Marketing *(n)*
marketing manager Verkaufsleiter *(m)*, Vertriebsleiter *(m)*, Marketing-Manager *(m)*
marmalade (Orangen-)Marmelade *(f)*
married verheiratet
marrow Mark *(n)*

marrow dumplings Markklößchen *(pl. n)*
marrowbone Markbein *(n)*, Markknochen *(m)*
mash Brei *(m)*
mashed potatoes Kartoffelbrei *(m)*
masked ball Maskenball *(m)*
mason Maurer *(m)*
mass (heilige) Messe *(f)*
massage Massage *(f)*
masseur Masseur *(m)*
masseuse Masseuse *(f)*
mast Mast *(m)*
master key Hauptschlüssel *(m)*
master scheduling Gesamtplanung *(f)*
mat Untersetzer *(m)*
match Zündholz *(n)*, Streichholz *(n)*; dazu passen, entsprechen, passend machen
match-box Streichholzschachtel *(f)*, Zündholzschachtel *(f)*
matching periodengerechte Gegenüberstellung *(f)* von Aufwand *(m)* und Ertrag *(m)*
matchstick potatoes Zündholzkartoffeln *(pl. f)*
material von Bedeutung *(f)*
materiality Kriterium der Wesentlichkeit *(f)* (Rechnungslegung)
matrix printer Matrixdrucker *(m)*
matron Hausdame *(f)*, Beschließerin *(f)*
matter Angelegenheit *(f)*
mattress Matratze *(f)*
mature reif
mature wine abgelagerter Wein *(m)*
matured coupon noch nicht eingelöster Gutschein *(m)*
maturity date Fälligkeitstermin *(m)*
Maundy Thursday Gründonnerstag *(m)*
maximum price Höchstpreis *(m)*
maximum speed Höchstgeschwindigkeit *(f)*
mayonnaise Mayonnaise *(f)*
mayonnaise eggs Russische Eier *(pl. n)*
mayonnaise of fish Fischmayonnaise *(f)*

mayonnaise of lobster
 Hummermayonnaise *(f)*
mayonnaise salad Mayonnaisesalat *(m)*
mayonnaise sauce Mayonnaisensoße *(f)*
mayor Bürgermeister *(m)*
Maypole Maibaum *(m)*
meadow Wiese *(f)*
meagre mager
meal Mahlzeit *(f)*, Speise *(f)*, Gericht *(n)*, Essen *(n)*
meal ticket Essensbon *(m)*, Essensgutschein *(m)*
meal ticket arrangement Essensabonnement *(n)*
meal time Essenszeit *(f)*, Tischzeit *(f)*
meals à la carte Essen *(n)* à la carte
meals on board (a) ship Mahlzeiten *(pl.f)* an Bord *(m)*
mean annual temperature mittlere Jahrestemperatur *(f)*
meaning Bedeutung *(f)*
means Mittel *(pl.n)*
means of transportation Beförderungsmittel *(pl.n)*
meanwhile inzwischen
measure Maßnahme *(f)*; Maß *(n)*
measurement Wertansatz *(m)*
measurement of performance Leistungsmessung *(f)*
meat Fleisch *(n)*
meat-ball Fleischklößchen *(n)*
meat-ball in white caper sauce Königsberger Klops *(m)*
meat broth Fleischbrühe *(f)*
meat croquette Frikadelle *(f)*
meat dish Fleischspeise *(f)*
meat dumpling Fleischknödel *(m)*
meat loaf Hackbraten *(m)*
meat pie Fleischpastete *(f)*
meat pudding Fleischkäse *(m)*
meat rice Reisfleisch *(n)*
meat tag Fleischanhänger *(m)*
meatless dish fleischloses Gericht *(n)*
meaty fleischig, gehaltvoll
mechanic Mechaniker *(m)*
mechanical mechanisch, maschinell
mechanical kitchen equipment Küchenausstattung *(f)*

mechanize mechanisieren
medallion of veal Kalbsmedaillon *(n)*
medical care ärztliche Betreuung *(f)*
medical certificate ärztliches Zeugnis *(n)*
medical identifification card Unfallschutzkarte *(f)*
medicinal bath medizinisches Bad *(n)*
medicinal mineral water Heilwasser *(n)*
medicinal spring Heilquelle *(f)*
medicine Medikament *(n)*
mediterranean Mittelmeer *(n)*, mittelmeerisch
medium mittel
medium done rosig gebraten
medium priced in mittlerer Preislage *(f)*
medium-range flight Mittelstreckenflug *(m)*
medium term mittelfristig
medlars Mispel *(f)*
meet treffen, sich versammeln, erfüllen
meet with an accident verunglücken
meeting Konferenz *(f)*, Sitzung *(f)*, Versammlung *(f)*
meeting-place Sammelstelle *(f)*, Sammelpunkt *(m)*, Treffpunkt *(m)*
meeting room rentals (schedule 2) Erträge *(pl.m)* aus der Vermietung *(f)* von Konferenzzimmern *(pl.n)* oder sonstigen Räumen *(pl.m)* (Umsatzbereich 2)
Melbatoast hartgeröstete Brotscheiben *(pl.f)*
melon Melone *(f)*
melted ausgelassen, geschmolzen, zerlassen
melted butter zerlassene Butter *(f)*
member Mitglied *(n)*
membership Mitgliedschaft *(f)*
membership card Mitgliedskarte *(f)*, Ausweis *(m)*
membership fee Mitgliederbeitrag *(m)*
memorable (stay) denkwürdig (Hotelaufenthalt)

memorandum Notiz *(f)*, Vermerk *(m)*
memorial Denkmal *(n)*
mention in the notes im Anhang *(m)* angeben
menu Speisenfolge *(f)*, Menü *(n)*; Speisekarte *(f)*
menu and wine list Speise- und Weinkarte *(f)*
menu at fixed prices Menü *(n)* zu festen Preisen *(pl. m)*
menu for motorists Menü *(n)* für Autofahrer *(pl. m)*
menu planning Menüplanung *(f)*, Planung *(f)* der Speisekarte *(f)*
men's hairdresser Herrenfriseur *(m)*
men's lavatory Herrentoilette *(f)*
merchandise Ware *(f)*, Handelsware *(f)*
merchandise Warenlager *(n)*
merchandise inventory Warenbestand *(m)*
merchandise on hand Warenbestand *(m)*
merchandising Merchandising *(n)*; Steuerung *(f)* von Vertrieb *(m)* und Verkauf *(m)*
merchandising policy Verkaufsgrundsätze *(pl. m)*
merchant ship Handelsschiff *(n)*
merge fusionieren, verschmelzen, mischen
merger Fusion *(f)*
meringue Sahnebaiser *(n)*, Baiser *(n)*
meringue cake Windtorte *(f)*
merit Verdienst *(n)*
merit rating Leistungsbeurteilung *(f)*
merry-go-round Karussell *(n)*
mess Verwirrung *(f)*, Durcheinander *(n)*
mess-tin Kochgeschirr *(n)*
message Nachricht *(f)*, Botschaft *(f)*
meteorological office Wetteramt *(n)*
meteorological services Wetterdienst *(m)*
meter maid Politesse *(f)*
method and procedures Ablauforganisation *(f)*
method of amortization Abschreibungsmethode *(f)*
method of payment Zahlungsmodus *(m)*, Zahlungsweise *(f)*

method of treatment Heilmethode *(f)*
metropolis Metropole *(f)*, Hauptstadt *(f)*
meunière sauce Soße *(f)* mit gebräunter Butter *(f)*, Zitrone *(f)*, Petersilie *(f)*
mew egg Möwenei *(n)*
mezzanine Zwischenstock *(m)*
micro computer Mikrocomputer *(m)*
microbus Kleinbus *(m)*
micromotion study Griff- und Bewegungsstudie *(f)*
mid station Mittelstation *(f)*
mid-morning break Frühstückspause *(f)*
mid-morning snack zweites Frühstück *(n)*, Brotzeit *(f)*
middle management mittleres Management *(n)*
midnight Mitternacht *(f)*
mignonette kleines Filetstück *(n)*
milage Meilenzahl *(f)*, Entfernung *(f)* in Meilen *(pl. f)*
mild mild, leicht
mild ale dunkles Ale *(n)*
mild climate mildes Klima *(n)*
mild diet Schonkost *(f)*
milestone Meilenstein *(m)*, Markstein *(m)*
milk Milch *(f)*
milk bar Milchbar *(f)*
milk dish Milchspeise *(f)*
milk jug Milchkännchen *(n)*
milk man Milchmann *(m)*
milk rice Milchreis *(m)*
milk roll Milchbrötchen *(n)*
milk shake Milchmixgetränk *(n)*
millet Hirse *(f)*
mince hacken, durchdrehen
mince-pie Pastetchen *(n)* mit gehackten Früchten gefüllt *(pl. f)*
minced kleingehackt
minced beef Hackfleisch *(n)*
minced meat Hackfleisch *(n)*
minced raw beef Tatar *(n)*
mincemeat gehackte Früchte zur Pastetenfüllung *(pl. f)*
mincer (Fleisch-)Hackmaschine *(f)*
mincing machine (Fleisch-)Hackmaschine *(f)*

mind beachten
mineral Mineralie *(f)*
mineral bath Mineralbad *(n)*
mineral spring Mineralquelle *(f)*, Heilquelle *(f)*
mineral water Mineralwasser *(f)*
minestrone Gemüsesuppe mit Einlagen *(f)*, Minestrone *(f)*
mingle sich mischen, mengen
mini computer Minicomputer *(m)*
miniature golf Minigolf *(n)*
miniature golf course Minigolfplatz *(m)*
minibus Kleinbus *(m)*
minicab Kleintaxi *(n)*
minimum number of participants Mindestteilnehmerzahl *(f)*
minimum rate Mindestpreis *(m)*
minimum stay Mindestaufenthalt *(m)*
minimum wage Mindestlohn *(m)*
minority interests Ausgleichsposten *(m)* für Anteile *(pl. m)* im Fremdbesitz *(m)*
minority stockholder Minderheitsaktionär *(m)*
mint Pfefferminze *(f)*
mint sauce Minzensoße *(f)*
mint tea Pfefferminztee *(m)*
minutes Protokoll *(n)*
mirabelle plum Mirabelle *(f)*
mirror Spiegel *(m)*
miscellaneous vermischt, verschiedenartig
miscellaneous banquet income (schedule 2) verschiedene Bankettumsätze *(pl. m)* (Umsatzbereich 2)
miscellaneous marketing expenses (schedule 11) sonstige Marketingkosten *(pl.)* (Service Center 11)
miscellaneous other income (schedule 2) verschiedene sonstige Umsätze *(pl. m)* (Umsatzbereich 2)
misconduct Mißverhalten *(n)*
misguide fehlleiten
misleading irreführend
mismanagement Mißwirtschaft *(f)*
miss verfehlen, vermissen
miss the train Zug *(m)* versäumen

missing fehlend, vermißt
mist Nebel *(m)*
mistake irren, Irrtum *(m)*
mistry neblig, unklar
misunderstanding Mißverständnis *(n)*
misuse mißbrauchen, Mißbrauch *(m)*
mitten Fausthandschuh *(m)*
mix mischen, vermischen, Mischung *(f)*
mix-up Verwechslung *(f)*
mixed gemischt
mixed bathing Familienbad *(n)*
mixed boiled meat gekochtes Fleischallerlei *(n)*
mixed fruit gemischtes Obst *(n)*
mixed grill Mixed Grill *(m)*
mixed ice gemischtes Eis *(n)*
mixed ice-cream gemischtes Eis *(n)*
mixed meat-stew with vegetables Pichelsteiner Fleisch *(n)*
mixed pickles Essiggemüse *(n)*
mixed salad gemischter Salat *(m)*
mixed vegetable gemischtes Gemüse *(n)*
mixture (of food) Allerlei *(n)*, Mischgericht *(n)*
moat Graben *(m)*
mock turtle soup falsche Schildkrötensuppe *(f)*
model Schema *(n)*, Modell *(n)*
moderate climate gemäßigtes Klima *(n)*
moderate rate mittlere Preislage *(f)*
modernize modernisieren
modest bescheiden
modesty Bescheidenheit *(f)*
modification Abänderung *(f)*, Modifizierung *(f)*
Modified American Plan (MAP) Zimmer *(n)* mit Halbpension *(f)*
modify abändern, modifizieren
moist feucht, naß
moisture Feuchtigkeit *(f)*
molasses Sirup *(m)*
molded cream bayrische Creme *(f)*
mole Mole *(f)*
molest belästigen
molestation Belästigung *(f)*
mollusk Weichtier *(n)*
monastery Kloster *(n)*

money contributed by a partner Geldeinlage *(f)* eines Gesellschafters *(m)*
monitor überwachen
month-to-date kumuliert zum Datum *(n)*
monthly consumption Monatsverbrauch *(m)*
monthly program Monatsprogramm *(n)*
monthly season ticket Monatskarte *(f)*
monument Denkmal *(n)*
mood Stimmung *(f)*
mood music Stimmungsmusik *(f)*
moon Mond *(m)*
moonlight boat-trip Mondscheinbootsfahrt *(f)*
moor anlegen
mooring Anlegen *(n)*
mooring pier Anlegestelle *(f)*
moral sittlich, moralisch
morale Moral *(f)*
morel Morchel *(f)*
morning concert Frühkonzert *(n)*
morning performance Matineevorstellung *(f)*
morning train Frühzug *(m)*
mortgage Hypothek *(f)*
mortgage bond Pfandbrief *(m)*
Moselle wine Moselwein *(m)*
mosque Moschee *(f)*
mosquito net Moskitonetz *(n)*
moss Moos *(n)*
motel Motel *(n)*
motion study Bewegungsstudie *(f)*
motivate motivieren
motor accident Autounfall *(m)*
motor ambulance Krankenwagen *(m)*, Rettungswagen *(m)*
motor boat Motorboot *(n)*
motor car Auto *(n)*, Wagen *(m)*
motor-car service Wagenpflege *(f)*
motor caravan Campingbus *(m)*
motor carrier Transportunternehmer *(m)*
motor-club Automobilclub *(m)*
motor coach Bus *(m)*, Omnibus *(m)*
motor hotel Motel *(n)*
motor inn Stadtmotel *(n)*

motor insurance Kraftfahrzeugversicherung
motor launch Motorboot *(n)*, Barkasse *(f)*
motor lorry Zugwagen *(m)*
motor race Autorennen *(n)*
motor ride Autofahrt *(f)*
motor road Autostraße *(f)*
motor scooter Motorroller *(m)*
motor sleigh Motorschlitten *(m)*
motor traffic Autoverkehr *(m)*
motor vehicle Kraftfahrzeug *(n)*
motor vehicle insurance Kraftfahrzeugversicherung *(f)*
motor vehicle licence Zulassung *(f)*
motor vehicle user Kraftfahrzeugbenutzer *(m)*
motor-vessel (MV) Motorschiff *(n)*
Motorail Autoreisezug-Service *(m)*
motorcycle Motorrad *(n)*
motoring guide Autoführer *(m)*
motoring journey Autoreise *(f)*
motoring offence Verkehrsdelikt *(n)*
motoring tourist Autoreisender *(m)*
motoring trip Autofahrt *(f)*, Autoreise *(f)*, Autotour *(f)*
motorist Autofahrer *(m)*, Kraftfahrer *(m)*
motorists' roadside assistance service Autohilfe *(f)*
motorship (MS) Motorschiff *(n)*
motorway Autobahn *(f)*
motorway feeder road Autobahnzubringer *(m)*
motorway hotel Autobahnhotel *(n)*
motorway restaurant Autobahnraststätte *(f)*
motorway toll Autobahngebühr *(f)*
mountain Berg *(m)*
mountain air Höhenluft *(f)*
mountain cabin Berghütte *(f)*
mountain climate Höhenklima *(n)*, Gebirgsklima *(n)*
mountain climber Bergsteiger *(m)*
mountain-climbing Klettern *(n)*, Klettersport *(m)*
mountain cock Auerhahn *(m)*
mountain guide Bergführer *(m)*
mountain hike Bergwanderung *(f)*
mountain hotel Berghotel *(n)*
mountain hut Berghütte *(f)*

mountain inn Berggasthof *(m)*
mountain lake Bergsee *(m)*
mountain lodge Hüttenhotel *(n)*
mountain meadow Bergwiese *(f)*
mountain pass Bergpaß *(m)*
mountain peak Berggipfel *(m)*
mountain railway Bergbahn *(f)*
mountain rescue service
   Bergwacht *(f)*
mountain restaurant
   Höhenrestaurant *(n)*, Bergrestaurant *(n)*
mountain road Bergstraße *(f)*, Hochstraße *(f)*
mountain top Berggipfel *(m)*
mountain tour Bergtour *(f)*
mountain village Bergdorf *(n)*
mountaineer Bergsteiger *(m)*
mountaineering Bergsteigen *(n)*, Hochtouristik *(f)*
mountaineering equipment
   Bergsteigerausrüstung *(f)*
mountaineering school
   Bergsteigerschule *(f)*
mountains Gebirge *(n)*, Gebirgswelt *(f)*
mousse Cremespeise *(f)*, Creme *(f)*
mouth wash Mundwasser *(n)*
movable beweglich
move bewegen, beantragen
movie Film *(m)*
movie performance
   Filmvorführung *(f)*, Filmvorstellung *(f)*
movie program Kinoprogramm *(n)*, Filmprogramm *(n)*
movie room Kinosaal *(m)*
movie show Filmvorstellung *(f)*
movie theater Filmtheater *(n)*, Kino *(n)*
movie ticket Kinokarte *(f)*
moving average acquisition costs
   fortgeschriebene durchschnittliche Anschaffungskosten *(pl.)*
moving average production costs
   fortgeschriebene durchschnittliche Herstellungskosten *(pl.)*
mow mähen
much frequented vielbesucht
mud bath Moorbad *(n)*, Schlammbad *(n)*

mud pack Fangopackung *(f)*, Schlammpackung *(f)*
mud therapy Fangotherapie *(f)*
mud treatment Moorbehandlung *(f)*, Fangobehandlung *(f)*
muffins Muffins *(pl.)* (engl. Teegebäck)
mug Krug *(m)*, Becher *(m)*
mulberry Maulbeere *(f)*
mule Maultier *(n)*, Maulesel *(m)*
mulled claret Glühwein *(m)*
mulled wine Glühwein *(m)*
mullet Meerbarbe *(f)*, Seebarbe *(f)*, Meeräsche *(f)*
mulligatawny Geflügelrahmsuppe *(f)* mit Curry *(m)*, Mulligatawny-Suppe *(f)*
multi-car garage Sammelgarage *(f)*
multi-purpose room
   Mehrzweckraum *(m)*
multi-storey garage Hochgarage *(f)*
multi-story car park Parkhochhaus *(n)*
multi-user system
   Mehrbenutzersystem *(n)*
multilateral vielseitig, multilateral
multilingual guide mehrsprachiger Führer *(m)*
multiple vielfach
multiple-unit train Triebwagenzug *(m)*
multiplier Multiplikator *(m)*
multiply multiplizieren
municipal städtisch
municipal district Stadtbezirk *(m)*
municipal museum Stadtmuseum *(n)*
municipal theatre Stadttheater *(n)*
muscatel (wine) Muskateller-Wein *(m)*
mushroom Edelpilz *(m)*, Pilz *(m)*
mushroom sauce Pilzsoße *(f)*
mushroom soup Pilzsuppe *(f)*
mushrooms on toast Pilze *(pl. m)* auf Toast *(m)*, Pilzschnitte *(f)*
music and entertainment Musik *(f)* und Unterhaltung *(f)*
musical Musical *(n)*
musical evening Musikabend *(m)*
musician Musiker *(m)*
mussel Muschel *(f)*
mussel soup Muschelsuppe *(f)*

mustard Senf *(m)*
mustard pot Senfglas *(n)*
mustard sauce Senfsoße *(f)*
musuem Museum *(n)*
mutton Hammel *(m)*
mutton chop Hammelrippchen *(n)*
mutton on skewers Hammelspießchen *(n)*
mutton stew Hammelragout *(n)*
mutual gegenseitig, wechselseitig
mutual agreement gegenseitiger Vertrag *(m)*
mystery tour Fahrt *(f)* ins Blaue *(n)*

N

name nennen, benennen, Name *(m)*
nap Mittagsschlaf *(m)*
napkin Serviette *(f)*
narrow eng, schmal
narrow film Schmalfilm *(m)*
narrow seas Ärmelkanal *(m)* und Irische See *(f)*
nasturtium Kapuzinerkresse *(f)*, Brunnenkresse *(f)*
national einheimisch, Staatsangehörige *(f)*, Staatsangehöriger *(m)*
national costume Nationaltracht *(f)*, Volkstracht *(f)*
national currency Landeswährung *(f)*
national holiday Nationalfeiertag *(m)*
national language Landessprache *(f)*
national park Reservat *(n)*, Nationalpark *(m)*
national tourist Inlandsgast *(m)*
nationality Staatsangehörigkeit *(f)*, Nationalität *(f)*
nationality sign Nationalitätszeichen *(n)*
nationalize verstaatlichen
native eingeboren, einheimisch, Einheimische (r) *(f)*, *(m)*
native language Muttersprache *(f)*
native town Heimatstadt *(f)*
natron kohlensaures Natron *(n)*
natural curative factor natürlicher Heilfaktor *(m)*
natural resources Bodenschätze *(pl. m)*

nature Natur *(f)*, natürliche Landschaft *(f)*
nature conservation Naturschutz *(m)*
nature cure Naturheilbehandlung *(f)*
nature reserve Naturschutzgebiet *(n)*, Reservat *(n)*
naturism Freikörperkultur *(f)*
naturopath Heilpraktiker *(m)*, Naturheilkundige *(m)*
naturopathy Naturheilmethode *(f)*, Naturheilverfahren *(n)*
nausea Übelkeit *(f)*, Brechreiz *(m)*, Seekrankheit *(f)*
nautical chart Seekarte *(f)*
nautical mile Seemeile (1.852km) *(f)*
navel orange Navelorange *(f)*
navigability Befahrbarkeit *(f)*, Schiffbarkeit *(f)*
navigable schiffbar
navigable river schiffbarer Fluß *(m)*
navigate schiffen, befahren
navigation Nautik *(f)*, Navigation *(f)*, Schiffahrtskunde *(f)*, Navigationskunde *(f)*, Schiffahrt *(f)*
navigation channel Fahrrinne *(f)*
navigation guide Navigationskarte *(f)*
navigation light Positionslicht *(n)*
navigator Steuermann *(m)*
near nahe, in der Nähe *(f)*
near at hand nahe, in der Nähe *(f)*, dicht dabei
near beer Dünnbier *(n)*
Near East Naher Osten
nearest nächster (Entfernung)
neat unverdünnt, pur, rein, sauber
necklace Halskette *(f)*
need Bedarf *(m)*, Bedürfnis *(n)*
negative Negativ *(n)*
neglect vernachlässigen, versäumen
negotiability Begebbarkeit *(f)*, Umlauffähigkeit *(f)*, Marktfähigkeit *(f)*, Indossierbarkeit *(f)*
negotiable begebbar, indossierbar
negotiable instrument begebbares Instrument *(n)* (z.B. Wechsel, Scheck)
negotiable note umlauffähiger kurz- bzw. mittelfristiger Schuldschein *(m)*
negotiate verhandeln, abschließen

negotiation Verhandlung *(f)*,
  Abschluß *(m)*
neighbourhood Nachbarschaft *(f)*
neighbouring country Nachbarland
  (n)
**net cost of food and beverage sales
  (schedule 2)** bereinigte
  Warenkosten *(pl.)* (Umsatzbereich 2)
net income Jahresüberschuß *(m)*
net other income (schedule 2)
  sonstige Umsätze *(pl. m)* – netto
  (Umsatzbereich 2)
net proceeds Reinertrag *(m)*
net property and equipment
  Sachanlagevermögen *(n)* abzüglich
  Abschreibungen *(pl. f)*
net receivables Forderungen *(pl. f)*
  abzüglich der uneinbringlichen
  Forderungen *(pl. f)*
net revenue Nettoumsatz *(m)*,
  Nettoerlös *(m)*
net weight Reingewicht *(n)*
net worth Eigenkapital *(n)*
net (offset) saldieren
neutrality Neutralität *(f)*
  (Rechnungslegung)
new-fallen snow Neuschnee *(m)*
new potatoes neue Kartoffeln
  (pl. f)
new wine junger Wein *(m)*
New Year's cruise Neujahrskreuzfahrt *(f)*, Silvesterreise *(f)*
New Year's Day Neujahrstag *(m)*
New Year's dinner
  Silvesterdiner *(n)*
New Year's Eve celebration
  Silvesterfeier *(f)*
news stall Zeitschriftenkiosk *(m)*
news stand Zeitungsstand *(m)*,
  Kiosk *(m)*
newspaper Zeitung *(f)*
newspaper advertising
  Zeitungswerbung *(f)*
newsreel Wochenschau *(f)*
next of kin nächster Verwandter *(m)*
night and sunday duty Nacht- und
  Sonntagsdienst *(m)*
night-cleaner
  Nachtreinigungspersonal *(n)*
night-club Nachtklub *(m)*,
  Nachtlokal *(n)*, Nachtbar *(f)*

night concierge Nachtportier *(m)*
night flight Nachtflug *(m)*
night life Nachtleben *(n)*
night manager Direktionsvertreter
  (m) während der Nacht *(f)*
night rate Nachttarif *(m)*
night rest Nachtruhe *(f)*
night run Nachtpiste *(f)*
night service Nachtverkehr *(m)*
night shift Nachtschicht *(f)*
night shift bonus Nachtschichtvergütung *(f)*
night shirt Herrennachthemd *(n)*
night-telephone operator
  Nachttelefonistin *(f)*
night traffic Nachtverkehr *(m)*
night train Nachtzug *(m)*
night trip Nachtfahrt *(f)*
night-watchman Nachtwächter *(m)*
nightdress Nachthemd *(n)*
nightwork Nachtarbeit *(f)*
night's lodging Übernachtung *(f)*,
  Schlafstelle *(f)*
ninepin Kegel *(m)*
no admittance kein Eintritt *(m)*
no entry Eintritt *(m)* verboten!,
  Einfahrt *(f)* verboten!
no honking (no hooting) hupen
  verboten!
no overtaking Überholverbot *(n)*
no right turn rechts abbiegen
  verboten
no stopping Halteverbot *(n)*
no stopping this side today
  Halteverbot *(n)* heute auf dieser
  Straßenseite *(f)*
no through road keine Durchfahrt *(f)*
no U-turn wenden verboten!
no waiting Parkverbot *(n)*
noise Lärm *(m)*, Geräusch *(n)*
noise control Lärmbekämpfung *(f)*
nominal account Erfolgskonto *(n)*
non-alcoholic alkoholfrei
non-alcoholic beverage
  alkoholfreies Getränk *(n)*
nonbusiness organization nicht
  unternehmerisch tätige
  Organisation *(f)*
nonconsolidated subsidiary
  nichtkonsolidiertes
  Beteiligungsunternehmen *(n)*

noncurrent assets langfristige Vermögenswerte *(pl. m)*, Vermögensteile *(pl. m)*
noncurrent receivables Forderungen *(pl. f)*, die nach einem Zeitraum *(m)* von 12 Monaten fällig sind; langfristige Forderungen *(pl. f)*
nondeductible nicht abzugsfähig
nondelivery Nichtlieferung *(f)*
nondurable goods Verbrauchsgüter *(pl. n)*
non-dutiable nicht zollpflichtig
nonfulfillment Nichterfüllung *(f)*
non-malted nicht gemälzt
nonproduction group produktionsunabhängige Stelle *(f)*
non-scheduled flight Sonderflug *(m)*
non-smoker Nichtraucher *(m)*
non-smoker compartment Nichtraucherabteil *(n)*
non-stop flight Non-Stop-Flug *(m)*, Flug *(m)* ohne Zwischenlandung *(f)*
non-swimmer Nichtschwimmer *(m)*
non-swimmers' pool Nichtschwimmerbecken *(n)*
nontrading corporation nicht handeltreibende Körperschaft *(f)*
noodle Nudel *(f)*
noodle-dish with grated cheese Teigwaren mit geriebenem Käse *(pl. f)*
noodle soup Nudelsuppe *(f)*
noon Mittag *(m)*
normal performance Normalleistung *(f)*
normal-fare ticket Vollpreisfahrkarte *(f)*
north wind Nordwind *(m)*
Norway Norwegen
Norway lobster Langustinen *(pl. f)*
nose-to-tail collision Auffahrunfall *(m)*
note aufzeichnen, vermerken, notieren, Mitteilung *(f)*, Aufzeichnung *(f)*, Notiz *(f)*
note-paper Briefpapier *(n)*, Schreibpapier *(n)*
notes Anhang *(m)*

notes accompanying the financial statements Anmerkungen *(pl. f)* zum Jahresabschluß *(m)*
notes payable Schuldwechsel *(m)*, Wechselverbindlichkeiten *(pl. f)*
notes receivable Besitzwechsel *(m)*, Wechselforderungen *(pl. f)*
notes receivable trade Handelswechsel *(m)*
notice bekanntgeben, wahrnehmen, Bekanntgabe *(f)*
notice of accident Unfallmeldung *(f)*
notice of claim Schadensanzeige *(f)*
notice of defects Mängelanzeige *(f)*
notice of departure Abmeldung *(f)*
notifiable meldepflichtig, anzeigepflichtig
notification Benachrichtigung *(f)*, Bekanntgabe *(f)*
notification of a loss Verlustanzeige *(f)*
notify avisieren
nourish ernähren
nourishment Nahrung *(f)*, Nahrungsmittel *(n)*
novelty Neuheit *(f)*
nudism FKK, Freikörperkultur *(f)*
nuisance Belästigung *(f)*, Unfug *(m)*, Störung *(f)*
null and void null und nichtig
number of arrivals Anzahl *(f)* der Ankünfte *(pl. f)*
number of food covers Anzahl *(f)* der Essensgedecke *(pl. n)*
number of participants Teilnehmerzahl *(f)*
number plate Nummernschild *(n)*
nurse Krankenschwester *(f)*
nursemaid Kindermädchen *(n)*
nursey Kinderzimmer *(n)*, Spielzimmer *(n)*
nut Nuß *(f)*
nut bun Nußbeugel *(n)*
nut butter Nußbutter *(f)*, braune Butter *(f)*
nut ice Nußeis *(n)*
nut pudding Nußpudding *(m)*
nut tart Nußtorte *(f)*
nutmeg Muskatnuß *(f)*
nutrition Ernährung *(f)*

O

oak Eiche *(f)*
oar Ruder *(n)*
oasis Oase *(f)*
oat Hafer *(m)*
oat flakes Haferflocken *(pl.f)*
oatmeal Hafermehl *(n)*
oatmeal cream soup
  Haferschleimsuppe *(f)*
oats Haferflocken *(pl.f)*
object Gegenstand *(m)*
object to beanstanden
objection Beanstandung *(f)*
objective Ziel *(n)*, Zielsetzung *(f)*
obligate verpflichten
obligation Verpflichtung *(f)*, Schuld *(f)*, Verbindlichkeit *(f)*
obligation to register with the police polizeiliche Meldepflicht *(f)*
obligatory verpflichtend, bindend
oblige verpflichten
observation Beobachtung *(f)*
observation platform
  Besucherbalkon *(m)*
observation tower Aussichtsturm *(m)*
observation window
  Aussichtsfenster *(n)*
observatory Sternwarte *(f)*, Observatorium *(n)*
observe beobachten
occasion Gelegenheit *(f)*
occasional customers
  Laufkundschaft *(f)*
occupancy Belegung *(f)*,
  Hotelbelegung *(f)*; Aneignung *(f)*
occupancy percentage
  Belegungsprozentsatz *(m)*
occupation Beruf *(m)*,
  Beschäftigung *(f)*
occupational illness
  Berufskrankheit *(f)*
occupied besetzt
ocean Ozean *(m)*
ocean-going hochseetüchtig
ocean liner Ozeandampfer *(m)*
odour Geruch *(m)*, Duft *(m)*
of age mündig, volljährig
off-licence inn Gassenschenke *(f)*
off limits Zutritt *(m)* verboten

off-peak fare Vor- und
  Nachsaisonfahrpreis *(m)*
off-peak period verkehrsarme Zeit *(f)*
off-peak season Vor- und
  Nachsaison *(f)*
off-season tote Saison *(f)*
off-time Freizeit *(f)*
off the beaten track abgelegen
off the peg von der Stange
off the road abseits der Straße *(f)*
offals Innereien *(pl.f)*
offend beleidigen
offer anbieten, offerieren, Angebot *(n)*, Offerte *(f)*
offer of employment Stellenangebot *(n)*
office Büro *(n)*, Service-Office *(n)*
office equipment Büroausstattung *(f)*
office furniture, fixtures and equipment Büromobiliar *(n)*, -einbauten *(pl.)* und -maschinen *(pl.f)*
office hours Geschäftszeit *(f)*
office supplies Büromaterial *(n)*
officer Vorstandsmitglied *(n)*,
  Mitglied *(n)* der Geschäftsleitung *(f)*
official offiziell, amtlich
oil Öl *(n)*
oil-changing Ölwechsel *(m)*
oil-fired central heating
  Ölzentralheizung *(f)*
oil heating Ölheizung *(f)*
oil level Ölstand *(m)*
old alt
old-fashioned altmodisch
old snow Altschnee *(m)*
old town Altstadt *(f)*
old wine alter Wein *(m)*
olive Olive *(f)*
olive oil Olivenöl *(n)*
olives, stuffed Oliven *(pl.f)* gefüllt
Olympic city Olympiastadt *(f)*
Olympic Games Olympische Spiele *(pl.n)*
omelet Omelett *(n)*
omelet soufflé Auflaufomelett *(n)*
omelet with fine herbs
  Kräuteromelett *(n)*
omelet with ham Schinkenomelett *(n)*
omelet with mushrooms
  Champignonomelett *(n)*

omnibus Omnibus *(m)*
on behalf of namens
on board an Bord *(m)*
on board ship auf dem Schiff *(n)*
on demand auf Verlangen *(n)*
on hand vorrätig, vorhanden
on hand (amount) Bestand *(m)*
on lease pachtweise, mietweise
on leaving the country bei der Ausreise *(f)*
on schedule planmäßig
on shore ans Land *(n)*
on short routes auf kurzen Strecken *(pl.f)*
on the high seas auf hoher See *(f)*
on the job training Ausbildung *(f)* am Arbeitsplatz *(m)*
on the quay am Kai *(n)*
on the rocks Getränk *(n)* mit Eis(-würfel) *(n)*
on the sea zur See *(f)*, an der See *(f)*
on the spit am Spieß gebraten *(m)*
on trial auf Probe *(f)*
oncoming traffic entgegenkommender Verkehr *(m)*, Gegenverkehr *(m)*
one-armed bandit Spielautomat *(m)*
one man operation Einmannbetrieb *(m)*
one-room flat Einzelzimmerappartement *(n)*
one-way street Einbahnstraße *(f)*
onion Zwiebel *(f)*
onion mash Zwiebelmus *(n)*
onion sauce Zwiebelsoße *(f)*
onward air journey Weiterflug *(m)*
open offen, öffnen
open-air bath Freibad *(n)*
open-air café Straßencafé *(n)*, Gartencafé *(n)*
open-air dance Tanz *(m)* im Freien
open-air rest cure Liegekur *(f)*
open-air restaurant Gartenlokal *(n)*, Gartenrestaurant *(n)*
open-air stage Freiluftbühne *(f)*
open-air swimming-pool Freibad *(n)*, Sommerbad *(n)*
open-air theatre Freiluftbühne *(f)*, Freilufttheater *(n)*
open-air ticket offener Flugschein *(m)*

open-air veranda Liegehalle *(f)*
open all the year round ganzjährig geöffnet
open an account Konto *(n)* eröffnen
open bar Open Bar *(f)*
open check Barscheck *(m)*
open market freier Markt *(m)*
open-door policy Politik *(f)* der offenen Tür *(f)*
open pie Pizza *(f)*
open price freier Preis *(m)*
open sandwich belegtes Brot *(n)* (einfach)
open season Jagdsaison *(f)*, Jagdzeit *(f)*
open space Grünfläche *(f)*
open-water port Hafen *(m)* am offenen Meer *(n)*
open wine offener Wein *(m)*
opening freie Stelle *(f)*, Eröffnung *(f)*
opening of the season Saisoneröffnung *(f)*
opera Oper *(f)*
Opera Ball Opernball *(m)*
opera house Opernhaus *(n)*
operate verkehren, funktionieren, in Betrieb *(m)* halten, Reisen *(pl.f)* abwickeln, Gäste *(pl.m)* bedienen
operates daily verkehrt täglich
operating all the year round ganzjährig in Betrieb *(m)*
operating cycle Geschäftszyklus *(m)*, Betriebskreislauf *(m)*
operating months Betriebszeit *(f)*
operating rate Beschäftigungsgrad *(m)*
operating supplies Betriebsstoffe *(pl.m)*
operating system Betriebssystem *(n)*
operational einsatzfähig, einsatzbereit
operational control Betriebskontrolle *(f)*
operational management Operational Management *(n)*, praktisches Hotelmanagement *(n)*, Betriebsführung *(f)*
operator Telefonistin *(f)*
operetta house Operettentheater *(n)*
opinion Meinung *(f)*, Prüfmeinung *(f)*
opinion survey Meinungsumfrage *(f)*

opportunity advertising Gelegenheitswerbung (f)
opposite gegenüber, entgegengesetzt, Gegenteil (n)
optical optisch
optimal lot size optimale Losgröße (f)
option Option (f), befristetes Kaufangebot (n)
option Optionsrecht (n)
option date Erklärungstag (m)
optional wahlfrei, fakultativ, freigestellt
oral mündlich
orange Orange (f), Apfelsine (f)
orange ice-cream Orangeneis (n)
orangeade Orangeade (f), natürliche Orangenlimonade (f)
orchestra Orchester (n)
order bestellen, beauftragen, Bestellung (f), Auftrag (m); Ordnung (f)
order by telephone telefonische Bestellung (f)
order copy Bestellkopie (f)
order form Bestellformular (n)
order pad Bestellscheinblock (m)
order quantity Bestellmenge (f)
order taking Bestellaufnahme (f)
ordering procedure Bestellverfahren (n)
ordering rate Bestellhäufigkeit (f)
orderly ordentlich, ordnungsgemäß
ordinary gewöhnlich
organization Organisation (f), Einrichtung (f), Betrieb (m)
organization chart Organigramm (n), Organisationsplan (m)
organize organisieren, einrichten
organized tour Gesellschaftsreise (f)
organizer Veranstalter (m), Organisator (m)
orient Osten (m), Morgenland (n)
orientation plan Orientierungstafel (f)
orientation training Einführungsschulung (f)
origin Herkunft (f), Ursprung (m), abstammung (f)
original historical acquisition or production costs ursprüngliche Anschaffungs- oder Herstellungskosten (pl.)

ornamental fountains Wasserspiele (pl. n)
other assets, at cost less amortization sonstiges Vermögen (n), zu Anschaffungskosten (pl.) abzüglich Abschreibungen (pl.f)
other assets, net sonstige Aktiva (pl.), netto
other catering operations sonstige Dienstleistungen (pl.f)
other cost of sales (schedule 2) sonstige Warenkosten (pl.) (Umsatzbereich 2)
other income (schedule 2) sonstige Umsätze (pl. m) (Umsatzbereich 2)
other operated departments Nebenbetriebe (pl. m), sonstige Betriebsabteilungen (pl.f)
ounce, o.z. Unze (f), 28,350g
out of date verfallen
out-of-line abweichend vom Üblichen (n)
out-of-pocket expense Barauslage (f)
out of the way abgelegen
outboard motor boat Außenbord-Motorboot (n)
outdoor advertising Außenwerbung (f)
outdoor bath Freibad (n)
outdoor dress Straßenkleidung (f)
outfit Ausstattung (f), Ausrüstung (f)
outing Ausflug (m), Ausfahrt (f), Exkursion (f)
outing in the country Landausflug (m)
outlet Betriebsstätte (f), Absatzmarkt (m), Großabnehmer (m), Auslaß (m), Steckdose (f)
outline umreißen, Umriß (m)
output Produktionsmenge (f), Arbeitsleistung (f)
outside representative Außenvertreter (m)
outside room Außenkabine (f)
outsider Außenseiter (m)
outstanding hervorragend
outstanding shares alle im Umlauf (m) befindlichen Aktien (pl.f)
outward äußerlich, Aus(wärts)...

outward and homeward voyage Hin- und Rückreise *(f)*
outward and inward flight Hin- und Rückflug *(m)*
outward and inward journey Hin- und Rückreise *(f)*, Hin- und Rückfahrt *(f)*
outward flight Hinflug *(m)*
outward journey Hinreise *(f)*, Hinflug *(m)*, Hinfahrt *(f)*
outward voyage Hinfahrt *(f)*, Hinreise *(f)*
oven Bratofen *(m)*, Backofen *(m)*
oven-baked im Ofen *(m)* gebacken
oven-baked apple im Ofen gebackener Apfel *(m)*
overall labor agreement Manteltarifvertrag *(m)*
overcapacity Überkapazität *(f)*
overcharge überfordern, zuviel berechnen
overcoat Mantel *(m)*, Überzieher *(m)*
overcome überwinden
overcook zu stark braten
overcrowded überfüllt, überlaufen
overdone übergar
overdraw überziehen
overdue überfällig
overestimate überschätzen, Überschätzung *(f)*
overflow Überlauf *(m)*
overhauls Generalüberholung *(f)*
overhead cost Gemeinkosten *(pl.)*
overhead expenses Gemeinkosten *(pl.)*
overhead railway Hochbahn *(f)*
overland transportation Überlandverkehr *(m)*
overlap überlappen, überlagern
overload überladen
overlooking mit Blick *(m)* auf
overnight accommodation Übernachtungsmöglichkeit *(f)*, Schlafstelle *(f)*
overnight bag Stadtkoffer *(m)*
overnight charge Übernachtungspreis *(m)*
overnight express Nachtschnellzug *(m)*
overnight stay Übernachtung *(f)*

overnight stay en route Zwischenübernachtung *(f)*
overpay überzahlen
overproduction Überproduktion *(f)*
overriding commission zusätzlicher Provisionssatz *(m)* für Vermittlungen *(pl.f)* über eine vereinbarte Menge *(f)* hinaus
overseas shipment Überseetransport *(m)*
overseas telegram Auslandstelegramm *(n)*
overseas tourist Auslandstourist *(m)*
overseas visitor Auslandsgast *(m)*
oversea(s) in (nach) Übersee
oversleep oneself verschlafen
overstaffed personell überbesetzt
overstocking Überbevorratung *(f)*
overtake überholen, einholen
overtime Überstunden *(pl.f)*
overture Ouvertüre *(f)*
overwhelm überwätigen, überwinden
owe verdanken, schuldig sein
own consumption Eigenverbrauch *(m)*
owner Eigentümer *(m)*
owner-driver Selbstfahrer *(m)*
ownership Eigentum *(n)*
owner's equity (proprietorship) Eigenkapital *(n)* (Einzelfirma)
owning company Eigentümergesellschaft *(f)*
ox Ochse *(m)*
ox-muzzle salad Ochsenmaulsalat *(m)*
ox-palate Ochsengaumen *(m)*
ox-tail Ochsenschwanz *(m)*
oxtail soup Ochsenschwanzsuppe *(f)*
oxtail stew Ochsenschwanzragout *(n)*
ox-tongue Ochsenzunge *(f)*
oxfords Straßenschuhe *(pl.m)*
oxygen bath Sauerstoffbad *(n)*
oyster Auster *(f)*
oyster bank Austernbank *(f)*
oyster bed Austernbank *(f)*
oyster farm Austernpark *(m)*
ozone Ozon *(n)*, reine Luft *(f)*
ozonic ozonisch
ozonic bath Ozonbad *(n)*
ozoniferous ozonhaltig
oz. (= ounce) Unze (28,350g) *(f)*

P

pace Schritt *(m)*, Tempo *(n)*, Leistung *(f)*
pack packen, verpacken, Packung *(f)*
package Paket *(n)*, Packung *(f)*, Programm *(n)*
package freight Stückgutfracht *(f)*
package tour Pauschalreise *(f)*
packaging Verpackung *(f)*, verpacken
packaging expenses Verpackungskosten *(pl.)*
packed lunch Lunchpaket *(n)*, Reiseproviant *(m)*
packing Verpackung *(f)*
paddle paddeln, planschen, Paddel *(n)*
paddle-steamer Raddampfer *(m)*
paddling-boat Paddelboot *(n)*
paddlingpool Planschbecken *(n)*
paddy roher Reis *(m)*
pagan Heide *(f)*
pageant Festumzug *(m)*, Trachtenfest *(n)*
pageboy Page *(m)*
paid holiday bezahlter Urlaub *(m)*
paid in advance (pia) Barzahlung *(f)* bei Ankunft *(f)* (des Gastes)
paid-in capital eingezahltes Kapital *(n)*, Grund- oder Stammkapital *(n)*
paid-up voll bezahlt, voll eingezahlt
painting and decorating Malerarbeiten *(pl.f)* und Dekoration *(f)*
palate Gaumen *(m)*
pale ale helles Bier *(n)*
Palm Sunday Palmsonntag *(m)*
pamphlet Broschüre *(f)*
pan Pfanne *(f)*, Topf *(m)*
pan fried pork sausage Bratwurst *(f)*
pancake Pfannkuchen *(m)*
pancake Emperor style Kaiserschmarrn *(m)*
pancake soup Pfannkuchensuppe *(f)*
pane Fensterscheibe *(f)*
panhandle Pfannenstiel *(m)*
pannikin Pfännchen *(n)*, (Trink-)Kännchen *(n)*
panorama Panorama *(n)*, Rundblick *(m)*, Rundsicht *(f)*
pantry Speisekammer *(f)*, Ausgabestelle *(f)* für Frühstück *(n)*

pantry girl Küchenhilfe *(f)*
pap (Kinder-)Brei *(m)*
paper bag cooking Kochen *(n)* in Folie *(f)*
paper napkin Papierserviette *(f)*
paper supplies Papierwaren *(pl.f)*
paper work Büroarbeiten *(pl.f)*
pappy breiig, pappig
paprika Paprika *(m)*
par value Nominalwert *(m)*, Nennwert *(m)*
par value capital stock Grundkapital *(n)*, dessen Aktien *(pl.f)* über einen bestimmten Nennbetrag *(m)* lauten
parasol Sonnenschirm *(m)*
parboil anbraten, ankochen
parcel Paket *(n)*
parcel post Paketpost *(f)*
parent company Muttergesellschaft *(f)*
parfait halbgefrorenes Eis *(n)*
park bench Ruhebank *(f)*
parka Anorak *(m)*, Parka *(m)*
parking attendant Parkwächter *(m)*
parking disk Parkscheibe *(f)*
parking facilities Parkmöglichkeit *(f)*, Parkgelegenheit *(f)*
parking lot Parkplatz *(m)*
parking meter Parkuhr *(f)*
parking place Parkplatz *(m)*
parlor Salon *(m)*, Wohnraum *(m)*
parlour Gastzimmer *(n)*
parlour game Gesellschaftsspiel *(n)*
parlour-maid Reinigungskraft *(f)*
Parmesan cheese Parmesankäse *(m)*
parsley Petersilie *(f)*
parsley potatoes Petersilienkartoffeln *(pl.f)*
Parsley sauce Petersiliensoße *(f)*
part teilen, auseinandergehen, einteilen, zuteilen, Stück *(n)*, Teil *(m)*, Bestandteil *(m)*
part payment Teilzahlung *(f)*
part-timer Teilzeitarbeiter *(m)*, Aushilfe *(f)*, Kurzarbeiter *(m)*
partial teilweise
partial board Teilverpflegung *(f)*
partial cancellation Teilstornierung *(f)*
partial massage Teilmassage *(f)*

partial payment Teilzahlung *(f)*, Abschlagszahlung *(f)*
participant Teilnehmer *(m)*, Teilhaber *(m)*
participate teilhaben, teilnehmen, sich beteiligen
participating certificate Genußschein *(m)*
participation Anteil *(m)*, Teilnahme *(f)*, Beteiligung *(f)*
particulars Einzelangaben *(pl.f)*
partition Trennwand *(f)*
partnership Personengesellschaft, etwa: Offene Handelsgesellschaft (OHG) *(f)*, Gesellschaft des bürgerlichen Rechts (GbR) *(f)*; Teilhaberschaft *(f)*, Sozietät *(f)* (Anwälte, Ärzte etc.)
partridge Rebhuhn *(n)*, Schnepfe *(f)*
partridge pie Rebhuhnpastete *(f)*
party flight Gesellschaftsflug *(m)*
party game Gesellschaftsspiel *(n)*
party outing Gesellschaftsfahrt *(f)*, Gruppenfahrt *(f)*, Sammelfahrt *(f)*
party rate Gruppentarif *(m)*
party ticket Sammelfahrschein *(m)*
party tour Gesellschaftsreise *(f)*, Gruppenreise *(f)*
party travel Gesellschaftsreisen *(pl.f)*, Gruppenreisen *(pl.f)*
party trip Gesellschaftsfahrt *(f)*, Gruppenfahrt *(f)*
pass übergeben, weiterreichen, übergehen, vergehen, Zugang *(m)*, Paß *(m)*, Durchgang *(m)*
pass in the Alps Alpenpaß *(m)*
pass on abwälzen
pass over übergehen, übergeben
passability Befahrbarkeit *(f)*
passable befahrbar
passage Durchfahrt *(f)*, Gang *(m)*
passenger Fahrgast *(m)*, Passagier *(m)*
passenger car Personenwagen *(m)*
passenger carriage Personentransport *(m)*, Personenverkehr *(m)*
passenger density Reisedichte *(f)*
passenger fare Passagenpreis *(m)*
passenger ferry Personenfähre *(f)*
passenger plane Passagierflugzeug *(n)*
passenger ship Passagierschiff *(n)*
passenger steamer Passagierdampfer *(m)*
passenger traffic Personenverkehr *(m)*
passenger train Reisezug *(m)*, Personenzug *(m)*
passenger's luggage Passagiergepäck *(n)*
passing place Ausweichstelle *(f)*
passionate hitzig, leidenschaftlich
passkey Hauptschlüssel *(m)*
passport Reisepaß *(m)*
passport and customs examination Zoll- und Paßabfertigung *(f)*
passport inspection Paßkontrolle *(f)*, Paßabfertigung *(f)*
passport office Paßstelle *(f)*
passport regulations Paßvorschriften *(pl.f)*
past due überfällig
paste Teig *(m)*
pasteurization Pasteurisierung *(f)*
pasteurized milk pasteurisierte Milch *(f)*
pastry Gebäck *(n)*
pastry board Nudelbrett *(n)*
pastry cook Patissier *(m)*, Zuckerbäcker *(m)*
pastry envelopes Teigtaschen *(pl.f)*
pastry envelopes filled with white cheese Quarktaschen *(pl.f)*
pasturage Weideland *(n)*
pasture Weide *(f)*
patchboard Schalttafel *(f)*
patchcord Steckschnur *(f)*
patent Patent *(n)*
patent violation Patentverletzung *(f)*
patron Gast *(m)*, Kunde *(m)*, Stammkunde *(m)*
patt Blätterteigpastetchen *(n)*, Pastetchen *(n)*
pattern Muster *(n)*, Probe *(f)*
paté Pastete *(f)*
paté de foie gras Gänseleberpastete *(f)*
pavement Bürgersteig *(m)*
pawn pfänden
pawpaw Baummelone *(f)*
pax Gast *(m)*, Passagier *(m)*

pay zahlen bezahlen, Lohn *(m)*, Gehalt *(n)*
pay cash bar bezahlen
pay damages Schadenersatz *(m)* leisten
pay day Zahltag *(m)*
pay load Nutzlast *(f)*
payable zahlbar, fällig
paying form Zahlkarte *(f)*
paying guest zahlender Gast *(m)*
paying habit Zahlungsgewohnheit *(f)*
paymaster Zahlmeister *(m)*
payment Zahlung *(f)*, Bezahlung *(f)*, Auszahlung *(f)*
payment in kind Naturalleistung *(f)*
payment of travellers Reisezahlungsverkehr *(m)*
payroll deductions einbehaltene Lohnsteuer *(f)* und Sozialabgaben *(pl.f)*
pea Erbse *(f)*
pea mash Erbsenpüree *(n)*
pea soup Erbsensuppe *(f)*; dichter Nebel *(m)* (scherzhafter Ausdruck); Waschküche *(f)*
peaceful friedlich, ungestört
peach Pfirsich *(m)*
peach Melba Pfirsich Melba *(m)*
peaches ice-cream Pfirsich-Eis *(n)*
peacock Pfau *(m)*
peak days Verkehrsspitze *(f)*
peak hour Zeit *(f)* der Spitzenbelastung *(f)*, Stoßzeit *(f)*
peak hour traffic Stoßverkehr *(m)*, Spitzenverkehr *(m)*
peak load Stoßarbeit *(f)*, Belastungsspitze *(f)*, Arbeitshäufung *(f)*
peak period Stoßzeit *(f)*
peak season Hochsaison *(f)*
peak season fare Hauptsaisonflugpreis *(m)*
peak tourist season Hauptreisezeit *(f)*
peak tourist traffic Hauptreiseverkehr *(m)*
peanut Erdnuß *(f)*
peanut butter Erdnußbutter *(f)*
pear Birne *(f)*
pebbly beach Kiesstrand *(m)*

pedestrian crossing Fußgängerübergang *(m)*
peel schälen, Schale *(f)*
peeled geschält
peeling Haut *(f)*, Rinde *(f)*, Schale *(f)*
pem(m)ican Pemmikan *(m)*
penalty Geldstrafe *(f)*, Strafstoß *(m)* (Sport)
peninsula Halbinsel *(f)*
penknife Taschenmesser *(n)*
penny-in-the-slot Automat *(m)*, Verkaufsautomat *(m)*
pension obligations Pensionsrückstellungen *(pl.f)*
pension reserves Pensionsrückstellungen *(pl.f)*
pension scheme Pensionsplan *(m)*
Pentecost Pfingsten *(n)*
penthouse Dachwohnung *(f)*, Nebengebäude *(n)*
pepper Pfeffer *(m)*, Pfefferschote *(f)*
pepper-box Pfeffergefäß *(n)*
pepper cake Ingwerkuchen *(m)*
pepper-castor Pfefferstreuer *(m)*
peppercorn Pfefferkorn *(n)*
pepper mill Pfeffermühle *(f)*
peppermint Pfefferminze *(f)*
pepper-pot Pfefferstreuer *(m)*
pepper-steak Pfeffersteak *(n)*
per annum im Jahr *(n)*, jährlich
per day pro Tag *(m)*, täglich
per diem allowance Reisespesen-Tagessatz *(m)*
perambulate durchwandern, bereisen, besichtigen
perambulation Durchwanderung *(f)*, Besichtigungsreise *(f)*
perch Barsch *(m)*
perch-pike Fogosch (Zander) *(m)*
percolate Kaffee *(m)* etc. filtern
percolator Perkolator *(m)*, Kaffee(filter)maschine *(f)*
peregrinate wandern, umherreisen
peregrination Wandern *(n)*, Wanderung *(f)*
performance Aufführung *(f)* (Theater); Leistung *(f)*, Leistungsgrad *(m)*
performance appraisal Arbeitsplatzbewertung *(f)*, Leistungsbewertung *(f)*

performance control
  Leistungskontrolle *(f)*
performance standard
  Leistungsmaßstab *(m)*
period of stay Aufenthaltsdauer *(f)*
period of validity Gültigkeitsdauer
  (f)
periodical Zeitschrift *(f)*
perishable leicht verderblich
  (Lebensmittel)
perishable goods verderbliche
  Waren *(pl.f)*
permanent dauernd, ständig
permanent residence ständiger
  Wohnsitz *(m)*
permanent resident Dauergast *(m)*
permanently open durchgehend
  geöffnet
permission Erlaubnis *(f)*
permit erlauben, gestatten, Erlaubnis
  (f), Genehmigung *(f)*, Passierschein
  (m)
perpendicular senkrecht
Persian blinds Jalousien *(pl.f)*
persimmon Kakipflaume *(f)*
personal belonging persönliche
  Gebrauchsgegenstände *(pl. m)*
personal computer
  Personalcomputer *(m)*
personal data Personenbeschreibung
  (f)
personal expenses persönliche
  Ausgaben *(pl.f)*
personal selling persönlicher
  Verkauf *(m)*
personal status Familienstand *(m)*
personnel Personal *(n)*
personnel department
  Personalabteilung *(f)*
personnel manager Personalchef *(m)*
personnel requisition
  Personalanforderung *(f)*
**PERT, Program Evaluation and
  Review Technique**
  Netzplantechnik *(f)*,
  Projektfortschrittsplanung *(f)*
pet Haustier *(n)*
petrol Benzin *(n)*
petrol can Benzinkanister *(m)*
petrol consumption
  Benzinverbrauch *(m)*

petrol station Tankstelle *(f)*
petrol tank Benzintank *(m)*
petrol voucher Benzinschein *(m)*
pettitoes Schweinsfüße *(pl.m)*
petty cash kleine Kasse *(f)*,
  Bargeldkasse *(f)*
pewit Kiebitz *(m)*
pharmacy Apotheke *(f)*
pheasant Fasan *(m)*
photo Foto *(n)*
photo safari Fotosafari *(f)*
photographic equipment
  Fotoausrüstung *(f)*
photographing not allowed
  Fotografieren *(n)* verboten!
physical inventory count
  körperliche Bestandsaufnahme *(f)*
  der Warenvorräte *(pl. m)*
physiotherapist Krankengymnast
  (m)
physiotherapy Heilgymnastik *(f)*,
  Krankengymnastik *(f)*
piano Klavier *(n)*
piccalilli scharf gewürztes
  Essiggemüse *(n)*
pick-me-up (Magen-)Stärkung *(f)*,
  Schnäpschen *(n)*
picking-up point
  Zusteigemöglichkeit *(f)*
pickle Essigsoße *(f)* (zum Einlegen),
  Gewürzgurke *(f)*, Essiggurke *(f)*
pickled gepökelt
pickled beef's muzzle
  Ochsenmaulsalat *(m)*
pickled cabbage Sauerkraut *(n)*,
  Weinkraut *(n)*
pickled cucumber saure Gurke *(f)*
pickled fish marinierter Fisch *(m)*
pickled fruit Senfobst *(n)*,
  Senffrüchte *(pl.f)*
pickled gherkin Gewürzgurke *(f)*
pickled onion Perlzwiebel *(f)*
pickled pork Pökelfleisch *(n)*,
  Eisbein *(n)*
pickled shank of pork Eisbein *(n)*
pickles in Essig *(m)* eingelegtes
  Gemüse *(n)*
pickpocket Taschendieb *(m)*
picnic Picknick *(n)*
picnic bag Picknicktasche *(f)*
picture gallery Gemäldegalerie *(f)*

picture postcard Ansichtskarte *(f)*
picturesque malerisch schön
piddock Dattelmuschel *(f)*
pie Pastete *(f)*
pie-crust Pastetenkruste *(f)*, Teigdecke *(f)*
piece Stück *(n)*
piece of cake Stück Kuchen *(n)*
piece of the ribs of beef Mittelrippenstück *(n)* (Rind)
pieplant Rhabarber (amerik.) *(m)*
pier Mole *(f)*
pig Schwein *(n)*
pigeon Taube *(f)*
pigeon hole Postfach *(n)*, Ablagefach *(n)*
pig's head Schweinskopf *(m)*
pig's trotters Schweinsfüße *(pl. m)*
pike Hecht *(m)*
pike dumplings Hechtklößchen *(pl. m)*
pike-perch Zander *(m)*
pilchard große Sardine *(f)*
pilfer stehlen, entwenden
pilferage Diebstahl *(m)*
pilgrimage Pilgerreise *(f)*
pilgrimage church Wallfahrtskirche *(f)*
pillow Kopfkissen *(n)*
pillow-case Kopfkissenbezug *(m)*
pillow-slip Kopfkissenbezug *(m)*
pilot Lotse *(m)*, Pilot *(m)*, steuern, lotsen
pilotage Lotsengebühr *(f)*
pilot's licence Flugschein *(m)*
pimento Jamaikapfeffer *(m)*
pinch Prise *(f)*
pine-apple Ananas *(f)*
pine-apple ice Ananaseis *(n)*
pine-apple-juice Ananassaft *(m)*
ping-pong Tischtennis *(n)*
ping-pong room Tischtennishalle *(f)*
pinpoint genau bestimmen (Ziel)
pint ca. 1/2 Liter *(m)*
pintail Wildente *(f)*
piquant sauce pikante Soße *(f)*
pitch a tent zelten
pitcher Kanne *(f)*, Krug *(m)*
pivotal question zentrale Frage *(f)*
pivotal role entscheidende Aufgabe *(f)*
pizza Pizza *(f)*

place a long-distance call ein Ferngespräch *(n)* anmelden
place an order einen Auftrag *(m)* erteilen
place-card Tischkarte *(f)*
place-name sign Ortstafel *(f)*
place of assembly Sammelstelle *(f)*, Treffpunkt *(m)*
place of birth Geburtsort *(m)*
place of delivery Erfüllungsort *(m)*
place of departure Abfahrtsstelle *(f)*
place of destination Bestimmungsort *(m)*
place of dispatch Versandort *(m)*
place of entertainment Vergnügungslokal *(n)*
place of interest Ausflugsort *(m)*, Sehenswürdigkeit *(f)*
place of issue Ausstellungsort *(m)*
place of payment Zahlungsort *(m)*
place of performance Erfüllungsort *(m)*
place of pilgrimage Wallfahrtsort *(m)*
place of residence Wohnort *(m)*
place on deck Deckplatz *(m)*
plaice Scholle *(f)*
plaid Plaid *(n)*
plain einfach, gutbürgerlich
plain boiled aus dem Wasser gezogen (gekocht)
plain boiled potatoes Salzkartoffeln *(pl. f)*
plain circle cake Gugelhupf *(m)*
plain cooking gutbürgerliche Küche *(f)*
plain fare Hausmannskost *(f)*
plain omelet einfaches Omelett *(n)*
plain sausage Knackwurst *(f)*
plain veal cutlet Kalbskotelett natur *(n)*
plain veal steak Naturschnitzel *(n)*
plan Plan *(m)*, planen
plane Flugzeug *(n)*, Maschine *(f)*
plane crash Flugzeugabsturz *(m)*
plane load Flugzeugladung *(f)*
plane ticket Flugkarte *(f)*, Flugschein *(m)*
plank Steg *(m)*
planning Planung *(f)*

plant oil Pflanzenöl *(n)*
plastic bag Plastikbeutel *(m)*
plate Teller *(m)*, Platte *(f)*
plate glass insurance Spiegel- und Fensterglasversicherung *(f)*
platform Bahnsteig *(m)*
platform ticket Bahnsteigkarte *(f)*
platter (Braten)-Platte *(f)*
play ninepine kegeln
play skittles kegeln
player Spieler *(m)*
playgoer Theaterbesucher *(m)*
playground Spielplatz *(m)*
playhouse Schauspielhaus *(n)*
playing-field Spielwiese *(f)*
playroom Spielzimmer *(n)*
please j-m gefallen, j-m zusagen, j-n erfreuen
please close the door bitte Tür *(f)* schließen
please do not touch bitte nicht berühren
pleasure Vergnügen *(n)*
pleasure boat Vergnügungsdampfer *(m)*
pleasure drive Vergnügungsfahrt *(f)*, Spazierfahrt *(f)*
pleasure trip Vergnügungsreise *(f)*
pleasures of the table kulinarische Genüsse *(pl. m)*
pledge Pfand *(n)*, verpfänden; Pfandrecht *(n)*
pledge of property gewährtes Pfandrecht *(n)*
plimsolls Tennisschuhe *(pl. m)*, Turnschuhe *(pl. m)*
plover Kiebitz *(m)*
plover's eggs Kiebitzeier *(pl. n)*
plug stecken, einstecken
plum Pflaume *(f)*, Zwetschge *(f)*
plum dumpling Zwetschgenknödel *(m)*
plum flan Pflaumenkuchen *(m)*
plum pudding engl. Weihnachtspudding *(m)*, Plumpudding *(m)*
plumber Klempner *(m)*, Installateur *(m)*
plumbing Zuleitung *(f)*
plummy reich an Pflaumen *(pl. f)* oder Rosinen *(pl. f)*

pluvial regnerisch
p.m. nachmittags
pneumatic boat Schlauchboot *(n)*
poached egg on toast verlorenes Ei auf Toast *(n)*
poached eggs verlorene Eier *(pl. n)*
pocket-lamp Taschenlampe *(f)*
pocket money Taschengeld *(n)*
pocket train schedule Taschenfahrplan *(m)*
point of origin Ausgangsort *(m)*
point of sale Verkaufsort *(m)*
point of turnaround Zielort *(m)*, Umkehrpunkt *(m)*
pointsman Verkehrspolizist *(m)*
poker Feuerhaken *(m)*; Poker(-spiel) *(n)*
police Polizei *(f)*
police headquarters Polizeipräsidium *(n)*
policeman Polizist *(m)*
police station Polizeirevier *(n)*
polish polieren
polite höflich
pollution of the air Luftverschmutzung *(f)*
pollution of the waters Gewässerverschmutzung *(f)*
polyglot vielsprachig
pomegranate Granatapfel *(m)*
pond Teich *(m)*
pone amerik. Maisbrot *(n)*
poolside room Zimmer *(n)* am Swimmingpool *(m)*
pop Brause *(f)*, Popmusik *(f)*
popcorn Puffmais *(m)*
poppy-seed bun Mohnbeugel *(n)*
popularity rate Beliebtheitsgrad *(m)*
population density Bevölkerungsdichte *(f)*
porcelain Porzellan *(n)*
porch (überdachte) Vorhalle *(f)*, Portal *(n)*
pork Schweinefleisch *(n)*
pork chop Schweinekotelett *(n)*
pork cutlet Schweinekotelett *(n)*
pork cutlet breaded Schweinskotelett *(n)* gebacken
pork galantine Schwartenmagen *(m)*
pork kidneys Schweinsnieren *(pl. f)*

pork knuckles Schweinshaxe (f)
porker Mastschwein (n)
porkling Ferkel (n)
porridge Haferbrei (m), Porridge (m)
port Hafen (m), Portwein (m)
port dues Hafengeld (n)
port entrance Hafeneinfahrt (f)
port installations Hafenanlagen (pl.f)
port of call Anlaufhafen (m), Anlegehafen (m), Bestimmungshafen (m)
port of registry Heimathafen (m)
port of transshipment Umschlaghafen (m)
portable luggage Handgepäck (n)
portable medicine case Reiseapotheke (f)
portable radio Kofferradio (n)
porter dunkles Bier (n); Hoteldiener (m), Gepäckträger (m)
porterhouse steak Zwischenrippenstück (n) mit Filet (n)
porthole Bullauge (n)
portion Portion (f), Teil (m)
portion chart Verzeichnis (n) der Soll-Portionsgrößen (pl.f)
portion size Portionsgröße (f)
position Stellung (f), Position (f), Lage (f)
possibility of travelling Anreisemöglichkeit (f)
post-mark Poststempel (m)
post office Postamt (n)
post-office box Postfach (n)
post-office bus Postbus (m)
post payment Nachzahlung (f)
post-paid franko, frankiert
postage Porto (n)
postage meter Frankiermaschine (f)
postal delivery Postzustellung (f)
postal district Postbezirk (n)
postal giro office Postscheckamt (n)
postal money order Postanweisung (f)
postal order Postanweisung (f)
postal rate Portogebühr (f)
postal savings account Postsparkonto (n)
postal stamp Briefmarke (f)

postal zone number Postleitzahl (f)
postale check account Postscheckkonto (n)
postcard Postkarte (f)
poste restante postlagernd
poste restante railway station bahnpostlagernd
poster Werbeplakat (n), Plakat (n), Poster (n)
poster board Anschlagtafel (f)
posting Übertragung (f)
posting to an account Verbuchung (f) auf einem Konto (n)
postman Briefträger (m)
postpone aufschieben, verschieben, vertagen
postponement Verschiebung (f), Vertagung (f)
pot Topf (m), Tiegel (m), einmachen
pot of broth with boiled meat Suppentopf mit Fleischeinlage (m)
pot roast Schmorbraten (m)
pot stew of fish Fischeintopfgericht (n)
pot stew of tripes gedämpfte Kutteln (pl.f)
pot-herb Küchenkraut (n)
potage (dicke) Suppe (f)
potation Trinken (n), Zecherei (f)
potato Kartoffel (f)
potato basket Kartoffelkörbchen (n)
potato chips Kartoffelchips (pl.)
potato crisps gebackene Kartoffelscheiben (pl.f)
potato croquettes Kartoffelkroketten (pl.f)
potato dumpling Kartoffelknödel (m)
potato fritters Reibekuchen (m)
potato mash Kartoffelbrei (m)
potato masher Kartoffelstampfer (m)
potato nest Kartoffelkörbchen (n)
potato pancake Kartoffelpuffer (m)
potato salad Kartoffelsalat (m)
potato soup Kartoffelsuppe (f)
potato straws Strohkartoffeln (pl.f)
potatoes, baked gebackene Kartoffeln (pl.f)
potatoes baked in their jackets gebackene Pellkartoffeln (pl.f)
potatoes, boiled Salzkartoffeln (pl.f)

potatoes, chipped Pommes frites *(pl.f)*
potatoes, fried Bratkartoffeln *(pl.f)*
potatoes in their jackets Kartoffeln in der Schale *(pl.f)*
potatoes, sauté Schwenkkartoffeln *(pl.f)*
potential of accommodation Aufnahmepotential *(n)*
pottage dicke Gemüsesuppe *(f)* (mit Fleisch)
potted beef Rinderschmorbraten *(m)*
pottery Keramik *(f)*
poulard Poularde *(f)*
poultry Geflügel *(n)*
pound engl. Pfund *(n)* (ca. 450g)
pound-cake Napfkuchen *(m)*
pour gießen
pour over darübergießen
poussin Küken *(n)*
powder Pulver *(n)*, Puder *(m)*, bestreuen
powder snow Pulverschnee *(m)*
power consumption Stromverbrauch *(m)*
power current Kraftstrom *(m)*
power supply Energieversorgung *(f)*
practice slope Übungshang *(m)*
practise üben, trainieren
prawn Garnele *(f)*, Krabbe *(f)*
prawn cocktail Krabbencocktail *(m)*
pre-opening management Voreröffnungsmanagement *(n)*
pre-preparation Grundzubereitung *(f)*
pre-season Vorsaison *(f)*
pre-/post-convention tour Einzel- oder Gruppenpreise *(f)* im Zusammenhang *(m)* mit einer Kongreßveranstaltung *(f)*
precede vorausgehen, vorangehen
precedence Priorität *(f)*, Vorrang *(m)*, Vorrecht *(n)*
precipitation Niederschlag *(m)*
precook vorkochen
precool vorkühlen
predicative value Voraussagetauglichkeit *(f)* (Rechnungslegung)
predict demand Prognose *(f)* der Nachfrage *(f)*
predominant vorherrschend

prefer bevorzugen, vorziehen
preference Vorzug *(m)*, Vorliebe *(f)*, Wahl *(f)*
preferential treatment Vorzugsbehandlung *(f)*, Sonderbehandlung *(f)*
preferred stock Vorzugsaktien *(pl.f)*
preheat vorwärmen
preliminary agreement Vorvertrag *(m)*
preopening expenses Voreröffnungskosten *(pl.)*
prepaid vorausbezahlt
prepaid expenses aktive Rechnungsabgrenzung *(f)*, transitorische Rechnungsabgrenzung *(f)*
prepaid rent vorausbezahlte Miete *(f)*
preparation Vorbereitung *(f)*, Zubereitung *(f)*
prepare vorbereiten, zubereiten
prepared at (guest's) table am Tisch *(m)* zubereitet
prepared with butter in Butter *(f)* zubereitet
prepayment Vorauszahlung *(f)*
prepayments geleistete Anzahlungen *(pl.f)*
prerequisite Voraussetzung *(f)*
present Geschenk *(n)*
present a bill Rechnung *(f)* vorlegen
present value Gegenwartswert *(m)*, Barwert *(m)*
present value of future cash flow diskontierte Nettoeinzahlungsüberschüsse *(pl.m)*
preservation of monuments Denkmalpflege *(f)*
preserves Eingemachtes *(n)*, Konserve *(f)*, eingemachte Früchte *(pl.f)*, Konfitüren *(pl.f)*
presidential suite Präsidenten-Suite *(f)*
press advertising Anzeigenwerbung *(f)*
press release Presseinformation *(f)*, Presseerklärung *(f)*
pressed hog's head Presskopf *(m)*
pressing service Bügelservice *(m)*, Büglerei *(f)*
pressure Druck *(m)*

prestige advertising
Repräsentationswerbung *(f)*
pretzel (Salz-)Bretzel *(f)*
prevent verhindern, verhüten
prevention Verhinderung *(f)*, Vorbeugung *(f)*
preventive vorbeugend
preview Vorschau *(f)*
previous season vorherige Saison *(f)*
previous year Vorjahr *(n)*
price allowance Preisnachlaß *(m)*
price category Preisklasse *(f)*
price ceiling Preisobergrenze *(f)*
price cut Preisermäßigung *(f)*
price for board and lodging Pensionspreis *(m)*
price increase Preiserhöhung *(f)*
price list Preisliste *(f)*
price policy Preispolitik *(f)*
price structure Preisgefüge *(n)*
price tag Preisschild *(n)*
prices include service charge and added-value tax Preise *(pl. m)* einschließlich Bedienungsgeld *(n)* und Mehrwertsteuer *(f)*
prices include the following services Preise *(pl. m)* schließen die folgenden Leistungen *(pl. f)* ein
prices on request Preise *(pl. m)* auf Anfrage *(f)*
prices per day and person Preise *(pl. m)* je Tag *(m)* und Person *(f)*
prices subject to alteration Preisänderung *(f)* vorbehalten
prices without guarantee Preise *(pl. m)* ohne Gewähr *(f)*
pricing Preisfestsetzung *(f)*
prime erstklassig
prime choice erste Wahl *(f)*
prime rib of beef Ochsenrippenstück *(n)*
principal payment Kapitalrückzahlung *(f)*, Tilgung *(f)*
print Abzug *(m)*, drucken
printed matter Drucksache *(f)*
printer Drucker *(m)*
printing and stationery Druck- und Büromaterial *(n)* und Drucksachen *(pl. f)*
prior to früher, älter, eher (als), vorher, vorausgehend

priority Vorzug *(m)*, Vorrang *(m)*, Priorität *(f)*
priority road Vorfahrtsstraße *(f)*
privacy Privatsphäre *(f)*
private bath Einzelbad *(n)*
private bathing-beach Privatbadestrand *(m)*
private car Privatwagen *(m)*
private hotel Hotelpension *(f)*
private house Privathaus *(n)*
private party geschlossene Gesellschaft *(f)*
private performance geschlossene Vorstellung *(f)*
private property Privatgrundstück *(n)*, Privatbesitz *(m)*
private room Privatzimmer *(n)*, Privatquartier *(n)*, Gesellschaftsraum *(m)*
private yacht Privatjacht *(f)*
privilege Vorrecht *(n)*
pro memoria item Erinnerungsposten *(m)*
pro rata depreciation anteilige Jahresabschreibung *(f)*
probable wahrscheinlich
probable losses from pending transactions drohende Verluste *(pl. m)* aus schwebenden Geschäften *(pl. f)*
probable time of arrival voraussichtliche Ankunftszeit *(f)*
procedure Verfahren *(n)*
proceed to the waiting room in good time sich frühzeitig in den Warteraum *(m)* begeben
process chart Arbeitsablaufdiagramm *(n)*
procession Umzug *(m)*
procession in national costumes Trachtenumzug *(m)*
produce herstellen, vorlegen
product Produkt *(n)*, Erzeugnis *(n)*
product liability claim Schadensersatzverpflichtung *(f)* (aus Produkthaftung)
product mix Sortiment *(n)*
product warranty Garantieverpflichtung *(f)*
production control Steuerung *(f)* der Produktion *(f)*

production planning
  Produktionsplanung *(f)*
production standard
  Leistungsmaßstab *(m)*,
  Leistungseinheit *(f)*
productivity Leistung *(f)*,
  Produktivität *(f)*
profession Beruf *(m)*
professional professionell, Profi *(m)*
profit Gewinn *(m)*
profit sharing plan
  Gewinnbeteiligung *(f)*, Tantiemen
  (pl.f)
profitability Rentabilität *(f)*
program (amerik.) Programm *(n)*
programme (brit.) Programm *(n)*
programming language
  Programmiersprache *(f)*
progress Fortgang *(m)*, Verlauf *(m)*
prohibit untersagen, verbieten
prohibited area Sperrgebiet *(n)*
prohibition of entry of vehicles
  Verkehrsverbot *(n)*
prohibition to overtake
  Überholverbot *(n)*
prohibition to park Parkverbot *(n)*
prohibition to stop Halteverbot *(n)*
projector Projektor *(m)*
prolong verlängern
prolongation Verlängerung *(f)*
promenade Promenade *(f)*
promenade deck Promenadendeck
  (n)
promise versprechen, Versprechen *(n)*
promissory note Schuldschein *(m)*,
  persönliches Schuldanerkenntnis
  (n), Solawechsel *(m)*
promontory Vorgebirge *(n)*
promote werben, fördern, Vorschub
  (m) leisten
promotion Werbung *(f)*,
  Verkaufsförderung *(f)*
promotion of the tourist trade
  Förderung *(f)* des Fremdenverkehrs
  (m)
prompt Eingabeaufforderung *(f)*
proof Unterlage *(f)*, Beweis *(m)*,
  Nachweis *(m)*
propan gas Propangas *(n)*
property Eigentum *(n)*
property manager Hotelmanager *(m)*

property right Eigentumsrecht *(n)*,
  Vermögensrecht *(n)*
property, plant and equipment, at cost Anlagevermögen *(n)*, zu
  Anschaffungs- bzw. Herstellkosten
  (pl.)
proposal Vorschlag *(m)*, Antrag *(m)*
propose vorschlagen, beantragen
proprietorship Einzelkaufmann *(m)*
prospectus Prospekt *(m)*
prosperity irregularity report, PIR
  Bestätigung *(f)* für abhanden
  gekommenes Gepäck *(n)*
protected against the wind
  windgeschützt
protected from geschützt gegen
protection of places of natural beauty Landschaftsschutz *(m)*
protective inoculation
  Schutzimpfung *(f)*
protective vaccination
  Schutzimpfung *(f)*
proven bewiesen, nachgewiesen
provide bereitstellen
provision Bestimmung *(f)*, Vorschrift
  (f), Klausel *(f)* (in Gesetzen,
  Verträgen etc.); Rückstellung *(f)*,
  Wertberichtigung *(f)*
provision dealer Feinkosthändler *(m)*
provisional vorläufig
provisions Lebensmittel *(pl. n)*,
  Proviant *(m)*
provoke hervorrufen, erregen,
  verursachen, provozieren
prune Pflaume *(f)*, Zwetschge *(f)*,
  Dörrpflaume *(f)*, Backpflaume *(f)*
prunelle Prünelle *(f)* (getrocknete,
  entkernte Pflaume)
pub Gasthaus *(n)*, Kneipe *(f)*,
  Ausschank *(m)*, Pub *(m)*
pub crawl Kneipenbummel *(m)*
public bar Stehbierhalle *(f)*
public bathroom Etagenbad *(n)*
public callroom öffentliche
  Fernsprechzelle *(f)*
public convenience öffentliche
  Toilette *(f)*
public corporation
  Aktiengesellschaft *(f)* mit breiter
  Streuung *(f)* des Aktienbesitzes *(m)*
public festival Volksfest *(n)*

public gardens öffentliche Anlagen *(pl.f)*
public health regulations Gesundheitsbestimmungen *(pl.f)*
public holiday gesetzlicher Feiertag *(m)*
public house Bierlokal *(n)*, Ausschank *(m)*, Wirtshaus *(n)*
public lavatory öffentliche Toilette *(f)*
public notices öffentliche Bekanntmachungen *(pl.f)*
public relations Öffentlichkeitsarbeit *(f)*, Public Relations (PR) *(pl.)*
public space and kitchen cleaning Reinigung *(f)* der Veranstaltungsräume *(pl.m)* und Küche *(f)*
public transport öffentliche Verkehrsmittel *(pl.n)*
publication Veröffentlichung *(f)*, Publikation *(f)*
publicity Publizität *(f)*, Öffentlichkeit *(f)*
publicity campaign Werbefeldzug *(m)*
publicity campaign abroad Auslandswerbung *(f)*
publicity department Werbeabteilung *(f)*
publish veröffentlichen
pudding Pudding *(m)*
puff omelet Omelette Soufflée *(n)*
puff pastry Blätterteiggebäck *(n)*
puff-paste Blätterteig *(m)*
puff-paste patty Blätterteigpastetchen *(n)*
puff-paste stick Blätterteigstengelchen *(n)*
puffed potatoes Auflaufkartoffeln *(pl.f)*
pull-down table Klapptisch *(m)*
pull the emergency brake Notbremse *(f)* ziehen
pull-out bed Ausziehbett *(n)*
Pullman(car) Pullmannwagen *(m)*, Salon-Schlafwagen *(m)*
pulse Hülsenfrüchte *(pl.f)*
pump room Trinkhalle *(f)*, Quellpavillon *(m)*, Wandelhalle *(f)*
pump-room cure Trinkkur *(f)*
pumpkin Kürbis *(m)*

punch Punsch *(m)*
purchase erwerben, einkaufen, Kauf *(m)*
purchase requisition Bedarfsmeldung *(f)*
purchasing agent Einkäufer *(m)*
purchasing department Einkaufsabteilung *(f)*
purchasing policy Einkaufspolitik *(f)*
purchasing procedure Einkaufsverfahren *(n)*
purchasing specifications Einkaufsrichtlinien *(pl.f)*
puree of beans Bohnenpüree *(n)*
puree of peas Erbsenpüree *(n)*
purse Geldbeutel *(m)*
purser Zahlmeister *(m)*
push stoßen
pusher Schieber *(m)* (Kinderlöffel)
put at ease j-n beruhigen
put off vertagen
put on a waitinglist auf eine Warteliste *(f)* setzen
put up absteigen, beherbergen
put up to sea auslaufen
put up with sich abfinden mit
PX (post exchange) Warenhaus *(n)* für amerik. Armeeangehörige

Q

quack doctor Kurpfuscher *(m)*, Quacksalber *(m)*
quaff zechen, schlürfen
quagmire Morast *(m)*
quail Wachtel *(f)*
qualification Tauglichkeit *(f)*, Qualifikation *(f)*, Eignung *(f)*
qualified qualifiziert
qualify befähigen, qualifizieren
quality Güte *(f)*, Beschaffenheit *(f)*, Qualität *(f)*
quality assurance program Qualitätsprüfungsprogramm *(n)*
quality checker Qualitätskontrolleur *(m)*
quality control Qualitätskontrolle *(f)*
quality evaluation Qualitätsbewertung *(f)*
quality label Gütezeichen *(n)*

quality standard Qualitätsstandard *(m)*
qualmish übel, unwohl
quantitative analysis quantitative Untersuchung *(f)*
quantity Menge *(f)*
quantity discount Rückvergütung *(f)*
quantity of available traffic Verkehrsaufkommen *(n)*
quantity standard Mengenstandard *(m)*, Mengenvorgabe *(f)*
quarantine Quarantäne *(f)*
quarrel streiten, zanken, Streit *(m)*
quart Quart *(n)* (1,136l)
quarter Viertel *(n)*, Vierteljahr *(n)*, Stadtviertel *(n)*, Himmelsrichtung *(f)*
quarterly vierteljährlich
quartermaster Quartiermeister *(m)*, Steuermannsmaat *(m)*
quarters Quartier *(n)*
quasi gleichkommend, quasi
quay Kai *(m)*
quay dues Kaigebühren *(pl.f)*, Liegegeld *(n)*
quayage Kaigeld *(n)*, Kaianlagen *(pl.f)*
queasy unwohl, empfindlich
queen olive große, grüne Olive *(f)*
quenelle Fleischknödel *(m)*
querulous unzufrieden
question Frage *(f)*, in Frage *(f)* stellen
questionary Fragebogen *(m)*
questionnaire Fragebogen *(m)*
queue Schlange *(f)*, Reihe *(f)*
queue up Schlange *(f)* stehen
quick schnell
quick-frozen tiefgekühlt
quick lunch restaurant Schnellgaststätte *(f)*
quick-service restaurant Schnellgaststätte *(f)*
quiet ruhig, still
quietly located in ruhiger Lage *(f)*
quilt Steppdecke *(f)*
quince Quitte *(f)*
quit aufgeben, verlassen, verzichten
quit claim verzichten, Verzicht *(m)*
quit rate Kündigungsquote *(f)*
quite ganz, ziemlich

quota Quote *(f)*, Anteil *(m)*, Kontingent *(n)*
quotation Kursnotierung *(f)*, Preisnotierung *(f)*, Preisangabe *(f)*
quotation of prices Preisangabe *(f)*
quote notieren, quotieren, ein Preisangebot *(n)* machen
quotient Quotient *(m)*

R

rabbit Kaninchen *(n)*
race Rennen *(n)*, rennen
race course Rennstrecke *(f)*
racing boat Rennboot *(n)*
rack Trockengestell *(n)*, Gläsergestell *(n)*
rack rate offizieller (höchster) Zimmerpreis *(m)*, Standard-Zimmerpreis *(m)*, Tarifpreis *(m)*
racket Tennisschläger *(m)*
radiator Kühler *(m)* (Auto)
radio sets in every room Radio *(n)* in allen Zimmern *(pl.n)*
radio taxi Funktaxi *(n)*
radish Radieschen *(n)*, Rettich *(m)*
radon spring Radonquelle *(f)*
raft Floß *(n)*
rag Lappen *(m)*
ragout Ragout *(n)*
ragout of chicken Geflügelragout *(n)*
rail Reling *(f)*
rail and steamship travel kombinierte Zug-Schiffsreise *(f)*
rail and water terminal Schiff-Eisenbahn-Umladeplatz *(m)*
railcar Triebwagen *(m)*
rail connection Bahnverbindung *(f)*, Zugverbindung *(f)*
railroad Eisenbahn *(f)*
railroad car Eisenbahnwagen *(m)*
railroad grade crossing Eisenbahnübergang *(m)*
railroad schedule Eisenbahnfahrplan *(m)*
railroad staff Bahnpersonal *(n)*
railroad terminal Eisenbahnendstation *(f)*
rail-steamer journey Bahn-Schiffsreise *(f)*

rail ticket Eisenbahnfahrkarte *(f)*
rail-ticket office Bahnschalter *(m)*
rail traffic Eisenbahnverkehr *(m)*
rail transport
    Eisenbahngütertransport *(m)*
railway Eisenbahn *(f)*
railway bookstand
    Bahnhofsbuchhandlung *(f)*
railway bus Bahnbus *(m)*
railway carriage Eisenbahnwagen *(m)*
railway coach Eisenbahnwagen *(m)*
railway guard Zugschaffner *(m)*
railway guide Kursbuch *(n)*
railway inquiry office Zugauskunft *(f)*
railway journey Bahnfahrt *(f)*, Bahnreise *(f)*
railway junction
    Eisenbahnknotenpunkt *(m)*
railway level Bahnübergang *(m)*
railway line Bahnstrecke *(f)*, Schienenweg *(m)*
railway network Bahnnetz *(n)*
railway rates Eisenbahntarif *(m)*
railway staff Bahnpersonal *(n)*
railway station Bahnhof *(m)*, Bahnstation *(f)*
railway system Eisenbahnnetz *(n)*
railway terminus
    Eisenbahnendstation *(f)*
railway ticket Eisenbahnfahrkarte *(f)*
railway timetable Eisenbahnfahrplan *(m)*
railway traffic Eisenbahnverkehr *(m)*
rails Gleise *(pl. n)*
rain insurance Regenversicherung *(f)*
rainbow trout Regenbogenforelle *(f)*
raincoat Regenmantel *(m)*
rainfall Niederschlag *(m)*, Regen *(m)*
rainproof regendicht
rainy regnerisch
rainy season Regenzeit *(f)*
raise erhöhen, aufnehmen
raise price Preis *(m)* erhöhen
raisin Rosine *(f)*
rally sammeln, Massenversammlung *(f)*; Rallye *(f)*, Sternfahrt *(f)*
ramble wandern, Wanderung *(f)*, Spaziergang *(m)*
rambler Wanderer *(m)*
ramblers' guide Wanderführer *(m)*

rambling Wandern *(n)*, Wandertourismus *(m)*, Wandersport *(m)*
rambling association Wanderverein *(m)*
ramp Rampe *(f)*
rancid ranzig
random access memory (ram)
    Speicher *(m)* mit wahlfreiem Zugriff *(m)*
random sampling
    Zufallsstichprobenuntersuchung *(f)*
random test Stichprobenprüfung *(f)*
range Palette *(f)*, Auswahl *(f)*, Herd *(m)*, Bereich *(m)*, Zone *(f)*
range finder Entfernungsmesser *(m)*
rank rangieren, einordnen, Rang *(m)*
rare blutig gebraten, halb durch
rare selten
raspberry Himbeere *(f)*
raspberry ice Himbeereis *(n)*
raspberry juice Himbeersaft *(m)*
raspberry syrup with soda water
    Soda-Himbeer *(n)*
rate schätzen; Rate *(f)*, Preis *(m)*, Anteil *(m)*
rate of exchange Devisenkurs *(m)*, Kurs *(m)*, Umrechnungskurs *(m)*
rate of mark-up Zuschlagssatz *(m)*
rate potential percentage relativer Ergiebigkeitsgrad *(m)*
rates on application Preise *(pl. m)* auf Anfrage *(f)*
rates restriction Preisbeschränkung *(f)*
ratio Verhältnis *(n)*, Anteilzahl *(f)*, Kennziffer *(f)*
rational vernünftig, zweckmäßig, praktisch
rationalization Rationalisierung *(f)*
rationalize rationalisieren
rauigote sauce Rauigote-Soße *(f)*
raw roh
raw ham Rohschinken *(m)*
raw material Rohmaterial *(n)*
raw yield Rohertrag *(m)*
ray Rochen *(m)*
razor point Steckdose *(f)* für Elektrorasierer *(pl. m)*
reacquire zurückkaufen
read-only memory (rom)

Lesespeicher *(m)*, Festwertspeicher *(m)*
readily prompt, leicht, ohne weiteres
readingroom Leseraum *(m)*, Lesezimmer *(n)*
ready fertig, bereit
ready for mail postfertig
ready for occupancy bezugsfertig
ready for shipment versandfertig
ready for use betriebsfertig
ready reckoner Rechentabelle *(f)*
ready-to-serve-dish Fertiggericht *(n)*, Tagesgericht *(n)*
ready-to-use gebrauchsfertig
real account Bestandskonto *(n)*
real property rights grundstücksgleiche Rechte *(pl. n)*
real time Echtzeit *(f)*
real turtle soup Schildkrötensuppe *(f)*
realizable value Veräußerungswert *(m)*, Gegenwartswert *(m)*
realize realisieren
rear of a train Zuganschluß *(m)*
reason urteilen; Vernunft *(f)*, Grund *(m)*
reasonable billig, angemessen
reasonable hour angemessene Stunde *(f)*
reasonable price angemessener Preis *(m)*
reasonable time angemessene Zeit *(f)*
reasonable user informationswilliger und vernünftiger Nutzer *(m)* von Rechnungslegungsinformationen *(pl.f)*
reasonably possible nicht unwahrscheinlich
reassuring beruhigend, ermutigend
rebate Preisnachlaß *(m)*, Rabatt *(m)*
recapitulation Zusammenfassung *(f)*
receipt quittieren, Empfangsbestätigung *(f)*, Quittung *(f)*
receipt for baggage to be deposited Gepäckannahme *(f)*, Gepäckannahmeschalter *(m)*
receipt for registered luggage Gepäckaufbewahrungsschein *(m)*

receipts Einnahmen *(pl.f)*
receivables Forderungen *(pl.f)*
receiving clerk Warenannehmer *(m)*
receiving department Warenannahme *(f)*
reception Empfang *(m)*, Anmeldung *(f)*, Aufnahme *(f)*
reception and information office Betreuung *(f)* und Information *(f)*
reception clerk Empfangssekretär *(m)*
reception desk Rezeption *(f)*, Empfangspult *(n)*
reception hall Empfangshalle *(f)*
reception office Empfangsbüro *(n)*, Rezeption *(f)*
receptionist Empfangsdame *(f)*, Empfangsherr *(m)*
recipe Rezept *(n)* (Küche)
recipient Empfänger *(m)*
reckon back zurückrechnen
reclaim reklamieren
reclassification Umbuchung *(f)*
reclassify umbuchen
recognition Anerkennung *(f)*, Realisationszeitpunkt *(m)*
recognition and measurement concept Realisierungs- und Bewertungsfragen *(pl.f)* (Rechnungswesen)
recognize anerkennen, erkennen
recommend empfehlen
recommendation Empfehlung *(f)*
reconcile abstimmen, zusammenstellen
reconciliation Abstimmung *(f)*
reconditioning Instandsetzung *(f)*, Generalüberholung *(f)*
reconfirm bestätigen
reconfirmation Rückbestätigung *(f)* (über eine erfolgte Buchung)
record eintragen, Eintragung *(f)*, Akte *(f)*; Schallplatte *(f)*
records Unterlagen *(pl.f)*
recover sich erholen
recovery Erholung *(f)*
recovery service Abschleppdienst *(m)*
recreation Erholung *(f)*
recreation centre Erholungszentrum *(n)*

recreation program
Erholungsprogramm *(n)*
recreation room Gemeinschaftsraum *(m)*
recreational area Erholungsgebiet *(n)*
recreational center for children Kindererholungsheim *(n)*
recreational facilities Erholungsanlage *(f)*, Erholungsmöglichkeiten *(pl.f)*
recreational holiday Erholungsurlaub *(m)*
recreational park Erholungspark *(m)*
recruitment Personalbeschaffung *(f)*
red rot
red beans rote Bohnen *(pl.f)*
red beef tongue Pökelzunge *(f)*
red beet rote Rübe *(f)*
red bilberry Preiselbeere *(f)*
red cabbage Rotkohl *(m)*
red currant rote Johannisbeere *(f)*
red currant-tartlets Cremetörtchen mit Johannisbeergelee *(n)*
red grits rote Grütze *(f)*
red herring Matjeshering *(m)*
red mullet Rotbarbe *(f)*
red pepper rote Pfefferschote *(f)*
red wine Rotwein *(m)*
red wine from the cask roter, offener Wein *(m)*
redcap Gepäckträger *(m)*
redirect nachsenden
reduce ermäßigen, herabsetzen, vermindern
reduce speed now langsam fahren!
reduced fare Fahrpreisermäßigung *(f)*
reduced fares for tourist groups Fahrpreisermäßigung *(f)* für Reisegesellschaften *(pl.f)*
reduced rates ermäßigter Tarif *(m)*, ermäßigter Preis *(m)*, Vergünstigungen *(pl.f)*
reduced-fare ticket Fahrkarte *(f)* zu ermäßigtem Preis *(m)*
reducing diet Abmagerungskur *(f)*
reduction Herabsetzung *(f)*, Ermäßigung *(f)*, Kürzung *(f)*
reduction for children Kinderermäßigung *(f)*

reduction for hotel guests Ermäßigung für Hausgäste *(pl.m)*
reduction of the rates Tarifsenkung *(f)*, Preissenkung *(f)*
re-educate umschulen
re-education Umschulung *(f)*
re-embark (sich) wieder einschiffen
re-entry visa Wiedereinreisevisum *(n)*
refer sich beziehen auf
reference Bezugnahme *(f)*, Hinweis *(m)*
referral business Geschäft *(n)* durch gegenseitige Empfehlung *(f)*
refreshed erfrischt
refreshing erholsam, erfrischend
refreshment Erfrischung *(f)*
refreshment bar Büffet *(n)*, Erfrischungsraum *(m)*
refreshment room Erfrischungsraum *(m)*
refreshment stall Erfrischungskiosk *(m)*
refrigerator Kühlschrank *(m)*
refrigerator car Kühlwagen *(m)*
refuel tanken
refuge Verkehrsinsel *(f)*, Schutzhütte *(f)*
refund Rückerstattung *(f)*, zurückerstatten, zurückzahlen
refusal Ablehnung *(f)*, Weigerung *(f)*
refusal to pay Zahlungsverweigerung *(f)*
refuse ablehnen, zurückweisen
region Gegend *(f)*
register eintragen, anmelden, einschreiben, Verzeichnis *(n)*
register luggage Gepäck *(n)* aufgeben
register with the police sich bei der Polizei *(f)* melden
registered letter Einschreibebrief *(m)*
registering of luggage Gepäckabgabe *(f)*
registration Abfertigung *(f)*, Anmeldung *(f)*, Eintragung *(f)*
registration fee Anmeldegebühr *(f)*, Registrierungsgebühr *(f)*
registration form Anmeldeformular *(n)*, Meldeschein *(m)*
registration of luggage Gepäckabfertigung *(f)*

registration office Meldeamt *(n)*
registry office Registratur *(f)*
regret bedauern
regroup umgruppieren
regular fahrplanmäßig
regular customer Stammgast *(m)*
regular depreciation planmäßige Abschreibung *(f)*
regular hotel guest Hotelstammgast *(m)*
regular time Normalarbeitszeit *(f)*
regular traffic Linienverkehr *(m)*
regulation Regel *(f)*, Richtlinie *(f)*, Ordnung *(f)*, Vorschrift *(f)*
regulations of the house Hausordnung *(f)*
regulatory body Regelungsinstitution *(f)*
reheat aufwärmen
rehire wiedereinstellen
reimburse zurückvergüten, zurückerstatten, ersetzen
reindeer Ren *(n)*, Rentier *(n)*
rejuvenation cure Verjüngungskur *(f)*
related verwandt
related to verbunden mit, verknüpft mit
relation Beziehung *(f)*, Verhältnis *(n)*
relative Verwandter *(m)*
relax sich erholen, entspannen
relaxation Erholung *(f)*, Ausspannen *(n)*
relaxation cure Entspannungskur *(f)*
relaxation time Erholungszeit *(f)*
relevance Relevanz *(f)* (Rechnungslegung)
reliability Zuverlässigkeit *(f)*
reliability criterion Reabilitätstest *(m)*
reliable zuverlässig
relief Erleichterung *(f)*
relief train Entlastungszug *(m)*, Sonderzug *(m)*
relieve unterstützen, entlasten, befreien
relieve measure Abhilfemaßnahme *(f)*
relish gern essen, sich schmecken lassen
reloading charge Umladungsgebühr *(f)*

relocate hier: umbuchen
relocation expenses (schedule 9) Versetzungskosten *(pl.)* (Service Center 9)
rely sich verlassen auf
remainder Rest *(m)*
remarkable bemerkenswert, sehenswert
remedial gymnastics Krankengymnastik *(f)*
remedy Medikament *(n)*, Heilmittel *(n)*, Abhilfe *(f)*
remind erinnern, mahnen
reminder Erinnerung *(f)*, Mahnung *(f)*
reminder advertising Erinnerungswerbung *(f)*
remit überweisen
remote entfernt; eher unwahrscheinlich
removal of waste matter (schedule 12) Abfallbeseitigung *(f)* (Service Center 12)
remove beseitigen, entfernen
render a service einen Dienst *(m)* leisten
renew erneuern, verlängern
renewal Erneuerung *(f)*, Verlängerung *(f)*
renounce aufgeben, verzichten, zurücktreten
renovate erneuern
renovation Erneuerung *(f)*
rent mieten, pachten, vermieten, verpachten, Miete *(f)*, Pacht *(f)*
rentable mietbar, pachtbar
rental charge Mietgebühr *(f)*
rental service Verleih *(m)*
rentals and other income (schedule 6) Miet- und sonstige Erträge *(pl. m)* (Umsatzbereich 6)
re-opening Wiedereröffnung *(f)*
reorder nachbestellen, Nachbestellung *(f)*
reorder system Bestellverfahren *(n)*
reorganization Umorganisation *(f)*
reorganize sanieren, umorganisieren
repair reparieren, instandsetzen, ausbessern
repair order Reparaturauftrag *(m)*
repair shop Reparaturwerkstätte *(f)*
repairs and maintenance Reparaturen *(pl. f)* und Instandhaltung *(f)*

repay zurückzahlen, zurückerstatten
repayable rückzahlbar
repayment amount
   Rückzahlungsbetrag *(m)*
repeat wiederholen, Wiederholung *(f)*
repeat business
   Wiederholungsgeschäft *(n)*
repeat order Wiederholungsauftrag *(m)*
repetition Wiederholung *(f)*
replace ersetzen
replacement value
   Wiederbeschaffungswert *(m)*
reply antworten, Antwort *(f)*
reply postcard Rückantwortkarte *(f)*
report berichten, Bericht *(m)*
report format Staffelform *(f)*
report to unterstellt sein
reporting time Meldezeit *(f)*
represent vertreten
representation Vertretung *(f)*, Stellvertretung *(f)*
representational faithfulness
   Abbildungstreue *(f)* (Rechnungslegung)
representative Beauftragter *(m)*, Vertreter *(m)*, Bevollmächtigter *(m)*
reputation Ruf *(m)*, Ansehen *(n)*
request bitten, auffordern, Bitte *(f)*, Aufforderung *(f)*
request for overtime
   Überstundenanforderung *(f)*
request stop Bedarfshaltestelle *(f)*
require erfordern, verlangen, brauchen
requirement Erfordernis *(n)*, Bedürfnis *(n)*, Anspruch *(m)*
requisition Anforderung *(f)*, Lageranforderung *(f)*, Bestellung *(f)*
rescue expedition
   Rettungsexpedition *(f)*
rescue party Rettungsmannschaft *(f)*
research forschen, Forschung *(f)*, Untersuchung *(f)*
research and development
   Forschung *(f)* und Entwicklung *(f)*
research department
   Forschungsabteilung *(f)*
reseller Wiederverkäufer *(m)*
reservation Reservierung *(f)*, Belegung *(f)*, Vorbehalt *(m)*; Reservat *(n)*

reservation clerk
   Reservierungsdame *(f)*
reservation number
   Buchungsnummer *(f)*
reservation of seats in advance
   Vorbestellung *(f)* von Plätzen *(pl. m)*
reservation service
   Reservierungssystem *(n)*
reservation supervisor Leiterin *(f)* der Reservierungsabteilung *(f)*
reservation system
   Reservierungssystem *(n)*
reserve Reserve *(f)*, reservieren, buchen, vorbestellen
reserve a table einen Tisch *(m)* reservieren
reserve by telephone telefonisch bestellen
reserved seat ticket Platzkarte *(f)*
reserves Rücklagen *(pl. f)*
reservoir Stausee *(m)*
reside wohnen, seinen Wohnsitz *(m)* haben
residence Wohnort *(m)*, Wohnsitz *(m)*, Aufenthaltsort *(m)*
residence permit
   Aufenthaltserlaubnis *(f)*, Aufenthaltsgenehmigung *(f)*
resident wohnhaft, Einwohner *(m)*, Bewohner *(m)*, Hausgast *(m)*, Pensionsgast *(m)*
resident guest Hausgast *(m)*
resident manager Hoteldirektor *(m)*
residential area Wohngebiet *(n)*
residential hotel Hotel garni *(n)*, Frühstückspension *(f)*, Familienpension *(f)*
residue Rest *(m)*
resignation Kündigung *(f)*
resolve (problem) lösen (Problem)
resource Hilfsquelle *(f)*, Reserve *(f)*
respectable seriös
respond to ansprechen auf, reagieren auf
responsibility Verantwortung *(f)*, Haftung *(f)*
responsible verantwortlich, haftbar
responsiveness Reaktionsfähigkeit *(f)*, Empfindlichkeit *(f)*
rest after treatment Nachkur *(f)*
rest-cure Erholungskur *(f)*,

Erholungsaufenthalt *(m)*, Liegekur *(f)*
rest-cure lawn Liegewiese *(f)*
rest-cure terrace Liegeterrasse *(f)*
rest-home Erholungsheim *(n)*
rest pause Erholungspause *(f)*
rest room Ruheraum *(m)*, Toilette *(f)* (USA), Waschraum *(m)*
restaurant car Speisewagen *(m)*
restaurant deck Restaurantdeck *(n)*
restaurant-keeper Gastwirt *(m)*, Gaststättenbesitzer *(m)*, Restaurateur *(m)*
restaurant manager Restaurantdirektor *(m)*
restful erholsam
restoration Wiederherstellung *(f)*
restore wiederherstellen
restraint of trade. Wettbewerbsbeschränkung *(f)*
restricted eingeschränkt, beschränkt, begrenzt
restricted cash funds flüssige Mittel *(pl. n)*, die einer Verfügungsbeschränkung *(f)* unterliegen
restricted money nicht verfügbares Geld *(n)*
restriction Einschränkung *(f)*, Beschränkung *(f)*
restrictive covenants Einschränkungen *(pl.f)*, eingeschränkende Vertragsklauseln *(pl.f)*
retain zurückbehalten
retained earnings Gewinnvortrag *(m)* einschließlich freie Rücklagen *(pl.f)*
retardation Verzögerung *(f)*
retire in Pension *(f)* gehen, zurücktreten
retirement Ruhestand *(m)*, Pension *(f)*
retraining Umschulung *(f)*
return Rückkehr *(f)*, Rückgabe *(f)*, zurückgeben, zurückkommen
return fare Fahrpreis *(m)* für die Hin- und Rückreise *(f)*
return flight Rückflug *(m)*
return home Heimkehr *(f)*
return journey Rückreise *(f)*, Rückfahrt *(f)*

return ticket Rückfahrkarte *(f)*, Hin- und Rückfahrschein *(m)*
return trip Rückreise *(f)*, Rückfahrt *(f)*
return voyage Rückreise *(f)*
reuse wiederverwenden, Wiederverwendung *(f)*
revalidate erneuern
revel schlemmen
revenue Einkommen *(n)*, Ertrag *(m)*, Umsatz *(m)*
review nachprüfen, überprüfen, Überprüfung *(f)*
revise verbessern, durchsehen, revidieren
reward belohnen, Belohnung *(f)*
Rhine salmon Rheinsalm *(m)*
Rhine wine Rheinwein *(m)*
rhubarb Rhabarber *(m)*
rhum-baba Rumbaba *(m)*
rib Rippchen *(n)*
rib of beef Ochsenrippenstück *(n)*
rib of beef boiled Beinfleisch *(n)*
rib of pork Schweinskarree *(n)*
rib roast of veal Kalbskarreebraten *(m)*
rib steak Kotelett *(n)*
ribbon macaroni Bandnudeln *(pl.f)*
ribs of veal Kalbskarreebraten *(m)*
rice Reis *(m)*
rice dish with grated cheese Reisgericht mit Reibkäse *(n)*
rice dish with peas Reisgericht mit Erbsen *(n)*
rice pie Reisgericht in Form *(n)*
rice pudding Milchreis *(m)*
rice soup Reissuppe *(f)*
rice timbale Reisgericht in Form *(n)*
riding-club Reitklub *(m)*
riding-course Reitkurs *(m)*
riding-facilities Reitgelegenheit *(f)*
riding-ground Reitgelände *(n)*
riding-ring Reitbahn *(f)*
riding school Reitschule *(f)*
riding-stable Reitstall *(m)*
riding-track Reitweg *(m)*
rigging Takelung *(f)*
right Recht *(n)*, Berechtigung *(f)*, Rechtsanspruch *(m)*; Lizenz *(f)*
right of rescission Rücktrittsrecht *(n)*
right of sublease Untervermietungsrecht *(n)*

right-hand traffic Rechtsverkehr *(m)*
right-of-way Vorfahrt *(f)*
rightful rechtmäßig
rightfulness Rechtmäßigkeit *(f)*
ring road Ringstraße *(f)*
rinse spülen
ripe reif
ripe olive reife Olive *(f)*
rise erhöhen, Erhöhung *(f)*, Aufstieg *(m)*
risk riskieren, Gefahr *(f)*, Risiko *(n)*, Wagnis *(n)*
risk of conveyance Transportgefahr *(f)*
risk of litigation Prozeßrisiko *(n)*
risk under guarantee Bürgschaftsrisiko *(n)*
risky risikoreich, gefährlich
risotto with saffron Safranreis *(m)*
rissole Fleischklöße (gebraten) *(pl. m)*
river Fluß *(m)*
river map Flußkarte *(f)*
river port Binnenhafen *(m)*
river steamer Flußdampfer *(m)*
river traffic Flußschiffahrt *(f)*
river-trout Flußforelle *(f)*
riverside hotel Flußhotel *(n)*
roach Plötze *(f)*
road atlas Straßenatlas *(m)*
road cleared of snow schneegeräumte Straße *(f)*
road closed gesperrte Straße *(f)*
road conditions Straßenzustand *(m)*
road construction Straßenbau *(m)*
road ditch Straßengraben *(m)*
road fork Straßengabelung *(f)*
road haulage Güterkraftverkehr *(m)*
road-hole Schlagloch *(n)*
road-house Raststätte *(f)*
road junction Straßenkreuzung *(f)*
road map Straßenkarte *(f)*, Autokarte *(f)*
road narrows Straßenverengung *(f)*
road network Straßennetz *(n)*
road-rail service Huckepackverkehr *(m)*
road report Straßenzustandsbericht *(m)*
road safety Verkehrssicherheit *(f)*
roadside café Ausflugslokal *(n)*
road sign Verkehrzeichen *(n)*

road site Straßenbaustelle *(f)*
road traffic Straßenverkehr *(m)*
road transport connection Zubringerverkehr *(m)*
road tunnel Straßentunnel *(m)*
road user Verkehrsteilnehmer *(m)*
roadway Fahrbahn *(f)*, Fahrdamm *(m)*
road works Straßenbauarbeiten *(pl. f)*
roast geröstet, gebraten, Braten *(m)*
roast beef Ochsenbraten *(m)*, Rostbraten *(m)*
roast beef English style englisches Roastbeef *(n)*
roast chicken Brathähnchen *(n)*
roast duck gebratene Ente *(f)*
roast fillet of beef Rindslendenbraten *(m)*
roast fillet of beef in puff-paste Filet Wellington *(n)*
roast goose Gänsebraten *(m)*
roast goose with sauerkraut Gänsebraten mit Sauerkraut *(m)*
roast hare Hasenbraten *(m)*
roast joint of pork Schweinebraten *(m)*
roast lamb Lammbraten *(m)*
roast loin of veal Kalbsbraten *(m)*
roast loin of veal with kidney Kalbsnierenbraten *(m)*
roast of veal Kalbsbraten *(m)*
roast pheasant Fasan *(m)* gebraten
roast pork Schweinebraten *(m)*
roast potatoes Schwenkkartoffeln *(pl. f)*
roast sausage Bratwurst *(f)*
roast sirloin Roastbeef *(n)*
roast sirloin of beef Nierstückbraten *(m)*
roast smoked spare rib of pork Kasseler Rippenspeer *(m, n)*
roast stuffed breast of veal gefüllte Kalbsbrust *(f)*
roast turkey Truthahn *(m)* gebraten
roast venison Rehbraten *(m)*
roasted gebraten
robe Morgenrock *(m)*
rock Felsen *(m)*
rock-climbing Bergsteigen *(n)*
rock garden Steingarten *(m)*
rock lobster Languste *(f)*
rockpartridge Steinhuhn *(n)*

rocky felsig
roe Rogen *(m)*
roebuck Rehbock *(m)*
roll ausrollen (Teig), Brötchen *(n)*, Semmel *(f)*
roll-a-way fahrbare Liege *(f)*
roll film Rollfilm *(m)*
roll on – roll off Autoverladung *(f)* bei Schiffen *(pl. n)*
rolled beef Rollbraten *(m)*
rolled braised beef Rindsroulade *(f)*
rolled fillets of sole Seezungenröllchen *(pl. n)*
rolled ham Rollschinken *(m)*
rolled herring Rollmops *(m)*
rolled pancake Palatschinken *(m)*
rolled stuffed cabbage leave Kohlroulade *(f)*
rolled veal on skewers Kalbsröllchen *(n)* am Spieß
rolled veal steak Kalbsroulade *(f)*
rolling pin Nudelholz *(n)*
rollmop herring Rollmops *(m)*
romaine Sommerendivie *(f)*
roof garage Dachgarage *(f)*
roof-garden Dachgarten *(m)*
roof rack Autodachgepäckträger *(m)*
room Zimmer *(n)*
room charge Zimmerpreis *(m)*
room clerk Empfangsdame *(f)*, Empfangsherr *(m)*
room facing south Südzimmer *(n)*
room facing the street Zimmer *(n)* zur Straße *(f)*
room loudness Zimmerlautstärke *(f)*
room night Logiernacht *(f)*
room nights available Zimmer *(pl. n)* vorhanden (im Berichtszeitraum)
room nights sold belegte Zimmer *(pl. n)* (im Berichtszeitraum)
room number Zimmernummer *(f)*
room rate Zimmerpreis *(m)*
room service Etagenservice *(m)*
room service headwaiter Etagenoberkellner *(m)*
room service ordertaking Bestellungsaufnahme *(f)* für den Etagenservice *(m)*
room service waiter Etagenkellner *(m)*, Zimmerkellner *(m)*

room telephone Zimmertelefon *(n)*
room with a view of the sea Zimmer *(n)* mit Blick *(m)* aufs Meer *(n)*
room with balcony Balkonzimmer *(n)*
room with private bath or shower Zimmer *(n)* mit Bad *(n)* oder Dusche *(f)*
room with two beds Zweibettzimmer *(n)*
rooming list Zimmerliste *(f)*
rooming (the guest) Zuweisung *(f)* eines Zimmers *(n)* (an den Gast)
rooms department Berherbergungsabteilung *(f)*
rooms division department Beherbergungsbereich *(m)*
rooms division manager Leiter *(m)* der Beherbergungsabteilung *(f)*
rooms occupied and vacant belegte und freie Zimmer *(pl. n)*
rooms statistic Beherbergungsstatistik *(f)*
rooms to let Zimmer *(pl. n)* zu vermieten, Fremdenzimmer *(pl. n)*
rooms vacant Zimmer *(pl. n)* frei
roomy geräumig
rooster Hahn *(m)*
rope down abseilen
rope railway Seilbahn *(f)*
rope tow Schlepplift *(m)*
rope-ladder Strickleiter *(f)*
Roquefort Roquefort-Käse *(m)*
rose wine hellroter Wein *(m)*, Roséwein *(m)*
rosemary Rosmarin *(m)*
rotate wechseln, rotieren
rotating shift Wechselschicht *(f)*
rotten faul, verfault, schlecht, gemein
rough stürmisch
rough calculation überschlägige Berechnung *(f)*
rough estimate grobe Schätzung *(f)*
round rund, Runde *(f)*
round off abrunden
round up aufrunden
round-trip Rundreise *(f)*
roundabout Kreisverkehr *(m)*, Karussell *(n)*

roundabout ticket Rückfahrkarte
  (f), Hin- und Rückfahrschein *(m)*
roundabout way Umweg *(m)*
route map Streckenkarte *(f)*
route network Flugnetz *(n)*,
  Streckennetz *(n)*
routine work Routinearbeit *(f)*
routing Streckenführung *(f)*
row rudern, Bootsfahrt *(f)*
rowboat Ruderboot *(n)*
rowing-boat Ruderboot *(n)*
rubber boots Gummistiefel *(pl. m)*
rubber dinghy Schlauchboot *(n)*
rubbish Müll *(m)*, Abfall *(m)*
rudder Steuerruder *(n)*
rug Vorleger *(m)*
rugged rauh, wild, zerklüftet
ruin Ruine *(f)*
rule regeln, entscheiden; Vorschrift
  (f), Regel *(f)*
rules and regulations of a hotel
  Hotelordnung *(f)*
rules of residents Hausordnung *(f)*
rum Rum *(m)*
rumpsteak Rumpsteak *(n)*
rumpsteak grilled Rumpsteak *(n)*
  vom Rost *(m)*
rumpsteak with fried onions
  Wiener Rostbraten *(m)*
run Abfahrt *(f)*, Abfahrtsstrecke *(f)*
run at regular times fahrplanmäßig
  fahren
run of the house rate Spezialpreis
  (m) für Reiseveranstalter *(pl. m)*
run the risk Gefahr *(f)* laufen
runner bean grüne Bohne *(f)*
running time Fahrzeit *(f)*
running water fließendes Wasser
  (n)
runway Rollbahn *(f)*, Piste *(f)*,
  Startbahn *(f)*, Landebahn *(f)*
rural ländlich
rural district Landbezirk *(m)*
rush Andrang *(m)*, Zustrom *(m)*, Eile
  (f)
rush hour traffic Stoßverkehr *(m)*
rush hours Hauptverkehrszeit *(f)*,
  Stoßzeit *(f)*
rush order Eilauftrag *(m)*
rusk Zwieback *(m)*
Russian bath Dampfbad *(n)*

Russian beetroot soup russische
  rote Rübensuppe *(f)*
Russian eggs russische Eier *(pl. n)*
rye Roggen *(m)*
rye-bread Roggenbrot *(n)*

S

sabayon warme Wein/Eiersoße *(f)*,
  Chaudeau *(n)*
sabbatical leave Bildungsurlaub *(m)*
saddle Rückenstück *(n)*, Rücken *(m)*
saddle of hare Hasenrücken *(m)*
saddle of mutton Hammelrücken
  (m)
saddle of veal Kalbsrücken *(m)*
saddle of vension Rehrücken *(m)*
safari Safari *(f)*
safe deposit box Stahlfach *(n)*,
  Schließfach *(n)*
safe deposit of valuables
  Aufbewahrung *(f)* von
  Wertgegenständen *(pl. m)*
safe for avalanches lawinensicher
safety Sicherheit *(f)*
safety binding Sicherheitsbindung *(f)*
safety regulation
  Unfallverhütungsvorschrift *(f)*
saffron Safran *(m)*
saffron-risotto Safranreis *(m)*
sage Salbei *(m)*
sail Segel *(n)*, segeln
sail near to the wind hart am Wind
  (m) segeln
sailing Abfahrt *(f)*, Fahrt *(f)*
sailing boat Segelboot *(n)*
sailing date Abfahrtstag *(m)* (Schiff)
sailing dinghy Jolle *(f)*
sailing plane Segelflugzeug *(n)*
sailing time Abfahrtszeit *(f)*
sailor Matrose *(m)*
salad Salat *(m)*
salad bowl Salatschüssel *(f)*
salad dressing Salatsoße *(f)*
salad of boiled beef
  Rindfleischsalat *(m)*
salad of ox-palate Ochsenmaulsalat
  (m)
salad plate Rohkostplatte *(f)*
salami Salami *(f)*

salary Gehalt *(n)*
sale Verkauf *(m)*, Absatz *(m)*, Ausverkauf *(m)*
sale agreement, conditional Kaufvertrag *(m)* unter Eigentumsvorbehalt *(m)*
sale of alcoholic drinks Ausschank *(m)* alkoholischer Getränke *(pl. n)*
sale of tickets Kartenverkauf *(m)*
sales argument Verkaufsargument *(n)*
sales department Verkaufsabteilung *(f)*
sales letter Werbebrief *(m)*
sales literature Werbematerial *(n)*
sales manager Verkaufsleiter *(m)*
sales mix Sortiment *(n)*
sales outlet Absatzstelle *(f)*
sales price Verkaufspreis *(m)*
sales promotion Verkaufsförderung *(f)*
sales representative Verkaufsvertreter *(m)*, Verkaufsrepräsentant *(m)*
salesman Verkäufer *(m)*, Vertreter *(m)*, Reisender *(m)*
salmon Salm *(m)*, Lachs *(m)*
salmon cut(let) Salmmittelstück *(n)*
salmon mayonnaise Salmmayonnaise *(f)*
salmon trout Lachsforelle *(f)*
saloon Ausschank *(m)*, Gastwirtschaft *(f)*
saloon bar Ausschank *(m)*, Kneipe *(f)*, Schenke *(f)*
saloon carriage Salonwagen *(m)*
saloonkeeper Wirt *(m)*, Schankwirt *(m)*
salsify Schwarzwurzel *(f)*
salt Salz *(n)*, salzen
salt-cellar Salzfäßchen *(n)*, Salzstreuer *(m)*
salt cod Stockfisch *(m)*
salt spring Solquelle *(f)*
salt water Sole *(f)*
salt-water bath Solbad *(n)*
salt-water fish Meerfisch *(m)*
salt-water resort Solbad *(n)* (Kurort) *(m)*
salted gesalzen, gepökelt

salted almonds Salzmandeln *(pl. f)*
salted beef Pökelrindfleisch *(n)*
salted codfish Stockfisch *(m)*
salted cucumber Salzgurke *(f)*
salted pig's knuckle Eisbein *(n)*
salted pig's trotter Eisbein *(n)*
salt(ed) herring Matjeshering *(m)*
salvage (schedule 6) Abfallverwertung *(f)* (Umsatzbereich 6)
Salzburg sweet dumpling Salzburger Nockerl *(n)*
sanatorium Sanatorium *(n)*, Kuranstalt *(f)*, Heilstätte *(f)*
sand bank Sandbank *(f)*
sand-bath Sandbad *(n)*
sandcastle competition Sandburgenwettbewerb *(m)*
sand-dune Sanddüne *(f)*
sandstone rock Sandsteinfelsen *(m)*
sandwich belegtes Brot *(n)*
sandy beach Sandstrand *(m)*
sanitary facilities sanitäre Anlagen *(pl. f)*
sanitary regulations Gesundheitsvorschriften *(pl. f)*
Santa Claus Weihnachtsmann *(m)*
sap Saft *(m)*
sardines Ölsardinen *(pl. f)*
sardines in oil Sardinen *(pl. f)* in Öl *(n)*
satisfactory zufriedenstellend
satisfy befriedigen, bezahlen
satisfying befriedigend, beruhigend, ausreichend
sauce Soße *(f)*, Tunke *(f)*
sauce-boat Sauciere *(f)*
saucepan Kochtopf *(m)*, Tiegel *(m)*
saucer Untersetzer *(m)*, Untertasse *(f)*
sauerbraten Sauerbraten *(m)*
sauerkraut Sauerkraut *(n)*
sauerkraut or string beans with meat and sausage Berner Platte *(f)*
sauerkraut with smoked meat, ham and sausage Sauerkrautplatte *(f)*
sauna Sauna *(f)*
sausage Wurst *(f)*, Würstchen *(n)*
sauteed gebraten
Sauterne Sauterne *(m)*
sauté potatoes Bratkartoffeln *(pl. f)*

saveloy Zervelat (f), Zervelatwurst (f), Knackwurst (f)
savings bank Sparkasse (f)
savoury schmackhaft; pikantes Vorgericht (n)
savoy cabbage Sommer- und Wirsingkohl (m)
scald brühen, abkochen (Milch)
scale Waage (f), Skala (f), staffeln
scallion Schalotte (f)
scallop Kammuschel (f)
scallop St. Jaques Jakobsmuschel (f)
scallop (mussel) Miesmuschel (f)
scallop (of meat) Schnitzel (n)
Scandinavian salmon Nordsalm (m)
scenery Landschaft (f)
scenic malerisch, landschaftlich schön
schedule planen, Aufstellung (f), Zeitplan (m), Verzeichnis (n), Fahrplan (m), Flugplan (m)
scheduled fahrplanmäßig, planmäßig
scheduled air line Fluglinie (f) mit fahrplanmäßigem Dienst (m)
scheduled bus Linienbus (m)
scheduled flight planmäßiger Flug (m)
scheduled plane Kursmaschine (f), Linienmaschine (f)
scheduled stop planmäßiger Halt (m)
scheduled train Regelzug (m)
schedulet halt planmäßiger Halt (m)
scheme Schema (n)
school holidays Schulferien (pl.)
school of hotel management Hotelfachschule (f)
school outing Schulausflug (m)
scientific management wissenschaftliche Betriebsführung (f)
scone (dreieckiger) Weizen- oder Gerstenmehlkuchen (m) (zum Tee)
scones Teegebäck (n)
scooter Motorroller (m)
Scotch broth dicke Gemüsesuppe (f) mit Hammelfleisch (n)
Scotch egg hartgekochtes Ei (n) (eingehüllt in Teig)
scouring cloth Scheuerlappen (m)
scrambled eggs Rühreier (pl. n)

screen Bildschirm (m)
screw Schiffsschraube (f)
scuba diving Unterwassersport (m)
sea See (f), Meer (n)
sea air Seeluft (f)
sea-air voyage See-Luft-Reise (f)
sea bag Seesack (m)
sea bath Seebad (n), Seeheilbad (n)
sea-bream Brasse (f), Rotbrasse (f)
seacaptain Schiffskapitän (m)
sea-climate Seeklima (n)
sea-fish Meerfisch (m)
sea-food Meeresfrüchte (pl. f), Seetiere (pl. n)
sea-front hotel Seehotel (n)
sea glider Wassersegelflugzeug (n)
sea-gull Möwe (f)
seaman Seemann (m), Schiffer (m)
seaplane Wasserflugzeug (n)
sea-perch Meerbarsch (m)
seaport Seehafen (m)
sea route Seeroute (f), Seeweg (m)
sea-shore Strand (m)
sea-sick seekrank
sea-sickness Seekrankheit (f)
sea-shells Muscheltiere (pl. n)
sea tourism Seetourismus (m), Seetouristik (f)
sea tourist Seetourist (m)
sea-water Meerwasser (n)
sear Sengen (n) (Geflügel), versengen, anbrennen
search suchen, durchsuchen
seaside Küste (f)
seaside gala Strandfest (n)
seaside health resort Seeheilbad (n)
seaside hotel Strandhotel (n), Seehotel (n)
seaside pleasures Badefreuden (pl. f)
seaside resort Seebad (n)
season Jahreszeit (f), Saison (f); würzen (Speisen)
season ticket Zeitkarte (f), Dauer-Abonnement (n)
season's salad Jahreszeitsalat (m)
seasonal business Saisongeschäft (n)
seasonal employment saisonale Beschäftigung (f)

seasonal establishment Saisonbetrieb (m)
seasonal fluctuation Saisonschwankung (f)
seasonal hotel Saisonhotel (n)
seasonal hotel trade Saisonhotellerie (f)
seasonal peak Saisonspitze (f)
seasonal price increase Saisonaufschlag (m)
seasonal service Saisonbetrieb (m)
seasonal surcharge Saisonzuschlag (m)
seasonal variation Saisonschwankung (f)
seat Platz (m), Sitz (m), Sessel (m)
seat belt Sicherheitsgürtel (m), Sicherheitsgurt (m)
seat reservation Platzreservierung (f), Platzbestellung (f)
seat reservation fee Platzkartengebühr (f)
seat taken besetzter Platz (m)
seating capacity Sitzplatzkapazität (f)
seats should be reserved in advance Platzkarten (pl.f) erforderlich
seawater bathing pool Seewasser-Badebecken (n)
seawater cure Meerwasserkur (f)
second class zweite Klasse (f)
second-class compartment Abteil (n) zweiter Klasse (f)
second course zweiter Gang (m)
second hand gebraucht
secretarial compartment Schreibabteil (n)
secretary rail Zugsekretärin (f)
secure sicher, decken, schützen
securities rendered gewährte Sicherheiten (pl.f)
security Wertpapier (n)
security deposit bei öffentlichen Versorgungsbetrieben (pl.m) hinterlegter Geldbetrag (m)
sedative factor Schonfaktor (m)
sediment Bodensatz (m)
select auswählen
selection Auswahl (f)
selection of cheese Käseplatte (f)
selection of cold cuts gemischter Aufschnitt (m)
selection of cold meat gemischter Aufschnitt (m)
self insurance Eigendeckung (f), freiwillige Selbstversicherung (f)
self-assured selbstbewußt, selbstvertrauend
self-contained flat Appartement (n)
self-drive car hire service Autovermietung (f) an Selbstfahrer (pl.m)
self-employed selbständig
self-esteem Selbstachtung (f), Eigendünkel (m)
self-service Selbstbedienung (f)
self-service cafeteria Selbstbedienungsrestaurant (n)
self-service restaurant Selbstbedienungsrestaurant (n)
self-service restaurant with slotmachines Automatenrestaurant (n)
self-service snack bar Schnellimbißstube (f)
self-service store Selbstbedienungsladen (m)
sell verkaufen
sell out ausverkaufen, (Lager) räumen
sellers' market Verkäufermarkt (m)
selling aid (schedule 11) Verkaufshilfe (f) (Service Center 11)
selling expenses Vertriebskosten (pl.)
sellingprice Verkaufspreis (m)
semiannual halbjährlich
semimonthly halbmonatlich
semolina Grieß (m)
semolina pie Grießstrudel (m)
semolina pudding Grießpudding (m)
semolina soup Grießsuppe (f)
send senden
send luggage in advance Gepäck (n) aufgeben
sensitive empfindlich
separate trennen
serious (matter) ernsthaft (Angelegenheit)
serve dienen, servieren, auftragen, bedienen

service Dienst *(m)*, Dienstleistung *(f)*, Verbindung *(f)*, Service *(m)*, Servierleistung *(f)*, Servieren *(n)*, Bedienungsgeld *(n)*, Gottesdienst *(m)*
service and taxes included Bedienung *(f)* und Steuern *(pl.f)* inbegriffen
service bureau fees (schedule 8) Kundendienstgebühren *(pl.f)* (Service Center 8)
service charge Bedienungsgeld *(n)*, Bedienungszuschlag *(m)*
service included Bedienung *(f)* inbegriffen
service lift Speisenaufzug *(m)*
service on board Service *(m)* an Bord *(m)*
service program Dienstprogramm
service staff Bedienungspersonal *(n)*
service station Reparaturdienst *(m)*, Tankstelle *(f)*
service station attendant Tankwart *(m)*
service trade Dienstleistungsgewerbe *(n)*
serviced hut bewirtschaftete Hütte *(f)*
servicing Wartung *(f)*
serving dish Platte *(f)*
set down passengers Fahrgäste *(pl.m)* aussteigen lassen
set off aufbrechen
set off again weiterfahren
set the table Tisch *(m)* decken
setting-up exercises Gymnastik *(f)*
settle an account ein Konto *(n)* ausgleichen
severe climate rauhes Klima *(n)*
sewer Abwasserkanal *(m)*
sewing kit Nähzeug *(n)*
shad Maifisch *(m)*, Alse *(f)*
shadow Schatten *(m)*
shady schattig
shaft Welle *(f)*
shake schütteln
shallot Schalotte *(f)*
shandy Schorle *(f)*, Radlermaß *(n)*
share a room with s.o. mit j-m ein Zimmer *(n)* teilen
shared bathroom gemeinsames Badezimmer *(n)*

shark's fins Haifischflossen *(pl.f)*
shark's fins soup Haifischflossensuppe *(f)*
sharp bend scharfe Kurve *(f)*
shaved cheese Hobelkäse *(m)*
shaver point Steckdose *(f)* für Elektrorasierer *(m)*
sheat-fish Wels *(m)*
shed Schuppen *(m)*
sheep's cheese Schafskäse *(m)*
sheet Laken *(n)*; Blatt *(n)*
shellfish Schalentier *(n)*
shelter Unterkunft *(f)*
sheltered geschützt
shepherd's pie Auflauf *(m)* aus Hackfleisch *(n)* und Kartoffeln *(pl.f)*
sherbet Scherbett *(m)*, Sorbett *(m)*
sherry Sherry *(m)*
shift Schicht *(f)*
shin of pork Schopfbraten *(m)*
ship versenden, Schiff *(n)*
ship game Bordspiel *(n)*
ship owner Reeder *(m)*
shipbuilding Schiffsbau *(m)*
shipment Versendung *(f)*, Verfrachtung *(f)*
shipping charges Verladekosten *(pl.)*
shipping clerk Expedient *(m)*
shipping company Reederei *(f)*
shipping cost Versandkosten *(pl.)*
shipping space Schiffsraum *(m)*
ship's cook Schiffskoch *(m)*
ship's doctor Schiffsarzt *(m)*
ship's newspaper Bordzeitung *(f)*
shirred eggs Spiegeleier *(pl.n)*
shoe cleaning Schuhputzen *(n)*
shoe-shining cloth Schuhputzlappen *(m)*
shoeblack Schuhputzer *(m)*
shoehorn Schuhanzieher *(m)*
shoestring potatoes Streichholzkartoffeln *(pl.f)*
shoot schießen, jagen, Jagdrevier *(n)*
shooting Jagd *(f)*
shooting box Jagdhütte *(f)*
shooting licence Jagdschein *(m)*
shooting lodge Jagdhütte *(f)*
shooting-match Schützenfest *(n)*
shooting season Jagdsaison *(f)*, Jagdzeit *(f)*
shooting trip Jagdreise *(f)*

shopping Einkaufen *(n)*
shopping center Geschäftsviertel *(n)*, Einkaufszentrum *(n)*
shopping street Geschäftsstraße *(f)*
shore Strand *(m)*, Küste *(f)*, Ufer *(n)*
shore excursion Landausflug *(m)*
short cut Abkürzung *(f)*
short-distance flight Kurzstreckenflug *(m)*
short-distance traffic Nahverkehr *(m)*
short-range kurzfristig
short-term kurzfristig
short-term investments kurzfristige Anlagen *(pl.f)*, Wertpapiere *(pl.n)* des Umlaufvermögens *(n)*
short-term parker Kurzparker *(m)*
shortage Manko *(n)*, Fehlbetrag *(m)*, Minus *(n)*
shortcake Mürbeteigkuchen *(m)*
shortcomings Unzulänglichkeiten *(pl.f)*, Mängel *(pl.m)*, Fehler *(pl.m)*
shortening Fett *(n)*, Pflanzenfett *(n)*
shoulder Schulter *(f)*
shoulder of pork Schweinsschulter *(f)*
shoulder of veal Kalbsschulter *(f)*
shoulder period Vor- oder Nachsaison *(f)*
show Vorführung *(f)*, Show *(f)*, zeigen
show case Schaukasten *(m)*, Vitrine *(f)*
show of national costumes Trachtenfest *(n)*
shower Brause *(f)*, Dusche *(f)*
shower-bath Dusche *(f)*
shower-bath cubicle Duschkabine *(f)*
shower of rain Regenschauer *(m)*
shower room Duschraum *(m)*
shower stall Duschnische *(f)*
showers Duschanlage *(f)*
shredded calf's liver geschnetzelte Kalbsleber *(f)*
shredded meat Geschnetzeltes *(n)*
shrimp Garnele *(f)*, Krabbe *(f)*
shrink schrumpfen, sich vermindern
shrinkage Schwundverlust *(m)*, Schwund *(m)*
Shrove Tuesday Fastnacht *(f)*, Faschingsdienstag *(m)*

Shrovetide Fastnachtszeit *(f)*, Karnevalszeit *(f)*
shrub Strauch *(m)*
shuffleboard Shuffleboard *(n)* (Unterhaltungsspiel auf Kreuzfahrt-Schiffen)
shunt rangieren
shutter Verschluß *(m)*
shutter-release Auslöser *(m)*
shuttle Flughafenbus *(m)*
shuttle cock Federball *(m)*
shuttle service Pendelverkehr *(m)*
sick leave Krankenurlaub *(m)*
sickness insurance Krankenversicherung *(f)*
side dish Beilage *(f)*, Vorspeise *(f)*, Vorgericht *(n)*
side-wheeler Raddampfer *(m)*
sidewalk Bürgersteig *(m)*
sidewalk café Straßencafé *(n)*
siesta Mittagsschlaf *(m)*
sieve Sieb *(n)*
sift sieben
sight Anblick *(m)*, Sehenswürdigkeit *(f)*
sight-seeing Besuchen *(n)* von Sehenswürdigkeiten *(pl.f)*
sight-seeing excursion Besichtigungsfahrt *(f)*
sight-seeing flight Rundflug *(m)*
sight-seeing tour Stadtrundfahrt *(f)*
signature Unterschrift *(f)*
significant bezeichnend, bedeutsam, wichtig, von Bedeutung *(f)*
signpost Wegweiser *(m)*
signs and symbols Zeichenerklärung *(f)*
silent partner stiller Gesellschafter *(m)*
silent partnership stille Beteiligung *(f)*
silver Silbergeschirr *(n)*, Silber *(n)*
silver hake Seehecht *(m)*
silver trout Silberfelchen *(m)*
simmer brodeln lassen, leicht sieden
simple einfach
simple breakfast einfaches Frühstück *(n)*
sincere aufrichtig, ehrlich, offen
single Einzelzimmer *(n)*, ledig, einfach

single bedroom Einbettzimmer *(n)*
single-berth compartment
  Einbettabteil *(n)*
single cabin Einzelkabine *(f)*
single-engined aircraft
  einmotoriges Flugzeug *(n)*
single file traffic einspurige
  Fahrbahn *(f)*
single market property auf
  bestimmten Gästetyp *(m)*
  spezialisiertes Hotel *(n)*
single passenger Einzelreisender *(m)*
single room Einzelzimmer *(n)*,
  Einbettzimmer *(n)*, Einzelkabine *(f)*
single room supplement
  Einzelzimmerzuschlag *(m)*
single ticket einfache Fahrkarte *(f)*
single tourist Einzelreisender *(m)*
single track eingleisig
sinking fund Tilgungsfonds *(m)*,
  Amortisationsfonds *(m)*
sinking fund payments
  Einzahlungen *(pl.f)* in einen
  Tilgungsfonds *(m)*
sinking fund requirements
  Rückzahlungsverpflichtungen *(pl.f)*
  (im Jahresabschluß)
sip nippen, schlürfen
sirloin Zwischenrippenstück *(n)*
sirloin steak with green pepper
  Zwischenrippenstück *(n)* mit
  grünem Pfeffer *(m)*
sirloin steak with onions
  Zwiebelrostbraten *(m)*
site Schauplatz *(m)*
sitting Besetzung *(f)* des Restaurants
  (n)
sitting-room Wohnzimmer *(n)*,
  Gästezimmer *(n)*, Tagesraum *(m)*
size of pary Personenzahl *(f)*
skate eislaufen, Schlittschuh *(m)*
  laufen
skateboard Skatebord *(n)*
skater Eisläufer *(m)*
skating Eislauf *(m)*, Eislaufen *(n)*
skating-rink Eishalle *(f)*,
  Rollschuhbahn *(f)*
skewer Spießchen *(n)*, Spieß *(m)*
ski Ski *(m)*, Ski *(m)* laufen
ski binding Skibindung *(f)*
ski boot Skistiefel *(m)*

ski carrier Skiträger *(m)*
ski center Skiort *(m)*, Skizentrum *(n)*
ski-coach Skilehrer *(m)*
ski equipment Skiausrüstung *(f)*
ski grounds Skigelände *(n)*
ski hire Skiverleih *(m)*
ski hotel Skihotel *(n)*
ski hut Skihütte *(f)*
ski jump Sprungschanze *(f)*
ski-jumping Skispringen *(n)*
ski-lift day ticket Skitages-Paß *(m)*
ski-lift season ticket Skipaß *(m)*
ski lodge Skihütte *(f)*
ski nursery slope Anfängerhang *(m)*
ski pole Skistock *(m)*
ski race Skirennen *(n)*
ski rental Skiverleih *(m)*
ski resort Skiort *(m)*
ski run Piste *(f)*
ski run maintenance Pistenpflege *(f)*
ski school Skischule *(f)*
ski slope Skihang *(m)*, Abfahrtshang
  (m)
ski stick Skistock *(m)*
ski tour Skitour *(f)*
ski tourist Skitourist *(m)*
ski tow Skischlepplift *(m)*
ski trousers Skihose *(f)*
ski wax Skiwachs *(n)*
ski wear Skikleidung *(f)*
skibob Skibob *(m)*
skid schleudern
skier Skifahrer *(m)*, Skiläufer *(m)*
skiing Skifahren *(n)*, Skilauf *(m)*,
  Skisport *(m)*
skiing club Skiklub *(m)*
skiing exercises Skigymnastik *(f)*
skiing guide Skiführer *(m)*
skiing holidays Skiurlaub *(m)*,
  Skiferien *(pl.)*
skiing instruction Skiunterricht *(m)*
skiing instructor Skilehrer *(m)*
skiing lessons Skiunterricht *(m)*
skiing trip Skireise *(f)*
skiing village Skidorf *(n)*
skiing-weekend Skiwochenende *(n)*
skill Fachkenntnis *(f)*, Fähigkeit *(f)*
skilled manpower gelernte
  Arbeitskräfte *(pl.f)*
skillet Bratpfanne *(f)*
skim milk Magermilch *(f)*

skim off abschöpfen
skimmed milk Magermilch *(f)*
skimmer Schaumlöffel *(m)*
skin Haut *(f)*
skins ski Steigfelle *(pl. n)*
skittle Kegel *(m)*
skittle-alley Kegelbahn *(f)*
sky Himmel *(m)*
skyline Horizont *(m)*
slack off nachlassen
sled Schlitten *(m)*
sledge tow Rodellift *(m)*, Schlittenlift *(m)*
sleep Schlaf *(m)*, schlafen
sleep late verschlafen
sleeper Schlafwagen *(m)*
sleeper section Schlafabteil *(n)*
sleeping accommodation Schlafgelegenheit *(f)*
sleeping bag Schlafsack *(m)*
sleeping berth Bett *(n)*, Schlafplatz *(m)*
sleeping car attendant Schlafwagenschaffner *(m)*
sleeping car charge Schlafwagenzuschlag *(m)*
sleeping car ticket Schlafwagenkarte *(f)*
sleeping compartment Schlafabteil *(n)*
sleeping cure Schlafkur *(f)*
sleigh-ride Schlittenfahrt *(f)*
slice Scheibe *(f)*, Schnitte *(f)*
slice of grilled (beef) meat grillierte Fleischschnitte *(f)*
sliced calf's liver Kalbsleberscheiben *(pl. f)*
sliced knuckle of veal Kalbshaxenscheiben *(pl. f)*
slices of sausage Wurstaufschnitt *(m)*
slide Diapositiv *(n)*
sliding roof Schiebedach *(n)*
slimming diet treatment Abmagerungskur *(f)*
slipper Hausschuh *(m)*
slippery glatt, rutschig
slippery when wet Schleudergefahr *(f)*
slips Badehose *(f)*
slope Abhang *(m)*, Hang *(m)*, Piste *(f)*

slope grooming Pistenpflege *(f)*
slopy abschüssig
slot machine (schedule 6) Automat *(m)*, Spielautomat *(m)* (Umsatzbereich 6)
slow down Schritt *(m)* fahren!
slow train Bummelzug *(m)*
sluice Schleuse *(f)*
slush Schneematsch *(m)*
small ad Kleinanzeige *(f)*
small cigar Zigarillo *(m)*
small cream puff Windbeutel *(m)*
small dumpling Klößchen *(n)*
small veal sausage Kalbfleischwürstchen *(n)*
small veal steak Kalbsnüßchen *(n)*
smell Geruch *(m)*, riechen
smelt Stint *(m)*
smoke room Rauchsalon *(m)*
smoked geräuchert
smoked beef Rauchfleisch *(n)*
smoked beef tongue Rindszunge *(f)*, geräuchert
smoked eel Räucheraal *(m)*
smoked ham Räucherschinken *(m)*
smoked herring Hering *(m)* geräuchert
smoked meat Rauchfleisch *(n)*
smoked pig's ears geräucherte Schweinsohren *(pl. n)*
smoked pork ribs Kasseler Rippenspeer *(m, n)*
smoked pork with pickled cabbage Rauchfleisch *(n)* mit Kraut *(n)*
smoked rib of pork with sauerkraut Schweinsrippchen *(n)* mit Sauerkraut *(n)*
smoked salmon Räucherlachs *(m)*
smoked sausage Mettwurst *(f)*
smoked (stuffed) pig's trotter Eisbein *(n)*
smoker Raucher *(m)*, Raucherabteil *(n)*
smoking compartment Raucherabteil *(n)*
smuggle schmuggeln
snack Imbiß *(m)*
snack-bar Imbißstube *(f)*, Snackbar *(f)*

snack-counter Imbißstube *(f)*
snail Weinbergschnecke *(f)*
snapshot Schnappschuß *(m)*
sneakers Turnschuhe *(pl. m)*
snipe Moorschnepfe *(f)*
snook Seebarsch *(m)*
snorkel Schnorchel *(m)*
snowball Schneeball *(m)*
snow-bound eingeschneit
snow break Schneeschmelze *(f)*
snow chains Schneeketten *(pl. f)*
snow-cleared schneegeräumt
snow-clearing Schneeräumung *(f)*
snow conditions Schneelage *(f)*, Schneeverhältnisse *(pl. n)*
snow-covered schneebedeckt, verschneit
snowdrift Schneewehe *(f)*
snow-fall Schneefall *(m)*
snowfield Schneefeld *(n)*
snow-goggles Schneebrille *(f)*
snow grouse Schneehuhn *(n)*
snowman Schneemann *(m)*
snowmobile Motorschlitten *(m)*
snow-plough Schneepflug *(m)*
snowplow Schneepflug *(m)*
snow report Schneebericht *(m)*
snowstorm Schneesturm *(m)*
snow train Wintersportzug *(m)*
snowed up eingeschneit, verschneit
snowy schneereich
snowy season Schneesaison *(f)*
snuff Schnupftabak *(m)*
snug behaglich, gemütlich
soak einweichen
sober nüchtern
soccer Fußball *(n)*
social activity gesellschaftliche Veranstaltung *(f)*
social evening Gesellschaftsabend *(m)*
social insurance Sozialversicherung *(f)*
social tourism Sozialtourismus *(m)*
society Gesellschaft *(f)*
socket Steckdose *(f)*, Fassung *(f)*
soda Soda *(n)*
soda fountain Erfrischungshalle *(f)*
soda water Selterswasser *(n)*
sodium sulphate spring Glaubersalzquelle *(f)*

soft weich
soft boiled egg weichgekochtes Ei *(n)*
soft drink alkoholfreies Getränk *(n)*
software Software *(f)*
solar radiation Sonnenstrahlung *(f)*, Sonnenbestrahlung *(f)*
sold out ausverkauft
sole Seezunge *(f)*
sole agent Alleinvertreter *(m)*
solicit sich bemühen, erstreben
solution Auflösung *(f)*, Lösung *(f)*, Erklärung *(f)*, Klärung *(f)*
sorrel Sauerampfer *(m)*
soufflé Auflauf *(m)*
soufflé of chocolate Schokoladenauflauf *(m)*
soufflé of rice Reisauflauf *(m)*
soufflé of vanilla Vanilleauflauf *(m)*
soufflé-potatoes Auflaufkartoffeln *(pl. f)*
sound equipment Tonwiedergabegeräte *(pl. n)*
sound proof schalldicht
soup Suppe *(f)*
soup ladle Schöpflöffel *(m)*
soup plate Suppenteller *(m)*
soup tureen Suppenschüssel *(f)*
soup with dumpling Knödelsuppe *(f)*
soup with egg dough drops Eintopfsuppe *(f)*
soup with fowl Geflügelsuppe *(f)*
soup with fried peas Bouillon *(f)* mit gedünsteten Erbsen *(pl. f)*
soup with ham dumplings Schinkenknödelsuppe *(f)*
soup with liver dumplings Leberknödelsuppe *(f)*
soup with liver rice Leberreissuppe *(f)*
soup with mushrooms Pilzsuppe *(f)*
soup with potatoes Kartoffelsuppe *(f)*
soup with semolina dumplings Grießklößchensuppe *(f)*
soup with tapioca Tapiocasuppe *(f)*
soup with white beans Bohnensuppe *(f)*
sour sauer

sour cream saurer Rahm *(m)*
source of information
  Informationsquelle *(f)*
sous-chef stellvertretender
  Küchenchef *(m)*
souse Marinade *(f)*
soused herring Bismarckhering *(m)*
souvenir shop Andenkengeschäft *(n)*
soy bean Sojabohne *(f)*
spa Mineralquelle *(f)*, Heilquelle *(f)*,
  Kurort *(m)*, Badeort *(m)*, Heilbad
  (n)
spa ballroom Tanzkasino *(n)*
spa concert Kurkonzert *(n)*
spa doctor Kurarzt *(m)*, Badearzt *(m)*
spa house Kurhaus *(n)*
spa open all the year round
  ganzjähriger Kurbetrieb *(m)*
spa orchestra Kurorchester *(n)*
spa park Kurpark *(m)*
spa treatment Kurbehandlung *(f)*
space rentals (schedule 6)
  Mieterträge *(pl.m)* aus der
  Vermietung *(f)* von Räumen *(pl.m)*
  im Hotel *(n)* (Umsatzbereich 6)
**spaghetti with minced meat
  sauce** Spaghetti *(pl.)* mit
  Hackfleischsoße *(f)*
spaghetti with tomato sauce
  Spaghetti *(pl.)* mit Tomatensoße *(f)*
Spain Spanien
span of control Kontrollspanne *(f)*
Spanish fish stew spanischer
  Fischeintopf *(m)*
Spanish meat-pot spanischer
  Suppentopf *(m)*
**Spanish rice dish with fish and
  meat** spanisches Reisgericht *(n)*
  mit Fisch *(m)* und Fleisch *(n)*
spare bed Reservebett *(n)*
spare part Ersatzteil *(n)*
spare rib Rippenspeer (m, n),
  Schopfbraten *(m)*
spare room Fremdenzimmer *(n)*,
  Gastzimmer *(n)*, Gästezimmer *(n)*
spare time Freizeit *(f)*
sparkling schäumend, perlend (Wein)
sparkling hock Schaumwein *(m)*,
  Sekt *(m)*,
sparkling wine Perlwein *(m)*
speaker Sprecher *(m)*

special arrangement
  Spezialarrangement *(n)*
special brochure Sonderprospekt *(m)*
special bus Sonderbus *(m)*
special folder Sonderprospekt *(m)*
special leave Sonderurlaub *(m)*
special plane Sonderflugzeug *(n)*
special price Vorzugspreis *(m)*
special quota Sonderkontingent *(n)*
special rate Sondertarif *(m)*,
  Sonderpreis *(m)*
special slalom Spezialslalom *(m)*
special weekend price
  Wochenend-Spezialpreis *(m)*
speciality of the house Spezialität
  (f) des Hauses *(n)*
specification Spezifikation *(f)*,
  Beschreibung *(f)*
specify spezifizieren
speed Geschwindigkeit *(f)*, Tempo *(n)*
speed limit
  Geschwindigkeitsbegrenzung *(f)*
speed skating Eisschnellauf *(m)*
spend ausgeben
spice Gewürz *(n)*
spicy pikant, scharf, würzig
spilt shift unterbrochene
  Arbeitsschicht *(f)*
spinach Spinat *(m)*
spinach beets Mangold *(m)*
spiny lobster Languste *(f)*
spirit stove Spirituskocher *(m)*
spirits Spirituosen *(pl.f)*, Alkohol *(m)*
spit-roasted am Spieß *(m)* gebraten
splash planschen
split 1/2 Flasche *(f)* Mineralwasser *(n)*
spoil verderben
spoilage Verderb *(m)* von Waren
  (pl.f)
sponge Schwamm *(m)*
sponge ice-cream
  Schaumgefrorenes *(n)*
sponge (Swiss)roll Biskuitrolle *(f)*
spoon Löffel *(m)*
sport clothes Sportkleidung *(f)*
sporting event Sportveranstaltung *(f)*
sporting goods Sportartikel *(pl.m)*
sporting plane Sportflugzeug *(n)*
sports car Sportwagen *(m)*
sports equipment Sportausrüstung
  (f)

sports facilities Sportanlagen *(pl.f)*
sports field Sportplatz *(m)*
sports hall Sporthalle *(f)*
sports hotel Sporthotel *(n)*
sportsman Sportler *(m)*
sportswear Sportkleidung *(f)*
spot buying rate Tagesankaufskurs *(m)*
spot check Überraschungsinventur *(f)*, Prüfung *(f)* an Ort *(m)* und Stelle *(f)*
spotted dick Sultaninenpudding *(m)*
spouse program Rahmenprogramm *(n)* für Begleitpersonen *(pl.f)*
spouses Eheleute *(pl.)*
sprat Sprotte *(f)*
spring Quelle *(f)*, Brunnen *(m)*, Frühling *(m)*, Frühjahr *(n)*
spring-board Sprungbrett *(n)*
spring chicken Masthähnchen *(n)*, Hähnchen *(n)*
spring cleaning Frühjahrsputz *(m)*, Hausreinigung *(f)*
spring holiday Frühjahrsferien *(pl.)*
spring onion kleine Zwiebel *(f)*
spring trade fair Frühjahrsmesse *(f)*
spring water Quellwasser *(n)*
sprinkle bestreuen
sprinkler Berieselungsapparat *(m)*, Rasensprenger *(m)*, Feuerlöschbrause *(f)*
sprinkler leakage Wasserschaden *(m)* durch Feuerlöschbrause *(f)*
spritzer gespritzter Wein *(m)*
sprouts Kohlsprossen *(pl.f)*, Brokkoli *(pl.)*
squab Taube *(f)*
square Platz *(m)*
squash Fruchtbrei *(m)*, Fruchtsaft *(m)*; Squash (Spiel) *(n)*
squid Tintenfisch *(m)*
stadium Stadion *(n)*
staff function Stabsfunktion *(f)*
staff holiday Betriebsferien *(pl.)*
staff position Stabsstelle *(f)*
staff responsibility Verantwortungsbereich *(m)* einer Stabsstelle *(f)*
staffing schedule Stellenbesetzungsplan *(m)*
stag Hirsch *(m)*

stage Teilstrecke *(f)*, Bühne *(f)*
stage of journey Reiseetappe *(f)*
staggered holidays Ferienstaffelung *(f)*
staggering of tourist traffic Streuung *(f)* des Fremdenverkehrs *(m)*
staggering scheduling gestaffelter Dienstplan *(m)*
staircase Treppenhaus *(n)*
stairs Treppe *(f)*
stale bread altbackenes Brot *(n)*
stall Sperrsitz *(m)*, Parkett *(n)*
stamp Briefmarke *(f)*, Stempel *(m)*, stempeln, frankieren
stamp machine Briefmarkenautomat *(m)*
stand-by Warteliste *(f)* (Abflug ohne feste Reservierung)
stand-by position Wartestellung *(f)*
standard Standard *(m)*, Vorgabe *(f)*, Wertmesser *(m)*
standard class Einheitsklasse *(f)*
standard of living Lebensstandard *(m)*
standard of performance Leistungsstandard *(m)*, Leistungsmaßstab *(m)*
standardization Normung *(f)*, Standardisierung *(f)*, Vereinheitlichung *(f)*
standardize standardisieren, vereinheitlichen
standardized menu item standardisierter Speiseartikel *(m)*
standing place Stehplatz *(m)*
starfish Seestern *(m)*
start Reisebeginn *(m)*, Abflug *(m)*, Start *(m)*
starting-point Ausgangsort *(m)*, Ausgangspunkt *(m)*
state Bundesstaat *(n)*
state forest Staatswald *(m)*
state frontier Staatsgrenze *(f)*
state of mind Geisteszustand *(m)*
stated value (capital stock) ursprünglich festgesetzter Wert *(m)* einer Aktie *(f)* (USA)
statement Aufstellung *(f)*, Verzeichnis *(n)*, Übersicht *(f)*, Behauptung *(f)*, Erklärung *(f)*

statement of capital stock and surplus Entwicklung *(f)* des Kapitals *(n)* und der Rücklagen *(pl.f)*
statement of financial position Bilanz *(f)*
statement of owner's equity Entwicklung des Eigenkapitals *(n)*, Eigenkapitalausweis *(m)*
statement of partners' equity Entwicklung *(f)* des Eigenkapitals *(n)* von Personenunternehmen *(pl.n)*
statement of retained earnings Bilanzgewinnentwicklungsrechnung *(f)*
statement of stockholders' equity Eigenkapitalspiegel *(m)*
station hall Bahnhofshalle *(f)*
station hotel Bahnhofshotel *(n)*
station locker Gepäckschließfach *(n)*
station-master Bahnhofsvorstand *(m)*, Bahnhofsvorsteher *(m)*
station post office Bahnpostamt *(n)*
station restaurant Bahnhofsgaststätte *(f)*
station superintendant Bahnhofsaufsicht *(f)*
station wagon Kombiwagen *(m)*
stationary stationär
stationery Bürobedarf *(m)*
statistic Statistik *(f)*
statistical statistisch
status Status *(m)*, Stand *(m)*
stay Aufenthalt *(m)*
stay abroad Auslandsaufenthalt *(m)*
stay at a spa Kuraufenthalt *(m)*
stay in the country Landaufenthalt *(m)*
stay over Bleibegast *(m)*
steak Beefsteak *(n)*, Steak *(n)*
steak and kidney pie warme Steak- und Nierenpastete *(f)*
steak, Vienna style Wiener Rostbraten *(m)*
steal stehlen, klauen
steam-ironing Dampfbügeln *(n)*
steamed gedämpft, gedünstet
steamed noodles with vanilla-cream Dampfnudeln *(pl.f)*
steamed potatoes Dampfkartoffeln *(pl.f)*

steamed rice with chopped pork (beef) Reisfleisch *(n)*
steamer Dampfer *(m)*
steamer service Schiffsverbindung *(f)*
steamer ticket Schiffskarte *(f)*
steamship Dampfer *(m)*
steamship connection Schiffsanschluß *(m)*
steep steil
steep coast Steilküste *(f)*
steep slope Steilhang *(m)*
steeple Kirchturm *(m)*
steer steuern
steerage Zwischendeck *(n)*
stencil Matrize *(f)*
stern Heck *(n)*
stew Ragout *(n)*
stew of pork Hungarian style Schweinsgulasch *(n)*
stew of veal with dumplings Kalbsgulasch *(n)* mit Klößen *(pl.m)*
stew of venison Rehragout *(n)*
stew of white beans Weißbohnengericht *(n)*
steward Steward *(m)*, Schiffskellner *(m)*, Leiter *(m)* der Spülküche *(f)*
stewardess Stewardeß *(f)*
stewarding department Spülküche *(f)*, Reinigungsabteilung *(f)*
stewed gedämpft
stewed apples Apfelkompott *(n)*
stewed beef Rinderschmorbraten *(m)*
stewed chicken in paprika (cream) sauce Paprikahühnchen *(n)*
stewed fruit Kompott *(n)*
stewed pork and sauerkraut in paprika sauce Szegedinergulasch *(n)*
stewed veal eingemachtes Kalbfleisch *(n)*
sticker Aufklebezettel *(m)*
sticky snow Pappschnee *(m)*
Stilton (cheese) Blauschimmelkäsesorte *(f)*
stock Aktie*(n)* *(pl.f)*, Wertpapier *(n)*; Lager *(n)*
stock in trade Warenbestand *(m)*
stock on hand Vorräte *(pl.m)*
stockholder Aktionär *(m)*
stockholder's equity Passiva *(pl.)*

insgesamt; Kapital *(n)*, Rücklagen *(pl.f)* und Gewinnvortrag *(m)*; Eigenkapital *(n)*
stomach Bauch *(m)*
stone Stein *(m)*, Kern *(m)*, auskernen, entsteinen
stool Barhocker *(m)*
stop Station *(f)*, Aufenthalt *(m)*, Haltestelle *(f)*, halten
stop en route Zwischenlandung *(f)*, Unterwegsaufenthalt *(m)*
stopover Reiseunterbrechung *(f)*, Zwischenlandung *(f)*
stoppage Stockung *(f)*
storage Lagerung *(f)*
storage space Lagerraum *(m)*
store lagern, speichern, Lager *(n)*
storekeeper Lagerhalter *(m)*
storeroom Lager *(n)*, Vorratsraum *(m)*
storeroom requisition Lageranforderung *(f)*
storing Lagerhaltung *(f)*
stout beer dunkles (schwächeres) Bier *(n)*
stove heating Ofenheizung *(f)*
straight line depreciation lineare Abschreibungsmethode *(f)*
straightforward (process) einfach, unkompliziert (Vorgang)
strain durchseien
stranger Fremder *(m)*
strategy Strategie *(f)*
straw Strohhalm *(m)*, Trinkhalm *(m)*
straw potatoes Strohkartoffeln *(pl.f)*
strawberry Erdbeere *(f)*
strawberry ice-cream Erdbeereis *(n)*
stream trout Flußforelle *(f)*
street hawker Straßenhändler *(m)*
street island Verkehrsinsel *(f)*
street plan Stadtplan *(m)*
street sign Straßenschild *(n)*
street-lamp Straßenlaterne *(f)*
streetcar Straßenbahn *(f)*
streetcar line Straßenbahnlinie *(f)*
stretch Strecke *(f)*
strike streiken, Streik *(m)*
string bean Stangenbohne *(f)*, junge Brechbohne *(f)*
strips of chicken breast Bruststreifen *(pl.m)* vom Huhn *(n)*

strips of sole fillets Streifen *(pl.m)* von Seezungen *(pl.f)*
stroll Bummel *(m)*
strong stark
stronghold Festung *(f)*, Burg *(f)*
structure bauliche Anlage *(f)*, Struktur *(f)*, Aufbau *(m)*
strudel Strudel *(m)*
student travel Studentenfahrt *(f)*, Studentenreiseverkehr *(m)*
student trip Studentenfahrt *(f)*
studio couch Bettcouch *(f)*
studio (executive room) Zimmer *(n)* mit zusätzlicher Schlafcouch *(f)*
study trip Studienreise *(f)*, Exkursion *(f)*
stuff füllen (mit Füllsel)
stuffed gefüllt
stuffed boar's head Wildschweinskopf *(m)* gefüllt
stuffed breast of veal Kalbsbrust *(f)* gefüllt
stuffed eggs gefüllte Eier *(pl.n)*
stuffed fritters Teigtaschen *(pl.f)*
stuffed green (sweet) peppers gefüllte Paprika *(pl.f)*
stuffed half-moon patty gefülltes Halbmondpastetchen *(n)*
stuffed olive gefüllte Olive *(f)*
stuffed pancakes Palatschinken *(m)*
stuffed shoulder gefüllte Schulter *(f)*
stuffed tomatoes Tomaten gefüllt *(pl.f)*
stuffed veal collop gefülltes Kalbsschnitzel *(n)*
stuffing Füllung *(f)*, Füllsel *(n)*
sturgeon Stör *(m)*, Sterlet *(m)*
subcontract Untervertrag *(m)*
subdivide unterteilen, aufteilen
subdivision Unterabteilung *(f)*, Aufteilung *(f)*
subject to alteration Änderungen *(pl.f)* vorbehalten
sublease Untervermietung *(f)*, Untermiete *(f)*
sublessee Untermieter *(m)*, Unterpächter *(m)*
sublessor Untervermieter *(m)*, Unterverpächter *(m)*
sublet untervermieten, unterverpachten

submeter gesondert erfassen (z. B. Strom)
submissive unterwürfig, ergeben, gehorsam
subordinate unterordnen, Untergebener *(m)*
subscribe abonnieren
subscription Abonnement *(n)*
subsequent payment Nachzahlung *(f)*
subsidiary company Tochtergesellschaft *(f)*
subsidy Zuschuß *(m)*
substantial meal reichliche Mahlzeit *(f)*
substitute ersetzen, Ersatz *(m)*, Stellvertreter *(m)*
subtenant Untermieter *(m)*, Unterpächter *(m)*
subtract abziehen
subtraction Abzug *(m)*
suburban train Vorortzug *(m)*
subway U-Bahn *(f)*, Fußgängertunnel *(m)*
suckling pig Spanferkel *(n)*
sudatory bath Schwitzbad *(n)*
sue klagen, verklagen
suet Fett *(n)*
sugar Zucker *(m)*
sugar basin Zuckerdose *(f)*
sugar bowl Zuckerschale *(f)*
sugar pea Zuckererbse *(f)*
sugar tong Zuckerzange *(f)*
sugared gezuckert
suggest vorschlagen, anregen
suggestion Vorschlag *(m)*, Anregung *(f)*
suit Anzug *(m)*, Kostüm *(n)*
suitcase Koffer *(m)*, Handkoffer *(m)*
suitcase label Kofferaufkleber *(m)*
suite Suite *(f)*
sulphur spring Schwefelquelle *(f)*
sultana Sultanine *(f)*
sultana (fruit) cake Englischer Kuchen *(m)*
sultry schwül
sum up zusammenfassen, summieren
summary Zusammenfassung *(f)*
summer fair Sommermesse *(f)*
summer festival Sommerspiele *(pl. n)*
summer health resort Sommerfrische *(f)*, Sommerkurort *(m)*
summer holiday resort Sommerfrische *(f)*
summer holiday village Sommerferiendorf *(n)*
summer holidays Sommerferien *(pl.)*
summer party Sommerfest *(n)*
summer residence Sommersitz *(m)*
summer resort Sommerfrische *(f)*
summer school Ferienkurs *(m)*
summer season Sommersaison *(f)*
summer stay Sommeraufenthalt *(m)*
summer terrace Sonnenterrasse *(f)*
summer time Sommerzeit *(f)*
summer timetable Sommerfahrplan *(m)*
summer tourist traffic Sommerreiseverkehr *(m)*, Sommerfremdenverkehr *(m)*
summer vacation Sommerferien *(pl.)*
summer visitor Sommergast *(m)*
summer-squash Zwergkürbis *(m)*
sunbath Sonnenbad *(n)*
sun-bathe ein Sonnenbad *(n)* nehmen
sun-bathing lawn Liegewiese *(f)*
sunburn Sonnenbrand *(m)*
sundae Eisbecher *(m)*
Sunday excursion Sonntagsausflug *(m)*
Sunday excursion ticket Sonntagsfahrkarte *(f)*
sun deck Sonnendeck *(n)*
sundry verschiedene
sun glasses Sonnenbrille *(f)*
sun-light treatment Heliotherapie *(f)*
sunny sonnig
sunrise Sonnenaufgang *(m)*
sunset Sonnenuntergang *(m)*
sunshade Sonnenschirm *(m)*
sunstroke Sonnenstich *(m)*
sunterrace Sonnenterrasse *(f)*
sun treatment Sonnenkur *(f)*
sun umbrella Sonnenschirm *(m)*
superior Vorgesetzter *(m)*
supermarket Selbstbedienungsladen *(m)*
supervise beaufsichtigen
supervision Aufsicht *(f)*
supervisor Aufsichtsperson *(f)*, Vorgesetzter *(m)*

supervisory body   Aufsichtsorgan
  (n), Überwachungsstelle *(f)*
supervisory training
  Vorgesetzenschulung *(f)*
supper   Abendessen *(n)*
supplement   Zuschlag *(m)*,
  Ergänzung *(f)*
supplementary accomodation
  Parahotellerie *(f)* (z. B.
  Privatquartiere, Ferienzentren,
  Campingplätze, Erholungsheime
  etc.)
supplementary charge   Zuschlag *(m)*
supplementary course of
  treatment   zusätzliche Kur *(f)*
supplementary cure   zusätzliche
  Kur *(f)*
supplementary fare   Zuschlag *(m)*
supplementary ticket
  Zusatzfahrkarte *(f)*
supplementary treatment
  Ergänzungsbehandlung *(f)*
supplier   Lieferant *(m)*, Lieferer *(m)*
supplies   Hilfs- und Betriebsstoffe
  (pl. m)
supply   liefern, versorgen, Lieferung
  (f), Angebot *(n)*
supply on credit   gegen Ziel *(n)*
  liefern
supplying industry   Zulieferindustrie
  (f)
support   unterstützen, Unterstützung
  (f)
surcharge   Aufschlag *(m)*
surf   Brandung *(f)*
surf-riding   Brandungsreiten *(n)*
surface connection   Anschluß *(m)*
  mit Bahn *(f)* oder Bus *(m)*
surface transport
  Bahn-Bus-Verkehr *(m)*
surfboard   Surfbrett *(n)*
surname   Zuname *(m)*, Familienname
  (m)
surpass   übersteigen, übertreffen
surplus   Gewinn *(m)*
surroundings   Umgebung *(f)*
survey   Untersuchung *(f)*, Erhebung
  (f), überblicken
survey sheet   Erhebungsbogen *(m)*,
  Fragebogen *(m)*
suspension railway   Schwebebahn *(f)*

swamp   Sumpf *(m)*
swap   tauschen, vertauschen,
  austauschen
sweat   Schweiß *(m)*, schwitzen
swede   weiße Rübe *(f)*
sweet   süß
sweet cheese cake   süßer
  Käsekuchen *(m)*
sweet cider   Süßmost *(m)*, Apfelsaft
  (m)
sweet cream   Rahm *(m)*, Sahne *(f)*
sweet curd-cheese strudel
  Topfenstrudel *(m)*
sweet curds pie   Topfenstrudel *(m)*
sweet dish   Dessert *(m)*, Süßspeise
  (f)
sweet potato   süße Kartoffel *(f)*,
  Süßkartoffel *(f)*
sweet shop   Konditorei *(f)*
sweet water fish   Süßwasserfisch *(m)*
sweet wine   Süßwein *(m)*, süßer
  Wein *(m)*
sweetbreads   Kalbsbries *(n)*
sweetcorn   Mais *(m)*
sweeten   zuckern
sweets   Süßigkeiten *(pl. f)*, Nachtisch
  (m), Nachspeise *(f)*
swim   schwimmen
swimmer   Schwimmer *(m)*
swimming   Schwimmen *(n)*
swimming-bath   Schwimmbad *(n)*
swimming-hall   Schwimmhalle *(f)*
swimming instructor
  Schwimmlehrer *(m)*
swimming-lessons
  Schwimmunterricht *(m)*
swimming master   Bademeister *(m)*
swimming-pool   Schwimmbad *(n)*,
  Badeanstalt *(f)*
swimsuit   Badeanzug *(m)*
Swiss Central Office of Tourism
  Schweizerische
  Fremdenverkehrszentrale *(f)*
Swiss chard   Mangold *(m)*
Swiss cheese   Schweizer Käse *(m)*
Swiss Hotel-Proprietors'
  Association   Schweizer
  Hotelier-Verein *(m)*
Swiss porridge with fresh fruit
  Birchermüsli *(n)*
switch   Lichtschalter *(m)*

switchback road Serpentinenstraße *(f)*
switchboard Telefonzentrale *(f)*
Switzerland Schweiz
swordfish Schwertfisch *(m)*
symbol Symbol *(n)*, Zeichen *(n)*
syrup Sirup *(m)*
system System *(n)*
systems and procedures (yield management) Informationstechnologie *(f)* (Yield Management)
S.O.S. message Reiseruf *(m)*

T

T-bar tow Schlepplift *(m)*
T-bone steak kleines Porterhousesteak *(n)*
T-junction Straßeneinmündung *(f)*
table Tisch *(m)*, Tafel *(f)*; Tabelle *(f)*, Schema *(n)*
table cloth Tischtuch *(n)*, Tischdecke *(f)*
table-cover Tischdecke *(f)*
table d'hote Table d'Hote *(n)*
table d'hote meal Tagesgericht *(n)*, gemeinsame Mahlzeit *(f)*
table knife Tafelmesser, Tischmesser *(n)*
table-lamp Tischlampe *(f)*
table linen Tischzeug *(n)*
table mat Untersatz *(m)*
table napkin Serviette *(f)*
table number Tischnummer *(f)*
table of calorific values Kalorientabelle *(f)*
table of distances Entfernungstabelle *(f)*
table reservation Tischreservierung *(f)*
table reserved for regular customers Stammtisch *(m)*
table salt Tafelsalz *(n)*
table spoon Eßlöffel *(m)*
table talk Tischgespräch *(n)*
table-tennis Tischtennis *(n)*
table-tennis room Tischtennishalle *(f)*
table top Tischplatte *(f)*

table ware Tischgeschirr *(n)*
table water Tafelwasser *(n)*, Mineralwasser *(n)*
table wine Tischwein *(m)*
tag Etikette *(f)*, Anhängezettel *(m)*
tail Schwanz *(m)*
tailcoat Frack *(m)*
tail-light Schlußlicht *(n)*
tail wind Rückenwind *(m)*
tailor Schneider *(m)*
take a holiday Ferien *(pl.)* machen
take a photo fotografieren
take a supplementary ticket nachlösen
take care Vorsicht!
take care of sorgen für
take in petrol tanken
take in tow abschleppen
take it out on s.o. seinen Zorn *(m)* an j-m auslassen
take notes sich Notizen *(pl.f)* machen
take off ausziehen
take-off Start *(m)*, Abflug *(m)*
take-off board Sprungbrett *(n)*
take part in teilnehmen an
take place stattfinden
take security precautions Sicherheitsvorkehrungen *(pl.f)* treffen
take shippings an Bord *(m)* nehmen, laden
take the lead Führung *(f)* übernehmen
taken besetzt
talk down herablassend reden; zum Schweigen bringen, unter den Tisch reden
tally sheet Inventuraufnahmeblatt *(n)*
tang Beigeschmack *(m)*
tangerine Mandarine *(f)*
tankard Deckelkrug *(m)*
tap Faßhahn *(m)*, Wasserhahn *(m)*
taproom Bierstube *(f)*, Schankstube *(f)*
tapster Schankkellner *(m)*
tardy säumig
target Vorgabe *(f)*, Planziel *(n)*
tariff Zolltarif *(m)*, Tarif *(m)*
tariff provision Tarifvorschriften *(f)*
tarragon Estragon *(m)*, Beifuß *(m)*

tart (cake) Torte *(f)*
tart (of taste) herb
tartare sauce Tartarensoße *(f)*
tartlet (Obst-)Törtchen *(n)*
task Aufgabe *(f)*
task force Arbeitsgruppe *(f)*
taste Geschmack *(m)*
tasteful geschmackvoll
tastefulness Geschmacksreichtum *(m)*
tasteless fade, unschmackhaft, geschmacklos
tastelessness Geschmacklosigkeit *(f)*
taster Probiergläschen *(n)* für Wein *(m)*
tastiness Schmackhaftigkeit *(f)*
tasty schmackhaft
tatare steak Beefsteak Tartar *(n)*
tattoo Zapfenstreich *(m)*, Abendparade *(f)* mit Musik *(f)* (Vorführungen)
tavern Lokal *(n)*, Wirtshaus *(n)*, Ausschank *(m)*
tavern keeper Schankwirt *(m)*
tax Steuer *(f)*, besteuern
tax de séjour Kurtaxe *(f)*
tax paid versteuert
taxation Besteuerung *(f)*
taxes payable Steuerverbindlichkeiten *(pl.f)*
taxi Taxi *(n)*
taxi rank Taxistand *(m)*
taxi-driver Taxifahrer *(m)*, Taxichauffeur *(m)*
tea Tee *(m)*
tea-caddy Teebüchse *(f)*
tea cakes Teegebäck *(n)*
tea-cart Teewagen *(m)*
tea-cloth kleine Tischdecke *(f)*, Geschirrtuch *(n)*
tea-cosy Teewärmer *(m)*
teacup Teetasse *(f)*
tea dance Tanztee *(m)*
tea garden Gartenrestaurant *(n)*
tea-house Teehaus *(n)* (in China und Japan)
tea-kettle Teekessel *(m)*
tea-party Teegesellschaft *(f)*
tea-pot Teekanne *(f)*
tea-room Frühstückszimmer *(n)*, Teestube *(f)*

tea-service Teegeschirr *(n)*
tea set Teeservice *(n)*
tea-shop Teerestaurant *(n)*, Imbißstube *(f)*
tea-spoon Teelöffel *(m)*
tea-time Teestunde *(f)*
tea-towel Geschirrtuch *(n)*
tea-trolley Teewagen *(m)*
tea-urn Teemaschine *(f)*, Warmhaltegerät *(n)* für das Teewasser *(n)*
tea with lemon Tee mit Zitrone
tea with milk Tee mit Milch
teaching method Lehrmethode *(f)*
teal Krickente *(f)*
team Arbeitsgruppe *(f)*, Team *(n)*
teamwork Gemeinschaftsarbeit *(f)*
technician Techniker *(m)*
tee Golf: künstlich erhöhte Abschlagstelle *(f)*, Ball *(m)* auf die Abschlagstelle *(f)* legen
tee off Golf: abschlagen, Spiel eröffnen *(n)*
TEE train, Trans-Europe-Express TEE-Zug *(m)*
teetotaller Abstinenzler *(m)*
telecommunication Telekommunikation *(f)*
telegram Telegramm *(n)*
telegram by telephone ein Telegramm *(n)* telefonisch aufgeben
telegram charges Telegrammkosten *(pl.)*
telegram form Telegrammformular *(n)*
telegraph office Telegrafenamt *(n)*
telegraphic telegrafisch
telegraphic address Telegrammadresse *(f)*
telegraphic order telegrafische Anweisung *(f)*
telephone Telefon *(n)*
telephone booth Fernsprechzelle *(f)*, Telefonzelle *(f)*
telephone box Telefonzelle *(f)*, Fernsprechzelle *(f)*
telephone directory Telefonbuch *(n)*, Telefonverzeichnis *(n)*
telephone exchange Telefonvermittlung *(f)*, Fernsprechamt *(n)*

telephone installation
Telefonanlage *(f)*
telephone on the train Zugtelefon *(n)*
telephone operator Telefonistin *(f)*
telephone receiver Telefonhörer *(m)*
telephoto lens Teleobjektiv *(n)*
teleprinter Fernschreiber *(m)*
teleprinter code Fernschreibercode *(m)*
teleregister elektronische Platzbelegung *(f)*
telescope Fernglas *(n)*
teletype Fernschreiber *(m)*
television (TV) Fernsehen (TV) *(n)*
television room Fernsehraum *(m)*
television set Fernsehgerät *(n)*, Fernsehapparat *(m)*
television tower Fernsehturm *(m)*
telex Fernschreibnetz *(n)*, Telex *(n)*
temperature Temperatur *(f)*, Fieber *(n)*
tempest Unwetter *(n)*
tempestuous stürmisch
template Schablone *(f)*
temporary vorläufig, vorübergehend, zeitweilig
temporary cash investments vorübergehend angelegte flüssige Mittel *(pl. n)*
temporary guest Logiergast *(m)*
temporary hotel guest Durchreisender *(m)*, Passant *(m)*
temporary residence visa Aufenthaltsvisum *(n)*
tenant Pächter *(m)*, Mieter *(m)*
tench Schleie *(f)*
tendency Tendenz *(f)*, Entwicklungsrichtung *(f)*
tender zart
tenderloin Lendenstück *(n)*, zartes
tenderloin of beef „Wellington" Rindsfilet im Blätterteig *(n)*
tenderloin steak Lendenschnitte *(f)*
tennis Tennis *(n)*
tennis ball Tennisball *(m)*
tennis club Tennisklub *(m)*
tennis court Tennisplatz *(m)*
tennis court fee Platzmiete *(f)*
tennis game Tennisspiel *(n)*
tennis racket Tennisschläger *(m)*

tennis tournament Tennisturnier *(n)*
tense (an-)gespannt, verkrampft
tent Zelt *(n)*
tent awning Zeltvordach *(n)*
tent camp Zeltlager *(n)*
tent-peg Zelthering *(m)*
tentative vorläufig
tentative agreement Vertragsentwurf *(m)*
tentative conclusion vorläufige Meinung *(f)*
tepid water lauwarmes Wasser *(n)*
term deposit Termingeld *(n)*, Termineinlage *(f)*
terminal Endstation *(f)*, Datenendstation *(f)*
terminal point Endhaltestelle *(f)*, Endstation *(f)*
terminate kündigen, beenden
termination Kündigung *(f)*, Beendigung *(f)*
terminus Endstation *(f)*
terms Vertragsbestimmungen *(pl. f)*, Vertragsbedingungen *(pl. f)*
terms of delivery Lieferbedingungen *(pl. f)*
terrace facing south Südterrasse *(f)*
terrace restaurant Terrassenrestaurant *(n)*
terrain treatment Terrainkur *(f)*
territorial waters Hoheitsgewässer *(pl. n)*
territory Gebiet *(n)*
test prüfen, untersuchen, Prüfung *(f)*, Untersuchung *(f)*
thached strohgedeckt
thalassotherapy Meerwasserkur *(f)*
Thanksgiving Day Erntedankfest *(n)*
thaw (auf)tauen, schmelzen, (Auf)Tauen *(n)*, Tauwetter *(n)*
the days dish Tagesplatte *(f)*
the days soup Tagessuppe *(f)*
theatre festival Bühnenfestspiele *(pl. n)*
theatre ticket Theaterkarte *(f)*
theatrical performance Theatervorstellung *(f)*
theatrical season Theatersaison *(f)*
theft Diebstahl *(m)*
theft insurance Diebstahlversicherung *(f)*

therapeutical therapeutsich
therapeutical facilities
 Kureinrichtungen *(pl.f)*
thermal baths Thermalbad *(n)*
thermal indoor swimming-pool
 Thermalhallenbad *(n)*
thermal water Thermalwasser *(n)*
thermal-water pool Thermalbecken *(n)*
Thermos flask Thermosflasche *(f)*
thermotherapy Thermotherapie *(f)*
thick ox-tail soup gebundene Ochsenschwanzsuppe *(f)*
thick soup legierte Suppe *(f)*
thieve stehlen
thin pancakes filled with jam Palatschinken *(m)*
third-party insurance Haftpflichtversicherung *(f)*
third-party liability Haftpflicht *(f)*
thirst Durst *(m)*
thirsty durstig
thoroughfare Durchgangsstraße *(f)*
three-bed room Dreibettzimmer *(n)*
three-berth compartment Dreibettabteil *(n)*
three-berth room Dreibettkabine *(f)*
three-mile zone Dreimeilenzone *(f)*
three-minute egg Dreiminutenei *(n)*
threshold Schwelle *(f)*
thrifty sparsam
throng of people Andrang *(m)*
through-carriage Kurswagen *(m)*
through connection Direktverbindung *(f)*
through fare Gesamtstreckenfahrpreis *(m)*
through flight Direktflug *(m)*
through passenger Durchgangsreisender *(m)*
through traffic Durchgangsverkehr *(m)*
through train durchgehender Zug *(m)*
throw overboard über Bord werfen
thunder donnern
thunderstorm Gewitter *(n)*
thyme Thymian *(m)*
ticket Fahrkarte *(f)*, Fahrschein *(m)*, Verwarnung *(f)*, Billett *(n)*
ticket barrier Bahnsteigsperre *(f)*

ticket clerk Schalterbeamter *(m)*
ticket-collector Bahnsteigschaffner *(m)*
ticket for reserved seat Platzkarte *(f)*
ticket inspection Fahrscheinkontrolle *(f)*
ticket inspector Kontrolleur *(m)*
ticket machine Fahrkartenautomat *(m)*
ticket of admission Eintrittskarte *(f)*
ticket office Fahrkartenschalter *(m)*, Bahnschalter *(m)*, Stadtbüro *(n)*
ticket office window Fahrkartenschalter *(m)*
tides Gezeiten *(pl.)*
tidy sauber, ordentlich
tie-in sale Kopplungsverkauf *(m)*
tilsit cheese Tilsiter Käse *(m)*
time Zeit *(f)*
time allowance Zeitvorgabe *(f)*
time and motion study Zeit- und Bewegungsstudie *(f)*
time exposure Zeitaufnahme *(f)*
time limit Frist *(f)*
time of arrival Ankunftszeit *(f)*
time of day Tageszeit *(f)*
time of delivery Lieferzeit *(f)*
time of departure Abfahrtszeit *(f)*, Abflugzeit *(f)*
time of sailing Abfahrtszeit *(f)*
time of stay Aufenthaltsdauer *(f)*
time signal Zeitansage *(f)*, Zeitzeichen *(n)*
timekeeper Personalpförtner *(m)*
timeliness Zeitnähe *(f)* (Rechnungslegung)
timetable Fahrplan *(m)*, Kursbuch *(n)*, Flugplan *(m)*
timing Zeitnahme *(f)*, Terminierung *(f)*
tin Konservenbüchse *(f)*
tin opener Büchsenöffner *(m)*
tinned beer Dosenbier *(n)*
tinned food Konserve *(f)*
tinned meat Büchsenfleisch *(n)*
tiny flour dumplings Spätzle *(pl.)*
tip Trinkgeld *(n)*, Trinkgeld *(n)* geben
tip-up seat Klappsitz *(m)*, Notsitz *(m)*
tipple zechen
tips included Bedienungsgeld *(n)* eingeschlossen (im Preis)

tissue paper Seidenpapier *(n)*
to zu (Richtung)
to your health Prosit!
toad-in-the-hole Schweinswürstchen *(n)* in gebackenem Eierteig *(m)*
toast Röstbrotschnitte *(f)*, Toast *(m)*
toast (to propose a toast) Trinkspruch *(m)*
toasted geröstet
toasted cheese Käseschnitte *(f)*
toaster Toaströster *(m)*, Toaster *(m)*
toastmaster Toastmeister *(m)*
tobacco Tabak *(m)*
tobacco pipe Tabakspfeife *(f)*
tobacco tax Tabaksteuer *(f)*
tobacconist Zigarettenverkäufer *(m)*
tobacconist's shop Tabakladen *(m)*
toboggan Schlitten *(m)*, rodeln
toboggan run Rodelbahn *(f)*
toboggan slide Rodelbahn *(f)*, Rodelhang *(m)*
toboggan tow Rodellift *(m)*, Schlittenlift *(m)*
tobogganing Rodeln *(n)*, Rodelsport *(m)*
toby jug Bierkrug (in Form eines Mannes) *(m)*
today heute
today's bill of fare Tageskarte *(f)*
today's menu Tageskarte *(f)*
today's program Tagesprogramm *(n)*
today's special dish Tagesspezialität *(f)*
today's speciality Tagesspezialität *(f)*
toddy Grog *(m)*
toiled soap Toilettenseife *(f)*
toilet Toilette *(f)*
toilet-paper Toilettenpapier *(n)*
toll Straßenzoll *(m)*, Maut *(f)*, Straßenbenutzungsgebühr *(f)*, Autobahngebühr *(f)*
toll road gebührenpflichtige Straße *(f)*
tomato Tomate *(f)*
tomato juice Tomatensaft *(m)*
tomato ketchup Tomatenketchup *(m)*
tomato pulp Tomatenmark *(n)*
tomato salad Tomatensalat *(m)*
tomato sauce Tomatensoße *(f)*
tomato soup Tomatensuppe *(f)*
tomorrow morgen
tongue Zunge *(f)*

tonic(water) Tonic(wasser) *(n)*
tonnage Schiffstonnage *(f)*
too zu, allzu
tool Handwerkszeug *(n)*, Gerät *(n)*
tools and dies Hand- und Maschinenwerkzeuge *(pl.n)*
tooth brush Zahnbürste *(f)*
toothpaste Zahnpaste *(f)*
toothpick Zahnstocher *(m)*
top cut roast Rindsrostbraten *(m)*
top executive leitender Angesteller *(m)*
top management Betriebsführung *(f)*, Geschäftsleitung *(f)*
top salary Spitzengehalt *(n)*
top secret streng geheim
top speed Höchstgeschwindigkeit *(f)*
top terminal Bergstation *(f)*
top up the radiator Kühlwasser *(n)* nachfüllen
tope trinken, saufen
topic Gesprächsstoff *(m)*
tornado Wirbelsturm *(m)*
tossed salad gemischter Salat *(m)*
tot Gläschen *(n)*, Schlückchen *(n)*
total cash flüssige Mittel *(pl.n)* insgesamt
total current assets Umlaufvermögen *(n)* insgesamt
total liabilities Passiva *(pl.)* insgesamt
total other assets sonstiges Vermögen *(n)* insgesamt
total receivables Forderungen *(pl.f)* insgesamt
touch anfassen, berühren
tough zäh
tour Tour *(f)*, Reise *(f)*, bereisen
tour conductor Reiseleiter *(m)*
tour management Reiseleitung *(f)*
tour manager Reiseleiter *(m)*, Reiseleiterin *(f)*
tour operator Reiseveranstalter *(m)*
tour program Ausflugsprogramm *(n)*
tour region Ausflugsgebiet *(n)*
tour round Rundgang *(m)*
tour ticket Ausflugskarte *(f)*
touring area Reisegebiet *(n)*
touring exhibition Wanderschau *(f)*
touring facilities Ausflugmöglichkeiten *(pl.f)*

touring itinerary Reisestrecke *(f)*,
  Reiseroute *(f)*, Reiseverlauf *(m)*
tourism Fremdenverkehr *(m)*,
  Tourismus *(m)*, Touristik *(f)*,
  Touristenverkehr *(m)*,
  Fremdenverkehrswesen *(n)*
tourist Tourist *(m)*, Reisender *(m)*,
  Ausflügler *(m)*
tourist abroad Auslandsreisender *(m)*
tourist advertising
  Fremdenverkehrswerbung *(f)*
tourist agency Reiseagentur *(f)*,
  Reisebüro *(n)*
tourist agent Reiseagent *(m)*,
  Reisemittler *(m)*
tourist area Reisegebiet *(n)*
tourist association
  Fremdenverkehrsverband *(m)*
tourist atlas Reiseatlas *(m)*
tourist-board Fremdenverkehrsamt
  (n)
tourist bus Reisebus *(m)*
tourist campaign
  Fremdenverkehrskampagne *(f)*
tourist card Touristenkarte *(f)*,
  Touristenausweis *(m)*
tourist centre Fremdenverkehrsort
  (m)
tourist class Touristenklasse *(f)*
tourist country
  Fremdenverkehrsland *(m)*
tourist court Motel *(n)*
tourist economy
  Fremdenverkehrswirtschaft *(f)*
tourist fare Touristenflugpreis *(m)*
tourist hotel Touristenhotel *(n)*
tourist industry
  Fremdenverkehrsindustrie *(f)*
tourist information office
  Verkehrsamt *(n)*, Verkehrsbüro *(n)*
tourist journal
  Fremdenverkehrszeitschrift *(f)*
tourist market Reisemarkt *(m)*
tourist office Fremdenverkehrsamt
  (n), Fremdenverkehrsbüro *(n)*
tourist party Reisegesellschaft *(f)*
tourist policy
  Fremdenverkehrspolitik *(f)*
tourist publicity
  Fremdenverkehrswerbung *(f)*
tourist region

Fremdenverkehrsgebiet *(n)*,
  Reisegebiet *(n)*, Touristengebiet *(n)*
tourist resort Fremdenverkehrsort *(m)*
tourist season
  Fremdenverkehrssaison *(f)*,
  Reisezeit *(f)*
tourist town Fremdenverkehrsstadt
  (f)
tourist trade Fremdenverkehr *(m)*
tourist trade establishment
  Fremdenverkehrsbetrieb *(m)*
tourist trade statistics
  Fremdenverkehrstatistik *(f)*
tourist traffic Fremdenverkehr *(m)*,
  Touristenverkehr *(m)*, Reiseverkehr
  (m), Ausflugsverkehr *(m)*
tourist traffic institution
  Fremdenverkehrsträger *(m)*
tourist visa Touristenvisum *(n)*
tourist weather insurance
  Reisewetterversicherung *(f)*
touristed überlaufen
touristic touristisch
touristic map Tourenkarte *(f)*
touristic poster Reiseplakat *(n)*
tourist's medicine-case
  Reiseapotheke *(f)*
tow abschleppen
tow-rope Abschleppseil *(n)*
towel Handtuch *(n)*
towel rack Handtuchhalter *(m)*
tower Turm *(m)*
tower room Turmzimmer *(n)*
towing Abschleppen *(n)*
town Stadt *(f)*, Ort *(m)*
town bus Linienbus *(m)*
town centre Innenstadt *(f)*,
  Stadtzentrum *(n)*
town hall Rathaus *(n)*
town office Stadtbüro *(n)*
town plan Stadtplan *(m)*
town terminal Autoabfahrtsstelle *(f)*,
  Flugplatzbahnhof *(m)*
town-wall Stadtmauer *(f)*
toxic(al) giftig, toxisch
toy Spielzeug *(n)*
trace zurückverfolgen,
  ausfindigmachen
track Gleis *(n)*
trade Handel *(m)*, Gewerbe *(n)*,
  handeln

trade custom Handelsbrauch *(m)*
trade discount Rabatt *(m)*
trade fair Fachmesse *(f)*
trademark Markenrecht *(n)*; Warenzeichen *(n)*
trading vessel Handelsschiff *(n)*
traffic Geschäftsverkehr *(m)*, Verkehr *(m)*, Handel *(m)*
traffic accident Verkehrsunfall *(m)*
traffic artery Verkehrsader *(f)*
traffic block Verkehrsstockung *(f)*
traffic circle Kreisverkehr *(m)*
traffic control Verkehrsüberwachung *(f)*
traffic density Verkehrsdichte *(f)*
traffic flow Verkehrsfluß *(m)*
traffic hold-up Verkehrsstockung *(f)*
traffic jam Verkehrsstockung *(f)*, Stau *(m)*
traffic light Verkehrsampel *(f)*
traffic police Verkehrspolizei *(f)*
traffic regulation Verkehrsregelung *(f)*, Verkehrsordnung *(f)*
traffic restriction Verkehrseinschränkung *(f)*
traffic safety Verkehrssicherheit *(f)*
traffic warden Politesse *(f)*
trail Pfad *(m)*, Spur *(f)*, Rennstrecke *(f)*, Abfahrt (Ski) *(f)*
trailer Autoanhänger *(m)*, Wohnwagen *(m)*
trailerite Wohnwagenfahrer *(m)*
trailtourist Caravaner *(m)*
train ausbilden, anlernen, trainieren; Zug *(m)*
train conductor Zugbegleiter *(m)*
train ferry Eisenbahnfähre *(f)*
train formation Zusammensetzung *(f)* der Züge *(pl. m)*
train indicator Aushangfahrplan *(m)*
train journey Bahnfahrt *(f)*, Bahnreise *(f)*
train number Zugnummer *(f)*
train set Zugteil *(m)*
train timings Zugzeiten *(pl. f)*
trainee Auszubildender *(m)*, Praktikant *(m)*
trainer Ausbilder *(m)*
training (schedule 9) Aus- und Weiterbildung *(f)* (Service Center 9)

training film Lehrfilm *(m)*
training ground Übungsgelände *(n)*
training hotel Schulungshotel *(n)*
training manager Ausbilder *(m)*, Ausbildungsleiter *(m)*
training method Lehrmethode *(f)*, Ausbildungsmethode *(f)*
training on the job Ausbildung *(f)* am Arbeitsplatz *(m)*
training suit Trainingsanzug *(m)*
tram Straßenbahn *(f)*
tram line Straßenbahnlinie *(f)*
tram stop Straßenbahnhaltestelle *(f)*
tram ticket Straßenbahnkarte *(f)*
tramcar Straßenbahnwagen *(m)*
tramp trampen, Landstreicher *(m)*, Tramper *(m)*, Trampschiff *(n)*
tramping Wandern *(n)*
tramway Straßenbahn *(f)*
transaction Verhandlung *(f)*, Geschäft *(n)*, Geschäftsvorfall *(m)*
transatlantic flight Ozeanflug *(m)*
transatlantic liner Ozeandampfer *(m)*
transfer übertragen, Übertrag *(m)*, Umbuchung *(f)*, Versetzung *(f)*, Transfer *(m)*, Umsteigekarte *(f)*
transfer free of charge kostenlose Zubringung *(f)*
transfer from airport to town terminal Transfer *(m)* vom Flughafen *(m)* zum Terminal *(m)*
transfer ticket Umsteigekarte *(f)*
transfer to hotel Transfer *(m)* zum Hotel *(n)*
transferable übertragbar
transient (guest) Durchreisender *(m)*, Passant *(m)*, Übernachtungsgast *(m)*
transient hotel Hotel *(n)* für Durchreisende *(pl. m)*, Passantenhotel *(n)*, Übernachtungshotel *(n)*
transient rate Übernachtungspreis *(m)* für Durchreisende *(pl. m)*
transire Zolldurchlaßschein *(m)*
transit Transit *(m)*
transit country Durchgangsland *(n)*
transit good Transitgut *(n)*
transit journey Transitreise *(f)*
transit passenger Transitreisender *(m)*

transit traffic Transitverkehr *(m),* Durchgangsverkehr *(m)*
transit visa Transitvisum *(n),* Durchreisevisum *(n)*
transition period Übergangszeit *(f)*
translate umrechnen, übersetzen
translation Übersetzung *(f),* Umrechnung *(f)*
transmission Getriebe *(n)* (Fahrzeug), Sendung *(f),* Radioübertragung *(f)*
transoceanic voyage Ozeanreise *(f),* Überseefahrt *(f)*
transport Transport *(m),* Beförderung *(f),* transportieren
transport charge Beförderungspreis *(m)*
transport charges Beförderungskosten *(pl.)*
transport company Transportunternehmen *(n)*
transport contractor Transportunternehmer *(m)*
transport insurance Transportversicherung *(f)*
transport planning Verkehrsplanung *(f)*
transport policy Verkehrsplanung *(f)*
transportable transportierbar
transportation Transport *(m),* Transportgewerbe *(n)*
transportation advertising Verkehrsmittelwerbung *(f)*
transportation cost Transportkosten *(pl.),* Versandkosten *(pl.)*
transportation industry Verkehrsgewerbe *(n)*
transshipment point Umschlagplatz *(m)*
trash Kitsch *(m),* Schund *(m)*
travel Reise *(f),* Reisen *(n),* Reiseverkehr *(m),* (be-)reisen
travel accident insurance Reiseunfallversicherung *(f)*
travel agency Reisebüro *(n)*
travel booklet Reiseprospekt *(m),* Fremdenverkehrsprospekt *(m)*
travel boom Reisewelle *(f)*
travel by train mit dem Zug *(m)* reisen
travel companion Reisebegleiter *(m)*

travel documents Reisepapiere *(pl.n)*
travel expenses Reisespesen *(pl.)*
travel information Reiseauskunft *(f)*
travel insurance Reiseversicherung *(f)*
travel market Reisemarkt *(m)*
travel organizer Reiseveranstalter *(m)*
travel poster Ferienplakat *(n),* Reiseplakat *(n)*
travel preparations Reisevorbereitungen *(pl.f)*
travel program Reiseprogramm *(n)*
travel research Fremdenverkehrsforschung *(f)*
travel service Reisebetreuung *(f)*
travel souvenir Reiseandenken *(n)*
travel statistics Fremdenverkehrstatistik *(f)*
travel supervisor Reiseleiter *(m)*
travel supplement Reisebeilage *(f)*
travel time Reisezeit *(f),* Fahrzeit *(f),* Wegzeit *(f)*
travel voucher Reisegutschein *(m)*
traveller Handelsvertreter *(m),* Reisender *(m)*
Travellers' Air Office Bahnhofsmission *(f)*
travellers' cheque Reisescheck *(m)*
travellers' letter of credit Reisekreditbrief *(m)*
travelling day Reisetag *(m)*
travelling provisions Reiseproviant *(m)*
travelling-bag Reisetasche *(f)*
tray Tablett *(n),* Ablagekorb *(m)*
treacle Sirup *(m)*
treasury stock eigene Aktien *(pl.f)* einer Unternehmung *(f)*
treatment Kur *(f)* (Behandlung), Kurmittel *(n)*
treatment at a spa Brunnenkur *(f)*
treatment with aerosols Aerosoltherapie *(f)*
trellis cake Linzertorte *(f)*
trend Tendenz *(f),* Trend *(m)*
trial balance Probebilanz *(f)*
trial run Probelauf *(m)*
trifle Mürbekuchen *(m)* (getaucht in Sirup, Sherry etc.)

trigger Auslöser *(m)*
trimmings Beilage *(f)*
trip Reise *(f)*, Fahrt *(f)*
tripe Kuttel *(f)*
tripe à la mode de Caen Kutteln *(pl.f)* gekocht in Weißwein *(pl.n)*
tripe and onions Rindsmagen *(m)* in Milch *(f)* und Wasser *(n)* gekocht mit Zwiebeln *(pl.f)*
tripes soup Kuttelnsuppe *(f)*
triple room Dreibettzimmer *(n)*
triplicate dreifach
tripod Stativ *(n)*
tripper Ausflügler *(m)*, Ausflüglerin *(f)*
tropical tropisch
tropics Tropen *(pl.)*
trotting race Trabrennen *(n)*
trouble maker Streithahn *(m)*, Querulant *(m)*
trout Forelle *(f)*
trout fishing Forellenfischen *(n)*
trout in champagne Forelle in Champagner *(f)*
truck Lastwagen *(m)*, Zugwagen *(m)*
truck trailer Lastwagenanhänger *(m)*
truffle Trüffel *(f)*
truffled getrüffelt
trunk Kabinenkoffer *(m)*, Kofferraum *(m)*
trunk call Ferngespräch *(n)*
trunk exchange Fernsprechamt *(n)*, Telefonvermittlung *(f)*
trunk road Fernverkehrsstraße *(f)*
trunks Badehose *(f)*
trustworthiness Vertrauenswürdigkeit *(f)*
trustworthy vertrauenswürdig
try versuchen, probieren
tub Wanne *(f)*
tub-bath Wannenbad *(n)*
tube U-Bahn *(f)*, Röhre *(f)*
tube post Rohrpost *(f)*
tug boat Schlepper *(m)*
tumbler Wasserglas *(n)*
tuna fish Thunfisch *(m)*
tunny Thunfisch *(m)*
turbo-ship (TS) Turbinenschiff *(n)*
turbo-steamship (TSS) Turbinendampfschiff *(n)*
turbot Steinbutt *(m)*

tureen Suppenschüssel *(f)*
turkey Truthahn *(m)*, Puter *(m)*
Turkish bath türkisches Bad *(n)*
Turkish coffee Kaffee türkisch *(m)*
Turkish towel Frottiertuch *(n)*
turn back kehrtmachen
turn off abbiegen, abschalten
turn on einschalten
turn round umkehren, wenden
turn upside down sich überschlagen
turning Straßenbiegung *(f)*
turnip weiße Rübe *(f)*
turnover Umsatz *(m)*, Umschlag *(m)*
turnpike Schlagbaum *(m)*
turtle Schildkröte *(f)*
turtle soup, real echte Schildkrötensuppe *(f)*
tuxedos Smoking *(m)*
twilight Zwielicht *(n)*
twin Zimmer *(n)* mit zwei einzelnen Betten *(pl.n)*
twin double Doppelzimmer *(n)* mit zwei großen Betten *(pl.n)*
two-berth compartment Zweibettabteil *(n)*
two-berth room Zweibettkabine *(f)*
two-lane road zweibahnige Straße *(f)*, zweispurige Straße *(f)*
two-way traffic Gegenverkehr *(m)*
type of customers Kundenkreis *(m)*, Kundengruppe *(f)*
typewriter Schreibmaschine *(f)*
typical typisch
tyre Reifen *(m)*
tyre chains Schneeketten *(pl.f)*
tyre pressure Reifendruck *(m)*

U

ugly häßlich
ultimative letztendlich
ultra-violet lamp Höhensonne *(f)*
ultrasinics Ultraschall *(m)*
ultrasound Ultraschall *(m)*
ultraviolet rays ultraviolette Strahlen *(pl.m)*
umber Umberfisch *(m)*
umbrella Schirm *(m)*
umbrella tent Hüttenzelt *(n)*
unappropriated retained earnings

offene Rücklagen *(pl.f)*; freie Rücklagen *(pl.f)* einschließlich Gewinn- oder Verlustvortrag *(m)*; Bilanzgewinn *(m)*
unappropriated surplus freie Rücklage *(f)* einschließlich Gewinn- oder Verlustvortrag *(m)*; Bilanzgewinn *(m)*
unattainable unerschwinglich
unauthorized unbefugt, unerlaubt, unberechtigt
unbilled receivables Forderungen *(pl.f)* aus noch nicht abgerechneten Leistungen *(pl.f)*
unbreakable unzerbrechlich
unclean unsauber
uncomfortable unbequem, ungemütlich
unconventional zwanglos
undated undatiert
under age minderjährig
under construction im Bau *(m)* befindlich
under penalty of interest bei entsprechendem Zinsverlust *(m)*
undercut unterschreiten, unterbieten
underdone blutig gebraten, fast roh
underestimate unterschätzen, unterbewerten
underground U-Bahn *(f)*
underground bar Kellerbar *(f)*
underground garage Tiefgarage *(f)*
underground restaurant Kellerlokal *(n)*
underlying zugrundeliegend, grundsätzlich
underpants Unterhose *(f)*
underpass Unterführung *(f)*
understand verstehen
understandability Verständlichkeit *(f)* (der Rechnungslegungsinformation)
understanding Verständnis *(n)*, Einsicht *(f)*
undertake unternehmen
underwater equipment Unterwasserausrüstung *(f)*
underwater exercises Unterwassergymnastik *(f)*
underwater massage Unterwassermassage *(f)*

underwear Unterwäsche *(f)*
underwriter Emissionsbank *(f)*, Konsortialbank *(f)*, Mitglied *(n)* eines Emissionskonsortiums *(n)*
underwriting vollständige Übernahme *(f)* einer Emission *(f)*
undisturbed ungestört
undisturbed possession ungestörter Besitz *(m)*
undivided (attention) ungeteilt (Aufmerksamkeit)
undress sich ausziehen
uneasiness Unbehagen *(n)*
unemployed arbeitslos
unexpired insurance vorausbezahlte Versicherungsbeiträge *(pl.m)*
unfamiliar unbekannt, fremd
unfriendly unfreundlich
uniform Uniform *(f)*
union Gewerkschaft *(f)*
union agreement Tarifvertrag *(m)*
unit Einheit *(f)*
unit price Preis *(m)* pro Einheit *(f)*
unknown unbekannt
unload ausladen
unloading station Bergstation *(f)*
unlock aufschließen
unmarried ledig, unverheiratet
unoccupied leerstehend, unbewohnt
unpack auspacken
unpaid unbezahlt
unripe unreif
unskilled manpower ungelernte Arbeitskräfte *(pl.f)*
unused credit nicht in Anspruch *(m)* genommener Kredit *(m)*
up-to-date auf dem laufenden, bis heute, aktuell, zeitgemäß
up-value aufwerten
upgrading Upgrading *(n)* (Verkaufsmethode)
uphill bergauf
upon arrival nach Ankunft *(f)*
upper berth Oberbett *(n)*
upper circle zweiter Rang *(m)* (Theater)
upper deck Oberdeck *(n)*
upper-bracket hotel Hotel *(n)* der gehobenen Mittelklasse *(f)*
upselling Upselling *(n)* (Verkaufsmethode)

upstream sales unrealisierte Gewinne *(pl.m)*, die aus einem Verkauf *(m)* der Tochter- an die Muttergesellschaft *(f)* resultieren
uptrend steigende Tendenz *(f)*
upward and downward journey Berg- und Talfahrt *(f)*
upward journey Auffahrt *(f)*, Bergfahrt *(f)*
urban städtisch
urban area Stadtgebiet *(n)*
urban bus service städtischer Autobusbetrieb *(m)*
urban express road Stadtschnellstraße *(f)*
urban freeway Stadtautobahn *(f)*
urban traffic Stadtverkehr *(m)*
urgent dringend
usable brauchbar, befahrbar
usage Brauch *(m)*
usage of trade Handelsbrauch *(m)*
use Gebrauch *(m)*
used gebraucht
useful zweckmäßig, nützlich
useful life of the asset betriebsgewöhnliche Nutzungsdauer *(f)*
user Verbraucher *(m)*, Benützer *(m)*
user group Interessengruppe *(f)* der Jahresabschlußverwender *(pl.m)*
usher Türsteher *(m)*, Platzanweiser *(m)*
usherette Platzanweiserin *(f)*
usual üblich
utilities Leistungen *(pl.f)* öffentlicher Versorgungsbetriebe *(pl.m)*
utility taxes (schedule 14) Gebühren *(pl.f)* für öffentliche Versorgungsbetriebe *(pl.m)* (Service Center 14)
utilization of capacity Beschäftigungsgrad *(m)*, Kapazitätsausnutzung *(f)*
utilize auslasten
utilty program Dienstprogramm *(n)*

V

vacancy offene Stelle *(f)*
vacant frei, unbesetzt
vacate räumen, freimachen
vacation Urlaub *(m)*
vacation apartment Ferienwohnung *(f)*, Ferienunterkunft *(f)*
vacation pay Urlaubsgeld *(n)*
vacation program Ferienprogramm *(n)*
vacation schedule Urlaubseinteilung *(f)*, Ferienordnung *(f)*
vacationer Urlauber *(m)*
vaccinate impfen
vaccination Impfung *(f)*
vacuum cleaner Staubsauger *(m)*
valet Hausdiener *(m)*, Etagendiener *(m)*, Bügel- und Reinigungsdienst *(m)*
valet (schedule 6) Bügel- und Reinigungsdienst *(m)* und Verkauf *(m)* von Herrenbekleidung *(f)* (Umsatzbereich 6)
valid wirksam, gültig
validation Gültigkeitserklärung *(f)*
validity Gültigkeit *(f)*, Geltungsdauer *(f)*
valley Tal *(n)*
valuables Wertsachen *(pl.f)*
valuation Bewertung *(f)*
valuation of current assets Bewertung *(f)* des Umlaufvermögens *(n)*
valuation of inventory Bewertung *(f)* des Vorratsvermögens *(n)*
value bewerten, Wert *(m)*
value added tax (V.A.T.) Mehrwertsteuer *(f)*
valve Ventil *(n)*
vanilla Vanille *(f)*
vanilla ice Vanilleeis *(n)*
vanilla ice-cream Vanilleeis *(n)*
vapour bath Dampfbad *(n)*, Schwitzbad *(n)*
variable veränderlich, variabel
variance Abweichung *(f)*, Veränderung *(f)*
varied diet abwechslungsreiche Kost *(f)*
variety Vielfalt *(f)*, Verschiedenheit *(f)*
variolization Pockenschutzimpfung *(f)*
various verschiedenartig
vary abwechseln, verändern

varying wechselnd, unterschiedlich
vase Vase *(f)*
veal Kalbfleisch *(n)*, Kalb *(n)*
veal bird Kalbfleischröllchen *(n)*
veal chop Kalbskotelett *(n)*
veal collop Kalbsschnitzel *(n)*
veal collop with fried egg
 Holsteiner Schnitzel *(n)*
veal cutlet Kalbskotelett *(n)*
veal olive Kalbsröllchen *(n)*
veal roll Kalbsroulade *(f)*
veal scallop Kalbsschnitzel *(n)*
veal steak Kalbssteak *(n)*
veal steak Hungarian style
 Paprikaschnitzel *(n)*
veal steak in sour cream
 Rahmschnitzel *(n)*
veal stew Kalbsragout *(n)*
veal stew with scrambled eggs
 Hoppel-Poppel *(n)*
veal with tuna kaltes Kalbfleisch *(n)* in Thunfischsauce *(f)*
vegetable Gemüse *(n)*
vegetable broth Gemüsesuppe *(f)*
vegetable dish Gemüsegericht *(n)*
vegetable marrow Speisekürbis *(m)*
vegetable plate Gemüseplatte *(f)*
vegetable salad Gemüsesalat *(m)*
vegetarian Vegetarier *(m)*, vegetarisch
vegetarian diet vegetarische Kost *(f)*
vegetarian dishes vegetarische Kost *(f)*
vegetarian food vegetarische Kost *(f)*
vegetarian restaurant
 Vegetarierrestaurant *(n)*
vehicle Fahrzeug *(n)*
vehicle Fahrzeug *(n)*, Verkehrsmittel *(n)*
vehicle traffic Fahrverkehr *(m)*
velouté sauce milde Sauce *(f)* (Hühner od. Kalbfleischbrühe mit Zusätzen)
vending machine (schedule 6)
 Verkaufsautomat *(m)* (Umsatzbereich 6)
venison Reh *(n)*, Rehbock *(m)*, Hirsch *(m)*
ventilation Lüftung *(f)*
ventilator Ventilator *(m)*
veranda deck Verandadeck *(n)*
verbal mündlich, wörtlich

verbalize formulieren, etwas geschickt in Worten *(pl. n)* ausdrücken
verifiability Nachprüfbarkeit *(f)* (Rechnungslegung)
verification Nachprüfung *(f)*, Überprüfung *(f)*
verify überprüfen, bestätigen
vermicelli Fadennudeln *(pl. f)*
vermin Ungeziefer *(n)*
verm(o)uth Wermut(wein) *(m)*
vertical drop Höhenunterschied *(m)*
vessel Schiff *(n)*
vestibule Vorhalle *(f)*
via über
vice-president Vizepräsident *(m)*
vicinity Nähe *(f)*
Vienna Wien
Vienna plum pudding Gugelhupf *(m)*
Vienna steak with fried onions
 Wiener Rostbraten *(m)*
Viennese Schnitzel Wiener Schnitzel *(n)*
view Aussicht *(f)*, Blick *(m)*, erblicken
view finder (Bild-)Sucher *(m)*
view of Blick *(m)* auf
village Dorf *(n)*, Ort *(m)*
village inn Dorfgasthaus *(n)*
village pub Dorfschenke *(f)*
vinaigrette (sauce)
 Vinaigrette-Sauce *(f)*
vine Rebstock *(m)*, Weinrebe *(f)*
vinegar Essig *(m)*
vineyard Weinberg *(m)*, Weingut *(n)*
vintage Weinlese *(f)*
vintage festival Weinlesefest *(n)*
vintage wine Spitzenwein *(m)*, naturreiner Wein *(m)*
vintagers' festival Winzerfest *(n)*
violate verletzen, brechen, übertreten
VIP (very important person)
 VIP-Gast *(m)* (besonders wichtiger Gast)
virgin forest Urwald *(m)*
visa Visum *(n)*, Sichtvermerk *(m)*
visa charge Visagebühr *(f)*
visibility Sicht *(f)*
visible sichtbar, mit dem Auge wahrnehmbar, (deutlich) erkennbar
visit Besuch *(m)*, besuchen

visit of relatives Verwandtenbesuch *(m)*
visiting hours Besuchszeiten *(pl.f)*
visitor Besucher *(m)*
visitors' book Gästebuch *(n)*, Fremdenbuch *(n)*
visitors' card Besucherkarte *(f)*
visitors' tax Kurtaxe *(f)*
visitors' visa Besuchervisum *(n)*
visual aid optisches Hilfsmittel *(n)*
visual merchandising Verkaufsförderung *(f)* durch Ausstellung *(f)* der Ware *(f)*
vocational training Berufsausbildung *(f)*
vodka Wodka *(m)*
void ungültig
vol-au-vent Blätterteigpastete *(f)*
volatile unbeständig, sprunghaft
voltage Spannung *(f)*
volume Volumen *(n)*, Beschäftigung *(f)*, Beschäftigungsgrad *(m)*, Band *(m)* (Buch)
volume bonus Abschlußvergütung *(f)*
volume of tourist traffic Reiseintensität *(f)*
voluntary freiwillig
vomit sich übergeben
voting right Stimmrecht *(n)*
voucher Beleg *(m)*, Gutschein *(m)*
voyage Seereise *(f)*, Schiffsreise *(f)*, Fahrt *(f)*, Reise *(f)*
voyage distance Fahrkilometer *(pl.m)*
voyage home Heimreise *(f)*
voyager Seereisender *(m)*, Reisender *(m)*

W

waffle Waffel *(f)*
wage Lohn *(m)*
wage incentive Lohnanreiz *(m)*
wage increase Lohnerhöhung *(f)*
wages according to agreement Tariflohn *(m)*
waggon Eisenbahnwagen *(m)*
waistcoat Weste *(f)*
wait warten
wait on bedienen

waiter Kellner *(m)*
waiter apprentice Kellnerlehrling *(m)*, Jungkellner *(m)*
waiting limited to Parkdauer *(f)* höchstens
waiting line Warteschlange *(f)*
waiting list Warteliste *(f)*
waiting period Wartezeit *(f)*
waiting prohibited Parken *(n)* verboten
waiting room Wartesaal *(m)*, Wartezimmer *(n)*
waitress Kellnerin *(f)*, Serviererin *(f)*, Bedienung *(f)*
waits Wartezeiten *(pl.f)*
wake up wecken, aufwachen
wake-up call Weckruf *(m)*
waking service Weckdienst *(m)*
walk gehen, spazierengehen, wandern, Spaziergang *(m)*, Spazierweg *(m)*
walk in the woods Waldspaziergang *(m)*
walk round Rundgang *(m)*
walking Wandern *(n)*
walking shoes Straßenschuhe *(pl.f)*
walking tour Wanderung *(f)*, Wanderfahrt *(f)*
walkway Laufgang *(m)*
wall Mauer *(f)*
wall map Wandkarte *(f)*
wall plug Steckdose *(f)*
wall socket Steckdose *(f)*
wallet Brieftasche *(f)*
walnut Walnuß *(f)*
waltz Walzer *(m)*
want Bedürfnis *(n)*, Mangel *(m)*, wünschen, wollen
wardrobe Garderobe *(f)*, Kleiderschrank *(m)*
wardrobe trunk Schrankkoffer *(m)*
warehouse Lagerhaus *(n)*
warm wärmen, erwärmen, warm
warmth Wärme *(f)*
warning Verwarnung *(f)*, Warnung *(f)*
warning sign Warnschild *(n)*
warrant officer Deckoffizier *(m)*
warranted garantiert
warranties without legal obligations Gewährleistung *(f)* ohne rechtliche Verpflichtung *(f)*

wash up spülen, abspülen
wash-basin Waschbecken *(n)*
washable waschbar, waschecht
washing and lavatory facilites
    Wasch- und Toilettenanlagen *(pl.f)*
washing basin Waschbecken *(n)*
washing tub Waschwanne *(f)*
washing-machine Waschmaschine *(f)*
washing-powder Waschpulver *(n)*
washroom Toilette *(f)*
washstand Waschtisch *(m)*
waste verderben, verfallen, Verderb *(m)*, Abfall *(m)*
waste-disposer Müllschlucker *(m)*
waste-paper basket Papierkorb *(m)*
watchman Wächter *(m)*
water Wasser *(n)*
water-borne traffic
    Schiffahrtsverkehr *(m)*
water-bottle Feldflasche *(f)*
water closet, W.C. Toilette *(f)*
water cress Kresse *(f)*
water cure Wasserkur *(f)*
waterfall Wasserfall *(m)*
water gliding Wasserfliegen *(n)*
water heater Heißwasserboiler *(m)*
water hen Bläßhuhn *(n)*, Wasserhuhn *(n)*
water level Wasserstand *(m)*
water pipe Wasserleitung *(f)*
water pollution
    Wasserverunreinigung *(f)*
water polo Wasserball *(m)*
water-ski Wasserski *(m)*
water sports Wassersport *(m)*
water-tap Wasserhahn *(m)*
water temperature
    Wassertemperatur *(f)*
water wave Wasserwelle *(f)*
watering place Wasserstelle *(f)*, Badeort *(m)*
watering place visitor Badegast *(m)*
watermelon Wassermelone *(f)*
waterproof wasserdicht
wave Welle *(f)*, winken, schwenken
wave damage insurance
    Hochwasserversicherung *(f)*
wavy wellig
wax wachsen, Wachs *(n)*
wax bean Wachsbohne *(f)*
wax-egg Wachsei *(n)*

way in Autoeinfahrt *(f)*
way out Ausgang *(m)*, Ausfahrt *(f)*
way up Aufgang *(m)*
wayside inn Dorfgasthaus *(n)*
wear and tear Abnutzung *(f)* durch Gebrauch *(m)*
weary (traveler) müde, matt, erschöpft (Reisender)
weather bureau Wetteramt *(n)*
weather chart Wetterkarte *(f)*
weather forecast Wettervorhersage *(f)*, Wetterbericht *(m)*
weather station Wetterwarte *(f)*
weatherproof wetterfest
wedding Hochzeit *(f)*
wedge strap Keilriemen *(m)*
week-day Wochentag *(m)*
week-end Wochenende *(n)*
week-end-excursion
    Wochenendausflug *(m)*
week-end guest-house
    Wochenendpension *(f)*
week-end-outing Wochenendfahrt *(f)*
week-end return ticket
    Sonntagsrückfahrkarte *(f)*
week-end ticket
    Wochenendfahrkarte *(f)*
week-end tourism
    Wochenendtourismus *(m)*
week-end tourist traffic
    Wochenendreiseverkehr *(m)*
week-end trip Wochenendfahrt *(f)*
weekly wöchentlich
weekly bill Wochenrechnung *(f)*
weekly market Wochenmarkt *(m)*
weigh wiegen
weigh anchor Anker *(m)* lichten
weight Gewicht *(n)*
welcome willkommen
well gut, wohl
well-cooked mürbe
well-done durchgebraten
well-furnished gut eingerichtet
well-groomed gepflegt
well-seasoned würzig
well-wooded waldreich
Welsh rabbit (rarebit) geröstetes Brot *(n)* mit heißem Käse *(m)*, Welsh rabbit *(n)* (walisische Käseschnitte)

Wensleydale Wensleydale-Käse *(m)*
Western European time
 westeuropäische Zeit (WEZ) *(f)*
Westphalian rye-bread
 Pumpernickel *(m)*
wet naß
wet paint frisch gestrichen
wetness Nässe *(f)*
wharf Schiffsanlegestelle *(f)*, Kai *(m)*
wheaten bread Weizenbrot *(n)*
wheel-chair Rollstuhl *(m)*
wheelage Rollgeld *(n)*
when shipped nach Verladung *(f)*
whereabouts Aufenthaltsort *(m)*
whet anregen (Appetit,
 Appetitanreger)
whipped cream Schlagsahne *(f)*
whisk Schneebesen *(m)*
whisky, Whiskey Whisky *(m)*
whistle pfeifen
white bass Meerbarsch *(m)*
white bean weiße Bohne *(f)*
white bean-soup weiße
 Bohnensuppe *(f)*
white beer Weißbier *(n)*
white bread Weißbrot *(n)*
white bread dumpling
 Semmelknödel *(m)*
white cabbage Weißkohl *(m)*,
 Weißkraut *(n)*
white cheese dumpling
 Quarkknödel *(m)*
white coffee Milchkaffee *(m)*
white collar worker
 Büroangestellter *(m)*
white fish Felchen *(m)*
white grape weiße Traube *(f)*
white sausage Weißwurst *(f)*
white stew weißes Ragout *(n)*
white wine Weißwein *(m)*
white wine from the cask
 Weißwein *(m)* offen
whitebait Breitling *(m)*
whiting Kohlfisch *(m)*, Weißling *(m)*
Whitsun holidays Pfingstferien *(pl.)*
Whitsunday Pfingsten *(n)*
whole-day tour Tagesausflug *(m)*
wholesale discount
 Großhandelsrabatt *(m)*
wholesome gesund
wholesome climate Heilklima *(n)*

whole(meal) bread Vollkornbrot *(n)*
wick Docht *(m)*
wide-vision window
 Aussichtsfenster *(n)*
width Breite *(f)*
Wieners Wiener Würstchen *(pl. n)*
wife Ehefrau *(f)*
wild wild
wild boar Wildschwein *(n)*
wild boar haunch
 Wildschweinkeule *(f)*
wild boar saddle
 Wildschweinrücken *(m)*
wild duck Wildente *(f)*
wild goose Wildgans *(f)*
wild rabbit Wildkaninchen *(n)*
wild strawberry Walderdbeere *(f)*
wilderness Wildnis *(f)*
wildlife conservation Naturschutz
 (m)
Winchester hard disk
 Winchesterplattenlaufwerk *(n)*
wind force Windstärke *(f)*
wind up aufziehen
windcheater Windjacke *(f)*
winding road Serpentinenstraße *(f)*
window Fenster *(n)*, Schalter *(m)*
window awning Markise *(f)*
window cleaner Fensterputzer *(m)*
window dressing Bilanzfrisur *(f)*
window pane Fensterscheibe *(f)*
window screen Sonnenblende *(f)*
window seat Fensterplatz *(m)*
window shade Fensterladen *(m)*
window-shopping
 Schaufensterbummel *(m)*
window technique Fenstertechnik *(f)*
windscreen Windschutzscheibe *(f)*
windshield Windschutzscheibe *(f)*
windshield wiper Scheibenwischer
 (m)
windsurfing Windsurfen *(n)*
windy windig
wine Wein *(m)*
wine bottle Weinflasche *(f)*
wine bouquet Weinblume *(f)*
wine by the glass Schoppenwein
 (m), offener Wein *(m)*
wine cellar Weinkeller *(m)*,
 Weinlokal *(n)*
wine cooler Weinkühler *(m)*

wine cup Bowle *(f)*
wine district Weingegend *(f)*
wine festival Weinfest *(n)*
wine glass Weinglas *(n)*
wine grower Winzer *(m)*
wine growing Weinbau *(m)*
wine house Weinschenke *(f)*
wine in a carafe offener Wein *(m)*
wine list Weinkarte *(f)*
wine merchant Weinhändler *(m)*
wine shop Weinhandlung *(f)*
wine tavern Weinstube *(f)*
wine test Weinprobe *(f)*
wine with sodawater Schorle *(f)*
wing Flügel *(m)*
winglet Flügelspitze vom Huhn *(f)*
winter cure Winterkur *(f)*
winter garden Wintergarten *(m)*
winter health resort Winterkurort *(m)*
winter holiday resort Winterfrische *(f)*
winter holiday village Winterferiendorf *(n)*
winter season Wintersaison *(f)*
winter sports Wintersport *(m)*
winter sports centre Wintersportort *(m)*
winter sports equipment Wintersportausrüstung *(f)*
winter sports event Wintersportveranstaltung *(f)*
winter sports facilities Wintersporteinrichtungen *(pl. f)*
winter sports resort Wintersportort *(m)*
winter sports season Wintersportsaison *(f)*
winter sports trip Wintersportreise *(f)*
winter stay Winteraufenthaltsort *(m)*
winter timetable Winterfahrplan *(m)*, Winterflugplan *(m)*
winter tourism Wintertourismus *(m)*
winter tourist traffic Winterreiseverkehr *(m)*
winter tyre Winterreifen *(m)*
wintry winterlich
wipe abtrocknen, wischen
wire Telegramm *(n)*, telegrafieren
wireless Radio *(n)*, Rundfunk *(m)*

withdrawal Abhebung *(f)*, Entnahme *(f)*
within the radius of im Umkreis *(m)* von
without delay unverzüglich
without fat fettlos, ohne Fett *(n)*
without obligation unverbindlich
without salt salzlos, ohne Salz *(n)*
wood Wald *(m)*, Holz *(n)*
wood cock Schnepfe *(f)*
wood fire Holzfeuer *(n)*
woodruff Waldmeister *(m)*, Maikräuter *(pl. n)*
wool blanket Wolldecke *(f)*
worcestersauce Worcestersoße *(f)*
word of mouth advertising Mund-zu-Mund-Werbung *(f)*
word processing Textverarbeitung *(f)*
work Arbeit *(f)*
work area Arbeitsbereich *(m)*
work flow analysis Arbeitsablaufanalyse *(f)*
work in process unfertige Erzeugnisse *(pl. n)*
work load Arbeitsbelastung *(f)*
work permit Arbeitserlaubnis *(f)*
work place Arbeitsplatz *(m)*
work place layout Arbeitsplatzgestaltung *(f)*
work sampling study Multimomentaufnahme *(f)*
work satisfaction Arbeitszufriedenheit *(f)*
work sheet Abschlußübersicht *(f)*, Betriebsübersicht *(f)*; Arbeitsunterlage *(f)*, Arbeitsbogen *(m)*
worksheet calculation Tabellenkalkulation *(f)*
workshop Fortbildungsseminar *(n)*, Werkstätte *(f)*
work simplification Arbeitsvereinfachung *(f)*
work terms Arbeitsbedingungen *(pl. f)*
working climate Betriebsklima *(n)*
working condition Arbeitsbedingung *(f)*
working instruction Dienstanweisung *(f)*
working knowledge praktisch verwertbare Kenntnisse *(pl. f)*

working papers Arbeitspapiere *(pl. n)*, Arbeitsunterlagen *(pl. f)*
World Association of Travel Agencies Weltverband *(m)* der Reisebüros *(pl. n)*
world exhibition Weltausstellung *(f)*
World Fair Weltausstellung *(f)*
world-wide fame Weltruf *(m)*
worn out abgenutzt
worry Kummer *(m)*, Unruhe *(f)*, Aufregung *(f)*, Verdruß *(m)*, sich sorgen
worth seeing sehenswert
worthless wertlos
wrapping paper Packpapier *(n)*
wreck Strandgut *(n)*, Wrack *(n)*
wrecking car Abschleppwagen *(m)*
write off abschreiben, ausbuchen
write out ausschreiben
writing case Schreibmappe *(f)*
writing kit Schreibzeug *(n)*
writing paper Schreibpapier *(n)*
written schriftlich
wrong falsch, verkehrt, Unrecht *(n)*
wrongly routed luggage verschlepptes Reisegepäck *(n)*

X

X-mas, Christmas Weihnachten *(n)*
X-ray photo Röntgenaufnahme *(f)*
xenophobia Fremdenfeindlichkeit *(f)*
xylose Holzzucker *(m)*

Y

y Flugscheinvermerk *(m)* für Touristenklasse *(f)*
yacht Segelboot *(n)*, Jacht *(f)*
yacht-race Segelregatta *(f)*
yachting Segelsport *(m)*
yachting school Segelschule *(f)*
yachting-season Segelsaison *(f)*
yachtsman Sportsegler *(m)*
yard Hof *(m)*
yardstick Maßstab *(m)*
yarn Garn *(n)*
yawl Segeljolle *(f)*
yawn gähnen

yeanling Lamm *(n)*, Zicklein *(n)*
year-round service Ganzjahresbetrieb *(m)*
yearly jährlich
yeast Hefe *(f)*
yeast extract Hefeextrakt *(m)*
yeast powder Backpulver *(n)*
yellow filter Gelbfilter *(m)*
yellow pea gelbe Erbse *(f)*
yellow plum Mirabelle *(f)*
yesterday gestern
yield management Yield Management *(n)*
yield management team Yield Management-Team *(n)*
yoghourt Joghurt *(m, n)*
yolk Eigelb *(n)*, Eidotter *(m)*
Yorkshire pudding gebackener Eierteig *(m)*
Yorkshire relish pikante fertige Soße *(f)*
young jung
young chicken Küken *(n)*
young wild boar Frischling *(m)*
youth Jugend *(f)*, Jugendlicher *(m)*
youth club Jugendklub *(m)*
youth fare Jugendfahrpreis *(m)*
youth group journey Jugendgruppenreise *(f)*
youth hostel Jugendherberge *(f)*
Youth Hostel Association Membership Card Jugendherbergsausweis *(m)*
youth travel Jugendreise *(f)*
yule Weihnachten *(n)*
zealous eifrig, hitzig

Z

zebra crossing Zebrastreifen *(m)*
zero Null *(f)*
zero balancing Nullkontrolle *(f)*
zest Würze *(f)*, Reiz *(m)*
zigzag cruise Kreuzundquerfahrt *(f)*
zinc Zink *(n)*
zip Reißverschluß *(m)*
zip code Postleitzahl *(f)*
zitherit Zitherspieler *(m)*
zone Zone *(f)*, Gebiet *(n)*
zone of rest Ruhezone *(f)*

zoned street Kurzparkzone *(f)*
zoo Tiergarten *(m)*, Zoo *(m)*
zoological garden zoologischer Garten *(m)*

zoom Steilflug *(m)*, steil hochziehen, zoomen
zoom lens Gummilinse *(f)*, Zoomobjektiv *(n)*

Teil III

Verzeichnis aller Aufwendungen (USAH)

Deutsch – Englisch

Part III

Expense and Payroll Dictionary (USAH)

German – English

Teil III: **Verzeichnis aller Aufwendungen (USAH)**
Deutsch – Englisch
Part III: Expense and Payroll Dictionary (USAH)
German – English

Abkürzungen

deutsch:

A	Abschreibungen
B	Beherbergung
E	Energie
F & B	Food und Beverage
MKT	Marketing
P	Personal
T	Technische Abteilung
Trans.	Transport
V	Verwaltung
Zinsaufw.	Zinsaufwendungen
zusätzliche, lohnabhängige (Personal-)Kosten	ohne Abkürzung

englisch:

D & A	depreciation and amortization
R	rooms
EC	energy cost
F & B	food and beverage
MKT	marketing
HR	human resources
POM	property, operation, and maintenance
Trans.	transportation
A & G	administrative and general
Int. Exp.	interest expense
PTEB	payroll taxes and employee benefits

Abfallbeseitigung (T) rubbish removal **(POM)**
Abfalltonnen (F & B) garbage cans **(F & B)**
Abfall, beim Sieben zurückbleibender (T) screening **(POM)**
Abhörgerät (beim Telefon) – Mietaufwendungen (V) dictograph – rentals **(A&G)**
Abschreibung – Einbauten in gemieteten (geleasten) Objekten (A) amortization – leasehold improvements **(D&A)**
Abschreibung – Emissionsdisagio (Zinsaufw.) ammortization – bond issue **(Int. Exp.)**
Abschreibung – Finanzierungskosten (Zinsaufw.) amortization – financing costs **(Int. Exp.)**
Abschreibung – geleaste Gebäude, Mietbesitz (A) amortization – leasehold **(D&A)**
Abschreibung auf Kosten der Anleiheemission (Zinsaufw.) bond expense amortization **(Int. Exp.)**
Abschreibungen – Gebäude (A) depreciation – buildings **(D&A)**
Abschreibungen auf zweifelhafte Forderungen (V) provision for doubtful accounts **(A&G)**
Abschrift, Kopie, Verhandlungsprotokoll (V) transcript **(A&G)**
Abwasserkanal – Reparaturen (T) sewer system – repairs **(POM)**
Abzeichen, Kennzeichen (B); (F & B) badges **(R); (F & B)**
Addiermaschine – Papierstreifen (T) adding machine – tape **(POM)**
Adressbuch, Telefonbuch (B) directory **(R)**
Adressenkartei (MKT) mailing list **(MKT)**
Adressiermaschine – Hilfs- und Betriebsstoffe (MKT) addressing machine – supplies **(MKT)**

Aktendeckel, Einband, Umschlag (B); (F & B); (V) binder **(R); (F & B); (A&G)**
Alarmvorrichtungen – Feuer und Einbruch (V) alarm service – fire and burglar **(A&G); (R); (F & B)**
Alkali, Laugensalz, alkalischer Stoff (Wasserenthärtungsmittel) (T) alkalies (water softener) **(POM)**
Alkohol – Brennstoff für Kochgeräte (F & B) alcohol – cooking fuel **(F & B)**
Alkohol – Reinigungszwecke (B); (F & B) alcohol – cleaning **(R); (F & B)**
alkoholfreies Getränk (F & B) soft drink **(F & B)**
Aluminium-Tablett (F & B) aluminium-tray **(F & B)**
Ammoniak – Kühlmittel (T) ammonia – refrigerant **(POM)**
Ammoniak – Reinigungszwecke (B); (F & B) ammonia – cleaning **(R); (F & B)**
Andenken, Souvenir (B) souvenir **(R)**
Anmeldeformulare – Gäste (B) registration cards – guests **(R)**
Annonce, Inserat – Aushilfskräfte (P) help wanted ad **(HR)**
(An-)Pflanzung (T) planting **(POM)**
Anschlagbrett (MKT) billboard **(MKT)**
Anschreibeblöcke (B) core pads **(R)**
Ansteckblumen, Anstecksträußchen (B) boutonnieres **(R)**
Ansteckbukett (Gäste) (B) corsage (guests) **(R)**
Anstecknadeln (Angestellte) (F & B); (B); (V) pins (employees) **(F & B); (R); (A&G)**
Anwaltskosten (V) attorney's fees **(A&G)**
Anzug (B) suit **(R)**
Arbeitskittel (B); (F & B) smock **(R); (F & B)**
Arbeitslosenversicherung (Arbeitgeberanteil) (zusätzliche,

**lohnabhängige
(Personal-)Kosten)** employee
benefits **(PTEB)**
**Arbeitslosenversicherung
(Arbeitgeberanteil) (zusätzliche,
lohnabhängige
(Personal-)Kosten)** federal
unemployment taxes **(PTEB)**
**Arzneimittel, Drogeriewaren und
sonstige pharmazeutische
Präparate (Angestellte) (P)**
drugs and other medical supplies
(employees) **(HR)**
**Arzneimittel, Drogeriewaren und
sonstige pharmazeutische
Präparate (Gäste) (B)** drugs and
other medical supplies (guests) **(R)**
Arzthonorare (Angestellte) (P); (V)
physician fees (employees) **(HR);
(A&G)**
**Arzthonorare (Leistungen für
Angestellte) (V)** medical fees
(service to employees) **(A&G)**
Arztkosten (Angestellte) (V) fees –
physician (employees) **(A&G)**
**Aschekasten, Abfalleimer,
Müllkübel (T)** ash can **(POM)**
Aschenbecher (B); (F & B) ash tray
(R); (F & B)
**Aufzeichnungen, Unterlagen,
Geschäftsbücher (B); (F & B);
(V)** record books **(R); (F & B);
(A&G)**
Aufzugkabel (T) elevator cable
(POM)
Aufzüge – Kontrolldienst (T)
elevator inspection service **(POM)**
Ausschußpapier (B); (F & B) waste
paper **(R); (F & B)**
Ausstellung – im Hotel (MKT)
exposition – local **(MKT)**
Austernmesser (F & B) knives –
oyster **(F & B)**
**Autoreparaturkosten (Gäste)
(Trans.); (B)** auto repairs (guest
use) **(Trans.); (R)**
**Autoreparaturkosten (Hotel)
(Trans.); (T)** auto repairs
(property use) **(Trans.); (POM)**
Ätznatron (B); (F & B) caustic soda
(R); (F & B)

Badematten (B) bath mats **(R)**
Bademützen (Gäste) (B) bathing
caps (guests) **(R)**
Bandsäge (T) band saw **(POM)**
Band, Borte (Geschenkladen)
ribbon **(gift shop)**
Bankettbericht (F & B) banquet
report **(F & B)**
Banner, Fahnen (B); (F & B) banner
(R); (F & B)
Bar – Geräte (F & B) bar – utensils
(F & B)
Batterien und Taschenlampen (T)
batteries and flashlights **(POM)**
Bauholz (T) lumber **(POM)**
Beeper – Mietkosten (V) beeper
rental **(A&G)**
**Beförderungskosten – Angestellte
(P)** employee transportation **(HR)**
**Beförderungskosten für Transport
zum Flughafen, die dem Gast
nicht berechnet werden
können (V)** airport transportation
– not chargeable to guest **(A&G);
(MKT)**
Behälter – Spülung (T) tank –
toilet floats **(POM)**
Behälter, Halter (F & B) holder
(F & B)
**Behang, Volant (am Bett oder
Baldachin) (T)** valance **(POM)**
**Beiträge – Hotel- und
Gaststättenverband (V)** dues –
hotel association **(A&G)**
**Beiträge, Gebühren – Fachpresse
(V)** subscriptions – trade
publications **(A&G)**
**Beiträge, Zuwendungen –
Kongreßbüro (MKT)**
contributions – convention bureau
(MKT)
**Beitrag, Gebühr – Kredit-
auskunfteien (V)** subscription –
mercantile agencies **(A&G)**
Beitrag, Spende (V) contribution
(A&G)
Benzin – Fahrzeuge (B); (V)
gasoline – motor vehicles **(R);
(A&G)**
Benzin-Reinigung (B)
benzine-cleaning **(R)**

Beratungskosten (V) consultant fees **(A&G)**
Bericht, Protokoll (V) report **(A&G)**
Beseitigung von Asche, Küchenabfall und Müll (T) removal of ashes, garbage, and waste matter **(POM)**
Besen (B); (F & B) broom **(R); (F & B)**
Betriebshaftpflichtversicherung (zusätzlich, lohnabhängige (Personal-)Kosten) workers' compensation insurance **(PTEB)**
Bettbezüge, farbige (B) color spreads **(R)**
Bettdecken, Tagesdecken (B) bedspreads **(R)**
Bettlaken – Leinen (B) sheets – linen **(R)**
Bettroste (T) bed springs **(POM)**
Beutel, Taschen – Schlüssel (B); (F & B) pouches – key **(R); (F & B)**
Bilderrahmen (T) picture frame **(POM)**
Bilder, Fotografien (MKT) photographs **(MKT)**
Bindfaden, Schnur (B); (F & B); (Geschenkladen) twine **(R); (F & B); (gift shop)**
Blaupause (MKT) blueprint **(MKT)**
Bleichmittel (Hotelwäscherei) bleach **(house laundry)**
Bleistifte (B); (F & B); (V) pencils **(R); (F & B); (A&G)**
Bleistiftspitzer (B); (F & B); (V) pencil sharpeners **(R); (F & B); (A&G)**
Blumentöpfe (B); (F & B) flower pots **(R); (F & B)**
Boilerinspektion (T) boiler inspection **(POM)**
Boilermanometer (T) boiler gauge **(POM)**
Boilerreparaturen (T) boiler-repairs **(POM)**
Borte, Litze, Tresse, Zierband, Flechtschnur für Uniformen (B); (F & B) braid for uniforms **(R); (F & B)**
Brennholz – Zimmer und Hotelhalle (B) fire wood – rooms and lobby **(R)**
Brennstoff (T) fuel **(POM)**
Briefmarken – allgemein (V) stamps – general **(A&G)**
Briefmarken – Werbung (MKT) stamps – advertising **(MKT)**
Briefpapier (B); (F & B); (V) stationery **(R); (F & B); (A&G)**
Briefumschläge (B); (V) envelopes **(R); (A&G)**
Briefumschläge – telefonische Nachrichten (B) envelopes – telephone messages **(R)**
Brikett, Presskohle (F & B) briquet **(F & B)**
Broschüre, Heft, Flugschrift (MKT) pamphlet **(MKT)**
Broschüre, Werbematerial (MKT) brochure **(MKT)**
Buchungsbeleg, Buchungsunterlage (auch: Gutschein) (B); (F & B); (V) voucher **(R); (F & B); (A&G)**
Büchsenöffner (F & B) can openers **(F & B)**
Bügelbrett (B) ironing board **(R)**
Bügelmaschine – Abdeckung (B) pressing machine – cover **(R)**
Bürger- und Gemeindeprojekt (MKT) civic and community project **(MKT)**
Büroausstattung – Reparaturen (T) office equipment – repairs **(POM)**
Bürobedarf (B); (F & B); (V) office supplies **(R); (F & B); (A&G)**
Büroklammer, Aktenklammer (B); (F & B); (V) paper clip **(R); (F & B); (A&G)**

Chemikalien – Feuerlöscher (V) chemical – fire extinguisher **(A&G)**
Chemikalien (Hotelwäscherei) chemicals **(house laundry)**
Chemische Reinigung (F & B) dry cleaning **(R); (F & B)**
Chintz, Möbelkattun (T) chintz **(POM)**
Chlor (T) chlorine **(POM)**

Chlorcalcium (Hotelwäscherei)
chloride of lime (**house laundry**)
Christbaum und
Christbaumschmuck (B);
(F & B) christmas tree and
decorations (**R**); (**F & B**)
Cocktail-Serviette – Papier (F & B)
cocktail napkin – paper (**F & B**)
Cocktailshaker (F & B) cocktail
shaker (**F & B**)
Computer (MVV) computer-rental
(**RTI**)
Computerdrucker (MVV) computer
printer (**RTI**)
Container – Flüssigkeiten, Papier
(F & B) containers – liquid, paper
(**F & B**)
Copyright – Lizenz (V); (F & B)
copyright – license (**A&G**);
(**F & B**)
Dachreparaturen (T) roof repairs
(**POM**)
Damenbinde (Gäste) (B) sanitary
napkin (guests) (**R**)
Dampf – Küche (F & B) steam –
kitchen (**F & B**)
Dampf (T) steam (**POM**)
Dampfkessel-Explosionsversicherung
(MVV) boiler explosion insurance
(**RTI**)
Datenverarbeitung – Hilfs- und
Betriebsstoffe (V) data
processing – supplies (**A&G**)
Datenverarbeitung –
Mietaufwendungen (MVV) data
processing – rentals (**RTI**)
Decken (B) blankets (**R**)
Dekorations- und Malerarbeiten
(T) decoration and painting
(**POM**)
Dekorationsarbeiten (B); (F & B)
decorations (**R**); (**F & B**)
Desinfektionsmittel (F & B)
disinfectants (**R**); (**F & B**)
Desinfektion, Entkeimen –
Vertragsfirmen (B); (F & B)
contract – disinfecting (**R**); (**F & B**)
Detektivleistungen (V) detective
service (**A&G**)
Disketten (V) floppy disks (**A&G**)
Docht (F & B) wick (**F & B**)

Draperie – Reinigung (B); (F & B)
drapery – cleaning (**R**); (**F & B**)
Draperie – Reparaturen (T) drapery
– repairs (**POM**)
Drell, Drillich (T) ticking (**POM**)
Drucksachen und Schreibbedarf
(B); (F & B); (V)
printing and stationery (**R**);
(**F & B**); (**A&G**)
Drucksachen (B); (F & B); (V)
printed matter (**R**); (**F & B**);
(**A&G**)
Duschpantoffeln (B) shower
slippers (**R**)
Duschvorhänge (B) shower curtains
(**R**)
Dynamo (Maschine) – Reparaturen
(T) dynamo – repairs (**POM**)

Eimer – Malerarbeiten und
Dekoration (T) pails – painting
and decorating (**POM**)
Eimer, Kübel (B) pails (**R**)
Einbauten (Ausbauten) in
gemieteten Räumen –
Abschreibung (A) leasehold
improvements – amortization
(**D&A**)
Einbruchsversicherung (V)
burglary insurance (**A&G**)
Einkommen- und Ertragssteuer
(Steuern auf Einkommen und
Ertrag) income tax – federal
(**income tax**)
Einkommen- und Ertragsteuer des
Bundes (Steuern auf
Einkommen und Ertrag)
federal income tax (**income tax**)
Einkommensteuer (Landesebene)
(Steuern auf Einkommen und
Ertrag) state income tax (**income**
tax)
Einpackfolie (F & B) wrapping foil
(**F & B**)
Eintrittskarten (Verkaufsförderung)
(MKT) tickets (for promotion)
(**MKT**)
Eis (F & B) ice (**F & B**)
Eisenbahnreklame (MKT) railroad
train advertising (**MKT**)

Eispfriem zum Zerkleinern von Eis (F & B) ice pick (F & B)
Eiszange (F & B) ice tong (F & B)
Ekrüstoff, Ekrü (Hotelwäscherei) ecru (house laundry)
Elektrizität – Küche (F & B) electricity – cooking (F & B)
Email- oder Glasurmasse (T) enamel (POM)
Emissionsdisagio (Zinsaufw.) bond discount (Int. Exp.)
Empfangsdame – Berichte (B) room clerk – reports (R)
Energiekosten (T) cost of power (POM)
Erlaubnis (B); (F & B) permit (R); (F & B)
Erste-Hilfe-Material (V) first aid supplies (A&G)
Eßbesteck (F & B) flatware (F & B)
Essig-/Ölfläschchen (F & B) cruet (F & B)

Fächer (Gäste) (B); (F & B) fans (guests) (R); (F & B)
Fachzeitschriften, Magazine – zum Verkauf (Miet- und sonstige Erträge – Warenkosten) periodicals – for sale (rentals and other income – cost of sales)
Fahrgeld, Fahrpreis (V) car fare (A&G)
Fahrpläne, Flugpläne (B) timetables (R)
Fahrpreise – Taxis (Angestellte) (P) taxicab fares (employees) (HR)
Fahrpreise – Taxis (Gäste) (B) taxicab fares (guests) (R)
Fahrzeugabschreibung (A) vehicle depreciation (D&A)
Färbeflüssigkeit für Teppiche und Brücken (T) dye for carpets and rugs (POM))
Farnkraut, Farn (B); (F & B) fern (R); (F & B)
Fensterscheiben, Ersatz von (T) replacement of window glass (POM)
Fernschreiber – Papier (V) teletype – paper (A&G)

Fernseher – Mietaufwendungen (MVV) television – rentals (RTI)
Feuerleiter – Reparaturen (T) fire escape – repairs (POM)
Feuerlöscher (V) fire extinguisher (A&G)
Feuerwehrschlauch (T) fire hose (POM)
Film (F & B) film (F & B)
Filterpapier (F & B) filter paper (F & B)
Filz (T) felt (POM))
Flaggentuch und Flaggen (B); (F & B) bunting and flags (R); (F & B)
Flaschenöffner (Gäste) (B) bottle openers (guests) (R)
Flaschenverkorkgerät (F & B) corking equipment (F & B)
Fleischspieß (F & B) skewer (F & B)
Fliegenklatsche (B); (F & B) fly swatter (R); (F & B)
Fliesen, Kacheln – Gummi (T) tiling – rubber (POM)
Flüssigkeitsbehälter (F & B) liquid container (F & B)
Forderungen, uneinbringliche (V) uncollectible accounts (A&G)
Form (für Speisen) (F & B) mold (F & B)
Formulare, vorgedruckte (B); (F & B); (V) printed forms (R); (F & B); (A&G)
Frachtkosten (V) freight charges (A&G)
Franchisegebühren (MKT) franchise fees (MKT)
Fremdenführerinformation (Gäste) (B) guides (guest use) (R)
Fremdreinigung – Desinfektion, Ausgasung, Fumigation (B); (F & B) contract cleaning – fumigation (R); (F & B)
Fremdreinigung – Empfangshalle, Foyer (B) contract cleaning – lobbies (R)
Fremdreinigung – Fenster (B) contract cleaning – windows (R); (F & B)
Fremdreinigung – Speisesaal

(F & B) contract cleaning – dining room **(F & B)**
Fundbüro – Berichte (V) lost & found reports **(A&G)**
Funkmeldung, Funktelegramm (V) radiogram **(A&G)**
Fußbodenpolitur (B); (F & B) floor polish **(R); (F & B)**
Fußbodenwachs (B); (F & B) floor wax **(R); (F & B)**
Fußgängerweg – Reparaturen (T) sidewalk – repairs **(POM)**
Füllfederhalter (B); (F & B); (V) fountain pens **(R); (F & B); (A&G)**

Gabeln (F & B) forks **(F & B)**
Garage (B); (F & B) garage **(R); (F & B)**
Gas- oder Elektroherd – Reparaturen (T) range – repairs **(POM)**
Gasofen – Mietaufwendungen (F & B) gas range – rentals **(F & B)**
Gästebuchhaltung (V) guest ledgers **(A&G)**
Gästerechnungen für Bedienungspersonal (F & B) servers' checks **(F & B)**
Gästerechnungen (F & B) restaurant checks **(F & B)**
Gästeseife (B) guest soap **(R)**
Gastrechnungen – Kellner (F & B) checks – waiter **(F & B)**
Gebäudereparaturen – Fremdaufträge building repairs – outside contract **(POM)**
Gebäudereparaturen (T) building repairs **(POM)**
Gebäudeversicherung (MVV) buildings and contents insurance **(RTI)**
Gebühren – Management (Management-Gebühren) fees – management **(management fees)**
Gegenstände, beschädigte – Gäste (V) damaged articles – guests **(A&G)**
Gehaltsprämien, Tantiemen für Angestellte (B); (F & B) employee bonuses **(R); (F & B)**

Geldstrafe, Geldbuße (V) fine **(A&G)**
Gemeinschaftsversicherung (gewerkschaftlich organisierte Arbeitnehmer) (zusätzliche, lohnabhängige (Personal-)Kosten) insurance – group (union) **(PTEB)**
Gemeinschaftsversicherung (nicht gewerkschaftlich organisierte Arbeitnehmer) (zusätzliche, lohnabhängige (Personal-)Kosten) insurance – group (non union) **(PTEB)**
Generator, Dynamo, Lichtmaschine – Reparaturen (T) generator – repairs **(POM)**
gepanzerte Fahrzeuge (Gebühren) (V) armored car service **(A&G)**
Gerichtskosten (V) court fees **(A&G)**
Geschenke (F & B) favors **(F & B)**
Geschenke (Gäste) (B); (F & B) gifts (guests) **(R); (F & B)**
Geschenke (V) donations **(A&G)**
Geschirr (F & B) dishes **(F & B)**
Geschirrspüler – Reparaturen (T) dish-washer – repairs **(POM)**
Gesetzliche Sozialabgaben (Arbeitgeberanteil) (zusätzliche, lohnabhängige (Personal-)Kosten) employee benefits **(PTEB)**
Gesetzliche Sozialversicherung des Bundes (Arbeitgeberanteil) (zusätzliche, lohnabhängige (Personal-)Kosten) federal retirement taxes **(PTEB)**
Getränke (kostenlos) – Musiker und Entertainer (F & B) complimentary beverage – musicians and entertainers **(F & B)**
Getränkemixer beverage mixer **(F & B)**
Getränkesteuer (F & B) beverage tax **(F & B)**
Getränke, kostenlose (MKT) complimentary beverage **(MKT)**
Gewerkschaft – Versicherungs- und Pensionskassenbeiträge (Arbeitgeberanteil) (zusätzliche,

**lohnabhängige
(Personal-)Kosten)** union –
insurance and pension fund
(employer's contribution) **(PTEB)**
Gips (T) plaster **(POM)**
**Glaserarbeiten (Ersatz von
Fensterglas) (T)** glazing
(replacing window glass) **(POM)**
Glaskanne (B); (F & B) glass pitcher
(R); (F & B)
Glasregal – Badezimmer (T)
bathroom – glass shelve **(POM)**
Glasschüsseln (F & B) glas bowls
(F & B)
Glastablett (B); (F & B) glass tray
(R); (F & B)
Glas, Glasgeschirr (B); (F & B)
glassware, glassdishes **(R); (F & B)**
Glückwunschkarten (MKT) greeting
cards **(MKT)**
Glühbirnen, elektrische (T) electric
bulbs **(POM)**
**Grundbesitz, Immobilien (Grund
und Boden) – Mietaufwendungen** real estate rent **(land
and buildings)**
Grundpacht (MVV) ground rent
(RTI)
Grundriß (B) floor plan **(R)**
Grundriß, Entwurf (MKT) sketch
(MKT)
Grundstückssteuer (MVV) real
estate taxes **(RTI)**
Gründungsaufwand (A)
organization expenses **(D&A)**
Guest History (MKT) guest history
(MKT)
Gummihandschuhe (B); (F & B)
rubber gloves **(R); (F & B)**
Gummimatten (T) rubber mats
(POM)
Gummistempel (B); (F & B); (V)
rubber stamps **(R); (F & B); (A&G)**
Gummistiefel (B); (F & B) rubber
boots **(R); (F & B)**

Haarnadeln (Gäste) (B) hairpins
(guests) **(R)**
**Haarnetze (Angestellte) (B);
(F & B)** hair nets (employees)
(R); (F & B)

**Haftpflichtversicherung für
Aufzüge (V)** elevator liability
insurance **(A&G)**
Haftpflichtversicherung (V) public
liability insurance **(A&G)**
Haken, Türangel (T) hook **(POM)**
**Handbuch, Leitfaden –
Servicepersonal
(Weiterbildungsmaterial) (B);
(F & B); (V)** manuals – service
(instructional materials) **(R);
(F & B); (A&G)**
**Handbücher für Personal (B);
(A&G)** service manuals **(R);
(A&G)**
**Handels-Kreditauskunftei –
Beiträge (V)** mercantile agency –
subscription **(A&G)**
Handschuhe (B); (F & B) gloves
(R); (F & B)
Handtücher – Leinen (B); (F & B)
towels – linen **(R); (F & B)**
**Hausdamenabteilung – Berichte
(B)** housekeeper – reports **(R)**
Heftmaschine (B); (F & B); (V)
stapler **(R); (F & B); (A&G)**
Heftpflaster (T) adhesive tape
(POM)
Heizungsanlage – Reparaturen (T)
heating plant – repairs **(POM)**
**Hilfsmittel, medizinische (für
Angestellte) (V)** medical
supplies (for employees) **(A&G)**
Hinweisschild (im Hotel) (MKT)
directional sign (inside bld.)
(MKT)
Holzkohle (F & B) charcoal **(F & B)**
**Honorar für Wirtschafts- und
Buchprüfer (V)** accountant's fees
(A&G)
**Honorare für Werbeagenturen
(MKT)** advertising agency fees
(MKT)
Hose (B) pants **(R)**
Hose (B); (F & B) trousers **(R);
(F & B)**
Hotelhallenreinigung (B) lobby
cleaning **(R)**
**Hypothekenzinsen auf die 1.
Hypothek (Zinsaufw.)** interest
on first mortgage **(Int. Exp.)**

Illustration, Grafik (MKT) art work
(MKT)
**Inhaltsverzeichnis, Tabelle,
Register, Index (B); (F & B);
(V)** index (R); (F & B); (A&G)
Inkasso-Einzugsspesen (V)
collection fees (A&G)
**Insektenvertilgung –
Vertragsfirmen (B)** contract
exterminating (R)
Insektenvertilgungsmittel
insecticide (R); (F & B)
**interne Prüfungsgebühren
(Kettenhotels) (V)** internal audit
fees (chain properties) (A&G)
Interviewkosten (P) interview
expense (HR)

Jackett für Uniformen (B); (F & B)
coat (uniforms) (R); (F & B)
Jalousie (T) Venetian blind (POM)

**Kabelfernsehen –
Mietaufwendungen (MVV)**
cable television – rentals (RTI)
Kabel, (Draht-)Seil – Aufzug (T)
cable – elevator (POM)
Kaffee – kostenlos (B) coffee –
free (R)
Kaffeekannen (F & B) coffee pots
(F & B)
Kaffeesack (F & B) coffee bag
(F & B)
Kalender (MKT) calendar (MKT)
**Kälteerzeugung – Elektrizität
(Kochnische in Apts.) (B)**
refrigeration – electricity
(kitchenette apts) (R)
Kalzium (T) calcium (POM)
Kämme (Gäste) (B) combs (guests)
(R)
Karaffe (B) carafe (R)
**Karte zur Verwendung im
Zimmerbelegungsplan (B)** rack
card (R)
Karteikarten (B); (F & B); (V) index
cards (R); (F & B); (A&G)
**Kassen-Überschuß und
-Fehlbetrag (V)** cash overage
and shortage (A&G)
Kassenzettel, Verkaufsschecks
(F & B); (Geschenkladen) sales
checks (F & B); (gift shop)
Kasserole, Auflaufform (F & B)
casserole (F & B)
Kassierer – Formulare (V) cashier
forms (A&G)
**Kaution(-sverpflichtung) des
Versicherers im Falle von
Veruntreuung (V)** bond fidelity
(A&B)
Kehrichtschaufel (B); (F & B) dust
pan (R); (F & B)
**Kehrmaschine – Teppich (B);
(F & B)** sweeper – carpet (R);
(F & B)
Kelch, Becher, Pokal (F & B) goblet
(F & B)
Kerzen (B); (F & B) candles (R);
(F & B)
**Kerzenhalter, Kerzenständer (B);
(F & B)** candlesticks (R); (F & B)
Kesselstein-Schutzmittel (T) boiler
compound (POM)
Kessel (aus Metall) (F & B) kettle
(F & B)
**Klavier-Mietkosten – Bankette
(F & B)** piano rentals – banquets
(F & B)
**Klavierstimmen – Appartement
(B)** piano tuning – apartment (R)
Klavierstimmen – Bankette (F & B)
piano tuning – banquets (F & B)
**Klebestreifen, durchsichtiger
(Geschenkladen); (V)** scotch
tape (gift shop); (A&G)
**Kleider-Reparaturen –
Fremdbetriebe (B); (F & B)**
clothing repairs – outside
establishments (R); (F & B)
Kleiderbügel (B) clothes hanger,
coat hanger, garment hanger (R)
Kleidersäcke (Gäste) (B) garment
bags (guests) (R)
**Kleidung (Uniformen) (B); (F & B);
(Hotelwäscherei)** dresses
(uniforms) (R); (F & B); (house
laundry)
**Klemptner – Installateurarbeiten
(T)** plumbing – repairs (POM)
**Klinik – Angestellte (Arztkosten)
(P)** clinic – employees (HR)

Klischeeherstellung, fotografische (MKT) photo – engraving (MKT)
Knöpfe – Uniformen (B); (F & B) buttons – uniforms (R); (F & B)
Knöpfe – Wäscherei (Hotelwäscherei) buttons – laundry (**house laundry**)
Knöpfe (Gäste) (B) buttons (guests) (R)
Kochnische – Aufwendungen (B) kitchenette expenses (R)
Kochtöpfe (F & B) pots (F & B)
Kohle – Heizung (T) coal – heating (POM)
Kohle – Küche (F & B) coal – cooking (F & B)
Kohlensäure (F & B) carbonated gas (F & B)
Kohlenschaufeln (T) coal shovels (POM)
Kohlepapier (B); (F & B); (V) carbon paper (R); (F & B); (A&G)
Kompottschalen (F & B) compotes (F & B)
Kontobuch (V) account-book (A&B)
Kopfkissen (B) pillow cases (R)
Korkenzieher (F & B) corkscrews (F & B)
Korkenzieher (Gäste) (B) corkscrews (guests) (R)
Körperpuder (Gäste) (B) talcum powder (guests) (R)
Kraftfahrzeugbedarf (Gäste) (z. B. Öl) (Garage) autosupplies (sold to guests) (**garage – cost of sales**)
Kraftfahrzeugbedarf – Hotel (Trans.) autosupplies (used by property) (**Trans.**)
Kragen (B) collar (R)
Kratzer, Schabeisen, Streichmesser – Farbe (T) scraper – paint (POM)
Krawatte (B) tie (POM)
Kreditinformationenbücher (V) credit information books (A&G)
Kreditkarten-Provision (V) credit card commission (A&G)
Kreditkosten und Inkassospesen (V) credit and collection expenses (A&G)

Kreide (B); (F & B) chalk (R); (F & B)
Krug (mit Henkel) (B); (F & B) pitcher (R); (F & B)
Kuchenschachteln (F & B) pastry boxes (F & B)
Kugellager (T) ball bearing (POM)
Kugelschreiber (Angestellte) (B); (F & B); (V) pens (employees) (R); (F & B); (A&G)
Kundendienstkosten für Addiermaschinen (T) adding machines – service (POM)
Kunstdünger, Düngemittel (T) fertilizer (POM)
Küchenausstattung – Reparaturen (T) kitchen equipment – repairs (POM)
Küchengeräte (einschließlich Messer, Gabeln, Schöpflöffel, und Löffel) (F & B) kitchen utensils (including knives, forks, ladles, and spoons) (F & B)
Küchengeräte (Kochnische in Appartements) (B) cooking utensils (in kitchenette apts.) (R)
Kühlmittel (T) refrigerant (POM)
Kühlvorrichtung – Faser, Fiber (F & B) cooler – fiber (F & B)
künstliche Blumen (B); (F & B) artificial flowers (R); (F & B)

Laborkosten (T) laboratory costs (POM)
Lack (T) varnish (POM)
Lackfarbe (T) lacquer (POM)
Lagerfachkarten – Spirituosen (F & B) bin cards – liquor (F & B)
Lagerkosten – Getränke (F & B) warehouse costs – beverage (F & B)
Lagerungsgebühren für Speisen und Getränke (F & B) storage charges on food and beverages (F & B)
Lampenschirm – Reinigung (B); (F & B) lamp shade – cleaning (R); (F & B)
Landkarte (MKT) map (MKT)
Landschaftsgestaltung (T) landscaping (POM)

Lappen – Reinigung (B);
(F & B) rags – cleaning (R);
(F & B)
Lastschriftzettel (B); (F & B) charge voucher (R); (F & B)
Lauge (B); (F & B) lye (R); (F & B)
Lautsprecheranlage (zur Übertragung von Ansagen etc. für eine große Zuhörerschaft) – Reparaturen (T) public address systems – repairs (POM)
Lebensversicherung (gewerkschaftlich organisierte Arbeitnehmer) (zusätzliche, lohnabhängige (Personal-)Kosten) insurance – life (union employees) (PTEB)
Leder (B) chamois (R)
Leim, Klebstoff, Gummilösung (B); (F & B); (A&G) mucilage (R); (F & B); (A&G)
Leine, Schnur (V); (F & B) cord (A&G); (F & B)
Leinwand – Malerarbeiten (T) canvas – painting (POM)
Leiter (T) ladder (POM)
Leitungsnetz, elektrisches – Reparaturen (T) wiring – repairs (POM)
Lieferkosten – Getränke (F & B) delivery charges on beverages (F & B)
Lieferkosten – Speisen (F & B) delivery charges on food (F & B)
Limousine (B) limousine (R)
Lineal (B); (F & B); (V) ruler (R); (F & B); (A&G)
Lizenzen – Schlosser (T) licenses – locksmith (POM)
Lizenzgebühr für Getränkeausschank (F & B) beverage license (F & B)
Logbuch, Reisetagebuch (B) log book (R)
Löffel – Getränke, Küche, Mixen (F & B) spoons – beverage, kitchen, mixing (F & B)
Löffel – Silber (F & B) spoons – silver (F & B)
Lösungsmittel (T) solvent (POM)

Luftkühlung – Reparaturen (T) air cooling system – repairs (POM)

Malerarbeiten und Dekorieren (T) painting and decorating (POM)
Malerpinsel (T) paint brush (POM)
Mantel – Türsteher (B) greatcoat – door attendant (R)
Marketinggebühren (MKT) marketing service fees (MKT)
Markise (über einem Hoteleingang) – Lizenz marquee license (A&G)
Markisen – Reinigung (B); (F & B) awnings – cleaning (R); (F & B)
Markisen – Reparaturen (B); (F & B) awnings – repairs (R); (F & B)
Maschinenöl (T) machine oil (POM)
Matratze (B) mattress (R)
Matten – Fußboden (T) mats – floor (POM)
Matte, Vorleger, Abtreter – Bad (B) mat – bath (R)
Mauerwerk – Reparaturen (T) masonry – repairs (POM)
Mausefalle (B) mouse trap (R)
Messen – am Ort (MKT) fairs – local (MKT)
Messer – Silber (F & B) knives – silver (F & B)
Meßinstrument, Meßwerkzeug –
Mietaufwendungen (T) meter – rentals (POM)
Mietaufwendungen – Fernschreiber (V) rentals – teletype (A&G)
Mietaufwendungen – Scheinwerfer (F & B) rentals – spotlights (F & B)
Mietautokosten (V); (MKT) auto rental (A&G); (MKT)
Mietkosten für Stühle – Bankette (F & B) chair rentals – banquets (F & B)
Mineralwasserausschank, Erfrischungshalle, Eisbar – Reparaturen (T) soda fountain – repairs (POM)
Mitgliedsbeiträge – Vereinigungen (V) membership dues – associations (A&G)

Mitteilungen – Briefumschläge
(Telefonzentrale) message
envelopes (telephone)
Mittel, desodorierende (B); (F & B)
deodorants (R); (F & B)
Mixer – Reparaturen (T) mixer –
repairs (POM)
Mobiliar für Veranstaltungsräume –
Mietaufwendungen (Bankette)
(F & B) furniture for public rooms
– rentals (banquets) (F & B)
Mop (B); (F & B) mop (R); (F & B)
Möbelpflegemittel, Möbelpolitur
(B); (F & B) furniture polish (R);
(F & B)
Musiker (F & B) musician (F & B)
Müllabfuhr (F & B) garbage removal
(F & B)
Müllbeseitigung (T) refuse removal
(POM)
Münzgeldbehälter (V) coin bag
(A&G)
Mütze (B) cap (R)

Nachtkleidung (B) night apparel (R)
Nadeln und Faden (T) needles and
thread (POM)
Nadeln und Faden (Gast) (B)
needles and thread (guests) (R)
Nähmaschinen – Reparaturen (T)
sewing machines – repairs (POM)
Notariatsgebühren (Honorare) (V)
notary fees (A&G)
Notenblatt (F & B) music-sheet
(F & B)
Notizblöcke (B); (F & B) desk pads
(R); (F & B)

Obligationszinsen (Zinsaufw.)
bond interest (Int. Exp.)
Obst (Gäste) (B) fruit (guests) (R)
Overall (B) overall (R)
Oxal-Kleesäure (Hotelwäscherei)
oxalic acid (house laundry)
Öl (zum Weiterverkauf) (Garage
und Parkplatz – Warenkosten)
oil (resale) (garage and parking –
cost of sales)
Öle und Schmierfette (T) oil and
greases – lubrication (POM)

Pachtbesitz, Mietbesitz,
Miet-Pachtland, Mietgrundstück
– Abschreibung (A) leasehold
amortization (D&A)
Packpapier (B); (F & B); (V)
wrapping paper (R); (F & B);
(A&G)
Paketpostversicherung (V)
insurance – parcel post (A&G)
Pannenservice, Service bei
Betriebsstörungen (T)
breakdown service (POM)
Papier – Küche (F & B) paper –
cooking (F & B)
Papierbecher (F & B);
(Geschenkladen) paper cups
(F & B); (gift shop)
Papierbeutel (F & B) paper bags
(F & B)
Papierhandtücher (Angestellte) (B);
(F & B); (V) paper towels
(employees) (R); (F & B); (A&G)
Papierhandtücher (Gäste) (B);
(F & B) paper towels (guests) (R);
(F & B)
Pappschachtel (F & B) cardboard
box (F & B)
Parken, kostenloses (B)
complimentary parking (R)
Pensionen (zusätzliche,
lohnabhängige
(Personal-)Kosten) pensions
(PTEB)
Pergament (F & B) parchment (F & B)
Personalbeherbergung (V); (P)
employee lodging (A&G); (HR)
Personalverpflegung (B); (F & B)
employee meals (R); (F & B)
Pfannen, Tiegel (F & B) pans (F & B)
Pflanze (B); (F & B) plant (R);
(F & B)
Pizzaschachteln (F & B) pizza boxes
(F & B)
Plakat – Sicherheitshinweise (V)
poster – safety (A&G)
Plakat, (Anschlag-)Zettel (MKT)
placard (MKT)
Platzkarte (B) place card (R)
Polier- und Reinigungsmasse (B);
(F & B) buffing compound (R);
(F & B)

**Poliermittel für Messing (B);
(F & B)** brass polish (R); (F & B)
Politur – Fußboden (B); (F & B)
polish – floor (R); (F & B)
**Polsterei – Hilfs- und
Betriebsstoffe (T)** upholstery –
supplies (POM)
Portiere, Türvorhang (T) portiere
(POM)
**Porto, Postgebühr, Postspesen
(V)** postage (A&G)
Porzellan für Hotelzimmer (B)
china – guestroom use (R)
**Porzellan für Umsatzbereich
Speisen (F & B)** china – F & B
use (F & B)
Postbriefbeutel (V) mail bag
(A&G)
Postfach – Mietaufwendungen (V)
post office box (P.O.B) – rentals
(A&G)
**Postkarten – zum Weiterverkauf
(Miet- und sonstige Erträge –
Warenkosten)** postcards – for
resale **(rentals and other income
– cost of sales)**
Postkarten (Gäste) (B) postcards
(guests) (R)
**Preis für Verbesserungsvorschlag
– Angestellte (P)** suggestion
award – employees **(HR)**
**Preise und Prämien – Angestellte
(P); (V)** awards – employees
(HR); (A & G)
Presse (F & B) squeezer (F & B)
Provisionen – Getränke (F & B)
commissions – beverage (F & B)
**Provisionen – Kreditkartenkosten
(V)** commissions – credit card
charge (A & G)
Provisionen für Angestellte (F & B)
commissions (employees) (F & B)
**Provisionen für
Bedienungspersonal (F & B)**
servers' commissions (F & B)
**Provisionen für Reiseagenturen
(B)** commissions – tour agencies
(R)
**Provisionen für Zimmervermittlung
(B)** commissions – rental agents
(R)

Puddingschalen (F & B) custard
cups (F & B)
**Puder-, Staubzuckerverzierung
(F & B)** icing sugar decoration
(F & B)
Pumpenreparaturen (T) pump
repairs (POM)
Pyjama, Schlafanzug (Gäste) (B)
pajamas (guests) (R)

Quasten, Troddeln (T) tassels
(POM)

Radiergummis (B); (F & B); (V)
erasers (R); (F & B); (A&G)
Radiowecker – Reparaturen (T)
clock radios – repairs (POM)
Rahmen (Bild) (T) frame (picture)
(POM)
**Ramequin, Käseauflauf (Geschirr)
(F & B)** ramekin (F & B)
Rasierklingen (Gäste) (B) razor
blades (guests) (R)
Räucherapparat (B); (F & B)
fumigator (R); (F & B)
Raumverteilungsplan (B) floor plan
(R)
**Rechenmaschine – laufende
Instandhaltung (T)** calculator –
maintenance (POM)
**Rechenschaftsbericht des
Nachtbuchhalters (V)** night
auditors' report (A&G)
Rechtsberatungskosten (V) legal
expenses (A&G)
Regenmantel (B) raincoat (R)
Regenschirme (für Türsteher) (B)
umbrellas (for door attendants) (R)
**Registrierkasse – Hilfs- und
Betriebsstoffe (B); (F & B)** cash
register – supplies (R); (F & B)
Registrierkasse – Reparaturen (T)
cash register – repairs (POM)
**Reinigung – Hilfs- und
Betriebsstoffe (B); (F & B)**
cleaning – supplies (R); (F & B)
**Reinigungsapparat und
Wasserenthärter (T)** purifier
and softener for water (POM)
Reinigungsflüssigkeit (B); (F & B)
cleaning fluid (R); (F & B)

Reinigungslappen (B); (F & B)
cleaning rags (R); (F & B)
Reinigungsmasse (B); (F & B)
cleaning compound (R); (F & B)
Reinigungsmittel, Waschmittel (B); (F & B) detergents (R); (F & B)
Reiseagentur – Provision (B) tour agency – commission (R)
Reisebüro – Provision (B) travel agent – commission (R)
Reisekosten für die wirtschaftliche Förderung (MKT) traveling expenses – business promotion (MKT)
Reisekosten (V) traveling expenses (A&G)
Reklamebeilage (zu Werbebriefen) (MKT) stuffer (MKT)
Reservierungsformulare (B) reservation forms (R)
Reservierungskosten (B) reservation expenses (R)
Restauranthinweisschild (F & B) restaurant sign (F & B)
Revision, Rechnungsprüfung, Buchprüfung, Jahresabschlußprüfung – Gebühren (V) audit fees (A&G)
Rohrleitung (T) tube (POM)
Rohrleitungen – Reparaturen (T) pipe – repairs (POM)
Rolladen, Rollo (T) blind (POM)
Room Service – Bestellformulare (F & B) room service – order blanks (F & B)
Rouleaus, Jalousien – Reinigung (B); (F & B) window shades – cleaning (R); (F & B)
Röhre, pneumatische (Rohrpost) – Reparaturen (T) pneumatic tube – repairs (POM)
Rundfunkübertragung (MKT) radio broadcasting (MKT)
Rupfen, grobe Leinwand, Sackleinen (T) burlap (POM)
Rührholz, Rührlöffel (F & B) stirrer (F & B)
Rührlöffel für Getränke – Glas (F & B) beverage stirrers – glass (F & B)

Safeschlüssel, Geldschrankschlüssel (B) safe deposit box keys (R)
Sägemehl, Sägespäne (F & B) saw dust (F & B)
Salatschüsseln (F & B) salad bowls (F & B)
Salz (Hotelwäscherei) salt (house laundry)
Sand – Feuereimer (V) sand – fire buckets (A&G)
Sand (T) sand (POM)
Sandpapier (T) sandpaper (POM)
sanitäre Überprüfung – privat (F & B) sanitary inspection – private (F & B)
Säure (B; F & B) acid (R; F & B)
Schablone, Matrize (B); (F & B); (V) stencil (R); (F & B); (A&G)
Schachteln – Konditorwaren, Backwaren, Torten, Pasteten (F & B) boxes – pastry (F & B)
Schachteln – Wäsche (Hotelwäscherei) boxes – laundry (house laundry)
Schallplatte (F & B) record (F & B)
Schaufeln (T) shovels (POM)
Scheck (V) bank check (A&G)
Scheren (B); (F & B); (V) scissors (R); (F & B); (A&G)
Schilder – auf dem Hotelgelände (MKT) signs – road (on premises) (MKT)
Schilder – Landstraße (nicht auf dem Hotelgelände) (MKT) signs – road (off premises) (MKT)
Schlüssel – Reparaturen (T) key – repairs (POM)
Schlüssel für Tresorfach, Stahlfach, Geldschrank (B) key for safe deposit boxes (R)
Schmiermittel, Schmierfett (T) grease (POM)
Schmieröl und Schmierfett (Garage und Parkplatz) lubricating oil and greases (garage and parking)
Schneebesen (F & B) eggbeaters (F & B)
Schneeräumung (T) snow removal (POM)
Schnittblumen (B) cut flowers (R)

Schonbezüge – Matratzen (B)
protectors – mattresses (**R**)
Schornstein – Reparaturen (T)
smoke stack – repairs (**POM**)
Schönheitsmittel, kosmetische Mittel (B) cosmetics (**R**)
Schöpflöffel (F & B) ladles (**F & B**)
Schuhputzlappen (Gäste) (B) shoe cloths (guests) (**R**)
Schutt, Müll (T) waste (**POM**)
Schüsseln – Porzellan, Glas, Salat (F & B) bowls – china, glass, salad (**F & B**)
Schwämme – Maler (T) sponges – painters (**POM**)
Schwämme – Reinigung (B); (F & B) sponges – cleaning (**R**); (**F & B**)
Seife für Reinigungszwecke (B); (F & B) soap for cleaning (**R**); (**F & B**)
Seife (Gäste) (B) soap (guests) (**R**)
Seiher, Sieb, Filter – Küche (F & B) strainer – kitchen (**F & B**)
Seil, Strick (T) rope (**POM**)
Servierplatten (F & B) platters (**F & B**)
Servietten – Papier (F & B) napkins – paper (**F & B**)
Servietten, Deckchen – Leinen (B); (F & B) doilies – linen (**R**); (**F & B**)
Shaker – Getränke (F & B) shaker – beverages (**F & B**)
Sicherheitszündhölzer (Gäste) (B); (F & B) safety matches (guests) (**R**); (**F & B**)
Sicherung des Hotels – Personal von Vertragsfirmen (V) security – contracted (**A&G**)
Sicherungen (T) fuses (**POM**)
Sieb, Seiher (F & B) colander (**F & B**)
Silber-Reinigungsmittel (F & B) silver cleaner (**F & B**)
Sitzplan (F & B) seating list (**F & B**)
Soda, kohlensaures Natrium (Hotelwäscherei) soda – laundry (**house laundry**)
Sonderaufwendungen für Arbeitnehmer (zusätzliche, lohnabhängige

(Personal-)Kosten) employee benefits (**PTEB**)
Sonnenschutz (Schirm) (T) sunshade (**POM**)
Soziale- und Sport-Veranstaltungen – Angestellte (P) social and sports activities – employees (**HR**)
Speise(n)karte (F&B) bill of fare, menu (**F & B**)
Spiegel-, Fensterglasversicherung (MVV) insurance – plate glass (**RTI**)
Spielkarten (B); (F & B) playing cards (**R**); (**F & B**)
Spielplatz – Instandhaltung (T) playground – maintenance (**POM**)
Spielzeug (B) toys (**R**)
Spitzenvorhänge (T) lace curtains (**POM**)
Sportgeräte für Angestellte (P); (V) athletic equipment for employees (**HR**); (**A&G**)
Spüllappen (B) wash cloth (**R**)
Stahlwolle (B); (F & B) steel wool (**R**); (**F & B**)
Stand – Messen und Ausstellungen (MKT) booth – trade shows (**MKT**)
Stangen – Vorhänge (T) poles – curtains (**POM**)
Stärke (Wäsche) (Hotelwäscherei) starch (**house laundry**)
Staubmop (B); (F & B) dust brush (**R**); (**F & B**)
Staubsaugerzubehör (B) vacuum cleaner accessories (**R**)
Staubtuch, Staublappen (B); (F & B) dust cloth (**R**); (**F & B**)
Staubtuch, Staublappen, Staubwedel (B); (F & B) duster (**R**); (**F & B**)
Stechuhr – Reparaturen (T) time clock – repairs (**POM**)
Stellenvermittlungsbüro (Beiträge) (P) employment agency fees (**HR**)
Stempelkissen (B); (F&B); (V) stamp pad (**R**); (**F&B**); (**A&G**)
Stöpsel, Propf (F & B) stopper (**F & B**)
Straße – Besprengen, Besprühen (T) street sprinkling (**POM**)

Straßenhinweisschild (MKT) road sign (**MKT**)
Straßenreinigung (T) street cleaning (**POM**)
Streichhölzer (Gäste) (B); (F & B) matches (guests) (**R**); (**F & B**)
Strohhalme – Bar (F & B) straws – bar (**F & B**)
Strom für Kühlung, Kälteerzeugung (Kochnischen in Apts.) (B) electricity for refrigerators (in kitchenette apts.) (**R**)
Strom, elektrischer (E) electric current (**EC**)
Suppentopf – Reparaturen (T) stock pot – repairs (**POM**)
Süßigkeit (B); (F & B) candy (guests) (**R**); (**F & B**)
Swimmingpool – Chemikalien, chemische Präparate (T) pool – chemicals (**POM**)
Swimmingpool – Zubehör (T) pool – accessories (**POM**)
Szenerie, Bühnenbildausstattung (Bankette) (F & B) scenery rental for public rooms (banquets) (**F & B**)

Tagesbericht (V) daily report (**A&G**)
Tantiemen und Gehaltsprämien – Angestellte (B); (F & B) bonuses – employees (**R**); (**F & B**)
Tantiemen, Ertragsgewinnanteil (F & B) royalties (**F & B**)
Tanzerlaubnis (F & B) dance license (**F & B**)
Tapete (T) wall paper (**POM**)
Taschenlampen und Batterien (T) flashlights and batteries (**POM**)
Technische Abteilung – Hilfs- und Betriebsstoffe (Z) engineering supplies (**POM**)
Teekannen (F & B) tea pots (**F & B**)
Teer (T) tar (**POM**)
Teigrührmaschinen (F & B) batter mixers (**F & B**)
Teigschüsseln (F & B) batter bowls (**F & B**)
Telefon – Buchungsbeleg (Telefon) telephone voucher (**telephone**)
Telefonanlage – Mietaufwendungen (MVV) telephone rentals (**RTI**)
Telefonanlagekosten (MVV) telephone equipment charges (**RTI**)
Telefonbuch – Werbung (MKT) telephone directory – advertising (**MKT**)
Telefonbücher (B) telephone directories (**R**)
Telefongebühren (Telefon – vom Hotel zu bezahlende Beträge) telephone charges (**telephone – cost of sales**)
Telefonzentrale – Reparaturen (T) switchboard – repairs (**POM**)
Telegramm (V) telegram (**A&G**)
Telegrammadresse, eingetragene (V) registered cable address (**A&G**)
Teller für Brot und Butter (F & B) bread and butter plates (**F & B**)
Teller (F & B) plates (**F & B**)
Teppiche und Bettvorleger – Reinigung (B) carpets and rugs – cleaning (**R**)
Teppiche, Läufer etc. – Reparaturkosten (T) carpet repairs (**POM**)
Teppichkehrmaschine (B); (F & B) carpet sweeper (**R**); (**F & B**)
Teppichstift (T) carpet tack (**POM**)
Terpentin (T) terpentine (**POM**)
(Tinten-)Löscher (B) blotter (**R**)
Tischtücher (F & B) table cloths (**F & B**)
Tischwäsche – Ersatzbeschaffung (in Kochnische-Apts.) (B) table linen – replacements (in kitchenette apts.) (**R**)
Tockeneis (F & B) dry ice (**F & B**)
Treppenhaus – Reparaturen (T) stairway – repairs (**POM**)
Treuhänder – Aufwendungen (V) trustee's expenses (**A&G**)
Trinkgelder und Weihnachtsgeschenke (V) gratuities and christmas presents (**A&G**)
Trinkgläser (B) drinking glasses (**R**)

Türschloß – Reparaturen (T) lock
– repairs **(POM)**
Türvorhänge (T) door hangings
(POM)
**Tüte für Back- und
Konditoreiwaren (Papier)
(F & B)** pastry bag (paper) **(F & B)**

Umfrage (F & B) survey – special
(F & B)
(Um-)Rührlöffel, Rührstab (F & B)
muddler **(F & B)**
Umsatzsteuer (MVV) sales tax **(RTI)**
uneinbringliche Forderungen (V)
bad debts **(A&G)**
**Unfallversicherung (zusätzliche,
lohnabhängige (Personal-)
Kosten)** insurance – accident
(PTEB)
Uniformjacke (B); (F & B) blouse
(R); (F & B)
**Unterhaltung – Vertragsfirmen
(F & B)** contract entertainment
(F & B)
Unterhaltung und Musik (F & B)
entertainment and music **(F & B)**
Unterhaltungsprogramm (F & B)
program – entertainment **(F & B)**
Untertassen (F & B) saucers **(F & B)**
Übernachtung, kostenlose (MKT)
complimentary rooms **(MKT)**
Überweisungsgebühren (V)
transfer fees **(A&G)**

Vase (B); (F & B) vase **(R); (F & B)**
**Ventilator, elektrischer –
Reparaturen (T)** electric fan –
repairs **(POM)**
**Ventil, Absperrvorrichtung, Klappe
– Reparaturen (T)** valve –
repairs **(POM)**
**Veranstaltungsräume (öffentlich
genutzte Räume) – Reinigung
(Vertragsfirmen) – Bankette
(F & B)** public rooms cleaning (on
contract) – banquets **(F & B)**
**Veräußerungsgewinne aus dem
Verkauf von Anlagevermögen
(Gewinne und Verluste aus
Anlageverkäufen)** gain on sale
of property **(gain or loss on sale
of property)**
**Veräußerungsverluste aus dem
Verkauf von Anlagevermögen
(Gewinne und Verluste aus
Anlageverkäufen)** loss on sale
of property **(gain or loss on sale
of property)**
**Verbrennungsofen – Reparaturen
(T)** incinerator – repairs **(POM)**
**Verbrennungsrückstände –
Beseitigungskosten (T)** ashes –
removal **(POM)**
**Vereinigungen – Gebühren und
Beiträge (V)** associations – dues
(A&G)
Verkaufsausrüstung (MKT) sales
kits **(MKT)**
Vermögenssteuer (MVV) personal
property tax **(RTI)**
**Verpackung – Hilfs- und
Betriebsstoffe (Geschenk-
laden)** packing supplies **(gift
shop)**
Verpackung (T) packing **(POM)**
Verpflegung, kostenlose (MKT)
complimentary food **(MKT)**
**Versandkosten für Lebensmittel
und Getränke (F & B)**
transportation charges on food and
beverage **(F & B)**
**Versicherung – Berufshaftpflicht
(zusätzliche, lohnabhängige
(Personal-)Kosten)** insurance –
workers' compensation **(PTEB)**
**Versicherung – Berufskrankheiten
(zusätzliche, lohnabhängige
(Personal-)Kosten)** insurance –
occupational disease **(PTEB)**
**Versicherung –
Betriebsunterbrechung (V)**
insurance – use and occupancy
(A&G)
Versicherung – Diebstahl (V)
insurance – theft **(A&G)**
Versicherung – Kassenraub (V)
insurance – robbery **(A&G)**
**Versicherung –
Krankenhausaufenthalt (nicht
gewerkschaftlich organisierte
Arbeitnehmer) (zusätzliche,**

lohnabhängige (Personal-)Kosten) insurance – hospitalization (non union employees) **(PTEB)**
Versicherung – Wetter (MVV) insurance – weather **(RTI)**
Vervielfältigungs- und Kopierarbeiten (V) duplicating and copying services **(A&G)**
Visitenkarten (B); (F & B) business cards **(R); (F & B)**
Voreröffnungskosten (A) preopening expenses **(D&A)**
Vorhänge – Hilfs- und Betriebsstoffe (B) curtains – supplies **(R)**
Vorhangreinigung (B) curtain cleaning **(R)**

Wachs (B); (F & B) wax **(R); (F & B)**
Wachspapier (F & B) wax paper **(F & B)**
Wandbehang (T) wall hanging **(POM)**
Wandbehang, Wandbekleidung, Tapete, Vorhang – Reparaturen (T) hanging – repairs **(POM)**
Warenanforderungsscheine – Berichte (F & B) storeroom issue – reports **(F & B)**
Warenanforderungsscheine (F & B) storeroom orders **(F & B)**
Wartungsvertrag (T) maintenance contract **(POM)**
Wäsche (B); (F & B) laundry **(R); (F & B)**
Wäschesäcke (Hotelwäscherei) laundry bags **(house laundry)**
Waschlappen (B) face cloth **(R)**
Waschpulver (B); (F & B) soap powder **(R); (F & B)**
Waschpulver, Waschmittel (B) washing powder **(R)**
Wasserglas (B); (F & B) tumbler **(R); (F & B)**
Weihnachtsfest – Kosten (V) christmas expenses **(A&G)**
Weihnachtsgeschenke – Angestellte (P) christmas gifts – employees **(HR)**
Weinkeller – Geräte, Gerätschaften (F & B) wine cellar – utensils **(F & B)**
Weinkeller – Hilfs- und Betriebsstoffe (F & B) wine cellar – supplies **(F & B)**
Weiter- und Fortbildung von Angestellten (V) educational activities for employees **(A&G)**
Werbeausgaben für Adressbücher, Einwohnerverzeichnisse (MKT) advertising – directories **(MKT)**
Werbeausgaben für Anzeigen (MKT) advertising – announcements **(MKT)**
Werbeausgaben für Außenwerbung, Straßenwerbung (MKT) advertising – outdoor **(MKT)**
Werbeausgaben für Beförderungskosten (MKT) advertising – transportation **(MKT)**
Werbeausgaben für Postwurfsendungen (MKT) advertising – direct mail **(MKT)**
Werbeausgaben für Radio und Fernsehen (MKT) advertising – Radio & TV **(MKT)**
Werbeausgaben für Werbegeschenkartikel (MKT) advertising – novelties **(MKT)**
Werbeausgaben für Werbeliteratur (MKT) advertising – publications **(MKT)**
Werbebroschüren (MKT) advrtising – booklets **(MKT)**
Werbegeschenkartikel (MKT) novelties (advertising) **(MKT)**
Werbematerial (Verkaufsförderung) (MKT) literature (promotional) **(MKT)**
Werbung in Tageszeitungen (MKT) newspaper advertising **(MKT)**
Werkzeuge (T) tools **(POM)**
Wetzstein, Gerät zum Messerschärfen (F & B) knife sharpening **(F & B)**
Winkeleisen (T) angle iron **(POM)**

**wirtschaftliche Förderung, Verkaufsförderung –
Reisekosten (MKT)** business promotion – traveling expenses (MKT)

Zahnbürsten (B) toothbrushes **(R)**
Zahnstocher (F & B) toothpicks **(F & B)**
Zeichentinte, Wäschetinte (Hotelwäscherei) marking ink – laundry **(house laundry)**
Zeitschriftenwerbung (MKT) magazine advertising **(MKT)**
Zeitung für (Zeitungs-)Ausschnitte (MKT) newspaper for clippings **(MKT)**
Zeitungen und Zeitschriften (für Angestellte) (P) house publications (for employees) **(HR)**
Zeitungen (zum Weiterverkauf) (Miet- und sonstige Erträge – Warenkosten) newspapers (for resale) **(rentals and other income – cost of sales)**
Zeitungsausschnitte (MKT) clippings **(MKT)**
Zellophan (F & B) cellophane **(F & B)**
Zement (T) cement **(POM)**
Zinsaufwendungen für rückständige Steuern (Zinsaufw.) interest on taxes in arrears **(Int. Exp.)**
Zinsaufwendungen (Zinsaufw.) interest **(Int. Exp.)**
Zinsen auf Schuldwechsel (Zinsaufw.) interest on notes **(Int. Exp.)**
Zirkular, Rundschreiben (MKT) circular **(MKT)**
Zitronenöl (B); (F & B) lemon oil **(R); (F & B)**
Zitronenpresse – Bar (F & B) lemon squeezer – bar **(F & B)**

Teil IV
Verzeichnis aller Aufwendungen (USAH)
Englisch – Deutsch

Part IV
Expense and Payroll Dictionary (USAH)
English – German

Teil IV: **Verzeichnis aller Aufwendungen (USAH)**
Englisch – Deutsch
Part IV: Expense and Payroll Dictionary (USAH)
English – German

Abbreviations

english:

D & A	depreciation and amortization
R	rooms
EC	energy cost
F & B	food and beverage
MKT	marketing
HR	human resources
POM	property, operation, and maintenance
Trans.	transportation
A & G	administrative and general
Int. Exp.	interest expense
PTEB	payroll taxes and employee benefits

german:

A	Abschreibungen
B	Beherbergung
E	Energie
F & B	Food und Beverage
MKT	Marketing
P	Personal
T	Technische Abteilung
Trans.	Transport
V	Verwaltung
Zinsaufw.	Zinsaufwendungen
zusätzliche, lohnabhängige (Personal-)Kosten	ohne Abkürzung

accountant's fee (A&G) Honorar
(n) für Wirtschafts- und
Buchprüfer *(m)* **(V)**
acid (R); (F & B) Säure *(f)* **(B); (F & B)**
adding machine – service (POM)
Kundendienstkosten *(pl.)* für
Addiermaschine *(f)* **(T)**
adding machine – tape (POM)
Addiermaschine *(f)* – Papierstreifen
(m) **(T)**
**addressing machine – supplies
(MKT)** Adressiermaschine *(f)* –
Hilfs- und Betriebsstoffe *(pl. m)*
(MKT)
adhesive tape (POM); (A&G)
Heftpflaster *(n)* **(T); (V)**
**advertising – announcements
(MKT)** Werbeausgaben *(pl. f)* für
Anzeigen *(pl. f)* **(MKT)**
advertising – direct mail (MKT)
Werbeausgaben *(pl. f)* für
Postwurfsendungen *(pl. f)* **(MKT)**
advertising – directories (MKT)
Werbeausgaben für Adressbücher
(pl. n), Einwohnerverzeichnisse
(pl. n) **(MKT)**
advertising – novelties (MKT)
Werbeausgaben *(pl. f)* für
Werbegeschenkartikel *(pl. m)*
(MKT)
advertising – out door (MKT)
Werbeausgaben *(pl. f)* für
Außenwerbung *(f)*, Straßenwerbung
(f) **(MKT)**
advertising – publications (MKT)
Werbeausgaben *(pl. f)* für
Werbeliteratur *(f)* **(MKT)**
advertising – radio & tv (MKT)
Werbeausgaben *(pl. f)* für Radio *(n)*
und Fernsehen *(n)* **(MKT)**
**advertising – transportation
(MKT)** Werbeausgaben *(pl. f)* für
Beförderungskosten *(pl.)* **(MKT)**
advertising agency fee (MKT)
Honorar *(n)* für Werbeagentur *(f)*
(MKT)
advertising booklet (MKT)
Werbebroschüre *(f)* **(MKT)**
**air cooling system – repairs
(POM)** Luftkühlung *(f)* –
Reparaturen *(pl. f)* **(T)**

**airport transportation – not
chargeable to guest (A&G);
(MKT)** Beförderungkosten *(pl.)*
für Transport *(m)* zum Flughafen
(m), die dem Gast *(m)* nicht
berechnet werden können **(V)**
**alarm service – fire and burglar
(A&G); (R); (F & B)**
Alarmvorrichtungen *(pl. f)* – Feuer
(n) und Einbruch *(m)* **(V)**
alcohol – cleaning (R); (F & B)
Alkohol *(m)* – Reinigungszwecke
(pl. m) **(B); (F & B)**
alcohol – cooking fuel (F & B)
Alkohol *(m)* – Brennstoff *(m)* für
Kochgeräte *(pl. n)* **(F & B)**
alkalies (water softener) (POM)
Alkali *(n)*, Laugensalz *(n)*,
alkalischer Stoff *(m)*
(Wasserenthärtungsmittel) **(T)**
aluminum trays (F & B)
Aluminiumtabletts *(pl. n)* **(F & B)**
ammonia – cleaning (R); (F & B)
Ammoniak *(n)* – Reinigungszwecke
(pl. m) **(B); (F & B)**
ammonia – refrigerant (POM)
Ammoniak *(n)* – Kühlmittel *(n)* **(T)**
**amortization – bond issue (Int.
Exp.)** Abschreibung *(f)* –
Emissionsdisagio *(n)* **(Zinsaufw.)**
**amortization – financing costs (Int.
Exp.)** Abschreibung *(f)* –
Finanzierungskosten *(pl.)*
(Zinsaufw.)
**amortization – leasehold
improvements (D&A)**
Abschreibung *(f)* – Einbauten
(pl. m) in gemieteten (geleasten)
Objekten *(pl. n)* **(A)**
amortization – leasehold (D&A)
Abschreibung *(f)* – geleaste
Gebäude *(pl. n)*, Mietbesitz *(m)* **(A)**
angle iron (POM) Winkeleisen *(n)* **(T)**
armored car service (A&G)
(Gebühren für) gepanzerte
Fahrzeuge *(pl. n)* **(V)**
art work (MKT) Illustration *(f)*,
Grafik *(f)* **(MKT)**
artificial flowers (R); (F & B)
künstliche Blumen *(pl. f)* **(B);
(F & B)**

ash can (POM) Aschekasten *(m)*,
Abfalleimer *(m)*, Mülleimer *(m)* **(T)**
ash trays (R); (F & B) Aschenbecher
(pl.m) **(B); (F & B)**
ashes – removal (POM)
Verbrennungsrückstände *(pl.m)* –
Beseitigungskosten *(pl.)* **(T)**
associations – dues (A&G)
Vereinigungen *(pl.f)* – Gebühren
(pl.f) und Beiträge *(pl.m)* **(V)**
**athletic equipment for employees
(HR); (A&G)** Sportgeräte *(pl.n)*
für Angestellte *(pl.)* **(P); (V)**
attorney's fees (A&G)
Anwaltskosten *(pl.)* **(V)**
audit fees (A&G) Gebühren *(pl.f)*
für Revision *(f)*, Rechnungsprüfung
(f), Buchprüfung *(f)*,
Jahresabschlußprüfung *(f)* **(V)**
auto rental (A&G); (MKT) Kosten
(pl.) für Mietwagen *(m)* **(V);
(MKT)**
**auto repairs – guest use (Trans.);
(R)** Autoreparaturkosten *(pl.)* –
Gäste **(Trans.); (B)**
**auto repairs – property use
(Trans.); (POM)**
Autoreparaturkosten *(pl.)* – Hotel
(Trans.); (T)
**autosupplies – sold to guests
(garage – cost of sales)**
Kraftfahrzeugbedarf *(m)* (z.B. Öl)
– Gäste **(Garage – Warenkosten)**
**autosupplies – used by property
(Trans.)** Kraftfahrzeugbedarf *(m)*
– Hotel **(Trans.)**
awards – employees (HR) Preise
(pl.m) und Prämien *(pl.f)* –
Angestellte *(pl.)* **(P); (V)**
awnings – cleaning (R); (F & B)
Markisen *(pl.f)* – Reinigung *(f)*
(B); (F & B)
awnings – repairs (R); (F & B)
Markisen *(pl.f)* – Reparaturen
(pl.f) **(B); (F & B)**

bad debts (A&G) uneinbringliche
Forderungen *(pl.f)* **(V)**
badges (R); (F & B) Abzeichen
(pl.n), Kennzeichen *(pl.n)* **(B);
(F & B)**

bag (house laundry) Wäschesack
(m) **(Hotelwäscherei)**
ball bearning (POM) Kugellager *(n)*
(T)
band saw (POM) Bandsäge *(f)* **(T)**
bank check (A&G) Scheck *(m)*
(Bank) **(V)**
banner (R); (F & B) Banner *(n)*,
Fahne *(f)* **(B); (F & B)**
banquet report (F & B)
Bankettbericht *(m)* **(F & B)**
bar – utensils (F & B) Bar *(f)* –
Geräte *(pl.n)* **(F & B)**
bath mats (R) Badematten *(pl.f)*
(B)
bathing caps (guests) (R)
Badehüten *(pl.f)* (Gäste) **(B)**
bathroom – glass shelve (POM)
Glasregal *(n)* – Badezimmer *(n)*
(T)
batter bowls (F & B) Teigschüsseln
(pl.f) **(F & B)**
batter mixers (F & B)
Teigrührmaschinen *(pl.f)* **(F & B)**
batteries and flashlights (POM)
Batterien *(pl.f)* und Taschenlampen
(pl.f) **(T)**
bed spreads (R) Bettdecken *(pl.f)*,
Tagesdecken *(pl.f)* **(B)**
bed springs (POM) Bettenroste
(pl.m) **(T)**
beeper rental (A&G) Mietkosten
(pl.) für Beeper *(m)* **(V)**
belt (POM) Treibriemen *(m)*,
Förderband *(n)* **(T)**
benzine-cleaning (R)
Benzin-Reinigung *(f)* **(B)**
beverage license (F & B)
Lizenzgebühr *(f)* für
Getränkeausschank *(m)* **(F & B)**
beverage mixer (F & B)
Getränkemixer *(m)* **(F & B)**
beverage stirrers – glass (F & B)
Rührlöffel *(pl.m)* für Getränke
(pl.n) – Glas *(n)* **(F & B)**
beverage tax (F & B) Getränkesteuer
(f) **(F & B)**
bill of fare (F & B) Speise(n)karte *(f)*
(F & B)
billboard (MKT) Anschlagbrett *(n)*
(MKT)

bin cards – liquor (F & B)
Lagerfachkarten *(pl.f)* –
Spirituosen *(pl.f)* **(F & B)**
binder (R); (F & B); (A & G)
Aktendeckel *(m)*, Einband *(m)* **(B)**;
(F & B); (V)
blankets (R) Decken *(pl.f)* **(B)**
bleach (house laundry)
Bleichmittel *(n)* **(Hotelwäscherei)**
blind (POM) Rolladen *(m)*, Rollo *(n)*
(T)
blotter (R) (Tinten-)Löscher **(B)**
blouse (R); (F & B) Uniformjacke *(f)*
(B); (F & B)
blueprint (MKT) Blaupause *(f)*
(MKT)
boiler – repairs (POM) Boiler *(m)* –
Reparaturen *(pl.f)* **(T)**
boiler compound (POM)
Kesselstein-Schutzmittel *(n)* **(T)**
boiler explosion insurance (RTI)
Dampfkessel-Explosionsversicherung
(f) **(MVV)**
boiler gauge (POM)
Boilermanometer *(n)* **(T)**
boiler inspection (POM)
Boilerinspektion *(f)* **(T)**
bond discount (Int. Exp.)
Emissionsdisagio *(n)*, Abschlag *(m)*
auf den Anleihekurs *(m)*
(Zinsaufw.)
**bond expense amortization (Int.
Exp.)** Abschreibung *(f)* auf
Kosten *(pl.)* der Anleiheemission
(f) **(Zinsaufw.)**
bond fidelity (A & G)
Kautionsverpflichtung *(f)* des
Versicherers *(m)* im Falle *(m)* von
Veruntreuung *(f)* **(V)**
bond interest (Int. Exp.)
Obligationszinsen *(pl.m)*
(Zinsaufw.)
bonuses – employees (R); (F & B)
Tantiemen *(pl.f)* und
Gehaltsprämien *(pl.f)* – Angestellte
(pl.) **(B); (F & B)**
booth – trade shows (MKT) Stand
(m) – Messen *(pl.f)* und
Ausstellungen *(pl.f)* **(MKT)**
bottle openers (R) Flaschenöffner
(pl.m) **(B)**

boutonnieres (R) Ansteckblumen
(pl.f), Anstecksträußchen *(pl.n)* **(B)**
**bowls – china, glass, salad
(F & B)** Schüsseln *(pl.f)* –
Porzellan *(n)*, Glas *(n)*, Salat *(m)*
(F & B)
boxes – laundry (house laundry)
Schachteln *(pl.f)* – Wäsche *(f)*
(Hotelwäscherei)
boxes – pastry (F & B) Schachteln
(pl.f) – Konditorwaren *(pl.f)*,
Backwaren *(pl.f)*, Torten *(pl.f)*,
Pasteten *(pl.f)* **(F & B)**
braid for uniforms (R); (F & B)
Borte *(f)*, Litze *(f)*, Tresse *(f)*,
Zierband *(n)*, Flechtschnur *(f)* für
Uniformen *(pl.f)* **(F & B)**
brass polish (R); (F & B)
Poliermittel *(n)* für Messing *(n)*
(B); (F & B)
bread and butter plates (F & B)
Teller *(pl.m)* für Brot *(n)* und
Butter *(f)* **(F & B)**
breakdown service (POM)
Pannenservice *(m)*, Service *(m)* bei
Betriebsstörungen *(pl.f)* **(T)**
briquet (F & B) Brikett *(n)*,
Presskohle *(f)* **(F & B)**
broad casting (MKT)
Rundfunkübertragung *(f)* **(MKT)**
brochure (MKT) Broschüre *(f)*,
Werbematerial *(n)* **(MKT)**
broom (R); (F & B) Besen *(m)* **(B);
(F & B)**
buffing compound (R); (F & B)
Polier- und Reinigungsmasse *(f)*
(B); (F & B)
**building repairs – outside contract
(POM)** Gebäudereparaturen *(pl.f)*
– Fremdaufträge *(pl.m)* **(T)**
building repairs (POM)
Gebäudereparaturen *(pl.f)* **(T)**
**buildings and contents insurance
(RTI)** Gebäudeversicherung *(f)*
(MVV)
bunting and flags (R); (F & B)
Flaggentuch *(n)* und Flaggen *(pl.f)*
(B); (F & B)
burglary insurance (A & G)
Einbruchs- und
Diebstahlversicherung *(f)* **(V)**

burlap (POM) grobe Leinwand *(f)*,
   Rupfen *(m)*, Sackleinen *(n)* **(T)**
business cards (R); (F & B)
   Visitenkarten *(pl.f)* **(B); (F & B)**
**business promotion – traveling
   expenses (MKT)** wirtschaftliche
   Förderung *(f)*, Verkaufsförderung
   (f) – Reisekosten *(pl.)* **(MKT)**
**buttons – laundry (house
   laundry)** Knöpfe *(pl. m)* –
   Wäscherei *(f)* **(Hotelwäscherei)**
buttons – uniforms (R); (F & B)
   Knöpfe *(pl. m)* – Uniformen *(pl.f)*
   (B); (F & B)
buttons (guests) (R) Knöpfe *(pl. m)*
   (Gäste) **(B)**

cable television – rental (RTI)
   Kabelfernsehen *(n)* –
   Mietaufwendungen *(pl.f)* **(MVV)**
cables – elevator Kabel *(pl. n)*,
   (Draht-)Seile *(pl. n)* – Aufzug *(m)*
   (T)
calcium (POM) Kalzium *(n)* **(T)**
calculator – maintenance (POM)
   Rechenmaschine *(f)* – laufende
   Instandhaltung *(f)* **(T)**
calendar (MKT) Kalender *(m)*
   (MKT)
can openers (F & B) Büchsenöffner
   (pl. m) **(F & B)**
candles (R); (F & B) Kerzen *(pl.f)*
   (B); (F & B)
candlesticks (R); (F & B)
   Kerzenhalter *(pl. m)*, Kerzenständer
   (pl. m) **(B); (F & B)**
candy (guests) (R); (F & B)
   Süßigkeit *(f)* **(B); (F & B)**
canvas – painting (POM) Leinwand
   (f) – Malerarbeiten *(pl.f)* **(T)**
cap (R) Mütze *(f)* **(B)**
car fare (A&G) Fahrgeld *(n)*,
   Fahrpreis *(m)* **(V)**
carafe (R) Karaffe *(f)* **(B)**
carbon paper (R); (F & B); (A&G)
   Kohlepapier *(n)* **(B); (F & B); (V)**
carbonated gas (F & B) Kohlensäure
   (f) **(F & B)**
cardboard box (F & B)
   Pappschachtel *(f)* **(F & B)**

carpet sweeper (R); (F & B)
   Teppichkkehrmaschine *(f)* **(B);
   (F & B)**
carpet tack (POM) Teppichstift *(m)*
   (T)
carpets – repairs (POM) Teppiche
   (pl. m), Läufer *(pl. m)* –
   Reparaturen *(pl.f)* **(T)**
carpets and rugs – cleaning (R)
   Teppiche *(pl. m)* und Bettvorleger
   (pl. m) – Reinigung *(f)* **(B)**
**cash overage and shortage
   (A&G)** Kassen-Überschuß *(m)*
   und -Fehlbetrag *(m)* **(V)**
cash register – repairs (POM)
   Registrierkasse *(f)* – Reparaturen
   (pl.f) **(T)**
**cash register – supplies (R);
   (F & B)** Registrierkasse *(f)* –
   Hilfs- und Betriebsstoffe *(pl. m)*
   (B); (F & B)
cashier forms (A&G) Formulare
   (pl. n) für den Kassierer *(m)* **(V)**
casserole (F & B) Kasserole *(f)*,
   Auflaufform *(f)* **(F & B)**
caustic soda (R); (F & B) Ätznatron
   (n) **(B); (F & B)**
cellophane (F & B) Zellophan *(n)*
   (F & B)
cement (POM) Zement *(m)* **(T)**
chair rentals – banquets (F & B)
   Mietkosten *(pl.)* für Stühle *(pl. m)*
   – Bankette *(pl. n)* **(F & B)**
chalk (R); (F & B) Kreide *(f)* **(B);
   (F & B)**
chamois (R) Leder *(n)* **(B)**
charcoal (F & B) Holzkohle *(f)* **(F & B)**
charge voucher (R); (F & B)
   Lastschriftzettel *(m)* **(B); (F & B)**
checks – waiter (F & B)
   Gastrechnungen *(pl.f)* – Kellner
   (m) **(F & B)**
**chemicals – fire extinguisher
   (A&G)** Chemikalien *(pl.f)* für
   Feuerlöscher *(m)* **(V)**
chemicals (house laundry)
   Chemikalien *(pl.f)*
   (Hotelwäscherei)
china – F & B use (F & B) Porzellan
   (n) für Umsatzbereich *(m)* Speisen
   (F & B)

china – guestroom use (R)
Porzellan *(n)* für Hotelzimmer *(n)* (**B**)
chintz (POM) Chintz *(m)*, Möbelkattun *(m)* (**T**)
chloride of lime (house laundry) Chlorcalcium *(n)* (**Hotelwäscherei**)
chlorine (POM) Chlor *(n)* (**T**)
christmas expenses (A&G) Kosten *(pl.)* für Weihnachtsfest *(n)* (**V**)
christmas gifts – employees (HR) Weihnachtsgeschenke *(pl. n)* – Angestellte *(pl.)* (**P**)
christmas tree and decorations (R); (F & B) Christbaum *(m)* und Christbaumschmuck *(m)* (**B**); (**F & B**)
circular (MKT) Rundschreiben *(n)* (**MKT**)
civic and community project (MKT) Bürger- und Gemeindeprojekt *(n)* (**MKT**)
cleaning – supplies (R); (F & B) Reinigung *(f)* – Hilfs- und Betriebsstoffe *(pl. m)* (**B**); (**F & B**)
cleaning compound (R); (F & B) Reinigungsmasse *(f)* (**B**); (**F & B**)
cleaning fluid (R); (F & B) Reinigungsflüssigkeit *(f)* (**B**); (**F & B**)
cleaning rags (R); (F & B) Reinigungslappen *(pl. m)* (**B**); (**F & B**)
clinic – employees (HR) Klinik *(f)* – Angestellte *(pl.)* (Arztkosten) (**P**)
clippings (MKT) Zeitungsausschnitte *(pl. m)* (**MKT**)
clock radio – repairs (POM) Radiowecker *(m)* – Reparaturen *(pl. f)* (**T**)
clothes hanger (guests) (R) Kleiderbügel *(m)* (Gäste) (**B**)
clothing repairs – outside establishments (R); (F & B) Kleiderreparaturen *(pl. f)* – Fremdbetriebe *(pl. m)* (**B**); (**F & B**)
coal – cooking (F & B) Kohle *(f)* für Küche *(f)* (**F & B**)
coal – heating (POM) Kohle *(f)* für Heizung *(f)* (**T**)

coal shovel (POM) Kohlenschaufel *(f)* (**T**)
coat hanger (guests) (R) Kleiderbügel *(m)* (Gäste) (**B**)
coat (uniforms) (R); (F & B) Jackett *(n)* für Uniformen *(pl. f)* (**B**); (**F & B**)
cocktail napkins – paper (F & B) Cocktail-Servietten *(pl. f)* – Papier *(n)* (**F & B**)
cocktail shaker (F & B) Cocktailshaker *(m)* (**F & B**)
coffee – free (R) Kaffee *(m)* – kostenlos (**R**)
coffee bag (F & B) Kaffeesack *(m)* (**F & B**)
coffee pots (F & B) Kaffeekannen *(pl. f)* (**F & B**)
coin bag (A&G) Behälter *(m)* für Münzgeld *(n)* (**V**)
colander (F & B) Sieb *(n)*, Seiher *(m)* (**F & B**)
collar (R) Kragen *(m)* (**B**)
collection fees (A&G) Inkasso-Einzugsspesen *(pl.)* (**V**)
color spreads (R) farbige Bettbezüge *(pl. m)* (**B**)
combs (guests) (R) Kämme *(pl. m)* (Gäste) (**B**)
commissions – beverage (F & B) Provisionen *(pl. f)* – Getränke *(pl. n)* (**F & B**)
commissions – credit card charge (A&G) Provisionen *(pl. f)* – Kreditkartenkosten *(pl.)* (**V**)
commissions – F & B employees (F & B) Provisionen *(pl. f)* für Angestellte *(pl.)* (**F & B**)
commissions – rental agents (R) Provisionen *(pl. f)* für Zimmervermittlung *(f)* (**B**)
commissions – tour agencies (R) Provisionen *(pl. f)* für Reiseagenturen *(pl. f)* (**B**)
complimentary beverage – musicians and entertainers (F & B) kostenlose Getränke *(pl. n)* – Musiker *(pl. m)* und Entertainer *(pl. m)* (**F & B**)
complimentary beverage (MKT) kostenlose Getränke *(pl. n)* (**MKT**)

complimentary food (MKT)
kostenlose Verpflegung *(f)* **(MTK)**
complimentary parking (R)
kostenloses Parken *(n)* **(B)**
complimentary rooms (MKT)
kostenlose Übernachtung *(f)* **(MKT)**
compotes (F & B) Kompottschalen *(pl. f)* **(F & B)**
computer printer (RTI)
Computerdrucker *(m)* **(MVV)**
consultant fees (A&G)
Beratungskosten *(pl.)* **(V)**
containers – liquid, paper (F & B)
Container *(pl. m)* – Flüssigkeit *(f)*, Papier *(n)* **(F & B)**
contract – disinfecting (R); (F & B)
Fremdreinigung *(f)* – Desinfektion *(f)*, Entkeimen *(n)* **(B); (F & B)**
contract cleaning – dining room (F & B) Fremdreinigung *(f)* – Speisesaal *(m)* **(F & B)**
contract cleaning – lobbies (R)
Fremdreinigung *(f)* – Empfangshalle *(f)* und Foyer *(n)* **(B)**
contract cleaning – windows (R); (F & B) Fremdreinigung *(f)* – Fenster *(pl. n)* **(B)**
contract entertainment (F & B)
Vertragsfirmen *(pl. f)* – Unterhaltung *(f)* **(F & B)**
contract exterminating (R)
Vertragsfirmen *(pl. f)* – Insektenvertilgung *(f)* **(B)**
contribution (A&G) Beitrag *(m)*, Spende *(f)* **(V)**
contributions – convention bureau (MKT) Beiträge *(pl. m)*, Zuwendungen *(pl. f)* – Kongreßbüro *(n)* **(MKT)**
cooking utensils (in kitchenette apts.) (R) Küchengeräte *(pl. n)* (Kochnische in Appartements) **(B)**
cooler – fiber (F & B)
Kühlvorrichtung *(f)* – Faser *(f)*, Fiber *(f)* **(F & B)**
copyright – license (A&G); (F & B)
Copyright *(n)* – Lizenzen *(pl. f)* **(V); (F & B)**
cord (A&G); (F & B) Leine *(f)*, Schnur *(f)* **(V); (F & B)**

corking equipment (F & B)
Flaschenverkorkgerät *(n)* **(F & B)**
corkscrews (F & B) Korkenzieher *(pl. m)* **(F & B)**
corkscrews (guests) (R)
Korkenzieher *(pl. m)* (Gäste) **(B)**
corsage (guests) (R) Ansteckbukett *(n)* (Gäste) **(B)**
cosmetics (R) kosmetische Mittel *(pl. n)*, Schönheitsmittel *(pl. n)* **(B)**
court fees (A&G) Gerichtskosten *(pl.)* **(V)**
creamers (F & B) Rahmtopf *(m)* **(F & B)**
credit and collection expenses (A&G) Kreditkosten *(pl.)* und Inkassospesen *(pl.)* **(V)**
credit card commission (A&G)
Kreditkarten-Provision *(f)* **(V)**
credit information books (A&G)
Kreditinformationenbücher *(pl. n)* **(V)**
cruet (F & B) Essig-/Ölfläschchen *(n)* **(F & B)**
cups – paper (F & B) Papierbecher *(pl. m)* **(F & B)**
curtain cleaning (R)
Vorhangreinigung *(f)* **(B)**
curtains – supplies (R) Vorhänge *(pl. m)* – Hilfs- und Betriebsstoffe *(pl. m)* **(B)**
custard cups (F & B)
Puddingschalen *(pl. f)* **(F & B)**
cut flowers (R) Schnittblumen *(pl. f)* **(B)**

daily report (A&G) Tagesbericht *(m)* **(V)**
damaged articles – guests (A&G)
beschädigte Gegenstände *(pl. m)* – Gäste **(V)**
dance license (F & B) Tanzerlaubnis *(f)* **(F & B)**
data processing – rentals (RTI)
Datenverarbeitung *(f)* – Mietaufwendungen *(pl. f)* **(MVV)**
data processing – supplies (A&G)
Datenverarbeitung *(f)* – Hilfs- und Betriebsstoffe *(pl. m)* **(V)**

decoration and painting (POM)
Dekorations- und Malerarbeiten
(pl.f) **(T)**
decorations (R); (F & B)
Dekorationsarbeiten *(pl.f)* **(B);**
(F & B)
deliver charges on food (F & B)
Lieferkosten *(pl.)* für Lebensmittel
(pl.n) **(F & B)**
**delivery charges on beverages
(F & B)** Lieferkosten *(pl.)* für
Getränke *(pl.n)* **(F & B)**
deodorants (R); (F & B)
desodorierende Mittel *(pl.n)* **(B);
(F & B)**
depreciation – buildings (D&A)
Abschreibungen *(pl.f)* – Gebäude
(pl.n) **(A)**
**desk pads (employees) (R);
(F & B)** Notizblöcke *(pl.m)*
(Angestellte) **(B); (F & B)**
desk pads (guests) (R); (F & B)
Notizblöcke *(pl.m)* (Gäste) **(B);
(F & B)**
detective service (A&G)
Detektivleistungen *(pl.f)* **(V)**
detergents (R); (F & B)
Reinigungsmittel *(pl.n)*,
Waschmittel *(pl.n)* **(B); (F & B)**
dictograph – rentals (A&G)
Abhörgerät *(n)* (beim Telefon) –
Mietaufwendungen *(pl.f)* **(V)**
**directional sign (inside bldg.)
(MKT)** Hinweisschild *(n)* (im
Hotel) **(MKT)**
directory (R) Adressbuch *(n)*,
Telefonbuch *(n)* **(B)**
dish-washer – repairs (POM)
Geschirrspüler *(m)* – Reparaturen
(pl.f) **(T)**
dishes (F & B) Geschirr *(n)* **(F & B)**
disinfectants (R); (F & B)
Desinfektionsmittel *(pl.n)*
(F & B)
doilies – linen (R); (F & B) kleine
Servietten *(pl.f)*, Zierdeckchen
(pl.n) – Leinen *(n)* **(B); (F & B)**
donations (A&G) Geschenke *(pl.n)*
(V)
door hangings (POM) Türvorhänge
(pl.m) **(T)**

drapery – cleaning (R); (F & B)
Draperie *(f)* – Reinigung *(f)* **(B);
(F & B)**
drapery – repairs (POM) Draperie
(f) – Reparaturen *(pl.f)* **(T)**
**dresses (uniforms) (R); (F & B);
(house laundry)** Kleidung *(f)*
(Uniformen) **(B); (F & B);**
(Hotelwäscherei)
drinking glasses (R) Trinkgläser
(pl.n) **(B)**
**drugs and other medical supplies
– employees (HR)** Arzneimittel
(pl.n), Drogeriewaren *(pl.f)* und
sonstige pharmazeutische Präparate
(pl.n) – Angestellte **(P)**
**drugs and other medical supplies
– guests (R)** Arzneimittel *(pl.n)*,
Drogeriewaren *(pl.f)* und sonstige
pharmazeutische Präparate *(pl.n)* –
Gäste **(B)**
dry cleaning (R); (F & B) chemische
Reinigung *(f)* **(F & B)**
dry ice (F & B) Trockeneis *(n)* **(F & B)**
dues – hotel association (A&G)
Beiträge *(pl.m)* – Hotel- und
Gaststättenverband *(m)* **(V)**
**duplicating and copying services
(A&G)** Vervielfältigungs- und
Kopierarbeiten *(pl.f)* **(V)**
dust brush (R); (F & B) Staubmop
(m) **(B); (F & B)**
dust cloth (R); (F & B) Staubtuch
(n), Staublappen *(m)* **(B); (F & B)**
dust pan (R); (F & B)
Kehrichtschaufel *(f)* **(B); (F & B)**
duster (R); (F & B) Staubwedel *(m)*,
Staubbesen *(m)* **(B); (F & B)**
dye for carpets and rugs (POM)
Färbeflüssigkeit *(f)* für Teppiche
(pl.m) und Brücken *(pl.f)* **(T)**
dynamo – repairs (POM) Dynamo
(m) (Maschine) – Reparaturen
(pl.f) **(T)**

ecru (house laundry) Ekrüstoff *(m)*,
Ekrü *(n)* **(Hotelwäscherei)**
**educational activities for
employees (A&G)** Weiter-,
Fortbildung *(f)* von Angestellten
(pl.) **(V)**

eggbeaters (F & B) Schneebesen
 (pl.m) **(F & B)**
electric bulbs (POM) Glühbirnen
 (pl.f) **(T)**
electric current (EC) elektrischer
 Strom *(m)* **(E)**
electric fan – repairs (POM)
 elektrischer Ventilator *(m)* –
 Reparaturen *(pl.f)* **(T)**
electricity – cooking (F & B)
 Elektrizität *(f)* – Küche *(f)* **(F & B)**
electricity for refrigerators (in kitchenette apts.) (R) Strom
 (m) für Kühlung *(f)*,
 Kälteerzeugung *(f)* (Kochnischen in
 Apts.) **(B)**
elevator cable (POM) Aufzugkabel
 (n) **(T)**
elevator inspection service (POM)
 Aufzüge *(pl.m)* – Kontrolldienst
 (m) **(T)**
elevator liability insurance (A&G)
 Haftpflichtversicherung *(f)* für
 Aufzüge *(pl.m)* **(V)**
employee benefits (PTEB)
 gesetzliche Sozialabgaben *(pl.f)*
 (Arbeitgeberanteil) **(zusätzliche, lohnabhängige (Personal-)Kosten)**
employee bonuses (R); (F & B)
 Angestellte *(pl.)* – Tantiemen
 (pl.f), Gehaltsprämien *(pl.f)* **(B);**
 (F & B)
employee lodging (A&G); (HR)
 Personalbeherbergung *(f)* **(V); (P)**
employee meals (R); (F & B)
 Personalverpflegung *(f)* **(B);**
 (F & B)
employee transportation (HR)
 Beförderungskosten *(pl.)* –
 Angestellte *(pl.)* **(P)**
employment agency fees (HR)
 Stellenvermittlungsbüro *(n)* –
 Gebühren *(pl.f)* **(P)**
enamel (POM) Email- oder
 Glasurmasse *(f)* **(T)**
engineering – supplies (POM)
 technische Abteilung *(f)* – Hilfs-
 und Betriebsstoffe *(pl.m)* **(T)**
entertainment and music (F & B)
 Unterhaltung *(f)* und Musik *(f)*
 (F & B)

**envelopes – telephone messages
 (R)** Briefumschläge *(pl.m)* –
 telefonische Nachrichten *(pl.f)* **(B)**
envelopes (R); (A&G)
 Briefumschläge *(pl.m)* **(B); (V)**
erasers (R); (F & B); (A&G)
 Radiergummis *(pl.m)* **(B); (F & B);**
 (V)
exposition – local (MKT)
 Ausstellung *(f)* im Hotel *(n)*
 (MKT)

face cloth (R) Waschlappen *(m)* **(B)**
fair – local (MKT) Messe *(f)* – am
 Ort *(m)* **(MKT)**
fan (guests) (R); (F & B) Fächer *(m)*
 (Gäste) **(B); (F & B)**
favors (F & B) Geschenke *(pl.n)*
 (F & B)
federal income tax (income tax)
 Einkommen- und Ertragsteuer *(f)*
 des Bundes *(m)* **(Steuern auf
 Einkommen und Ertrag)**
federal retirement taxes (PTEB)
 Arbeitgeberanteile *(pl.m)* zur
 gesetzlichen Sozialversicherung *(f)*
 des Bundes *(m)* **(zusätzliche
 lohnabhängige (Personal-)
 Kosten)**
**federal unemployment taxes
 (PTEB)** Arbeitslosenversicherung
 (f) (Arbeitgeberanteile)
 **(zusätzliche, lohnabhängige
 (Personal-)Kosten)**
**fees – management (management
 fees)** Gebühren *(pl.f)* –
 Management *(n)*
 (Management-Gebühren)
**fees – physician (employees)
 (A&G)** Arztkosten *(pl.)*
 (Angestellte) **(V)**
felt (POM) Filz *(m)* **(T)**
fern (R); (F & B) Farnkraut *(n)*, Farn
 (n) **(B); (F & B)**
fertilizer (POM) Kunstdünger *(m)*,
 Düngemittel *(n)* **(T)**
film (F & B) Film *(m)* **(F & B)**
filter paper (F & B) Filterpapier *(n)*
 (F & B)
fine (A&G) Geldstrafe *(f)*, Geldbuße
 (f) **(V)**

fire escape – repairs (POM)
Feuerleiter *(f)* – Reparaturen *(pl.f)*
(T)
fire extinguisher (A&G)
Feuerlöscher *(m)* **(V)**
fire hose (POM) Feuerwehrschlauch
(m) **(T)**
fire wood – rooms and lobby (R)
Brennholz *(n)* – Zimmer *(pl.n)* und
Hotelhalle *(f)* **(B)**
first aid supplies (A&G)
Erste-Hilfe-Material *(n)* **(V)**
flashlights and batteries (POM)
Taschenlampen *(pl.f)* und Batterien
(pl.f) **(T)**
flatware (F&B) Eßbesteck *(n)* **(F&B)**
floor plan (R) Grundriß *(m)* ;
Raumverteilungsplan *(m)* **(B)**
floor polish (R); (F&B)
Fußbodenpolitur *(f)* **(B); (F&B)**
floor wax (R); (F&B)
Fußbodenwachs *(n)* **(B); (F&B)**
floppy disks (A&G) Disketten *(pl.f)*
(V)
flower pots (R); (F&B)
Blumentöpfe *(pl.m)* **(B); (F&B)**
fly swatter (R); (F&B)
Fliegenklatsche *(f)* **(B); (F&B)**
forks (F&B) Gabeln *(pl.f)* **(F&B)**
forms (R); (F&B); (A&G)
Formulare *(pl.n)* **(B); (F&B); (V)**
fountain pens (R); (F&B); (A&G)
Füllfederhalter *(pl.m)* **(B); (F&B);**
(V)
frames (picture) (POM) Rahmen
(pl.m) (Bild) **(T)**
franchise fees (MKT)
Franchisegebühren *(pl.f)* **(MKT)**
freight charges (A&G) Frachtkosten
(pl.) – Gebühren *(pl.f)* **(V)**
fruit (guests) (R) Obst *(n)* (Gäste)
(B)
fuel (POM) Brennstoff *(m)* **(T)**
fumigator (R); (F&B)
Räucherapparat *(m)* **(B); (F&B)**
furniture for public rooms
(banquets) – rentals (F&B)
Mobiliar *(n)* für
Veranstaltungsräume *(pl.m)*
(Bankette) – Mietaufwendungen
(pl.f) **(F&B)**

furniture polish (R); (F&B)
Möbelpflegemittel *(n)*,
Möbelpolitur *(f)* **(B); (F&B)**
fuses (POM) Sicherungen *(pl.f)* **(T)**

gain on sale of property (gain or
loss on sale of property)
Veräußerungsgewinne *(pl.m)* aus
dem Verkauf *(m)* von
Anlagevermögen *(n)* **(Gewinne**
oder Verluste aus
Anlageverkäufen)
garage (R); (F&B) Garage *(f)* **(B);**
(F&B)
garbage cans (F&B) Abfalltonnen
(pl.f) **(F&B)**
garbage removal (F&B)
Müllabfuhr *(f)* **(F&B)**
garment bags (guests) (R)
Kleidersäcke *(pl.m)* (Gäste) **(B)**
garment hangers (guests) (R)
Kleiderbügel *(pl.m)* (Gäste) **(B)**
gas range – rentals (F&B)
Gasofen *(m)* – Mietaufwendungen
(pl.f) **(F&B)**
gasoline – motor vehicles (R);
(A&G) Benzin *(n)* – Fahrzeuge
(pl.n) **(B); (V)**
generator – repairs (POM)
Generator *(m)*, Dynamo *(m)*,
Lichtmaschine *(f)* – Reparaturen
(pl.f) **(T)**
gifts (guests) (R); (F&B)
Geschenke *(pl.n)* (Gäste) **(B);**
(F&B)
glas bowls (F&B) Glasschüsseln
(pl.f) **(F&B)**
glass dishes (F&B) Glasgeschirr
(n) **(F&B)**
glass pitcher (R); (F&B) Glaskanne
(f) **(B); (F&B)**
glass tray (R); (F&B) Glastablett
(n) **(B); (F&B)**
glassware (R); (F&B) Glas *(n)*,
Glasgeschirr *(n)* **(B); (F&B)**
glazing (replacing window glass)
(POM) Glaserarbeiten *(pl.f)*
(Ersatz von Fensterglas) **(T)**
gloves (R); (F&B) Handschuhe
(pl.m) **(B); (F&B)**

goblet (F & B) Kelch *(m)*, Becher *(m)*, Pokal *(m)* **(F & B)**
gratuities and christmas presents (A&G) Trinkgelder *(pl.n)* und Weihnachtsgeschenke *(pl.n)* **(V)**
grease (POM) Schmiermittel *(n)*, Schmierfett *(n)* **(T)**
greatcoat – door attendants (R) dekorativer Mantel *(m)* – Türsteher *(pl.m)* **(B)**
greeting cards (MKT) Glückwunschkarten *(pl.f)* **(MKT)**
ground rent (RTI) Grundpacht *(f)* **(MVV)**
guest history (MKT) Guest History *(f)* **(MKT)**
guest ledgers (A&G) Gästebuchhaltung *(f)* **(V)**
guest soap (R) Gästeseife *(f)* **(B)**
guides (guest use) (R) Berg-, Reise-, Fremdenführer *(pl.m)* (Gäste) **(B)**

hair nets (employees) (R); (F & B) Haarnetze *(pl.n)* (Angestellte) **(B); (F & B)**
hairpins (guests) (R) Haarnadeln *(pl.f)* (Gäste) **(B)**
hangers (guests) (R) Kleiderbügel *(pl.m)* (Gäste) **(B)**
hanging – repairs (POM) Wandbehang *(m)*, Wandbekleidung *(f)*, Tapete *(f)*, Vorhang *(m)* – Reparaturen *(pl.f)* **(T)**
heating plant – repairs (POM) Heizungsanlage *(f)* – Reparaturen *(pl.f)* **(T)**
help wanted – ad (HR) Annonce *(f)*, Inserat *(n)* – Aushilfskräfte **(P)**
holder (F & B) Behälter *(m)* **(F & B)**
hooks (POM) Haken *(m)*, Türangel *(f)* **(T)**
house publications (for employees) (HR) hauseigene Zeitungen *(pl.f)* und Zeitschriften *(pl.f)* (für Angestellte) **(P)**
housekeeper – reports (R) Hausdamenabteilung *(f)* – Berichte *(pl.m)* **(B)**
housing (employees) (HR) Personalbeherbergung *(f)* **(P)**

ice pick (F & B) Eispfriem *(m)* zum Zerkleinern *(n)* von Eis *(n)* **(F & B)**
ice tong (F & B) Eiszange *(f)* **(F & B)**
ice (F & B) Eis *(n)* **(F & B)**
icing sugar decoration (F & B) Puder-, Staubzuckerverzierung *(f)* **(F & B)**
incinerator – repairs (POM) Verbrennungsofen *(m)* – Reparaturen *(pl.f)* **(T)**
income tax – federal (income tax) Einkommen- und Ertragssteuer *(f)* **(Steuern auf Einkommen und Ertrag)**
index (R); (F & B); (A&G) Inhaltsverzeichnis *(n)*, Tabelle *(f)*, Register *(n)*, Index *(m)* **(B); (F & B); (V)**
index cards (R); (F & B); (A&G) Karteikarten *(pl.f)* **(B); (F & B); (V)**
insecticide (R); (F & B) Insektenvertilgungsmittel *(n)* **(B); (F & B)**
insurance – accident (PTEB) Unfallversicherung *(f)* **(zusätzliche, lohnabhängige (Personal-)Kosten)**
insurance – burglary (A&G) Einbruchsversicherung *(f)* **(V)**
insurance – group (non union) (PTEB) Gemeinschaftsversicherung *(f)* (nicht gewerkschaftlich organisierte Arbeitnehmer) **(zusätzliche, lohnabhängige (Personal-)Kosten)**
insurance – group (union) (PTEB) Gemeinschaftsversicherung *(f)* (gewerkschaftlich organisierte Arbeitnehmer) **(zusätzliche, lohnabhängige (Personal-)Kosten)**
insurance – hospitalization (non union employees) (PTEB) Krankenhausversicherung *(f)* (nicht gewerkschaftlich organisierte Arbeitnehmer) **(zusätzliche, lohnabhängige (Personal-)Kosten)**
insurance – life (union employees) (PTEB) Lebensversicherung *(f)* (gewerkschaftlich organisierte Arbeitnehmer) **(zusätzliche lohnabhängige (Personal-)Kosten)**

insurance – occupational disease (PTEB) Versicherung *(f)* – Berufskrankheiten *(pl.f)* (zusätzliche, lohnabhängige (Personal-)Kosten)
insurance – parcel post (A&G) Paketpostversicherung *(f)* **(V)**
insurance – plate glass (RTI) Spiegel-, Fensterglasversicherung *(f)* **(MVV)**
insurance – robbery (A&G) Versicherung *(f)* – Kassenraub *(m)* **(V)**
insurance – theft (A&G) Versicherung *(f)* – Diebstahl *(m)* **(V)**
insurance – use and occupancy (A&G) Versicherung *(f)* – Betriebsunterbrechung *(f)* **(V)**
insurance – weather (RTI) Versicherung *(f)* – Wetter *(n)* **(MVV)**
insurance – workers' compensation (PTEB) Versicherung *(f)* – Berufshaftpflicht *(f)* (zusätzliche, lohnabhängige (Personal-)Kosten)
interest (Int. Exp.) Zinsaufwendungen *(pl.f)* **(Zinsaufw.)**
interest on bonds (Int. Exp.) Obligationenzinsen *(pl.m)* **(Zinsaufw.)**
interest on first mortgage (Int. Exp.) Hypothekenzinsen *(pl.m)* auf die 1. Hypothek *(f)* **(Zinsaufw.)**
interest on notes (Int. Exp.) Zinsen *(pl.m)* auf Schuldwechsel *(pl.m)* **(Zinsaufw.)**
interest on taxes in arrears (Int. Exp.) Zinsaufwendungen *(pl.f)* für rückständige Steuern *(pl.f)* **(Zinsaufw.)**
internal audit fees (chain properties) (A&G) interne Prüfungsgebühren *(pl.f)* (Kettenhotels) **(V)**
interview expenses (HR) Interviewkosten *(pl.)* **(P)**
ironing board (R) Bügelbrett *(n)* **(B)**

kettel (F & B) Kessel *(m)* (aus Metall) **(F & B)**
key – repairs (POM) Schlüssel *(m)* – Reparaturen *(pl.f)* **(T)**
key for safe deposit box (R) Schlüssel *(m)* für Tresorfach *(n)*, Stahlfach *(n)*, Geldschrank *(m)* **(B)**
kitchen equipment – repairs (POM) Küchenausstattung *(f)* – Reparaturen *(pl.f)* **(T)**
kitchen utensils (including knives, forks, ladles, and spoons) (F & B) Küchengeräte *(pl.n)* (einschließlich Messer, Gabeln, Schöpflöffel und Löffel) **(F & B)**
kitchenette expenses (R) Kochnische *(f)* – Aufwendungen *(pl.f)* **(B)**
knife sharpening (F & B) Wetzstein *(m)*, Gerät *(n)* zum Messerschärfen *(n)* **(F & B)**
knives – silver (F & B) Messer *(pl.n)* – Silber *(n)* **(F & B)**

laboratory costs (POM) Laborkosten *(pl.)* **(T)**
lace curtains (POM) Spitzenvorhänge *(pl.m)* **(T)**
lacquer (POM) Lackfarbe *(f)* **(T)**
ladder (POM) Leiter *(f)* **(T)**
ladles (F & B) Schöpflöffel *(pl.m)* **(F & B)**
lamp shades – cleaning (R); (F & B) Lampenschirme *(pl.m)* – Reinigung *(f)* **(B); (F & B)**
landscaping (POM) Landschaftsgestaltung *(f)* **(T)**
laundry bags (house laundry) Wäschesäcke *(pl.m)* **(Hotelwäscherei)**
laundry (R); (F & B) Wäsche *(f)* **(B); (F & B)**
leasehold improvements – amortization (D&A) Ein- und Ausbauten *(pl.m)* in gemieteten Räumen *(pl.m)* – Abschreibung *(f)* **(A)**
legal expenses (A&G) Rechtsberatungskosten *(pl.)* **(V)**
lemon oil (R); (F & B) Zitronenöl *(n)* **(B); (F & B)**

lemon squeezer – bar (F & B)
Zitronenpresse *(f)* – Bar *(f)* **(F & B)**
licenses – lock smith (POM)
Lizenzen *(pl.f)* – Schlosser *(m)* **(T)**
limousine (R) Limousine *(f)* **(B)**
liquid container (F & B)
Flüssigkeitsbehälter *(m)* **(F & B)**
literature (promotional) (MKT)
Werbematerial *(n)*
(Verkaufsförderung) **(MKT)**
lobby cleaning (R)
Hotelhallenreinigung *(f)* **(B)**
lock repairs (POM) Türschloß *(n)* –
Reparaturen *(pl.f)* **(T)**
lodging of employees (HR)
Personalbeherbergung *(f)* **(P)**
log book (R) Logbuch *(n)*,
Reisetagebuch *(n)* **(B)**
loss on sale of property (gain or loss on sale of property)
Veräußerungsverluste *(pl. m)* aus dem Verkauf *(m)* von Anlagevermögen *(n)* **(Gewinne oder Verluste aus Anlageverkäufen)**
lost & found – reports (A&G)
Fundbüro *(n)* – Berichte *(pl. m)* **(V)**
lubricating oil and greases (garage and parking) Schmieröl *(n)* und Schmierfett *(n)* **(Garage und Parkplatz)**
lumber (POM) Bauholz *(n)* **(T)**
lye (R); (F & B) Lauge *(f)* **(B); (F & B)**

machine oil (POM) Maschinenöl *(n)* **(T)**
magazine advertising (MKT)
Zeitschriftenwerbung *(f)* **(MKT)**
mail bag (A&G) Postbeutel *(m)* **(V)**
mailing list (MKT) Adressenkartei *(f)* **(MKT)**
maintenance contract (POM)
Wartungsvertrag *(m)* **(T)**
manual – service (instructional materials) (R); (F & B); (A&G)
Handbuch *(n)*, Leitfaden *(m)* – Servicepersonal *(n)* (Weiterbildungsmaterial) **(B); (F & B); (V)**
map (MKT) Landkarte *(f)* **(MKT)**

marketing service fees (MKT)
Marketing-Gebühren *(pl.f)* **(MKT)**
marking ink (house laundry)
(unauslöschliche) Zeichentinte *(f)*, Wäschetinte *(f)* **(Hotelwäscherei)**
marquee licence (A&G) Markise *(f)* (über einem Hoteleingang) – Lizenzgebühr *(f)* **(V)**
masonry – repairs (POM)
Mauerwerk *(n)* – Reparaturen *(pl.f)* **(T)**
mat – bath (R) Matte *(f)*, Vorleger *(m)*, Abtreter *(m)* – Bad *(n)* **(B)**
mat – floor (POM) Matte *(f)* – Fußboden *(m)* **(T)**
matches (guests) (R); (F & B)
Streichhölzer *(pl. n)* **(B); (F & B)**
mattress (R) Matratze *(f)* **(B)**
meals – employees (R); (F & B)
Personalverpflegung *(f)* **(B); (F & B)**, etc.
medical fees (service to employees) (A&G) Arzthonorare *(pl. n)* (Leistungen für Angestellte) **(V)**
medical supplies (for employees) (A&G) medizinische Hilfsmittel *(pl. n)* (für Angestellte) **(V)**
membership dues – associations (A&G) Mitgliedsbeiträge *(pl. m)* – Vereinigungen *(pl.f)* **(V)**
menu (F & B) Speise(n)karte *(f)* **(F & B)**
mercantile agency – subscription (A&G) Handels-Kreditauskunftei *(f)* – Beiträge *(pl. m)* **(V)**
message envelopes (telephone)
Briefumschläge *(pl. m)* – Mitteilungen *(pl.f)* **(Telefonzentrale)**
meter – rentals (POM)
Meßinstrument *(n)*, Meßwerkzeug *(n)* – Mietaufwendungen *(pl.f)* **(T)**
mixer – repairs (POM) Mixer *(m)* – Reparaturen *(pl.f)* **(T)**
mold (F & B) Form *(f)* (für Speisen) **(F & B)**
mop (R); (F & B) Mop *(m)*, Staubbesen *(m)* **(B); (F & B)**
mortgage interest on first mortgage (Int. Exp.)

Hypothekenzinsen *(pl.m)* auf die 1. Hypothek *(f)* **(Zinsaufw.)**
mouse trap (R) Mausefalle *(f)* **(B)**
mucilage (R); (F & B); (A&G) Leim *(m)*, Klebstoff *(m)*, Gummilösung *(f)* **(B); (F & B); (A&G)**
muddler (F & B) (Um-)Rührlöffel, (Um-)Rührstab **(F & B)**
music-sheet (F & B) Notenblatt *(n)* **(F & B)**
musician (F & B) Musiker *(m)* **(F & B)**

napkins – paper (F & B) Servietten *(pl.f)* – Papier *(n)* **(F & B)**
needles and thread (guests) (R) Nadeln *(pl.f)* und Faden *(m)* (Gäste) **(B)**
needles and thread (POM) Nadeln *(pl.f)* und Faden *(m)* **(T)**
newspaper advertising (MKT) Werbung *(f)* in Tageszeitungen *(pl.f)* **(MKT)**
newspaper for clippings (MKT) Zeitung *(f)* für (Zeitungs-)Ausschnitte *(pl.m)* **(MKT)**
newspapers (for resale) (rentals and other income – cost of sales) Zeitungen *(pl.f)* (zum Weiterverkauf) **(Miet- und sonstige Erträge – Warenkosten)**
night apparel (R) Nachtkleidung *(f)* **(B)**
night auditors' report (A&G) Rechenschaftsbericht *(m)* des Nachtbuchhalters *(m)* **(V)**
notary fees (A&G) Notariatsgebühren *(pl.f)* **(V)**
novelties (advertising) (MKT) Werbegeschenkartikel *(pl.m)* **(MKT)**

office equipment – repairs (POM) Büroausstattung *(f)* – Reparaturen *(pl.f)* **(T)**
office supplies (R); (F & B); (A&G) Bürobedarf *(m)* **(B); (F & B); (V)**
oil (resale) (garage and parking – cost of sales) Öl *(n)* (zum Weiterverkauf) **(Garage und Parkplatz – Warenkosten)**

organization expenses (D&A) Gründungsaufwand *(m)* **(A)**
overages and shortages – cash (A&G) Kassen-Überschüsse *(pl.m)* und -Fehlbeträge *(pl.m)* **(V)**
overall (R) Overall *(m)* **(B)**
oxalic acid (house laundry) Oxal-Kleesäure *(f)* **(Hotelwäscherei)**
oyster knives (F & B) Austernmesser *(pl.n)* **(F & B)**

packing – supplies (gift shop) Verpackung *(f)* – Hilfs- und Betriebsstoffe *(pl.m)* **(Geschenkladen)**
packing – (POM) Verpackung *(f)* **(T)**
pails – painting and decorating (POM) Eimer *(pl.m)* – Malerarbeiten *(pl.f)* und Dekoration *(f)* **(T)**
pails (R) Eimer *(pl.m)*, Kübel *(pl.m)* **(B)**
paint brush (POM) Malerpinsel *(m)* **(T)**
painting and decorating (POM) Malerarbeiten *(pl.f)* und Dekoration *(f)* **(T)**
pajama (guests) (R) Pyjama *(m)*, Schlafanzug *(m)* (Gäste) **(B)**
pamphlet (MKT) Broschüre *(f)*, Heft *(n)*, Flugschrift *(f)* **(MKT)**
pans (F & B) Pfannen *(pl.f)*, Tiegel *(pl.m)* **(F & B)**
pants (R) Hose *(f)* **(B)**
paper – cooking (F & B) Papier *(n)* – Küche *(f)* **(F & B)**
paper bags (F & B) Papierbeutel *(pl.m)* **(F & B)**
paper clips (R); (F & B); (A&G) Büroklammern *(pl.f)*, Aktenklammern *(pl.f)* **(B); (F & B); (V)**
paper cups (F & B); (giftshop) Papierbecher *(pl.m)* **(F & B); (Geschenkladen)**
paper towels (employees) (R); (F & B); (A&G) Papierhandtücher *(pl.n)* (Angestellte) **(B); (F & B); (V)**

paper towels (guests) (R); (F & B)
Papierhandtücher *(pl. n)* (Gäste)
(B); (F & B)
parchment (F & B) Pergament *(n)*
(F & B)
paste (R); (F & B); (A&G) Paste *(f)*,
Brei *(m)* (B); (F & B); (V)
pastry bags (paper) (F & B) Tüten
(pl. f) für Back- und
Konditoreiwaren *(pl. f)* (Papier)
(F & B)
pastry boxes (F & B)
Kuchenschachteln *(pl. f)* (F & B)
**pencil sharpeners (R); (F & B);
(A&G)** Bleistiftspitzer *(pl. m)* (B);
(F & B); (V)
pencils (R); (F & B); (A&G)
Bleistifte *(pl. m)* (B); (F & B);
(V)
**pens (employees) (R); (F & B);
(A&G)** Kugelschreiber *(pl. m)*
(Angestellte) (B); (F & B); (V)
pensions (PTEB) Pensionen *(pl. f)*
(zusätzliche, lohnabhängige
(Personal-)Kosten)
**periodicals – for sale (rentals and
other income – cost of sales)**
Fachzeitschriften *(pl. f)*, Magazine
(pl. n) – zum Verkauf (Miet- und
sonstige Erträge – Warenkosten)
permit (R); (F & B) Erlaubnis *(f)* (B);
(F & B)
personal property tax (RTI)
Vermögenssteuer *(f)* (MVV)
photo – engraving (MKT)
(fotografische) Klischeeherstellung
(f) (MKT)
photographs (MKT) Bilder *(pl. n)*,
Fotografien *(pl. f)* (MKT)
**physician – fees (employees) (HR);
(A&G)** Arzthonorare *(pl. n)*
(Angestellte) (P); (V)
piano rentals – banquets (F & B)
Klavier-Mietkosten *(pl.)* – Bankette
(pl. n) (F & B)
piano tuning – apartment (R)
Klavierstimmen *(n)* – Appartement
(n) (B)
piano tuning – banquets (F & B)
Klavierstimmen *(n)* – Bankette
(pl. n) (F & B)

picture frame (POM) Bilderrahmen
(m) (T)
pillow cases (R) Kopfkissen *(pl. n)*
(B)
**pins (employees) (F & B); (R);
(A&G)** Anstecknadeln *(pl. f)*
(Angestellte) (F & B); (B); (V)
pipe – repairs (POM) Rohrleitungen
(pl. f) – Reparaturen *(pl. f)* (T)
pitcher (R); (F & B) Krug *(m)* (B);
(F & B)
pizza box (F & B) Pizzaschachtel *(f)*
(F & B)
placard (MKT) Plakat *(n)*,
(Anschlag-)Zettel *(m)* (MKT)
place card (R) Platzkarte *(f)* (B)
plant (R); (F & B) Pflanze *(f)* (B);
(F & B)
planting (POM) (An-)Pflanzung *(f)*
(T)
plaster (POM) Gips *(m)* (T)
plates (F & B) Teller *(pl. m)* (F & B)
platters (F & B) Servierplatten *(pl. f)*
(F & B)
playground – maintenance (POM)
Spielplatz *(m)* – Instandhaltung *(f)*
(T)
playing cards (R); (F & B)
Spielkarten *(pl. f)* (B); (F & B)
plumbing – repairs (POM)
Klemptner *(m)* –
Installateurarbeiten *(pl. f)* (T)
pneumatic tube – repairs (POM)
pneumatische Röhre *(f)* (Rohrpost)
– Reparaturen *(pl. f)* (T)
poles – curtains (POM) Stangen
(pl. f) – Vorhänge *(pl. m)* (T)
polish – floor (R); (F & B) Politur
(f) – Fußboden *(m)* (B); (F & B)
pool – accessories (POM)
Swimmingpool *(m)* – Zubehör *(n)*
(T)
pool – chemicals (POM)
Swimmingpool *(m)* – Chemikalien
(pl. f), chemische Präparate *(pl. n)*
(T)
portiere (POM) Portiere *(f)*,
Türvorhang *(m)* (T)
**post office box (P.O.B.) – rentals
(A&G)** Postfach *(n)* –
Mietaufwendungen *(pl. f)* (V)

postage (A&G) Porto *(n)*,
Postgebühr *(f)*, Postspesen *(pl.)* **(V)**
postcards – for resale (rentals and other income – cost of sales)
Postkarten *(pl.f)* – zum Weiterverkauf *(m)* **(Miet- und sonstige Erträge – Warenkosten)**
postcards (guests) (R) Postkarten *(pl.f)* (Gäste) **(B)**
poster – safety (A&G) Plakat *(n)* – Sicherheitshinweise *(pl.m)* **(V)**
pots (F & B) Kochtöpfe *(pl.m)* **(F & B)**
pouches – key (R); (F & B) Beutel *(pl.m)*, Taschen *(pl.f)* – Schlüssel *(pl.m)* **(B); (F & B)**
power, cost of (POM) Energiekosten *(pl.)* **(T)**
preopening expenses (D&A) Voreröffnungskosten *(pl.)* **(A)**
pressing machine – cover (R) Bügelmaschine *(f)* – Abdeckung *(f)* **(B)**
printed forms (R); (F & B); (A&G) vorgedruckte Formulare *(pl.n)* **(B); (F & B); (V)**
printed matter (R); (F & B); (A&G) Drucksachen *(pl.f)* **(B); (F & B); (V)**
printing and stationery (R); (F & B); (A&G) Drucksachen *(pl.f)* und Schreibbedarf *(m)* **(B); (F & B); (V)**
prizes (employees) (HR) Preise *(pl.m)*, Gewinne *(pl.m)* (Angestellte) **(P)**
program – entertainment (F & B) Unterhaltungsprogramm *(n)* **(F & B)**
protectors – mattresses (R) Schonbezüge *(pl.m)* – Matratzen *(pl.f)* **(B)**
provision for doubtful accounts (A&G) Abschreibungen *(pl.f)* auf zweifelhafte Forderungen *(pl.f)* **(V)**
public address system – repairs (POM) Lautsprecheranlage *(f)* (zur Übertragung von Ansagen etc. für eine große Zuhörerschaft) – Reparaturen *(pl.f)* **(T)**
public liability insurance (A&G) Haftpflichtversicherung *(f)* **(V)**
public rooms cleaning (on contract) – banquets (F & B)
Veranstaltungsräume *(pl.m)* – Reinigung *(f)* (Vertragsfirmen) – Bankette *(pl.n)* **(F & B)**
pump repairs (POM) Pumpenreparaturen *(pl.f)* **(T)**
purifier and softener for water (POM) Reinigungsapparat *(m)* und Wasserenthärter *(m)* **(T)**

rack card (R) Karte *(f)* zur Verwendung *(f)* im Zimmerbelegungsplan *(m)* **(B)**
radio broadcasting (MKT) Rundfunkübertragung *(f)* **(MKT)**
radiogram (A&G) Funkmeldung *(f)*, Funktelegramm *(m)* **(V)**
rags – cleaning (R); (F & B) Lappen *(pl.m)* – Reinigung *(f)* **(B); (F & B)**
railroad train advertising (MKT) Eisenbahnreklame *(f)* **(MKT)**
raincoat (R) Regenmantel *(m)* **(B)**
ramekins (F & B) Ramequin *(n)*, Käseauflauf *(m)* (Geschirr) **(F & B)**
range repairs (POM) Gas- oder Elektroherd *(m)* – Reparaturen *(pl.f)* **(T)**
razor blades (guests) (R) Rasierklingen *(pl.f)* (Gäste) **(B)**
real estate rent (land and buildings) Grundbesitz *(m)*, Immobilien *(pl.f)* **(Grund und Boden – Mietaufwendungen)**
real estate tax (RTI) Grundstückssteuer *(f)* **(MVV)**
record (F & B) Schallplatte *(f)* **(F & B)**
record books (R); (F & B); (A&G) Aufzeichnungen *(pl.f)*, Unterlagen *(pl.f)*, Geschäftsbücher *(pl.n)* **(B); (F & B); (V)**
refrigerant (POM) Kühlmittel *(n)* **(T)**
refrigeration – electricity (kitchenette apts) (R) Kälteerzeugung *(f)* – Elektrizität *(f)* (Kochnische in Apts.) **(B)**
refuse removal (POM) Müllbeseitigung *(f)* **(T)**
registered cable address (A&G) eingetragene Telegrammadresse *(f)* **(V)**

registration cards – guests (R)
Anmeldeformulare *(pl. n)* – Gäste
(pl. m) **(B)**
removal of ashes, garbage, and waste matter (POM)
Beseitigung *(f)* von Asche *(f)*,
Küchenabfall *(m)* und Müll *(m)* **(T)**
rentals – spotlights (F & B)
Mietaufwendungen *(pl. f)* –
Scheinwerfer *(pl. m)* **(F & B)**
rentals – teletype (A&G)
Mietaufwendungen *(pl. f)* –
Fernschreiber *(pl. m)* **(V)**
replacement of window glass (POM) Ersatz *(m)* von
Fensterscheiben *(pl. f)* **(T)**
report (A&G) Bericht *(m)*, Protokoll *(n)* **(V)**
reservation expenses (R)
Reservierungskosten *(pl.)* **(B)**
reservation forms (R)
Reservierungsformulare *(pl. n)* **(B)**
restaurant checks (F & B)
Gästerechnungen *(pl. f)* **(F & B)**
restaurant sign (F & B)
Restauranthinweisschild *(n)* **(F & B)**
ribbon (gift shop) Band *(n)*, Borte *(f)* **(Geschenkladen)**
road sign (MKT)
Straßenhinweisschild *(n)* **(MKT)**
roof repairs (POM) Dachreparaturen *(pl. f)* **(T)**
room clerk – reports (R)
Empfangsdame *(f)* – Berichte *(pl. m)* **(B)**
room service – order blanks (F & B) Room Service *(m)* –
Bestellformulare *(pl. n)* **(F & B)**
rope (POM) Seil *(n)*, Strick *(m)* **(T)**
royalties (F & B) Tantiemen *(pl. f)*, Ertragsgewinnanteil *(m)* **(F & B)**
rubber boots (R); (F & B)
Gummistiefel *(pl. m)* **(B); (F & B)**
rubber gloves (R); (F & B)
Gummihandschuhe *(pl. m)* **(B); (F & B)**
rubber mats (POM) Gummimatten *(pl. f)* **(T)**
rubber stamps (R); (F & B); (A&G)
Gummistempel *(pl. m)* **(B); (F & B); (V)**

rubbish removal (POM)
Abfallbeseitigung *(f)* **(T)**
ruler (R); (F & B); (A&G) Lineal *(n)* **(B); (F & B); (V)**
safe deposit box keys (R)
Safeschlüssel *(pl. m)*,
Geldschrankschlüssel *(pl. m)* **(B)**
safety matches (guests) (R); (F & B) Sicherheitszündhölzer *(pl. n)* (Gäste) **(B); (F & B)**
salad bowls (F & B) Salatschüsseln *(pl. f)* **(F & B)**
sales checks (F & B); (gift shop)
Kassenzettel *(m)*, Verkaufsscheck *(m)* **(F & B); (Geschenkladen)**
sales kits (MKT) Verkaufsausrüstung *(f)* **(MKT)**
sales tax (RTI) Umsatzsteuer *(f)* **(MVV)**
salt (house laundry) Salz *(n)* **(Hotelwäscherei)**
sand – fire buckets (A&G) Sand *(m)* – Feuereimer *(pl. m)* **(V)**
sand (POM) Sand *(m)* **(T)**
sandpaper (POM) Sandpapier *(n)* **(T)**
sanitary inspection (F & B) sanitäre Überprüfung *(f)* **(F & B)**
sanitary napkin (guests) (R)
Damenbinde *(f)* (Gäste) **(B)**
saucers (F & B) Untertassen *(pl. f)* **(F & B)**
saw dust (F & B) Sägemehl *(n)*, Sägespäne *(pl. m)* **(F & B)**
scenery rental for public rooms (banquets) (F & B) Szenerie *(f)*, Bühnenbildausstattung *(f)* (Bankette) **(F & B)**
scissors (R); (F & B); (A&G)
Scheren *(pl. f)* **(B); (F & B); (V)**
score pads (R) Anschreibeblöcke *(pl. m)* **(B)**
scotch tape (gift shop); (A&G)
(durchsichtiger) Klebestreifen *(m)* **(Geschenkladen); (V)**
scraper – paint (POM) Kratzer *(m)*, Schabeisen *(n)*, Streichmesser *(n)* – Farbe *(f)* **(T)**
screening (POM) (beim Sieben zurückbleibender) Abfall *(m)* **(POM)**

seating list (F & B) Sitzplan *(m)* (F & B)
security – contracted (A&G) Sicherung *(f)* des Hotels *(n)* – Personal *(n)* von Vertragsfirmen *(pl.f)* (V)
servers' checks (F & B) Gästerechnungen *(pl.f)* – Bedienungspersonal *(n)* (F & B)
servers' commissions (F & B) Provisionen *(pl.f)* – Bedienungspersonal *(n)* (F & B)
service manuals (R); (A&G) Handbücher *(pl.n)* – Personal *(n)* (B); (A&G)
sewer system – repairs (POM) Abwasserkanal *(m)* – Reparaturen *(pl.f)* (T)
sewing machines – repairs (POM) Nähmaschinen *(pl.f)* – Reparaturen *(pl.f)* (T)
shaker – beverages (F & B) Shaker *(m)* – Getränke *(pl.n)* (F & B)
sheets – linen (R) Bettlaken *(pl.n)* – Leinen *(n)* (B)
shoe cloths (guests) (R) Schuhputzlappen *(pl.m)* (Gäste) (B)
shortages and overages – cash (A&G) Kassen-Fehlbeträge *(pl.m)* und Überschüsse *(pl.m)* (V)
shovels (POM) Schaufeln *(pl.f)*, Schippen *(pl.f)* (T)
shower curtains (R) Duschvorhänge *(pl.m)* (B)
shower slippers (R) Duschpantoffeln *(pl.f)* (B)
sidewalk – repairs (POM) Fußgängerweg *(m)* – Reparaturen *(pl.f)* (T)
signs – road (off premises) (MKT) Schilder *(pl.n)* – Landstraße *(f)* (nicht auf dem Hotelgelände) (MKT)
signs – road (on premises) (MKT) Schilder *(pl.n)* – auf dem Hotelgelände *(n)* (MKT)
silver cleaner (F & B) Silber-Reinigungsmittel *(n)* (F & B)
sketch (MKT) Grundriß *(m)*, Entwurf *(m)* (MKT)

skewer (F & B) Fleischspieß *(m)* (F & B)
smock (R); (F & B) Arbeitskittel *(m)* (B); (F & B)
smoke stack – repairs (POM) Schornstein *(m)* – Reparaturen *(pl.f)* (T)
snow removal (POM) Schneeräumung *(f)* (T)
soap for cleaning (R); (F & B) Seife *(f)* für Reinigungszwecke *(pl.m)* (B); (F & B)
soap powder (R); (F & B) Waschpulver *(n)* (B); (F & B)
soap (guests) (R) Seife *(f)* (Gäste) (B)
social and sports activities – employees (HR) Soziale und Sportveranstaltungen *(pl.f)* – Angestellte *(pl.)* (P)
soda – laundry (house laundry) Soda *(n)*, kohlensaures Natrium *(n)* (Hotelwäscherei)
soda fountain – repairs (POM) Mineralwasserausschank *(m)*, Erfrischungshalle *(f)*, Eisbar *(f)* – Reparaturen *(pl.f)* (T)
soft drink (F & B) alkoholfreies Getränk *(n)* (F & B)
solvent (POM) Lösungsmittel *(n)* (T)
souvenir (R) Andenken *(n)*, Souvenir *(n)* (B)
sponges – cleaning (R); (F & B) Schwämme *(pl.m)* – Reinigung *(f)* (B); (F & B)
sponges – painters (POM) Schwämme *(pl.m)* – Maler *(pl.m)* (T)
spoons – beverage, kitchen, mixing (F & B) Löffel *(pl.m)* – Getränke *(pl.n)*, Küche *(f)*, Mixen *(n)* (F & B)
spoons – silver (F & B) Löffel *(pl.m)* – Silber *(n)* (F & B)
squeezer (F & B) Presse *(f)* (F & B)
stairway – repairs (POM) Treppenhaus *(n)* – Reparaturen *(pl.f)* (T)
stamp pad (R); (F & B); (A&G) Stempelkissen *(n)* (B); (F & B); (V)

stamps – advertising (MKT)
 Briefmarken *(pl.f)* – Werbung *(f)*
 (**MKT**)
stamps – general (A&G)
 Briefmarken *(pl.f)* – allgemein (**V**)
stapler (R); (F & B); (A&G)
 Heftmaschine *(f)* (**B**); (**F & B**); (**V**)
starch (house laundry) Stärke *(f)*
 (Wäsche) (**Hotelwäscherei**)
state income tax (income tax)
 Einkommensteuer *(f)*
 (Landesebene) (**Steuern auf**
 Einkommen und Ertrag)
stationery (R); (F & B); (A&G)
 Briefpapier *(n)* (**B**); (**F & B**); (**V**)
steam (POM) Dampf *(m)* (**T**)
steam – kitchen (F & B) Dampf *(m)*
 – Küche *(f)* (**F & B**)
steel wool (R); (F & B) Stahlwolle
 (f) (**B**); (**F & B**)
stencil (R); (F & B); (A&G)
 Schablone *(f)*, Matrize *(f)* (**B**);
 (**F & B**); (**V**)
stirrer (F & B) Rührholz *(n)*,
 Rührlöffel *(m)* (**F & B**)
stock pot – repairs (POM)
 Suppentopf *(m)* – Reparaturen
 (pl.f) (**T**)
stoppers (F & B) Stöpsel *(m)*, Propf
 (m) (**F & B**)
storage charges on food and
 beverages (F & B)
 Lagerungsgebühren *(pl.f)* für
 Lebensmittel *(pl.n)* und Getränke
 (pl.n) (**F & B**)
storeroom issue – reports (F & B)
 Warenanforderungsscheine *(pl.m)* –
 Berichte *(pl.m)* (**F & B**)
storeroom orders (F & B)
 Warenanforderungsscheine *(pl.m)*
 (**F & B**)
strainer – kitchen (F & B) Seiher
 (m), Sieb *(n)*, Filter *(m)* – Küche
 (f) (**F & B**)
straws – bar (F & B) Strohhalme
 (pl.m) – Bar *(f)* (**F & B**)
street cleaning (POM)
 Straßenreinigung *(f)* (**T**)
street sprinkling (POM) Straße *(f)* –
 Besprengen *(n)*, Besprühen *(n)*
 (**T**)

stuffer (MKT) Reklamebeilage *(f)* (zu
 Werbebriefen) (**MKT**)
subscription – mercantile agencies
 (A&G) Beitrag *(m)*, Gebühr *(f)* –
 Kreditauskunfteien *(pl.f)* (**V**)
subscriptions – trade publications
 (A&G) Gebühren *(pl.f)* –
 Fachpresse *(f)* (**V**)
suggestion award – employees
 (HR) Preis für
 Verbesserungsvorschlag *(m)* –
 Angestellte *(pl.)* (**P**)
suit (R) Anzug *(m)* (**B**)
sunshade (POM) Sonnenschutz *(m)*
 (Schirm) (**T**)
survey (F & B) Umfrage *(f)* (**F & B**)
switchboard – repairs (POM)
 Telefonzentrale *(f)* – Reparaturen
 (pl.f) (**T**)

table cloths (F & B) Tischtücher
 (pl.n) (**F & B**)
table linen – replacements (in
 kitchenette apts.) (R)
 Tischwäsche *(f)* – Ersatzbeschaffung
 (f) (in Kochnische Apts.) (**B**)
talcum powder (guests) (R)
 Körperpuder *(m)* (Gäste) (**B**)
tank – toilet floats (POM) Behälter
 (m) – Spülung *(f)* (**T**)
tar (POM) Teer *(m)* (**T**)
tassels (POM) Quasten *(pl.f)*,
 Troddeln *(pl.f)* (**T**)
taxicab fares (employees) (HR)
 Fahrpreise *(pl.m)* – Taxis *(pl.n)*
 (Angestellte) (**P**)
taxicab fares (guests) (R)
 Fahrpreise *(pl.m)* – Taxis *(pl.n)*
 (Gäste) (**B**)
tea pots (F & B) Teekannen *(pl.f)*
 (**F & B**)
telegram (A&G) Telegramm *(n)* (**V**)
telephone charges (telephone –
 cost of sales) Telefongebühren
 (pl.f) (**Telefon – vom Hotel zu**
 bezahlende Beträge)
telephone directories (R)
 Telefonbücher *(pl.n)* (**B**)
telephone directory – advertising
 (**MKT**) Telefonbuch *(n)* –
 Werbung *(f)* (**MKT**)

**telephone equipment charges
(RTI)** Telefonanlagekosten *(pl.)*
(MVV)
telephone rentals (RTI)
Telefonanlage *(f)* –
Mietaufwendungen *(pl.f)* **(MVV)**
telephone vouchers (telephone)
Telefon *(n)* – Buchungsbeleg *(m)*
(Telefon)
teletype – paper (A&G)
Fernschreiber *(m)* – Papier *(n)* **(V)**
television – rentals (RTI) Fernseher
(m) – Mietaufwendungen *(pl.f)*
(MVV)
terpentine (POM) Terpentin *(n)* **(T)**
tickets (for promotion) (MKT)
Eintrittskarten *(pl.f)*
(Verkaufsförderung) **(MKT)**
ticking (POM) Drell *(m)*, Drillich
(m) **(T)**
tie (R) Krawatte *(f)* **(B)**
tiling – rubber (POM) Fliesen *(pl.f)*,
Kacheln *(pl.f)* – Gummi *(n)* **(T)**
time clock – repairs (POM)
Stechuhr *(f)* – Reparaturen *(pl.f)*
(T)
timetables (R) Fahrpläne *(pl.m)*
Flugpläne *(pl.m)* **(B)**
tools (POM) Werkzeug *(n)* **(T)**
toothbrushes (R) Zahnbürsten *(pl.f)*
(B)
toothpicks (F & B) Zahnstocher
(pl.m) **(F & B)**
tour agency – commission (R)
Reiseagentur *(f)* – Provision *(f)* **(B)**
towels – linen (R); (F & B)
Handtücher *(pl.n)* – Leinen *(n)*
(B); (F & B)
toys (R) Spielzeug *(n)* **(B)**
transcript (A&G) Abschrift *(f)*,
Kopie *(f)*, Verhandlungsprotokoll *(n)*
(V)
transfer fees (A&G)
Überweisungsgebühren *(pl.f)* **(V)**
**transportation charges on food
and beverage (F & B)**
Versandkosten *(pl.)* für
Lebensmittel *(pl.n)* und Getränke
(pl.n) **(F & B)**
travel agent – commission (R)
Reisebüro *(n)* – Provision *(f)* **(B)**

traveling expenses (A&G)
Reisekosten *(pl.)* **(V)**
**traveling expenses – business
promotion (MKT)** Reisekosten
(pl.) für die wirtschaftliche
Förderung *(f)* **(MKT)**
trousers (R); (F & B) Hose *(f)* **(B);
(F & B)**
trustee's expenses (A&G)
Treuhänder *(m)* – Aufwendungen
(pl.f) **(V)**
tube (POM) Rohrleitung *(f)* **(T)**
tumbler (R); (F & B) Wasserglas *(n)*
(B); (F & B)
twine (R); (F & B); (gift shop)
starker Bindfaden *(m)*, Schnur *(f)*
(B); (F & B); (Geschenkladen)

**umbrellas (for door attendants)
(R)** Regenschirme *(pl.m)* (für
Türsteher) **(B)**
uncollectible accounts (A&G)
uneinbringliche Forderungen *(pl.f)*
(V)
**union – insurance and pension
fund (employer's contribution)
(PTEB)** Gewerkschaft –
Versicherungs- und
Pensionskassenbeiträge *(pl.m)*
(Arbeitgeberanteil) **(zusätzliche
lohnabhängige (Personal-)Kosten)**
upholstery – supplies (POM)
Polsterei *(f)* – Hilfs- und
Betriebsstoffe *(pl.m)* **(T)**

vacuum cleaner accessories (R)
Staubsaugerzubehör *(n)* **(B)**
valance (POM) kurzer Behang *(m)*,
Volant *(m)* (am Bett oder
Baldachin) **(T)**
valve – repairs (POM) Ventil *(n)*,
Absperrvorrichtung *(f)*, Klappe *(f)*
– Reparaturen *(pl.f)* **(T)**
varnish (POM) Lack *(m)* **(T)**
vase (R); (F & B) Vase *(f)* **(B);
(F & B)**
vehicle depreciation (D&A)
Fahrzeugabschreibung *(f)* **(A)**
Venetian blind (POM) Jalousie *(f)*
(T)

voucher (R); (F & B); (A&G)
Buchungsbeleg *(m)*,
Buchungsunterlage *(f)*, (auch:
Gutschein) **(B); (F & B); (V)**

wall hanging (POM) Wandbehang *(m)* **(T)**
wall paper (POM) Tapete *(f)* **(T)**
warehouse costs – beverage (F & B) Lagerkosten *(pl.)* – Getränke *(pl. n)* **(F & B)**
wash cloth (R) Spüllappen *(m)* **(B)**
washing powder (R) Waschpulver *(n)*, Waschmittel *(n)* **(B)**
waste paper (R); (F & B) Abfall *(m)*, Ausschußpapier *(n)* **(B); (F & B)**
waste (POM) Schutt *(m)*, Müll *(m)* **(T)**
wax paper (F & B) Wachspapier *(n)* **(F & B)**
wax (R); (F & B) Wachs *(n)* **(B); (F & B)**

wick (F & B) Docht *(m)* **(F & B)**
window shades – cleaning (R); (F & B) Rouleaus *(pl. n)*, Jalousien *(pl. f)* – Reinigung *(f)* **(B); (F & B)**
wine cellar – supplies (F & B) Weinkeller *(m)* – Hilfs- und Betriebsstoffe *(pl. m)* **(F & B)**
wine cellar – utensils (F & B) Weinkeller *(m)* – Gerätschaften *(pl. f)* **(F & B)**
wiring – repairs (POM) elektrisches Leitungsnetz *(n)* – Reparaturen *(pl. f)* **(T)**
workers' compensation insurance (PTEB) Betriebshaftpflichtversicherung *(f)* **(zusätzliche, lohnabhängige (Personal-)Kosten)**
wrapping foil (F & B) Einpackfolie *(f)* **(F & B)**
wrapping paper (R); (F & B); (A&G) Packpapier *(n)* **(B); (F & B); (V)**

Anhang

Regelungsinstitutionen (Bilanzrecht) in den USA

Appendix

Regulatory Bodies (accounting legislaton) in the USA

Accounting and Review Service Committee (ARSC) Ausschuß des „AICPA", der Richtlinien für die Rechnungslegung nicht geprüfter, nicht öffentlicher Einheiten (unaudited, nonpublic entities) festlegt.
Accounting Interpretations Verlautbarungen, die zwecks schnellerer Behandlung von aktuellen Fragen herausgegeben wurden.
Accounting Principles Board (APB) Gremium von amerikanischen Fachleuten, das 1959 vom „AICPA" ins Leben gerufen wurde. Es befaßt sich mit offiziellen Verlautbarungen zu Fragen der Rechnungslegung.
Accounting Research Bulletin 43 wichtige Veröffentlichung des Committee on Accounting Prodecures, das eine Zusammenfassung von wesentlichen Bilanzierungs- und Bewertungsvorschriften enthält.
Accounting Review weltweit führende wissenschaftliche Zeitschrift, die von der „AAA" herausgegeben wird.
Accounting Series Release 150 die „SEC" bekräftigt hier die rechtsverbindliche Wirkung der FASB-Verlautbarungen.
Accounting Series Releases (ASR) Verlautbarungen zu verschiedenen Problembereichen des Rechnungswesens; Rechnungslegungsnormen.
Accounting Standards Board (ASB) Ausschuß des „AICPA", der die „Statements on Auditing Standards" (SAS) und die dazugehörigen Interpretationen erläßt. Diese „Statements" bilden in ihrer Gesamtheit die Grundsätze ordnungsmäßiger Prüfung.
Accounting Standards Executive Committee (ASEC) Ausschuß, der unter anderem die Statements of Position (SOP), die Stellungnahmen des Berufsstandes der Wirtschaftsprüfer zu Einzelfragen, erläßt. Sie sind nicht verbindlich im Sinne der Rule 203.
American Accounting Association (AAA) Vertretung der Hochschullehrer und theoretisch interessierter Praktiker des Fachs Accounting.
American Institute of Certified Public Accountants (AICPA) wichtigste Berufsstandvereinigung der amerikanischen Wirtschaftsprüfer.
APB-Opinions offizielle Verlautbarungen des „APB" zu Fragen der Rechnungslegung. Es wurde 1973 aufgelöst.
Authoritative Support Gesetzeskraft; alle Verlautbarungen des „FAS" haben „Authoritative Support", d.h. sie werden von der „SEC" anerkannt und haben damit Gesetzescharakter.
Basic Concepts and Accounting Principles underlying Financial Statements of Business Enterprises Formulierung einer Grundlagentheorie des Rechnungswesens.
Certified Management Accountant (CMA) das unternehmensinterne Gegenstück zum „CPA", d.h. dem Wirtschaftsprüfer.
Concepts Statements (SFAC) theoretische Grundlagen des Rechnungswesens. Diese Veröffentlichungen sind für den ausländischen Beobachter von besonderem Interesse, da er sich dort einen guten Überblick über die derzeitige und künftige Situation der US-Rechnungslegung verschaffen kann.
consensus Consensus-Lösung; man spricht von einer Consensus-Lösung, wenn weniger als 3 Personen der „Emergency Task Force" (EITF) einer Lösung widersprechen. Der Problemkreis (issue) gilt dann als gelöst.
Cost Accounting Standards Board (CASB) Ausschuß mit dem Ziel

der Entwicklung einer einheitlichen Kostenrechnungspraxis.

due process stark formalisierter Ablauf des Verabschiedungsverfahrens bei den Verlautbarungen.

entity theory Einheitstheorie (betrachtet den Konzern als selbständige Einheit).

fair presentation Bewertungsgrundsatz, der besagt, daß die wirtschaftliche Lage eines Unternehmens nicht der Form, sondern dem Inhalt nach wahrheitsgemäß darzustellen ist.

Financial Accounting Concepts (SFAC) diese Concept-Statements bilden einen theoretischen Rahmen, die sogenannte ,,Conceptional Framework", innerhalb dessen sich die zukünftigen Rechnungslegungsregelungen weiterentwickeln sollen.

Financial Accounting Standards Advisory Council (FASAC) Beratungsgremium mit der Aufgabe, das ,,FASB" über die aktuellen Probleme der Jahresabschlußersteller und -nutzer zu informieren.

Financial Accounting Standards Board (FASB) Nachfolgegremium des ,,APB", das sich mit offiziellen Verlautbarungen zu Fragen der Rechnungslegung befaßt. Alle Verlautbarungen des ,,FASB" genießen ,,Authoritative Support", haben also Gesetzescharakter.

Generally Accepted Auditing Standards (GAAS) Grundsätze ordnungsmäßiger Prüfung.

Governmental Accounting Standards Advisory Council (GASAC) Organ, das dem GASB zur Unterstützung bei der Aufgabenbewältigung zur Verfügung steht.

Governmental Accounting Standards Board (GASB) Parallelorganisation zum ,,FASB", die die Rechnungslegung von öffentlichen Einheiten (governmental entities) regelt.

Industry Audit and Accounting Guides diese Industrieführer des ,,AICPA" sind Anleitungsbücher zur Bilanzierung und Prüfung in bestimmten Branchen.

Institute of Internal Auditors (IIA) Organisation, die auch die Berufsbezeichnung ,,CIA" (Certified Internal Auditor) vergibt; es handelt sich hier um den Berufsstand der internen Revisoren.

International Accounting Standards Committee (IASC) 1973 gegründetes Komitee, das sich zur Aufgabe gemacht hat, Rechnungslegungsverlautbarungen zu erarbeiten, die weltweite Anerkennung finden.

International Accounting Standards (IAS) Rechnungslegungsverlautbarungen, die in den USA nicht direkt rechtsverbindlich sind. Der ,,FASB" versucht bei der Formulierung seiner Standards jedoch, die ,,IAS" zu integrieren.

International Auditing Guidelines (IAG) Verlautbarungen zu Prüfungsfragen, die aber keine direkte Bindungswirkung für die Mitgliedsstaaten haben. Das ,,AICPA" berücksichtigt jedoch den Inhalt der internationalen Erarbeitungen zur Erstellung neuer ,,Statements on Auditing Standards" (SAS).

International Auditing Practice Committee (IFAC) Gremium, das Verlautbarungen zu Prüfungsfragen erläßt.

International Federation of Accountants (IFAC) 1977 in München gegründete Organisation, die Organisationen im Bereich des Rechnungswesens aus über 60

Staaten vereinigt. Ziel ist eine weltweite Entwicklung des Rechnungswesens und des Berufstandes.
interpretations Informationen, die sich meist auf Einzelprobleme vorher erlassener „Statements" beziehen. Diese Veröffentlichungen haben rechtsverbindliche Wirkung.

National Association of Accountants (NAA) Interessenorganisation für primär mit internem Rechnungswesen befaßte Praktiker.

parent company (or proprietary) theory Interessentheorie (Konzernrechnungslegung).

percentage of completion method steuerliche Gewinnermittlungsmethode, bei der die aus langfristigen Verträgen resultierenden Gewinne anteilig zu der prozentualen Fertigstellung des Projekts berücksichtigt werden.

Prevalent Industry Practices Vorschriften für das Rechnungswesen, die aus der Praxis der einzelnen Branchen stammen.

Regulation S-X SEC-Bestimmungen zu Form und Inhalt der von Emittenten vorzulegenden Finanzausweise (Ausführungsbestimmungen zum Securities Act (SA) und Securities Exchange Act (SEA)). Die Bestimmungen enthalten detaillierte Regelungen zu Form, Fristen und Inhalt der Jahresabschlüsse.

restatements Zusammenfassung aller von der „EITF" bearbeiteten Problemkreise und deren Lösungen, die von dritter Seite erhältlich sind.

Rule 203 Richtlinie, die von allen Wirtschaftsprüfern, die Mitglieder des „AICPA" sind, verlangt, daß sie bei der Formulierung einer Prüfmeinung (opinion) die vom „FASB" formulierten Grundsätze ordnungsmäßiger Buchführung beachten.

Rules and Regulations Verordnungen und Formvorschriften mit Gesetzeskraft, mit deren Hilfe die „SEC" die dem Gesetz unterworfenen Unternehmen kontrolliert.

Securities Exchange Act (SEA) US-Börsengesetz, das das Börsengeschehen in den USA regelt, z.B. die Errichtung einer Wertpapier- und Börsenaufsichtsbehörde (SEC).

Security and Exchange Commission (SEC) amerikanische Börsenaufsichtsbehörde, die beauftragt wurde, den „Securities Act" (SA) und den „Securities Exchange Act" (SEA) zu verwalten.

Staff Accounting Bulletins (SAB) administrative Richtlinien für das Vorgehen der „SEC" im Zusammenhang mit der Überprüfung der vorgelegten Abschlüsse und Rechenschaftsberichte. Vergleichbar mit den Richtlinien einer Finanzbehörde.

Statements of Financial Accounting Standards (SFAS) APB-Opinions entsprechende Verlautbarungen des „FASB".

Statements on Auditing Standards in ihrer Gesamtheit die Grundsätze ordnungsmäßiger Prüfung.

Statements on Standards for Accounting and Review Services (SSARS) diese Statements regeln die sogenannten „Compilation and Review Services" seitens der „CPA" (Wirtschaftsprüfer). Unter Compilation ist die Erstellung von Jahresabschlüssen zu verstehen.

technical bulletin veröffentlichte Rechnungslegungsprobleme mit Empfehlungscharakter.

Alles Gute für Ihr
Verpflegungs-Management

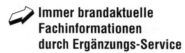

Ihre Vorteile auf einen Blick:

➪ Immer brandaktuelle Fachinformationen durch Ergänzungs-Service

➪ Moderne Lösungen von Experten aus der Praxis

➪ Mit zahlreichen Tips und Formularen, die Sie gleich einsetzen können

➪ Jede Menge kostenlose Service-Leistungen für Sie

Bethge / Bolten / Dörsam (Hrsg.)
Modernes Küchenmanagement

Loseblattwerk auf dem neuesten Stand, 2 Ordner mit 800 Seiten
Ergänzungslieferungen 4 Mal im Jahr, Seitenpreis 43,5 Pfennig
Bestell-Nr. 29119

Fordern Sie Ihr Test-Exemplar an. Prüfen Sie 20 Tage ohne Verpflichtung die Vorteile dieses Beraters.

Am besten gleich anfordern bei:
**Deutscher Fachverlag GmbH
Buchverlag**
z. Hd. Frau Manus
Mainzer Landstr. 251
60326 Frankfurt

Am schnellsten geht's per:

☎ 069 / 75 95 21 24/25
FAX 069 / 75 95 21 10

VERLAGSGRUPPE
DEUTSCHER
FACHVERLAG

Fachbücher für Ihren Erfolg ...
... da steckt viel Praxis drin!

Alles rund um das GV-Management!

- Gästebedürfnisse richtig erkennen
- Konzepte erfolgreich durchziehen
- Mit zahlreichen Tips, Checklisten und Anleitungen

Siegfried Bober
Marketing-Praxis in der Gemeinschafts-Gastronomie
Analysieren, Planen, Gestalten, Kontrollieren
265 Seiten, broschiert
Bestell-Nr. 50359

DM 68,-

Die Geheimnisse erfolgreicher Führung!

- Über 100 Praxis-Beispiele aus der Gastronomie
- Schritt-für-Schritt Beispiele
- Spielend leicht und sofort anwendbar

Ulla Thombansen
Teamgeist als Trumpf
Erfolgreiche Mitarbeiterführung in Hotellerie, Gastronomie und Gemeinschaftsverpflegung
288 Seiten, gebunden
Bestell-Nr. 50395

DM 78,-

Profitieren Sie vom Know-how von über 40 erfolgreichen Service-Spezialisten!

Der Aufbau:
- Hervorragend bebildert
- mit umfangreichem Kostenmaterial
- Klare Ablaufdiagramme

Schweizer Wirte Verband (Hrsg.)
Service-Lehrbuch
560 Seiten, viele Abbildungen,
umfangreiches Kartenmaterial, Hardcover
Bestell-Nr. 29088

DM 98,-

Der Inhalt:
- Was Gäste erwarten
- Wie Sie den Service im Gastronomie-Betrieb richtig organisieren
- Wie die Arbeit im Service-Bereich professionell abläuft
- Alles, was Sie bei Getränken beachten müssen

Die richtige Technik spart viel Geld!

Willi Schwebel
Technische Arbeitsblätter Großverpflegung und Küchentechnik

DM 168,-

Systematisch gegliedert finden Sie folgende Themen:
- Küchentechnologie
- Küchen und Verpflegungseinrichtung
- Küchenplanung
- Gerätetechnik, Anlagen, Einrichtungsteile
- Haustechnik
- Richtlinien, Normen, Vorschriften
- Weiterführende Literatur

Willi Schwebel
Technische Arbeitsblätter Großverpflegung und Küchentechnik
Praktischer Ringbuchordner,
Format A4, über 250 Seiten
Bestell-Nr. 50333

dfv VERLAGSGRUPPE DEUTSCHER FACHVERLAG